SHELLY CASHMAN SERIES®

Systems Analysis and Design

ELEVENTH EDITION

TILLEY | **ROSENBLATT**

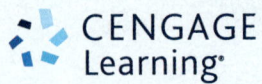

Systems Analysis and Design, Eleventh Edition
Scott Tilley and Harry Rosenblatt

SVP, GM Skills & Global Product Management: Dawn Gerrain

Product Director: Kathleen McMahon

Product Team Manager: Kristin McNary

Senior Director, Development: Marah Bellegarde

Senior Content Developer: Kate Mason

Developmental Editor: Deborah Kaufmann

Product Assistant: Abigail Pufpaff

Senior Production Director: Wendy Troeger

Production Director: Patty Stephan

Senior Content Project Manager: Stacey Lamodi

Designer: Diana Graham

Cover Template Designer: Lisa Kuhn, Curio Press, LLC

Cover image(s): robuart/Shutterstock.com

For product information and technology assistance, contact us at
Cengage Learning Customer & Sales Support, 1-800-354-9706

For permission to use material from this text or product, submit all requests online at **www.cengage.com/permissions**. Further permissions questions can be e-mailed to **permissionrequest@cengage.com**

Library of Congress Control Number: 2015958228

ISBN: 978-1-305-49460-2

Cengage Learning
20 Channel Center Street
Boston, MA 02210
USA

Cengage Learning is a leading provider of customized learning solutions with employees residing in nearly 40 different countries and sales in more than 125 countries around the world. Find your local representative at **www.cengage.com**

Cengage Learning products are represented in Canada by Nelson Education, Ltd.

To learn more about Cengage Learning, visit **www.cengage.com**

Purchase any of our products at your local college store or at our preferred online store **www.cengagebrain.com**

Printed in the United States of America
Print Number: 03 Print Year: 2017

BRIEF CONTENTS

TABLE OF CONTENTS

PHASE 1: SYSTEMS PLANNING

Chapter 10

System Architecture

PHASE 4 : SYSTEMS IMPLEMENTATION

Chapter 11

Managing Systems Implementation

Toolkit Part B
CASE Tools

Toolkit Part C
Financial Analysis Tools

Toolkit Part D
Internet Resource Tools

DEDICATION

To Harry

FOREWORD

Harry Rosenblatt was a teacher, a mentor, and textbook author. His dedication to writing the previous editions of this book was grounded in the desire to help students understand the material, and to provide the foundation for becoming future systems analysts and designers. He sought input from students on how to make the textbook better, even going as far as putting together a team of students to help him. Harry's work has enabled thousands of students to gain an understanding of systems analysis and design.

While Harry was writing the previous editions of this text, he was actively teaching at several colleges. Harry's experience with teaching this material led him to develop an extensive selection of supplemental resources to assist instructors who used the text in their courses. The format of each edition was an iterative revision of his pedagogical views of the subject matter stemming from his teaching experience.

Farewell, Harry. Your legacy will live on through the continued publication of this text. Systems analysis and design is a timeless topic in the field of information technology, and thousands of students will continue to be touched by your work.

Ronald R. Savilla, MBA
Carolinas Healthcare System
Former student and textbook assistant

PREFACE

The Shelly Cashman Series® offers the finest textbooks in computing education. We are proud that our previous editions of *Systems Analysis and Design* have been so well received by instructors and students. *Systems Analysis and Design, Eleventh Edition* continues with the innovation, quality, and reliability you have come to expect.

The Shelly Cashman Series development team carefully reviewed our pedagogy and analyzed its effectiveness in teaching today's student. Contemporary students read less, but need to retain more. As they develop and perform skills, students must know how to apply the skills to different settings. Today's students need to be continually engaged and challenged to retain what they're learning. With this book, we continue our commitment to focusing on the user and how they learn best.

Facing a challenging global marketplace, companies need strong IT resources to survive and compete effectively. Many of today's students will become the systems analysts, managers, and IT professionals of tomorrow. This textbook will help prepare them for those roles.

Overview

Systems Analysis and Design, Eleventh Edition offers a practical, streamlined, and updated approach to information systems development. The book emphasizes the role of the systems analyst in a dynamic, business-related environment. Throughout the book, real-world examples emphasize critical thinking and IT skills in a dynamic, business-related environment.

Many two- and four-year colleges and schools use this book in information systems, computer science, and ecommerce curriculums. The *Eleventh Edition* includes expanded coverage of emerging technologies, such as agile methods, cloud computing, and mobile applications. This new material compliments the updated treatment of traditional approaches to systems analysis and design.

Using this book, students learn how to translate business requirements into information systems that support a company's short- and long-term objectives. Case studies and assignments teach analytical reasoning, critical thinking, and problem-solving skills. Numerous projects, assignments, and end-of-chapter exercises are accessible online, along with detailed instructor support material.

Objectives of This Textbook

Systems Analysis and Design, Eleventh Edition is intended for a three credit-hour introductory systems analysis and design course. This textbook is designed to:

- Explain systems analysis and design using an appealing full-color format, numerous screen shots and illustrations, and an easy-to-read style that invites students to learn.

- Introduce project management concepts early in the systems development process, with a new chapter that explains project management tools and techniques.

- Challenge students with a Question of Ethics mini-case in each chapter that asks them to respond to real-life ethical issues in an IT environment.

- Provide multi-method coverage, including a comparison of structured, object-oriented, and agile systems development methods.

- Explain how IT supports business requirements in today's intensely competitive environment, and describe major IT developments and trends.

New and Updated Features in This Edition

Systems Analysis and Design, Eleventh Edition offers these exciting new and expanded features:

- Streamlined presentation of material throughout the book, helping students focus on the main content quickly and easily. There is less visual distraction and a clearer flow of topics. Much of the additional material has been moved online.

- Expanded coverage of emerging technologies, such as agile methods, cloud computing, and mobile applications, making topics more aligned with today's business environments and student interests. New developments are placed in historical context.

- Updated examples of CASE tools reflecting web-based and/or open source offerings. These tools are often free and are representative of modern systems analysis solutions.

- Revised Toolkits reflecting changes in systems analysis tools and resources.

- Glossary of key terms now appears at the end of each chapter, helping students remember concepts in context.

Organization of This Textbook

Systems Analysis and Design, Eleventh Edition contains 16 learning units in twelve chapters and a four-part Systems Analyst's Toolkit that teaches valuable cross-functional skills. The twelve chapters are organized into five phases: planning, analysis, design, implementation, and support and security.

Phase 1: Systems Planning

- **Chapter 1 – Introduction to Systems Analysis and Design:** Chapter 1 provides an introduction to systems analysis and design by describing the role of information technology in today's dynamic business environment.

- **Chapter 2 – Analyzing the Business Case:** Chapter 2 explains how systems projects get started and how to evaluate a project proposal to determine its feasibility.

- **Chapter 3 – Managing Systems Projects:** Chapter 3 describes how to use project management tools and techniques, and how to plan, schedule, monitor, and report on IT projects.

Phase 2: Systems Analysis

- **Chapter 4 – Requirements Modeling:** Chapter 4 describes the requirements modeling process: gathering facts about a systems project, preparing documentation, and creating models that will be used to design and develop the system.

- **Chapter 5 – Data and Process Modeling:** Chapter 5 discusses data and process modeling techniques that analysts use to show how the system transforms data into useful information.

- **Chapter 6 – Object Modeling:** Chapter 6 discusses object modeling techniques that analysts use to create a logical model.

- **Chapter 7 – Development Strategies:** Chapter 7 considers various development strategies for the new system, and plans for the transition to the systems design phase.

Phase 3: Systems Design

- **Chapter 8 – User Interface Design:** Chapter 8 explains how to design an effective user interface, and how to handle data security and control issues.

- **Chapter 9 – Data Design:** Chapter 9 focuses on the data design skills that are necessary for a systems analyst to construct the physical model of the information system.

- **Chapter 10 – System Architecture:** Chapter 10 describes system architecture, which translates the logical design of an information system into a physical blueprint.

Phase 4: Systems Implementation

- **Chapter 11 – Managing Systems Implementation:** Chapter 11 describes application development, documentation, testing, training, data conversion, and system change-over.

Phase 5: Systems Support and Security

- **Chapter 12 – Managing Systems Support and Security:** Chapter 12 describes systems support and security tasks that continue throughout the useful life of the system, including maintenance, security, backup and disaster recovery, performance measurement, and system obsolescence.

Toolkits

- **Toolkit Part A – Communication Tools:** Part A of the Toolkit discusses communication tools that can help the analyst write clearly, speak effectively, and deliver powerful presentations.

- **Toolkit Part B – CASE Tools:** Part B describes CASE tools that be can used to design, construct, and document an information system.

- **Toolkit Part C – Financial Analysis Tools:** Part C demonstrates financial analysis tools that can used to measure project feasibility, develop accurate cost-benefit estimates, and make sound decisions.

- **Toolkit Part D – Internet Resource Tools:** Part D describes Internet resource tools that can be used to locate information, obtain reference material, and monitor IT trends and developments.

FOR THE STUDENT

The Shelly Cashman Series wants all students to have a valuable learning experience that will provide the knowledge and skills you need to be successful. With that goal in mind, the presentation of material has been significantly streamlined throughout the book. There is now less distraction on the page and a clearer flow of topics. This should help students focus on the main content quickly and easily.

CHAPTER LEARNING TOOLS AND HOW THEY WILL HELP YOU

Dilbert: There is a saying that a picture is worth a thousand words. To illustrate this concept, each phase of the textbook begins with an eye-catching Dilbert© cartoon. If you're not familiar with Scott Adams' characters, you will quickly recognize their behavior in the workplace.

Case In Point: Each chapter includes four brief cases that focus on key issues.

A Question of Ethics: A realistic ethical issue is presented at the end of each chapter. These examples force you to examine your reactions and how you would respond to common workplace situations.

Chapter Exercises: Your answers to the ten Questions will show that you understand the key points. Five Discussion Topics and five Projects offer opportunities to dig deeper and learn even more.

Learn Online: CengageBrain.com is the premier destination for purchasing or renting Cengage Learning textbooks, eBooks, eChapters, and study tools at a significant discount. In addition, CengageBrain.com provides direct access to MindTap, which gives you the tools you need to get better grades, all in one place, all there when you need them.

FOR THE INSTRUCTOR

The Shelly Cashman Series is dedicated to providing you all of the tools you need to make your class a success. Information on all supplementary materials is available through your Cengage Learning representative or by calling one of the following telephone numbers: Colleges, Universities, Continuing Education Departments, Post-Secondary Vocational Schools, Career Colleges, Business, Industry, Government, Trade, Retailer, Wholesaler, Library, and Resellers, call Cengage Learning at 800-354-9706; K-12 Schools, Secondary and Vocational Schools, Adult Education, and School Districts, call Cengage Learning at 800-354-9706. In Canada, call Nelson Cengage Learning at 800-268-2222.

INSTRUCTOR COMPANION SITE

The Instructor Companion Site for this textbook includes both teaching and testing aids, and all are available for download at *sso.cengage.com*. The Instructor Resources include:

- **Instructor's Manual:** Includes lecture notes summarizing the chapter sections, figures and boxed elements found in every chapter, teacher tips, classroom activities, lab activities, and quick quizzes in Microsoft Word files.

- **Syllabus:** Easily customizable sample syllabus that covers policies, assignments, exams, and other course information. Also included is a Microsoft Project file used to create the five Phase Opener Gantt charts. An instructor can use this project file to create a visual syllabus that could include additional tasks, quizzes, and projects. The file also can be used to track class progress through the course. Instructors are welcome to distribute this file to students, and show them how to manage tasks, resources, and deadlines for team projects that might be assigned.

- **PowerPoint Presentations:** A multimedia lecture presentation system provides slides for each chapter, based on chapter objectives.

- **Figure Files:** Illustrations for every figure in the textbook in electronic form.

- **Solutions to Exercises:** Includes solutions for end-of-chapter exercises.

- **Test Bank & Test Engine:** Test Banks include questions for every chapter, and featuring objective-based and critical thinking question types, page number references, and figure references when appropriate. Cengage Learning Testing powered by Cognero is a flexible, online system that allows you to:

- Author, edit, and manage test bank content from multiple Cengage Learning solutions.

- Create multiple test versions in an instant.

- Deliver tests from your LMS, your classroom, or wherever you want!

- **Additional Activities for Students:** The forms that students can use to complete the Case Studies are included. Two additional case studies are also provided for every chapter, to be assigned as homework, extra credit, or assessment tools. Chapter Reinforcement Exercises, which are true/false, multiple-choice, and short answer questions that help students gain confidence in the material learned are included.

- **Additional Faculty Files:** Several sample solutions to case study tasks also are included. To install this program, you follow a simple registration process that entitles you to use the software and obtain support. Detailed instructions are provided on the Instructor Companion Site. Also included are Word document versions of the email and voice mail messages posted for students on the SCR website and the Interview Summaries for the New Century Case Study.

MINDTAP

MindTap is a personalized teaching experience with relevant assignments that guide students to analyze, apply, and improve thinking, allowing you to measure skills and outcomes with ease.

- Personalized Teaching: Becomes yours with a Learning Path that is built with key student objectives. Control what students see and when they see it. Use it as-is or match to your syllabus exactly—hide, rearrange, add, and create your own content.

- Guide Students: A unique learning path of relevant readings, multimedia and activities that move students up the learning taxonomy from basic knowledge and comprehension to analysis and application.

- Promote Better Outcomes: Empower instructors and motivate students with analytics and reports that provide a snapshot of class progress, time in course, engagement, and completion rates.

The MindTap for *Systems Analysis and Design* includes study tools, critical thinking challenges, and interactive quizzing, all integrated into an eReader that contains the full content from the printed text.

AUTHOR'S NOTE

Systems analysis and design is a disciplined process for creating high-quality enterprise information systems. An information system is an amalgam of people, data, and technology to provide support for business functions. As technology evolves, so does systems analysis.

A systems analyst is a valued team member who helps plan, develop, and maintain information systems. Analysts must be excellent communicators with strong analytical and critical thinking skills. They must also be business-savvy and technically competent, and be equally comfortable working with managers and programmers.

With the eleventh edition of *Systems Analysis and Design*, I have striven to cover the fundamental aspects of modern systems analysis and design, including both technical and non-technical issues. By far the most significant change with the eleventh edition of this textbook has been the streamlining of subject coverage, helping students focus on the main content quickly and easily. There is less distraction and a clearer flow of topics. That said, there is still a lot of material to cover, so students and faculty should not be surprised if they have to be judicious in their selection of topics to discuss in a typical semester.

On personal note, I would be remiss if I did not express my sincere gratitude to Harry Rosenblatt for involving me in this project several years ago. Our talks at the local coffee shop led to plans for co-authorship of the eleventh edition. Little did I know that Harry would be cruelly taken from us before work on the eleventh edition could begin. While writing this book I didn't have access to Harry's experience or wisdom to advise me, but I did have his enduring vision to guide me. Any errors or omissions in this edition of the textbook are purely my responsibility.

PUBLISHER'S NOTE

With the eleventh edition we are thrilled to welcome Scott Tilley to The Shelly Cashman Series author team. Scott is a professor at the Florida Institute of Technology (FIT), where he is director of computing education. He has a Ph.D. from the University of Victoria. He is an ACM Distinguished Lecturer. He writes the weekly "Technology Today" column for the *Florida Today* newspaper (Gannett). In addition to this book, he is the author of *Software Testing in the Cloud: Migration & Execution* (Springer, 2012), *Hard Problems in Software Testing: Solutions Using Testing as a Service* (Morgan & Claypool, 2014), *Testing iOS Apps with Hadoop Unit: Rapid Distributed GUI Testing* (Morgan & Claypool, 2014). Scott recently taught the Systems Analysis and Design course in the College of Business at FIT and used *Systems Analysis and Design, Tenth Edition*. He incorporated his students' feedback from this offering of the course to help shape his revision of the textbook.

ACKNOWLEDGMENTS

A book like *Systems Analysis and Design* would not be possible without the help and support of a great many people. First and foremost, I want to thank Harry Rosenblatt for providing the solid foundation upon which the eleventh edition of this textbook was built.

A very special "Thank You" to Deb Kaufmann, the textbook's development editor, whose insight and suggestions were extremely valuable. Thanks also to the reviewers who provided feedback that shaped each chapter: Melisa "Joey" Bryant, Forsyth Technical Community College; Paul Dadosky, Ivy Technical Community College; Barbara Myers, Dakota State University; and Teresa Shorter, Guilford Technical Community College.

The support of the entire production team is greatly appreciated. Thanks to Kate Mason, Alyssa Pratt, and Stacey Lamodi at Cengage Learning, and Arul Joseph Raj at Lumina Datamatics.

Finally, sincere thanks to the instructors and students who offered feedback and comments. I have tried to address your concerns and incorporate your suggestions. I will certainly continue to listen carefully. Feel free to contact me via email at scott@srtilley.com.

ABOUT OUR COVERS

The Shelly Cashman Series is continually updating our approach and content to reflect the way today's students learn and experience new technologies. This focus on student success is reflected on this textbook's cover, which features imagery informed by new technologies, such as apps and mobile devices, cloud computing, and ubiquitous networks. When you use the Shelly Cashman Series, you can be assured that you are learning computing skills using the most effective courseware available.

PHASE

SYSTEMS PLANNING

DELIVERABLE
Preliminary investigation report

TOOLKIT SUPPORT
Communications and financial analysis tools

As the Dilbert cartoon suggests, it is always a good idea to know whether a project fits the company's overall strategy. A systems project that does not align with corporate strategies should not be approved. The role of an information system is to support business goals.

Systems planning is the first of five phases in the systems development life cycle. Chapter 1 provides an introduction to systems analysis and design by describing the role of information technology in today's dynamic business environment. Chapter 2 explains how systems projects get started and how to evaluate a project proposal to determine its feasibility. Chapter 3 describes how to use project management tools and techniques, and how to plan, schedule, monitor, and report on IT projects.

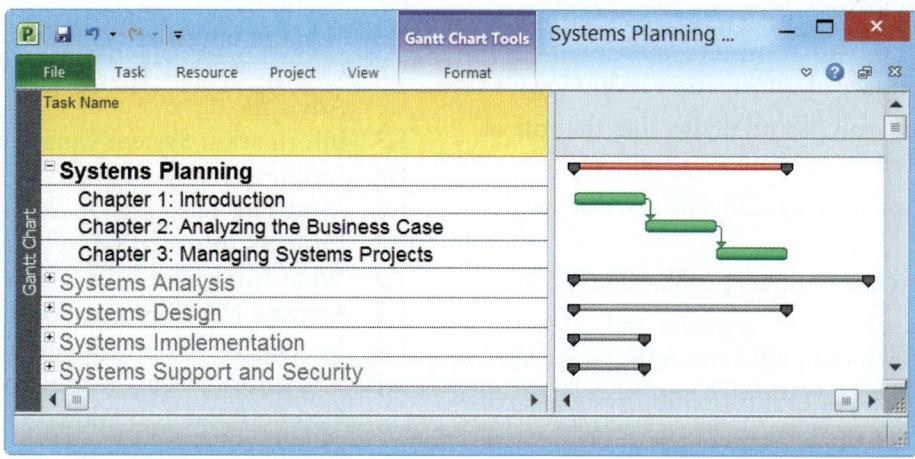

1

CHAPTER 1

Introduction to Systems Analysis and Design

Chapter 1 is the first of three chapters in the systems planning phase. This chapter describes the role of information technology in today's dynamic business environment. This chapter describes the development of information systems, systems analysis and design concepts, and various systems development methods. This chapter also describes the role of the information technology department and its people.

The chapter includes four "Case in Point" discussion questions to help contextualize the concepts described in the text. The "Question of Ethics" invites examination of the ACM's code of ethics and those of a developing systems analyst.

LEARNING OBJECTIVES

When you finish this chapter, you should be able to:

- Describe the impact of information technology

- Define systems analysis and design and the role of a systems analyst

- Define an information system and describe its components

- Explain how to use business profiles and models

- Explain Internet business strategies and relationships, including B2C and B2B

- Identify various types of information systems and explain who uses them

- Distinguish among structured analysis, object-oriented analysis, and agile methods

- Explain the waterfall model, and how it has evolved

- Discuss the role of the information technology department and the systems analysts who work there

CHAPTER CONTENTS

1.1 INTRODUCTION

The headlines in Figure 1-1 offer dramatic examples of how information technology affects our society. Companies use information as a way to increase productivity, deliver quality products and services, maintain customer loyalty, and make sound decisions. In a global economy with intense competition, information technology can mean the difference between success and failure.

1.2 WHAT IS INFORMATION TECHNOLOGY?

Information technology (IT) refers to the combination of hardware, software, and services that people use to manage, communicate, and share information. Although fictitious, the bold headlines in Figure 1-1 illustrate the huge impact of IT on our society.

FIGURE I-I These headlines illustrate the enormous impact of information technology on our lives.

More than ever, business success depends on information technology. IT is driving a new digital economy, where advances in hardware, software, and connectivity can provide enormous benefits to businesses and individuals. Although economic trends affect IT spending levels, most companies give IT budgets a high priority, in good times or bad. The reason is simple: During periods of growth, companies cannot afford to lag behind the IT curve. Conversely, when the economy slows down, firms often use IT to reduce operating costs and improve efficiency.

The following sections provide a sense of IT history, an overview of systems analysis and design, and a description of the system analyst's role.

1.2.1 The Changing Nature of Information Technology

The history of IT is a fascinating study of human progress and achievement. We are dazzled by the latest and greatest technology, just as our parents and grandparents were astonished by the arrival of television, space flight, and personal computing. It is important for IT professionals, who live and work in this exciting world, to realize that each technology advance is part of a long-term process that often brings dramatic change, but never really ends. The story of IBM is a good example.

As its name suggests, International Business Machines was a major supplier of office equipment and typewriters long before the modern computer era. Herman Hollerith, who invented a card that identified characters by the location of punched holes, founded IBM's predecessor company in 1896. A deck of hundreds or even thousands of these cards could store data that was easily sorted, queried, and printed by machines. This system sounds archaic now, but punch card technology was a huge advance that revolutionized the business world, and was in use into the 1960s and beyond.

Today, IBM is a globe-spanning company with several hundred thousand employees. It has succeeded in part by constantly adapting to its changing business environment. For example, while it was once known primarily as a hardware company, today IBM makes a significant part of its revenue from software and services. It also invests

FIGURE 1-2 An employee clocking in with a punch card in 1953.

ClassicStock.com/Superstock

in its people and tries to hire the best talent available. It has more patents and more Noble Prize winners than any other IT company in history.

Figure 1-2 shows an employee clocking in with a punch card in 1953. Nowadays, most forward-thinking IT firms do not require their employees to "punch in" at all. Working from home, "hoteling" using random offices as needed, and global contracting has dramatically changed the definition of "being at work." No doubt future students will view our current technology the same way we smile at punched cards.

1.2.2 Systems Analysis and Design

Systems analysis and design is a step-by-step process for developing high-quality information systems. An information system combines technology, people, and data to provide support for business functions such as order processing, inventory control, human resources, accounting, and many more. Some information systems handle routine day-to-day tasks, while others can help managers make better decisions, spot marketplace trends, and reveal patterns that might be hidden in stored data.

Talented people, including a mix of managers, users, network administrators, web designers, programmers, and systems analysts, typically develop information systems. Capable IT professionals like these are always in demand, even in a slow economy. For example, notice how many positions related to information technology and information systems are available in the Melbourne, Florida area, as shown on Monster .com's job search website in Figure 1-3.

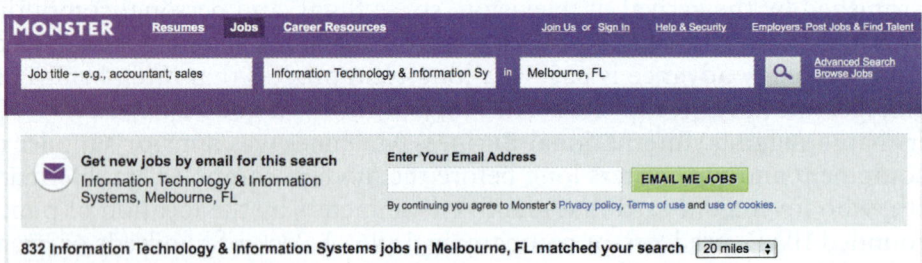

FIGURE 1-3 Monster.com is an example of an online job search website that IT professionals can use.

Source: Monster.com

1.2.3 What Does a Systems Analyst Do?

A systems analyst is a valued member of the IT department team who helps plan, develop, and maintain information systems. Analysts must be excellent communicators with strong analytical and critical thinking skills. Because systems analysts transform business requirements into IT projects, they must be business-savvy as well as technically competent, and be equally comfortable with managers and programmers, who sometimes have different points of view.

Most companies assign systems analysts to the IT department, but analysts also can report to a specific user area such as marketing, sales, or accounting. As a member of a functional team, an analyst is better able to understand the needs of that group and how IT supports the department's mission. Smaller companies often use consultants to perform systems analysis work on an as-needed basis.

On any given day, an analyst might be asked to document business processes, test hardware and software packages, design input screens, train users, and plan ecommerce websites. A systems analyst may occasionally manage IT projects, including tasks, resources, schedules, and costs. To keep managers and users informed, the analyst conducts meetings, delivers presentations, and writes memos, reports, and documentation.

The last section in this chapter lists typical skills and education requirements, certifications, career opportunities, and the possible impact of future IT trends for systems analysts.

CASE IN POINT 1.1:   CLOUD NINE FINANCIAL ADVISORS

Cloud Nine provides its clients with a monthly newsletter that offers recommendations about stocks to buy or sell. Doug Layton, Cloud Nine's president, has asked your opinion on whether dot-com stocks might be good investments for the future. He specifically mentioned Google, eBay, Amazon.com, and Yahoo!, but he said you could suggest other companies. Doug wants you to do some Internet research to learn more about these web-based companies and their future prospects. You can use a search engine or start by visiting the websites of publications such as *Forbes*, *Fortune Magazine*, *Business Week*, or *The Wall Street Journal*, among others.

1.3 INFORMATION SYSTEM COMPONENTS

A system is a set of related components that produces specific results. For example, specialized systems route Internet traffic, manufacture microchips, and control complex entities like the Hubble Telescope, which took the amazing image shown in Figure 1-4. A mission-critical system is one that is vital to a company's operations. An order processing system, for example, is mission-critical because the company cannot do business without it.

Every system requires input data. For example, a computer receives data when a key is pressed or when a menu command is selected. In an information system, data consists of basic facts that are the system's raw material. Information is data that has been transformed into output that is valuable to users.

An information system has five key components, as shown in Figure 1-5: hardware, software, data, processes, and people.

FIGURE I-4 Consider the amazing technology that enabled the Hubble telescope to capture this image.
Courtesy of The Hubble Heritage Team (AURA/STScI/NASA)

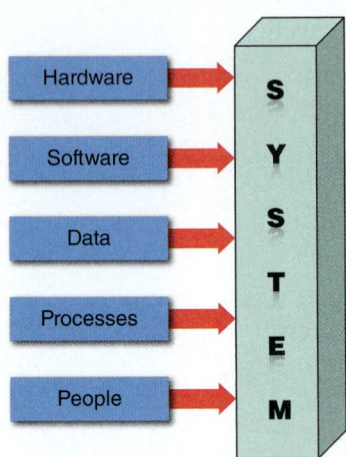

FIGURE 1-5 An information system needs these components.

1.3.1 Hardware

Hardware consists of everything in the physical layer of the information system. For example, hardware can include servers, workstations, networks, telecommunications equipment, fiber-optic cables, mobile devices, scanners, digital capture devices, and other technology-based infrastructure. A large concentration of servers working together is called a server farm. As new technologies emerge, manufacturers race to market the innovations and reap the rewards.

Hardware purchasers today face a wide array of technology choices and decisions. In 1965, Gordon Moore, a cofounder of Intel, predicted that the number of transistors on an integrated circuit chip would double about every 24 months. His concept, called Moore's Law, has remained valid for 50 years. Fortunately, as hardware became more powerful, it also became much less expensive. Large businesses with thousands or millions of sales transactions require company-wide information systems and powerful servers, which are often now in the cloud, such as those shown in Figure 1-6.

FIGURE 1-6 Server farms provide the enormous power and speed that modern IT systems need.
dotshock/Shutterstock.com

1.3.2 Software

Software refers to the programs that control the hardware and produce the desired information or results. Software consists of system software and application software.

System software manages the hardware components, which can include a single computer or a global network with many thousands of clients. Either the hardware manufacturer supplies the system software or a company purchases it from a vendor. Examples of system software include the operating system, security software that protects the computer from intrusion, device drivers that communicate with hardware such as printers, and utility programs that handle specific tasks such as data backup and disk management. System software also controls the flow of data, provides data security, and manages network operations. In today's interconnected business world, network software is vitally important.

Application software consists of programs that support day-to-day business functions and provide users with the information they need. Examples of company-wide applications, called enterprise applications, include order processing systems, payroll systems, and company communications networks. On a smaller scale, individual users can boost productivity with tools such as spreadsheets, presentation software, and database management systems.

Application software includes horizontal and vertical systems. A horizontal system is a system, such as an inventory or a payroll application, that can be adapted for use in many different types of companies. A vertical system is designed to meet the unique requirements of a specific business or industry, such as an online retailer, a medical practice, or an auto dealership.

Most companies use a mix of software that is acquired at various times. When planning an information system, a company must consider how a new system will interface with older systems, which are called legacy systems. For example, a new human resources system might need to exchange data with a legacy payroll application.

1.3.3 Data

Data is the raw material that an information system transforms into useful information. An information system can store data in various locations, called tables. By linking the tables, the system can display the specific information that the user needs—no more, and no less. Figure 1-7 shows a payroll system that stores data in four separate tables. Notice that the linked tables work together to supply 19 different data items to the screen. A user can display any or all data items and filter the data to fit defined limits. In this example, the user requested a list of employees who live in a certain city and worked more than 40 hours in the last pay period. Jane Doe's name was the first to display.

1.3.4 Processes

Processes describe the tasks and business functions that users, managers, and IT staff members perform to achieve specific results. Processes are the building blocks of an information system because they represent actual day-to-day business operations. To build a successful information system, analysts must understand business processes and document them carefully.

1.3.5 People

People who have an interest in an information system are called stakeholders. Stakeholders include the management group responsible for the system, the users (sometimes called end users) inside and outside the company who will interact with the system, and IT staff members, such as systems analysts, programmers, and network administrators who develop and support the system.

Each stakeholder group has a vital interest in the information system, but most experienced IT professionals agree that the success or failure of a system usually depends on whether it meets the needs of its users. For that reason, it is essential to understand user requirements and expectations throughout the development process.

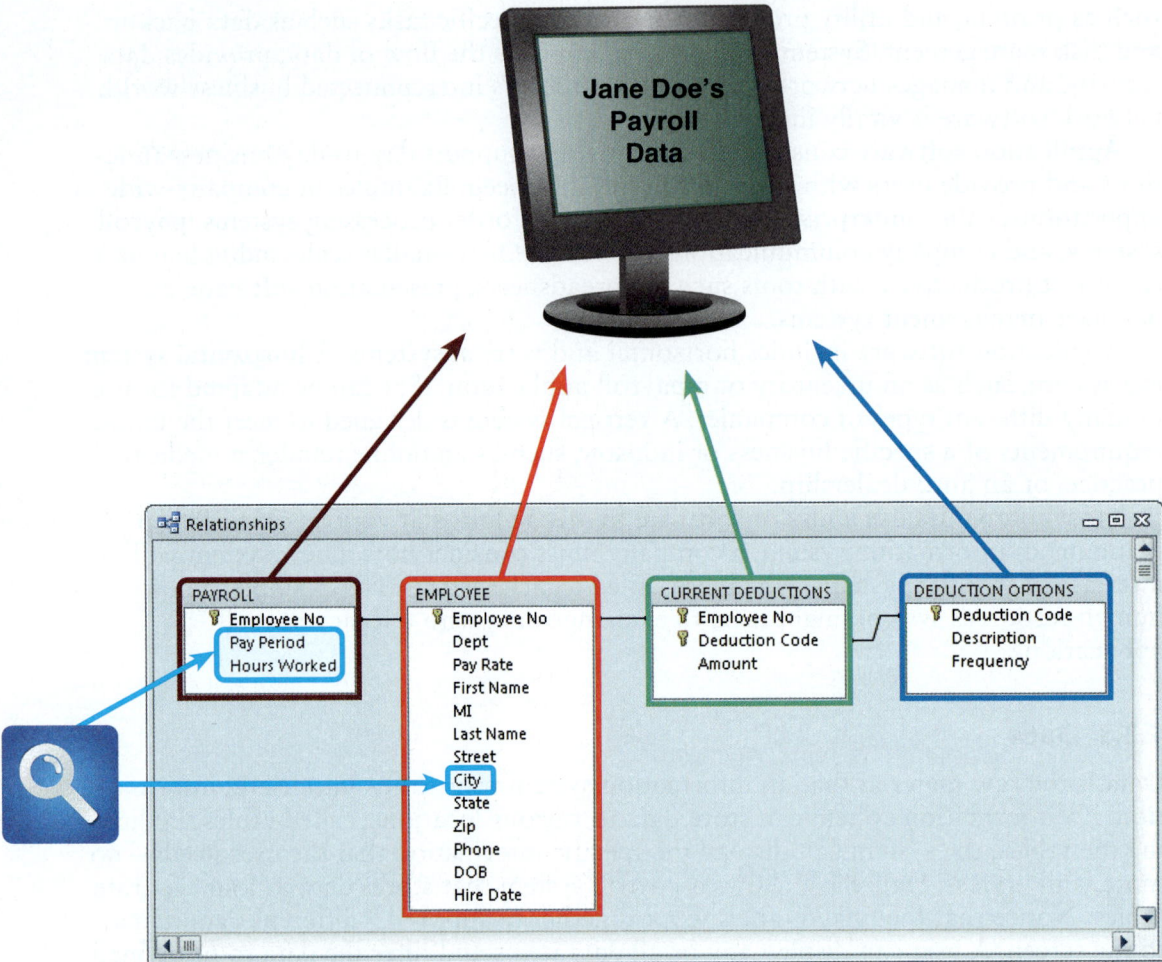

FIGURE 1-7 In a typical payroll system, data is stored in separate tables that are linked to form an overall database.

1.4 BUSINESS TODAY

To design successful systems, systems analysts must understand a company's business operations. Each situation is different. For example, a retail store, a medical practice, and a hotel chain all have unique information systems requirements. As the business world changes, systems analysts can expect to work in new kinds of companies that will require innovative IT solutions.

Business today is being shaped by three major trends: rapidly increasing globalization, technology integration for seamless information access across a wide variety of devices such as laptops and smartphones, and the rapid growth of cloud-based computing and software services. These trends are being driven by the immense power of the Internet.

1.4.1 The Internet Model

Internet-based commerce is called **ecommerce (electronic commerce)**. Internet-based systems involve various hardware and software designs, but a typical model is a series of webpages that provides a user interface, which communicates with database management software and a web-based data server. On mobile devices, the user interacts with the system with an **app**, but the same back-end services are accessed. As Internet-based commerce continues to grow, career opportunities will expand significantly for IT professionals such as web designers, database developers, and systems analysts.

Ecommerce includes two main sectors: **B2C (business-to-consumer)** and **B2B (business-to-business)**. Within these broad categories, competition is dynamic, extreme, and global. Every day brings new ideas, new players, and new ways to involve customers, suppliers, and hordes of social network participants. The following sections discuss this rapidly changing environment.

1.4.2 B2C (Business-to-Consumer)

Using the Internet, consumers can go online to purchase an enormous variety of products and services. This new shopping environment allows customers to do research, compare prices and features, check availability, arrange delivery, and choose payment methods in a single convenient session. Many companies, such as airlines, offer incentives for online transactions because web-based processing costs are lower than traditional methods. By making flight information available online to last-minute travelers, some airlines also offer special discounts on seats that might otherwise go unfilled.

B2C commerce is changing traditional business models and creating new ones. For example, a common business model is a retail store that sells a product to a customer. To carry out that same transaction on the Internet, the company must develop an online store and deal with a totally different set of marketing, advertising, and profitability issues.

Some companies have found new ways to use established business models. For example, eBay.com has transformed a traditional auction concept into a popular and successful method of selling goods and services. Other retailers seek to enhance the online shopping experience by offering gift advisors, buying guides, how-to clinics, and similar features. In the ecommerce battles, the real winners are online consumers, who have more information, better choices, and the convenience of shopping at home.

1.4.3 B2B (Business-to-Business)

Although the business-to-consumer (B2C) sector is more familiar to retail customers, the volume of business-to-business (B2B) transactions is many times greater. Industry observers predict that B2B sales will increase sharply as more firms seek to improve efficiency and reduce costs.

Initially, electronic commerce between two companies used a data sharing arrangement called **electronic data interchange (EDI)**. EDI enabled computer-to-computer data transfer, usually over private telecommunications lines. Firms used EDI to plan production, adjust inventory levels, or stock up on raw materials using data from another company's information system. As B2B volume soared, company-to-company transactions migrated to the Internet, which offered standard protocols, universal availability, and low communication costs. The main advantage of the web is that it offers seamless communication between different hardware and software environments, anywhere and anytime.

Because it allows companies to reach the global marketplace, B2B is especially important to smaller suppliers and customers who need instant information about prices and availability. In an approach that resembles an open marketplace, some B2B sites invite buyers, sellers, distributors, and manufacturers to offer products, submit specifications, and transact business.

Most large firms and government agencies use supply chain management (SCM) software. A supply chain refers to all the companies who provide materials, services, and functions needed to provide a product to a customer. For example, a Sherwin-Williams customer who buys a gallon of paint is at the end of a chain that includes the raw material sources, packaging suppliers, manufacturers, transporters, warehouses, and retail stores. Because SCM is complex and dynamic, specialized software helps businesses manage inventory levels, costs, alternate suppliers, and much more.

1.5 MODELING BUSINESS OPERATIONS

Systems analysts use modeling to represent company operations and information needs. Business process modeling involves a business profile and a set of models that document business operations.

1.5.1 Business Profiles

A business profile is an overview of a company's mission, functions, organization, products, services, customers, suppliers, competitors, constraints, and future direction. Although much of this information is readily available, a systems analyst usually needs to do additional research and fact-finding. A business profile is the starting point for the modeling process.

1.5.2 Business Processes

A business process is a specific set of transactions, events, and results that can be described and documented. A business process model (BPM) graphically displays one or more business processes, such as handling an airline reservation, filling a product order, or updating a customer account. The sales order example in Figure 1-8 shows a simple model that includes an event, three processes, and a result.

A rough sketch might be sufficient to document a simple business process. For complex models, analysts can choose computer-based tools that use business process modeling notation (BPMN). BPMN includes standard shapes and symbols to represent events, processes, workflows, and more. Multipurpose application such as Microsoft Visio, CASE tools such as Visible Analyst, or online diagramming tools such as draw.io can be used to create BPMN models. Notice that the draw.io model in Figure 1-9 uses BPMN symbols to represent the same sales order process shown in Figure 1-8.

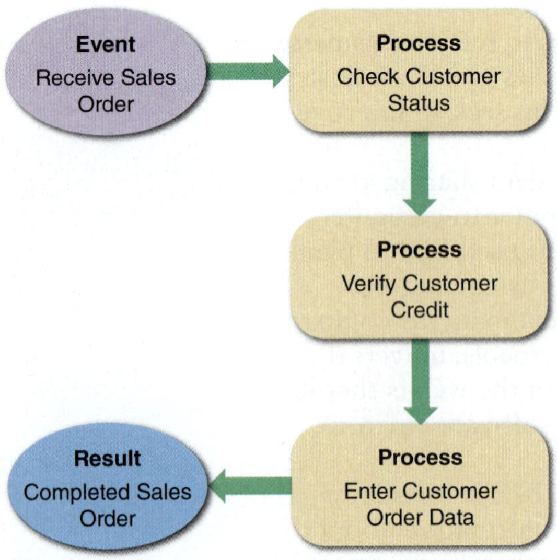

1.6 BUSINESS INFORMATION SYSTEMS

In the past, IT managers identified an information system based on its primary users. For example, administrative staff used *office systems*, operational people used *operational systems*, middle managers used *decision support systems*, and top managers used *executive information systems*.

Event
Receive Sales Order

Process
Check Customer Status

Process
Verify Customer Credit

Process
Enter Customer Order Data

Result
Completed Sales Order

FIGURE 1-8 A simple business model might consist of an event, three processes, and a result.

Today, those traditional labels no longer apply. For example, all employees, including top managers, use office productivity systems to do their jobs. Similarly, operational users often require decision support systems to do their jobs. As business changes, information use also changes, and now it makes more sense to identify a system by its functions and features, rather than by its users. A new set of system definitions includes enterprise computing systems, transaction processing systems, business support systems, knowledge management systems, and user productivity systems.

1.6.1 Enterprise Computing

Enterprise computing refers to information systems that support company-wide operations and data management requirements. Wal-Mart's inventory control system, Boeing's production control system, and Hilton Hotels' reservation system are examples of enterprise computing systems. The main objective of enterprise computing is to integrate a company's primary functions (such as production, sales, services, inventory control, and accounting) to improve efficiency, reduce costs, and help managers make key decisions. Enterprise computing also improves data security and reliability by imposing a company-wide framework for data access and storage.

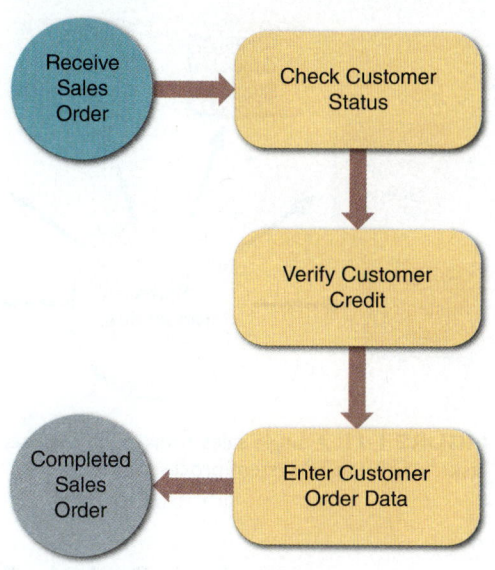

FIGURE 1-9 This sample uses business process modeling notation (BPMN) to represent the same events, processes, and workflow shown in Figure 1-8.
Source: Drawio.com

In many large companies, applications called **enterprise resource planning (ERP)** systems provide cost-effective support for users and managers throughout the company. For example, a car rental company can use ERP to forecast customer demand for rental cars at hundreds of locations. Because of its growth and potential, many hardware and software vendors target the enterprise computing market and offer a wide array of products and services. For example, Figure 1-10 highlights Microsoft Dynamics as an ERP solution that can boost productivity.

By providing a company-wide computing environment, many firms have been able to achieve dramatic cost reductions. Other companies have been disappointed in the time, money, and commitment necessary to implement ERP successfully. A potential disadvantage is that ERP systems generally impose an overall structure that might or might not match the way a company operates. ERP is described in more detail in Chapter 7, which discusses development strategies.

1.6.2 Transaction Processing

Transaction processing (TP) systems process data generated by day-to-day business operations. Examples of TP systems include customer order processing, accounts receivable, and warranty claim processing.

FIGURE 1-10 Microsoft Dynamics is an example of an ERP solution that can boost productivity.
Source: Microsoft Corporation

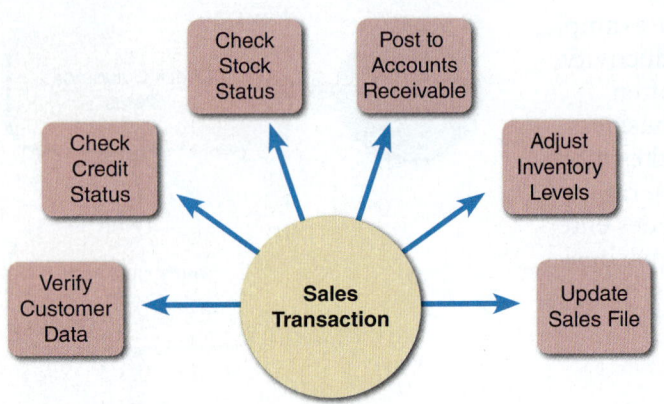

FIGURE 1-11 A single sales transaction consists of six separate tasks, which the TP system processes as a group.

TP systems perform a series of tasks whenever a specific transaction occurs. In the example shown in Figure 1-11, a TP system verifies the customer's data, checks the customer's credit status, checks the stock status, posts to accounts receivable, adjusts the inventory level, and updates the sales file. TP systems typically involve large amounts of data and are mission-critical systems because the enterprise cannot function without them.

TP systems are efficient because they process a set of transaction-related commands as a group rather than individually. To protect data integrity, however, TP systems ensure that if any single element of a transaction fails, the system does not process the rest of the transaction.

1.6.3 Business Support

Business support systems provide job-related information support to users at all levels of a company. These systems can analyze transactional data, generate information needed to manage and control business processes, and provide information that leads to better decision making.

The earliest business computer systems replaced manual tasks, such as payroll processing. Companies soon realized that computers also could produce valuable information. The new systems were called **management information systems (MIS)** because managers were the primary users. Today, employees at *all* levels need information to perform their jobs, and they rely on information systems for that support.

A business support system can work hand in hand with a TP system. For example, when a company sells merchandise to a customer, a TP system records the sale, updates the customer's balance, and makes a deduction from inventory. A related business support system highlights slow- or fast-moving items, customers with past-due balances, and inventory levels that need adjustment.

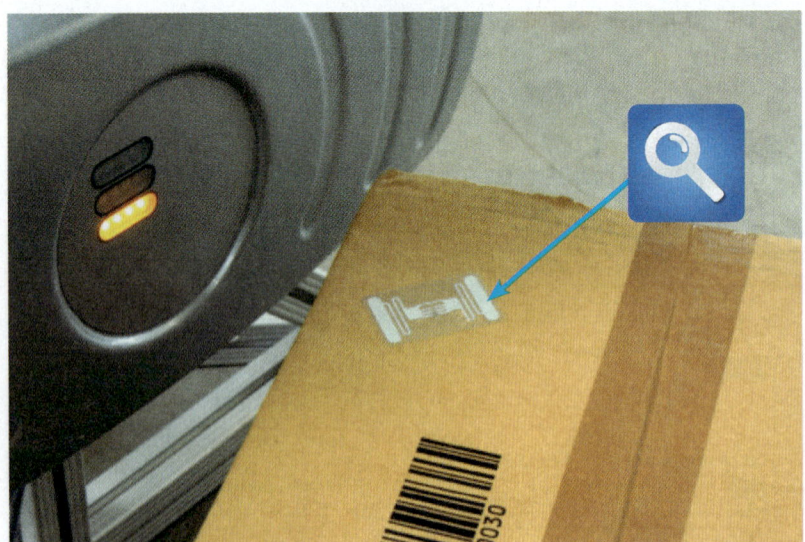

FIGURE 1-12 With an RFID tag, items can be tracked and monitored throughout the shipping process.

© nullplus/photos.com

To compete effectively, firms must collect production, sales, and shipping data and update the company-wide business support system immediately. The newest development in data acquisition is called **radio frequency identification (RFID)** technology, which uses high-frequency radio waves to track physical objects, such as the item shown in Figure 1-12. Major retailers such as Wal-Mart, which requires its suppliers to add RFID tags to all items, have fueled RFID's dramatic growth.

An important feature of a business support system is decision support capability. Decision support helps users make decisions by creating a computer model and applying a set of variables. For example, a truck fleet dispatcher might run a series of what-if scenarios to determine the impact of increased shipments or bad weather. Alternatively, a retailer might use what-if analysis to determine the price it must charge to increase profits by a specific amount while volume and costs remain unchanged.

1.6.4 Knowledge Management

Knowledge management systems use a large database called a **knowledge base** that allows users to find information by entering keywords or questions in normal English phrases. A knowledge management system uses **inference rules**, which are logical rules that identify data patterns and relationships.

The WolframAlpha website, shown in Figure 1-13, describes itself as a "computational knowledge engine." It has a sophisticated natural language front end that understands user queries in several

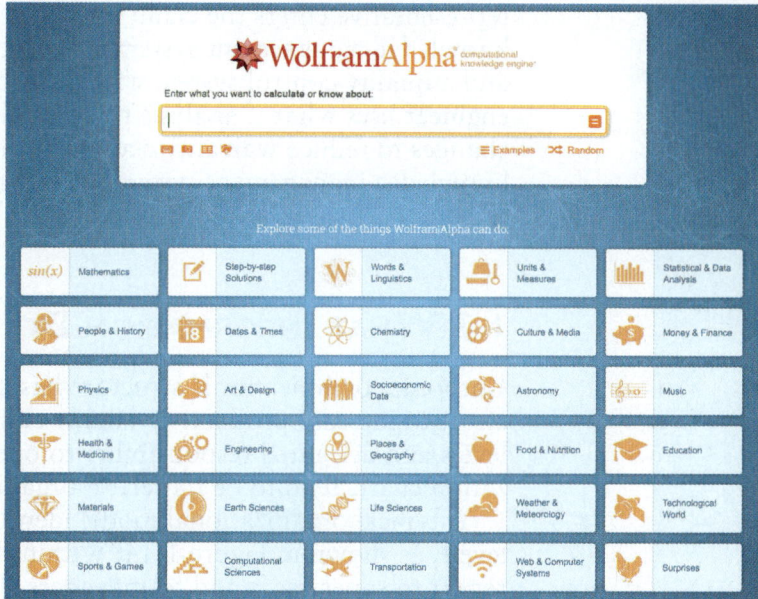

FIGURE 1-13 WolframAlpha describes itself as a "computational knowledge engine."
Source: WolframAlpha

domains (shown in the figure). It relies upon a large knowledge base spanning multiple websites and its own proprietary algorithms to provide users with detailed answers to their questions on many different topics. The results are displayed using a mix of multimedia, including mathematical equations if appropriate.

1.6.5 User Productivity

Companies provide employees at all levels with technology that improves productivity. Examples of **user productivity systems** include email, voice mail, video and web conferencing, word processing, automated calendars, database management, spreadsheets, desktop publishing, presentation graphics, company intranets, and integrated mobile computing systems. User productivity systems also include groupware. **Groupware** programs enable users to share data, collaborate on projects, and work in teams.

When companies first installed word processing systems, managers expected to reduce the number of employees as office efficiency increased. That did not happen, primarily because the basic nature of clerical work changed. With computers performing the repetitive work, office personnel were able to handle tasks that required more judgment, decision making, and access to information.

Computer-based office work expanded rapidly as companies assigned more responsibility to employees at lower organizational levels. Relatively inexpensive hardware, powerful networks, corporate downsizing, and a move toward employee empowerment also contributed to this trend. Today, administrative assistants and company presidents alike are networked, use computer workstations, and share corporate data to perform their jobs.

1.6.6 Systems Integration

Most large companies require systems that combine transaction processing, business support, knowledge management, and user productivity features. For example, suppose an international customer makes a warranty claim. A customer service representative enters the claim into a TP system, which updates two other systems: a knowledge management system that tracks product problems and warranty activity, and a quality control system with decision support capabilities. A quality control engineer uses what-if analysis to determine if the firm should make product design changes to reduce warranty claims. In this example, a TP system is integrated with a knowledge management system and a business support system with decision support features.

1.7 WHAT INFORMATION DO USERS NEED?

Corporate organizational structure has changed considerably in recent years. In an effort to increase productivity, many companies reduced the number of management levels and delegated responsibility to operational personnel. Although modern organization charts tend to be flatter, an organizational hierarchy still exists in most firms.

A typical organizational model identifies business functions and organizational levels, as shown in Figure 1-14. Within the functional areas, operational personnel report to supervisors and team leaders. The next level includes middle managers and knowledge workers, who, in turn, report to top managers. In a corporate structure, the top managers report to a board of directors elected by the company's shareholders.

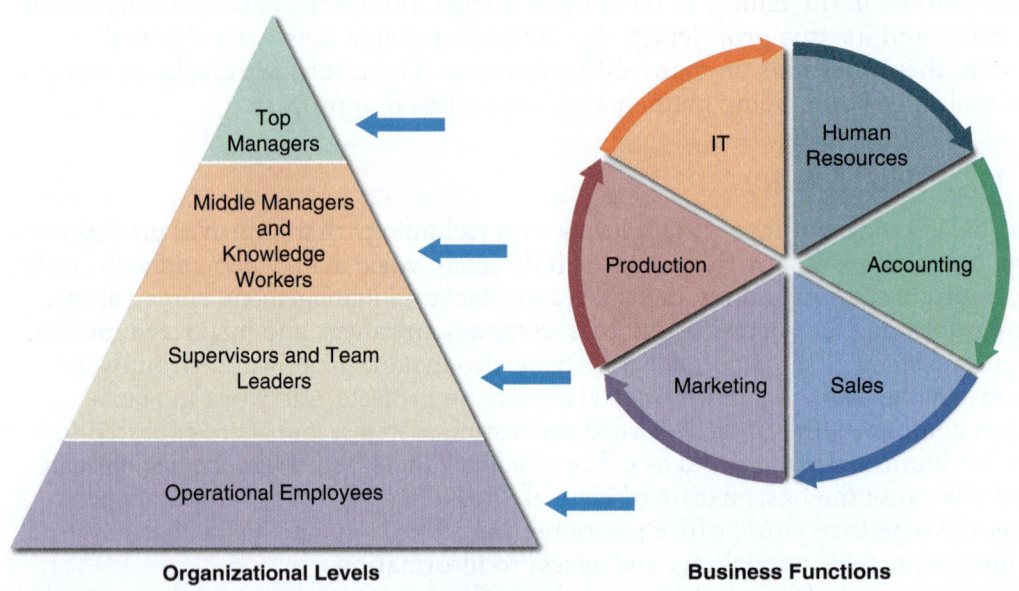

Organizational Levels   **Business Functions**

FIGURE 1-14 A typical organizational model identifies business functions and organizational levels.

A systems analyst must understand the company's organizational model to recognize who is responsible for specific processes and decisions and to be aware of what information is required by whom.

1.7.1 Top Managers

Top managers develop long-range plans, called strategic plans, which define the company's overall mission and goals. To plot a future course, top managers ask questions such as "How much should the company invest in information technology?" or

"How much will Internet sales grow in the next five years?" or "Should the company build new factories or contract out production functions?"

Strategic planning affects the company's future survival and growth, including long-term IT plans. Top managers focus on the overall business enterprise and use IT to set the company's course and direction. To develop a strategic plan, top managers also need information from outside the company, such as economic forecasts, technology trends, competitive threats, and governmental issues.

1.7.2 Middle Managers and Knowledge Workers

Just below the top management level, most companies have a layer of middle managers and knowledge workers. Middle managers provide direction, necessary resources, and performance feedback to supervisors and team leaders. Because they focus on a somewhat shorter time frame, middle managers need more detailed information than top managers, but somewhat less than supervisors who oversee day-to-day operations. For example, a middle manager might review a weekly sales summary for a three-state area, whereas a local sales team leader would need a daily report on customer sales at a single location.

In addition to middle managers, every company has people called knowledge workers. Knowledge workers include systems analysts, programmers, accountants, researchers, trainers, human resource specialists, and other professionals. Knowledge workers also use business support systems, knowledge management systems, and user productivity systems. Knowledge workers provide support for the organization's basic functions. Just as a military unit requires logistical support, a successful company needs knowledge workers to carry out its mission.

1.7.3 Supervisors and Team Leaders

Supervisors, often called team leaders, oversee operational employees and carry out day-to-day functions. They coordinate operational tasks and people, make necessary decisions, and ensure that the right tools, materials, and training are available. Like other managers, supervisors and team leaders need decision support information, knowledge management systems, and user productivity systems to carry out their responsibilities.

1.7.4 Operational Employees

Operational employees include users who rely on transaction processing systems to enter and receive data they need to perform their jobs. In many companies, operational users also need information to handle tasks and make decisions that were assigned previously to supervisors. This trend, called empowerment, gives employees more responsibility and accountability. Many companies find that empowerment improves employee motivation and increases customer satisfaction.

1.8 SYSTEMS DEVELOPMENT TOOLS

In addition to understanding business operations, systems analysts must know how to use a variety of techniques, such as modeling, prototyping, and computer-aided systems engineering tools to plan, design, and implement information systems. Systems analysts work with these tools in a team environment, where input from users, managers, and IT staff contributes to the system design.

1.8.1 Modeling

Modeling produces a graphical representation of a concept or process that systems developers can analyze, test, and modify. A systems analyst can describe and simplify an information system by using a set of business, data, object, network, and process models.

A **business model** describes the information that a system must provide. Analysts also create models to represent data, objects, networks, and other system components. Although the models might appear to overlap, they actually work together to describe the same environment from different points of view.

System developers often use multipurpose charting tools such as Microsoft Visio to display business-related models. Visio is a popular tool that systems analysts can use to create business process diagrams, flowcharts, organization charts, network diagrams, floor plans, project timelines, and work flow diagrams, among others. Figure 1-15 shows how to drag and drop various symbols from the left pane into the drawing on the right, and connect them to show a business process. There are similar online tools for drawing business-related models, such as draw.io.

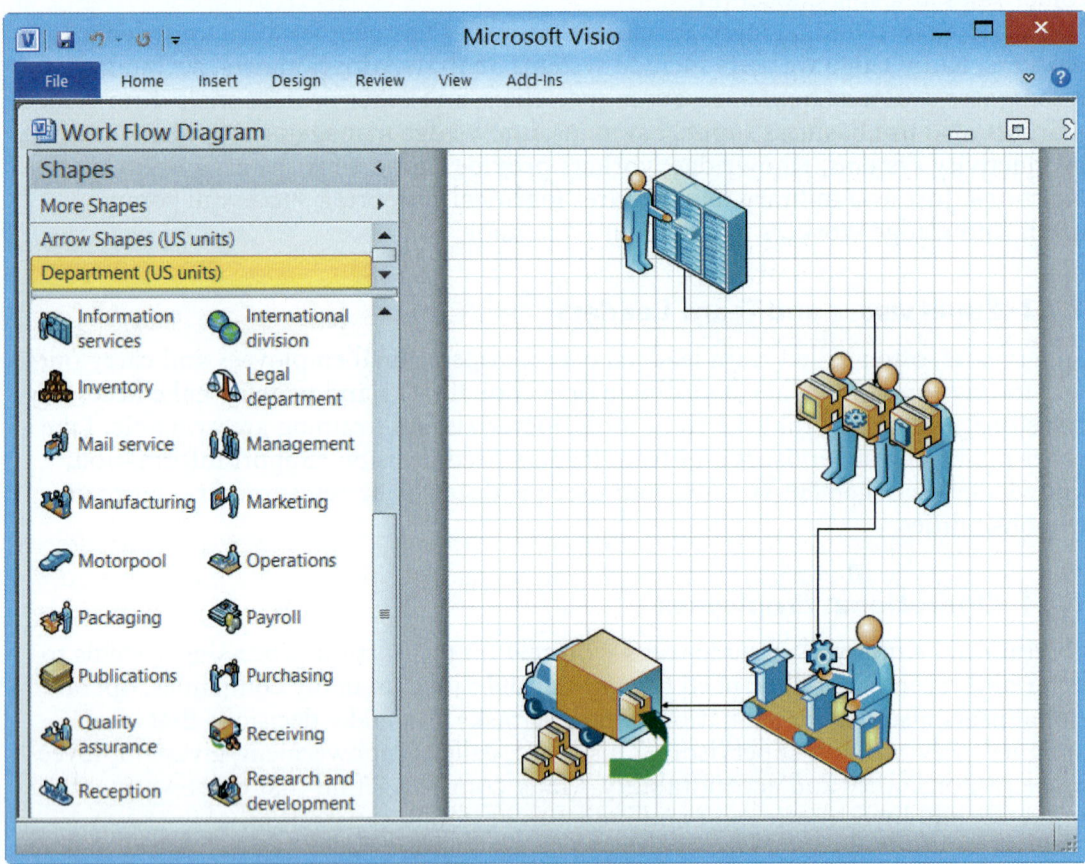

FIGURE 1-15 Microsoft Visio allows you to drag and drop various symbols and connect them to model a business process.
Source: Microsoft Visio 2010

1.8.2 Prototyping

Prototyping tests system concepts and provides an opportunity to examine input, output, and user interfaces before final decisions are made. A **prototype** is an early working version of an information system. Just as an aircraft manufacturer tests a new design in a wind tunnel, systems analysts construct and study information system prototypes. A prototype can serve as an initial model that is used as a benchmark to evaluate the finished system, or the prototype itself can develop into the final version of the system. Either way, prototyping speeds up the development process significantly.

A possible disadvantage of prototyping is that important decisions might be made too early, before business or IT issues are understood thoroughly. A prototype based on careful fact-finding and modeling techniques, however, can be an extremely valuable tool.

1.8.3 Computer-Aided Systems Engineering (CASE) Tools

Computer-aided systems engineering (CASE), also called **computer-aided software engineering**, is a technique that uses powerful software, called **CASE tool**, to help systems analysts develop and maintain information systems. CASE tools provide an overall framework for systems development and support a wide variety of design methodologies, including structured analysis and object-oriented analysis.

Because CASE tools make it easier to build an information system, they boost IT productivity and improve the quality of the finished product. After developing a model, many CASE tools can generate program code, which speeds the implementation process. Figure 1-16 shows the website for Visible Systems Corporation, a CASE tool vendor.

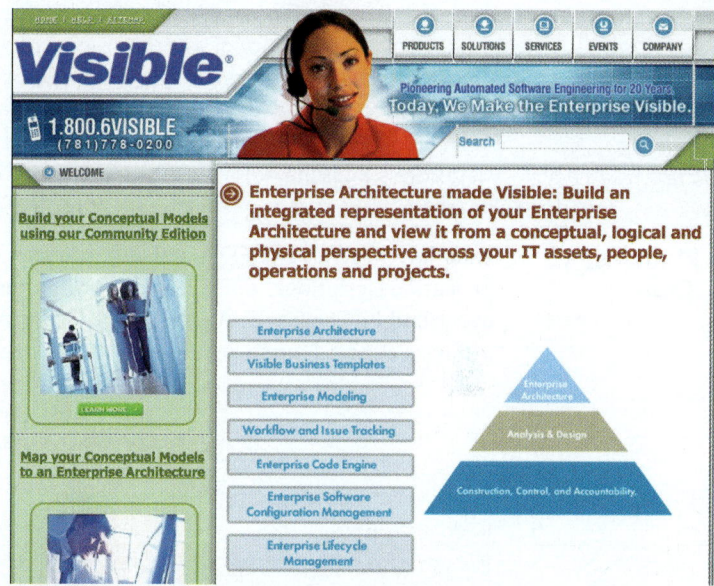

FIGURE 1-16 Visible Systems Corporation offers several software engineering tools, including Visible Analyst, a popular CASE tool.
Source: Visible Systems Corporation

1.9 SYSTEMS DEVELOPMENT METHODS

Many options exist for developing information systems, but the most popular alternatives are **structured analysis**, which is a traditional method that still is widely used, **object-oriented (O-O) analysis**, which is a more recent approach that many analysts prefer, and **agile methods**, also called **adaptive methods**, which include the latest trends in software development. Figure 1-17 provides an overview of the three methods, which are discussed in the following sections.

Although most projects utilize one approach, it is not unusual for system developers to mix and match methods to gain a better perspective. In addition to these three main development methods, some organizations choose to develop their own in-house approaches or use techniques offered by software suppliers, CASE tool vendors, or consultants. Many alternatives exist, and IT experts agree that no single development method is best in all cases. An approach that works well for one project might have disadvantages or risks in another situation. The important thing is to understand the various methods and the strengths and weaknesses of each approach.

Regardless of the development strategy, people, tasks, timetables, and costs must be managed effectively. Complex projects can involve dozens of people, hundreds of tasks, and many thousands of dollars. Project management is the process of planning, scheduling, monitoring, controlling, and reporting upon the development of an information system. Chapter 3 describes project management tools and techniques in detail.

	STRUCTURED ANALYSIS	OBJECT-ORIENTED ANALYSIS	AGILE METHODS
Description	Represents the system in terms of data and the processes that act upon that data. System development is organized into phases, with deliverables and milestones to measure progress. The waterfall model typically consists of five phases: requirements, design, construction, testing, and maintenance & evolution. Iteration is possible among the phases.	Views the system in terms of objects that combine data and processes. The objects represent actual people, things, transactions, and events. Compared to structural analysis, O-O phases tend to be more interactive. Can use the waterfall model or a model that stresses greater iteration.	Stresses intense team-based effort. Breaks development into cycles, or iterations, that add functionality. Each cycle is designed, built, and tested in an ongoing process. Attempts to reduce major risks by incremental steps in short time intervals.
Modeling Tools	Data flow diagrams (DFDs) and process descriptions, which are described in Chapter 5. Also, business process modeling.	Various object-oriented diagrams depict system actors, methods, and messages, which are described in Chapter 6. Also, business process modeling.	Tools that enhance communication, such as collaborative software, brainstorming, and whiteborads. Business process modeling works well with agile methods.
Pros	Traditional method that has been very popular over time. Relies heavily on written documentation. Frequent phase iteration can provide flexibility comparable to other methods. Well-suited to traditional project management tools and techniques.	Integrates easily with object-oriented programming languages. Code is modular and reusable, which can reduce cost and development time. Easy to maintain and expand because new objects can be created using inherited properties.	Very flexible and efficient in dealing with change. Stresses team interaction and reflects a set of community-based values. Frequent deliverables constantly validate the project and reduce risk.
Cons	Changes can be costly, especially in later phases. Requirements are defined early, and can change during development. Users might not be able to describe their needs until they can see examples of features and functions.	Somewhat newer method might be less familiar to development team members. Interaction of objects and classes can be complex in larger systems.	Team members need a high level of technical and communications skills. Lack of structure and documentation can introduce risk factors. Overall project might be subject to scope change as user requirements change.

FIGURE 1-17 Comparison of structured, object-oriented, and agile development methods.

1.9.1 Structured Analysis

Structured analysis is a traditional systems development technique that is time-tested and easy to understand. Structured analysis uses a series of phases, called the systems development life cycle (SDLC), to plan, analyze, design, implement, and support an information system. Although structured analysis evolved many years ago, it remains a popular systems development method. Structured analysis is based on an overall plan, similar to a blueprint for constructing a building, so it is called a predictive approach.

Structured analysis uses a set of process models to describe a system graphically. Because it focuses on processes that transform data into useful information, structured analysis is called a process-centered technique. In addition to modeling the processes, structured analysis also addresses data organization and structure, relational database design, and user interface issues.

A process model shows the data that flows in and out of system processes. Inside each process, input data is transformed by **business rules** that generate the output. Figure 1-18 shows a process model that was created with the Visible Analyst CASE tool. The model, which represents a school registration system, is called a **data flow diagram (DFD)** because it uses various symbols and shapes to represent data flow, processing, and storage. DFDs are discussed in more detail in Chapter 5.

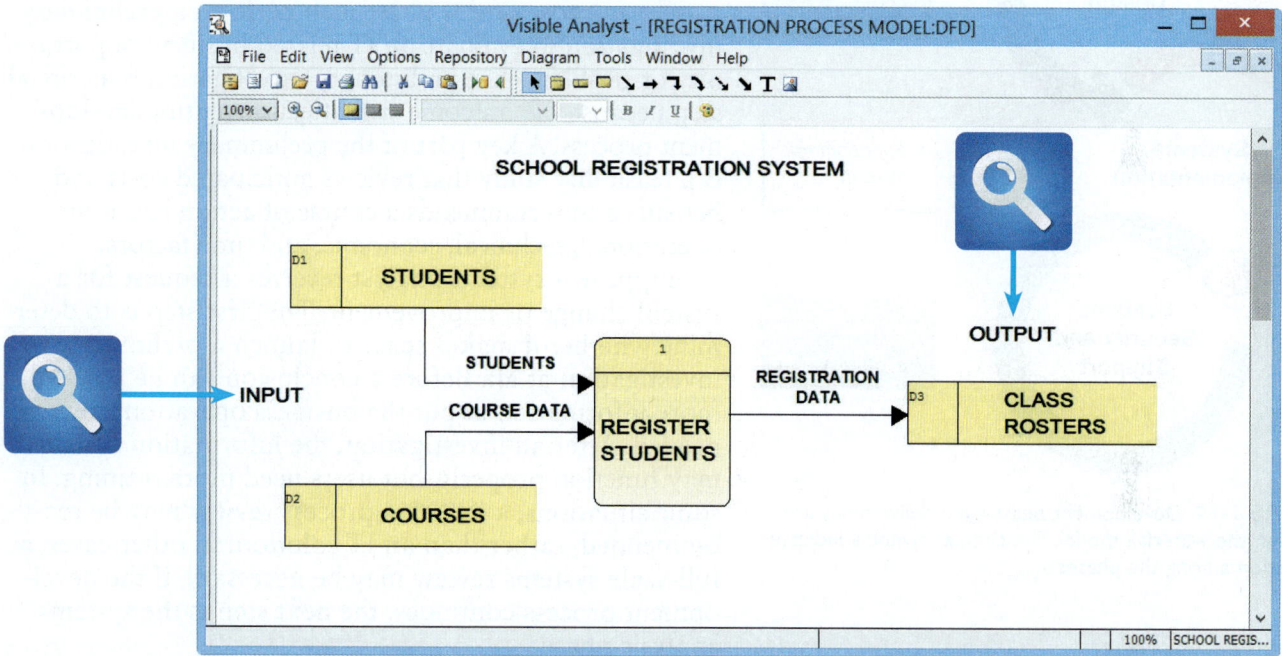

FIGURE I-18 This Visible Analyst screen shows a process model for a school registration system. The REGISTER STUDENTS process accepts input data from two sources and transforms it into output data.
Source: Visible Systems Corporation

Structured analysis uses the SDLC to plan and manage the systems development process. The SDLC describes activities and functions that all systems developers perform, regardless of which approach they use. In the **waterfall model**, the result of each phase is called a **deliverable**, which flows into the next phase.

Some analysts see a disadvantage in the built-in structure of the SDLC, because the waterfall model does not emphasize interactivity among the phases. This criticism can be valid if the SDLC phases are followed too rigidly. However, adjacent phases can and do interact, as shown by the circular arrows in Figure 1-19, and interaction among several phases is not uncommon. Used in this manner, the traditional model is not as different from agile methods as it might appear to be.

The SDLC model usually includes five steps, which are described in the following sections: systems planning, systems analysis, systems design, systems implementation, and systems support and security.

SYSTEMS PLANNING: The systems planning phase usually begins with a formal request to the IT department, called a systems request, which describes problems or desired changes in an information system or a business process. In many companies, IT systems planning is an integral part of overall business planning. When managers and users develop their business plans, they usually include IT requirements that generate systems requests. A systems request can come from a top manager, a planning team, a department head, or the IT department itself. The request can be very significant or relatively minor. A major request might involve a new information system or the upgrading of an existing system. In contrast, a minor request might ask for a new feature or a change to the user interface.

The purpose of this phase is to perform a preliminary investigation to evaluate an IT-related business opportunity or problem. The preliminary investigation is a critical step because the outcome will affect the entire development process. A key part of the preliminary investigation is a feasibility study that reviews anticipated costs and benefits and recommends a course of action based on operational, technical, economic, and time factors.

Suppose a systems analyst receives a request for a system change or improvement. The first step is to determine whether it makes sense to launch a preliminary investigation at all. Before a conclusion can be reached, more information about the business operations may be needed. After an investigation, the information system may function properly, but users need more training. In some situations, a business process review may be recommended, rather than an IT solution. In other cases, a full-scale systems review may be necessary. If the development process continues, the next step is the systems analysis phase.

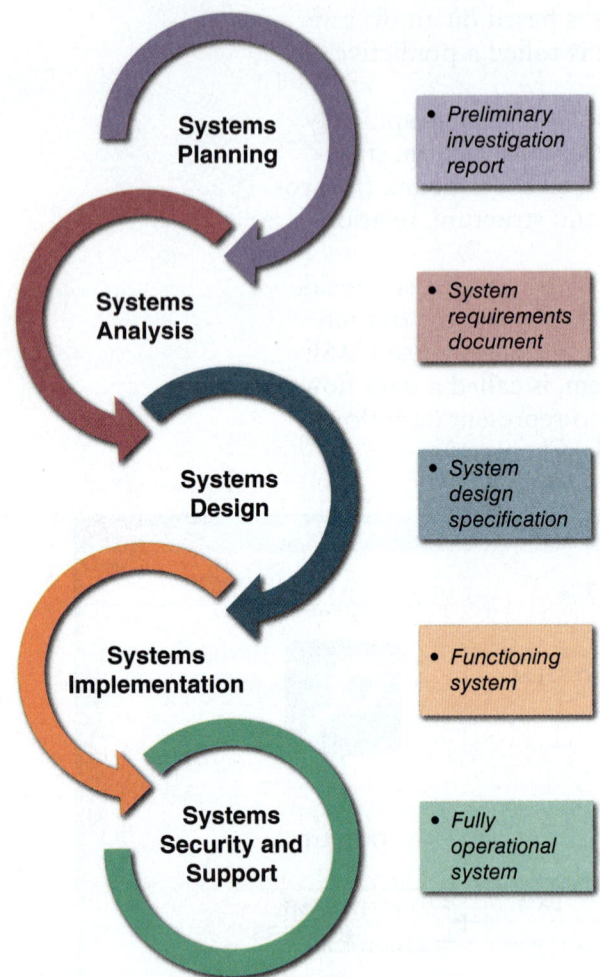

FIGURE 1-19 Development phases and deliverables are shown in the waterfall model. The circular symbols indicate interaction among the phases.

SYSTEMS ANALYSIS: The purpose of the systems analysis phase is to build a logical model of the new system. The first step is requirements modeling, where the analyst investigates business processes and documents what the new system must do to satisfy users. Requirements modeling continues the investigation that began during the systems planning phase. To understand the system, fact-finding using techniques such as interviews, surveys, document review, observation, and sampling is performed. The fact-finding results are used to build business models, data and process models, and object models.

The deliverable for the systems analysis phase is the system requirements document. The system requirements document describes management and user requirements, costs and benefits, and outlines alternative development strategies.

SYSTEMS DESIGN: The purpose of the systems design phase is to create a physical model that will satisfy all documented requirements for the system. At this stage, the user interface is designed and necessary outputs, inputs, and processes are identified. In addition, internal and external controls are designed, including computer-based and manual features to guarantee that the system will be reliable, accurate, maintainable, and secure. During the systems design phase, the application architecture is also determined, which programmers will use to transform the logical design into program modules and code.

The deliverable for this phase is the system design specification, which is presented to management and users for review and approval. Management and user involvement is critical to avoid any misunderstanding about what the new system will do, how it will do it, and what it will cost.

SYSTEMS IMPLEMENTATION: During the systems implementation phase, the new system is constructed. Whether the developers use structured analysis or O-O methods, the procedure is the same—programs are written, tested, and documented, and the system is installed. If the system was purchased as a package, systems analysts configure the software and perform any necessary modifications. The objective of the systems implementation phase is to deliver a completely functioning and documented information system. At the conclusion of this phase, the system is ready for use. Final preparations include converting data to the new system's files, training users, and performing the actual transition to the new system.

The systems implementation phase also includes an assessment, called a systems evaluation, to determine whether the system operates properly and if costs and benefits are within expectations.

SYSTEMS SUPPORT AND SECURITY: During the systems support and security phase, the IT staff maintains, enhances, and protects the system. Maintenance changes correct errors and adapt to changes in the environment, such as new tax rates. Enhancements provide new features and benefits. The objective during this phase is to maximize return on the IT investment. Security controls safeguard the system from both external and internal threats. A well-designed system must be secure, reliable, maintainable, and scalable. A scalable design can expand to meet new business requirements and volumes. Information systems development is always a work in progress. Business processes change rapidly, and most information systems need to be updated significantly or replaced after several years of operation. For example, a web-based system may need more servers added to cope with increased workload.

1.9.2 Object-Oriented Analysis

Whereas structured analysis treats processes and data as separate components, object-oriented analysis combines data and the processes that act on the data into things called objects. Systems analysts use O-O to model real-world business processes and operations. The result is a set of software objects that represent actual people, things, transactions, and events. Using an O-O programming language, a programmer then writes the code that creates the objects.

An object is a member of a class, which is a collection of similar objects. Objects possess characteristics called properties, which the object inherits from its class or possesses on its own. As shown in Figure 1-20, the class called PERSON includes INSTRUCTOR and STUDENT. Because the

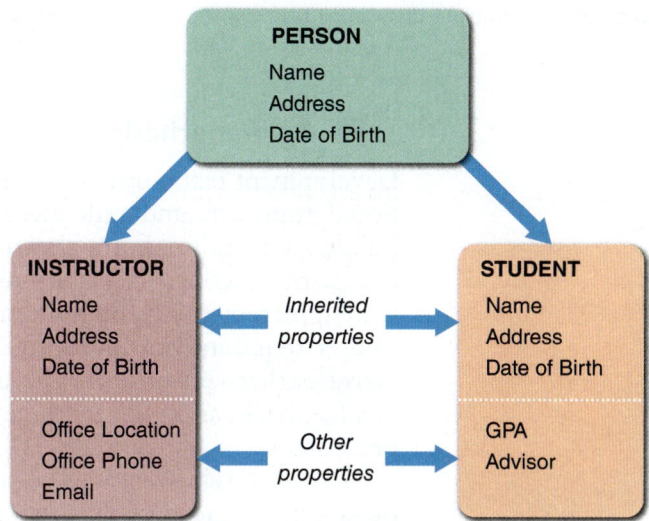

FIGURE 1-20 The PERSON class includes INSTRUCTOR and STUDENT objects, which have their own properties and inherited properties.

PERSON class has a property called Address, a STUDENT inherits the Address property. A STUDENT also has a property called Major that is not shared by other members of the PERSON class.

In O-O design, built-in processes called *methods* can change an object's properties. For example, in an online catalog store, an ORDER object might have a property called STATUS that changes when a CUSTOMER object clicks to place, confirm, or cancel the order.

One object can send information to another object by using a message. A *message* requests specific behavior or information from another object. For example, an ORDER object might send a message to a CUSTOMER object that requests a shipping address. When it receives the message, the CUSTOMER object supplies the information. The ORDER object has the capability to send the message, and the CUSTOMER object knows what actions to perform when it receives the message. O-O analysis uses object models to represent data and behavior, and to show how objects affect other objects. By describing the objects and methods needed to support a business operation, a system developer can design reusable components that speed up system implementation and reduce development cost.

Object-oriented methods usually follow a series of analysis and design phases that are similar to the SDLC, although there is less agreement on the number of phases and their names. In an O-O model, the phases tend to be more interactive. Figure 1-21 shows an O-O development model where planning, analysis, and design tasks interact to produce prototypes that can be tested and implemented. The result is an interactive model that can accurately depict real-world business processes.

O-O methodology is popular because it provides an easy transition to O-O programming languages such as C++, Java, and Swift. Chapter 6 covers O-O analysis and design, with a detailed description of O-O terms, concepts, tools, and techniques.

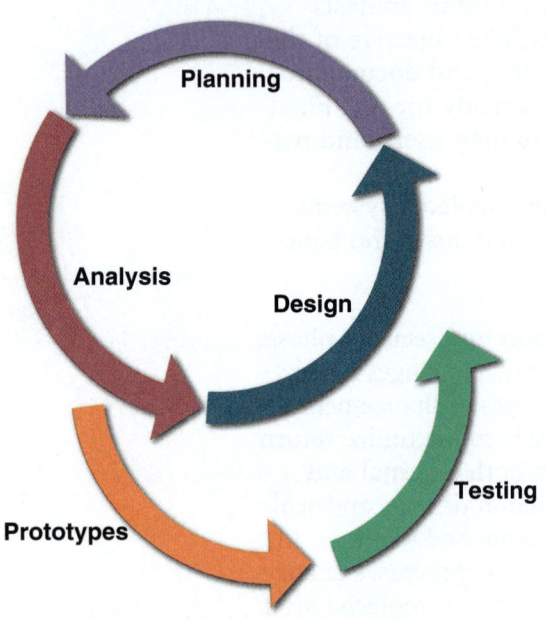

FIGURE 1-21 In a typical O-O development model, planning, analysis, and design tasks interact continuously to generate prototypes that can be tested.

1.9.3 Agile Methods

Development techniques change over time. For example, structured analysis is a traditional approach, and agile methods are the newest development. Structured analysis builds an overall plan for the information system, just as a contractor might use a blueprint for constructing a building. Agile methods, in contrast, attempt to develop a system incrementally, by building a series of prototypes and constantly adjusting them to user requirements. As the agile process continues, developers revise, extend, and merge earlier versions into the final product. An agile approach emphasizes continuous feedback, and each incremental step is affected by what was learned in the prior steps.

Although relatively new to software development, the notion of iterative development can be traced back to Japanese auto firms that were able to boost productivity by using a flexible manufacturing system, where team-based effort and short-term milestones helped keep quality up and costs down. Agile methods have attracted a wide following and an entire community of users, as shown in Figure 1-22.

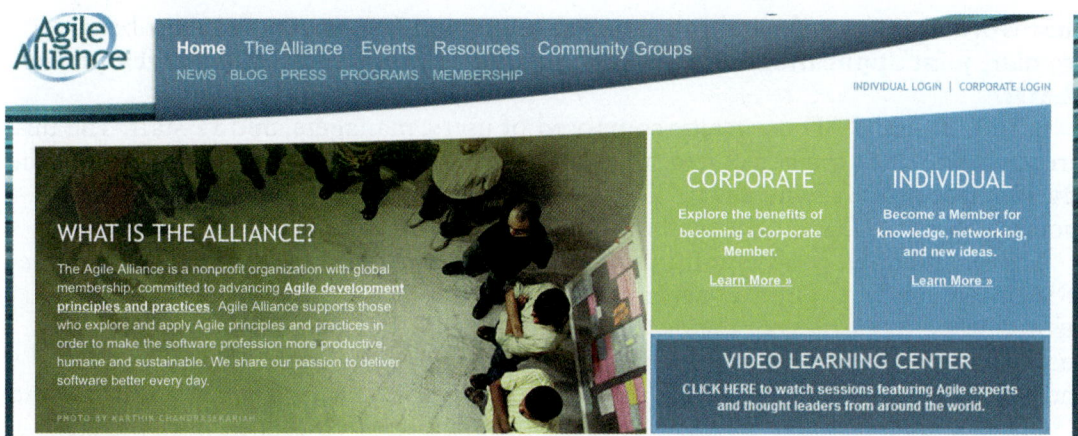

FIGURE 1-22 Agile methods have attracted a wide following and an entire community of users.
Source: Agile Alliance

Agile methods typically use a spiral model, which represents a series of iterations, or revisions, based on user feedback. As the process continues, the final product gradually evolves. An agile approach requires intense interactivity between developers and individual users, and does not begin with an overall objective. Instead, the agile process determines the end result. Proponents of the spiral model believe that this approach reduces risks and speeds up software development.

Barry Boehm, a noted software engineering professor, initially suggested spiral models in the 1990s. He stated that each iteration, or phase, of the model must have a specific goal that is accepted, rejected, or changed by the user or client. Thus, each iteration produces feedback and enhancements, which enable the team to reach the overall project goal. Typically, each iteration in a spiral model includes planning, risk analysis, engineering, and evaluation. The repeated iterations produce a series of prototypes, which evolve into the finished system. Notice that these phases resemble SDLC tasks, which also can be iterative.

Numerous other adaptive variations and related methods exist, and most IT developers expect this trend to continue in the future. Two examples are Scrum, which is discussed in Chapter 4, and Extreme Programming (XP), which is discussed in Chapter 11.

Although agile methods are becoming popular, analysts should recognize that these approaches have advantages and disadvantages. By their nature, agile methods can allow developers to be much more flexible and responsive, but can be riskier than more traditional methods. For example, without a detailed set of system requirements, certain features requested by some users might not be consistent with the company's larger game plan.

Other potential disadvantages of agile methods can include weak documentation, blurred lines of accountability, and too little emphasis on the larger business picture. Also, unless properly implemented, a long series of iterations might actually add to project cost and development time. The bottom line is that systems analysts should understand the pros and cons of any approach before selecting a development method for a specific project.

1.9.4 Other Development Methods

IT professionals know that the key to success is user input—before, during, and after a system is developed. Over time, many companies discovered that systems development teams composed of IT staff, users, and managers could complete their work more rapidly and produce better results. Two methodologies became popular: joint application development (JAD) and rapid application development (RAD).

Both JAD and RAD use teams composed of users, managers, and IT staff. The difference is that JAD focuses on team-based fact-finding, which is only one phase of the development process, whereas RAD is more like a compressed version of the entire process. JAD, RAD, and agile methods are described in more detail in Chapter 4.

Companies often choose to follow their own methodology. Using CASE tools, an IT team can apply a variety of techniques rather than being bound to a single, rigid methodology. Regardless of the development model, it will be necessary to manage people, tasks, timetables, and expenses by using various project management tools and techniques.

1.10 THE INFORMATION TECHNOLOGY DEPARTMENT

The IT department develops and maintains information systems. The structure of the IT department varies among companies, as does its name and placement within the organization. In a small firm, one person might handle all computer support activities and services, whereas a large corporation might require many people with specialized skills to provide information systems support. Figure 1-23 shows a typical IT organization in a company that has networked PCs, enterprise-wide databases, centralized processing, and web-based operations.

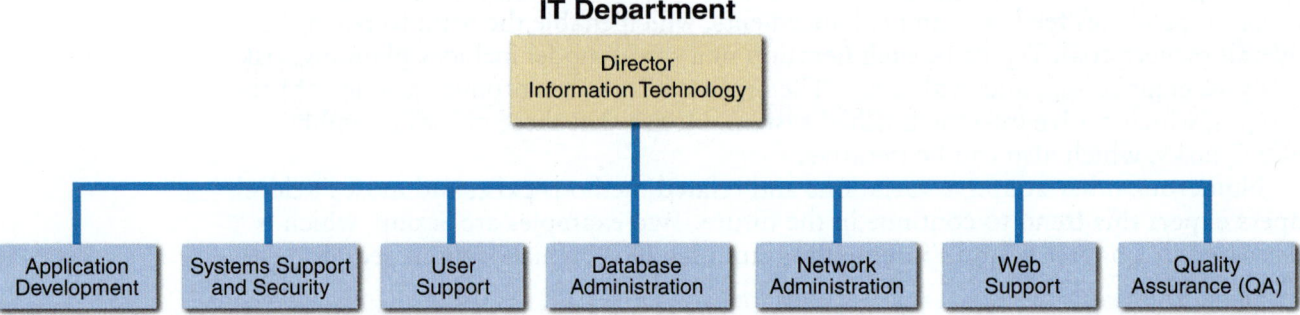

FIGURE 1-23 Depending on its size, an IT department might have separate organization units for these functions, or they might be combined into a smaller number of teams.

The IT group provides technical support, which includes seven main functions: application development, systems support and security, user support, database administration, network administration, web support, and quality assurance. These functions overlap considerably and often have different names in different companies.

1.10.1 Application Development

The IT application development group typically provides leadership and overall guidance, but teams consisting of users, managers, and IT staff members develop the systems themselves. A popular model for information systems development is a project-oriented team using RAD or JAD, with IT professionals providing overall coordination, guidance, and technical support.

CASE IN POINT 1.2: GLOBAL HOTELS AND MOMMA'S MOTELS

Suppose you work in the IT department of Global Hotels, a multinational hotel chain. Global Hotels runs several specialized business support systems, including a guest reservations system that was developed in-house to meet the requirements of a large company with worldwide operations. Guests can make one-stop online reservations by visiting Global's website, which has links to all major travel industry sites.

Global Hotels just acquired Momma's, a regional chain of 20 motels in western Canada. Momma's uses a vertical reservations package suitable for small- to medium-sized businesses, and a generic accounting and finance package. Should Momma's use Global Hotels' information systems or continue with its own? In your answer, consider issues such as business profiles, business processes, system interactivity, EDI, ecommerce, and the characteristics of both information systems. What additional information would be helpful to you in making a recommendation?

1.10.2 Systems Support and Security

Systems support and security provides vital protection and maintenance services for system hardware and software, including enterprise computing systems, networks, transaction processing systems, and corporate IT infrastructure. The systems support and security group implements and monitors physical and electronic security hardware, software, and procedures. This group also installs and supports operating systems, telecommunications software, and centralized database management systems. In addition, systems support and security technicians provide technical assistance to other groups in the IT department. If a site has a large number of remote clients, the systems support group often includes a deployment team that installs and configures the workstations.

1.10.3 User Support

User support provides users with technical information, training, and productivity support. The user support function usually is called a **help desk**. A help desk's staff trains users and managers on application software such as email, word processing, spreadsheets, and graphics packages. User support specialists answer questions, troubleshoot problems, and serve as a clearinghouse for user problems and solutions.

1.10.4 Database Administration

Database administration involves data design, management, security, backup, and access. In small- and medium-sized companies, an IT support person performs those roles in addition to other duties. Regardless of company size, mission-critical database applications require continuous attention and technical support.

1.10.5 Network Administration

Business operations depend on networks that enable company-wide information systems. Network administration includes hardware and software maintenance, support, and security. In addition to controlling user access, network administrators install, configure, manage, monitor, and maintain network applications. Network administration is discussed in more detail in Chapter 10.

1.10.6 Web Support

Web support is a vital technical support function. Web support specialists design and construct webpages, monitor traffic, manage hardware and software, and link web-based applications to the company's information systems. Reliable, high-quality web support is especially critical for companies engaged in ecommerce.

1.10.7 Quality Assurance (QA)

Many large IT departments also use a quality assurance (QA) team that reviews and tests all applications and systems changes to verify specifications and software quality standards. The QA team usually is a separate unit that reports directly to IT management.

CASE IN POINT 1.3:   What Should Lisa Do?

Lisa Jameson has two job offers. One is from Pembroke Boats, a boat manufacturer that employs 200 people in a small Ohio town. Pembroke does not have an IT department and wants her to create one. The job position is called information coordinator, but she would be the only IT person.

   The other offer, which pays about $7500 more annually, is from Albemarle Express, a nationwide trucking firm located in Detroit. At Albemarle Express, Lisa would be a programmer-analyst, with the promise that if she does well in her position, she eventually will move into a systems analyst position and work on new systems development. Lisa has heard a rumor that another company might acquire Albemarle Express, but that rumor has occurred before and nothing has ever happened. What should Lisa do, and why?

1.11 The Systems Analyst

A systems analyst investigates, analyzes, designs, develops, installs, evaluates, and maintains a company's information systems. To perform those tasks, a systems analyst constantly interacts with users and managers within and outside the company. The following sections describe a system analyst's role, knowledge, skills, education, certifications, and career opportunities.

1.11.1 Role

A systems analyst helps develop IT systems that support business requirements. To succeed, analysts often must act as translators. For example, when they describe business processes to programmers, they must speak a language that programmers will understand clearly. Typically, the analyst builds a series of models, diagrams, decision tables, and uses other descriptive tools and techniques. Similarly, when communicating with managers, the analyst often must translate complex technical issues into words and images that nontechnical people can grasp. To do this, the analyst uses various presentation skills, models, and communication methods.

   Analysts are often the company's best line of defense against an IT disaster—a system that is technically sound but fails because it does not meet the needs of users and managers. When this occurs, poor communication is usually to blame. For an analyst, the most valuable skill is the ability to listen. An effective analyst will involve users in every step of the development process, and listen carefully to what they have to say. As the process continues, the analyst will seek feedback and comments from the users. This input can provide a valuable early warning system for projects that might otherwise go off the track.

The chapters on project management, modeling, and user interface design are especially valuable to the user-focused analyst.

1.11.2 Knowledge, Skills, and Education

A successful systems analyst needs technical knowledge, oral and written communication skills, an understanding of business operations, and critical thinking skills. Educational requirements vary widely depending on the company and the position. In a rapidly changing IT marketplace, a systems analyst must manage his or her own career and have a plan for professional development.

TECHNICAL KNOWLEDGE: State-of-the-art knowledge is extremely important in a rapidly changing business and technical environment. The Internet offers numerous opportunities to update technical knowledge and skills. Many IT professionals go online to learn about technical developments, exchange experiences, and get answers to questions. For example, the IEEE Computer Society, shown in Figure 1-24, is one of the leading computing organizations offering systems analysts a wealth of information, news, training, support communities, and more. Analysts also maintain their skills by attending training courses, both onsite and online. Networking with colleagues is another way to keep up with new developments, and membership in professional associations also is important.

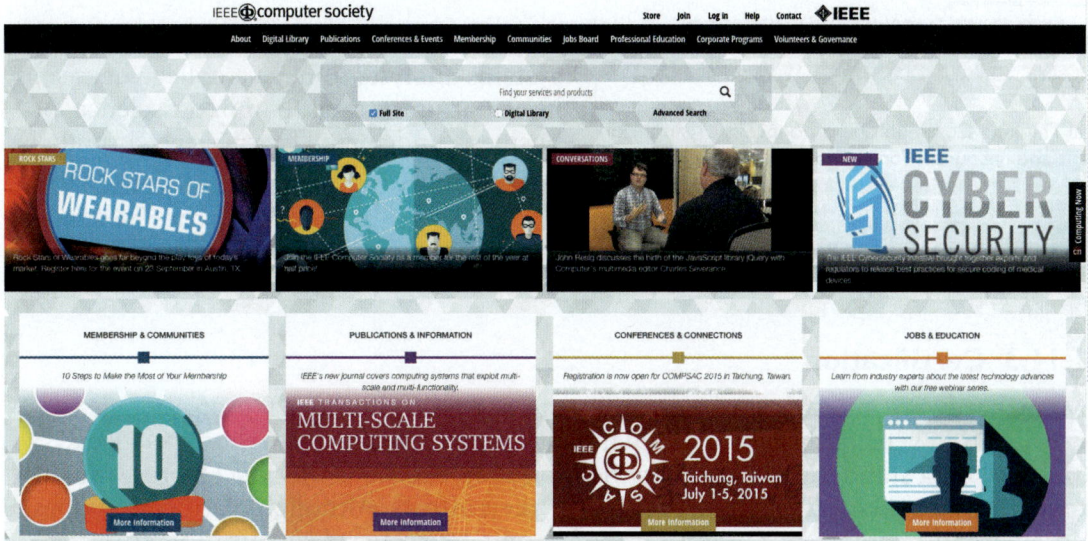

FIGURE 1-24 The IEEE Computer Society is one of the leading computing organizations offering systems analysts a wealth of information, news, training, communities, and more.
Source: IEEE Computer Society

COMMUNICATION SKILLS: A systems analyst needs strong oral and written communication skills, and the ability to interact with people at all levels, from operational staff to senior executives. Often, the analyst must work with people outside the company, such as software and hardware vendors, customers, and government officials.

Analysts often coordinate IT project teams, where they use communication skills to guide and motivate team members.

BUSINESS SKILLS: A systems analyst works closely with managers, supervisors, and operational employees. To be effective, he or she must understand business operations and processes, communicate clearly, and translate business needs into requirements that can be understood by programmers and systems developers. A successful analyst is business-oriented, curious, comfortable with financial tools, and able to see the big picture. Chapter 2 describes some basic concepts, including strategic planning, SWOT analysis, and feasibility tests.

CRITICAL THINKING SKILLS: Most educators agree that critical thinking skills include the ability to compare, classify, evaluate, recognize patterns, analyze cause-and-effect, and apply logic. Critical thinkers often use a *what-if* approach, and they have the ability to evaluate their own thinking and reasoning.

Critical thinking skills are valuable in the IT industry, where employers seek job candidates who can demonstrate these skills and bring them to the workplace. Figure 1-25 shows the website for Critical Thinking Community, a nonprofit organization that provides encouragement and resources for critical thinkers.

FIGURE 1-25 The Critical Thinking Community is a nonprofit organization that provides encouragement and resources for critical thinkers.
Source: The Critical Thinking Community

EDUCATION: Companies typically require systems analysts to have a college degree in information systems, computer science, or business, and some IT experience usually is required. For higher-level positions, many companies require an advanced degree. Sometimes, educational requirements can be waived if a candidate has significant experience, skills, or professional certifications.

1.11.3 Certification

Many hardware and software companies offer certification for IT professionals. Certification verifies that an individual demonstrated a certain level of knowledge and skill on a standardized test. Certification is an excellent way for IT professionals to learn new skills and gain recognition for their efforts. Although certification does not guarantee competence or ability, many companies regard certification as an important credential for hiring or promotion. Certification is discussed in more detail in Chapter 12.

In addition to traditional hardware and software certifications, some firms are exploring ways to assess critical thinking skills, as shown in Figure 1-26. These skills include perception, organization, analysis, problem solving, and decision making. Whether or not formal certification is involved, these skills are extremely valuable to IT professionals and the employers who hire them.

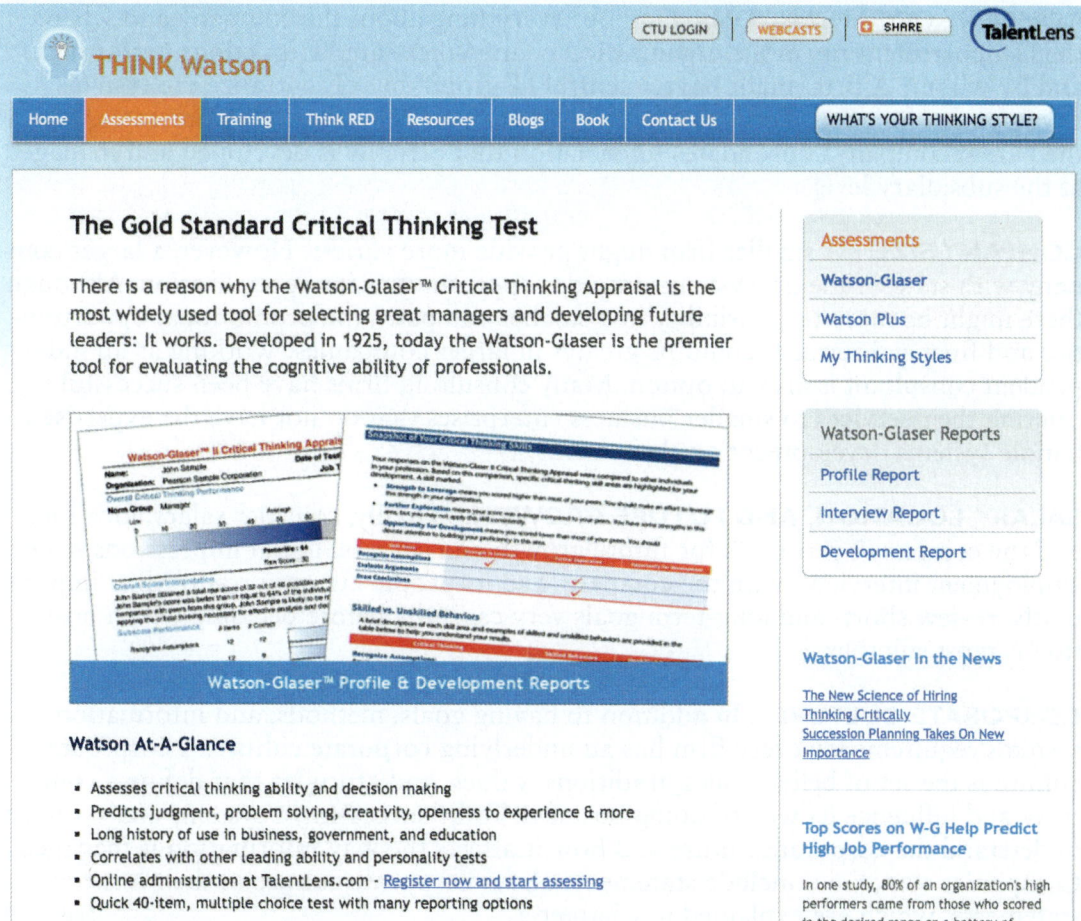

FIGURE 1-26 Employers like to hire people who can think logically and effectively.
Source: Think Watson/Pearson Education, Inc.

1.11.4 Career Opportunities

The demand for systems analysts is expected to remain strong. Companies will need systems analysts to apply new information technology, and the explosion in ecommerce will fuel IT job growth. The systems analyst position is a challenging and rewarding one that can lead to a top management position. With an understanding of technical and business issues, a systems analyst has an unlimited horizon. Many companies have presidents and senior managers who started in IT departments as systems analysts.

The responsibilities of a systems analyst at a small firm are different from those at a large corporation. Working at a small or large company is a matter of personal choice.

JOB TITLES: First, do not rely on job titles alone. Some positions are called systems analysts, but involve only programming or technical support. In other cases, systems analyst responsibilities are found in positions titled computer specialist, programmer, programmer/analyst, systems designer, software engineer, and various others. Be sure the responsibilities of the job are stated clearly when considering a position.

COMPANY ORGANIZATION: Find out everything about the company and where the IT department fits in the organization chart. Where are IT functions performed, and by whom? A firm might have a central IT group, but decentralize the systems development function. This situation sometimes occurs in large conglomerates, where the parent company consolidates information that actually is developed and managed at the subsidiary level.

COMPANY SIZE: A smaller firm might provide more variety. However, a larger company with state-of-the-art systems provides opportunities for specialization. Although there might be more responsibility in a smaller company, the promotional opportunities and financial rewards could be greater in larger companies. Working as an independent consultant is also an option. Many consulting firms have been successful in offering their services to smaller business enterprises that do not have the expertise to handle systems development on their own.

SALARY, LOCATION, AND FUTURE GROWTH: Finally, consider salary, location, and the company's prospects for future growth and success. Initial impressions from employment interviews with the company and its people are important. Most importantly, review short- and long-term goals very carefully before deciding which position is most suitable.

CORPORATE CULTURE: In addition to having goals, methods, and information systems requirements, every firm has an underlying corporate culture. A corporate culture is the set of beliefs, rules, traditions, values, and attitudes that define a company and influence its way of doing business. To be successful, a systems analyst must understand the corporate culture and how it affects the way information is managed. Companies sometimes include statements about corporate culture in their mission statements, which are explained in Chapter 2.

A systems analyst must understand the firm's culture and find it comfortable. If the company encourages personal growth and empowerment, work is much more enjoyable. For example, consider the Google corporate culture described in Figure 1-27. A company like Google is likely to attract, retain, and motivate the best and brightest people.

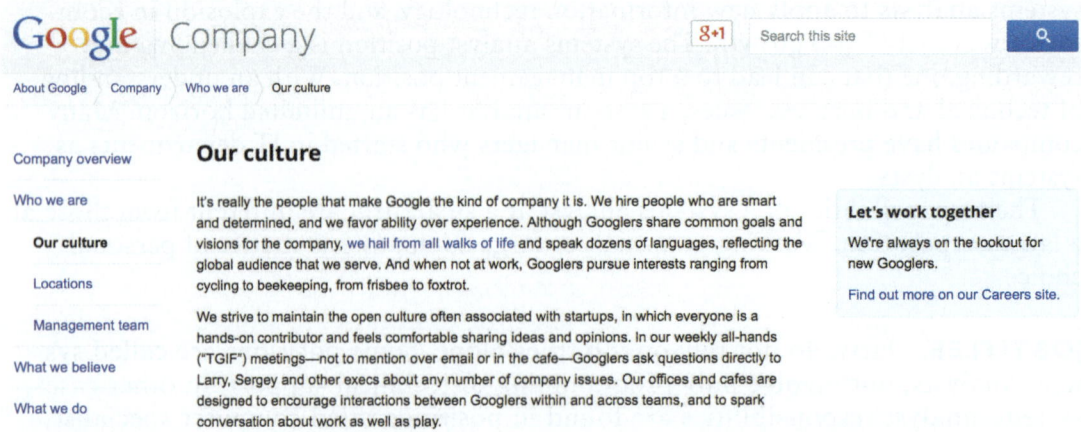

FIGURE 1-27 A corporate culture like Google's is likely to attract, retain, and motivate the best and brightest people.
Source: Google

CASE IN POINT 1.4:   JUST-IN-TIME AIRFREIGHT, INC.

Suppose you are the IT director at Just-in-Time Airfreight, and you have received authorization to hire another systems analyst. This will be an entry-level position, and the person will assist senior systems analysts on various projects involving the reservations and the human resources systems. Using the information in this chapter, draft an ad that would appear in *The Wall Street Journal*, local newspapers, and online. You can get some ideas by visiting monster.com or a similar site. In your ad, be sure to list desired skills, experience, and educational requirements.

1.12 TRENDS IN INFORMATION TECHNOLOGY

Very few areas evolve as fast as information technology. Each year sees evolutionary developments in current technology, such as faster processors, wider network bandwidth, and increased storage capabilities. Once in a while a truly transformative change occurs, such as the ongoing shift to cloud computing across the enterprise, or a revolution in the basic tenets of computation with the nascent introduction of quantum computing.

Systems analysts should be aware of current trends in information technology, so that they can better serve their organizations and so that they can adapt their skill sets going forward. Some of the key trends that are disrupting information technology include agile methods, cloud computing, mobile devices, service orientation, and social media networks.

Agile methods have already been discussed in this chapter and are covered in more detail later in the book. The agile movement is a significant trend in information technology that all systems analysts should follow. It started as a response to the heavy-weight process models and was initially used for smaller teams, but interest in agile methods has grown to encompass almost all application areas and business organizations.

Cloud computing is in many ways a return to the past: a model of shared computing and data storage resources accessed from remote clients, rather like the mainframe era. However, cloud computing is different in that it offers virtualized resources that can grow to accommodate increased requirements as needed. It is also different in that buying capacity on demand from a thriving vendor marketplace can reduce the capital costs needed for in-house computing infrastructure. And it is different in that it presents additional security needs to address.

Mobile devices and the app ecosystem that goes with them are a revolutionary development in information technology. The shift of computing capabilities to "the edge" of the network has put unprecedented power in the hands of end users. Smartphones are the most common computing device on the planet, and systems analysts will need to know about the role of apps and the effect of the **bring your own device (BYOD)** movement in the enterprise.

Traditionally, IT companies were identified as product-oriented or service-oriented. **Product-oriented** firms manufactured computers, routers, or microchips, while **service-oriented** companies included consultants, vendors, software developers, and service providers. Today, those distinctions are gone. Most successful IT companies offer a mix of products, services, and support. Value-added services such as consulting, software, and technical support often are more profitable than hardware sales.

Social media rides on some of the trends mentioned above, such as cloud computing, mobile devices, and service orientation. However, social media has had arguably the most profound influence on society. Witness the popularity of Facebook, with over 1 billion users worldwide. Companies tap into the power of social media, coupled with location-aware apps, to create truly innovative solutions that are changing the face of information technology.

A QUESTION OF ETHICS

iStockphoto.com/faberfoto_it

You are enjoying your job as a summer intern in the IT department of a local company. At lunch yesterday, several people were discussing ethical issues. You learned that some of them belong to IT organizations that have ethical codes to guide members and set professional standards. For example, Ann, your supervisor, belongs to the Association for Computing Machinery (ACM), which has over 100,000 members from more than 100 countries and a website at *acm.org*. Ann said that the ACM code of ethics is important to her, and would definitely influence her views. On the other hand, Jack, a senior programmer, believes that his own personal standards would be sufficient to guide him if ethical questions were to arise.

Because you are excited about your career as an IT professional, you decide to visit ACM's website to examine the code of ethics and make up your own mind. After you do so, would you tend to agree more with Ann or with Jack?

1.13 CHAPTER SUMMARY

Information technology (IT) refers to the combination of hardware, software, and services that people use to manage, communicate, and share information. Technology is changing rapidly, and IT professionals must prepare for the future. IT supports business operations, improves productivity, and helps managers make decisions. Systems analysis and design is the process of developing information systems that transform data into useful information, and systems analysts are IT team members who help plan, develop, and maintain information systems.

The essential components of an information system are hardware, software, data, processes, and people. Hardware consists of everything in the physical layer of the information system. Software consists of system software, which manages the hardware components, and application software, which supports day-to-day business operations. Data is the raw material that an information system transforms into useful information. Processes describe the tasks and functions that users, managers, and IT staff members perform. People who interact with a system include users, from both within and outside the company.

Most successful companies offer a mix of products, technical and financial services, consulting, and customer support. A rapidly growing business category is the Internet-dependent firm, which relies solely on Internet-based operations. Ecommerce includes business-to-consumer (B2C) sales and business-to-business (B2B) transactions that use Internet-based digital marketplaces or private electronic data interchange (EDI) systems.

A systems analyst starts with a business profile, which is an overview of company functions, and then he or she creates a series of business models that represent business processes, which describe specific transactions, events, tasks, and results. Analysts use business process modeling tools to document complex operations.

Based on their functions and features, business information systems are identified as enterprise computing systems, transaction processing systems, business support systems, knowledge management systems, or user productivity systems. In most companies, significant overlap and integration exists among the various types of information systems.

A typical organization structure includes top managers, middle managers and knowledge workers, supervisors and team leaders, and operational employees. Top managers develop strategic plans, which define an overall mission and goals.

Middle managers provide direction, resources, and feedback to supervisors and team leaders. Knowledge workers include various professionals who function as support staff. Supervisors and team leaders oversee operational employees. Each organizational level has a different set of responsibilities and information needs.

Systems analysts use modeling, prototyping, and computer-aided systems engineering (CASE) tools. Modeling produces a graphical representation of a concept or process, whereas prototyping involves the creation of an early working model of the information or its components. A systems analyst uses CASE tools to perform various systems development tasks.

Three popular system development approaches are structured analysis, which is a traditional method that still is widely used, object-oriented analysis (O-O), which is a more recent approach that many analysts prefer, and agile methods, also called adaptive methods, which include the latest trends in software development.

Structured analysis uses a series of phases, called the systems development life cycle (SDLC) that usually is shown as a waterfall model. Structured analysis uses an overall plan, similar to a blueprint for constructing a building, so it is called a predictive approach. This method uses a set of process models to describe a system graphically, and also addresses data organization and structure, relational database design, and user interface issues.

Object-oriented analysis combines data and the processes that act on the data into things called objects that represent people, things, transactions, and events. Objects have characteristics, called properties, built-in processes called methods, and can send information to other objects by using messages. Using an O-O programming language, a programmer then writes the code that creates the objects. Object-oriented methods usually follow a series of analysis and design phases similar to the SDLC, but the phases are more interactive.

Agile methods are the newest development approach, and attempt to develop a system incrementally by building a series of prototypes and constantly adjusting them to user requirements. Agile methods typically use a spiral model, which represents a series of iterations, or revisions, based on user feedback. The repeated iterations produce a series of prototypes, which evolve into the finished system.

Regardless of the development strategy, people, tasks, timetables, and costs must be managed effectively using project management tools and techniques, which are described in detail in Chapter 3.

Some firms choose to develop their own in-house methods or adopt techniques offered by software suppliers, CASE tool vendors, or consultants. Companies also use team-based strategies called joint application development (JAD) and rapid application development (RAD). JAD focuses on team-based fact-finding, whereas RAD is more like a compressed version of the entire process. JAD and RAD are described in more detail in Chapter 4.

The IT department develops, maintains, and operates a company's information systems. IT staff members provide technical support, including application development, systems support, user support, database administration, network administration, web support, and quality assurance. These functions overlap considerably and often have different names in different companies.

In addition to technical knowledge, a systems analyst must understand the business, think critically, and communicate effectively. Valuable credentials such as certifications are available to systems analysts. A systems analyst's responsibilities depend on a company's organization, size, and culture. Systems analysts need to consider salary, location, and future growth potential when making a career decision.

Five key trends in information technology are agile methods, cloud computing, mobile devices, service orientation, and social media networks.

Key Terms

adaptive method A systems development method that typically uses a spiral development model, which builds on a series of iterations, to make adapting to changes easier for all stakeholders.

agile method Systems development method that attempts to develop a system incrementally, by building a series of prototypes and constantly adjusting them to user requirements. Related to adaptive method.

app A software application that runs on a mobile device, such as a smartphone or tablet.

application software Software programs, such as email, word processors, spreadsheets, and graphics packages, used by employees in typical office scenarios.

B2B (business-to-business) A commercial exchange (e.g., products or services) between businesses, typically enabled by the Internet or electronic means.

B2C (business-to-consumer) A commercial exchange (e.g., products or services) between businesses and consumers conducted over the Internet.

bring your own device (BYOD) An equipment management model where employees are in charge of their devices (e.g., computers, tablets, smartphones) at work, not the IT department. This includes device selection and setup, program installation and updating, and network connectivity (including security).

business model A graphical representation of business functions that consist of business processes, such as sales, accounting, and purchasing.

business process A description of specific events, tasks, and desired results.

business process model (BPM) A graphical representation of one or more business processes.

business process modeling notation (BPMN) A standard set of shapes and symbols used to represent events, processes, and workflows in computer-based modeling tools.

business profile A definition of a company's overall functions, processes, organization, products, services, customers, suppliers, competitors, constraints, and future direction.

business rules How a system handles data and produces useful information. Business rules, also called business logic, reflect the operational requirements of the business. Examples include adding the proper amount of sales tax to invoices, calculating customer balances and finance charges, and determining whether a customer is eligible for a volume-based discount.

business support system Provide job-related information support to users at all levels of a company.

CASE tool Powerful software used in computer-aided systems engineering (CASE) to help systems analysts develop and maintain information systems.

certification A credential an individual earns by demonstrating a certain level of knowledge and skill on a standardized test.

class A term used in object-oriented modeling to indicate a collection of similar objects.

computer-aided software engineering (CASE) A technique that uses powerful programs called CASE tools to provide an overall framework for systems development. The tools support a wide variety of design methodologies, including structured analysis and object-oriented analysis. Also referred to as computer-aided systems engineering.

computer-aided systems engineering (CASE) *See* computer-aided software engineering (CASE).

corporate culture A set of beliefs, rules, traditions, values, and attitudes that define a company and influence its way of doing business.

critical thinking skill The ability to compare, classify, evaluate, recognize patterns, analyze cause and effect, and apply logic. Such skills are valued in the IT industry.

data The raw material or basic facts used by information systems.

data flow diagram (DFD) Graphical representation of the system, showing it stores, processes, and transforms data into useful information.

deliverable A polished, final product, suitable for its intended use. End products or deliverables often coincide with the completion of each SDLC phase.

ecommerce (electronic commerce) Transactions (e.g., buying and selling of goods and information) that occur on the Internet. Includes both business-to-consumer and business-to-business.

electronic data interchange (EDI) A process that involves the computer-to-computer transfer of data between companies.

empowerment A business practice that places more responsibility and accountability throughout all levels of an organization.

enterprise application Company-wide applications, such as order processing systems, payroll systems, and company communications networks.

enterprise computing Information systems that support company-wide data management requirements, such as airline reservations or credit card billing systems.

enterprise resource planning (ERP) A process that establishes an enterprise-wide strategy for IT resources. ERP defines a specific architecture, including standards for data, processing, network, and user interface design.

feasibility study An initial investigation to clearly identify the nature and scope of the business opportunity or problem. Also called a preliminary investigation.

groupware Programs that run on a network that enable users to share data, collaborate on projects, and work in teams. Also called workgroup software.

hardware The physical layer of the information system, to include computers, networks, communications equipment, and other technology-based infrastructure.

help desk A centralized resource staffed by IT professionals that provides users with the support they need to do their jobs. A help desk has three main objectives: to show people how to use system resources more effectively, to provide answers to technical or operational questions, and to make users more productive by teaching them how to meet their own information needs.

horizontal system A basic system, such as an inventory or payroll package that is commonly used by a variety of companies.

inference rule Instruction that directs a knowledge management system to identify data patterns and relationships.

information Data that has been changed into a useful form of output.

information system A combination of information technology, people, and data to support business requirements. The five key components are hardware, software, data, processes, and people.

information technology (IT) A combination of hardware, software, and telecommunications systems that support business operations, improve productivity, and help managers make decisions.

iterative An adaptive method typically uses a spiral development model, which builds on a series of iterations.

joint application development (JAD) A popular systems development technique that uses a group of users, managers and IT professionals that work together to gather information, discuss business needs, and define the new system requirements.

knowledge base A popular systems development technique that uses a group of users, managers, and IT professionals that work together to gather information, discuss business needs, and define the new system requirements.

legacy system An older system that is typically less technologically advanced than currently available systems.

management information system (MIS) A computer-based information system used in business planning, control, decision making, and problem solving.

mission-critical system An information system that is vital to a company's operations.

modeling A process that produces a graphical representation of a concept or process that systems developers can analyze, test, and modify.

Moore's Law A prediction that computing power would double every 18 to 24 months due to increased miniaturization of electronic components.

object In object-oriented analysis or programming, an object represents a real person, place, event, or transaction.

object-oriented (O-O) analysis The act of understanding an information system by identifying things called objects. An object represents a real person, place, event, or transaction. Object-oriented analysis is a popular approach that sees a system from the viewpoint of the objects themselves as they function and interact with the system.

preliminary investigation An initial analysis to clearly identify the nature and scope of the business opportunity or problem. Also called a feasibility study.

process Procedure or task that users, managers, and IT staff members perform. Also, the logical rules of a system that are applied to transform data into meaningful information. In data flow diagrams, a process receives input data and produces output that has a different content, form, or both.

product-oriented Companies that manufacture computers, routers, or microchips.

properties In object-oriented (O-O) analysis, characteristics that objects inherit from their class or possess on their own.

prototype An early, rapidly constructed working version of the proposed information system.

radio frequency identification (RFID) Technology that uses high-frequency radio waves to track physical objects.

rapid application development (RAD) A team-based technique that speeds up information systems development and produces a functioning information system. RAD is similar in concept to joint application development (JAD), but goes further by including all phases of the System Development Life Cycle (SDLC).

requirements modeling Used in the systems planning phase of the SDLC. It involves using various fact-finding techniques, such as interviews, surveys, observation, and sampling, to describe the current system and identify the requirements for the new system.

scalable The ability of a system to expand to meet new business requirements and volumes.

server farm A large concentration of networked computers working together.

service-oriented A company that primarily offers information or services, or sells goods produced by others.

software A program run by computers for a specific function or task.

spiral model A development model with a series of iterations, or revisions, based on user feedback.

stakeholder Anyone who is affected by the company's performance, such as customers, employees, suppliers, stockholders, and members of the community.

strategic plan The long-range plan that defines the corporate mission and goals. Typically defined by top management, with input from all levels.

structured analysis A traditional systems development technique that uses phases to plan, analyze, design, implement, and support an information system. Processes and data are treated as separate components.

supply chain A traditional systems development technique that uses phases to plan, analyze, design, implement, and support an information system. Processes and data are treated as separate components.

system A set of related components that produces specific results.

system design specification A document that presents the complete design for the new information system, along with detailed costs, staffing, and scheduling for completing the next SDLC phase, systems implementation. Also called the technical design specification or the detailed design specification.

system requirements document A document that contains the requirements for the new system, describes the alternatives that were considered, and makes a specific recommendation to management. It is the end product of the systems analysis phase.

system software Programs that control the computer, including the operating system, device drivers that communicate with hardware, and low-level utilities.

systems analysis and design The process of developing information systems that effectively use hardware, software, data, processes, and people to support the company's business objectives.

systems analysis phase The second SDLC phase. The purpose of this phase is to build a logical model of the new system.

systems analyst A person who plans, analyzes, and implements information systems. He or she may work internally within a company's IT department, or be hired by a company as an independent consultant.

systems design phase The third SDLC phase. The purpose of systems design is to create a blueprint for the new system that will satisfy all documented requirements, whether the system is being developed in-house or purchased as a package.

systems development life cycle (SDLC) Activities and functions that systems developers typically perform, regardless of how those activities and functions fit into a particular methodology. The SDLC model includes five phases: 1. Systems planning, 2. Systems analysis, 3. Systems design, 4. Systems implementation, and 5. Systems support and security.

systems implementation phase The fourth phase of SDLC. During this phase the new system is constructed, programs are written, tested, and documented, and the system is installed.

systems planning phase The first phase of the SDLC. During this phase the systems project gets started. The project proposal is evaluated to determine its feasibility. The project management plan is formulated, with the help of CASE tools where appropriate.

systems request A formal request to the IT department that describes problems or desired changes in an information system or business process. It might propose enhancements for an existing system, the correction of problems, or the development of an entirely new system.

systems support and security phase During the systems support and security phase of the SDLC, the IT staff maintains, enhances, and protects the system.

technical support Technical support is necessary to support the wide variety of IT systems and users. It includes six main functions: application development, systems support, user support, database administration, network administration, and web support. These functions overlap considerably and often have different names in different companies.

transaction processing (TP) system Operational system used to process day-to-day recurring business transactions, such as customer billing.

user productivity system Application that provides employees of all levels a wide array of tools to improve job performance. Examples include email, word processing, graphics, and company intranets.

user Stakeholder inside or outside the company who will interact with the system.

vertical system A system designed to meet the unique requirements of a specific business or industry, such as a web-based retailer or auto-supply store.

waterfall model The traditional model of software development. A graph that depicts the result of each SDLC phase flowing down into the next phase.

Chapter Exercises

Questions

1. What is information technology and why is it important? Suggest three fictitious headlines that might be added to Figure 1-1.
2. Why would a systems analyst have to act as a translator? What groups might be involved?
3. Write a business profile for a large business in your town. You can use your imagination to supply details you might not know.
4. What strategies are Wal-Mart and Lowe's using to gain more online customers?
5. Identify the main components of an information system. What is a mission-critical system?
6. Compare enterprise computing systems to transaction processing systems. Provide three examples of each type of system.
7. What are the four organizational levels common to many businesses? Which level typically requires data that supports long-term strategic planning and the overall business enterprise? What level of worker might rely heavily on transaction processing systems?
8. Describe three systems development tools and three development methods.
9. What are the phases of the SDLC waterfall model? Who was Barry Boehm, and what did he have to say about spiral models?
10. Review the IBM history. Describe three distinct phases the company has gone through in reaction to changing mark conditions.

Discussion Topics

1. Some experts believe that the growth in ecommerce will cause states and local governments to lose tax revenue, unless Internet transactions are subject to sales tax. What is one argument that supports this view and one that opposes it?
2. Are top managers likely to be more effective if they have IT experience? Why or why not?
3. Should the IT director report to the company president, or somewhere else? Does it matter?
4. Will online transactions eventually replace person-to-person contact? Why or why not?
5. The BYOD movement has serious implications for IT professionals, such as managing applications on user devices and security implications. Do you think BYOD is a net positive or a net negative for the enterprise? Explain your answer.

Projects

1. Contact four people at your school who use information systems. List their positions, the systems they use, and the business functions they perform.
2. Research newspaper, business magazine articles, or the web to find IT companies whose stock is traded publicly. Choose a company and *pretend* to buy $5,000 of its stock. Why did you choose that company? What is the current price per share? Report each week to your class.
3. Visit at least three websites to learn more about agile system development and spiral models. Prepare a list of the sites you visited and a summary of the results.
4. Explore the *Critical Thinking Community* website at *criticalthinking.org*. Identify three important topics currently being discussed, and describe your findings.
5. Read about the corporate culture of three leading IT companies, such as that from Google shown in Figure 1-27. Compare each statement of values and describe the type of employee you think each company is looking for.

CHAPTER 2 Analyzing the Business Case

Chapter 2 explains how to analyze a business case. This chapter also explains why it is important to understand business operations and requirements, how IT projects support a company's overall strategic plan, how systems projects get started, and how systems analysts conduct a preliminary investigation and feasibility study.

The chapter includes four "Case in Point" discussion questions to help contextualize the concepts described in the text. The "Question of Ethics" asks the systems analyst to consider the implications of granting preferential treatment to a system enhancement request when the request originates with a friend of the project's manager.

LEARNING OBJECTIVES

When you finish this chapter, you should be able to:

- Explain the concept of a business case and how a business case affects an IT project
- Describe the strategic planning process and why it is important to the IT team
- Explain the purpose of a mission statement
- Conduct a SWOT analysis and describe the four factors involved
- Explain how the SDLC serves as a framework for systems development
- List reasons for systems projects and factors that affect such projects
- Describe systems requests and the role of the systems review committee
- Define operational, technical, economic, and schedule feasibility
- Explain the factors that affect project priorities
- Describe the steps and the end product of a preliminary investigation

CHAPTER CONTENTS

2.1 INTRODUCTION

During the systems planning phase, the IT team reviews a proposal to determine if it presents a strong business case. The term **business case** refers to the reasons, or justification, for a proposal. To analyze the business case for a specific proposal, the analyst must consider the company's overall mission, objectives, and IT needs.

This chapter begins with a discussion of a framework for strategic planning because the IT team must understand and support the firm's long-term strategic goals.

Systems development typically starts with a systems request, followed by a preliminary investigation, which includes a feasibility study. This chapter explains how systems requests originate, how a request is evaluated, and how a preliminary investigation is conducted. Fact-finding techniques that begin at this point and carry over into later development phases are also described. The preliminary investigation concludes with the report to management.

2.2 A FRAMEWORK FOR IT SYSTEMS DEVELOPMENT

The future will see new industries, new products, and new services — all spurred by huge advances in technology. There will also be a surge in Internet commerce, a cloud computing explosion, and a new business environment that is global, dynamic, and incredibly challenging. To some firms, these changes will be very threatening. Other companies will see great opportunities and take advantage of them by creating strategic plans.

Strategic planning is the process of identifying long-term organizational goals, strategies, and resources. A strategic plan looks beyond day-to-day activities and focuses on a horizon that is three, five, ten, or more years in the future. A company requires information technology to support its strategic goals. Because the firm's IT group will be expected to deliver IT resources, IT managers must understand and participate in strategic planning. IT managers have to prepare for long-range needs, such as a new data warehouse, even as they handle immediate problems, such as a logic bug in the payroll system. In most companies, the IT team reviews each IT-related proposal, project, and systems request to determine if it presents a strong business case, or justification.

The following sections provide an overview of strategic planning, a description of SWOT analysis, and a look at the changing role of the IT department.

2.2.1 Strategic Planning Overview

Why should a systems analyst be interested in strategic planning? The answer might be found in an old story about two stonecutters who were hard at work when a passerby asked them what they were doing. "I'm cutting stones," said the first worker. The second worker replied, "I'm building a cathedral."

So it is with information technology: One analyst might say, "I am using a CASE tool," while another might say, "I am helping the company succeed in a major new business venture." The difference is clear: Systems analysts should focus on the larger, strategic role of IT even as they carry out their day-to-day technical tasks.

Strategic planning starts with a **mission statement** that reflects the firm's vision, purpose, and values. Mission statements usually focus on long-term challenges and goals, the importance of the firm's stakeholders, and a commitment to the firm's role as a corporate citizen. For example, Google's mission statement posted on their website is stated succinctly as, "… to organize the world's information and make it universally accessible and useful."

With the mission statement as a backdrop, a firm develops short-term goals and objectives. For example, the company might establish one-year, three-year, and five-year goals for expanding market share. To achieve those goals, the company might develop a list of shorter-term objectives. If it wants to increase web-based orders by 30% next year, a company might set quarterly objectives with monthly milestones. High-priority objectives are called critical success factors. A critical success factor is one that must be achieved to fulfill the company's mission.

Objectives also might include tactical plans, such as creating a new website and training a special customer support group to answer email inquiries. Finally, the objectives translate into day-to-day business operations, supported by IT and other corporate resources. The outcome is a set of business results that affect company stakeholders.

2.2.2 What Is SWOT Analysis?

The letters SWOT stand for strengths, weaknesses, opportunities, and threats. A SWOT analysis can focus on a specific product or project, an operating division, the entire company, or the mission statement itself. The overall aim is to avoid seeking goals that are unrealistic, unprofitable, or unachievable.

An enterprise SWOT analysis usually begins with these questions:

- What are our strengths, and how can we use them to achieve our business goals?

- What are our weaknesses, and how can we reduce or eliminate them?

- What are our opportunities, and how do we plan to take advantage of them?

- What are our threats, and how can we assess, manage, and respond to the possible risks?

A SWOT analysis examines a firm's technical, human, and financial resources. In Figure 2-1, the bulleted lists show samples of typical strengths, weaknesses, opportunities, and threats for an organization considering expanding their web-based online operations.

As the SWOT process continues, management reviews specific resources, business operations, and valuable assets. For example, suppose that the company owns an important patent. A SWOT review for the patent might resemble Figure 2-2.

There is no standard approach to strategic planning. Some managers believe that a firm's mission statement should contain an inspirational message to its stakeholders. Others feel that unless a firm starts with a realistic SWOT assessment, it might develop a mission statement that is unachievable. Most companies view the strategic

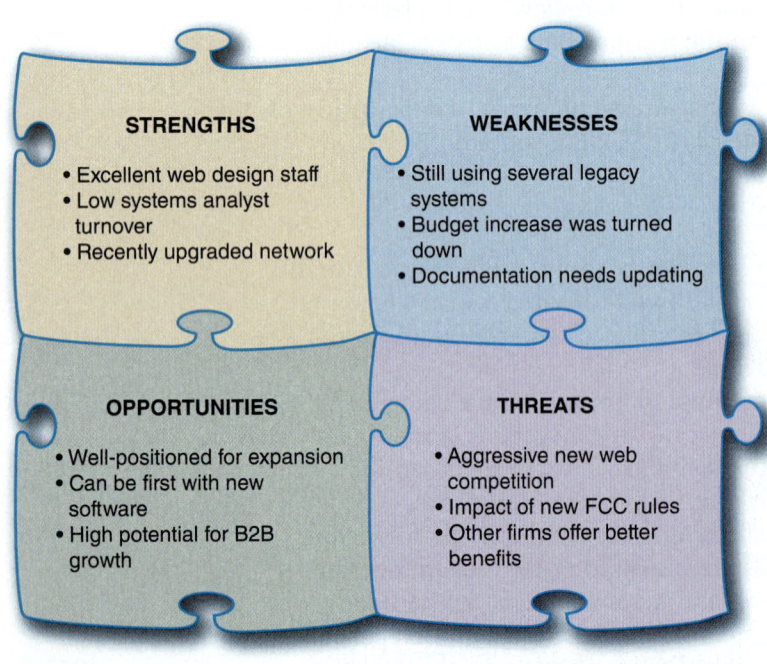

FIGURE 2-1 A SWOT analysis might produce results similar to those shown here.

planning process as a dynamic interaction, where the company's mission statement reflects a long-term horizon, but sets forth goals that are achievable and consistent with real-world conditions.

2.2.3 Strategic Planning for IT Projects

Experienced analysts know that planning is essential for IT project success, and it must start as early as possible. Careful planning can help assure that:

- The project supports overall business strategy and operational needs.

- The project scope is well defined and clearly stated.

- The project goals are realistic, achievable, and tied to specific statements, assumptions, constraints, factors, and other inputs.

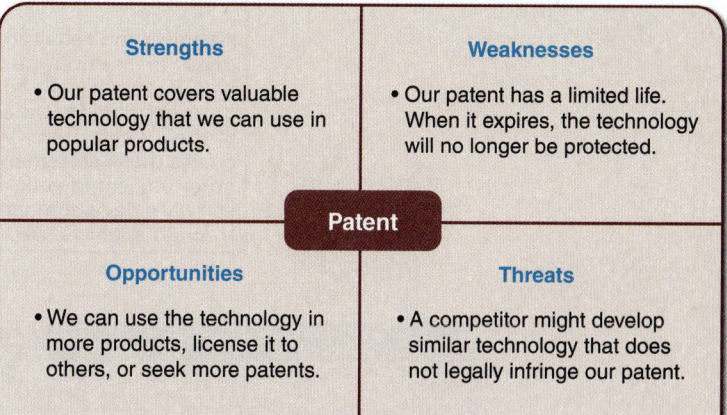

SWOT Analysis of a Corporate Patent

Strengths
- Our patent covers valuable technology that we can use in popular products.

Weaknesses
- Our patent has a limited life. When it expires, the technology will no longer be protected.

Patent

Opportunities
- We can use the technology in more products, license it to others, or seek more patents.

Threats
- A competitor might develop similar technology that does not legally infringe our patent.

FIGURE 2-2 This SWOT analysis example focuses on a specific asset: a company patent.

CASE IN POINT 2.1:   Lo Carb Meals

Lo Carb is a successful new company that has published several cookbooks and marketed its own line of low-carbohydrate meals. Joe Turner, Lo Carb's president, has asked your opinion. He wants to know whether a mission statement really is necessary. After you review the chapter material, write a brief memo with your views. Be sure to include good (and not-so-good) examples of actual mission statements that you find on the web.

The first step is to select a planning tool. Some developers stick to traditional text-based methods, using Microsoft Word tables to provide structure and clarity. Others prefer a spreadsheet, such as Microsoft Excel, because it is easy to display priorities and the relative importance of planning assumptions. However, another approach is to use a computer-aided systems engineering (CASE) tool to define and document the overall environment. To understand why this is so, consider the following scenario and illustration:

As a systems analyst in the IT department of a large hotel chain, your task is to review the Visible Analyst CASE tool to see whether it would be helpful in planning a new marketing system. After opening the program, you navigate to the Help section for an overview, which is shown in Figure 2-3a.

Next, you create a sample project and enter an assumption about the target date for a new network, as shown in Figure 2-3b. You see that many types of planning statements are possible, including goals, objectives, and critical success factors, among others. Planning statements also can document strengths, weaknesses, opportunities, and threats, as shown in Figure 2-3c.

After entering the planning statement, you open the strategic planning screen and see the new statement displayed, as shown in Figure 2-3d. You can see that Visible Analyst has embedded the planning statement directly into the project, so it can be accessed at any point in the development process.

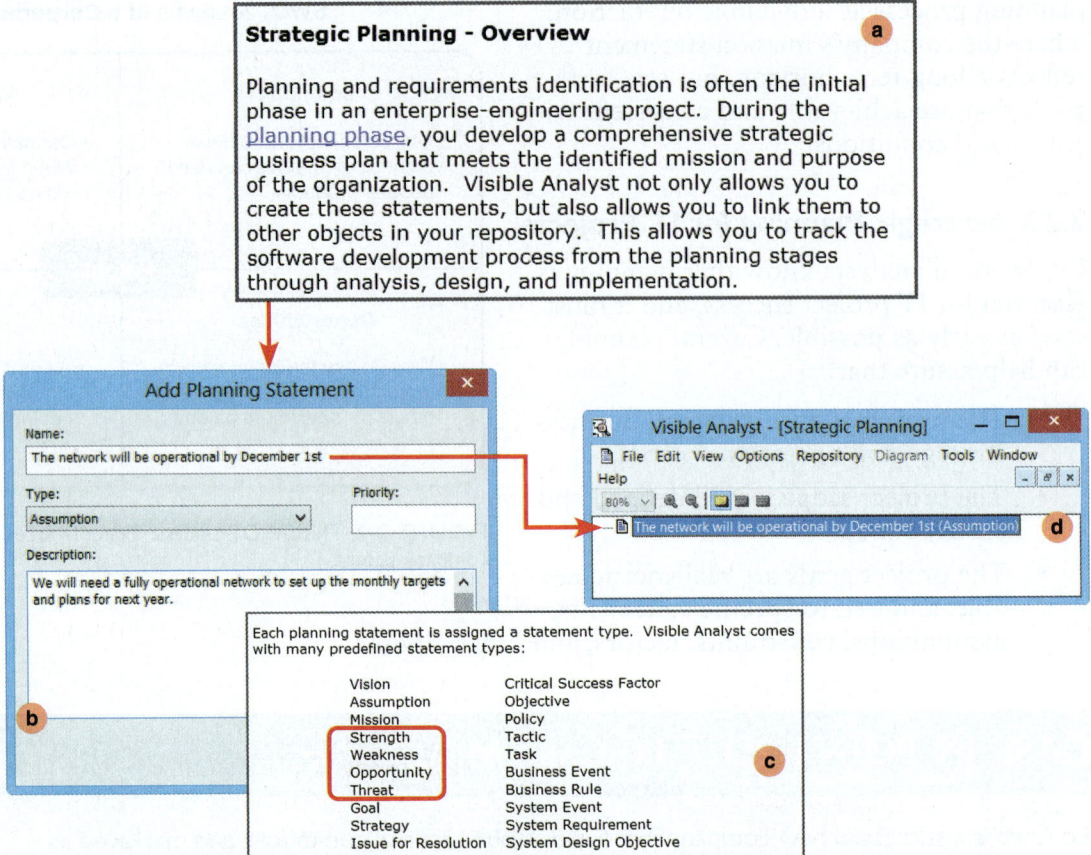

FIGURE 2-3 The Visible Analyst CASE tool supports strategic planning and allows a user to enter many kinds of planning statements. Notice the four SWOT categories highlighted in the list.
Source: Visible Systems Corporation.

This example shows how a CASE tool can integrate various statements, entities, data elements, and graphical models into an overall structure. The result is more consistency, better quality, and much less effort for the system analyst.

2.2.4 The Changing Role of the IT Department

Management and IT are linked closely, and remarkable changes have occurred in both areas. In the past a typical IT department handled all aspects of systems development and consulted users only when, and if, the department wanted user input. Today, systems development is much more team oriented. New approaches to systems development, such as agile methods and rapid application development (RAD), typically involve groups of users, managers, and IT staff working together right from the start of the project.

Although team-oriented development is the norm, some companies still see the role of the IT department as a gatekeeper, responsible for screening and evaluating systems requests. Should the IT department perform the initial evaluation, or should a cross-functional team do it? The answer probably depends on the company's size, the nature of the system request, and the scale of the project. For example, in smaller companies or firms where only one person has IT skills, that person acts as a coordinator and consults closely with users and managers to evaluate systems requests. Larger firms are more likely to use an evaluation team or a systems review committee.

CASE IN POINT 2.2:   ATTAWAY AIRLINES, PART ONE

You are the IT director at Attaway Airlines, a small regional air carrier. You chair the company's systems review committee, and you currently are dealing with strong disagreements about two key projects. Dan Esposito, the marketing manager, says it is vital to have a new computerized reservation system that can provide better customer service and reduce operational costs. Molly Kinnon, vice president of finance, is equally adamant that a new accounting system is needed immediately because it will be very expensive to adjust the current system to new federal reporting requirements. Molly outranks Dan, and she is your boss. The next meeting, which promises to be a real showdown, is set for 9:00 a.m. tomorrow. How will you prepare for the meeting? What questions and issues should be discussed?

2.3 WHAT IS A BUSINESS CASE?

As mentioned earlier, the term *business case* refers to the reasons, or justification, for a proposal. A business case should be comprehensive yet easy to understand. It should describe the project clearly, provide the justification to proceed, and estimate the project's financial impact. The business case should answer questions such as the following:

- Why are we doing this project?
- What is the project about?
- How does this solution address key business issues?
- How much will it cost and how long will it take?
- Will we suffer a productivity loss during the transition?
- What is the return on investment and payback period?
- What are the risks of doing the project? What are the risks of not doing the project?
- How will we measure success?
- What alternatives exist?

Examples of business cases, both good and bad, can be found online. Just search for "sample business case" and examine the structure and content of some of the samples available. It is particularly instructive to compare and contrast business cases for different areas, such as those for government contracts versus private enterprises.

2.4 INFORMATION SYSTEMS PROJECTS

This section discusses reasons for systems projects and the internal and external factors that affect systems projects. The section also includes a preview of project management, which is discussed in detail in Chapter 3.

2.4.1 Main Reasons for Systems Projects

The starting point for most projects is called a systems request, which is a formal way of asking for IT support. A systems request might propose enhancements for an existing system, the correction of problems, the replacement of an older system, or the

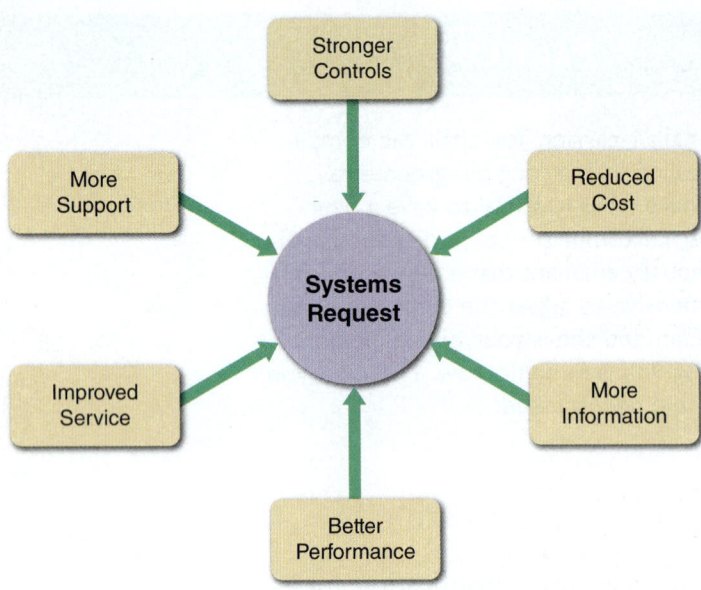

FIGURE 2-4 Six main reasons for systems requests.

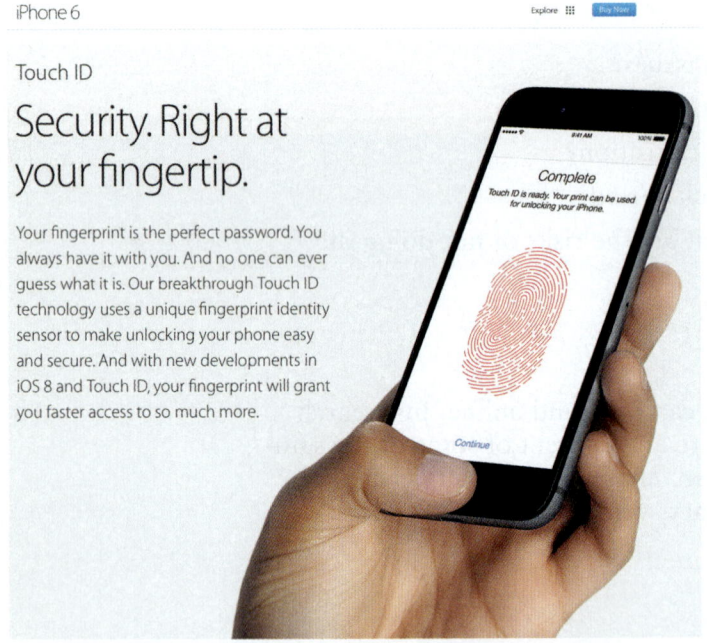

FIGURE 2-5 Apple Touch ID uses a unique fingerprint identity sensor.
Source: www.apple.com

development of an entirely new information system that is needed to support a company's current and future business needs.

As Figure 2-4 shows, the six main reasons for systems requests are stronger controls, reduced cost, more information, better performance, improved service to customers, and more support for new products and services.

STRONGER CONTROLS: A system must have effective controls to ensure that data is secure and accurate. Some common security controls include passwords, various levels of user access, and encryption, or coding data to keep it safe from unauthorized users. Hardware-based security controls include biometric devices that can identify a person by a retina scan or by mapping a fingerprint pattern. The technology uses infrared scanners that create images with thousands of measurements of hand and finger characteristics, as shown in Figure 2-5, which displays Apple's Touch ID security mechanism on the iPhone.

In addition to being secure, data also must be accurate. Controls should minimize data entry errors whenever possible. For example, if a user enters an invalid customer number, the order processing system should reject the entry immediately and prompt the user to enter a valid number. Data entry controls must be effective without being excessive. If a system requires users to confirm every item with an "Are you sure? Y/N" message, internal users and customers might complain that the system is not user-friendly.

REDUCED COST: The current system could be expensive to operate or maintain as a result of technical problems, design weaknesses, or the changing demands of the business. It might be possible to adapt the system to newer technology or upgrade it. On the other hand, cost-benefit analysis might show that a new system would be more cost effective and provide better support for long-term objectives.

MORE INFORMATION: The system might produce information that is insufficient, incomplete, or unable to support the company's changing information needs. For example, a system that tracks customer orders might not be capable of analyzing and predicting marketing trends. In the face of intense competition and rapid product development cycles, managers need the best possible information to make major decisions on planning, designing, and marketing new products and services.

BETTER PERFORMANCE: The current system might not meet performance requirements. For example, it might respond slowly to data inquiries at certain times, or it might be unable to support company growth. Performance limitations also result when a system that was designed for a specific hardware configuration becomes obsolete when new hardware is introduced.

IMPROVED SERVICE: Systems requests often are aimed at improving service to customers or users within the company. For instance, allowing mutual fund investors to check their account balances on a website, storing data on rental car customer preferences, or creating an online college registration system are all examples of providing valuable services and increased customer satisfaction.

MORE SUPPORT FOR NEW PRODUCTS AND SERVICES: New products and services often require new types or levels of IT support. For example, a software vendor might offer an automatic upgrade service for subscribers, or a package delivery company might add a special service for radio frequency identification (RFID)-tagged shipments. In situations like these, it is most likely that additional IT support will be required. At the other end of the spectrum, product obsolescence can also be an important factor in IT planning. As new products enter the marketplace, vendors often announce that they will no longer provide support for older versions. A lack of vendor support would be an important consideration in deciding whether or not to upgrade.

CASE IN POINT 2.3:   TRENT COLLEGE

Trent College is a private school in a small Maryland town. The college has outgrown its computerized registration system and is considering a new system. Althea Riddick, the college president, has asked you to list the reasons for systems projects, which are described in Section 2.4.1, and assign a relative weight to each reason, using a scale of 1–10, low to high. She said to use your best judgment and support your conclusions in a brief memo to her. She also wants you to create a Microsoft Excel spreadsheet that will calculate the weighted values automatically for each reason.

2.4.2 Factors That Affect Systems Projects

Internal and external factors affect every business decision that a company makes, and IT projects are no exception. Figure 2-6 shows internal and external factors that shape corporate IT choices.

2.4.3 Internal Factors

Internal factors include the strategic plan, top managers, user requests, information technology department, existing systems and data, and company finances.

STRATEGIC PLAN: A company's strategic plan sets the overall direction for the firm and has an important impact on IT projects. Company goals and objectives that need IT support will generate systems requests and influence IT priorities. A strategic plan that stresses technology tends to create a favorable climate for IT projects that extends throughout the organization.

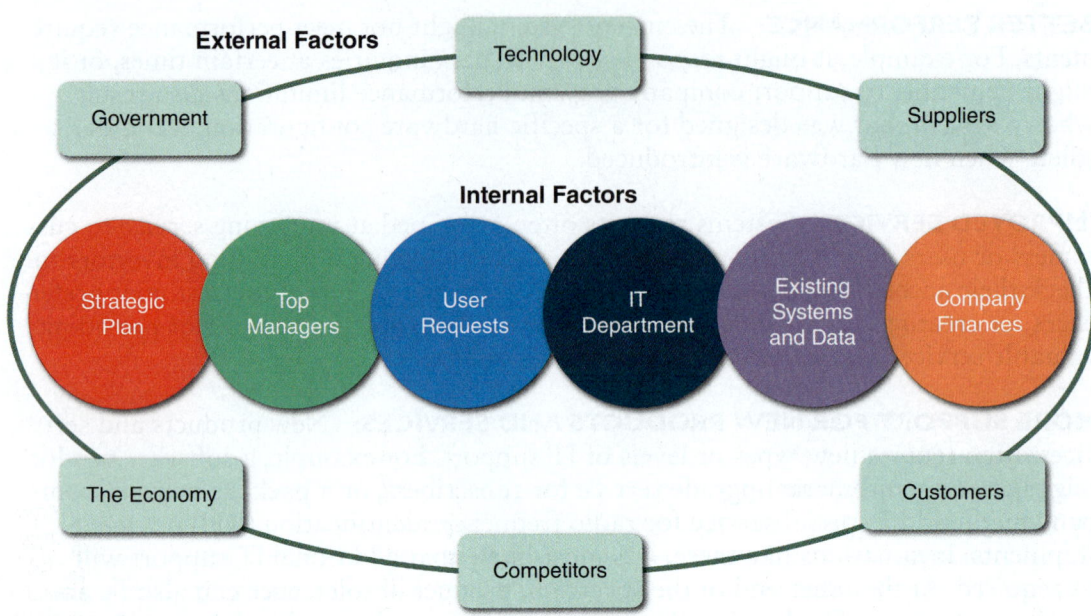

FIGURE 2-6 Internal and external factors that affect IT projects.

TOP MANAGERS: Because significant resources are required, top management usually initiates large-scale projects. Those decisions often result from strategic business goals that require new IT systems, more information for decision-making processes, or better support for mission-critical information systems.

USER REQUESTS: As users rely more heavily on information systems to perform their jobs, they are likely to request even more IT services and support. For example, sales reps might request improvements to the company's website, a more powerful sales analysis report, a network to link all sales locations, or an online system that allows customers to obtain the status of their orders instantly. Or, users might not be satisfied with the current system because it is difficult to learn or lacks flexibility. They might want information systems support for business requirements that did not even exist when the system was first developed.

INFORMATION TECHNOLOGY DEPARTMENT: Systems project requests come also from the IT department itself. IT staff members often make recommendations based on their knowledge of business operations and technology trends. IT proposals might be strictly technical matters, such as replacement of certain network components, or suggestions might be more business oriented, such as proposing a new reporting or data collection system.

EXISTING SYSTEMS AND DATA: Errors or problems in existing systems can trigger requests for systems projects. When dealing with older systems, analysts sometimes spend too much time reacting to day-to-day problems without looking at underlying causes. This approach can turn an information system into a patchwork of corrections and changes that cannot support the company's overall business needs. This problem typically occurs with legacy systems, which are older systems that are less technologically advanced. When migrating to a new system, IT planners must plan the conversion of existing data, which is described in detail in Chapter 11.

COMPANY FINANCES: A company's financial status can affect systems projects. If the company is going through a difficult time, the project may be postponed until there is more cash available to finance the effort. On the other hand, if the company is enjoying financial success, the decision to embark on a new project may be easier to make.

2.4.4 External Factors

External factors include technology, suppliers, customers, competitors, the economy, and government.

TECHNOLOGY: Changing technology is a major force affecting business and society in general. For example, the rapid growth of telecommunications, coupled with increased computing power and continuous miniaturization of electronic components, has created entire new industries and technologies, including the proliferation of smartphones and the app ecosystem.

Technology also dramatically reshapes existing business operations. The success of scanner technology resulted in universal bar coding that now affects virtually all products. Some industry experts predict that bar code technology, which is over 40 years old, will be overshadowed in the future by **electronic product code (EPC)** technology that uses RFID tags to identify and monitor the movement of each individual product, from the factory floor to the retail checkout counter.

Quick Response codes (QR codes), as shown in Figure 2-7, are like bar codes but square in shape. They contain more information than traditional bar codes, but less than RFID tags. They do have the advantage of being less expensive to use than RFID tags, and they can be printed on almost anything — including online advertisements.

FIGURE 2-7 QR code

Source: www.qrstuff.com

SUPPLIERS: With the growth of electronic data interchange (EDI), relationships with suppliers are critically important. For example, an automobile company might require that suppliers code their parts in a certain manner to match the auto company's inventory control system. EDI also enables **just-in-time (JIT)** inventory systems that rely on computer-to-computer data exchange to minimize unnecessary inventory. The purpose of a JIT system is to provide the right products at the right place at the right time.

CUSTOMERS: Customers are vitally important to any business. Information systems that interact with customers usually receive top priority. Many companies implement **customer relationship management (CRM)** systems that integrate all customer-related events and transactions, including marketing, sales, and customer service activities. Vendor-oriented CRM systems often interconnect with supply chain management (SCM) systems, which were discussed in Chapter 1. CRM components can provide automated responses to sales inquiries, online order processing, and inventory tracking. Because an efficient warehouse is just as important as a successful website, suppliers use *smart* forklifts that can read RFID tags or UPC numbers and transmit data to a CRM system, as shown in Figure 2-8. Some suppliers also use robots for order fulfillment, such as the Kiva robots shown in Figure 2-9 that Amazon.com uses in their warehouses.

Another RFID application is called **electronic proof of delivery (EPOD)**. Using EPOD, a supplier uses RFID tags on each crate, case, or shipping unit to create a digital shipping list. The customer receives the list and scans the incoming shipment. If a

FIGURE 2-8 In an efficient warehouse, smart forklifts can read RFID tags or UPC numbers and transmit data to a CRM system.

Courtesy of Intermec Technologies

discrepancy is detected, it is reported and adjusted automatically. Because they would be expensive to investigate manually, small shipping inconsistencies might not otherwise be traced. This is an example of technology-related cost control.

COMPETITORS: Competition drives many information systems decisions. For example, if one cellular telephone provider offers a new type of digital service, other firms must match the plan in order to remain competitive. New product research and development, marketing, sales, and service all require IT support.

THE ECONOMY: Economic activity has a powerful influence on corporate information management. In a period of economic expansion, firms need to be ready with scalable systems that can handle additional volume and growth. Predicting the business cycle is not an exact science, and careful research and planning are important.

GOVERNMENT: Federal, state, and local government regulations directly affect the design of corporate information systems. For example, up-to-date IRS reporting requirements must be designed into a payroll package.

FIGURE 2-9 Kiva robots used in an Amazon.com warehouse.

Justin Sullivan/Getty Images

2.5 Evaluation of Systems Requirements

In most organizations, the IT department receives more systems requests than it can handle. Many organizations assign responsibility for evaluating systems requests to a group of key managers and users. Many companies call this group a **systems review committee** or a **computer resources committee**. Regardless of the name, the objective is to use the combined judgment and experience of several analysts to evaluate systems projects.

2.5.1 Systems Request Forms

Many organizations use a special form for systems requests, similar to the online sample shown in Figure 2-10. A properly designed form streamlines the request process and ensures consistency. The form must be easy to understand and include clear instructions. It should include enough space for all required information and should indicate what supporting documents are needed. Most companies use online systems request forms that users submit electronically because the form can be processed automatically.

When a systems request form is received, a systems analyst or IT manager examines it to determine what IT resources are required for the preliminary investigation. A designated person or a committee then decides whether to proceed with a preliminary investigation. Sometimes, a situation requires an immediate response. For example, if the problem involves a mission-critical system, an IT maintenance team must restore normal operations immediately. When the system is functioning properly, the team conducts a review and prepares a systems request to document the work that was performed.

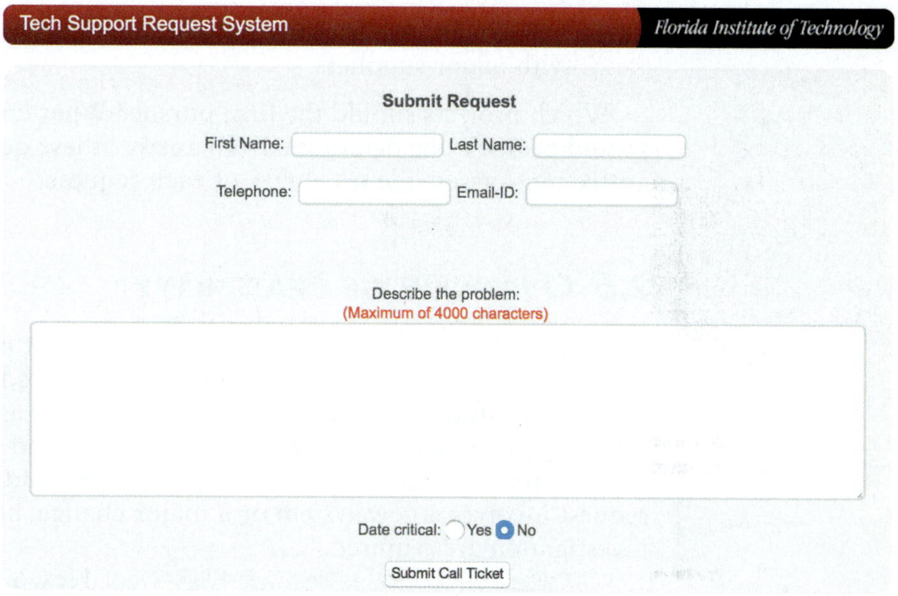
Tech Support Request System
Florida Institute of Technology
Submit Request
First Name: Last Name:
Telephone: Email-ID:
Describe the problem:
(Maximum of 4000 characters)
Date critical: Yes No
Submit Call Ticket

FIGURE 2-10 Example of an online systems request form.
Source: Florida Institute of Technology

2.5.2 Systems Review Committee

Most large companies use a systems review committee to evaluate systems requests. Instead of relying on a single individual, a committee approach provides a variety of experience and knowledge. With a broader viewpoint, a committee can establish priorities more effectively than an individual, and one person's bias is less likely to affect the decisions. A typical committee consists of the IT director and several managers or representatives from other departments. The IT director usually serves as a technical consultant to ensure that committee members are aware of crucial issues, problems, and opportunities.

Although a committee offers many advantages, some disadvantages exist. For example, action on requests must wait until the committee meets. Another potential disadvantage of a committee is that members might favor projects requested by their own departments, and internal political differences could delay important decisions.

Many smaller companies rely on one person to evaluate system requests instead of a committee. If only one person has the necessary IT skills and experience, that person must consult closely with users and managers throughout the company to ensure that business and operational needs are considered carefully.

Whether one person or a committee is responsible, the goal is to evaluate the requests and set priorities. Suppose four requests must be reviewed:

1. The marketing group wants to analyze current customer spending habits and forecast future trends.

2. The technical support group wants a cellular link so service representatives can download technical data instantly.

3. The accounting department wants to redesign customer statements and allow Internet access.

4. The production staff wants an inventory control system that can exchange data with major suppliers.

Which projects should the firm pursue? What criteria should be applied? How should priorities be determined? To answer these questions, the individual or the committee must assess the feasibility of each request.

2.6 OVERVIEW OF FEASIBILITY

As described in Chapter 1, a systems request must pass several tests, called a feasibility study, to see whether it is worthwhile to proceed further. As shown in Figure 2-11, a feasibility study uses four main yardsticks to measure a proposal: operational feasibility, economic feasibility, technical feasibility, and schedule feasibility.

Sometimes a feasibility study is quite simple and can be done in a few hours. If the request involves a new system or a major change, however, extensive fact-finding and investigation are required.

How much effort should go into a feasibility study depends on nature of the request. For example, if a department wants an existing report sorted in a different order, the analyst can decide quickly whether the request is feasible. On the other hand, a proposal by the marketing department for a new market research system to predict sales trends would require much more effort. In both cases, the systems analyst asks these important questions:

- Is the proposal desirable in an operational sense? Is it a practical approach that will solve a problem or take advantage of an opportunity to achieve company goals?

- Is the proposal technically feasible? Are the necessary technical resources and people available for the project?

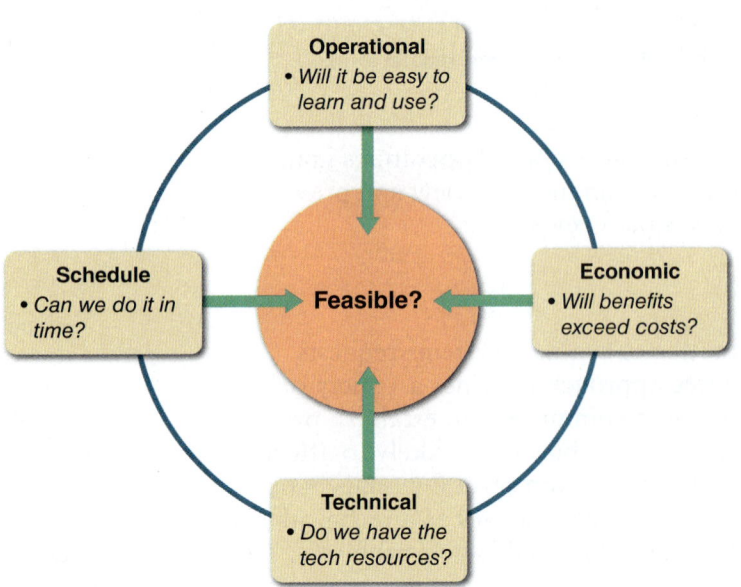

FIGURE 2-11 A feasibility study examines operational, technical, economic, and schedule factors.

- Is the proposal economically desirable? What are the projected savings and costs? Are other intangible factors involved, such as customer satisfaction or company image? Is the problem worth solving, and will the request result in a sound business investment?

- Can the proposal be accomplished within an acceptable time frame?

To obtain more information about a systems request, initial fact-finding might be accomplished by studying organization charts, performing interviews, reviewing current documentation, observing operations, and surveying users. If the systems request is approved, more intensive fact-finding will continue during the systems analysis phase.

2.6.1 Operational Feasibility

Operational feasibility means that a proposed system will be used effectively after it has been developed. If users have difficulty with a new system, it will not produce the expected benefits. Organizational culture can also affect operational feasibility. For instance, a system that works well in a highly structured workplace might be very unpopular in a more relaxed corporate culture. Operational feasibility is difficult to measure with precision, but must be studied very carefully. The following questions would help predict a system's operational feasibility:

- Does management support the project? Do users support the project? Is the current system well liked and effectively used? Do users see the need for change?

- Will the new system result in a workforce reduction? If so, what will happen to the affected employees?

- Will the new system require training for users? If so, is the company prepared to provide the necessary resources for training current employees?

- Will users be involved in planning the new system right from the start?

- Will the new system place any new demands on users or require any operating changes? For example, will any information be less accessible or produced less frequently? Will performance decline in any way? If so, will an overall gain to the organization outweigh individual losses?

- Will customers experience adverse effects in any way, either temporarily or permanently?

- Will any risk to the company's image or goodwill result?

- Does the development schedule conflict with other company priorities?

- Do legal or ethical issues need to be considered?

2.6.2 Economic Feasibility

Economic feasibility means that the projected benefits of the proposed system outweigh the estimated costs usually considered the total cost of ownership (TCO), which includes ongoing support and maintenance costs, as well as acquisition costs. To determine TCO, the analyst must estimate costs in each of the following areas:

- People, including IT staff and users

- Hardware and equipment

- Software, including in-house development as well as purchases from vendors
- Formal and informal training, including peer-to-peer support
- Licenses and fees
- Consulting expenses
- Facility costs
- The estimated cost of not developing the system or postponing the project

Tangible costs, such as those listed above, usually can be measured in dollars. But **intangible costs** also must be considered. For example, low employee morale might not have an immediate dollar impact, but certainly will affect the company's performance.

In addition to costs, tangible and intangible benefits to the company must be assessed. The systems review committee will use those figures, along with the cost estimates, to decide whether to pursue the project beyond the preliminary investigation phase.

Tangible benefits are benefits that can be measured in dollars. Tangible benefits result from a decrease in expenses, an increase in revenues, or both. Examples of tangible benefits include the following:

- A new scheduling system that reduces overtime
- An online package tracking system that improves service and decreases the need for clerical staff
- A sophisticated inventory control system that cuts excess inventory and eliminates production delays

Intangible benefits are advantages that are difficult to measure in dollars but are important to the company. Examples of intangible benefits include the following:

- A user-friendly system that improves employee job satisfaction
- A sales tracking system that supplies better information for marketing decisions
- A new website that enhances the company's image

The development timetable must also be considered, because some benefits might occur as soon as the system is operational, but others might not take place until later.

2.6.3 Technical Feasibility

Technical feasibility refers to the technical resources needed to develop, purchase, install, or operate the system. When assessing technical feasibility, an analyst should consider the following points:

- Does the company have the necessary hardware, software, and network resources? If not, can those resources be acquired without difficulty?
- Does the company have the needed technical expertise? If not, can it be acquired?
- Does the proposed platform have sufficient capacity for future needs? If not, can it be expanded?
- Will a prototype be required?

- Will the hardware and software environment be reliable? Will it integrate with other company information systems, both now and in the future? Will it interface properly with external systems operated by customers and suppliers?

- Will the combination of hardware and software supply adequate performance? Do clear expectations and performance specifications exist?

- Will the system be able to handle future transaction volume and company growth?

2.6.4 Schedule Feasibility

Schedule feasibility means that a project can be implemented in an acceptable time frame. When assessing schedule feasibility, a systems analyst must consider the interaction between time and costs. For example, speeding up a project schedule might make a project feasible, but much more expensive.

Other issues that relate to schedule feasibility include the following:

- Can the company or the IT team control the factors that affect schedule feasibility?

- Has management established a firm timetable for the project?

- What conditions must be satisfied during the development of the system?

- Will an accelerated schedule pose any risks? If so, are the risks acceptable?

- Will project management techniques be available to coordinate and control the project?

- Will a project manager be appointed?

Chapter 3 describes various project management tools and techniques.

2.7 EVALUATING FEASIBILITY

The first step in evaluating feasibility is to identify and weed out systems requests that are not feasible. For example, a request would not be feasible if it required hardware or software that the company already had rejected.

Even if the request is feasible, it might not be necessary. For example, a request for multiple versions of a report could require considerable design and programming effort. A better alternative might be to download the server data to a personal computer-based software package and show users how to produce their own reports. In this case, training users would be a better investment than producing reports for them.

Also keep in mind that systems requests that are not currently feasible can be resubmitted as new hardware, software, or expertise becomes available. Development costs might decrease, or the value of benefits might increase enough that a systems request eventually becomes feasible. Conversely, an initially feasible project can be rejected later.

As the project progresses, conditions often change. Acquisition costs might increase, and the project might become more expensive than anticipated. In addition, managers and users sometimes lose confidence in a project. For all those reasons, feasibility analysis is an ongoing task that must be performed throughout the systems development process.

2.8 SETTING PRIORITIES

After rejecting systems requests that are not feasible, the systems review committee must establish priorities for the remaining items. The highest priority goes to projects that provide the greatest benefit, at the lowest cost, in the shortest period of time. Many factors, however, influence project evaluation.

2.8.1 Factors That Affect Priority

When assessing a project's priority, a systems analyst should consider the following:

- Will the proposed system reduce costs? Where? When? How? By how much?
- Will the system increase revenue for the company? Where? When? How? By how much?
- Will the systems project result in more information or produce better results? How? Are the results measurable?
- Will the system serve customers better?
- Will the system serve the organization better?
- Can the project be implemented in a reasonable time period? How long will the results last?
- Are the necessary financial, human, and technical resources available?

Few projects will score high in all areas. Some proposals might not reduce costs but will provide important new features. Other systems might reduce operating costs substantially but require the purchase or lease of additional hardware. Some systems might be very desirable but require several years of development before producing significant benefits.

Whenever possible, the analyst should use tangible costs and benefits that can be measured in dollars. However, the proposal might involve intangible benefits, such as enhancing the organization's image, raising employee morale, or improving customer service. These examples would be harder to measure, but should also be considered.

2.8.2 Discretionary and Nondiscretionary Projects

Projects where management has a choice in implementing them are called discretionary projects. Projects where no choice exists are called nondiscretionary projects. Creating a new report for a user is an example of a discretionary project; adding a report required by a new federal law is an example of a nondiscretionary project.

If a particular project is not discretionary, the systems analyst should ask if it is really necessary for the systems review committee to evaluate it. Some people believe that waiting for committee approval delays critical nondiscretionary projects unnecessarily. Others believe that submitting all requests to the systems review keeps the committee aware of all projects that compete for IT resources. As a result, the committee can review priorities and create realistic schedules.

Many nondiscretionary projects are predictable. Examples include annual updates to payroll, tax percentages, or quarterly changes in reporting requirements for an insurance processing system. By planning ahead for predictable projects, the IT department manages its resources better and keeps the systems review committee fully informed without needing prior approval in every case.

Back at Attaway Airlines, the morning meeting ended with no agreement between Dan Esposito and Molly Kinnon. In fact, a new issue arose. Molly now says that the new accounting system is entitled to the highest priority because the federal government soon will require the reporting of certain types of company-paid health insurance premiums. Because the current system will not handle this report, she insists that the entire accounting system is a nondiscretionary project. As you might expect, Dan is upset. Can part of a project be nondiscretionary? What issues need to be discussed? The committee meets again tomorrow, and the members will look to you, as the IT director, for guidance.

2.9 PRELIMINARY INVESTIGATION OVERVIEW

A systems analyst conducts a preliminary investigation to study the systems request and recommend specific action. After obtaining an authorization to proceed, the analyst interacts with managers, users, and other stakeholders, as shown in the model in Figure 2-12. The analyst gathers facts about the problem or opportunity, project scope and constraints, project benefits, and estimated development time and costs. The end product of the preliminary investigation is a report to management.

2.9.1 Interaction with Managers, Users, and Other Stakeholders

Before starting a preliminary investigation, it is important to let people know about the investigation and explain the role of the system analyst. Meetings with key managers, users, and other stakeholders such as the IT staff should be scheduled, to describe the project, explain roles and responsibilities, answer questions, and invite comments. Interactive communication with users starts at this point and continues throughout the development process.

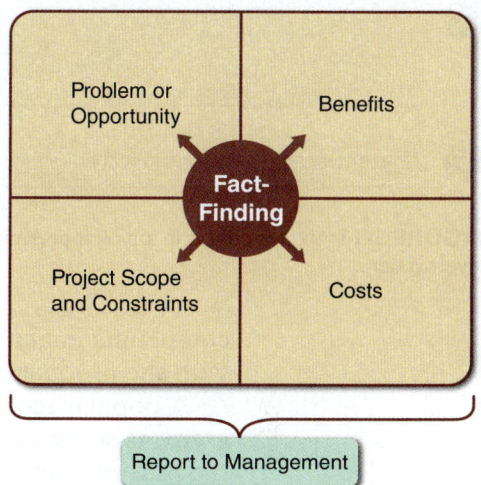

FIGURE 2-12 Model of a preliminary investigation. Note the importance of fact-finding in each of the four areas.

   A systems project often produces significant changes in company operations. Employees may be curious, concerned, or even opposed to those changes. It is not surprising to encounter some user resistance during a preliminary investigation. Employee attitudes and reactions are important and must be considered.

   When interacting with users, use the word *problem* carefully, because it has a negative meaning. When users are asked about *problems*, some will stress current system limitations rather than desirable new features or enhancements. Instead of focusing on difficulties, question users about additional capability they would like to have. This approach highlights ways to improve the user's job, provides a better understanding of operations, and builds better, more positive relationships with users.

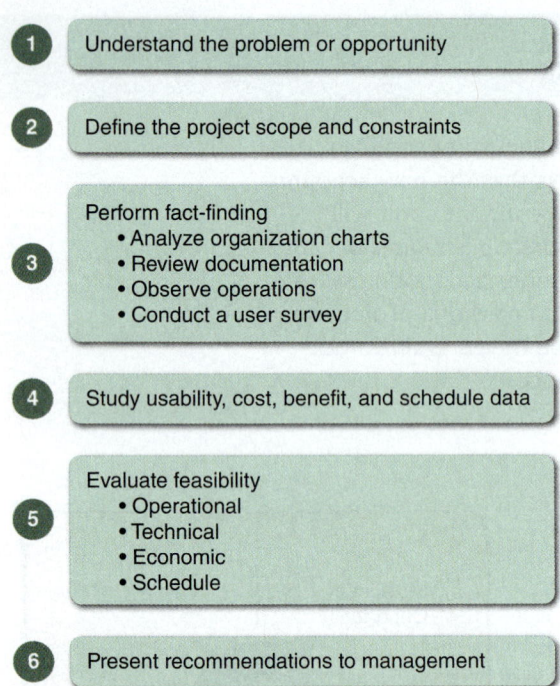

1. Understand the problem or opportunity

2. Define the project scope and constraints

3. Perform fact-finding
   • Analyze organization charts
   • Review documentation
   • Observe operations
   • Conduct a user survey

4. Study usability, cost, benefit, and schedule data

5. Evaluate feasibility
   • Operational
   • Technical
   • Economic
   • Schedule

6. Present recommendations to management

FIGURE 2-13 Six main steps in a typical preliminary investigation.

2.9.2 Planning the Preliminary Investigation

During a preliminary investigation, a systems analyst typically follows a series of steps, as shown in Figure 2-13. The exact procedure depends on the nature of the request, the size of the project, and the degree of urgency.

STEP 1: UNDERSTAND THE PROBLEM OR OPPORTUNITY: If the systems request involves a new information system or a substantial change in an existing system, systems analysts might need to develop a business profile that describes current business processes and functions, as explained in Chapter 1. Even where the request involves relatively minor changes or enhancements, how those modifications will affect business operations and other information systems must be understood. Often a change in one system has an unexpected ripple effect on another system. When a systems request is analyzed, which departments, users, and business processes are involved must be determined.

In many cases, the systems request does not reveal the underlying problem, but only a symptom. For example, a request to investigate centralized processing delays might reveal improper scheduling practices rather than hardware problems. Similarly, a request for analysis of customer complaints might disclose a lack of sales representative training, rather than problems with the product.

A popular technique for investigating causes and effects is called a **fishbone diagram,** as shown in Figure 2-14. A fishbone diagram is an analysis tool that represents the possible causes of a problem as a graphical outline. When using a fishbone diagram, an analyst first states the problem and draws a main bone with sub-bones that represent possible causes of the problem. In the example shown in Figure 2-14, the problem is *Low Morale*, and the analyst has identified four areas to investigate: *Environment, People, Management,* and *Machines.* In each area, the analyst identifies possible causes and draws them as horizontal sub-bones. For example, *Temp too hot or cold* is a possible cause in the *Environment* bone. For each cause, the analyst must dig deeper and ask the question: What could be causing *this* symptom to occur? For example, *why* is it too hot? If the answer is a *Faulty thermostat,* the analyst indicates this as a sub-bone to the *Temp too hot or cold* cause. In this manner, the analyst adds additional sub-bones to the diagram, until he or she uncovers root causes of a problem, rather than just the symptoms.

STEP 2: DEFINE THE PROJECT SCOPE AND CONSTRAINTS: Determining the **project scope** means defining the specific boundaries, or extent, of the project. For example, a statement that, *payroll is not being produced accurately* is very general, compared with the statement, *overtime pay is not being calculated correctly for production workers on the second shift at the Yorktown plant.* Similarly, the statement, *the project scope is to modify the accounts receivable system,* is not as specific as the statement, *the project scope is to allow customers to inquire online about account balances and recent transactions.*

Some analysts find it helpful to define project scope by creating a list with sections called *Must Do, Should Do, Could Do,* and *Won't Do.* This list can be reviewed later, during the systems analysis phase, when the systems requirements document is developed.

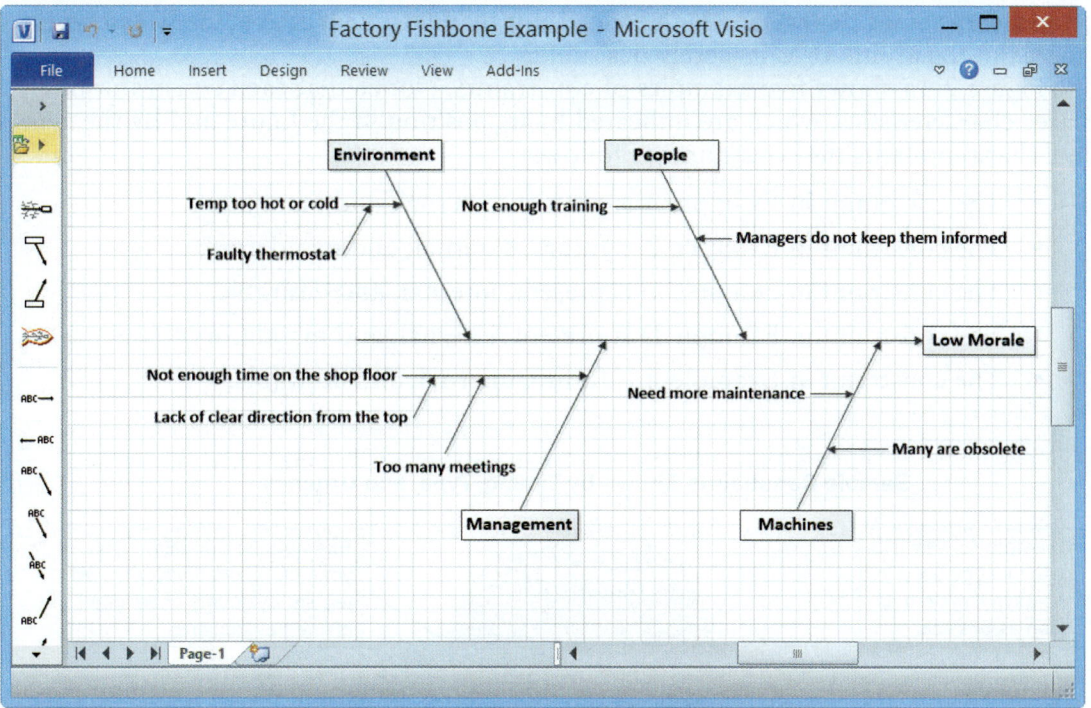

FIGURE 2-14 A fishbone diagram displays the causes of a problem. Typically, you must dig deeper to identify actual causes rather than just symptoms.

Projects with very general scope definitions are at risk of expanding gradually, without specific authorization, in a process called **project creep**. To avoid this problem, project scope should be defined as clearly as possible. A graphical model that shows the systems, people, and business processes that will be affected is sometimes useful. The scope of the project also establishes the boundaries of the preliminary investigation itself. A systems analyst should limit the focus to the problem at hand and avoid unnecessary expenditure of time and money.

Along with defining the scope of the project, any constraints on the system must be identified. A **constraint** is a requirement or condition that the system must satisfy or an outcome that the system must achieve. A constraint can involve hardware, software, time, policy, law, or cost. System constraints also define project scope. For example, if the system must operate with existing hardware, that is a constraint that affects potential solutions. Other examples of constraints are:

- The order entry system must accept input from 15 remote sites.
- The human resources information system must produce statistics on hiring practices.
- The new website must be operational by March 1.

When examining constraints, their characteristics should be identified, as follows.

Present versus future.   Is the constraint something that must be met as soon as the system is developed or modified, or is the constraint necessary at some future time?

Internal versus external.   Is the constraint due to a requirement within the organization, or does some external force, such as government regulation, impose it?

Mandatory versus desirable.   Is the constraint mandatory? Is it absolutely essential to meet the constraint, or is it merely desirable?

Figure 2-15 shows five examples of constraints. Notice that each constraint has three characteristics, which are indicated by its position in the figure and by the symbol that represents the constraint, as follows:

- The constraint in Example A is present, external, and mandatory.
- The constraint in Example B is future, external, and mandatory.
- The constraint in Example C is present, internal, and desirable.
- The constraint in Example D is present, internal, and mandatory.
- The constraint in Example E is future, internal, and desirable.

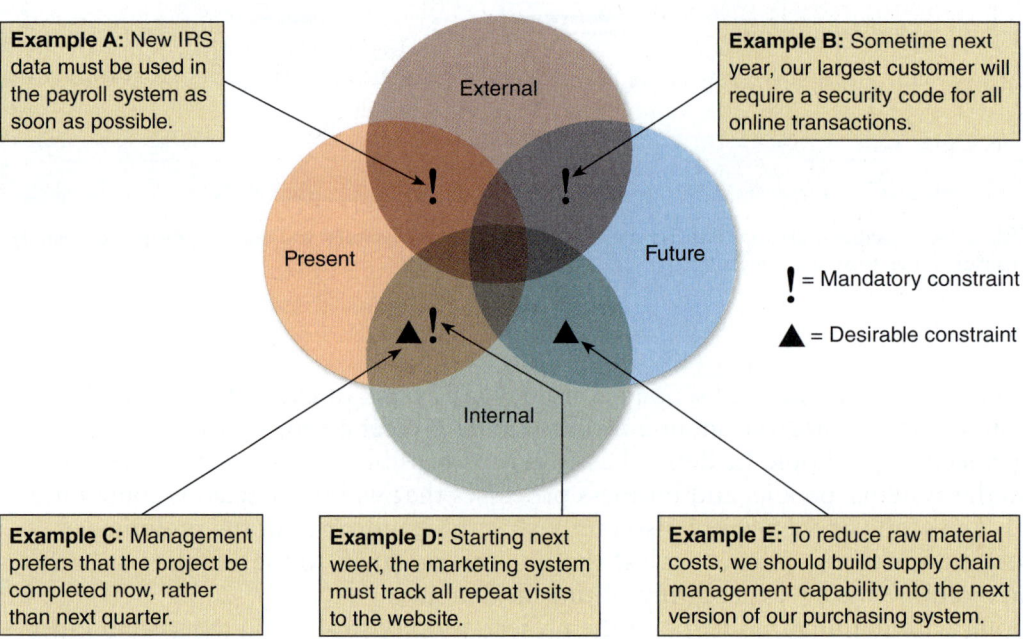

FIGURE 2-15 Examples of various types of constraints.

Regardless of the type, all constraints should be identified as early as possible to avoid future problems and surprises. A clear definition of project scope and constraints avoids misunderstandings that arise when managers assume that the system will have a certain feature or support for a project, but later find that the feature is not included.

STEP 3: PERFORM FACT-FINDING: The objective of fact-finding is to gather data about project usability, costs, benefits, and schedules. Fact-finding involves various techniques, which are described below. Depending on what information is needed to investigate the systems request, fact-finding might consume several hours, days, or weeks. For example, a change in a report format or data entry screen might require a single telephone call or email message to a user, whereas a new inventory system would involve a series of interviews. During fact-finding, the analyst might analyze organization charts, conduct interviews, review current documentation, observe operations, and carry out a user survey.

Analyze organization charts. An analyst will not always know the organizational structure of departments involved in the study. Organization charts should be obtained to understand the functions and identify people to interview.

If organization charts are not available, or are out of date, the necessary information should be obtained from department personnel and construct the charts, as shown in Figure 2-16.

Even when charts are available, their accuracy should be verified. Keep in mind that an organization chart shows formal reporting relationships but not the informal alignment of a group, which also is important.

Customer Service Department

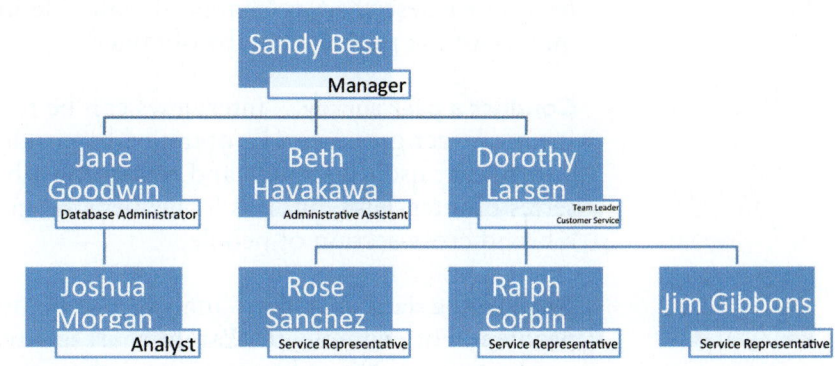

FIGURE 2-16 Specialized tools such as Microsoft Visio can be used to draw organizational charts, but general purpose presentation tools such as Microsoft PowerPoint shown here can also be used.

Conduct interviews. The primary method of obtaining information during the preliminary investigation is the interview. The interviewing process involves a series of steps:

1. Determine the people to interview.
2. Establish objectives for the interview.
3. Develop interview questions.
4. Prepare for the interview.
5. Conduct the interview.
6. Document the interview.
7. Evaluate the interview.

These seven steps are discussed in detail in Chapter 4, which describes fact-finding techniques that occur during the systems analysis phase of the systems development life cycle (SDLC).

Remember that the purpose of the interview, and of the preliminary investigation itself, is to uncover facts, not to convince others that the project is justified. The analyst's primary role in an interview is to ask effective questions and listen carefully. If several people will be asked about the same topic, a standard set of questions for all the interviews should be prepared. Also be sure to include open-ended questions, such as "What else do you think I should know about the system?" or "Is there any other relevant information that we have not discussed?"

When conducting interviews during the preliminary investigation, interview managers and supervisors who have a broad knowledge of the system and can provide an overview of the business processes involved. Depending on the situation, talking to operational personnel to learn how the system functions on a day-to-day basis may also be helpful.

Review documentation. Although interviews are an extremely important method of obtaining information, investigating the current system documentation is also useful. The documentation might not be up to date, so check with users to confirm that the information is accurate and complete.

Observe operations.   Another fact-finding method is to observe the current system in operation. Observe how workers carry out typical tasks. Trace or follow the actual paths taken by input source documents or output reports. In addition to observing operations, consider sampling the inputs or outputs of the system. Using sampling techniques described in Chapter 4, valuable information about the nature and frequency of the problem can be obtained.

Conduct a user survey.   Interviews can be time consuming. Sometimes information from a larger group can be obtained by conducting a user survey. In this case, design a form that users complete and return for tabulation. A survey is not as flexible as a series of interviews, but it is less expensive, generally takes less time, and can involve a broad cross-section of people.

Analyze the data.   Systems analysts use many techniques to locate the source of a problem. For example, the Pareto chart is a widely used tool for visualizing issues that need attention. Named for a nineteenth-century economist, a Pareto chart is drawn as a vertical bar graph, as shown in Figure 2-17. The bars, which represent various causes of a problem, are arranged in descending order, so the team can focus on the most important causes. In the example shown, a systems analyst might use a Pareto chart to learn more about the causes of inventory system problems, so that necessary improvements can be made.

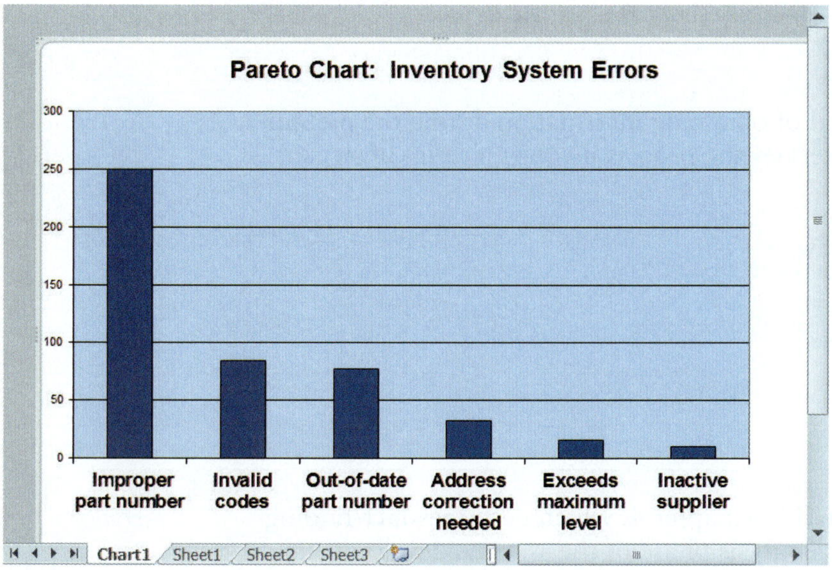

The XY chart, sometimes called a scatter diagram, is another problem-solving tool. Often, an analyst looks for a correlation between two variables. For example, suppose complaints are received about network response time, and the cause needs to be determined. The analyst would try to identify variables, such as the number of users, to see whether there is a correlation, or pattern. Figure 2-18 shows two XY charts with data samples. The first chart sample would suggest that there is no correlation between the delays and the number of users, so the analyst would continue to look for the source of the problem. However, if the data resembles the second XY sample, it indicates a strong relationship between the number of users and the longer response times. That information would be extremely valuable in the problem-solving process.

FIGURE 2-17 A Pareto chart displays the causes of a problem, in priority order, so an analyst can tackle the most important cases first. In this example, the part number issue would be the obvious starting point.

STEP 4: ANALYZE PROJECT USABILITY, COST, BENEFIT, AND SCHEDULE DATA: During fact-finding, data is gathered about the project's predicted costs, anticipated benefits, and schedule issues that could affect implementation. Before feasibility can be evaluated, this data must be analyzed carefully. If interviews were conducted or surveys used, the data should be tabulated to make it easier to understand. If current operations were observed, the results should be reviewed and key facts that will be

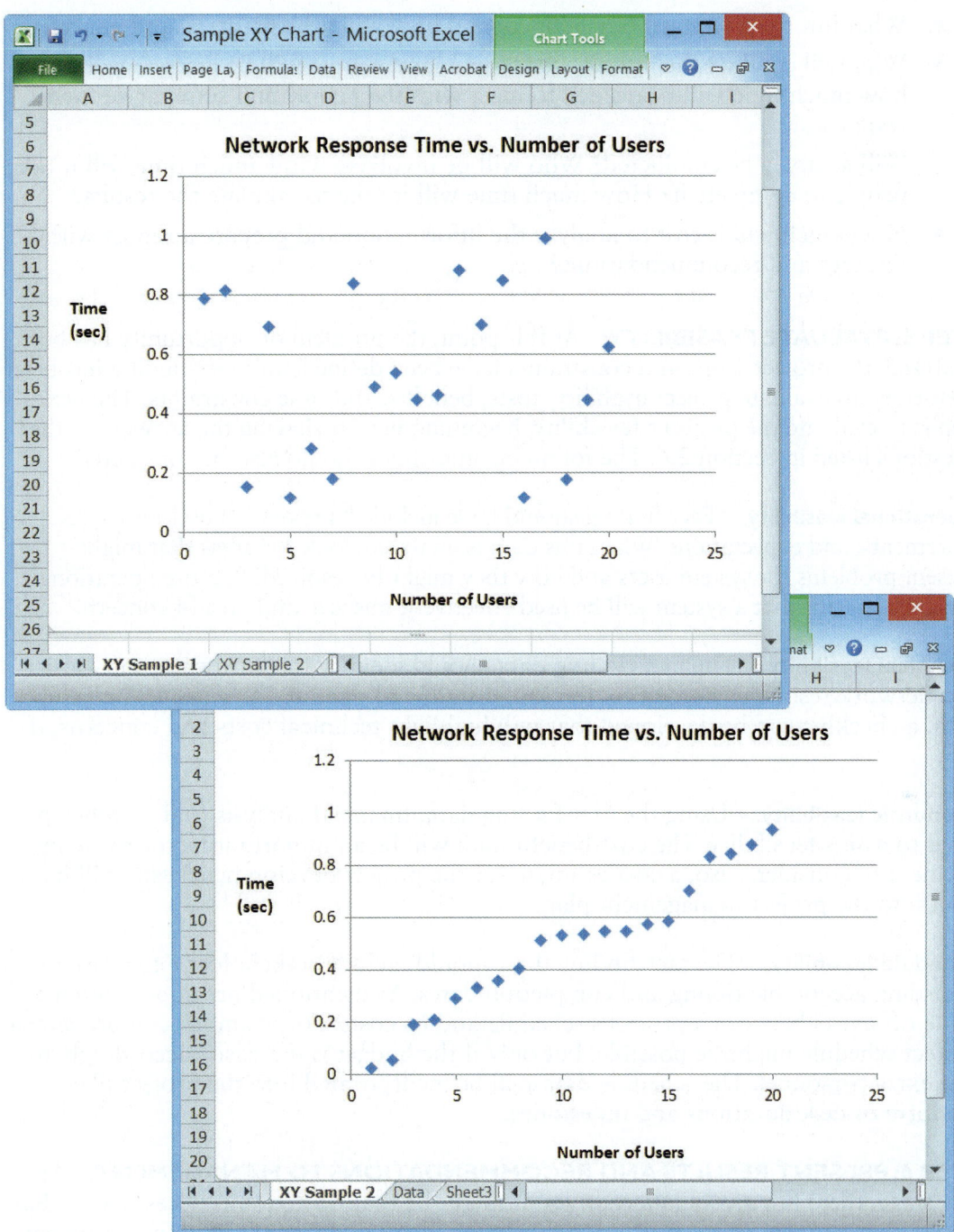

FIGURE 2-18 An XY chart shows correlation between variables, which is very important in problem solving. Conversely, a lack of correlation suggests that the variables are independent and that you should look elsewhere for the cause.

useful in the feasibility analysis highlighted. If cost and benefit data were gathered, financial analysis and impact statements can be prepared using spreadsheets and other decision-support tools.

Also, time and cost estimates should be developed for the requirements modeling tasks for the next SDLC phase, systems analysis. Specifically, the following should be considered:

- What information must be obtained, and how will it be gathered and analyzed?

- Who will conduct the interviews? How many people will be interviewed, and how much time will be needed to meet with the people and summarize their responses?

- Will a survey be conducted? Who will be involved? How much time will it take people to complete it? How much time will it take to tabulate the results?

- How much will it cost to analyze the information and prepare a report with findings and recommendations?

STEP 5: EVALUATE FEASIBILITY: At this point, the problem or opportunity has been analyzed, the project scope and constraints have been defined, and fact-finding has been performed to evaluate project usability, costs, benefits, and time constraints. The next step is to evaluate the project's feasibility, beginning with reviewing the answers to the questions listed in Section 2.6. The following guidelines should also be considered:

Operational feasibility.   Fact-finding should have included a review of user needs, requirements, and expectations. When this data is analyzed, look for areas that might present problems for system users and how they might be resolved. Because operational feasibility means that a system will be used effectively, this is a vital area of concern.

Technical feasibility.   The fact-finding data should identify the hardware, software, and network resources needed to develop, install, and operate the system. With this data, a checklist can be developed that will highlight technical costs and concerns, if any.

Economic feasibility.   Using the fact-finding data, financial analysis tools can be applied to assess feasibility. The cost-benefit data will be an important factor for management to consider. Also, a cost estimate for the project development team will be built into the project management plan.

Schedule feasibility.   The fact-finding data should include stakeholder expectations regarding acceptable timing and completion dates. As mentioned previously, often a trade-off exists between a project's schedule and its costs. For example, compressing a project schedule might be possible, but only if the budget is increased accordingly to add extra personnel. The schedule data will be incorporated into the project plan in the form of task durations and milestones.

STEP 6: PRESENT RESULTS AND RECOMMENDATIONS TO MANAGEMENT: At this stage, there are several alternatives. It might be that no action is necessary or that some other strategy, such as additional training, is needed. To solve a minor problem, a simple solution might be chosen without performing further analysis. In other situations, it will be recommended that the project proceed to the next phase, which is systems analysis.

The final task in the preliminary investigation is to prepare a report to management, and possibly deliver a presentation. The written report and the oral presentation are examples of the need for systems analysts to develop strong communications skills. The report includes an evaluation of the systems request, an estimate of costs and benefits, and a case for action, which is a summary of the project request and a specific recommendation.

The specific format of a preliminary investigation report varies. A typical report might consist of the following sections:

- *Introduction* — the first section is an overview of the report. The introduction contains a brief description of the system, the name of the person or group who performed the investigation, and the name of the person or group who initiated the investigation.

- *Systems Request Summary* — the summary describes the basis of the systems request.

- *Findings* — the findings section contains the results of the preliminary investigation, including a description of the project's scope, constraints, and feasibility.

- *Recommendations* — a summary of the project request and a specific recommendation. Management will make the final decision, but the IT department's input is an important factor.

- *Project Roles* — this section lists the people who will participate in the project, and describes each person's role.

- *Time and Cost Estimates* — this section describes the cost of acquiring and installing the system, and the total cost of ownership during the system's useful life. Intangible costs also should be noted.

- *Expected Benefits* — this section includes anticipated tangible and intangible benefits and a timetable that shows when they are to occur.

- *Appendix* — an appendix is included in the report if supporting information must be attached. For example, the interviews conducted might be listed, the documentation reviewed, and other sources for the information obtained. Detailed interview reports do not need to be included, but those documents that support the report's findings should be retained for future reference.

A QUESTION OF ETHICS

iStockphoto.com/faberfoto_it

As a new systems analyst at Premier Financial Services, you are getting quite an education. You report to Mary, the IT manager, who also chairs the systems review committee. Several months ago, the committee rejected a request from Jack, the finance director, for an expensive new accounts payable system because the benefits did not appear to outweigh the costs.

Yesterday, Mary's boss called her in and asked her to reconsider Jack's request, and to persuade the other members to approve it. Mary wanted to discuss the merits of the request, but he cut her off rather abruptly. Mary happens to know that Jack and her boss are longtime friends.

Mary has confided in you. She is very uncomfortable about the meeting with her boss, and she believes that his request would undermine the integrity of the systems review process. Mary feels it would be unethical to grant preferred treatment just because a friendship is involved. She is thinking of submitting a request to step down as review committee chair, even though that might harm her career at the company.

Is this an ethical question, or just a matter of office politics? What would you say to Mary?

2.10 CHAPTER SUMMARY

Systems planning is the first phase of the systems development life cycle. Effective information systems help an organization support its business processes, carry out its mission, and serve its stakeholders. During strategic planning, a company examines its purpose, vision, and values and develops a mission statement, which leads to goals, objectives, day-to-day operations, and business results that affect company stakeholders. SWOT analysis examines strengths, weaknesses, opportunities, and threats. SWOT analysis can be used at the enterprise level and for individual projects.

During the systems planning phase, an analyst reviews the business case, which is the basis, or reason, for a proposed system. A business case should describe the project clearly, provide the justification to proceed, and estimate the project's financial impact.

Systems projects are initiated to improve performance, provide more information, reduce costs, strengthen controls, or provide better service. Various internal and external factors affect systems projects, such as user requests, top management directives, existing systems, the IT department, software and hardware vendors, technology, customers, competitors, the economy, and government.

During the preliminary investigation, the analyst evaluates the systems request and determines whether the project is feasible from an operational, technical, economic, and schedule standpoint. Analysts evaluate systems requests on the basis of their expected costs and benefits, both tangible and intangible.

The steps in the preliminary investigation are to understand the problem or opportunity; define the project scope and constraints; perform fact-finding; analyze project usability, cost, benefit, and schedule data; evaluate feasibility; and present results and recommendations to management. During the preliminary investigation, analysts often use investigative tools such as fishbone diagrams, Pareto charts, and XY charts. The last task in a preliminary investigation is to prepare a report to management. The report must include an estimate of time, staffing requirements, costs, benefits, and expected results for the next phase of the SDLC.

Key Terms

biometric device A mechanism used to uniquely identify a person by a retina scan or by mapping a facial pattern.

business case Refers to the reasons, or justification, for a proposal.

case for action A part of the preliminary investigation report to management that summarizes project requests and makes specific recommendations.

computer resources committee A group of key managers and users responsible for evaluating systems requests. The term *systems review committee* is also used.

constraint A requirement or a condition that the system must satisfy or an outcome that the system must achieve.

critical success factor Vital objective that must be achieved for the enterprise to fulfill its mission.

customer relationship management (CRM) Many companies implement systems to integrate all customer-related events and transactions including marketing, sales, and customer service activities.

discretionary project Where management has a choice in implementing a project, they are called discretionary. For example, creating a new report for a user is an example of a discretionary project.

economic feasibility Achieved if the projected benefits of the proposed system outweigh the estimated costs involved in acquiring, installing, and operating it.

electronic product code (EPC) Technology that uses RFID tags to identify and monitor the movement of each individual product, from the factory floor to the retail checkout counter.

electronic proof of delivery (EPOD) A supplier uses RFID tags on each crate, case, or shipping unit to create a digital shipping list to verify receipt of goods.

encryption A process where data is coded (converted into unreadable characters) so that only those with the required authorization can access the data.

fishbone diagram An analysis tool that represents the possible causes of a problem as a graphical outline. Also called an *Ishikawa diagram*.

intangible benefit Positive outcome that is difficult to measure in dollars. However, intangible benefits can be very important in the calculation of economic feasibility. An example of an intangible benefit might be a new website that improves a company's image.

intangible cost Item that is difficult to measure in dollar terms, such as employee dissatisfaction.

just-in-time (JIT) The exchange or delivery of information when and where it is needed. For example, just-in-time inventory systems rely on computer-to-computer data exchange to minimize unnecessary inventory.

mission statement A document or statement that describes the company for its stakeholders and briefly states the company's overall purpose, products, services, and values.

nondiscretionary project Where management has no choice in implementing a project, it is called nondiscretionary. For example, adding a report required by a new federal law.

operational feasibility A system that that will be used effectively after it has been developed.

Pareto chart A vertical bar graph named for a nineteenth-century economist. The bars, which represent various causes of a problem, are arranged in descending order, so the team can focus on the most important causes.

project creep The process by which projects with very general scope definitions expand gradually, without specific authorization.

project scope A specific determination of a project's boundaries or extent.

scatter diagram A tool used by system analysts to graphically show the correlation between two variables. Also called an *XY chart*.

schedule feasibility A project can be implemented in an acceptable time frame.

strategic planning The process of identifying long-term organizational goals, strategies, and resource.

SWOT analysis An examination of a company's strengths (S), weaknesses (W), opportunities (O), and threats (T).

systems review committee A group of key managers and users responsible for evaluating systems requests. The *term computer resources committee* is sometimes also used.

tangible benefit Positive outcome that can be measured in dollars. It can result from a decrease in expenses, an increase in revenues, or both.

tangible cost Expense that has a specific dollar value. Examples include employee salaries and hardware purchases.

technical feasibility When an organization has the resources to develop or purchase, install, and operate the system.

total cost of ownership (TCO) A number used in assessing costs, which includes ongoing support and maintenance costs, as well as acquisition costs.

XY chart A tool used by system analysts to graphically show the correlation between two variables. Also called a *scatter diagram*.

Chapter Exercises

Questions

1. How does strategic planning influence day-to-day business operations? Why is it important for systems analysts to understand a company's strategic plan?
2. What is a SWOT analysis? Prepare a SWOT analysis of your school or your employer.
3. What is an effective way to assess user requests for additional features and functions?
4. What are four types of feasibility? Which type focuses on total cost of ownership? Which type do users primarily influence?
5. Describe the six steps in a typical preliminary investigation. Why should an analyst be careful when using the word *problem*?
6. What is project scope? What are constraints? Provide an example of a mandatory, external, future constraint. Also provide an example of a discretionary, internal, present constraint.
7. Identify and briefly describe five common fact-finding methods.
8. What fact-finding methods are well suited for complex technical issues? Which might be appropriate for the pursuit of new, cutting-edge features?
9. What type of tool might a systems analyst use to identify a relationship between two variables? What tool is useful for identifying and prioritizing causes of problems?
10. What is a fishbone diagram, and why would you use one? Think of a problem you have experienced at school or work, and draw a sample fishbone diagram with at least two levels.

Discussion Topics

1. Suppose that the vice president of marketing asks you to write a program to create labels for a one-time advertising promotion. As IT manager, you know that the labels can be prepared more efficiently by exporting the data to a word processing program and using a mail merge feature. How would you handle this situation?
2. The vice president of accounting says to you, the IT director, "This request procedure takes too long. My people know what they are doing and their systems requests are necessary and important." She suggests that the IT department bypass the initial steps and immediately get to work on her requests. What would you say to her?
3. One of your coworkers says, "Mission statements are nice, but they really don't change things down here where the work gets done." How would you reply?
4. Would you continue to work for a company if you disagreed with the firm's mission statement? Why or why not?
5. If an organization currently lacks the skills necessary to make a project technically feasible, how would you rectify the situation?

Projects

1. Use the Internet to find two examples of corporate mission statements.
2. Many articles have been written on how to develop, understand, and evaluate a business case. Visit the website for an IT magazine and find an article that discusses business cases. Describe the article and what you learned from it.
3. Suppose you own a travel agency in a large city. You have many corporate clients, but growth has slowed somewhat. Some long-term employees are getting discouraged, but you feel that there might be a way to make technology work in your favor. Use your imagination and do a SWOT analysis: Suggest at least one strength, one weakness, one opportunity, and one threat that your business faces.
4. Write a mission statement and three goals for the travel agency in Project 3.
5. Identify a situation where one of the external factors (as shown in Figure 2-6) that affected a system project was a natural disaster.

CHAPTER 3 Managing Systems Projects

Chapter 3 is the final chapter in the systems planning phase of the SDLC. This chapter describes project management and explains how to plan, schedule, monitor, and report on IT projects.

The chapter includes four "Case in Point" discussion questions to help contextualize the concepts described in the text. The "Question of Ethics" considers the implications of raising awareness of a project going astray even when the project manager is reluctant to do so.

LEARNING OBJECTIVES

When you finish this chapter, you should be able to:

- Explain project planning, scheduling, monitoring, and reporting
- Draw a project triangle that shows the relationship among project cost, scope, and time
- Create a work breakdown structure, identify task patterns, and calculate a critical path
- Explain techniques for estimating task completion times and costs
- Describe various scheduling tools, including Gantt charts and PERT/CPM charts
- Analyze task dependencies, durations, start dates, and end dates
- Describe project management software and how it can be of assistance
- Control and manage project changes as they occur
- Discuss the importance of managing project risks
- Understand why projects sometimes fail

CHAPTER CONTENTS

3.1 Introduction

Many professionals manage business and personal projects every day, but do not always give it much thought. To manage a large-scale IT project, specific tools and techniques are needed. A project manager is also needed, someone who is responsible for overseeing all relevant tasks. No matter which tools are used, the idea is to break the project down into individual tasks, determine the order in which the tasks need to be performed, and figure out how long each task will take. With this information, Gantt charts or PERT/CPM charts can be used to schedule and manage the work. Microsoft Project is a popular project management tool that can help create and then monitor the project plan, report progress, and use risk management to make the whole process easier for everyone.

3.2 Overview of Project Management

The management process for developing an information system or working on a construction project is much the same. The only difference is the nature of the project. **Project management** for IT professionals includes planning, scheduling, monitoring and controlling, and reporting on information system development.

3.2.1 What Shapes a Project?

A successful project must be completed on time, within budget, and deliver a quality product that satisfies users and meets requirements. Project management techniques can be used throughout the SDLC. System developers can initiate a formal project as early as the preliminary investigation stage, or later on, as analysis, design, and implementation activities occur.

Systems development projects tend to be dynamic and challenging. There is always a balance between constraints, which was discussed in Chapter 2, and interactive elements such as project cost, scope, and time.

FIGURE 3-1 You can't get everything you want; you have to make choices.

3.2.2 What Is a Project Triangle?

Figure 3-1 shows a very simple example of a project triangle. For each project, it must be decided what is most important, because the work cannot be good *and* fast *and* cheap.

When it comes to project management, things are not quite so simple. Decisions do not need to be all-or-nothing, but recognize that any change in one leg of the triangle will affect the other two legs. Figure 3-2 represents a common view of a **project triangle**, where the three legs are cost, scope, and time. The challenge is to find the optimal balance among these factors. Most successful project managers rely on personal experience, communication ability, and resourcefulness. For example, if an extremely time-critical project starts to slip, the project manager might have to trim some features, seek approval for a budget increase, add new personnel, or a combination of all three actions.

On its website, Microsoft offers an interesting suggestion for project managers who have a project at risk: Find the "stuck side" of the triangle. Microsoft states that in most projects, at

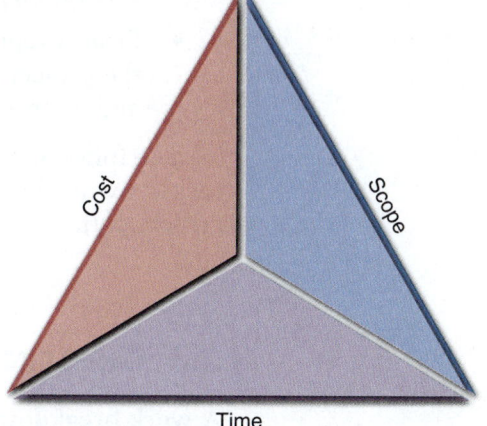

FIGURE 3-2 A typical project triangle includes cost, scope, and time.

least one side of the triangle is fixed and unlikely to change. It might be a budget cast in stone, a scope that is inflexible, or a schedule driven by factors beyond the firm's control. Whichever side is fixed is probably critical to the project's success. The leg where the problem resides must also be identified: cost, scope, or time. Microsoft suggests that if the problem is in the fixed leg, work on the other two legs. For example, if the project must not exceed the budget and it is starting to run over, adjust the schedule, or the scope, or both. However, if the problem is not related to the fixed leg, the adjustment might have to be in the remaining leg. So, when faced with an inflexible budget (fixed leg) and the schedule is slipping (problem leg), the project's scope (remaining leg) might have to be adjusted. Explaining this situation to management is sometimes the most difficult task of all.

3.2.3 What Does a Project Manager Do?

Whether a project involves a new office building or an information system, good leadership is essential. In a systems project, the **project manager**, or **project leader**, usually is a senior systems analyst or an IT department manager if the project is large. An analyst or a programmer/analyst might manage smaller projects. In addition to the project manager, most large projects have a project coordinator. A **project coordinator** handles administrative responsibilities for the team and negotiates with users who might have conflicting requirements or want changes that would require additional time or expense.

Project managers typically perform four activities, or functions: planning, scheduling, monitoring, and reporting:

- **Project planning** includes identifying all project tasks and estimating the completion time and cost of each.

- **Project scheduling** involves the creation of a specific timetable, usually in the form of charts that show tasks, task dependencies, and critical tasks that might delay the project. Scheduling also involves selecting and staffing the project team and assigning specific tasks to team members. Project scheduling uses Gantt charts and PERT/CPM charts, which are explained in the following sections.

- **Project monitoring** requires guiding, supervising, and coordinating the project team's workload. The project manager must monitor the progress, evaluate the results, and take corrective action when necessary to control the project and stay on target.

- **Project reporting** includes regular progress reports to management, users, and the project team itself. Effective reporting requires strong communication skills and a sense of what others want and need to know about the project.

The following sections describe the project planning and scheduling steps: how to create a work breakdown structure, identify task patterns, and calculate the project's critical path.

3.3 CREATING A WORK BREAKDOWN STRUCTURE

A **work breakdown structure (WBS)** involves breaking a project down into a series of smaller tasks. Before creating work breakdown structures, the two primary chart types should be understood: Gantt charts and PERT/CPM charts.

3.3.1 Gantt Charts

Henry L. Gantt, a mechanical engineer and management consultant, developed Gantt charts almost 100 years ago. His goal was to design a chart that could show planned and actual progress on a project. A **Gantt chart** is a horizontal bar chart that represents a set of tasks. For example, the Gantt chart in Figure 3-3 displays five tasks in a vertical array, with time shown on the horizontal axis. The position of the bar shows the planned starting and ending time of each task, and the length of the bar indicates its duration. On the horizontal axis, time can be shown as elapsed time from a fixed starting point, or as actual calendar dates. A Gantt chart also can simplify a complex project by combining several activities into a **task group** that contains subsidiary tasks. This allows a complex project to be viewed as a set of integrated modules.

A Gantt chart can show task status by adding a contrasting color to the horizontal bars. For example, a vertical red arrow marks the current date in Figure 3-3. With a fixed reference point, it is easy to see that Task 1 is way behind schedule, Task 2 is only about 80% done and is running behind schedule, Task 3 should have started, but no work has been done, Task 4 actually is running ahead of schedule, and Task 5 will begin in several weeks.

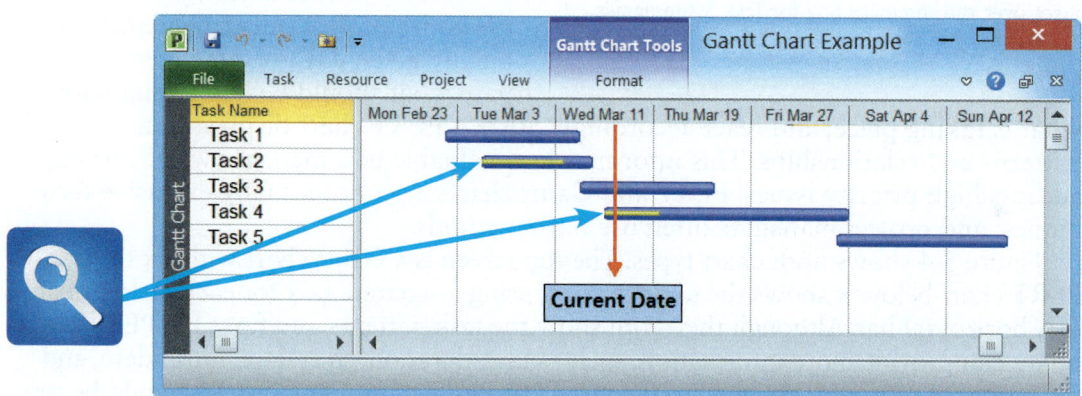

FIGURE 3-3 In this Gantt chart, notice the yellow bars that show the percentage of task completion.

Gantt charts can present an overview of the project's status, but they do not provide enough detailed information, which is necessary when managing a complex project. Some project managers may find that PERT/CPM charts, which are discussed in the following section, are better tools for managing large projects.

3.3.2 PERT/CPM Charts

The **Program Evaluation Review Technique (PERT)** was developed by the U.S. Navy to manage very complex projects, such as the construction of nuclear submarines. At approximately the same time, the **Critical Path Method (CPM)** was developed by private industry to meet similar project management needs. The distinction between the two methods has disappeared over time, and today the technique is called either PERT, CPM, or **PERT/CPM**. This textbook will use the term *PERT chart*.

PERT is a **bottom-up technique** because it analyzes a large, complex project as a series of individual tasks, just as a pyramid is built from the bottom up using individual blocks. To create a PERT chart, first identify all the project tasks and estimate how much time each task will take to perform. Next, determine the logical order in which the tasks must

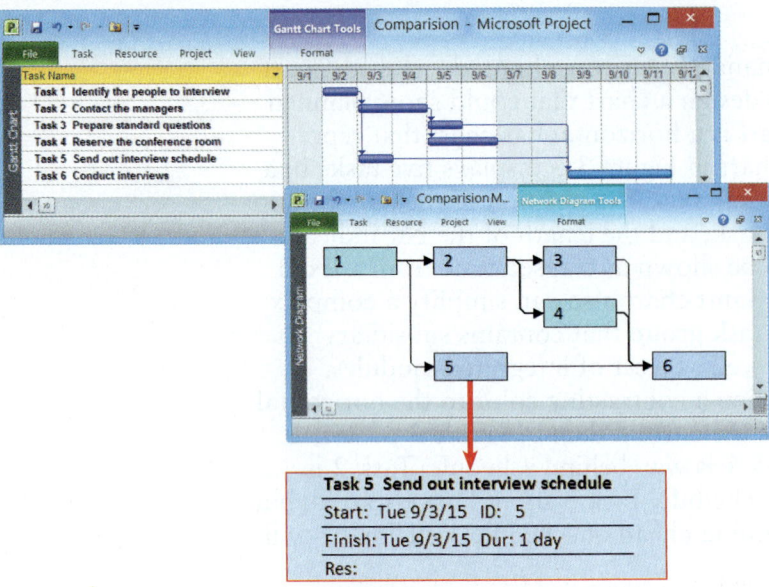

FIGURE 3-4 The top screen shows a Gantt chart with six tasks. The PERT chart in the bottom screen displays an easy-to-follow task pattern for the same project. When the user mouses over the summary box for Task 5, the details become visible.

be performed. For example, some tasks cannot start until other tasks have been completed. In other situations, several tasks can be performed at the same time.

Once the tasks are known, their durations, and the order in which they must be performed, calculate the time that it will take to complete the project. The specific tasks that will be critical to the project's on-time completion can also be identified. An example of a PERT chart, which Microsoft calls a **network diagram**, is shown in the lower screen in Figure 3-4.

Although a Gantt chart offers a valuable snapshot view of the project, PERT charts are more useful for scheduling, monitoring, and controlling the actual work. With a PERT chart, a project manager can convert task start and finish times to actual dates by laying out the entire project on a calendar. Then, on any given day, the manager can compare what should be happening with what is taking place, and react accordingly. Also, a PERT chart displays complex task patterns and relationships. This information is valuable to a manager who is trying to address high priority issues. PERT and Gantt charts are not mutually exclusive techniques, and project managers often use both methods.

Figure 3-4 shows both chart types. The top screen is a Gantt chart with six tasks. The PERT chart below it shows the same project, using a separate box for each task instead of a horizontal bar. Although they both show the task patterns and flow, the PERT chart boxes can provide more information, such as task duration, start date, finish date, and the names of resources assigned to the task. The PERT chart in Figure 3-4 would be too small to view the actual details, which are shown in the expanded text box at the bottom of the figure. How to create PERT charts is explained in a later section.

3.3.3 Identifying Tasks in a Work Breakdown Structure

A work breakdown structure must clearly identify each task and include an estimated duration. A **task**, or **activity**, is any work that has a beginning and an end and requires the use of company resources such as people, time, or money. Examples of tasks include conducting interviews, designing a report, selecting software, waiting for the delivery of equipment, or training users. Tasks are basic units of work that the project manager plans, schedules, and monitors—so they should be relatively small and manageable.

In addition to tasks, every project has **events**, or **milestones**. An event, or milestone, is a recognizable reference point that can be used to monitor progress. For example, an event might be the start of user training, the conversion of system data, or the completion of interviews. A milestone such as "complete 50% of program testing" would not be useful information unless it could be determined exactly when that event will occur.

Figure 3-5 shows tasks and events that might be involved in the creation, distribution, and tabulation of a questionnaire. Notice that the beginning and end of each task are marked by a recognizable event. It would be virtually impossible to manage a project as one large task. Instead, the project is broken down into smaller tasks, creating a WBS. The first step in creating a WBS is to list all the tasks.

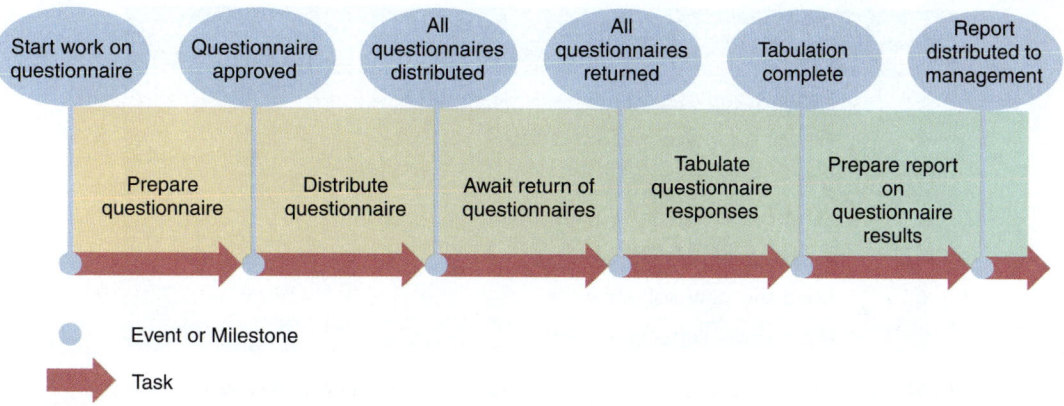

FIGURE 3-5 Using a questionnaire requires a series of tasks and events to track the progress. The illustration shows the relationship between the tasks and the events, or milestones that mark the beginning and end of each task.

LISTING THE TASKS: While this step sounds simple, it can be challenging because the tasks might be embedded in a document, such as the one shown in the first version of Figure 3-6. One trick is to start by highlighting the individual tasks, as shown in the second version. Adding bullets makes the tasks stand out more clearly, as shown in the third version. The next step is to number the tasks and create a table, similar to the one shown in Figure 3-7, with columns for task number, description, duration, and **predecessor tasks**, which must be completed before another task can start.

ESTIMATING TASK DURATION: Task duration can be hours, days, or weeks—depending on the project. Because the following example uses days, the units of measurement are called person-days. A **person-day** represents the work that one person can complete in one day. This approach, however, can present some problems. For example, if it will take one person 20 days to perform a particular task, it might not be true that two people could complete the same task in 10 days or that 10 people could perform the task in two days. Some tasks can be divided evenly so it is possible to use different combinations of time and people—up to a point—but not all. In most systems analysis tasks, time and people are not interchangeable. If one analyst needs two hours to interview a user, two analysts also will need two hours to do the same interview.

Project managers often use a weighted formula for estimating the duration of each task. The project manager first makes three time estimates for each task: an optimistic, or **best-case estimate** (B), a **probable-case estimate** (P), and a pessimistic, or **worst-case estimate** (W). The manager then assigns a **weight**, which is an importance value, to each estimate. The weight can vary, but a common approach is to use a ratio of B = 1, P = 4, and W = 1. The expected task duration is calculated as follows:

$$\frac{(B + 4P + W)}{6}$$

First version

First, reserve the meeting room. Then order the marketing materials and brief the managers. After the briefings, send out customer emails and burn sample DVDs. When the emails are sent and the DVDs are ready, load the new software. When the marketing materials have arrived and the software is ready, do a dress rehearsal.

Second version

First, *reserve the meeting room*. Then *order the marketing materials* and *brief the managers*. After the briefings, *send out customer emails* and *burn sample DVDs*. When the emails are sent and the DVDs are ready, *load the new software*. When the marketing materials have arrived and the software is ready, *do a dress rehearsal*.

Third version

- First, *reserve the meeting room*.
- Then *order the marketing materials* and *brief the managers*.
- After the briefings, *send out customer emails* and *burn sample DVDs*.
- When the emails are sent and the DVDs are ready, *load the new software*.
- When the marketing materials have arrived and the software is ready, *do a dress rehearsal*.

FIGURE 3-6 The three versions show how to transform a task statement into a list of specific tasks for a work breakdown structure.

Task No.	Description	Duration (Days)	Predecessor Tasks
1	Reserve the meeting room		
2	Order the marketing materials		
3	Brief the managers		
4	Send out customer emails		
5	Burn sample DVDs		
6	Load the new software		
7	Do a dress rehearsal		

FIGURE 3-7 In this table, columns have been added for task number, description, duration, and predecessor tasks, which must be completed before another task can start.

For example, a project manager might estimate that a file-conversion task could be completed in as few as 20 days or could take as many as 34 days, but most likely will require 24 days. Using the formula, the expected task duration is 25 days, calculated as follows:

$$\frac{(20 + (4*24) + 34)}{6} = 25$$

CASE IN POINT 3.1: PARALLEL SERVICES

The project management team at Parallel Services is having a debate about how to define tasks in the work breakdown structure (WBS). Ann, the project manager, wants to break tasks down into the smallest possible units. For example, she objected to a broad task statement called Develop a training schedule. Instead, she suggested three subtasks: (1) Determine availability of training room, (2) Determine availability of attendees, and (3) Select specific dates and training times.

Karen, another project team member, disagrees. She feels that the broader task statement is better because it allows more flexibility and will produce the same result. Karen says that if you break tasks into pieces that are too small, you risk over-managing the work and spending more time on monitoring than actually performing the tasks. As a member of the team, would you tend to agree more with Ann or Karen? What are the pros and cons of each approach?

3.3.4 Factors Affecting Duration

When developing duration estimates, project managers consider four factors:

1. Project size
2. Human resources
3. Experience with similar projects
4. Constraints

PROJECT SIZE: As described in Chapter 1, information systems have various characteristics that affect their complexity and cost. In addition to considering those factors, a project manager must estimate the time required to complete each project phase.

To develop accurate estimates, a project manager must identify all project tasks, from initial fact-finding to system implementation. Regardless of the systems development methodology used, the project manager must determine how much time will be needed to perform each task. In developing an estimate, the project manager must allow time for meetings, project reviews, training, and any other factors (e.g., scheduled vacations or unscheduled medical leave) that could affect the productivity of the development team.

HUMAN RESOURCES: Companies must invest heavily in cutting-edge technology to remain competitive in a connected world. In many areas, skilled IT professionals are in great demand, and firms must work hard to attract and retain the talent they need. A project manager must assemble and guide a development team that has the skill and experience to handle the project. If necessary, additional systems analysts or programmers must be hired or trained, and this must be accomplished within a specific time frame. After a project gets under way, the project manager must deal with turnover, job vacancies, and escalating salaries in the technology sector—all of which can affect whether the project can be completed on time and within budget. The project manager also has to accommodate official holidays, family emergencies, and other events that may affect the schedule.

EXPERIENCE WITH SIMILAR PROJECTS: A project manager can develop time and cost estimates based on the resources used for similar, previously developed information systems. The experience method works best for small- or medium-sized projects where the two systems are similar in size, basic content, and operating environment. In large systems with more variables, the estimates are less reliable.

CONSTRAINTS: Chapter 2 explained that constraints are defined during the preliminary investigation. A constraint is a condition, restriction, or requirement that the system must satisfy. For example, a constraint might involve maximums for one or more resources, such as time, dollars, or people. A project manager must define system requirements that can be achieved realistically within the required constraints. In the absence of constraints, the project manager simply calculates the resources needed. However, if constraints are present, the project manager must adjust other resources or change the scope of the project. This approach is similar to the what-if analysis described in Chapter 12.

CASE IN POINT 3.2: SUNRISE SOFTWARE

A lively discussion is under way at Sunrise Software, where you are a project manager. The main question is whether the person-days concept has limitations. In other words, if a task will require 100 person-days, does it matter whether two people in 50 days, five people in 20 days, 10 people in 10 days, or some other combination that adds up to 100 performs the work?

Programmers Paula and Ethan seem to think it does not matter. On the other hand, Hector, a systems analyst, says it is ridiculous to think that any combination would work. To support his point, he offers this extreme example: Could 100 people accomplish a task estimated at 100 person-days in one day?

Is Hector correct? If so, what are the limits in the "people versus days" equation? Taking the concept a step further, is there an optimum number of people to be assigned to a task? If so, how would that number be determined? You need to offer some guidance at the next project team meeting. What will you say?

3.3.5 Displaying the Work Breakdown Structure

After the task durations are entered, the work breakdown structure will look like Figure 3-8. Task groups can be used to manage a complex project with many tasks, just as with a Gantt chart, to simplify the list. Note that the WBS shown in Figure 3-8 is still

Task No.	Description	Duration (Days)	Predecessor Tasks
1	Reserve the meeting room	1	
2	Order the marketing materials	9	
3	Brief the managers	2	
4	Send out customer emails	3	
5	Burn sample DVDs	3	
6	Load the new software	2	
7	Do a dress rehearsal	1	

FIGURE 3-8 Task durations have been added, and the WBS is complete except for predecessor task information. The predecessor tasks will determine task patterns and sequence of performance.

incomplete: It does not show fields such as Start Date, End Date, Task Name, Duration, and Predecessors—fields that can be key for project managers. With Microsoft Project, the WBS (including some of these missing fields) might resemble Figure 3-9.

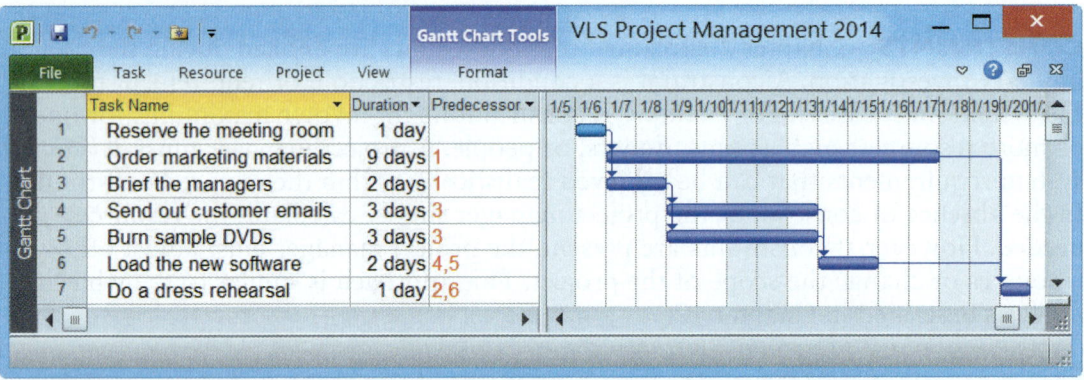

FIGURE 3-9 This Microsoft Project screen displays the same WBS, including task number, task name, duration, and predecessor tasks.

3.4 IDENTIFYING TASK PATTERNS

Tasks in a work breakdown structure must be arranged in a logical sequence called a task pattern. This section explains how to understand and create graphical models of these patterns.

3.4.1 Task Patterns

In any project, large or small, tasks depend on each other and must be performed in a sequence, not unlike the commands in a software program. Task patterns can involve dependent tasks, multiple successor tasks, and multiple predecessor tasks. In larger projects, these patterns can be very complex, and an analyst must study the logical flow carefully.

3.4.2 Using Task Boxes to Create a Model

In a PERT/CPM chart, project tasks are shown as rectangular boxes, arranged in the sequence in which they must be performed. Each rectangular box, called a **task box**, has five sections, as shown in Figure 3-10. Each section of the task box contains important information about the task, including the Task Name, Task ID, Task Duration, Start Day/Date, and Finish Day/Date.

TASK NAME: The **task name** should be brief and descriptive, but it does not have to be unique in the project. For example, a task named Conduct Interviews might occur in several phases of the project.

TASK ID: The **task ID** can be a number or code that provides unique identification.

TASK DURATION: The **duration** is the amount of time it will take to complete a task, which is not necessarily the same as the elapsed time. For example, a task that takes eight hours of effort to complete would be done in one day by a person dedicated 100%, but if the person assigned this task is only working 50% on this project, the task would take two days elapsed time to complete. All tasks must use the same time units, which can be hours, days, weeks, or months, depending on the project. An actual project starts on a specific date, but can also be measured from a point in time, such as Day 1.

START DAY/DATE: The **start day/date** is the time that a task is scheduled to begin. For example, suppose that a simple project has two tasks: Task 1 and Task 2. Also suppose that Task 2 cannot begin until Task 1 is finished. An analogy might be that a program cannot run until the computer is turned on. If Task 1 begins on Day 1 and has duration of three days, it will finish on Day 3. Because Task 2 cannot begin until Task 1 is completed, the start time for Task 2 is Day 4, which is the day after Task 1 is finished.

FINISH DAY/DATE: The **finish day/date** is the time that a task is scheduled for completion. To calculate the finish day or date, add the duration to the start day or date. When doing this, be very careful not to add too many days. For example, if a task starts on Day 10 and has duration of 5 days, then the finish would be on Day 14—not Day 15.

3.4.3 Task Patterns

A project is based on a pattern of tasks. In a large project the overall pattern would be quite complex, but it can be broken down into three basic patterns: dependent tasks, multiple successor tasks, and multiple predecessor tasks.

DEPENDENT TASKS: When tasks must be completed one after another, like the relay race shown in Figure 3-11, they

---

TASK BOX FORMAT

Task Name	
Start Day/Date	Task ID
Finish Day/Date	Task Duration

FIGURE 3-10 Each section of the task box contains important information about the task, including the Task Name, Task ID, Task Duration, Start Day/Date, and Finish Day/Date.

FIGURE 3-11 In a relay race, each runner is dependent on the preceding runner and cannot start until the earlier finishes.

William Perugini/Shutterstock.com

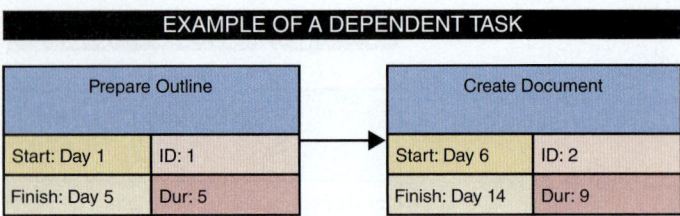

EXAMPLE OF A DEPENDENT TASK

Prepare Outline		Create Document	
Start: Day 1	ID: 1	Start: Day 6	ID: 2
Finish: Day 5	Dur: 5	Finish: Day 14	Dur: 9

FIGURE 3-12 This example of a dependent task shows that the finish time of Task 1, Day 5 controls the start date of Task 2, which is Day 6.

EXAMPLE OF MULTIPLE SUCCESSOR TASKS

Develop Plan		Arrange Interviews	
		Start: Day 31	ID: 2
Start: Day 1	ID: 1	Finish: Day 60	Dur: 30
Finish: Day 30	Dur: 30	Design Survey	
		Start: Day 31	ID: 3
		Finish: Day 40	Dur: 10

FIGURE 3-13 This example of multiple successor tasks shows that the finish time for Task 1 determines the start time for both Tasks 2 and 3.

EXAMPLE OF MULTIPLE PREDECESSOR TASKS

Obtain Authorization		Conduct Interviews	
Start: Day 1	ID: 1		
Finish: Day 15	Dur: 15	Start: Day 16	ID: 3
Create Job Description		Finish: Day 45	Dur: 30
Start: Day 1	ID: 2		
Finish: Day 5	Dur: 5		

FIGURE 3-14 This example of multiple predecessor tasks shows that the start time for a successor task must be the latest (largest) finish time for any of its preceding tasks. In the example shown, Task 1 ends of Day 15, while Task 2 ends on Day 5, so Task 1 controls the start time for Task 3.

are called **dependent tasks** because one depends on the other. For example, Figure 3-12 shows that Task 2 depends on Task 1, because Task 2 cannot start until Task 1 is completed. In this example, the finish time of Task 1, Day 5, controls the start date of Task 2, which is Day 6.

MULTIPLE SUCCESSOR TASKS: When several tasks can start at the same time, each is called a **concurrent task**. Often, two or more concurrent tasks depend on a single prior task, which is called a predecessor task. In this situation, each concurrent task is called a **successor task**. In the example shown in Figure 3-13, successor Tasks 2 and 3 both can begin as soon as Task 1 is finished. Notice that the finish time for Task 1 determines the start time for both Tasks 2 and 3. In other words, the earliest that Task 1 can finish is Day 30, so Day 31 is the earliest that Tasks 2 and 3 can start.

MULTIPLE PREDECESSOR TASKS: Suppose that a task requires two or more prior tasks to be completed before it can start. Figure 3-14 shows that example because Task 3 cannot begin until Tasks 1 and 2 are both completed. Since the two tasks might not finish at the same time, the longest (latest) predecessor task becomes the controlling factor. Notice that the start for Task 3 is Day 16, not Day 6. Why is this so? Because Task 3 depends on two predecessor tasks, Tasks 1 and 2, Task 3 cannot begin until the later of those tasks is complete. Therefore, the start time for a successor task must be the latest (largest) finish time for any of its preceding tasks. In the example shown, Task 1 ends on Day 15, while Task 2 ends on Day 5, so Task 1 controls the start time for Task 3.

3.4.4 Identifying Task Patterns

Task patterns are identified by looking carefully at the wording of the task statement. Words like *then*, *when*, or *and* are action words that signal a sequence of events. Here are three simple examples:

- Do Task 1, *then* do Task 2 describes dependent tasks that must be completed one after the other.

- *When* Task 2 is finished, start two tasks: Task 3 *and* Task 4 describes multiple successor tasks that can both start as soon as Task 2 is finished.

- *When* Tasks 5 *and* 6 are done, start Task 7 indicates that Task 7 is a multiple predecessor task because it cannot start until two or more previous tasks all are completed.

3.4.5 Working with Complex Task Patterns

When several task patterns combine, the facts must be studied very carefully to understand the logic and sequence. A project schedule will not be accurate if the underlying task pattern is incorrect. For example, consider the following three fact statements and the task patterns they represent. Examples of the task patterns are shown in Figure 3-15, Figure 3-16, and Figure 3-17.

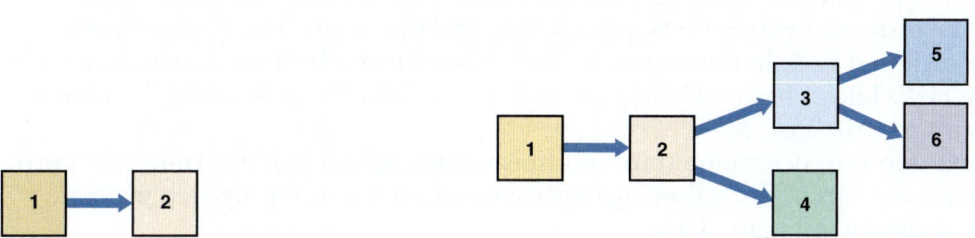

FIGURE 3-15 Dependent tasks.

FIGURE 3-16 Dependent tasks and multiple successor tasks.

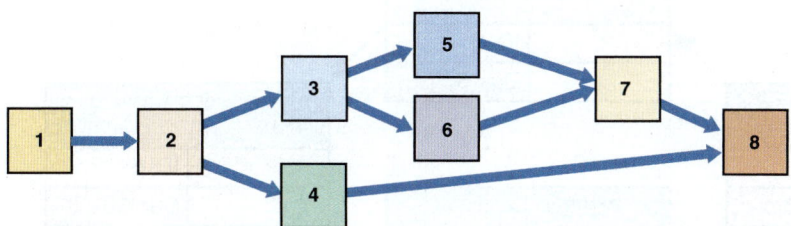

FIGURE 3-17 Dependent tasks, multiple successor tasks, and multiple predecessor tasks.

DEPENDENT TASKS: Perform Task 1. When Task 1 is complete, perform Task 2.

DEPENDENT TASKS AND MULTIPLE SUCCESSOR TASKS: Perform Task 1. When Task 1 is complete, perform Task 2. When Task 2 is finished, start two tasks: Task 3 and Task 4. When Task 3 is complete, start two more tasks: Task 5 and Task 6.

DEPENDENT TASKS, MULTIPLE SUCCESSOR TASKS, AND MULTIPLE PREDECESSOR TASKS: Perform Task 1. When Task 1 is complete, perform Task 2. When Task 2 is finished, start two Tasks: Task 3 and Task 4. When Task 3 is complete, start two more tasks: Task 5 and Task 6. When Tasks 5 and 6 are done, start Task 7. Then, when Tasks 4 and 7 are finished, perform Task 8.

3.5 CALCULATING THE CRITICAL PATH

Task patterns determine the order in which the tasks are performed. Once the task sequence has been defined, a project manager can schedule the tasks and calculate the critical path.

3.5.1 Critical Path

A critical path is a series of tasks that, if delayed, would affect the completion date of the overall project. If any task on the critical path falls behind schedule, the entire project will be delayed. For example, suppose that Joan and Jim are invited to someone's home for dinner. Joan arrives on time, but Jim arrives 30 minutes late. Jim's arrival is part of the critical path because the host does not want to start without him, so the meal will be served 30 minutes later than originally planned.

Project managers always must be aware of the critical path, so they can respond quickly to keep the project on track. Microsoft Project and other project management software can highlight the series of tasks that form the critical path.

3.5.2 Calculating the Critical Path

Figure 3-18 shows a training project with five tasks. Notice that the analyst has arranged the tasks and entered task names, IDs, and durations. The task patterns should be reviewed first. In this example, Task 1 is followed by Task 2, which is a dependent task. Task 2 has two successor tasks: Task 3 and Task 4. Tasks 3 and 4 are predecessor tasks for Task 5.

The next step is to determine start and finish dates, which will determine the critical path for the project. The following explanation outlines a step-by-step process. The result is shown in Figure 3-19.

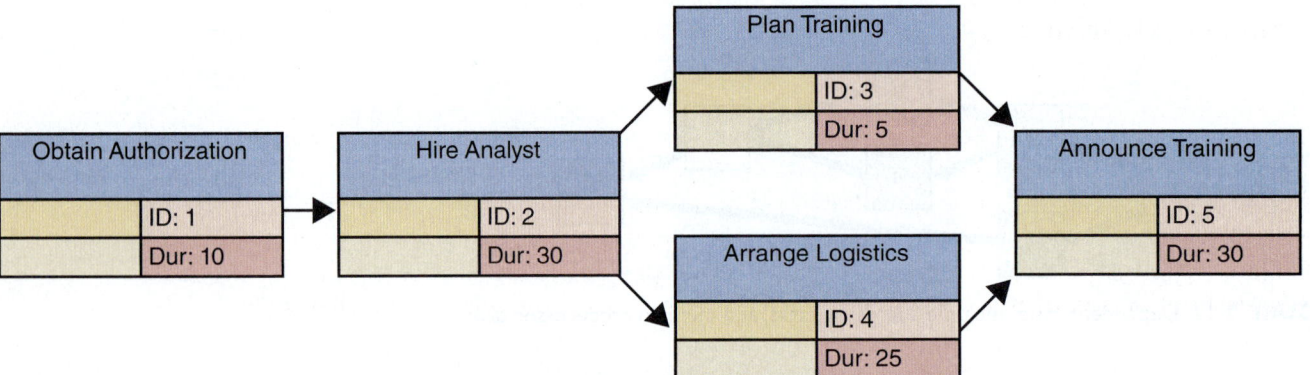

FIGURE 3-18 Example of a PERT/CPM chart with five tasks. Task 2 is a dependent task that has multiple successor tasks. Task 5 has multiple predecessor tasks. In this figure, the analyst has arranged the tasks and entered task names, IDs, and durations.

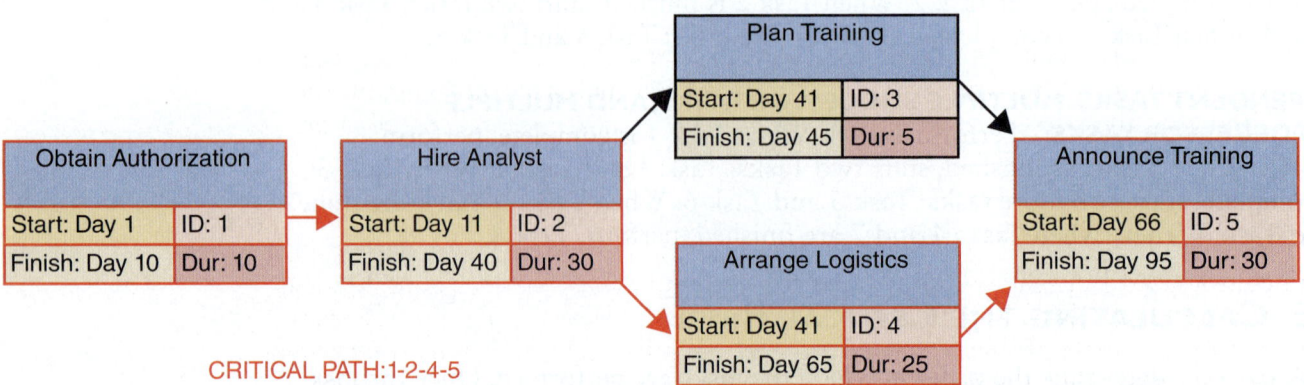

FIGURE 3-19 Now the analyst has entered the start and finish times, using the rules explained in this section. Notice that the overall project has duration of 95 days.

- Task 1 starts on Day 1 and has duration of 10 days, so the finish date is Day 10.

- Task 2, which is dependent on Task 1, can start on Day 11—the day after Task 1 ends. With duration of 30 days, Task 2 will end on Day 40.

- Tasks 3 and 4 are multiple successor tasks that can start after Task 2 is done. Task 2 ends on Day 40, so Tasks 3 and 4 both can start on Day 41. Task 3 has duration of 5 days, and will end on Day 45. Task 4 has duration of 25 days, and will not end until Day 65.

- Task 5 depends on Tasks 3 and 4, which are multiple predecessors. Because Task 5 depends on both tasks, it cannot start until the later of the two tasks is complete. In this example, Task 3 ends earlier, but Task 4 will not be completed until Day 65, so Task 5 cannot start until Day 66.

Recall that the critical path is a series of tasks that, if delayed, would affect the final completion date of the overall project. In this example, Tasks 1 and 2 are the first tasks on the critical path. Now look at Task 5, which cannot start until both Tasks 3 and 4 are done. In this case, Task 4 is the controlling factor because Task 4 finishes on Day 65, which is 20 days later than Task 3, which is completed on Day 45. Therefore, the start date for Task 5 is determined by the finish date for Task 4.

In contrast, Task 3 has slack time, and could be delayed up to 20 days without affecting Task 5. Slack time is the amount of time that the task could be late without pushing back the completion date of the entire project. Tasks 1, 2, 4, and 5 represent the critical path, which is highlighted with red arrows in Figure 3-19.

3.6 PROJECT MONITORING AND CONTROL

Regardless of whether the project was planned and scheduled with project management software or in some other manner, the project manager must keep track of the tasks and progress of team members, compare actual progress with the project plan, verify the completion of project milestones, and set standards and ensure that they are followed.

3.6.1 Monitoring and Control Techniques

To help ensure that quality standards are met, many project managers institute structured walk-throughs. A structured walk-through is a review of a project team member's work by other members of the team. Generally, systems analysts review the work of other systems analysts, and programmers review the work of other programmers, as a form of peer review. Structured walk-throughs take place throughout the SDLC and are called design reviews, code reviews, or testing reviews, depending on the phase in which they occur.

3.6.2 Maintaining a Schedule

Maintaining a project schedule can be challenging, and most projects run into at least some problems or delays. By monitoring and controlling the work, the project manager tries to anticipate problems, avoid them or minimize their impact, identify potential solutions, and select the best way to solve the problem.

The better the original plan, the easier it will be to control the project. If clear, verifiable milestones exist, it will be simple to determine if and when those targets are achieved. If enough milestones and frequent checkpoints exist, problems will be detected rapidly. A project that is planned and scheduled with PERT/CPM or in a WBS with Gantt chart can be tracked and controlled using these same techniques. As work continues, the project manager revises the plan to record actual times for completed tasks and revises times for tasks that are not yet finished.

Project managers spend most of their time tracking the tasks along the critical path because delays in those tasks have the greatest potential to delay or jeopardize the project. Other tasks cannot be ignored, however. For example, suppose that a task not on the critical path takes too long and depletes the allotted slack time. At that point, the task actually becomes part of the critical path, and any further delay will push back the overall project.

3.7 REPORTING

Members of the project team regularly report their progress to the project manager, who in turn reports to management and users. The project manager collects, verifies, organizes, and evaluates the information he or she receives from the team. Then the manager decides which information needs to be passed along, prepares a summary that can be understood easily, adds comments and explanations if needed, and submits it to management and users.

3.7.1 Project Status Meetings

Project managers, like the one shown in Figure 3-20, schedule regular meetings to update the team and discuss project status, issues, problems, and opportunities. Although meetings can be time consuming, most project managers believe they are

FIGURE 3-20 Project managers schedule regular meetings to update the project team and discuss project status, issues, problems, and opportunities

Hero Images/Getty Images

worth the effort. The sessions give team members an opportunity to share information, discuss common problems, and explain new techniques. The meetings also give the project manager an opportunity to seek input and conduct brainstorming sessions.

3.7.2 Project Status Reports

A project manager must report regularly to his or her immediate supervisor, upper management, and users. Although a progress report might be given verbally to an immediate supervisor, reports to management and users usually are written. Gantt charts often are included in progress reports to show project status graphically.

Deciding how to handle potential problems can be difficult. At what point should management be informed about the possibility of cost overruns, schedule delays, or technical problems? At one extreme is the overly cautious project manager who alerts management to every potential snag and slight delay. The danger here is that the manager loses credibility over a period of time, and management might ignore potentially serious situations. At the other extreme is the project manager who tries to handle all situations single-handedly and does not alert management until a problem is serious. By the time management learns of the problem, little time might remain in which to react or devise a solution.

A project manager's best course of action lies somewhere between the two extremes, but is probably closer to the first. If the consequences are unclear, the analyst should err on the side of caution and warn management about the possibility of a problem.

When the situation is reported, explain what is being done to handle and monitor the problem. If the situation is beyond the analyst's control, suggest possible actions that management can take to resolve the situation. Most managers recognize that problems do occur on most projects; it is better to alert management sooner rather than later.

3.8 PROJECT MANAGEMENT EXAMPLES

These examples can be used to practice the skills described in this chapter. The examples also illustrate the use of project management software to help manage and display tasks.

3.8.1 PERT/CPM Examples

Figure 3-21 shows a work breakdown structure with 11 tasks. The example is more complex than previous ones, but the same guidelines apply. Notice that each task has an ID, a description, duration, and a reference to predecessor tasks, if any, which must be completed before the task can begin. Also notice that dependent tasks can have one predecessor task, or several. A PERT/CPM chart can be constructed from this task list in a two-step process:

Task No.	Description	Duration (Days)	Predecessor Tasks
1	Develop Plan	1	-
2	Assign Tasks	4	1
3	Obtain Hardware	17	1
4	Programming	70	2
5	Install Hardware	10	3
6	Program Test	30	4
7	Write User Manual	25	5
8	Convert Files	20	5
9	System Test	25	6
10	User Training	20	7, 8
11	User Test	25	9, 10

FIGURE 3-21 Example of a work breakdown structure listing 11 tasks, together with their descriptions, durations, and predecessor tasks.

STEP 1: DISPLAY THE TASKS AND TASK PATTERNS: In the first step, as shown in Figure 3-22, identify the tasks, determine task dependencies, and enter the task name, ID, and duration. Notice that this example includes dependent tasks, multiple successor tasks, and multiple predecessor tasks.

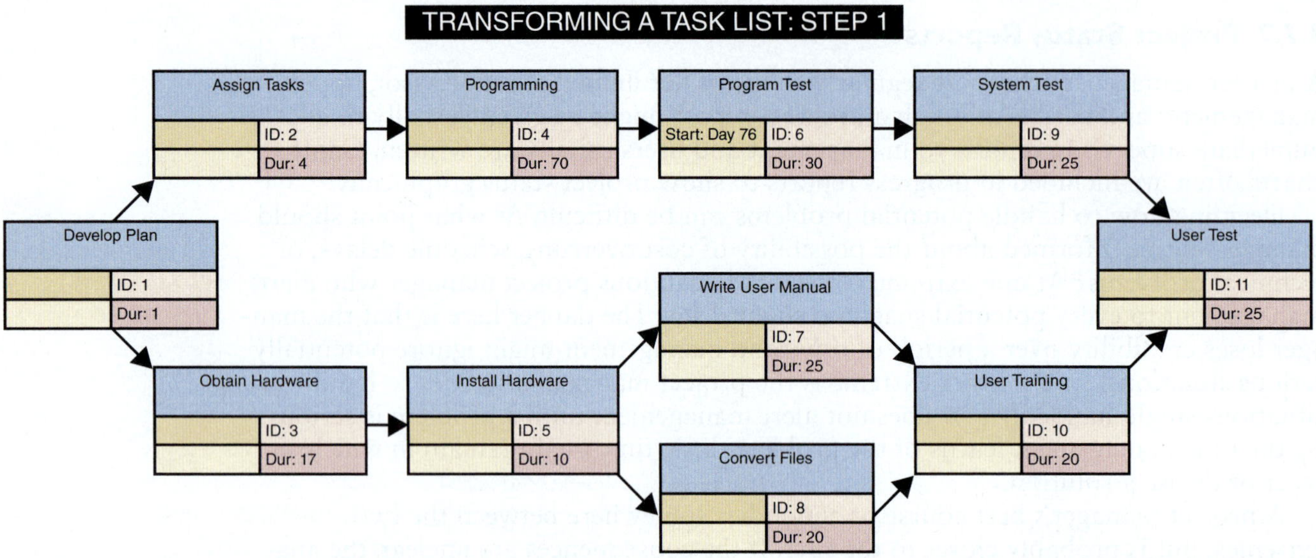

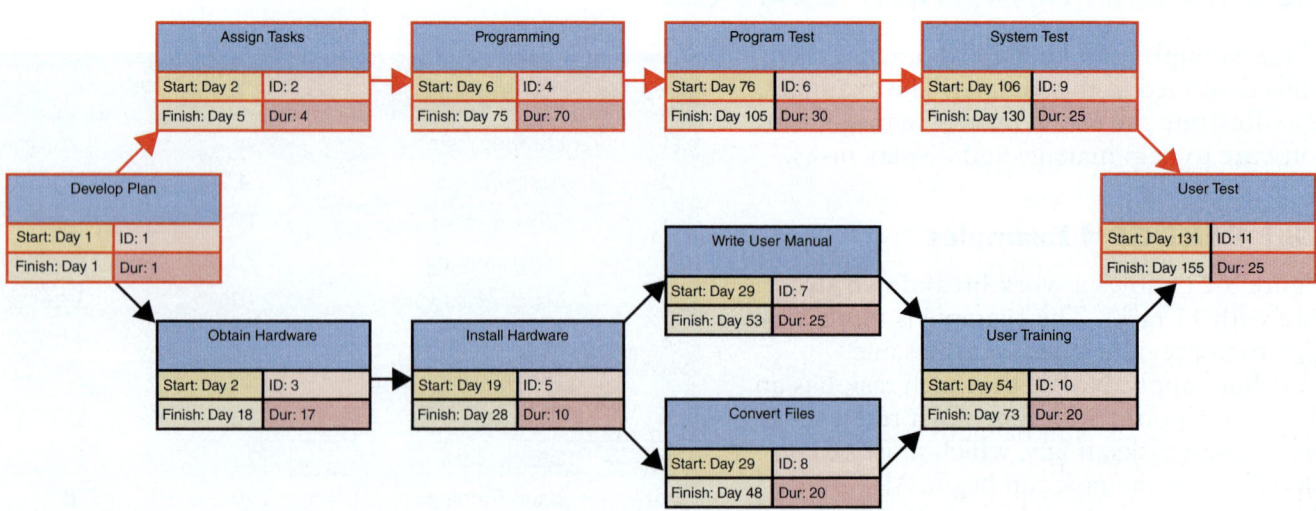

FIGURE 3-22 To transform a task list into a PERT/CPM chart, you first enter the task name, ID, duration, and predecessors for each task. Notice that this example includes dependent tasks, tasks with multiple successors, and tasks with multiple predecessors.

STEP 2: ENTER START AND FINISH TIMES: In the second step, as shown Figure 3-23, enter the start and finish times by applying the guidelines in this section. For example, Task 1 has a one-day duration, so the start and finish times for Task 1 are entered as Day 1. Then enter Day 2 as the start time for successor Tasks 2 and 3. Continuing from left to right, add the task duration for each task to its start time to determine its finish time.

FIGURE 3-23 To complete the PERT/CPM chart, you apply the guidelines explained in this section. For example, Task 1 has a one-day duration, so you enter the start and finish for Task 1 as Day 1. Then you enter Day 2 as the start for successor Tasks 2 and 3.

There are three important rules to must keep in mind during this process:

1. If a successor task has more than one predecessor task, use the latest finish time of the predecessor tasks to determine the start time for the successor task.

2. If a predecessor task has more than one successor task, use the predecessor task's finish time to determine the start time for all successor tasks.

3. Continuing from left to right, add the task duration for each task to its start time to determine and enter its finish time. Again, be very careful not to add too many days. For example, if a task starts on Day 10 and has duration of five days, then the finish would be Day 14—not Day 15.

When all the start and finish times have been entered, it is determined that the project will be completed on Day 155. Also, note that Tasks 1, 2, 4, 6, 9, and 11 represent the critical path shown by the red arrows.

3.9 PROJECT MANAGEMENT SOFTWARE

Project managers use software applications to help plan, schedule, monitor, and report on a project. Most programs offer features such as PERT/CPM, Gantt charts, resource scheduling, project calendars, and cost tracking. As shown in Figure 3-24, Microsoft Project is a full-featured program that holds the dominant share of the market. It is available as a software product for Windows and as an online service as part of Microsoft's Office 365.

Irrespective of which project management tool used, a step-by-step process is followed to develop a WBS, work with task patterns, and analyze the critical path. The main difference is that the software does most of the work automatically, which enables much more effective management.

The following sections explain how Microsoft Project could be used to handle the sample task summary for a preliminary investigation shown in Figure 3-25.

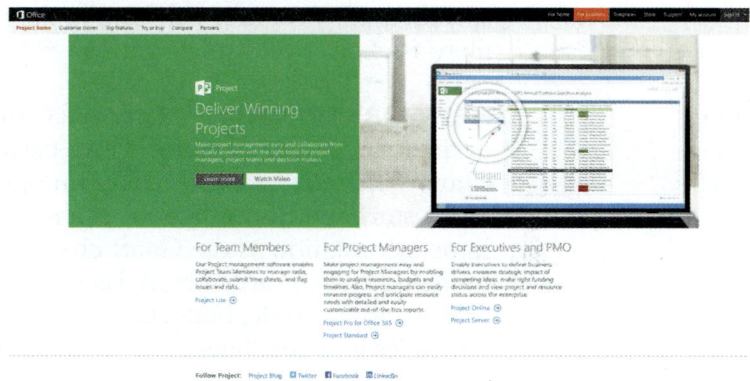

FIGURE 3-24 Microsoft Project.
Source: Microsoft Corporation

This example illustrates that project management is dynamic and challenging. One significant advantage of integrated project management software is that it allows the project manager to adjust schedules, estimates, and resource assignments rapidly to response to real-world events.

WORK BREAKDOWN STRUCTURE: Creating a work breakdown structure using Microsoft Project is much the same as creating it manually. The tasks, durations, and task patterns must still be identified. This information might have to be developed, or a task summary like the one in Figure 3-25 might be used. The goal is to document all tasks, dependencies, dates, and total project duration. The first step is to create a Gantt chart showing the necessary information. As the information for each task is entered into Microsoft Project, the duration and the predecessor tasks, if any, should also be noted.

Please study the following task summary:

- First, we need to spend one day studying potential problems or opportunities.

- Then, we will define the project scope and constraints. That will take two days.

- Next, we will analyze the organization charts. That will take one day.

- After we analyze the charts, four fact-finding tasks can start at once:

  ○ Observe operations (two days)

  ○ Conduct a user survey (three days)

  ○ Conduct interviews (two days)

  ○ Review documentation (one day)

- When all four fact-finding tasks are finished, we will spend one day evaluating feasibilty.

- Then we will spend one day presenting the results and recommendations to management.

FIGURE 3-25 A sample task summary for a preliminary investigation.

GANTT CHART: As tasks are entered, the program automatically performs the calculations, detects the task patterns, and creates a Gantt chart. The chart consists of horizontal bars, connected with arrows that indicate task dependencies. If a typical workweek is selected, tasks will not be scheduled on Saturdays and Sundays. However, for a mission-critical project, a 24/7 calendar might be created. Whatever is specified, the program will handle the tasks accordingly. Microsoft Project offers numerous choices of display settings, formats, and calculation methods.

NETWORK DIAGRAM: After the Gantt chart is completed, the data can be viewed in the form of a Microsoft Project network diagram, which is similar to a PERT chart. When the Network Diagram option is selected, the project tasks, dependencies, and a start and finish date for each task are shown. A network diagram displays the same information as the Gantt chart, including task dependencies, but use task boxes to include much more detail. Using Microsoft Project, each task can be assigned to one or more people, budgets can be assigned targets, progress reports produced, and schedules and deadlines readjusted as necessary.

CALENDAR VIEW: Calendar view is a good way to manage day-to-day activity. This view shows the tasks, similar to a PERT chart, as an overlay on the actual calendar. Because the critical path is highlighted in red, it is easy for a project manager to determine priorities at any point in time.

Suppose the project manager wants to view the preliminary investigation in Figure 3-25 as a Gantt chart, a PERT chart, and a day-to-day calendar. All three views are shown in Figure 3-26. Each view shows the tasks, the timing, the dependencies, and the critical path. Notice that of the four tasks scheduled for September 25, only the user survey is on the critical path, therefore that should be the project manager's primary concern.

In addition to Microsoft Project, there are a number of other project management tools available. For example, *GanttProject* is a free open source Java-based project management tool that is available on multiple platforms (Windows, Mac OS X, and Linux). It can produce Gantt charts, PERT/CPM charts, calculate the critical path automatically, and read/write Microsoft Project files. Figure 3-27 shows GanttProject displaying a Gantt chart for the same information shown by Microsoft Project in Figure 3-26.

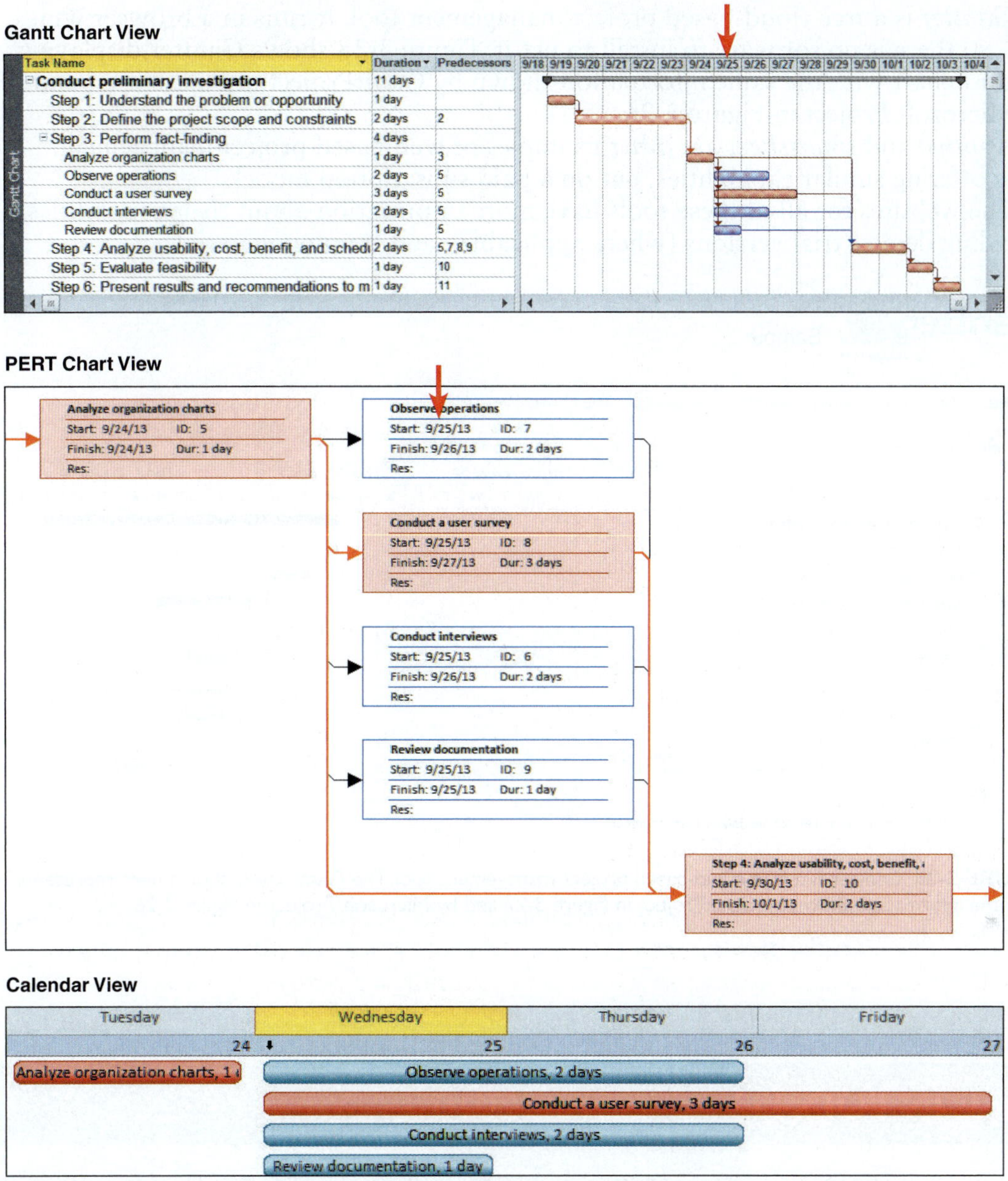

Gantt Chart View
Task Name
Duration
Predecessors
9/18 9/19 9/20 9/21 9/22 9/23 9/24 9/25 9/26 9/27 9/28 9/29 9/30 10/1 10/2 10/3 10/4
Conduct preliminary investigation 11 days
Step 1: Understand the problem or opportunity 1 day
Step 2: Define the project scope and constraints 2 days 2
Step 3: Perform fact-finding 4 days
Analyze organization charts 1 day 3
Observe operations 2 days 5
Conduct a user survey 3 days 5
Conduct interviews 2 days 5
Review documentation 1 day 5
Step 4: Analyze usability, cost, benefit, and schedu 2 days 5,7,8,9
Step 5: Evaluate feasibility 1 day 10
Step 6: Present results and recommendations to m 1 day 11
Gantt Chart
PERT Chart View
Analyze organization charts
Start: 9/24/13 ID: 5
Finish: 9/24/13 Dur: 1 day
Res:
Observe operations
Start: 9/25/13 ID: 7
Finish: 9/26/13 Dur: 2 days
Res:
Conduct a user survey
Start: 9/25/13 ID: 8
Finish: 9/27/13 Dur: 3 days
Res:
Conduct interviews
Start: 9/25/13 ID: 6
Finish: 9/26/13 Dur: 2 days
Res:
Review documentation
Start: 9/25/13 ID: 9
Finish: 9/25/13 Dur: 1 day
Res:
Step 4: Analyze usability, cost, benefit,
Start: 9/30/13 ID: 10
Finish: 10/1/13 Dur: 2 days
Res:
Calendar View
Tuesday
Wednesday
Thursday
Friday
24
25
26
27
Analyze organization charts, 1
Observe operations, 2 days
Conduct a user survey, 3 days
Conduct interviews, 2 days
Review documentation, 1 day

FIGURE 3-26 Notice how each view displays the project and highlights the critical path. If you were the project manager on September 25, your primary concern should be conducting the user survey.

Resources Chart
PERT chart
Zoom Out
Today
Show critical path
Baselines...
Week 49
Week 50
Name
Conduct preliminary investigation
Step 1: Understand the problem or opportunity
Step 2: Define the project scope and constraints
Step 3: Perform fact-finding
Analyze organization charts
Observe operations
Conduct a user survey
Conduct interviews
Review documentation
Step 4: Analyze usability, cost, benefit, and schedule
Step 5: Evaluate feasibility
Step 6: Present results and recommendations to management

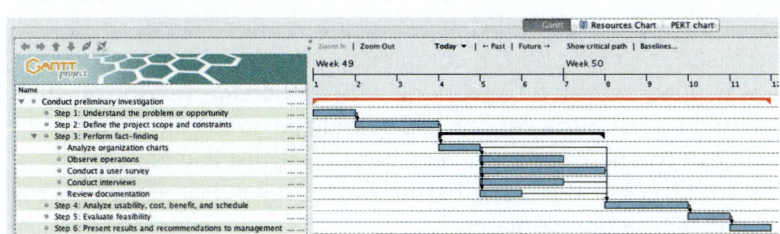

FIGURE 3-27 GanttProject is a free open source Java-based program. The Gantt chart shown here represents the same information shown by Microsoft Project in Figure 3-26.

Courtesy of GanttProject Team

Gantter is a free cloud-based project management tool. It runs in a browser window, so there is no software to install to use it. Figure 3-28 shows Gantter displaying a Gantt chart with the same information shown by GanttProject in Figure 3-27 and by Microsoft Project in Figure 3-26.

Apptivo and *smartsheet* are other examples of web-based project management tools offering similar capabilities, but on a paid subscription model.

The websites for all of these tools have more information about their capabilities, including demos, trial versions (where applicable), and training material.

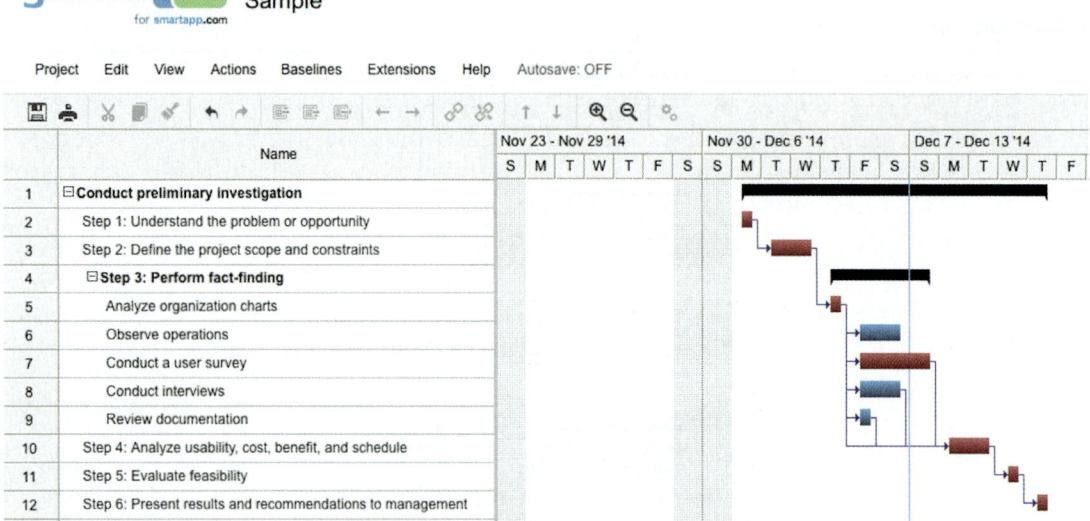

FIGURE 3-28 Gantter is a free cloud-based project management tool. The Gantt chart shown here represents the same information shown by GanttProject in Figure 3-27 and by Microsoft Project in Figure 3-26.
Source: Courtesy of InQuest Technologies, Inc.

CASE IN POINT 3.3:   CENSUS 2010

Just before the 2010 census, the U.S. Commerce Department canceled a plan to acquire 500,000 handheld computers they had ordered to tabulate data. According to Commerce Secretary Carlos Gutierrez, costs had skyrocketed. He blamed the problem on "a lack of effective communications with one of our major suppliers."

Apparently, there was plenty of blame to go around. Secretary Gutierrez noted that the Census Bureau had submitted numerous technical changes to the vendor, Harris Corporation. This greatly increased the cost and the complexity of the devices. Gutierrez stated, "The Census Bureau was unaccustomed to working with an outside vendor on such a large contract." He also pointed out that the vendor had submitted an initial estimate of $36 million to operate a help desk to assist census-takers, but that figure had jumped to $217 million. "It was a bad estimate. I can't think of a better way to say it. Harris gave us the number. We accepted it. It was totally underestimated."

What can be learned from the failure of this project, and could it have been prevented? Suppose you were asked to head up a similar project. What would you do to prevent a similar outcome?

3.10 RISK MANAGEMENT

Every IT project involves risks that systems analysts and project managers must address. A **risk** is an event that could affect the project negatively. **Risk management** is the process of identifying, analyzing, anticipating, and monitoring risks to minimize their impact on the project.

3.10.1 Steps in Risk Management

The first step in risk management is to develop a specific plan. Although project management experts differ with regard to the number of steps or phases, a basic list would include the following tasks:

- *Develop a risk management plan.* A **risk management plan** includes a review of the project's scope, stakeholders, budget, schedule, and any other internal or external factors that might affect the project. The plan should define project roles and responsibilities, risk management methods and procedures, categories of risks, and contingency plans.

- *Identify the risks.* **Risk identification** lists each risk and assesses the likelihood that it could affect the project. The details would depend on the specific project, but most lists would include a means of identification, and a brief description of the risk, what might cause it to occur, who would be responsible for responding, and the potential impact of the risk.

- *Analyze the risks.* This typically is a two-step process: Qualitative risk analysis and quantitative risk analysis. **Qualitative risk analysis** evaluates each risk by estimating the probability that it will occur and the degree of impact. Project managers can use a formula to weigh risk and impact values, or they can display the results in a two-axis grid. For example, a Microsoft Excel XY chart can be used to display the matrix, as shown in Figure 3-29. In the chart, notice

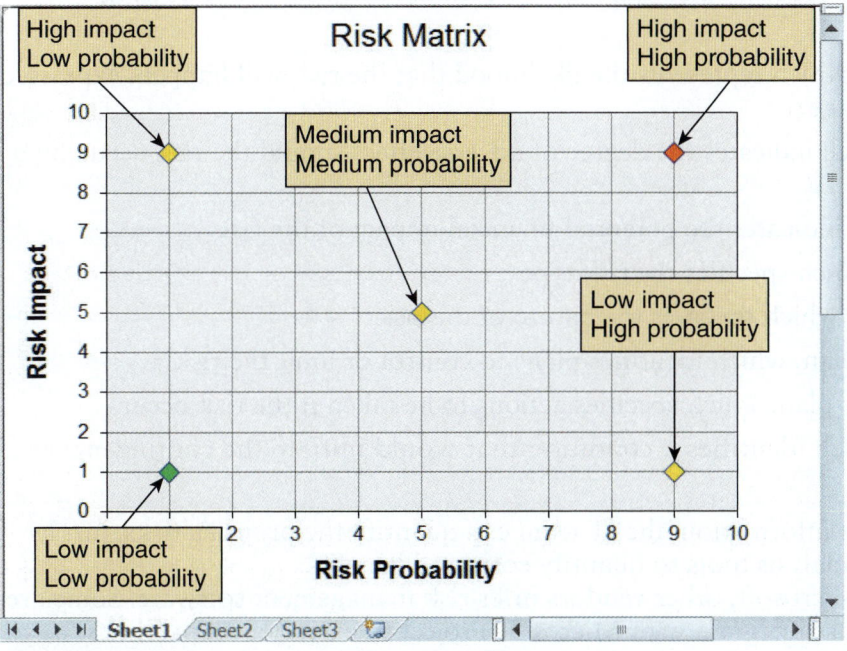

FIGURE 3-29 You can use a Microsoft Excel XY Chart type to display a risk matrix that shows risk probability and potential impact.

the various combinations of risk and impact ratings for the five sample values. This tool can help a project manager focus on the most critical areas, where risk probability and potential impact are high.

The purpose of quantitative risk analysis is to understand the actual impact in terms of dollars, time, project scope, or quality. Quantitative risk analysis can involve a modeling process called what-if analysis, which allows a project manager to vary one or more element(s) in a model to measure the effect on other elements. This topic is discussed in more detail in Chapter 12.

- *Create a risk response plan.* A risk response plan is a proactive effort to anticipate a risk and describe an action plan to deal with it. An effective risk response plan can reduce the overall impact by triggering timely and appropriate action.

- *Monitor risks.* This activity is ongoing throughout the risk management process. It is important to conduct a continuous tracking process that can identify new risks, notice changes in existing risks, and update any other areas of the risk management plan.

3.10.2 Risk Management Software

Most project management software includes powerful features that allow a project manager to assign specific dates as constraints, align task dependencies, note external factors that might affect a task, track progress, and display tasks that are behind schedule.

For example, the enterprise edition of Microsoft Project has a built-in risk management capability that can be used for large, corporate-wide projects. Microsoft claims that the software can link risks with specific tasks and projects, specify probability and impact, assign ownership, and track progress to manage projects more efficiently. Microsoft's risk management model includes the following factors:

- Probability, which represents the likelihood that the risk will happen, expressed as a percentage

- Impact, which indicates the degree of adverse effect should the risk occur, on a scale of 1 to 10

- Cost, which indicates the potential financial impact of the risk

- Category, which specifies the risk type

- Description, which specifies the nature of the risk

- Mitigation plan, which identifies plans to control or limit the risk

- Contingency plan, which specifies actions to be taken if the risk occurs

- Trigger, which identifies a condition that would initiate the contingency plan

Armed with this information, the IT team can quantify the project's risks, just as they use financial analysis tools to quantify costs and benefits.

In addition to Microsoft, other vendors offer risk management software. Some are add-on packages that integrate with Microsoft Project to extend its capabilities. Others are stand-alone applications that provide similar functionality to the core Microsoft Project program.

3.11 MANAGING FOR SUCCESS

To be successful, an information system must satisfy business requirements, stay within budget, be completed on time, and—most important of all—be managed effectively. When a project develops problems, the reasons typically involve business, budget, or schedule issues, as explained in the following sections. In addition to planning and managing the project, a project manager must be able to recognize these problems and deal with them effectively.

3.11.1 Business Issues

The major objective of every system is to provide a solution to a business problem or opportunity. If the system does not do this, then it is a failure—regardless of positive reaction from users, acceptable budget performance, or timely delivery. When the information system does not meet business requirements, causes can include unidentified or unclear requirements, inadequately defined scope, imprecise targets, shortcuts or sloppy work during systems analysis, poor design choices, insufficient testing or inadequate testing procedures, and lack of change control procedures. Systems also fail because of changes in the organization's culture, funding, or objectives. A system that falls short of business needs also produces problems for users and reduces employee morale and productivity.

As explained in Chapter 2, projects without clear scope definitions are risky because they tend to expand gradually, without specific authorization, in a process called *project creep*. However, even when a project is clearly described, it must be managed constantly.

3.11.2 Budget Issues

Cost overruns typically result from one or more of the following:

- Unrealistic estimates that are too optimistic or based on incomplete information
- Failure to develop an accurate forecast that considers all costs over the life of the project
- Poor monitoring of progress and slow response to early warning signs of problems
- Schedule delays due to factors that were not foreseen
- Human resource issues, including turnover, inadequate training, and motivation

3.11.3 Schedule Issues

Problems with timetables and project milestones can indicate a failure to recognize task dependencies, confusion between effort and progress, poor monitoring and control methods, personality conflicts among team members, or turnover of project personnel. The failure of an IT project also can be caused by poor project management techniques.

If the project manager fails to plan, staff, organize, supervise, communicate, motivate, evaluate, direct, and control properly, then the project is certain to fail. Even when factors outside his or her control contribute to the failure, the project manager is responsible for recognizing the early warning signs and handling them effectively.

CASE IN POINT 3.4:   SPRING FORWARD PRODUCTS

After three years with the company, you recently were asked to manage several IT projects. You are confident that you have the technical skills you need, but you are concerned about morale at the company. There has been some downsizing, and many employees are worried about the future.

As a longtime fan of the Dilbert cartoon strip, you know that maintaining morale can be a real challenge. Your current project involves a team of a dozen people, several of whom remind you of Dilbert and his coworkers. What are some techniques that you might use to motivate the team and inspire its members? What are some things you might not want to do?

3.12 THE BOTTOM LINE

Project management is a challenging task. Project managers must be alert, technically competent, and highly resourceful. They also must be good communicators with strong human resource skills. Project managers can be proud when they handle a successful project that helps the company achieve its business objectives.

Unfortunately, projects can and do get derailed for a wide variety of reasons. When problems occur, the project manager's ability to handle the situation becomes the critical factor. When a project manager first recognizes that a project is in trouble, what options are available? Alternatives can include trimming the project requirements, adding to the project resources, delaying the project deadline, and improving management controls and procedures. Sometimes, when a project experiences delays or cost overruns, the system still can be delivered on time and within budget if several less critical requirements are trimmed. The system can be delivered to satisfy the most necessary requirements, and additional features can be added later as a part of a maintenance or enhancement project.

If a project is in trouble because of a lack of resources or organizational support, management might be willing to give the project more commitment and higher priority. For example, management might agree to add more people to a project that is behind schedule. Adding staff, however, will reduce the project's completion time only if the additional people can be integrated effectively into the development team. If team members lack experience with certain aspects of the required technology, temporary help might be obtained from IT consultants or part-time staff. Adding staff can mean training and orienting the new people, however. In some situations, adding more people to a project actually might increase the time necessary to complete the project because of a principle called **Brooks' Law**. Frederick Brooks, Jr., an IBM engineer, observed that adding manpower to a late software project only makes it later. Brooks reached this conclusion when he saw that new workers on a project first had to be educated and instructed by existing employees whose own productivity was reduced accordingly.

A QUESTION OF ETHICS

iStockphoto.com/faberfoto_it

"Better blow the whistle," says Roy, your friend and project teammate at Final Four Industries. "The project is out of control, and you know it!" "Maybe so," you respond, "But that's not my call—I'm not the project manager." What you do not say is that Stephanie, the project manager, feels like her career is on the line and she is reluctant to bring bad news to management at this time. She honestly believes that the project can catch up, and says that a bad report on a major project could result in bad publicity for the firm and frighten potential customers.

To be fair, the next management progress report is scheduled in three weeks. It is possible that the team could catch up, but you doubt it. You wonder if there is an ethical question here: Even though the report is not due yet, should a significant problem be reported to management as soon as possible? You are concerned about the issue, and you decide to discuss it with Stephanie. What will you say to her?

3.13 CHAPTER SUMMARY

Project management is the process of planning, scheduling, monitoring, and reporting on the development of an information system. Planning includes identifying all project tasks and estimating the completion time and cost of each. Project scheduling involves the creation of a specific timetable, usually in the form of charts that show tasks, task dependencies, and critical tasks that might delay the project. Project monitoring requires guiding, supervising, and coordinating the project team's workload. The project manager must monitor the progress, evaluate the results, and take corrective action when necessary to control the project and stay on target. Project reporting includes regular progress reports to management, users, and the project team itself. Effective reporting requires strong communication skills and a sense of what others want and need to know about the project. A successful project must be completed on time, within budget, and deliver a quality product that satisfies users and meets requirements.

A project triangle shows three legs: project cost, scope, and time. A project manager must find the best balance among these elements because a change in any leg of the triangle will affect the other two legs. Project management techniques can be used throughout the SDLC.

Planning, scheduling, monitoring and reporting all take place within a larger project development framework, which includes three key steps: creating a work breakdown structure, identifying task patterns, and calculating the critical path. A work breakdown structure must clearly identify each task and include an estimated duration. A task, or activity, is any work that has a beginning and an end and requires the use of company resources such as people, time, or money. Time and cost estimates for tasks usually are made in person-days. A person-day represents the work that one person can accomplish in one day. Estimating the time for project activities is more difficult with larger systems. Project managers must consider the project size and scope, IT resources, prior experience with similar projects or systems, and applicable constraints. In addition to tasks, every project has events, or milestones. An event, or milestone, is a recognizable reference point that can be used to monitor progress.

Task patterns establish the sequence of work in a project. Task patterns involve dependent tasks, multiple successor tasks, and multiple predecessor tasks. In larger projects, these patterns can be very complex.

A critical path is a series of tasks that, if delayed, would affect the completion date of the overall project. If any task on the critical path falls behind schedule, the entire project will be delayed. Tasks on the critical path cannot have slack time. To identify the critical path, calculate the start and finish date for each task, which will determine the critical path for the project.

In project scheduling, the project manager develops a specific time for each task, based on available resources and whether or not the task is dependent on other predecessor tasks. The manager can use graphical tools such as Gantt charts and PERT charts to assist in the scheduling process.

A Gantt chart is a horizontal bar chart that represents the project schedule with time on the horizontal axis and tasks arranged vertically. It shows individual tasks and task groups, which include several tasks. In a Gantt chart, the length of the bar indicates the duration of the tasks. A Gantt chart can display progress, but does not show task dependency details or resource assignment unless the chart was created with a project management program that supports dependency linking and the entry of other information.

A PERT/CPM chart shows the project as a network diagram with tasks connected by arrows. Using a prescribed calculation method, the project manager uses a PERT chart to determine the overall duration of the project and provide specific information for each task, including the task IDs, their durations, start and finish times, and the order in which they must be performed. With this information, the manager can determine the critical path, which is the sequence of tasks that have no slack time and must be performed on schedule in order to meet the overall project deadline.

Most project managers use software applications such as Microsoft Project to plan, schedule, and monitor projects. Project managers are responsible for risk management, which is the process of identifying, analyzing, anticipating, and monitoring risks to minimize their impact on the project.

In the end, project management involves the same skills as any other management. The project manager must be perceptive, analytical, well organized, and a good communicator. If the project manager senses that the project is off-track, he or she must take immediate steps to diagnose and solve the problem. If the project manager fails to plan, staff, organize, supervise, communicate, motivate, evaluate, direct, and control properly, then the project is certain to fail. Even when factors outside his or her control contribute to the failure, the project manager is responsible for recognizing the early warning signs and handling them effectively.

Key Terms

activity Any work that has a beginning and an end, and requires the use of company resources including people, time, and/or money. Examples include conducting a series of interviews, designing a report, selecting software, waiting for the delivery of equipment, and training users. *See also* **task**.

best-case estimate The most optimistic outcome.

bottom-up technique A method for analyzing a large, complex project as a series of individual tasks, called project tasks.

Brooks' Law Frederick Brooks, an IBM engineer, observed that adding more manpower to a late software project only makes it later.

code review *See* **structured walk-through**.

concurrent task A task that can be completed at the same time as (in parallel with) another task.

critical path A series of events and activities with no slack time. If any activity along the critical path falls behind schedule, the entire project schedule is similarly delayed. As the name implies, a critical path includes all activities that are vital to the project schedule.

Critical Path Method (CPM) Shows a project as a network diagram. The activities are shown as vectors, and the events are displayed graphically as nodes. Although CPM developed separately from the Program Evaluation Review Technique (PERT), the two methods are essentially identical. *See also* **PERT/CPM**.

dependent task A task is said to be dependent when it has to be completed in a serial sequence.

design review *See* **structured walk-through**.

duration The amount of time it will take to complete a task.

event A reference point that marks a major occurrence. Used to monitor progress and manage a project. *See also* **milestone**.

finish day/date The day or date when a task is scheduled to be finished.

Gantt chart A horizontal bar chart that illustrates a schedule. Developed many years ago by Henry L. Gantt as a production control technique. Still are in common use today.

milestone A reference point that marks a major occurrence. Used to monitor progress and manage a project. *See also* **event**.

network diagram A PERT chart also is referred to as a network diagram.

open source Software that is supported by a large group of users and developers. The source code is made freely available.

person-day The amount of work that one person can complete in one day.

PERT/CPM The Program Evaluation Review Technique (PERT) was developed by the U.S. Navy to manage very complex projects, such as the construction of nuclear submarines. At approximately the same time, the Critical Path Method (CPM) was developed by private industry to meet similar project management needs. The important distinctions between the two methods have disappeared over time, and today the technique is called either PERT, CPM, or PERT/CPM.

predecessor task A single prior task upon which two or more concurrent tasks depend.

probable-case estimate The most likely outcome is called a probable-case estimate.

Program Evaluation Review Technique (PERT) *See* **PERT/CPM**.

project coordinator The person who handles administrative responsibilities for the development team and negotiates with users who might have conflicting requirements or want changes that would require additional time or expense.

project leader The person charged with leading a project from a technical perspective.

project management The process of planning, scheduling, monitoring, controlling, and reporting upon the development of an information system.

project manager The person charged with managing a project from an administrative perspective.

project monitoring Guiding, supervising, and coordinating the project team's workload.

project planning Identifying project tasks and estimating completion time and costs.

project reporting Providing regular progress reports to management, users, and the project team itself.

project scheduling The creation of a specific timetable to facilitate completion of a project. Also involves selecting and staffing the project team and assigning specific tasks to team members.

project triangle The three major components of a project: cost, scope, and time. A project manager tries to find the optimal balance among these factors.

qualitative risk analysis Evaluating risk by estimating the probability that it will occur and the degree of impact.

quantitative risk analysis Evaluating risk in terms of the actual impact in terms of dollars, time, project scope, or quality.

risk An event that could affect the project negatively.

risk identification Listing each risk and assessing the likelihood that it could affect a project.

risk management The process of identifying, evaluating, tracking, and controlling risks to minimize their impact.

risk management plan Includes a review of the project's scope, stakeholders, budget, schedule, and any other internal or external factors that might affect the project. The plan should define project roles and responsibilities, risk management methods and procedures, categories of risks, and contingency plans.

risk response plan A proactive effort to anticipate a risk and describe an action plan to deal with it. An effective risk response plan can reduce the overall impact by triggering a timely and appropriate action.

slack time The amount of time by which an event can be late without delaying the project. The difference between latest completion time (LCT) and earliest completion time (ECT).

start day/date The day or date when a task is scheduled to begin.

structured walk-through A review of a project team member's work by other members of the team. Generally, systems analysts review the work of other systems analysts, and programmers review the work of other programmers, as a form of peer review. Should take place throughout the SDLC and are called requirements reviews, design reviews, code reviews, or testing reviews, depending on the phase in which they occur.

successor task Each of the concurrent tasks of a predecessor task.

task Any work that has a beginning and an end, and requires the use of company resources including people, time, and/or money. Examples include conducting a series of interviews, designing a report, selecting software, waiting for the delivery of equipment, and training users. *See also* **activity**.

task box A component of a PERT/CPM chart that contains important scheduling and duration information about a task. Each task in a project is represented by its own task box in the PERT/CPM chart.

task group A task that represents several activities.

task ID A number or code that uniquely identifies a task.

task name A brief descriptive name for a task, which does not have to be unique in the project. For example, a task named Conduct Interviews might appear in several phases of the project.

task pattern A logical sequence of tasks in a work breakdown structure. Can involve sequential tasks, multiple successor tasks, and multiple predecessor tasks.

testing review *See* **structured walk-through**.

weight An important multiplier that managers factor into estimates so they can be analyzed.

work breakdown structure (WBS) A project broken down into a series of smaller tasks. *See also* **Gantt chart; PERT/CPM chart**.

worst-case estimate The most pessimistic outcome.

Chapter Exercises

Questions

1. Write the script for a one-minute explanation of basic project management concepts.
2. What is a task? What is an event? What is a milestone?
3. What specific information do you need to create a work breakdown structure?
4. What are the three main task patterns? Provide an example of each.
5. Explain the differences between a Gantt chart and a PERT/CPM chart.
6. What formula can a project manager use to estimate task duration? Provide an example.
7. What is a common problem in calculating start and finish times? Provide an example.
8. Why is the critical path important? Why would a task be on the critical path?
9. Why is it important to deliver effective project reports and communications?
10. What is risk management, and why is it important? Provide an example.

Discussion Topics

1. In Poor Richard's Almanac, Benjamin Franklin penned the familiar lines: "For the want of a nail the shoe was lost, for the want of a shoe the horse was lost, for the want of a horse the rider was lost, for the want of a rider the battle was lost, for the want of a battle the kingdom was lost—and all for the want of a horseshoe nail." Looking at the outcome in hindsight, could project management concepts have avoided the loss of the kingdom? How?
2. Microsoft Project is powerful, but quite expensive. As a manager, how would you justify the purchase of this software?
3. Suppose you want to manage a small project, but you do not have access to project management software. Could you use a spreadsheet or database program instead? How?
4. Some managers believe that they have "seat of the pants" intuition and do not need project management tools. Does that make sense to you? Why or why not?
5. Consider a scenario where a task is dependent on another task being started but not necessarily completed. For example, a project may depend on a task being started and 25% being completed before the group could start their portion of the project. Do you think this situation occurs frequently in systems analysis projects? Why or why not?

Projects

1. Think of all the tasks that you perform when you purchase a car. Include any research, decisions, or financial issues that relate to the purchase. Create a work breakdown structure that shows all the tasks, their estimated duration, and any predecessor tasks.
2. Perform an Internet research to learn more about project risk management, and write a summary of the results. Be sure to search for the classic book titled *Waltzing with Bears: Managing Risk on Software Projects*, by Tom Demarco and Timothy Lister.
3. Go to the websites for project management tools (besides Microsoft Project), such as Apptivo (*www.apptivo.com*), GanttProject (*www.ganttproject.biz*), Gantter (*www.gantter.com*), and smartsheet (*www.smartsheet.com/product-tour/gantt-charts*). Explore each program's features and describe what you like and do not like.
4. Describe three personal experiences where project management would have helped you avoid a problem or take advantage of an opportunity. Be specific.
5. Many of today's projects involve team members scattered across different time zones and in different physical locations. Moreover, the projects may have adopted an agile methodology, which reduces cycle time dramatically. Write a brief report that summarizes some of the key differences a manager would face managing this type of project, as opposed to a traditional project.

PHASE 2 SYSTEMS ANALYSIS

DILBERT © 1997 Scott Adams. Used By permission of UNIVERSAL UCLICK. All rights reserved.

As the Dilbert cartoon suggests, a successful project manager must determine the requirements before starting the design process, not the other way around. It may be tempting to "just do something" to give the appearance of productivity, but a systems project that does not satisfy business requirements serves no useful purpose.

Systems analysis is the second of five phases in the systems development life cycle. In the previous phase, systems planning, a preliminary investigation was conducted to determine the project's feasibility. The output of that phase, the preliminary investigation report, is used as input to the system analysis phase, where a system requirements document is created that captures the needs of the all stakeholders.

Chapter 4 describes the requirements modeling process: gathering facts about a systems project, preparing documentation, and creating models that will be used to design and develop the system. Chapter 5 discusses data and process modeling techniques that analysts use to show how the system transforms data into useful information. Chapter 6 discusses object modeling techniques that analysts use to create a logical model. Chapter 7 considers various development strategies for the new system, and plans for the transition to the systems design phase.

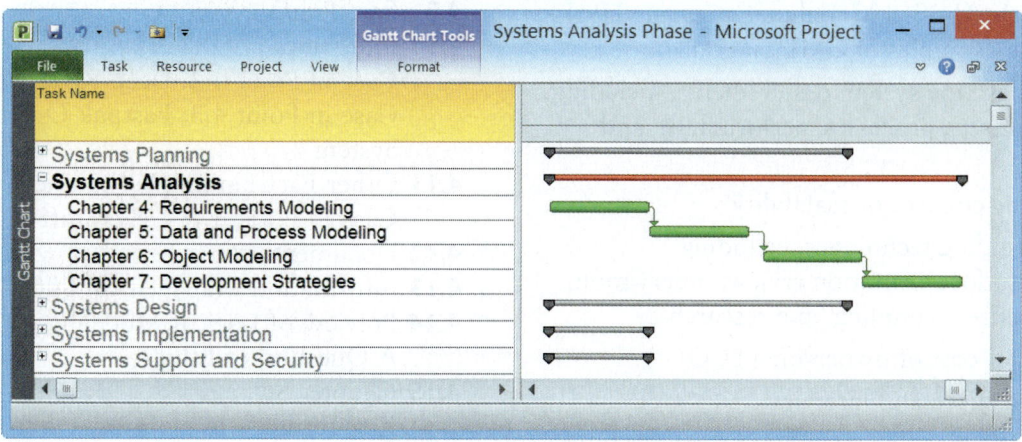

CHAPTER 4 Requirements Modeling

Chapter 4 is the first of four chapters in the systems analysis phase. This chapter describes the requirements modeling process: gathering facts about a systems project, preparing documentation, and creating models that will be used to design and develop the system.

The chapter includes four "Case in Point" discussion questions to help contextualize the concepts described in the text. The "Question of Ethics" raises the issue of considering a request by a supervisor to identify departments that reported the lowest ratings in a survey that was supposed to be kept anonymous.

LEARNING OBJECTIVES

When you finish this chapter, you should be able to:

- Describe systems analysis phase activities
- Explain joint application development (JAD), rapid application development (RAD), and agile methods
- Use a functional decomposition diagram (FDD) to model business functions and processes
- Describe the Unified Modeling Language (UML) and create examples of UML diagrams
- List and describe system requirements, including outputs, inputs, processes, performance, and controls
- Explain the concept of scalability
- Use fact-finding techniques, including interviews, documentation review, observation, questionnaires, sampling, and research
- Define total cost of ownership (TCO)
- Conduct a successful interview
- Develop effective documentation methods to use during systems development

CHAPTER CONTENTS

4.1 INTRODUCTION

After an overview of the systems analysis phase, this chapter describes requirements modeling techniques and team-based methods that systems analysts use to visualize and document new systems. The chapter then discusses system requirements and fact-finding techniques, which include interviewing, documentation review, observation, surveys and questionnaires, sampling, and research.

The Dilbert© cartoon shown in Figure 4-1 comically illustrates the challenges of getting system requirements correct. Customers often find it difficult to clearly describe what they want the system to do, and when they do list the requirements, the result tends to be an unprioritized set of conflicting capabilities. The canonical example is requesting that a system be "extremely usable" but also "completely secure." No system can meet both requirements satisfactorily: A completely secure system would have to be locked in a vault, disconnected from the outside world, and inaccessible to the user — hardly very usable.

FIGURE 4-1 An illustration of the challenges inherent in understanding system requirements.

4.2 SYSTEMS ANALYSIS PHASE OVERVIEW

The overall objective of the systems analysis phase is to understand the proposed project, ensure that it will support business requirements, and build a solid foundation for system development. In this phase, the analyst uses models and other documentation tools to visualize and describe the proposed system.

4.2.1 Systems Analysis Activities

The systems analysis phase includes the four main activities shown in Figure 4-2: requirements modeling, data and process modeling, object modeling, and consideration of development strategies.

Although the waterfall model shows sequential SDLC phases, it is not uncommon for several phases (or certain tasks within a phase) to interact during the development process, just as they would in an adaptive model. For example, this occurs whenever new facts are learned or system requirements change during the modeling process. Figure 4-2 shows typical interaction among the three modeling tasks: requirements modeling, data and process modeling, and object modeling.

Systems Analysis Phase Tasks

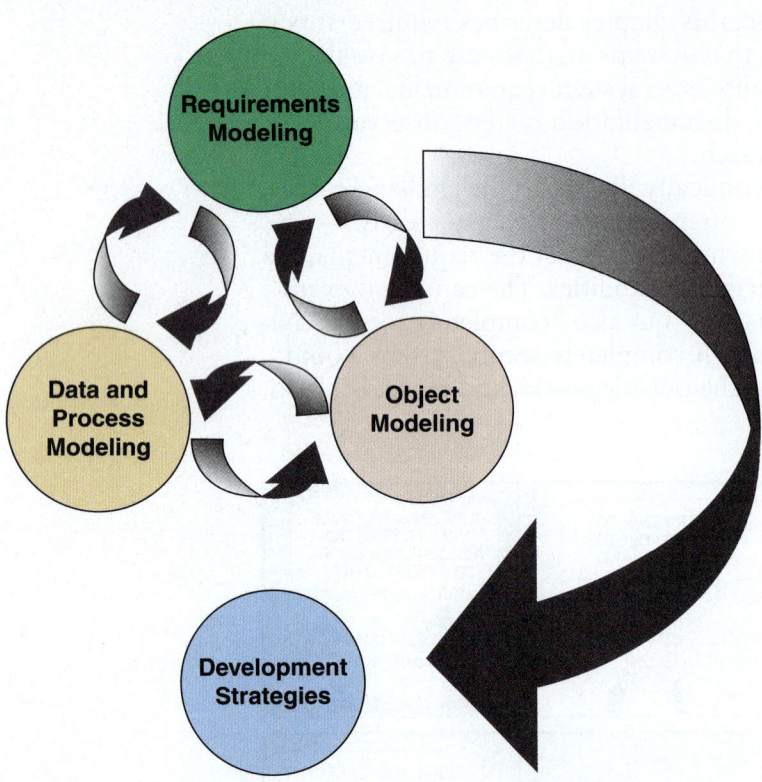

FIGURE 4-2 The systems analysis phase consists of requirements modeling, data and process modeling, object modeling, and consideration of development strategies. Notice that the systems analysis tasks are interactive, even though the waterfall model generally depicts sequential development.

REQUIREMENTS MODELING: This chapter describes requirements modeling, which involves fact-finding to describe the current system and identification of the requirements for the new system, such as outputs, inputs, processes, performance, and security.

- **Output** refers to electronic or printed information produced by the system.

- **Input** refers to necessary data that enters the system, either manually or in an automated manner.

- **Process** refers to the logical rules that are applied to transform the data into meaningful information.

- **Performance** refers to system characteristics, such as speed, volume, capacity, availability, and reliability.

- **Security** refers to hardware, software, and procedural controls that safeguard and protect the system and its data from internal or external threats.

DATA AND PROCESS MODELING:
Chapter 5 continues the modeling process by showing how to represent graphically system data and processes using traditional structured analysis techniques. As described in Chapter 1, structured analysis identifies the data flowing into a process, the business rules that transform the data, and the resulting output data flow.

OBJECT MODELING: Chapter 6 discusses object modeling, which is another popular modeling technique. While structured analysis treats processes and data as separate components, object-oriented (O-O) analysis combines data and the processes that act on the data into things called objects. These objects represent actual people, things, transactions, and events that affect the system. During the system development process, analysts often use both modeling methods to gain as much information as possible.

DEVELOPMENT STRATEGIES: Chapter 7 considers various development options and prepares for the transition to the systems design phase of the SDLC. Topics in Chapter 7 include software trends, acquisition and development alternatives, outsourcing, and formally documenting requirements for the new system.

The deliverable, or end product, of the systems analysis phase is a system requirements document, which is an overall design for the new system. In addition, each activity within the systems analysis phase has an end product and one or more milestones. As described in Chapter 3, project managers use various tools and techniques to coordinate people, tasks, timetables, and budgets.

4.2.2 Systems Analysis Skills

A systems analyst needs strong analytical and interpersonal skills to build an accurate model of the new system. Analytical skills enable the analyst to identify a problem, evaluate the key elements, and develop a useful solution. Interpersonal skills are especially valuable to a systems analyst who must work with people at all organizational levels, balance conflicting needs of users, and communicate effectively.

Because information systems affect people throughout the company, team-oriented strategies should be considered at the start of the systems analysis phase.

4.2.3 Team-Based Techniques: JAD, RAD, and Agile Methods

The IT department's goal is to deliver the best possible information system, at the lowest possible cost, in the shortest possible time. To achieve the best results, system developers view users as partners in the development process. Greater user involvement usually results in better communication, faster development times, and more satisfied users.

The traditional model for systems development was an IT department that used structured analysis and consulted users only when their input or approval was needed. Although the IT staff still has a central role, and structured analysis remains a popular method of systems development, most IT managers invite system users to participate actively in various development tasks.

As described in Chapter 1, team-based approaches have been around for some time. A popular example is joint application development (JAD), which is a user-oriented technique for fact-finding and requirements modeling. Because it is not linked to a specific development methodology, systems developers use JAD whenever group input and interaction are desired.

Another popular user-oriented method is rapid application development (RAD). RAD resembles a condensed version of the entire SDLC, with users involved every step of the way. While JAD typically focuses only on fact-finding and requirements determination, RAD provides a fast-track approach to a full spectrum of system development tasks, including planning, design, construction, and implementation.

Finally, as described in Chapter 1, agile methods represent a recent trend that stresses intense interaction between system developers and users. JAD, RAD, and agile methods are discussed in the following sections.

4.3 JOINT APPLICATION DEVELOPMENT

Joint application development (JAD) is a popular fact-finding technique that brings users into the development process as active participants.

4.3.1 User Involvement

Users have a vital stake in an information system, and they should participate fully in the development process. Many years ago, the IT department usually had sole responsibility for systems development, and users had a relatively passive role. During the development process, the IT staff would collect information from users, define system requirements, and construct the new system. At various stages of the process, the IT staff might ask users to review the design, offer comments, and submit changes.

Today, users typically have a much more active role in systems development. IT professionals now recognize that successful systems must be user-oriented, and users need to be involved, formally or informally, at every stage of system development.

One popular strategy for user involvement is a JAD team approach, which involves a task force of users, managers, and IT professionals who work together to gather information, discuss business needs, and define the new system requirements.

4.3.2 JAD Participants and Roles

A JAD team usually meets over a period of days or weeks in a special conference room or at an off-site location. Either way, JAD participants should be insulated from the distraction of day-to-day operations. The objective is to analyze the existing system, obtain user input and expectations, and document user requirements for the new system.

The JAD group usually has a project leader, who needs to have strong interpersonal and organizational skills, and one or more members who can document and record the results and decisions. Figure 4-3 describes typical JAD participants and their roles. IT staff members often serve as JAD project leaders, but that is not always the case. Systems analysts on the JAD team participate in discussions, ask questions, take notes, and provide support to the team. If CASE tools are available, analysts can develop models and enter documentation from the JAD session directly into the CASE tool.

JAD PARTICIPANT	ROLE
JAD project leader	Develops an agenda, acts as a facilitator, and leads the JAD session
Top management	Provides enterprise-level authorization and support for the project
Managers	Provide department-level support for the project and understanding of how the project must support business functions and requirements
Users	Provide operational-level input on current operations, desired changes, input and output requirements, user interface issues, and how the project will support day-to-day tasks
Systems analysts and other IT staff members	Provide technical assistance and resources for JAD team members on issues such as security, backup, hardware, software, and network capability
Recorder	Documents results of JAD sessions and works with systems analysts to build system models and develop CASE tool documentation

FIGURE 4-3 Typical JAD participants and roles.

A typical JAD session agenda is shown in Figure 4-4. The JAD process involves intensive effort by all team members. Because of the wide range of input and constant interaction among the participants, many companies believe that a JAD group produces the best possible definition of the new system.

4.3.3 JAD Advantages and Disadvantages

Compared with traditional methods, JAD is more expensive and can be cumbersome if the group is too large relative to the size of the project. Many companies find, however, that JAD allows key users to participate effectively in the requirements modeling

Project leader	• Introduce all JAD team members • Discuss ground rules, goals, and objectives for the JAD sessions • Explain methods of documentation and use of CASE tools, if any
Top management (sometimes called the project owner or sponsor)	• Explain the reason for the project and express top management authorization and support
Project leader	• Provide overview of the current system and proposed project scope and constraints • Present outline of specific topics and issues to be investigated
Open discussion session, moderated by project leader	• Review the main business processes, tasks, user roles, input, and output • Identify specific areas of agreement or disagreement • Break team into smaller groups to study specific issues and assign group leaders
JAD team members working in smaller group sessions, supported by IT staff	• Discuss and document all system requirements • Develop models and prototypes
Group leaders	• Report on results and assigned tasks and topics • Present issues that should be addressed by the overall JAD team
Open discussion session, moderated by project leader	• Review reports from small group sessions • Reach consensus on main issues • Document all topics
Project leader	• Present overall recap of JAD session • Prepare report that will be sent to JAD team members

FIGURE 4-4 Typical agenda for a JAD session.

process. When users participate in the systems development process, they are more likely to feel a sense of ownership in the results and support for the new system. When properly used, JAD can result in a more accurate statement of system requirements, a better understanding of common goals, and a stronger commitment to the success of the new system.

4.4 RAPID APPLICATION DEVELOPMENT

Rapid application development (RAD) is a team-based technique that speeds up information systems development and produces a functioning information system. Like JAD, RAD uses a group approach but goes much further. While the end product of JAD is a requirements model, the end product of RAD is the new information system. RAD is a complete methodology, with a four-phase life cycle that parallels the traditional SDLC phases. Companies use RAD to reduce cost and development time and increase the probability of success.

RAD relies heavily on prototyping and user involvement. The RAD process allows users to examine a working model as early as possible, determine if it meets their needs, and suggest necessary changes. Based on user input, the prototype is modified and the interactive process continues until the system is completely developed and users are satisfied. The project team uses CASE tools to build the prototypes and create a continuous stream of documentation.

4.4.1 RAD Phases and Activities

The RAD model consists of four phases: requirements planning, user design, construction, and cutover, as shown in Figure 4-5. Notice the continuous interaction between the user design and construction phases.

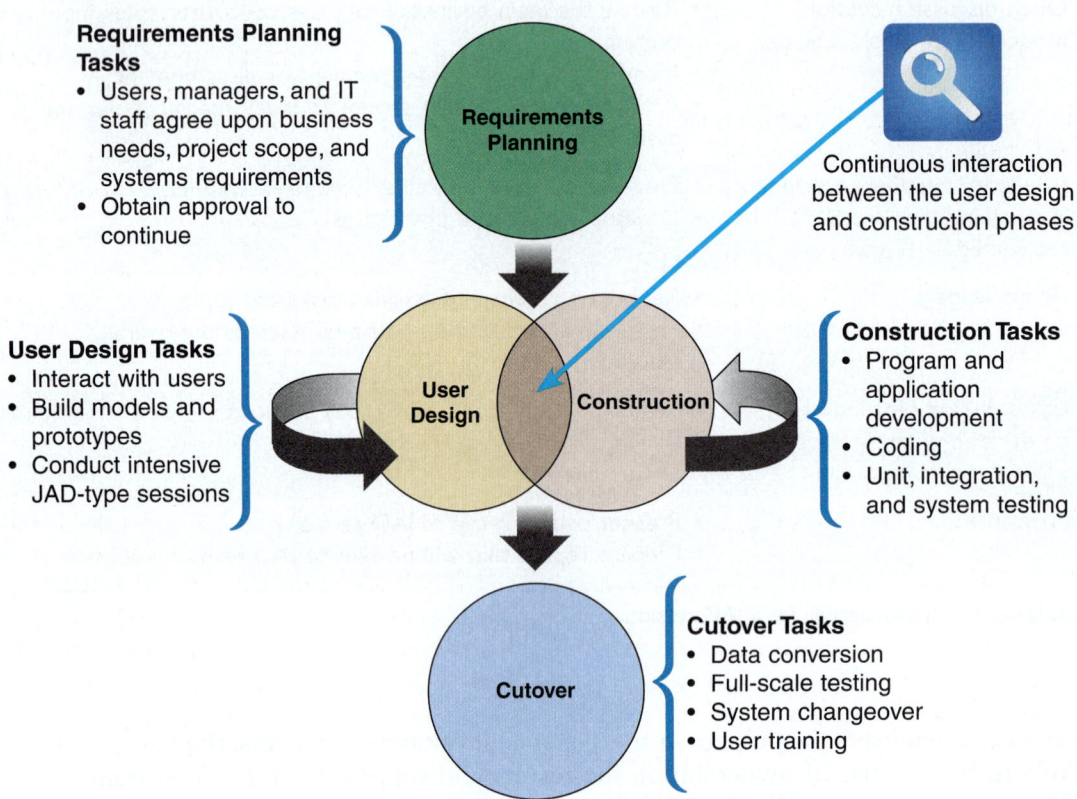

FIGURE 4-5 The four phases of the RAD model are requirements planning, user design, construction, and cutover. Notice the continuous interaction between the user design and construction phases.

REQUIREMENTS PLANNING: The **requirements planning phase** combines elements of the systems planning and systems analysis phases of the SDLC. Users, managers, and IT staff members discuss and agree on business needs, project scope, constraints, and system requirements. The requirements planning phase ends when the team agrees on the key issues and obtains management authorization to continue.

USER DESIGN: During the **user design phase**, users interact with systems analysts and develop models and prototypes that represent all system processes, outputs, and inputs. The RAD group or subgroups typically use a combination of JAD techniques and CASE tools to translate user needs into working models. User design is a continuous, interactive process that allows users to understand, modify, and eventually approve a working model of the system that meets their needs.

CONSTRUCTION: The construction phase focuses on program and application development tasks similar to the SDLC. In RAD, however, users continue to participate and still can suggest changes or improvements as actual screens or reports are developed.

CUTOVER: The cutover phase resembles the final tasks in the SDLC implementation phase, including data conversion, testing, changeover to the new system, and user training. Compared with traditional methods, the entire process is compressed. As a result, the new system is built, delivered, and placed in operation much sooner.

4.4.2 RAD Objectives

The main objective of all RAD approaches is to cut development time and expense by involving users in every phase of systems development. Because it is a continuous process, RAD allows the development team to make necessary modifications quickly, as the design evolves. In times of tight corporate budgets, it is especially important to limit the cost of changes that typically occur in a long, drawn-out development schedule.

In addition to user involvement, a successful RAD team must have IT resources, skills, and management support. Because it is a dynamic, user-driven process, RAD is especially valuable when a company needs an information system to support a new business function. By obtaining user input from the beginning, RAD also helps a development team design a system that requires a highly interactive or complex user interface.

4.4.3 RAD Advantages and Disadvantages

RAD has advantages and disadvantages compared with traditional structured analysis methods. The primary advantage is that systems can be developed more quickly with significant cost savings. A disadvantage is that RAD stresses the mechanics of the system itself and does not emphasize the company's strategic business needs. The risk is that a system might work well in the short term, but the corporate and long-term objectives for the system might not be met. Another potential disadvantage is that the accelerated time cycle might allow less time to develop quality, consistency, and design standards. RAD can be an attractive alternative, however, if an organization understands the possible risks.

4.5 AGILE METHODS

Chapter 1 explained that agile methods attempt to develop a system incrementally, by building a series of prototypes and constantly adjusting them to user requirements. As the agile process continues, developers revise, extend, and merge earlier versions into the final product. An agile approach emphasizes continuous feedback, and each incremental step is affected by what was learned in the prior steps.

As agile methods become more popular, a large community of agile-related software and services has evolved. Many agile developers prefer not to use CASE tools at all, and as shown in Figure 4-6 rely instead on whiteboard displays and arrangements of movable sticky notes. This approach, they believe, reinforces the agile strategy: simple, rapid, flexible, and user-oriented.

Scrum is another agile approach. The name comes from the rugby term *scrum*, where team members lunge at each other to achieve their objectives, as shown in Figure 4-7. The systems development version of Scrum involves the same intense interaction, though it is more mental than physical. In a Scrum session, agile team

FIGURE 4-6 Reinforcing the agile strategy: simple, rapid, flexible, and user-oriented.

Sam Edwards/Getty Images

FIGURE 4-7 In a rugby scrum, team members prepare to lunge at each other to achieve their objectives.

fotograf.lv / Shutterstock.com

members play specific roles, including colorful designations such as pigs or chickens. These roles are based on the old joke about the pig and chicken who discuss a restaurant where ham and eggs would be served. However, the pig declines, because that role would require a total commitment, while for the chicken, it would only be a contribution.

In the agile world, the pigs include the product owner, the facilitator, and the development team; while the chickens include users, other stakeholders, and managers. Scrum sessions have specific guidelines that emphasize time blocks, interaction, and team-based activities that result in deliverable software. An agile team uses a series of scrums to pause the action and allow the players to reset the game plan, which remains in effect until the next scrum.

4.5.1 Agile Method Advantages and Disadvantages

Agile, or adaptive, methods are very flexible and efficient in dealing with change. They are popular because they stress team interaction and reflect a set of community-based values. Also, frequent deliverables constantly validate the project and reduce risk.

However, some potential problems exist. For example, team members need a high level of technical and interpersonal skills. Also, a lack of structure and documentation can introduce risk factors, such as blurring of roles and responsibilities, and loss of corporate knowledge. Finally, the overall project may be subject to significant change in scope as user requirements continue to evolve during the project.

CASE IN POINT 4.1:   NORTH HILLS COLLEGE

North Hills College has decided to implement a new registration system that will allow students to register online, as well as in person. As IT manager, you decide to set up a JAD session to help define the requirements for the new system. The North Hills organization is fairly typical, with administrative staff that includes a registrar, a student support and services team, a business office, an IT group, and a number of academic departments. Using this information, you start work on a plan to carry out the JAD session. Who would you invite to the session, and why? What would be your agenda for the session, and what would take place at each stage of the session?

4.6 MODELING TOOLS AND TECHNIQUES

Models help users, managers, and IT professionals understand the design of a system. Modeling involves graphical methods and nontechnical language that represent the system at various stages of development. During requirements modeling, the analyst can use various tools to describe business processes, requirements, and user interaction with the system.

Systems analysts use modeling and fact-finding interactively — first they build fact-finding results into models, then they study the models to determine whether additional fact-finding is needed. To help them understand system requirements, analysts use functional decomposition diagrams, business process models, data flow diagrams, and Unified Modeling Language diagrams. Any of these diagrams can be created with CASE tools or stand-alone drawing tools if desired.

4.6.1 Functional Decomposition Diagrams

A functional decomposition diagram (FDD) is a top-down representation of a function or process. Using an FDD, an analyst can show business functions and break them down into lower-level functions and processes. Creating an FDD is similar to drawing an organization chart: Start at the top and work downwards. Figure 4-8 shows an FDD of a library system drawn with the Visible Analyst CASE tool. FDDs can be used at several stages of systems development. During requirements modeling, analysts use FDDs to model business functions and show how they are organized into lower-level processes. Those processes translate into program modules during application development.

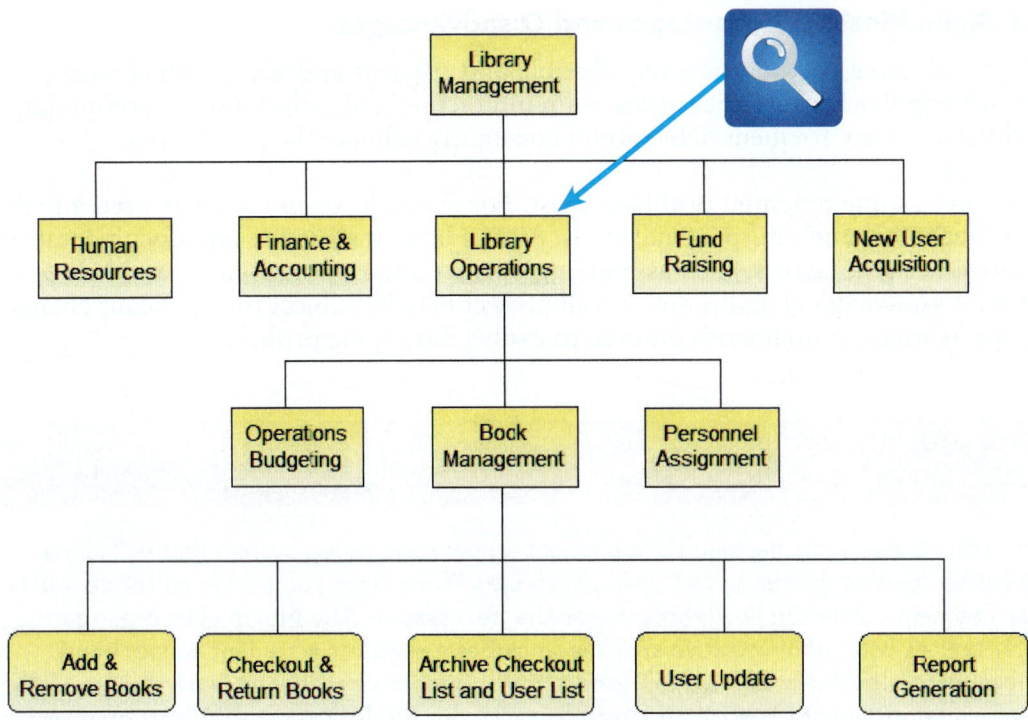

FIGURE 4-8 This Visible Analyst FDD shows a library system with five top-level functions. The Library Operations function includes two additional levels of processes and sub-processes.
Source: Visible Systems Corporation.

4.6.2 Business Process Modeling

As described in Chapter 1, a business process model (BPM) represents one or more business processes, such as handling an airline reservation, filling a product order, or updating a customer account. During requirements modeling, analysts often create models that use a standard language called business process modeling notation (BPMN). BPMN includes various shapes and symbols to represent events, processes, and workflows.

When creating a business process model using a CASE tool such as Visible Analyst, the diagram automatically becomes part of the overall model. In the example shown in Figure 4-9, using BPMN terminology, the overall diagram is called a pool, and the designated customer areas are called swim lanes. Integrating BPM into the CASE development process leads to faster results, fewer errors, and reduced cost.

4.6.3 Data Flow Diagrams

Working from a functional decomposition diagram, analysts can create data flow diagrams (DFDs) to show how the system stores, processes, and transforms data. The DFD in Figure 4-10 describes adding and removing books, which is a function shown in the Library Management diagram in Figure 4-8. Notice that the two boxes in the DFD represent processes, each with various inputs and outputs. Additional levels of information and detail are depicted in other, related DFDs. Data and process modeling is described in detail in Chapter 5.

4.6.4 Unified Modeling Language

The **Unified Modeling Language (UML)** is a widely used method of visualizing and documenting software systems design. UML uses object-oriented design concepts, but it is independent of any specific programming language and can be used to describe business processes and requirements generally.

UML provides various graphical tools, such as use case diagrams and sequence diagrams. During requirements modeling, a systems analyst can utilize the UML to represent the information system from a user's viewpoint. Use case diagrams, sequence diagrams, and other UML concepts are discussed in more detail in Chapter 6, along with other object-oriented analysis concepts. A brief description of each technique follows.

USE CASE DIAGRAMS: During requirements modeling, systems analysts and users work together to document requirements and model system functions. A **use case diagram** visually represents the interaction between users and the information system. In a use case diagram, the user becomes an **actor**, with a specific role that describes how he or she interacts with the system. Systems analysts can draw use case diagrams freehand or use CASE tools that integrate the use cases into the overall system design.

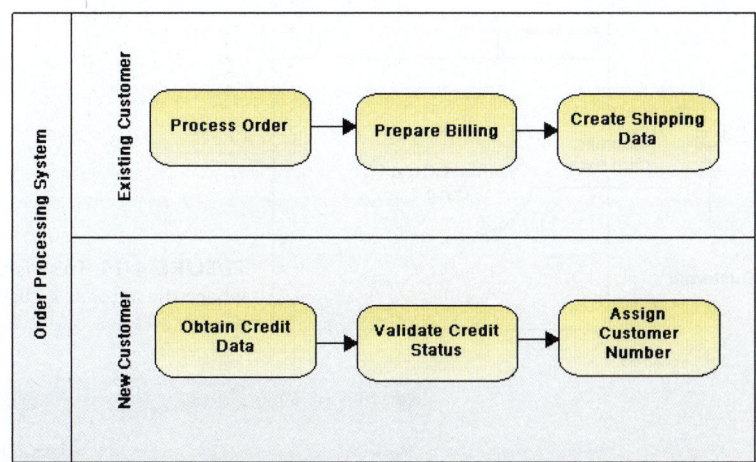

FIGURE 4-9 Using the Visible Analyst CASE tool, an analyst can create a business process diagram. The overall diagram is called a pool, and the two separate customer areas are called swim lanes.
Source: Visible Systems Corporation.

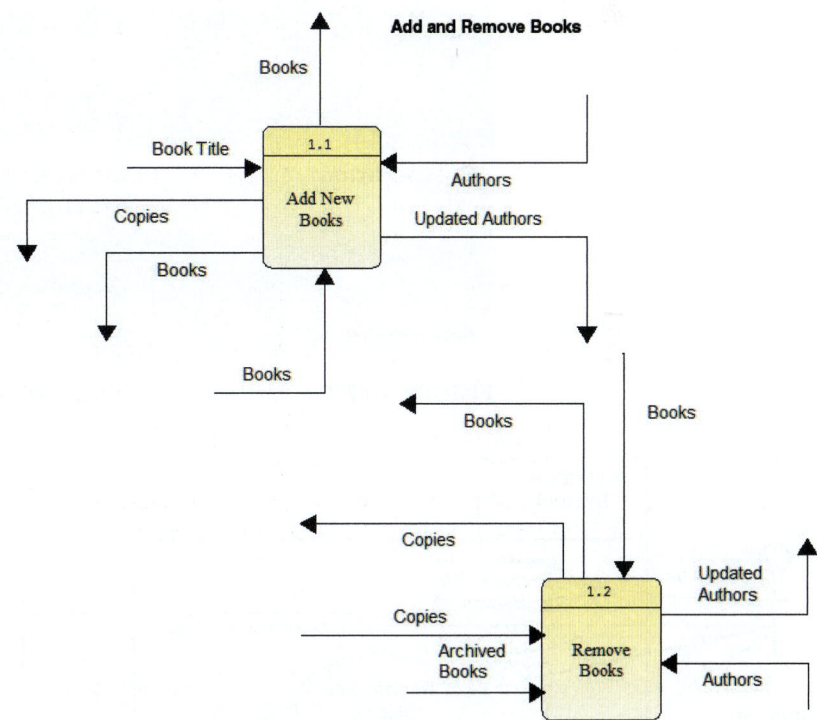

FIGURE 4-10 This Visible Analyst DFD shows how books are added and removed in a library system.
Source: Visible Systems Corporation.

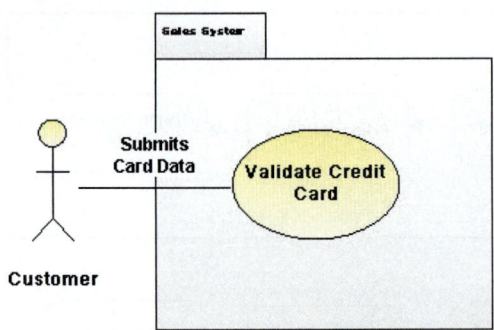

FIGURE 4-11 This Visible Analyst use case diagram shows a sales system, where the actor is a customer and the use case is a credit card validation.
Source: Visible Systems Corporation.

Name of Use Case:	Credit card validation process
Actor:	Customer
Description:	Describes the credit card validation process
Successful Completion:	1. Customer clicks the input selector and enters credit card number and expiration date 2. System verifies card 3. System sends authorization message
Alternative:	1. Customer clicks the input selector and enters credit card number and expiration date 2. System rejects card 3. System sends rejection message
Precondition:	Customer has selected at least one item and has proceeded to checkout area
Postcondition:	Credit card information has been validated Customer can continue with order
Assumptions:	None

FIGURE 4-12 This table documents the credit card validation use case shown in Figure 4-11.

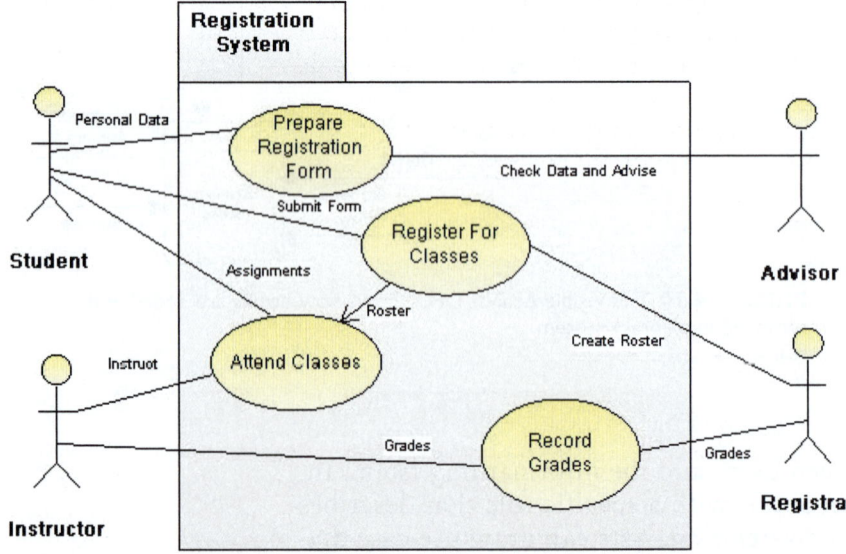

FIGURE 4-13 This Visible Analyst use case diagram shows a student records system.
Source: Visible Systems Corporation.

Figure 4-11 shows a simple use case diagram for a sales system where the actor is a customer and the use case involves a credit card validation that is performed by the system. Because use cases depict the system through the eyes of a user, common business language can be used to describe the transactions. For example, Figure 4-12 shows a table that documents the credit card validation use case, and Figure 4-13 shows a student records system, with several use cases and actors.

SEQUENCE DIAGRAM: A sequence diagram shows the timing of interactions between objects as they occur. A systems analyst might use a sequence diagram to show all possible outcomes, or focus on a single scenario. Figure 4-14 shows a simple sequence diagram of a successful credit card validation. The interaction proceeds from top to bottom along a vertical timeline, while the horizontal arrows represent messages from one object to another.

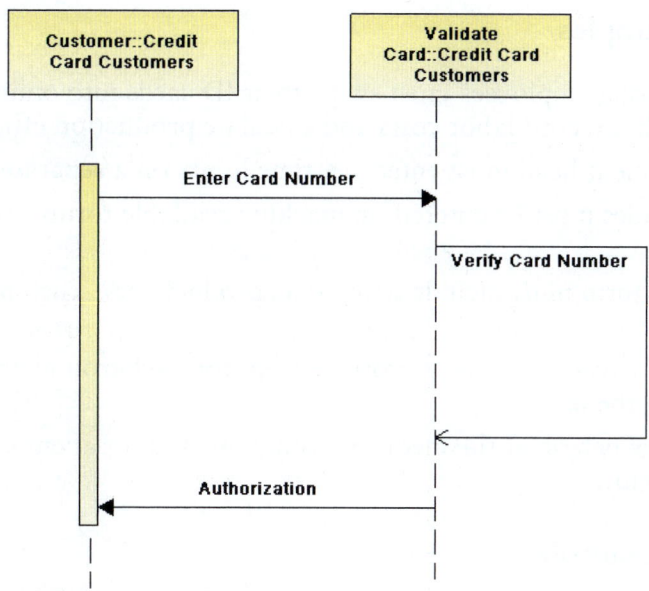

FIGURE 4-14 This Visible Analyst sequence diagram shows a credit card validation process.
Source: Visible Systems Corporation.

4.7 SYSTEM REQUIREMENTS CHECKLIST

During requirements modeling, systems developers must identify and describe all system requirements. A system requirement is a characteristic or feature that must be included in an information system to satisfy business requirements and be acceptable to users. System requirements serve as benchmarks to measure the overall acceptability of the finished system.

System requirements fall into five general categories: outputs, inputs, processes, performance, and controls. Typical examples of system requirements for each category are listed below.

4.7.1 Output Examples

- The website must report online volume statistics every four hours, and hourly during peak periods.
- The inventory system must produce a daily report showing the part number, description, quantity on hand, quantity allocated, quantity available, and unit cost of all sorted by part number.
- The contact management system must generate a daily reminder list for all sales reps.
- The purchasing system must provide suppliers with up-to-date specifications.

- The sales tracking system must produce a daily fast-moving-item report, listing all products that exceed the forecasted sales volume grouped by style, color, size, and reorder status.
- The customer analysis system must produce a quarterly report that identifies changes in ordering patterns or trends with statistical comparisons to the previous four quarters.

4.7.2 Input Examples

- Manufacturing employees must swipe their ID cards into online data collection terminals that record labor costs and calculate production efficiency.
- The department head must enter overtime hours on a separate screen.
- Student grades must be entered on machine-readable forms prepared by the instructor.
- Each input form must include date, time, product code, customer number, and quantity.
- Data entry screens must be uniform, except for background color, which can be changed by the user.
- A data entry person at the medical group must input patient services into the billing system.

4.7.3 Process Examples

- The student records system must calculate the GPA at the end of each semester.
- As the final step in year-end processing, the payroll system must update employee salaries, bonuses, and benefits and produce tax data required by the IRS.
- The warehouse distribution system must analyze daily orders and create a routing pattern for delivery trucks that maximizes efficiency and reduces unnecessary mileage.
- The human resources system must interface properly with the existing payroll system.
- The equipment rental system must not execute new rental transactions for customers who have overdue accounts.
- The prescription system must automatically generate an insurance claim form.

4.7.4 Performance Examples

- The system must support 25 users online simultaneously.
- Response time must not exceed four seconds.
- The system must be operational seven days a week, 365 days a year.
- The accounts receivable system must prepare customer statements by the third business day of the following month.
- The student records system must produce class lists within five hours after the end of registration.
- The online inventory control system must flag all low-stock items within one hour after the quantity falls below a predetermined minimum.

4.7.5 Control Examples

- The system must provide logon security at the operating system level and at the application level.

- An employee record must be added, changed, or deleted only by a member of the human resources department.

- The system must maintain separate levels of security for users and the system administrator.

- All transactions must have audit trails.

- The manager of the sales department must approve orders that exceed a customer's credit limit.

- The system must create an error log file that includes the error type, description, and time.

4.8 FUTURE GROWTH, COSTS, AND BENEFITS

In addition to the system requirements, systems analysts must consider scalability, which determines how a system will handle future growth and demands, and the total cost of ownership, which includes all future operational and support costs.

4.8.1 Scalability

Scalability refers to a system's ability to handle increased business volume and transactions in the future. Because it will have a longer useful life, a scalable system offers a better return on the initial investment.

To evaluate scalability, information is needed about projected future volume for all outputs, inputs, and processes. For example, for a web-based order processing system, one needs to know the maximum projected number of concurrent users, the periods of peak online activity, the number and types of data items required for each transaction, and the method of accessing and updating customer files.

Even to print customer statements, the analyst needs to know the number of active accounts and have a forecast for one, two, or five years because that information affects future hardware decisions. In addition, with realistic volume projections, reliable cost estimates for related expenses, such as postage and online charges, can be provided.

Similarly, to ensure that a web-based hotel reservation system is sufficiently scalable, the analyst would need to project activity levels for several years of operation. For example, one might forecast the frequency of online queries about room availability and estimate the time required for each query and the average response time. With that information, server transaction volume and network requirements could be estimated.

Transaction volume has a significant impact on operating costs. When volume exceeds a system's limitations, maintenance costs increase sharply. Volume can change dramatically if a company expands or enters a new line of business. For example, a new Internet-based marketing effort might require an additional server and 24-hour technical support.

Data storage is also an important scalability issue. The analyst must determine how much data storage is required currently and predict future needs based on system activity and growth. Those requirements affect hardware, software, and network bandwidth needed to maintain system performance. Data retention requirements must also be considered to determine whether data can be deleted or archived on a specific timetable.

4.8.2 Total Cost of Ownership

In addition to direct costs, systems developers must identify and document indirect expenses that contribute to the total cost of ownership (TCO). TCO is especially important if the development team is assessing several alternatives. After considering the indirect costs, which are not always apparent, a system that seems inexpensive initially might actually turn out to be the most costly choice. One problem is that cost estimates tend to understate indirect costs, such as user support and downtime productivity losses. Even if accurate figures are unavailable, systems analysts should try to identify indirect costs and include them in TCO estimates.

Because cost control is so important, vendors often claim that their products or services will reduce TCO significantly. For example, one of the most common reasons to migrate a legacy system to the cloud is reduced TCO. As shown in Figure 4-15, cloud computing offers the opportunity for lower operational costs due to the outsourcing of expenses such as capital investment in exchange for a pay-as-you-go pricing model.

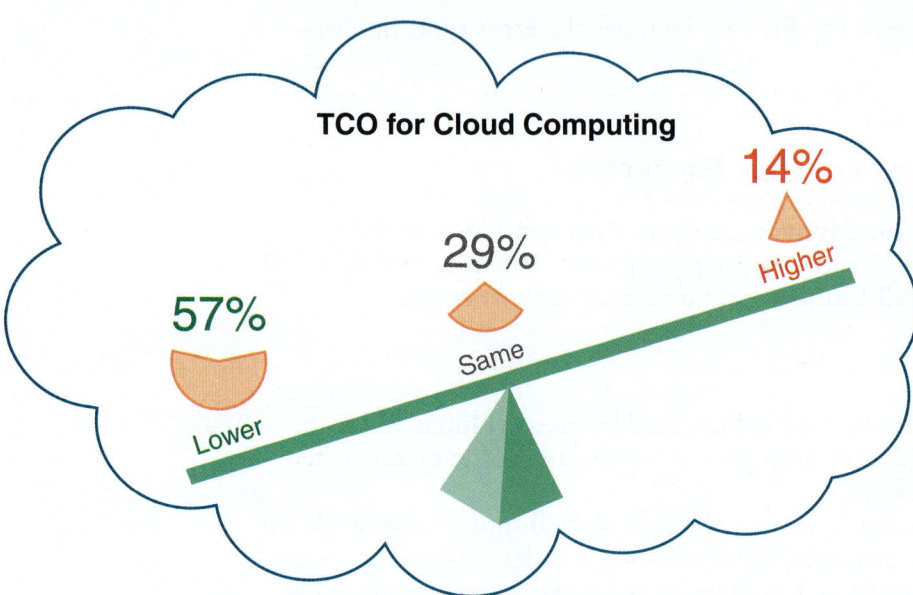

FIGURE 4-15 Total cost of ownership when migrating to the cloud can be significantly less than current computing platforms.

4.9 Fact-Finding

After mastering the categories of system requirements, scalability, and TCO, the next step is fact-finding: collecting information. Whether working solo or as a member of a JAD team, during requirements modeling the analyst will use various fact-finding techniques, including interviews, document review, observation, surveys and questionnaires, sampling, and research.

4.9.1 Fact-Finding Overview

Although software can help gather and analyze facts, no program actually performs fact-finding automatically. First, the information needed must be identified. Typically, this activity begins by asking a series of questions, such as these:

- What business functions are supported by the current system?
- What strategic objectives and business requirements must be supported by the new system?

- What are the benefits and TCO of the proposed system?
- What transactions will the system process?
- What information do users and managers need from the system?
- Must the new system interface with legacy systems?
- What procedures could be eliminated by business process reengineering?
- What security issues exist?
- What risks are acceptable?
- What budget and timetable constraints will affect system development?

To obtain answers to these questions, the analyst develops a fact-finding plan, which can involve another series of questions (who, what, where, when, and how), or use a more structured approach, such as the Zachman Framework described in Section 4.9.3. Either way, the analyst will develop a strategy, carry out fact-finding techniques, document the results, and prepare a system requirements document, which is presented to management.

4.9.2 Who, What, Where, When, How, and Why?

Fact-finding involves answers to five familiar questions: who, what, where, when, and how. For each of those questions, one also must ask another very important question: why. Some examples of these questions are:

1. *Who?* Who performs each of the procedures within the system? Why? Are the correct people performing the activity? Could other people perform the tasks more effectively?

2. *What?* What is being done? What procedures are being followed? Why is that process necessary? Often, procedures are followed for many years and no one knows why. Question why a procedure is being followed at all.

3. *Where?* Where are operations being performed? Why? Where could they be performed? Could they be performed more efficiently elsewhere?

4. *When?* When is a procedure performed? Why is it being performed at this time? Is this the best time?

5. *How?* How is a procedure performed? Why is it performed in that manner? Could it be performed better, more efficiently, or less expensively in some other manner?

There is a difference between asking what is being done and what could or should be done. The systems analyst first must understand the current situation. Only then

CURRENT SYSTEM		PROPOSED SYSTEM
Who does it?	Why does this person do it?	Who should do it?
What is done?	Why is it done?	What should be done?
Where is it done?	Why is it done there?	Where should it be done?
When is it done?	Why is it done then?	When should it be done?
How is it done?	Why is it done this way?	How should it be done?

FIGURE 4-16 Sample questions during requirements modeling as the focus shifts from the current system to the proposed system.

can he or she tackle the question of what should be done. Figure 4-16 lists the basic questions and when they should be asked. Notice that the first two columns relate to the current system, but the third column focuses on the proposed system.

4.9.3 The Zachman Framework

In the 1980s, John Zachman observed how industries such as architecture and construction handled complex projects, and he suggested that the same ideas could be applied to information systems development. His concept, the Zachman Framework for Enterprise Architecture, is a model that asks the traditional fact-finding questions in a systems development context, as shown in Figure 4-17.

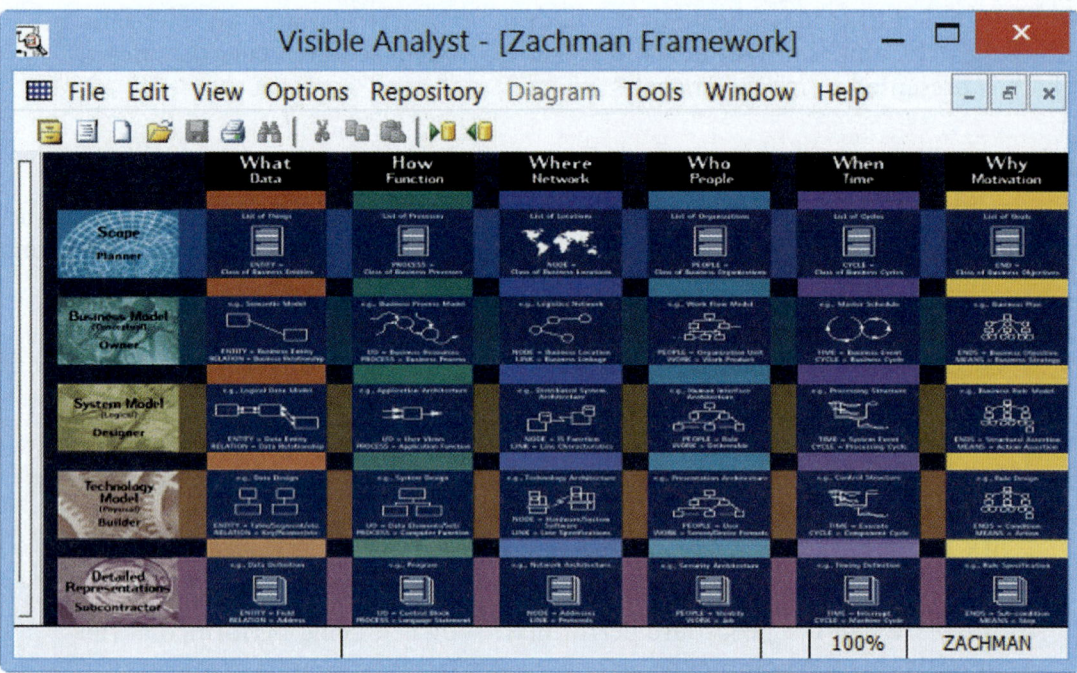

FIGURE 4-17 Visible Analyst uses the Zachman Framework for Enterprise Architecture. The Zachman concept presents traditional fact-finding questions in a systems development context.
Source: Visible Systems Corporation.

The Zachman Framework is a popular approach to modeling enterprise architectures. It helps managers and users understand the model and ensures that overall business goals translate into successful IT projects. The framework has evolved over time, particularly refinements to its graphical elements and clarifications to its modeling language, but the fundamental concepts remain essentially the same.

4.10 INTERVIEWS

Interviewing is an important fact-finding tool during the systems analysis phase. An interview is a planned meeting during which the analyst obtains information from another person. The skills needed to plan, conduct, document, and evaluate interviews successfully must be understood.

After identifying the information needed, as described earlier in the chapter, the interviewing process commences, which consists of seven steps for each interview:

1. Determine the people to interview.
2. Establish objectives for the interview.
3. Develop interview questions.
4. Prepare for the interview.
5. Conduct the interview.
6. Document the interview.
7. Evaluate the interview.

STEP 1: DETERMINE THE PEOPLE TO INTERVIEW: To get an accurate picture, the analyst must select the right people to interview and ask them the right questions. The preliminary investigation involved mainly middle managers or department heads. Now, during the systems analysis phase, people from all levels of the organization should be interviewed. In some situations, it might be prudent to interview stakeholders that are not members of the organization, because their opinion is valuable.

Although interview candidates can be selected from the formal organization charts reviewed earlier, one must also consider any informal structures that exist in the organization. **Informal structures** usually are based on interpersonal relationships and can develop from previous work assignments, physical proximity, unofficial procedures, or personal relationships such as the informal gathering shown in Figure 4-18. In an informal structure, some people have more influence or knowledge than appears on an organization chart. The analyst's knowledge of the company's formal and informal structures helps determine the people to interview during the systems analysis phase.

Should several people be interviewed at the same time? Group interviews can save time and provide an opportunity to observe interaction among the participants. Group interviews can also present problems. One person might dominate the conversation, even when questions are addressed specifically to others. Organization level can also present a problem because the presence of senior managers in an interview might prevent lower-level employees from expressing themselves candidly.

STEP 2: ESTABLISH OBJECTIVES FOR THE INTERVIEW: After deciding on the people to interview, objectives for the session must be established. First, the general areas to be discussed should be determined, and then the facts to be gathered should be listed. Soliciting ideas, suggestions, and opinions during the interview is also a good idea.

The objectives of an interview depend on the role of the person being interviewed. Upper-level managers can provide the big picture to help understand the system as a whole. Specific details about operations and business processes are best learned from people who actually work with the system on a daily basis.

FIGURE 4-18 When setting up interviews, an analyst should look outside a formal organization chart to identify people who might provide valuable information.

iStockphoto.com/mammamart

In the early stages of systems analysis, interviews usually are general. As the fact-finding process continues, however, the interviews focus more on specific topics. Interview objectives also vary at different stages of the investigation. Interviews should be as brief as possible (though as long as needed), since time is so valuable to employees, especially managers. By setting specific objectives, a framework is created that helps the analyst decide what questions to ask and how to phrase them.

STEP 3: DEVELOP INTERVIEW QUESTIONS: Creating a standard list of interview questions helps to keep the session on track and avoid unnecessary tangents. Also, if several people who perform the same job are interviewed, a standard question list permits a comparison of their answers. Although there may be a list of specific questions, the interviewer might decide to depart from it because an answer to one question leads to another topic that warrants pursuing. That question or topic then should be included in a revised set of questions used to conduct future interviews. If the question proves to be extremely important, it may be needed to return to a previous interviewee to query him or her on the topic.

The interview should consist of several different kinds of questions: open-ended, closed-ended, or questions with a range of responses. When phrasing questions, avoid leading questions that suggest or favor a particular reply. For example, rather than asking, "What advantages do you see in the proposed system?" ask instead, "Do you see any advantages in the proposed system?"

Open-ended questions. Open-ended questions encourage spontaneous and unstructured responses. Such questions are useful to understand a larger process or draw out the interviewee's opinions, attitudes, or suggestions. Here are some examples of open-ended questions:

- What are users saying about the new system?
- How is this task performed?
- Why do you perform the task that way?
- How are the checks reconciled?
- What added features would you like to have in the new billing system?

Also, an open-ended question can be used to probe further by asking: Is there anything else you can tell me about this topic?

Closed-ended questions. Closed-ended questions limit or restrict the response. Closed-ended questions are used when information that is more specific is needed, or when facts must be verified. Examples of closed-ended questions include the following:

- How many personal computers do you have in this department?
- Do you review the reports before they are sent out?
- How many hours of training does a clerk receive?
- Is the calculation procedure described in the manual?
- How many customers ordered products from the website last month?

Range-of-response questions. Range-of-response questions are closed-ended questions that ask the person to evaluate something by providing limited answers to specific responses or on a numeric scale. This method makes it easier to tabulate the answers and interpret the results. Range-of-response questions might include these:

- On a scale of 1 to 10, with 1 the lowest and 10 the highest, how effective was your training?

- How would you rate the severity of the problem: low, medium, or high?

- Is the system shutdown something that occurs never, sometimes, often, usually, or always?

STEP 4: PREPARE FOR THE INTERVIEW: After setting the objectives and developing the questions, preparing for the interview is next. Careful preparation is essential because an interview is an important meeting and not just a casual chat. When the interview is scheduled, suggest a specific day and time and let the interviewee know how long the meeting is expected to last. It is also a good idea to send an email or place a reminder call the day before the interview.

Remember that the interview is an interruption of the other person's routine, so the interview should be limited to no more than one hour. If business pressures force a postponement of the meeting, schedule another appointment as soon as it is convenient. Remember to keep department managers informed of meetings with their staff members. Sending a message to each department manager listing planned appointments is a good way to keep them informed. Figure 4-19 is an example of such a message.

A list of topics should be sent to an interviewee several days before the meeting, especially when detailed information is needed, so the person can prepare for the interview and minimize the need for a follow-up meeting. Figure 4-20 shows a sample message that lists specific questions and confirms the date, time, location, purpose, and anticipated duration of the interview.

If there are questions about documents, ask the interviewee to have samples available at the meeting. The advance memo should include a list of the documents to discuss (if it is known what they are). Also, a general request for documents can be made, as the analyst did in the email shown in Figure 4-20.

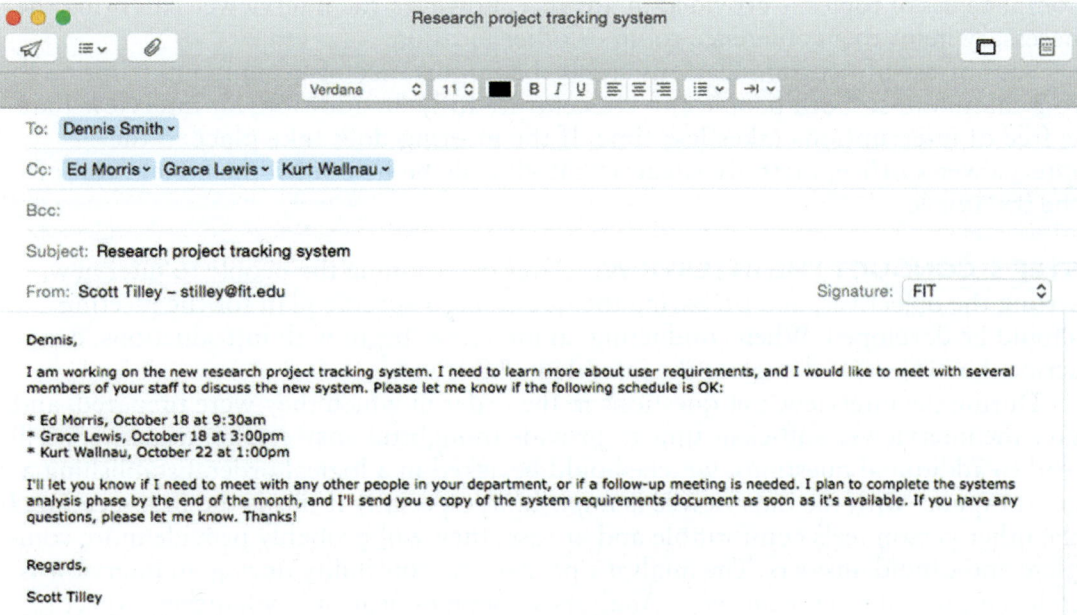

FIGURE 4-19 Sample message to a department head about interviews.

Source: 2015 Apple

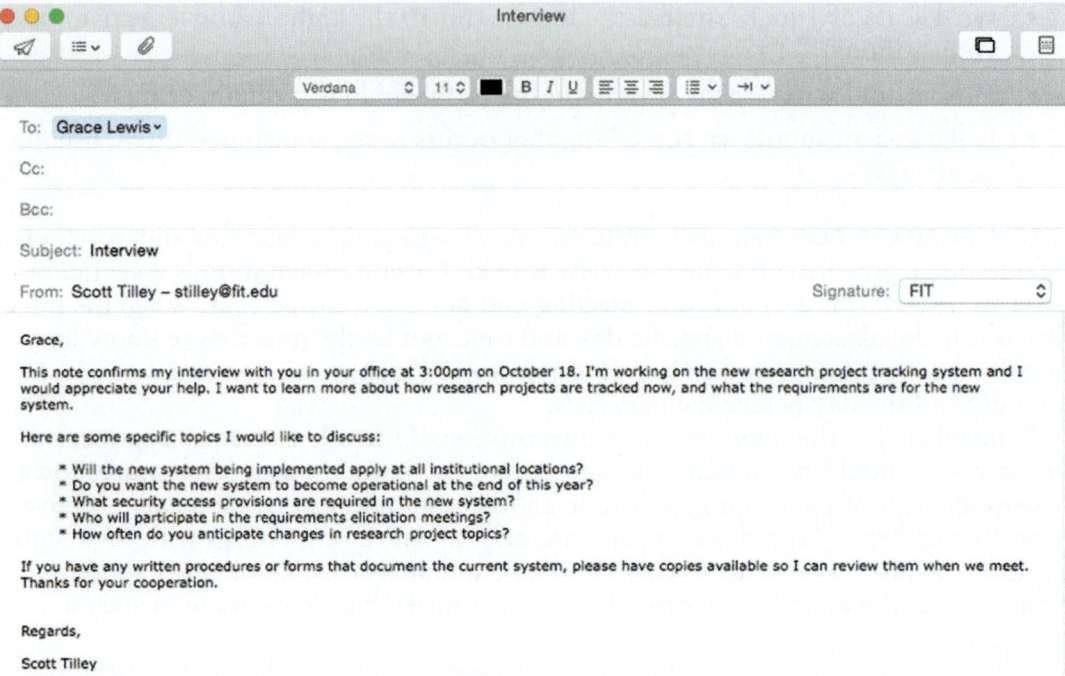

FIGURE 4-20 Sample message to confirm an interview.
Source: 2015 Apple

Two schools of thought exist about the best location for an interview. Some analysts believe that interviews should take place in the interviewee's office, whereas other analysts feel that a neutral location such as a conference room is better.

Supporters of interviews in the interviewee's office believe that is the best location because it makes the interviewee feel comfortable during the meeting. A second argument in favor of the interviewee's office is that the office is where he or she has the easiest access to supporting material that might be needed during the discussion. If a complete list of topics is provided in advance, however, the interviewee can bring the necessary items to a conference room or other location.

Supporters of neutral locations stress the importance of keeping interruptions to a minimum so both people can concentrate fully. In addition, an interview that is free of interruptions takes less time. If the meeting does take place in the interviewee's office, tactfully suggest that all calls be held until the conclusion of the interview.

STEP 5: CONDUCT THE INTERVIEW: After determining the people to interview, setting the objectives, and preparing the questions, a specific plan for the meeting should be developed. When conducting an interview, begin with introductions, describe the project, and explain the interview objectives.

During the interview, ask questions in the order in which they were prepared, and give the interviewee sufficient time to provide thoughtful answers. Some answers will lead to additional questions, which should be asked in a logical order. Establishing a good rapport with the interviewee is important, especially if this is the first meeting. If the other person feels comfortable and at ease, they will probably provide more complete and candid answers. The analyst's primary responsibility during an interview is to listen carefully to the answers. Analysts sometimes hear only what they expect to hear. Concentrate on what is said and notice any nonverbal communication that takes place. This process is called **engaged listening**.

After asking a question, allow the person enough time to think about the question and arrive at an answer. Studies have shown that the maximum pause during a conversation is usually three to five seconds. After that interval, one person will begin talking. An analyst needs to be patient and practice their skills in many actual interview situations to be successful.

When all the questions have been asked, summarize the main points covered in the interview and explain the next course of action. For example, mention that a follow-up memo will be sent, or that the interviewee should send certain requested information after the meeting. When the interview has concluded, thank the person and encourage him or her to reach out with any questions or additional comments. Also, when the interview ends, it is a good idea to ask the interviewee whether he or she can suggest any additional topics that should be discussed.

After an interview, summarize the session and seek a confirmation from the other person. By stating the interviewer's understanding of the discussion, the interviewee can respond and provide corrections, if necessary. One approach is to rephrase the interviewee's answers. For example, the analyst could say, "If I understand you correctly, you are saying that ..." and then reiterate the information given by the interviewee.

STEP 6: DOCUMENT THE INTERVIEW: Although taking notes during an interview has both advantages and disadvantages, it should be kept to a minimum. It is a good idea to write down a few notes to remember key points after the interview, but avoid writing down everything that is said. Too much writing distracts the other person and makes it harder to establish a good rapport.

After conducting the interview, record the information quickly. Set aside time right after the meeting to record the facts and evaluate the information. For that reason, try not to schedule back-to-back interviews. Studies have shown that 50% of a conversation is forgotten within 30 minutes. Therefore, use the notes to record the facts immediately so they will not be forgotten. Summarize the facts by preparing a narrative describing what took place, or by recording the answers received next to each question on the prepared list.

Small, portable recorders are effective tools for interviews, but some people are uncomfortable when they are used. Before using a recorder, discuss its use with the interviewee. Assure them that the recording will be erased after its contents are transcribed into note form, and that the interview can be stopped at anytime at the interviewee's request. If sensitive questions are asked, or the interviewee wants to answer a question without being recorded, explain that the recorder can be turned off for a period of time during the interview.

Instead of using a traditional recorder that calls attention to its presence, an interviewer can use built-in audio (or even video) recording features on a notebook or mobile device. Also, as pointed out in Section 4.12, Documentation, an interviewer can use powerful information management software, such as Microsoft OneNote, to record the meeting, store the results, and create a searchable file for easy access. Irrespective of the mechanism used to record the meeting, all participants should be aware that what they say is being recorded.

Whether or not the meeting is recorded, listen carefully to the interviewee's responses so good follow-up questions can be asked. Otherwise, a second visit might be needed to ask the questions missed the first time. Also, remember that each recorded interview takes twice the amount of time, because the analyst must listen to or view the recorded meeting again after conducting the interview itself.

After the meeting, a memo should be sent to the interviewee, expressing appreciation for his or her time and cooperation. In the memo, note the date, time, location, purpose of the interview, and the main points discussed, so the interviewee has a written summary and can offer additions or corrections.

STEP 7: EVALUATE THE INTERVIEW: In addition to recording the facts obtained in an interview, try to identify any possible biases. For example, an interviewee who tries to protect his or her own area or function might give incomplete answers or refrain from volunteering information. Or, an interviewee with strong opinions about the current or future system might distort the facts. Some interviewees might answer questions in an attempt to be helpful even though they do not have the necessary experience to provide accurate information.

CASE IN POINT 4.2:   DEEP RIVER COLLEGE

Deep River College is a two-year school in Southern California. Twice a year, the fund-raising office at Deep River mails requests for donations to the alumni. The staff uses a word processing program and a personal information database to create personalized letters. Data on past contributions and other alumni information, however, is stored manually. The dean, Alexandra Ali, recently submitted a systems request asking the college's IT department to develop a computerized alumni information system. The school does not have a formal systems review committee, and each department has an individual budget for information services.

Eddie Bateman, a systems analyst, performed a preliminary investigation and he concluded that the system met all the feasibility tests. After reading his report, Alexandra asked him to proceed with the systems analysis phase. Eddie has scheduled an interview with her, and he has asked you to help him prepare for the meeting. Specifically, he wants you to list all the topics he should cover during the interview. Eddie also wants you to prepare a list of specific questions that he should ask. Be sure to include open-ended, closed-ended, and range-of-response questions.

4.10.1 Unsuccessful Interviews

Some interviews are unsuccessful irrespective of the amount of preparation. One of the main reasons could be that the interviewer and the interviewee did not get along well. Such a situation can be caused by several factors. For example, a misunderstanding or personality conflict could affect the interview negatively, or the interviewee might be afraid that the new system will eliminate or change his or her job.

In other cases, the interviewee might give only short or incomplete responses to the open-ended questions. If so, switching to closed-ended questions, or questions with a range of replies, may elicit more favorable responses. If that still does not help, find a tactful way to conclude the meeting.

Continuing an unproductive interview is difficult. The interviewee could be more cooperative later, or the analyst might find the information required elsewhere. If failure to obtain specific information will jeopardize the success of the project, the supervisor should be informed; they can help decide what action to take. The supervisor might contact the interviewee's supervisor, ask another systems analyst to interview the person, or find some other way to get the needed information.

CASE IN POINT 4.3:   FASTPAK OVERNIGHT PACKAGE SYSTEM

FastPak, the nation's fourth-largest overnight package system, is headquartered in Los Angeles, California. Jesse Evans is a systems analyst on an IT team that is studying ways to update FastPak's package tracking system. Jesse prepared well for her interview with Jason Tanya, FastPak's executive vice president. Mr. Tanya did not ask his assistant to hold his calls during the meeting, however. After several interruptions, Jesse tactfully suggested that she could come back another time, or perhaps that Mr. Tanya might ask his assistant to hold his calls. "No way," he replied. "I'm a very busy man and we'll just have to fit this in as we can, even if it takes all day." Jesse was unprepared for his response. What are her options? Is an analyst always in control of this kind of situation? Why or why not?

4.11 OTHER FACT-FINDING TECHNIQUES

In addition to interviewing, systems analysts use other fact-finding techniques, including document review, observation, questionnaires and surveys, sampling, and research. Such techniques are used before interviewing begins to obtain a good overview and to help develop better interview questions.

4.11.1 Document Review

Document review can help the analyst understand how the current system is supposed to work. Remember that system documentation sometimes is out of date. Forms can change or be discontinued, and documented procedures often are modified or eliminated. It is prudent to obtain copies of actual forms and operating documents currently in use, and to review blank copies of forms, as well as samples of actual completed forms. Document samples can be obtained during interviews with the people who perform that procedure. If the system uses a software package, review the documentation for that software.

4.11.2 Observation

The observation of current operating procedures is another fact-finding technique. Seeing the system in action provides additional perspective and a better understanding of system procedures. Personal observation also allows the analyst to verify statements made in interviews and determine whether procedures really operate as they are described. Through observation, it might be discovered that neither the system documentation nor the interview statements are accurate.

Personal observation can also provide important advantages as the development process continues. For example, recommendations often are better accepted when they are based on personal observation of actual operations. Observation can also provide the knowledge needed to test or install future changes and can help build relationships with the users who will work with the new system.

Plan observations in advance by preparing a checklist of specific tasks to observe and questions to ask. Consider the following issues when preparing the list:

- Ask sufficient questions to ensure a complete understanding of the present system operation. A primary goal is to identify the methods of handling situations that are not covered by standard operating procedures. For example, what happens in a payroll system if an employee loses a time card? What is the procedure if an employee starts a shift 10 minutes late but then works 20 minutes overtime? Often, the rules for exceptions such as these are not written or formalized; therefore, try to document any procedures for handling exceptions.

- Observe all the steps in a transaction and note the documents, inputs, outputs, and processes involved.

- Examine each form, record, and report. Determine the purpose each item of information serves.

- Consider each user who works with the system and the following questions: What information does that person receive from other people? What information does this person generate? How is the information communicated? How often do interruptions occur? How much downtime occurs? How much support does the user require, and who provides it?

- Talk to the people who receive current reports to see whether the reports are complete, timely, accurate, and in a useful form. Ask whether information can be eliminated or improved and whether people would like to receive additional information.

As people are observed at work, as shown in Figure 4-21, consider a factor called the **Hawthorne Effect**. The name comes from a well-known study performed in the Hawthorne plant of the Western Electric Company in the 1920s. The purpose of the study was to determine how various changes in the work environment would affect employee productivity. The surprising result was that productivity improved during

FIGURE 4-21 The Hawthorne study suggested that worker productivity improves during observation. Always consider the Hawthorne Effect when observing the operation of an existing system.

Monkey Business Images/Shutterstock.com

observation whether the conditions were made better or worse. Researchers concluded that productivity seemed to improve whenever the workers knew they were being observed.

Although some recent studies have raised questions about the original findings, be aware that observation can and does have an effect on normal operations. With this in mind, always give advance notice to the supervisor in that area. In some situations, it might be helpful to explain the purpose of the visit to the people being observed.

4.11.3 Questionnaires and Surveys

In projects where it is desirable to obtain input from a large number of people, a questionnaire can be a valuable tool. A **questionnaire**, also called a **survey**, is a document containing a number of standard questions that can be sent to many individuals.

Questionnaires can be used to obtain information about a wide range of topics, including workloads, reports received, volumes of transactions handled, job duties, difficulties, and opinions of how the job could be performed better or more efficiently. Figure 4-22 shows a sample questionnaire that includes several different question and response formats.

A typical questionnaire starts with a heading, which includes a title, a brief statement of purpose, the name and telephone number of the contact person, the deadline date for completion, and how and where to return the form. The heading usually is followed by general instructions that provide clear guidance on how to answer the questions. Headings are also used to introduce each main section or portion of the survey and include instructions when the type of question or response changes. A long questionnaire might end with a conclusion that thanks the participants and reminds them how to return the form.

What about the issue of anonymity? Should people be asked to sign the questionnaire, or is it better to allow anonymous responses? The answer depends on two questions. First, does an analyst really need to know who the respondents are in order to match or correlate information? For example, it might be important to know what percentage of users need a certain software feature, but specific usernames might not be relevant. Second, does the questionnaire include any sensitive or controversial topics? Many people do not want to be identified when answering a question such as "How well has your supervisor explained the system to you?" In such cases, anonymous responses might provide better information.

When designing a questionnaire, the most important rule of all is to make sure that the questions collect the right data in a form that can be used to further the fact-finding effort. Here are some additional ideas to keep in mind when designing the questionnaire:

- Keep the questionnaire brief and user-friendly.
- Provide clear instructions that will answer all anticipated questions.

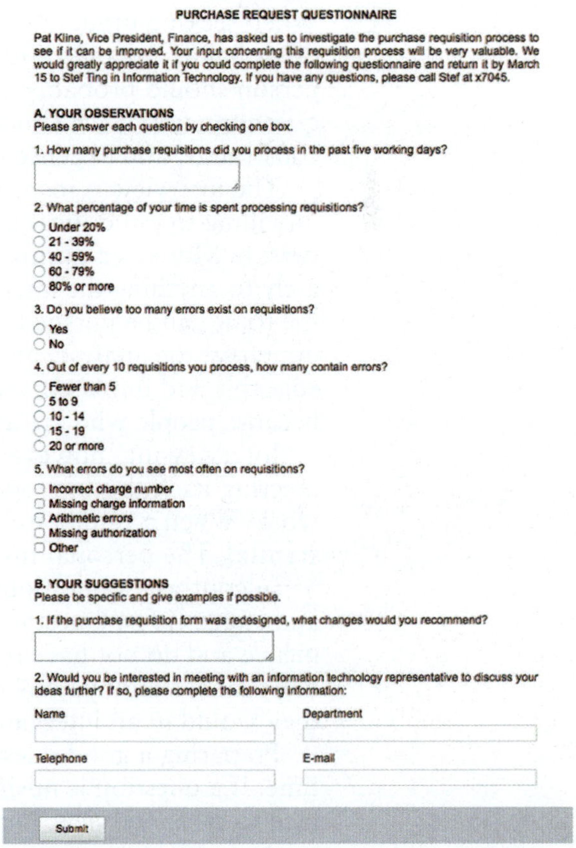

PURCHASE REQUEST QUESTIONNAIRE

Pat Kline, Vice President, Finance, has asked us to investigate the purchase requisition process to see if it can be improved. Your input concerning this requisition process will be very valuable. We would greatly appreciate it if you could complete the following questionnaire and return it by March 15 to Stef Ting in Information Technology. If you have any questions, please call Stef at x7045.

A. YOUR OBSERVATIONS
Please answer each question by checking one box.

1. How many purchase requisitions did you process in the past five working days?

2. What percentage of your time is spent processing requisitions?
- Under 20%
- 21 - 39%
- 40 - 59%
- 60 - 79%
- 80% or more

3. Do you believe too many errors exist on requisitions?
- Yes
- No

4. Out of every 10 requisitions you process, how many contain errors?
- Fewer than 5
- 5 to 9
- 10 - 14
- 15 - 19
- 20 or more

5. What errors do you see most often on requisitions?
- Incorrect charge number
- Missing charge information
- Arithmetic errors
- Missing authorization
- Other

B. YOUR SUGGESTIONS
Please be specific and give examples if possible.

1. If the purchase requisition form was redesigned, what changes would you recommend?

2. Would you be interested in meeting with an information technology representative to discuss your ideas further? If so, please complete the following information:

Name Department

Telephone E-mail

Submit

FIGURE 4-22 Online version of a sample questionnaire. Does it follow the suggested guidelines?

Created by author using Adobe Online Forms, Adobe Systems Incorporated

- Arrange the questions in a logical order, going from simple to more complex topics.

- Phrase questions to avoid misunderstandings; use simple terms and wording.

- Try not to lead the response or use questions that give clues to expected answers.

- Limit the use of open-ended questions that are difficult to tabulate.

- Limit the use of questions that can raise concerns about job security or other negative issues.

- Include a section at the end of the questionnaire for general comments.

- Test the questionnaire whenever possible on a small test group before finalizing it and distributing to a large group.

A questionnaire can be a traditional paper form, or it can be created as a **fill-in form** and collect data on the Internet or a company intranet. For example, Adobe tools such as Acrobat Pro or Forms Central can be used to create form fields, including text boxes and drop-down lists where users can click selections. Before publishing the form, protect it so users can fill it in but cannot change the layout or design. The sample questionnaire shown in Figure 4-22 was created using Adobe Forms Central online. Online survey websites, such as Survey Monkey and Zoomerang, can also be used to create and manage questionnaires.

4.11.4 Interviews versus Questionnaires

When seeking input from a large group, a questionnaire is a very useful tool. On the other hand, if detailed information is required from only a few people, then each person should probably be interviewed individually. Is it better to interview or use a questionnaire? Each situation is different; consider the type of information, time constraints, and expense factors.

The interview is more familiar and personal than a questionnaire. People who are unwilling to put critical or controversial comments in writing might talk more freely in person. Moreover, during a face-to-face interview, the interviewer can react immediately to anything the interviewee says. If surprising or confusing statements are made, the topic can be pursued with additional questions. In addition, during a personal interview, the analyst can watch for clues to help determine if responses are knowledgeable and unbiased. Participation in interviews can also affect user attitudes because people who are asked for their opinions often view the project more favorably.

Interviewing, however, is a costly and time-consuming process. In addition to the meeting itself, both people must prepare, and the interviewer has to do follow-up work. When a number of interviews are planned, the total cost can be quite substantial. The personal interview usually is the most expensive fact-finding technique.

In contrast, a questionnaire gives many people the opportunity to provide input and suggestions. Questionnaire recipients can answer the questions at their convenience and do not have to set aside a block of time for an interview. If the questionnaire allows anonymous responses, people might offer more candid responses than they would in an interview.

Preparing a good questionnaire, however, like a good interview, requires skill and time. If a question is misinterpreted, its meaning cannot be clarified as easily as in a face-to-face interview. Furthermore, unless questionnaires are designed well, recipients might view them as intrusive, time-consuming, and impersonal. The analyst should select the technique that will work best in a particular situation.

4.11.5 Brainstorming

Another popular method of obtaining input is called **brainstorming**, which refers to a small group discussion of a specific problem, opportunity, or issue. This technique encourages new ideas, allows team participation, and enables participants to build on each other's inputs and thoughts. Brainstorming can be structured or unstructured. In **structured brainstorming**, each participant speaks when it is his or her turn, or passes. In **unstructured brainstorming**, anyone can speak at any time. At some point, the results are recorded and made part of the fact-finding documentation process.

4.11.6 Sampling

When studying an information system, examples of actual documents should be collected using a process called **sampling**. The samples might include records, reports, operational logs, data entry documents, complaint summaries, work requests, and various types of forms. Sampling techniques include systematic sampling, stratified sampling, and random sampling.

Suppose there is a list of 200 customers who complained about errors in their statements, and a representative sample of 20 customers will be reviewed. A **systematic sample** would select every tenth customer for review. To ensure that the sample is balanced geographically, however, a **stratified sample** could be used to select five customers from each of four postal codes. Another example of stratified sampling is to select a certain percentage of transactions from each postal code, rather than a fixed number. Finally, a **random sample** selects any 20 customers.

The main objective of a sample is to ensure that it represents the overall population accurately. If inventory transactions are being analyzed, for example, select a sample of transactions that are typical of actual inventory operations and do not include unusual or unrelated examples. For instance, if a company performs special processing on the last business day of the month, that day is not a good time to sample typical daily operations. To be useful, a sample must be large enough to provide a fair representation of the overall data.

Sampling should also be considered when using interviews or questionnaires. Rather than interviewing everyone or sending a questionnaire to the entire group, a sample of participants can be used. Sound sampling techniques must be used to reflect the overall population and obtain an accurate picture.

4.11.7 Research

Research is another important fact-finding technique. Research can include the Internet, IT magazines, and books to obtain background information, technical material, and news about industry trends and developments. In addition, attending professional meetings, seminars, and discussions with other IT professionals can be very helpful in problem solving.

The Internet is an extremely valuable resource. Using the Internet, the analyst can also access information from federal and state governments, as well as from publishers, universities, and libraries around the world. Online forums and newsgroups are good resources for exchanging information with other professionals, seeking answers to questions, and monitoring discussions that are of mutual interest.

FIGURE 4-23 The *Wall Street Journal's* Technology website contains valuable information for IT professionals.
Source: *Wall Street Journal*

All major hardware and software vendors maintain websites with information about products and services offered by the company. There are also websites maintained by publishers and independent firms that provide links to hundreds of hardware and software vendors. Examples of popular websites for IT professionals include Ars Technica, CNET, InfoWorld, Techchrunch, and the *Wall Street Journal's* Technology pages (shown in Figure 4-23).

Research can also involve a visit to a physical location, called a site visit, where the objective is to observe a system in use at another location. For example, if a firm's human resources information system is the subject of study, it might be beneficial to see how another company's system works. Site visits also are important when considering the purchase of a software package. If the software vendor suggests possible sites to visit, be aware that such sites might constitute a biased sample. A single site visit seldom provides true pictures, so try to visit more than one installation.

Before a site visit, prepare just as for an interview. Contact the appropriate manager and explain the purpose of the visit. Decide what questions will be asked and what processes will be observed. During the visit, observe how the system works and note any problems or limitations. Also learn about the support provided by the vendor, the quality of the system documentation, and so on.

CASE IN POINT 4.4: CyberStuff

Ann Ellis is a systems analyst at CyberStuff, a large company that sells computer hardware and software via telephone, mail order, and the Internet. CyberStuff processes several thousand transactions per week on a three-shift operation and employs 50 full-time and 125 part-time employees. Lately, the billing department has experienced an increase in the number of customer complaints about incorrect bills. During the preliminary investigation, Ann learned that some CyberStuff representatives did not follow established order entry procedures. She feels that with more information, she might find a pattern and identify a solution for the problem.

Ann is not sure how to proceed. She came to you, her supervisor, with two separate questions. First, is a questionnaire the best approach, or would interviews be better? Second, whether she uses interviews, a questionnaire, or both techniques, should she select the participants at random, include an equal number of people from each shift, or use some other approach? As Ann's supervisor, what would you suggest, and why?

4.12 DOCUMENTATION

Keeping accurate records of interviews, facts, ideas, and observations is essential to successful systems development. The ability to manage information is the mark of a successful systems analyst and an important skill for all IT professionals.

4.12.1 The Need for Recording the Facts

As information is gathered, the importance of a single item can be overlooked or complex system details can be forgotten. The basic rule is to write it down. An analyst should document their work according to the following principles:

- Record information as soon as it is obtained.
- Use the simplest recording method possible.
- Record findings in such a way that someone else can understand them.
- Organize documentation so related material is located easily.

Often, systems analysts use special forms for describing a system, recording interviews, and summarizing documents. One type of documentation is a narrative list with simple statements about what is occurring, apparent problems, and suggestions for improvement. Other forms of documentation that are described in this chapter include data flow diagrams, flowcharts, sample forms, and screen captures.

4.12.2 Software Tools

Many software programs are available to help record and document information. Some examples are described here.

CASE TOOLS: CASE tools can be used at every stage of systems development. This chapter contains several examples of CASE tools.

PRODUCTIVITY SOFTWARE: Productivity software includes word processing, spreadsheet, database management, presentation graphics, and collaboration software programs. Although Microsoft Office is the best-known set of productivity software programs, other vendors offer products in each of these categories.

Using word processing software such as Microsoft Word, the analyst can create reports, summaries, tables, and forms. In addition to standard document preparation, the program can help organize a presentation with templates, bookmarks, annotations, revision control, and an index. The program's Help system provides more information about those and other features. Fill-in forms can also be created to conduct surveys and questionnaires, as described earlier in this chapter.

Spreadsheet software, such as Microsoft Excel, can help track and manage numeric data or financial information. Graphs and charts can also be generated that display the data and show possible patterns. The statistical functions in a spreadsheet can be used to tabulate and analyze questionnaire data. A graphical format often is used in quality control analysis because it highlights problems and their possible causes, and it is effective when presenting results to management. A common tool for showing the distribution of questionnaire or sampling results is a vertical bar chart called a histogram. Most spreadsheet programs can create histograms and other charts that can display the data collected. Figure 4-24 displays a typical histogram that might have resulted from the questionnaire shown in Figure 4-22.

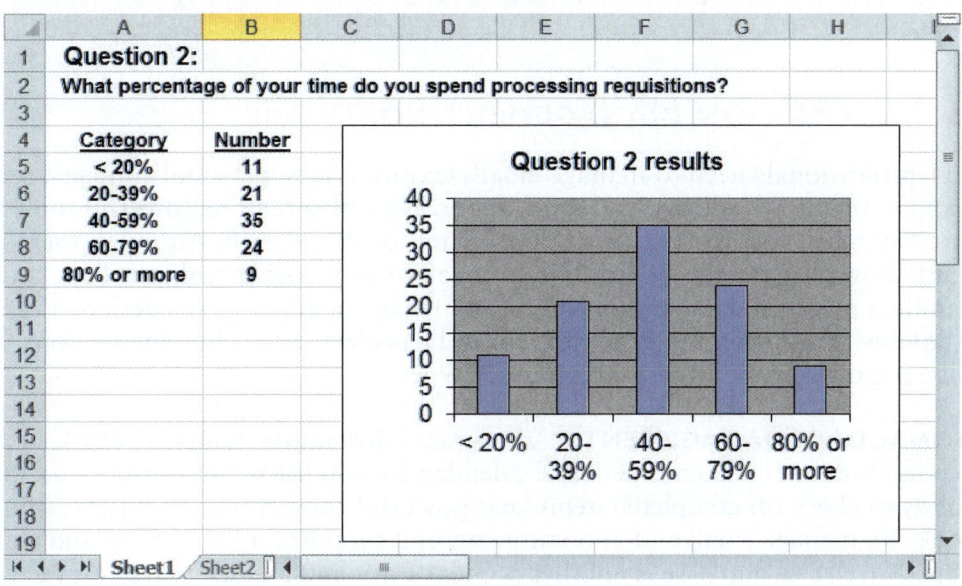

FIGURE 4-24 This histogram displays the results from Question 2 in the questionnaire shown in Figure 4-22.

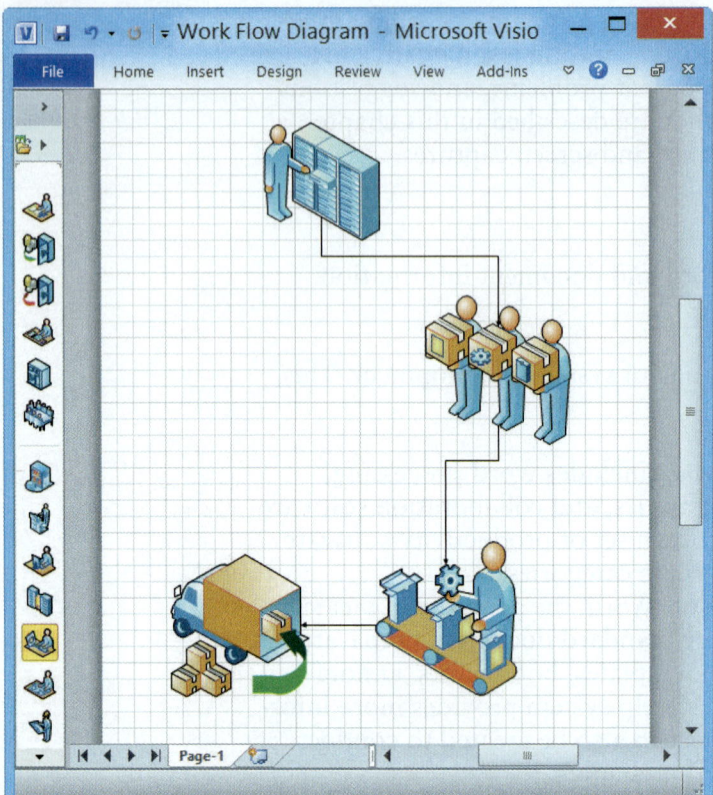

FIGURE 4-25 This Microsoft Visio drawing uses drag-and-drop shapes to represent a business process.
Source: Microsoft, LLC

Database management software allows the analyst to document and organize fact-finding results, such as events, observations, and data samples. A database program such as Microsoft Access can be used to manage the details of a complex project, create queries to retrieve specific information, and generate custom reports.

Presentation graphics software, such as Microsoft PowerPoint, is a powerful tool for organizing and developing formal presentations. Presentation graphics programs enable the creation of organization charts that can be used in a preliminary investigation and later during requirements modeling. These high-quality charts can also be included in written reports and management presentations.

Collaboration software is the latest weapon in the struggle to boost productivity. People work in teams and use web-based software such as Google Docs and Microsoft Office 365 to access data and share files. Google and others are betting that cloud computing will create a virtual workplace, where people will be able to interact in real time, with all the benefits of a traditional face-to-face workplace, but none of the limitations.

GRAPHIC MODELING SOFTWARE: Microsoft Visio is a popular graphic modeling tool that can produce a wide range of charts and diagrams. Visio includes a library of templates, stencils, and shapes. An analyst can use Visio to create many types of visual models, including business processes, flowcharts, network diagrams, organization charts, and many more. For example, in Figure 4-25, the analyst used drag-and-drop shapes to represent a business process.

4.13 INFORMATION MANAGEMENT SOFTWARE

Busy IT professionals need to manage email, text messages, personal contacts, meetings, appointments, deadlines, and much more. They also require powerful tools to capture, organize, and access project documentation and details. Although there is a substantial overlap, two broad categories have evolved: Software that is better-suited for handling personal data; and information management programs designed for the large amount of information generated by an IT project. The following sections describe popular examples of both software types.

PERSONAL DATA MANAGEMENT: A personal information manager (PIM), such as Microsoft Outlook, includes a personal calendar, a to-do list with priorities and the capability to check off completed items, and powerful contact management features. Outlook can manage email and appointments, and supports collaboration and team projects. Novell's GroupWise is another popular PIM, and a quick search on the web will reveal many other options, including pay-ware, shareware, and some free programs.

PROJECT DATA MANAGEMENT: Although a PIM such as Microsoft Outlook can handle day-to-day activities, tasks, and schedules, it is not the best way to capture and organize large amounts of information. Instead, analysts use information management software such as Microsoft OneNote, which is a powerful, flexible tool that can handle many different types of input, including text, handwritten notes, images, audio and video recording, web links, and much more. OneNote is included in several versions of the Office suite.

Recent versions of Microsoft Word also provide a capable note-taking feature. When a document is viewed in "Notebook Layout," as shown in Figure 4-26, tabs are available to separate content into topics. Audio commentary can also be recorded using the built-in tool and saved as annotations in the document.

Figure 4-27 shows another popular personal information manager called Evernote. It is available for free on most computing platforms, including smartphones and on the web. There are also premium versions available on a monthly subscription model. Evernote does a great job of handling all sorts of multimedia content, adding free-form notes, and providing templates for organizing projects. It also syncs files across all devices.

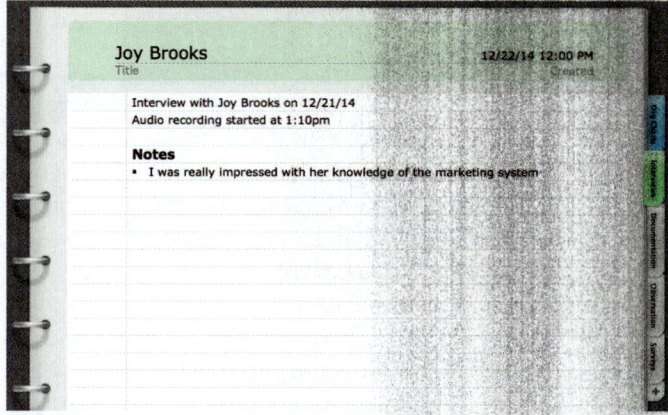

FIGURE 4-26 The analyst is using Microsoft Word to store fact-finding results. During the interview with Joy Brooks, the analyst recorded part of the discussion and stored it as a document annotation.
Source: Microsoft Corporation.

FIGURE 4-27 Evernote offers a free version of its popular information management software for most computing platforms, including smartphones and on the web.
Source: www.evernote.com

4.14 PREVIEW OF LOGICAL MODELING

At the conclusion of requirements modeling, systems developers should have a clear understanding of business processes and system requirements. The next step is to construct a logical model of the system.

Data and process modeling, which is described in Chapter 5, uses a structured analysis approach. Structured analysis is a popular, traditional technique that describes the system in terms of data and the processes that act on that data.

An alternative to structured analysis modeling is object modeling, which is described in Chapter 6. Object modeling is a methodology that combines data and processes into things called objects that represent actual people, things, transactions, and events. Systems analysts use object models to visualize and document real-world business processes and operations.

IT professionals have differing views about systems development methodologies, and no universally accepted approach exists. By studying both structured analysis and object-oriented methods, valuable knowledge, skills, and perspective can be gained. This information can then be used to determine what method, or combination of methods, is best for the different situations all analysts will face in their careers.

A QUESTION OF ETHICS

iStockphoto.com/faberfoto_it

Your supervisor manages the corporate office where you work as a systems analyst. Several weeks ago, after hearing rumors of employee dissatisfaction, he asked you to create a survey for all IT employees. After the responses were returned and tabulated, he was disappointed to learn that many employees assigned low ratings to morale and management policies.

This morning he called you into his office and asked whether you could identify the departments that submitted the lowest ratings. No names were used on the individual survey forms. However, with a little analysis, you probably could identify the departments because several questions were department-related.

Now you are not sure how to respond. The expectation was that the survey would be anonymous. Even though no individuals would be identified, would it be ethical to reveal which departments sent in the low ratings? Would your supervisor's motives for wanting this information matter?

4.15 CHAPTER SUMMARY

The systems analysis phase includes three activities: requirements modeling, data and process modeling, and consideration of development strategies. The main objective is to understand the proposed project, ensure that it will support business requirements, and build a solid foundation for the systems design phase.

During requirements modeling, the business-related requirements for the new information system are identified, including outputs, inputs, processes, performance, and controls. Scalability is considered to ensure that the system can support future growth and expansion. The total cost of ownership (TCO) is also estimated to identify all costs, including indirect costs.

Popular team-based approaches include JAD, RAD, and agile methods. Joint application development (JAD) is a popular, team-based approach to fact-finding and requirements modeling. JAD involves an interactive group of users, managers, and IT professionals who participate in requirements modeling and develop a greater commitment to the project and to their common goals.

Rapid application development (RAD) is a team-based technique that speeds up information systems development and produces a functioning information system. RAD is a complete methodology, with a four-phase life cycle that parallels the traditional SDLC phases.

Agile methods attempt to develop a system incrementally, by building a series of prototypes and constantly adjusting them to user requirements. Tools are often avoided and replaced with simpler aids, such as whiteboards and sticky notes to facilitate communication.

Systems analysts use various tools and techniques to model system requirements. Unified Modeling Language (UML) is a widely used method of visualizing and documenting software design through the eyes of the business user. UML tools include use case diagrams and sequence diagrams to represent actors, their roles, and the sequence of transactions that occurs.

A functional decomposition diagram (FDD) is a model of business functions and processes. A CASE tool can generate a set of data flow diagrams directly from an FDD.

The fact-finding process includes interviewing, document review, observation, questionnaires, sampling, and research. Successful interviewing requires good planning and strong interpersonal and communication skills. The systems analyst must decide on the people to interview, set interview objectives, and prepare for, conduct, and analyze interviews. The analyst might also find it helpful to use one or more software tools during fact-finding.

Systems analysts should carefully record and document factual information as it is collected, and various software tools can help an analyst visualize and describe an information system. The chapter concluded with a preview of logical modeling. Data and process modeling is a structured analysis approach that views the system in terms of data and the processes that act on that data. Object modeling is an approach that views the system in terms of data and the processes that act on that data.

Key Terms

actor An external entity with a specific role. In a use case model, actors are used to model interaction with the system.

brainstorming A fact-finding technique for gaining information through the use of a small group discussion of a specific problem, opportunity, or issue.

closed-ended question Query that limits or restricts the range of responses. Used in the interview process when specific information or fact verification is desired.

construction phase A phase that focuses on program and application development tasks similar to the SDLC.

cutover phase A phase that resembles the final tasks in the SDLC implementation phase, including data conversion, testing, changeover to the new system, and user training.

document review A review of baseline documentation. A useful fact-finding technique that helps an analyst understand how the current system is supposed to work.

engaged listening The ability to really concentrate on what someone is saying and avoid the temptation to hear what is expected. Also includes noticing nonverbal communication.

fact-finding A step in the requirements modeling process that involves gathering facts about a systems project using techniques such as interviews, documentation review, observation, questionnaires, sampling, and research.

fill-in form A template used to collect data on the Internet or a company intranet

functional decomposition diagram (FDD) A top-down representation of business functions and processes. Also called a structure chart.

Hawthorne Effect A phenomenon where employees who know they are being observed are more productive.

Histogram A common tool for showing the distribution of questionnaire or sampling results. It takes the form of a vertical bar chart.

informal structure An organization based on interpersonal relationships, which can develop from previous work assignments, physical proximity, unofficial procedures, or personal relationships.

input Necessary data that enters a system, either manually or in an automated manner.

interview A planned meeting during which information is obtained from another person.

leading question Query that suggests or favors a particular reply.

observation A fact-finding technique where an analyst sees a system in action. Observation allows the verification of statements made in interviews.

open-ended question Query that allows for a range of answers. It encourages spontaneous and unstructured responses, and is useful in understanding a larger process.

output Electronic or printed information produced by an information system.

performance System characteristics such as speed, volume, capacity, availability, and reliability.

personal information manager (PIM) A tool that helps manage tasks and schedules. Many handheld devices also include this function.

pool The overall diagram In business process modeling notation (BPMN).

process Procedure or task that users, managers, and IT staff members perform. The logical rules of a system that are applied to transform data into meaningful information. In data flow diagrams, a process receives input data and produces output that has a different content, form, or both.

productivity software Applications such as word processing, spreadsheet, database management, and presentation graphics programs.

questionnaire A document containing a number of standard questions that can be sent to many individuals. Also called a survey.

random sample A selection taken in a random, unplanned manner. For example, a random sample might be a sample that selects any 20 customers.

range-of-response question Closed-ended question that asks the person to evaluate something by providing limited answers to specific responses or on a numeric scale.

requirements planning phase A phase that combines elements of the systems planning and systems analysis phases of the SDLC.

research An important fact-finding technique that include the review of journals, periodicals, and books to obtain background information, technical material, and news about industry trends and developments.

sampling A process where an analyst collects examples of actual documents, which could include records, reports, or various forms.

scalability A characteristic of a system, implying that the system can be expanded, modified, or downsized easily to meet the rapidly changing needs of a business enterprise.

Scrum A popular technique for agile project management. Derived from a rugby term. In Scrum, team members play specific roles and interact in intense sessions.

security Hardware, software, and procedural controls that safeguard and protect a system and its data from internal or external threats.

sequence diagram A UML diagram that shows the timing of transactions between objects as they occur during system execution.

site visit A trip to a physical location to observe a system in use at another location.

stratified sample A set metric is collected across functional areas. For example, a certain percentage of transactions from every work shift, or five customers from each of four zip codes, could be a stratified sample.

structured brainstorming A group discussion where each participant speaks when it is his or her turn, or passes.

survey A document containing a number of standard questions that can be sent to many individuals. Also called a questionnaire.

swim lane In a business process diagram, the overall diagram is called a pool, and the designated customer areas are called swim lanes.

system requirement A characteristic or feature that must be included in an information system to satisfy business requirements and be acceptable to users.

systematic sample A sample that occurs at a predetermined periodicity. For example, every tenth customer record might be selected as a systematic sample for review.

Unified Modeling Language (UML) A widely used method of visualizing and documenting software systems design. UML uses object-oriented design concepts, but it is independent of any specific programming language and can be used to describe business processes and requirements generally.

unstructured brainstorming A group discussion where any participant can speak at any time.

use case diagram A visual representation that represents the interaction between users and the information system in UML.

user design phase In this phase, users interact with systems analysts and develop models and prototypes that represent all system processes, outputs, and inputs.

Zachman Framework for Enterprise Architecture A model that asks the traditional fact-finding questions in a systems development context.

Chapter Exercises

Questions

1. What five questions typically are used in fact-finding? What other question does the Zachman Framework include? Is the additional question important?
2. What is a system requirement, and how are system requirements classified?
3. What are JAD and RAD, and how do they differ from traditional fact-finding methods? What are the main advantages of team-based methods?
4. What is total cost of ownership (TCO)? What costs often are underestimated?
5. Provide three examples each of closed-ended, open-ended, and range-of-response questions.
6. What are three types of sampling? Which one would you use to analyze data input errors?
7. What is the Hawthorne Effect? Have you ever experienced it? When and where?
8. What is a functional decomposition diagram (FDD) and why would you use one? Explain how to create an FDD.
9. What are agile methods? Are they better than traditional methods? Why or why not?
10. To what three different audiences might you have to give a presentation? How would the presentation differ for each? Which one would be the most challenging for you?

Discussion Topics

1. A group meeting sometimes is suggested as a useful compromise between interviews and questionnaires. In a group meeting, a systems analyst meets with a number of users at one time. Discuss the advantages and disadvantages of group meetings.
2. JAD requires strong interpersonal and communication skills on the part of the systems analyst. Are those skills different from the ones that an analyst needs when conducting one-to-one interviews? Explain your answer.
3. Agile methods use rapid development cycles to iteratively produce running versions of the system. How would these shorter cycles affect the ability of the analyst to manage system's requirements?
4. Research the Internet, magazines, or textbooks to find examples of visual aids, including a bar chart, pie chart, line chart, table, diagram, and bulleted list. How effective was each example? Find at least one example that you could improve. Explain your choice.
5. Review Part A of the Systems Analyst's Toolkit, and then attend a speech or presentation and analyze its effectiveness. Consider the speaker's delivery and how he or she organized the material, used visual aids, and handled audience questions. Was the speech or presentation effective? How could it have been improved?

Projects

1. Design a questionnaire to learn what students think of the registration process at your school. Apply the guidelines you learned in this chapter.

2. Use Adobe Online Forms or Microsoft Word to design a simple fill-in form with at least five fields.

3. Create a functional decomposition diagram similar to the one in Figure 4-8 but showing your school instead of the library example.

4. Use the Internet to find a site that contains current IT industry news, information, and links. Write a brief description of what you liked and didn't like.

5. Research TCO in the context of migrating software systems to the cloud. Identify some of the benefits and shortcomings of the cloud computing environment for a traditional information system.

CHAPTER 5 Data and Process Modeling

Chapter 5 is the second of four chapters in the systems analysis phase of the SDLC. This chapter discusses data and process modeling techniques that analysts use to show how the system transforms data into useful information. The deliverable, or end product, of data and process modeling is a logical model that will support business operations and meet user needs.

The chapter includes four "Case in Point" discussion questions to help contextualize the concepts described in the text. The "Question of Ethics" raises the issue of how to respond to subtle but insistent requests by an IT manager in a systems analyst's new organization for proprietary information related to the business processes used by the analyst's previous employer, which is a competitor of the analyst's current company.

LEARNING OBJECTIVES

When you finish this chapter, you should be able to:

- Describe data and process modeling concepts and tools, including data flow diagrams, a data dictionary, and process descriptions

- Describe the symbols used in data flow diagrams and explain the rules for their use

- Draw data flow diagrams in a sequence, from general to specific

- Explain how to level and balance a set of data flow diagrams

- Describe how a data dictionary is used and what it contains

- Use process description tools, including structured English, decision tables, and decision trees

- Describe the relationship between logical and physical models

CHAPTER CONTENTS

5.1 INTRODUCTION

During the requirements modeling process described in Chapter 4, fact-finding techniques were used to investigate the current system and identify user requirements. Chapters 5 and 6 explain how that information is used to develop a logical model of the proposed system and document the system requirements. A **logical model** shows *what* the system must do, regardless of how it will be implemented physically. Later, in the systems design phase, a **physical model** is built that describes *how* the system will be constructed. Data and process modeling involves three main tools: data flow diagrams, a data dictionary, and process descriptions.

5.2 OVERVIEW OF DATA AND PROCESS MODELING TOOLS

Systems analysts use many graphical techniques to describe an information system. One popular method is to draw a set of data flow diagrams. As seen in Chapter 4, a data flow diagram (DFD) uses various symbols to show how the system transforms input data into useful information. Other graphical tools include object models, which are explained in Chapter 6, and entity-relationship diagrams, which are described in Chapter 9.

5.3 DATA FLOW DIAGRAMS

During the systems analysis phase of the SDLC, the systems analyst creates a visual model of the information system using a set of data flow diagrams. In his seminal book *The Visual Display of Quantitative Information*, author and renowned academic Edward Tufte provides guidance on creating effective diagrams to concisely convey complex information. A DFD is an example of this type of visual explanation of system behavior.

A DFD shows how data moves through an information system but does not show program logic or processing steps. A set of DFDs provides a logical model that shows *what* the system does, not *how* it does it. That distinction is important because focusing on implementation issues at this point would restrict the search for the most effective system design.

5.3.1 DFD Symbols

DFDs use four basic symbols that represent processes, data flows, data stores, and entities. Several different versions of DFD symbols exist, but they all serve the same purpose. DFD examples in this textbook use the **Gane and Sarson** symbol set. Another popular symbol set is the **Yourdon** symbol set. Figure 5-1 shows examples of both versions. In this text, symbols are referenced using all capital letters for the symbol name.

PROCESS SYMBOL: A process receives input data and produces output that has a different content, form, or both. For instance, the process for calculating pay uses two inputs (pay rate and hours worked) to produce one output (total pay). Processes can be very simple or quite complex. In a typical company, processes might include calculating sales trends, filing online insurance claims, ordering inventory from a supplier's system, or verifying email addresses for web customers. Processes contain the **business logic**, also called **business rules**, which transform the data and produce the required results.

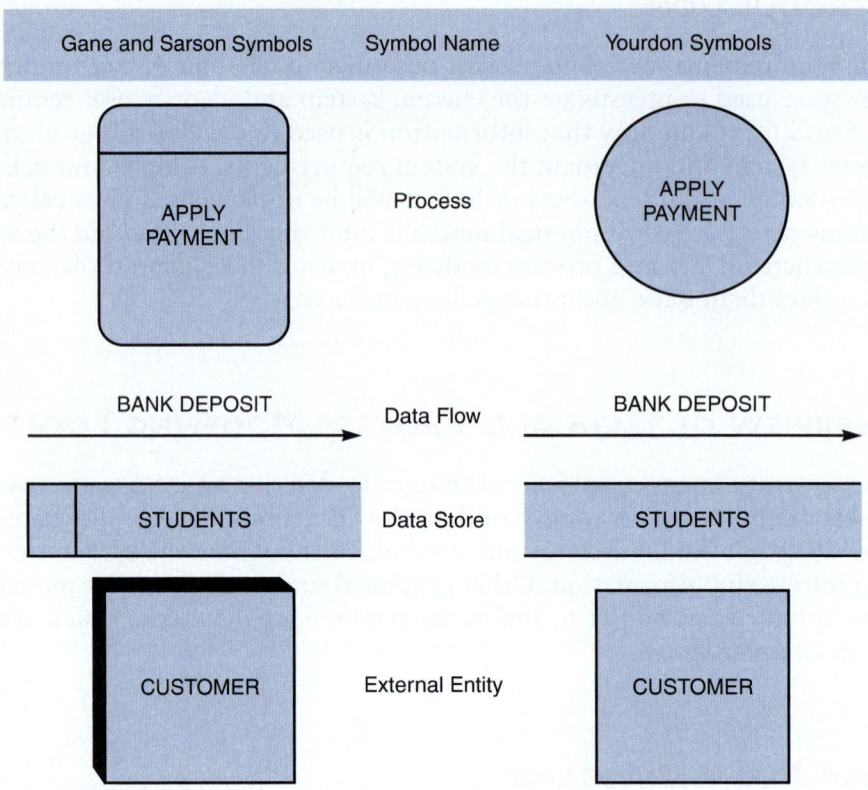

Gane and Sarson Symbols	Symbol Name	Yourdon Symbols
APPLY PAYMENT	Process	APPLY PAYMENT
BANK DEPOSIT →	Data Flow	BANK DEPOSIT →
STUDENTS	Data Store	STUDENTS
CUSTOMER	External Entity	CUSTOMER

FIGURE 5-1 Data flow diagram symbols, symbol names, and examples of the Gane and Sarson, and Yourdon, symbol sets.

The symbol for a process is a rectangle with rounded corners. The name of the process appears inside the rectangle. The process name identifies a specific function and consists of a verb (and an adjective, if necessary) followed by a singular noun. Examples of process names are APPLY RENT PAYMENT, CALCULATE COMMISSION, ASSIGN FINAL GRADE, VERIFY ORDER, and FILL ORDER.

Processing details are not shown in a DFD. For example, there might be a process named DEPOSIT PAYMENT. The process symbol does not reveal the business logic for the DEPOSIT PAYMENT process. To document the logic, a process description is created, which is explained later in this chapter.

In DFDs, a process symbol can be referred to as a **black box**, because the inputs, outputs, and general functions of the process are known, but the underlying details and logic of the process are hidden. By showing processes as black boxes, an analyst can create DFDs that show how the system functions but avoid unnecessary detail and clutter. When the analyst wishes to show additional levels of detail, he or she can zoom in on a process symbol and create a more in-depth DFD that shows the process's internal workings — which might reveal even more processes, data flows, and data stores. In this manner, the information system can be modeled as a series of increasingly detailed pictures.

The network router shown in Figure 5-2 is an example of a black box. An observer can see cables that carry data into and out of the router, but the router's internal operations are not revealed — only the results are apparent.

DATA FLOW SYMBOL: A **data flow** is a path for data to move from one part of the information system to another. A data flow in a DFD represents one or more data items. For example, a data flow could consist of a single data item (such as a student

ID number) or it could include a set of data (such as a class roster with student ID numbers, names, and registration dates for a specific class). Although the DFD does not show the detailed contents of a data flow, that information is included in the data dictionary, which is described later in this chapter.

The symbol for a data flow is a line with a single or double arrowhead. The data flow name appears above, below, or alongside the line. A data flow name consists of a singular noun and an adjective, if needed. Examples of data flow names are DEPOSIT, INVOICE PAYMENT, STUDENT GRADE, ORDER, and COMMISSION. Exceptions to the singular name rule are data flow names, such as GRADING PARAMETERS, where a singular name could mislead the analyst into thinking a single parameter or single item of data exists.

Figure 5-3 shows correct examples of data flow and process symbol connections. Because a process changes the data's content or form, at least one data flow must enter and one data flow must exit each process symbol, as they do in the CREATE INVOICE process. A process symbol can have more than one outgoing data flow, as shown in the GRADE STUDENT WORK process, or more than one incoming data flow, as shown in the CALCULATE GROSS PAY process. A process can also connect to any other symbol, including another process symbol, as shown by the connection between VERIFY ORDER and ASSEMBLE ORDER in Figure 5-3. A data flow, therefore, *must* have a process symbol on at least one end.

FIGURE 5-2 A router acts like a *black box* for network data. Cables carry data and out, but internal operations are hidden inside the case.
Martin Bobrovsky/Insadco Photography/Alamy

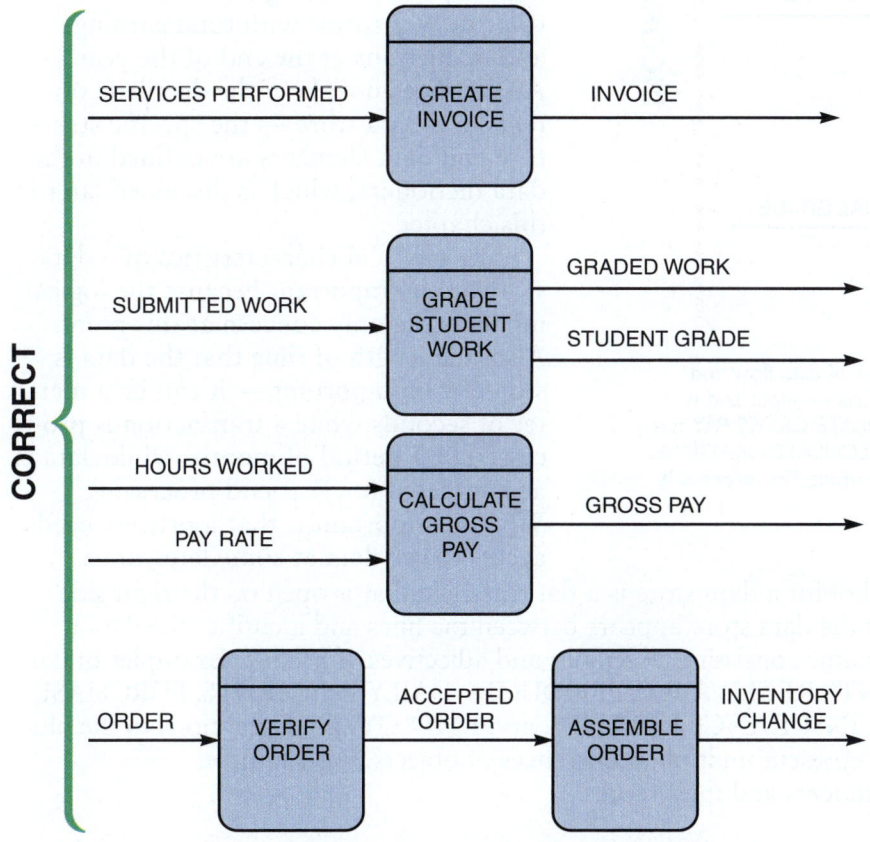

FIGURE 5-3 Examples of correct combinations of data flow and process symbols.

Figure 5-4 shows three data flow and process combinations that must be avoided:

- **Spontaneous generation.** The APPLY INSURANCE PREMIUM process, for instance, produces output, but has no input data flow. Because it has no input, the process is called a spontaneous generation process.

- **Black hole.** CALCULATE GROSS PAY is called a black hole process, which is a process that has input, but produces no output.

- **Gray hole.** A gray hole is a process that has at least one input and one output, but the input obviously is insufficient to generate the output shown. For example, a date of birth input is not sufficient to produce a final grade output in the CALCULATE GRADE process.

Spontaneous generation, black holes, and gray holes are impossible logically in a DFD because a process must act on input, shown by an incoming data flow, and produce output, represented by an outgoing data flow.

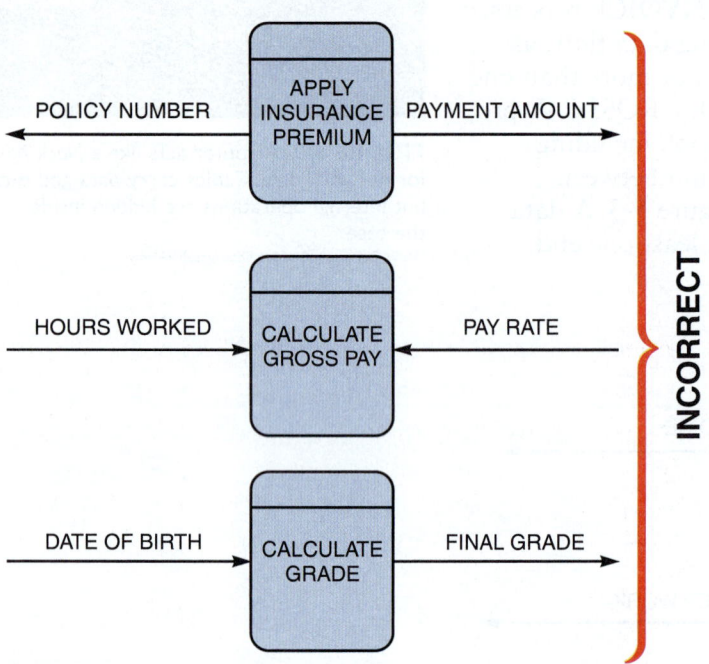

FIGURE 5-4 Examples of incorrect combinations of data flow and process symbols. APPLY INSURANCE PREMIUM has no input and is called a spontaneous generation process. CALCULATE GROSS PAY has no outputs and is called a black hole process. CALCULATE GRADE has an input that is obviously unable to produce the output. This process is called a gray hole.

DATA STORE SYMBOL: A **data store** is used in a DFD to represent data that the system stores because one or more processes need to use the data at a later time. For instance, instructors need to store student scores on tests and assignments during the semester so they can assign final grades at the end of the term. Similarly, a company stores employee salary and deduction data during the year in order to print W-2 forms with total earnings and deductions at the end of the year. A DFD does not show the detailed contents of a data store — the specific structure and data elements are defined in the data dictionary, which is discussed later in this chapter.

The physical characteristics of a data store are unimportant because the logical model is the only concern at this point. Also, the length of time that the data is stored is unimportant — it can be a matter of seconds while a transaction is processed or a period of months while data is accumulated for year-end processing. What is important is that a process needs access to the data at some later time.

In a DFD, the Gane and Sarson symbol for a data store is a flat rectangle that is open on the right side and closed on the left side. The name of the data store appears between the lines and identifies the data it contains. A data store name is a plural name consisting of a noun and adjectives, if needed. Examples of data store names are STUDENTS, ACCOUNTS RECEIVABLE, PRODUCTS, DAILY PAYMENTS, PURCHASE ORDERS, OUTSTANDING CHECKS, INSURANCE POLICIES, and EMPLOYEES. Exceptions to the plural name rule are collective nouns that represent multiple occurrences of objects. For example, GRADEBOOK represents a group of students and their scores.

A data store must be connected to a process with a data flow. Figure 5-5 illustrates typical examples of data stores. Since data stores represent data storage for use by another process in the future, in each case, the data store has at least one incoming and one outgoing data flow and is connected to a process symbol with a data flow.

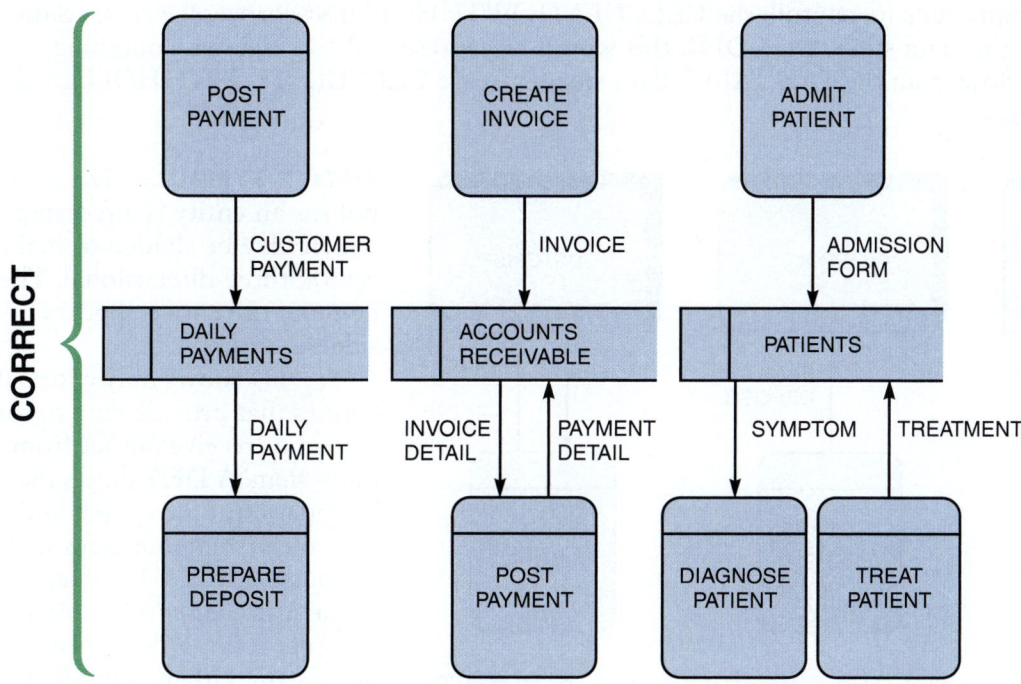

FIGURE 5-5 Examples of correct use of data store symbols in a data flow diagram.

Violations of the rule that a data store must have at least one incoming and one outgoing data flow are shown in Figure 5-6. In the first example, two data stores are connected incorrectly because no process is between them. Also, COURSES has no incoming data flow and STUDENTS has no outgoing data flow. In the second and third examples, the data stores lack either an outgoing or incoming data flow.

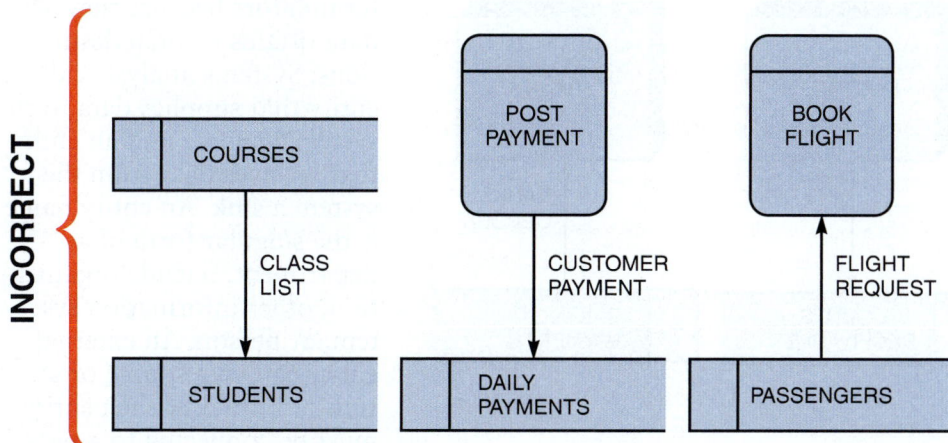

FIGURE 5-6 Examples of incorrect use of data store symbols in a data flow diagram. Two data stores cannot be connected by a data flow without an intervening process, and each data store should have an outgoing and incoming data flow.

There is an exception to the requirement that a data store must have at least one incoming and one outgoing data flow. In some situations, a data store has no input data flow because it contains fixed reference data that is not updated by the system. For example, consider a data store called TAX TABLE, which contains withholding tax data that a company downloads from the Internal Revenue Service. When the company runs its payroll, the CALCULATE WITHHOLDING process accesses data from this data store. On a DFD, this would be represented as a one-way outgoing data flow from the TAX TABLE data store into the CALCULATE WITHHOLDING process.

ENTITY SYMBOL: The symbol for an **entity** is a rectangle, which may be shaded to make it look three-dimensional. The name of the entity appears inside the symbol.

A DFD shows only external entities that provide data to the system or receive output from the system. A DFD shows the boundaries of the system and how the system interfaces with the outside world. For example, a customer entity submits an order to an order processing system. Other examples of entities include a patient who supplies data to a medical records system, a homeowner who receives a bill from a city property tax system, or an accounts payable system that receives data from the company's purchasing system.

DFD entities are also called **terminators** because they are data origins or final destinations. Systems analysts call an entity that supplies data to the system a **source** and an entity that receives data from the system a **sink**. An entity name is the singular form of a department, outside organization, other information system, or person. An external entity can be a source or a sink or both, but each entity must be connected to a process by a data flow. Figure 5-7 and Figure 5-8 show correct and incorrect examples of this rule, respectively.

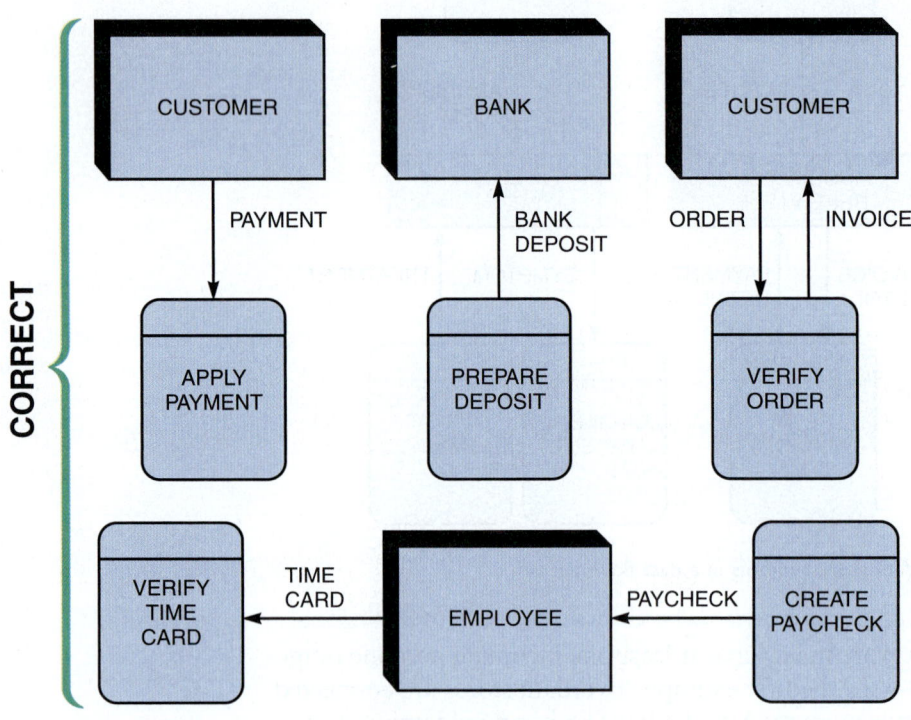

FIGURE 5-7 Examples of correct uses of external entities in a data flow diagram.

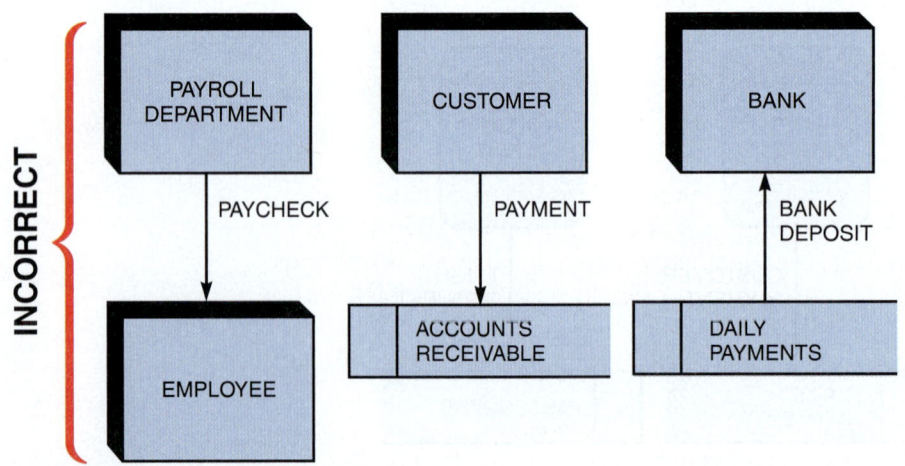

FIGURE 5-8 Examples of incorrect uses of external entities in a data flow diagram. An external entity must be connected by a data flow to a process and not directly to a data store or to another external entity.

With an understanding of the proper use of DFD symbols, the next step is to construct diagrams that use these symbols. Figure 5-9 shows a summary of the rules for using DFD symbols.

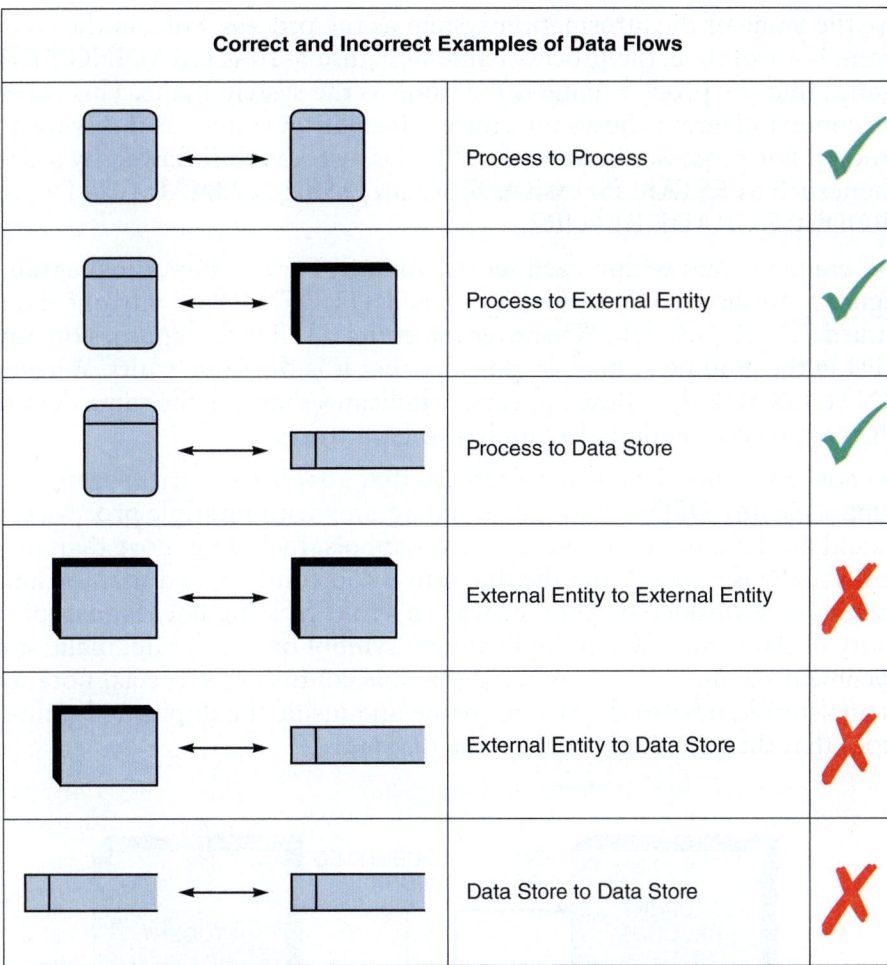

Correct and Incorrect Examples of Data Flows		
	Process to Process	✔
	Process to External Entity	✔
	Process to Data Store	✔
	External Entity to External Entity	✘
	External Entity to Data Store	✘
	Data Store to Data Store	✘

FIGURE 5-9 Examples of correct and incorrect uses of data flows.

5.4 CREATING A SET OF DFDs

During requirements modeling, interviews, questionnaires, and other techniques were used to gather facts about the system, and it was explained how the various people, departments, data, and processes fit together to support business operations. Now a graphical model of the information system is created based on the fact-finding results.

To learn how to construct DFDs, examples of two information systems will be used. The first example is a grading system that instructors use to assign final grades based on the scores that students receive during the term. The second example is an order system that a company uses to enter orders and apply payments against a customer's balance. First, review a set of guidelines for drawing DFDs. Then, learn how to apply these guidelines and create a set of DFDs using a three-step process.

5.5 GUIDELINES FOR DRAWING DFDs

When drawing a context diagram and other DFDs, these guidelines should be followed:

- Draw the context diagram so it fits on one page.

- Use the name of the information system as the process name in the context diagram. For example, the process name in Figure 5-10 is GRADING SYSTEM. Notice that the process name is the same as the system name. This is because the context diagram shows the entire information system as if it were a single process. For processes in lower-level DFDs, use a verb followed by a descriptive noun, such as ESTABLISH GRADEBOOK, ASSIGN FINAL GRADE, or PRODUCE GRADE REPORT.

- Use unique names within each set of symbols. For instance, the diagram in Figure 5-10 shows only one entity named STUDENT and only one data flow named FINAL GRADE. Whenever the entity STUDENT appears on any other DFD in the grading system, it indicates that it is the same entity. Whenever the FINAL GRADE data flow appears, it indicates that it is the same data flow. The naming convention also applies to data stores.

- Do not cross lines. One way to achieve that goal is to restrict the number of symbols in any DFD. On lower-level diagrams with multiple processes, there should not be more than nine process symbols. Including more than nine symbols usually is a signal that the diagram is too complex and that the analysis should be reconsidered. Another way to avoid crossing lines is to duplicate an entity or data store. When duplicating a symbol on a diagram, make sure to document the duplication to avoid possible confusion. A special notation, such as an asterisk, next to the symbol name and inside the duplicated symbols signifies that they are duplicated on the diagram.

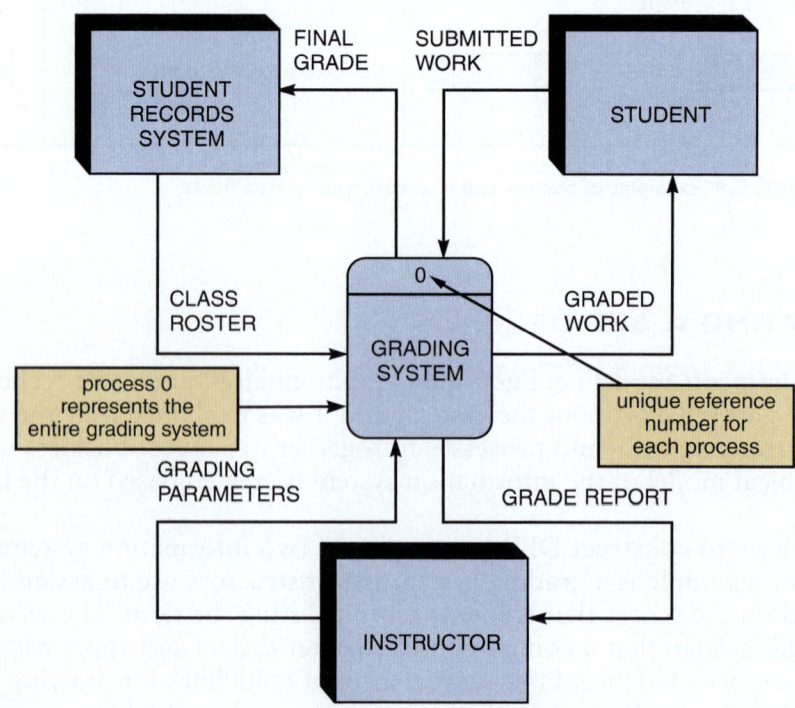

FIGURE 5-10 Context diagram DFD for a grading system.

- Provide a unique name and reference number for each process. Because it is the highest-level DFD, the context diagram contains process 0, which represents the entire information system, but does not show the internal workings. To describe the next level of detail inside process 0, create a DFD named diagram 0, which will reveal additional processes that must be named and numbered. As lower-level DFDs are created, assign unique names and reference numbers to all processes, until the logical model is completed.

- Obtain as much user input and feedback as possible. The main objective is to ensure that the model is accurate, easy to understand, and meets the needs of its users.

STEP 1: DRAW A CONTEXT DIAGRAM: The first step in constructing a set of DFDs is to draw a context diagram. A **context diagram** is a top-level view of an information system that shows the system's boundaries and scope. To draw a context diagram, start by placing a single process symbol in the center of the page. The symbol represents the entire information system, and it is identified as **process 0** (the numeral zero, and not the letter O). Then place the system entities around the perimeter of the page and use data flows to connect the entities to the central process. Data stores are not shown in the context diagram because they are contained within the system and remain hidden until more detailed diagrams are created.

To determine which entities and data flows to place in the context diagram, begin by reviewing the system requirements to identify all external data sources and destinations. During that process, identify the entities, the name and content of the data flows, and the direction of the data flows. If that is done carefully, and the job of fact-finding was done well in the previous stage, drawing the context diagram should be relatively easy. Now review the following context diagram examples.

Example: Context diagram for a grading system. The context diagram for a grading system is shown in Figure 5-10. The GRADING SYSTEM process is at the center of the diagram. The three entities (STUDENT RECORDS SYSTEM, STUDENT, and INSTRUCTOR) are placed around the central process. Interaction among the central process and the entities involves six different data flows. The STUDENT RECORDS SYSTEM entity supplies data through the CLASS ROSTER data flow and receives data through the FINAL GRADE data flow. The STUDENT entity supplies data through the SUBMITTED WORK data flow and receives data through the GRADED WORK data flow. Finally, the INSTRUCTOR entity supplies data through the GRADING PARAMETERS data flow and receives data through the GRADE REPORT data flow.

Example: Context diagram for an order system. The context diagram for an order system is shown in Figure 5-11. Notice that the ORDER SYSTEM process is at the center of the diagram and five entities surround the process. Three of the entities, SALES REP, BANK, and ACCOUNTING, have single incoming data flows for COMMISSION, BANK DEPOSIT, and CASH RECEIPTS ENTRY, respectively. The WAREHOUSE entity has one incoming data flow — PICKING LIST — that is, a report that shows the items ordered and their quantity, location, and sequence to pick from the warehouse. The WAREHOUSE entity has one outgoing data flow: COMPLETED ORDER. Finally, the CUSTOMER entity has two outgoing data flows, ORDER and PAYMENT, and two incoming data flows, ORDER REJECT NOTICE and INVOICE.

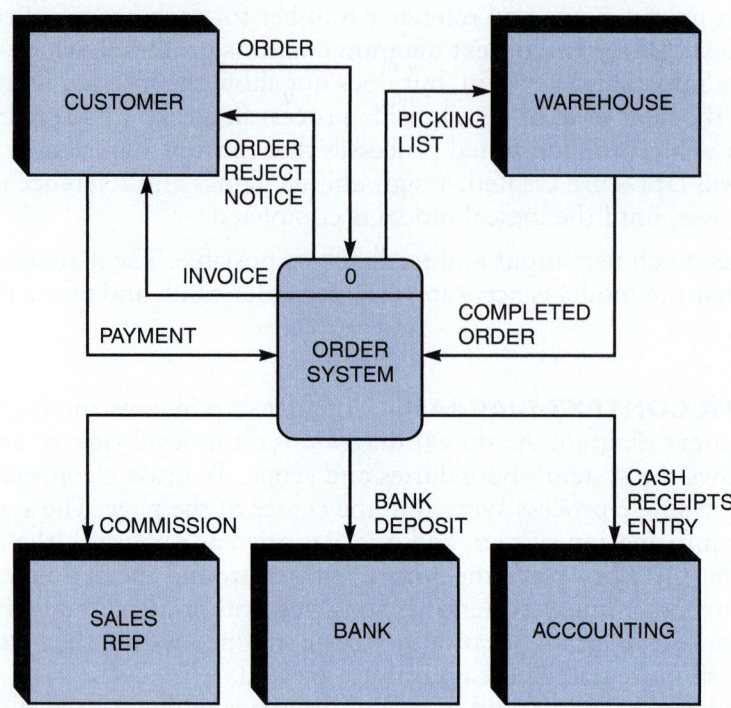

FIGURE 5-11 Context diagram DFD for an order system.

The context diagram for the order system appears more complex than the grading system because it has two more entities and three more data flows. What makes one system more complex than another is the number of components, the number of levels, and the degree of interaction among its processes, entities, data stores, and data flows.

STEP 2: DRAW A DIAGRAM 0 DFD: In the previous step, it was explained how a context diagram provides the most general view of an information system and contains a single process symbol, which is like a black box. To show the detail inside the black box, a DFD diagram 0 is created. **Diagram 0** (the numeral zero, and not the letter O) provides an overview of all the components that interact to form the overall system. It zooms in on the system and shows major internal processes, data flows, and data stores. Diagram 0 also repeats the entities and data flows that appear in the context diagram. When the context diagram is expanded into DFD diagram 0, all the connections that flow into and out of process 0 must be retained.

Example: Diagram 0 DFD for a grading system. Figure 5-12 shows a context diagram at the top and diagram 0 beneath it. Notice that diagram 0 is an expansion of process 0. Also notice that the three same entities (STUDENT RECORDS SYSTEM, STUDENT, and INSTRUCTOR) and the same six data flows (FINAL GRADE, CLASS ROSTER, SUBMITTED WORK, GRADED WORK, GRADING PARAMETERS, and GRADE REPORT) appear in both diagrams. In addition, diagram 0 expands process 0 to reveal four internal processes, one data store, and five additional data flows.

Notice that each process in diagram 0 has a reference number: ESTABLISH GRADEBOOK is 1, ASSIGN FINAL GRADE is 2, GRADE STUDENT WORK is 3, and PRODUCE GRADE REPORT is 4. These reference numbers are important

Context Diagram for Grading System

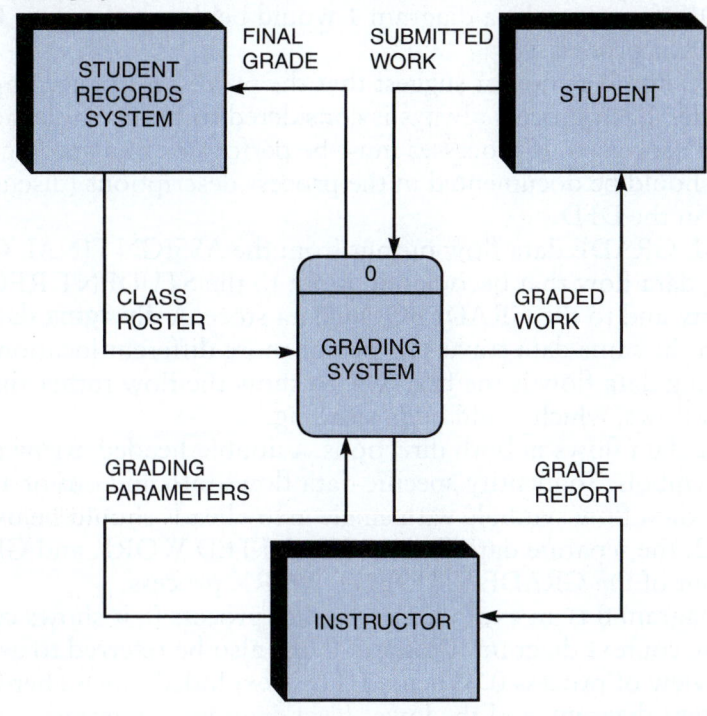

Diagram 0 for Grading System

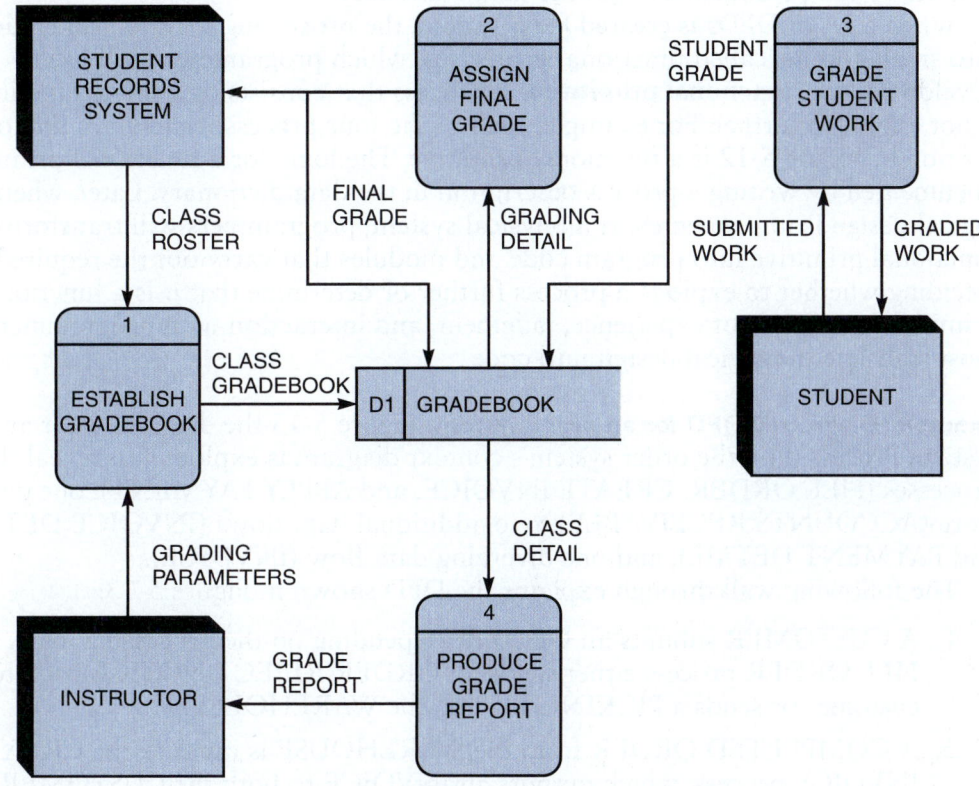

FIGURE 5-12 Context diagram and diagram 0 for the grading system.

because they identify a series of DFDs. If more detail were needed for ESTABLISH GRADEBOOK, for example, a diagram 1 would be drawn, because ESTABLISH GRADEBOOK is process 1.

The process numbers do not suggest that the processes are accomplished in a sequential order. Each process always is considered to be available, active, and awaiting data to be processed. If processes must be performed in a specific sequence, the information should be documented in the process descriptions (discussed later in this chapter), not in the DFD.

The FINAL GRADE data flow output from the ASSIGN FINAL GRADE process is a diverging data flow that becomes an input to the STUDENT RECORDS SYSTEM entity and to the GRADEBOOK data store. A **diverging data flow** is a data flow in which the same data travels to two or more different locations. In that situation, a diverging data flow is the best way to show the flow rather than showing two identical data flows, which could be misleading.

If the same data flows in both directions, a double-headed arrow can be used to connect the symbols. To identify specific data flows into and out of a symbol, however, separate data flow symbols with single arrowheads should be used. For example, in Figure 5-12, the separate data flows (SUBMITTED WORK and GRADED WORK) go into and out of the GRADE STUDENT WORK process.

Because diagram 0 is an exploded version of process 0, it shows considerably more detail than the context diagram. Diagram 0 can also be referred to as a partitioned or decomposed view of process 0. When a DFD is exploded, the higher-level diagram is called the **parent diagram**, and the lower-level diagram is referred to as the **child diagram**. The grading system is simple enough that no additional DFDs are needed to model the system. At that point, the four processes, the one data store, and the 10 data flows can be documented in the data dictionary.

When a set of DFDs is created for a system, the processing logic is broken down into smaller units, called functional primitives, which programmers will use to develop code. A **functional primitive** is a process that consists of a single function that is not exploded further. For example, each of the four processes shown in the lower portion of Figure 5-12 is a functional primitive. The logic for a functional primitive is documented by writing a process description in the data dictionary. Later, when the logical design is implemented as a physical system, programmers will transform each functional primitive into program code and modules that carry out the required steps. Deciding whether to explode a process further or determine that it is a functional primitive is a matter of experience, judgment, and interaction with programmers who must translate the logical design into code.

Example: Diagram 0 DFD for an order system. Figure 5-13 the diagram 0 for an order system. Process 0 on the order system's context diagram is exploded to reveal three processes (FILL ORDER, CREATE INVOICE, and APPLY PAYMENT), one data store (ACCOUNTS RECEIVABLE), two additional data flows (INVOICE DETAIL and PAYMENT DETAIL), and one diverging data flow (INVOICE).

The following walkthrough explains the DFD shown in Figure 5-13:

1. A CUSTOMER submits an ORDER. Depending on the processing logic, the FILL ORDER process either sends an ORDER REJECT NOTICE back to the customer or sends a PICKING LIST to the WAREHOUSE.

2. A COMPLETED ORDER from the WAREHOUSE is input to the CREATE INVOICE process, which outputs an INVOICE to both the CUSTOMER process and the ACCOUNTS RECEIVABLE data store.

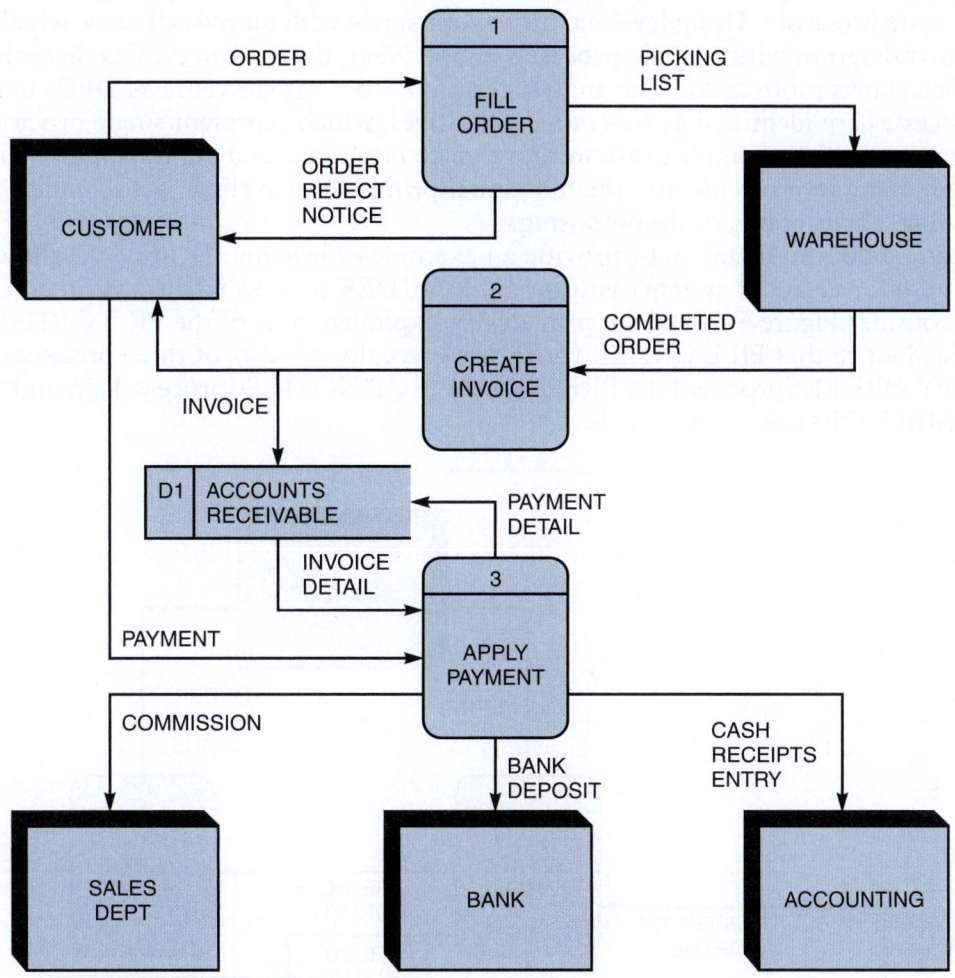

FIGURE 5-13 Diagram 0 DFD for the order system.

3. A CUSTOMER makes a PAYMENT that is processed by APPLY PAYMENT.
   APPLY PAYMENT requires INVOICE DETAIL input from the ACCOUNTS
   RECEIVABLE data store along with the PAYMENT. APPLY PAYMENT also
   outputs PAYMENT DETAIL back to the ACCOUNTS RECEIVABLE data
   store and outputs COMMISSION to the SALES DEPT, BANK DEPOSIT to the
   BANK, and CASH RECEIPTS ENTRY to ACCOUNTING.

The walkthrough of diagram 0 illustrates the basic requirements of the order system. Examine the detailed description of each separate process to learn more.

STEP 3: DRAW THE LOWER-LEVEL DIAGRAMS: This set of lower-level DFDs is
based on the order system. To create lower-level diagrams, leveling and balancing
techniques must be used. **Leveling** is the process of drawing a series of increasingly
detailed diagrams, until all functional primitives are identified. **Balancing** maintains
consistency among a set of DFDs by ensuring that input and output data flows
align properly. Leveling and balancing are described in more detail in the following
sections.

Leveling examples. Leveling uses a series of increasingly detailed DFDs to describe an
information system. For example, a system might consist of dozens, or even hundreds,

of separate processes. Using leveling, an analyst starts with an overall view, which is a context diagram with a single process symbol. Next, the analyst creates diagram 0, which shows more detail. The analyst continues to create lower-level DFDs until all processes are identified as functional primitives, which represent single processing functions. More complex systems have more processes, and analysts must work through many levels to identify the functional primitives. Leveling is also called **exploding, partitioning**, or **decomposing**.

Figure 5-13 and Figure 5-14 provide an example of leveling. Figure 5-13 shows diagram 0 for an order system, with the FILL ORDER process labeled as process 1. Now consider Figure 5-14, which provides an exploded view of the FILL ORDER process. Notice that FILL ORDER (process 1) actually consists of three processes: VERIFY ORDER (process 1.1), PREPARE REJECT NOTICE (process 1.2), and ASSEMBLE ORDER (process 1.3).

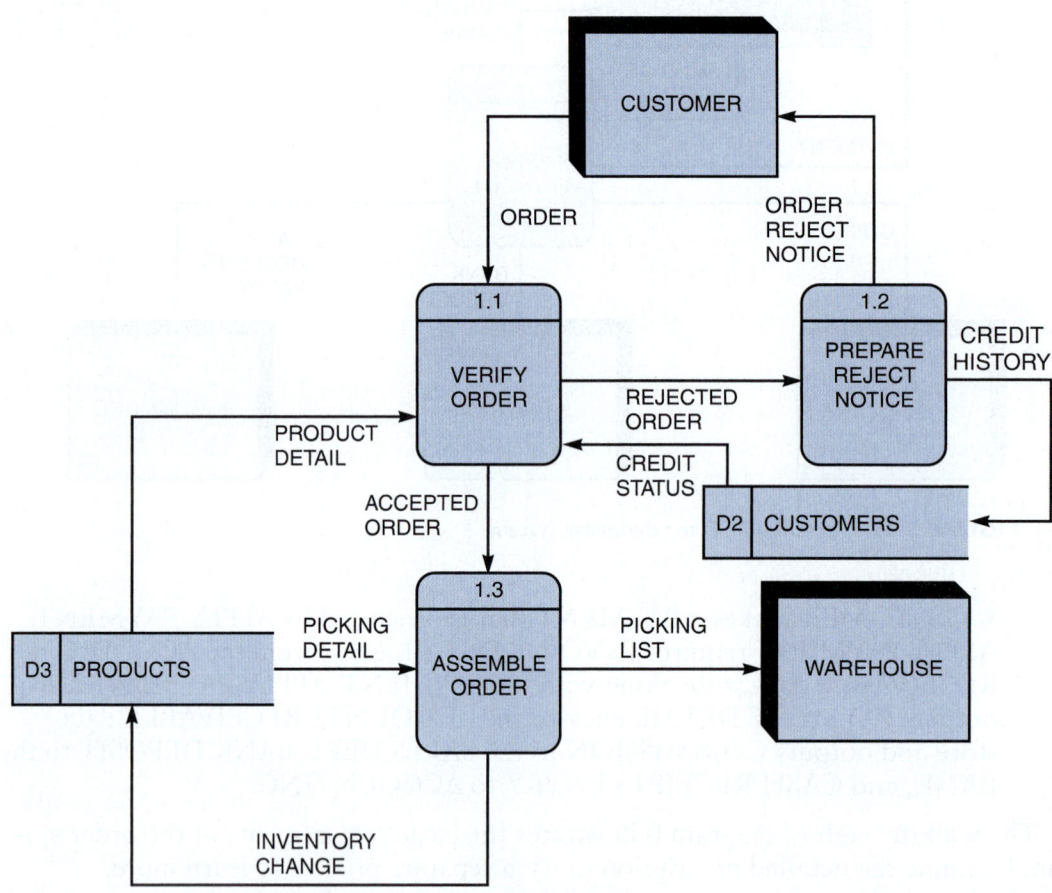

FIGURE 5-14 Diagram I DFD shows details of the FILL ORDER process in the order system.

As Figure 5-14 shows, all processes are numbered using a decimal notation consisting of the parent's reference number, a decimal point, and a sequence number within the new diagram. In Figure 5-14, the parent process of diagram 1 is process 1, so the processes in diagram 1 have reference numbers of 1.1, 1.2, and 1.3. If process 1.3, ASSEMBLE ORDER, is decomposed further, then it would appear in diagram 1.3 and the processes in diagram 1.3 would be numbered as 1.3.1, 1.3.2, 1.3.3, and so on. This numbering technique makes it easy to integrate and identify all DFDs.

When Figure 5-13 and Figure 5-14 are compared, it is apparent that Figure 5-14 (the exploded FILL ORDER process) shows two data stores (CUSTOMER and PRODUCTS) that do not appear on Figure 5-13, which is the parent DFD. Why not? The answer is based on a simple rule: When drawing DFDs, a data store is shown only when two or more processes use that data store. The CUSTOMER and PRODUCTS data stores were internal to the FILL ORDER process, so the analyst did not show them on diagram 0, which is the parent. When the FILL ORDER process is exploded into a diagram 1 DFD, however, three processes (1.1, 1.2, and 1.3) interacting with the two data stores are now shown.

Now compare Figure 5-14 and Figure 5-15. Notice that Figure 5-15 shows the same data flows as Figure 5-14, but does not show the CUSTOMER and WAREHOUSE entities. Analysts often use this technique to simplify a DFD and reduce unnecessary clutter. Because the missing symbols appear on the parent DFD, that diagram can be used to identify the source or destination of the data flows.

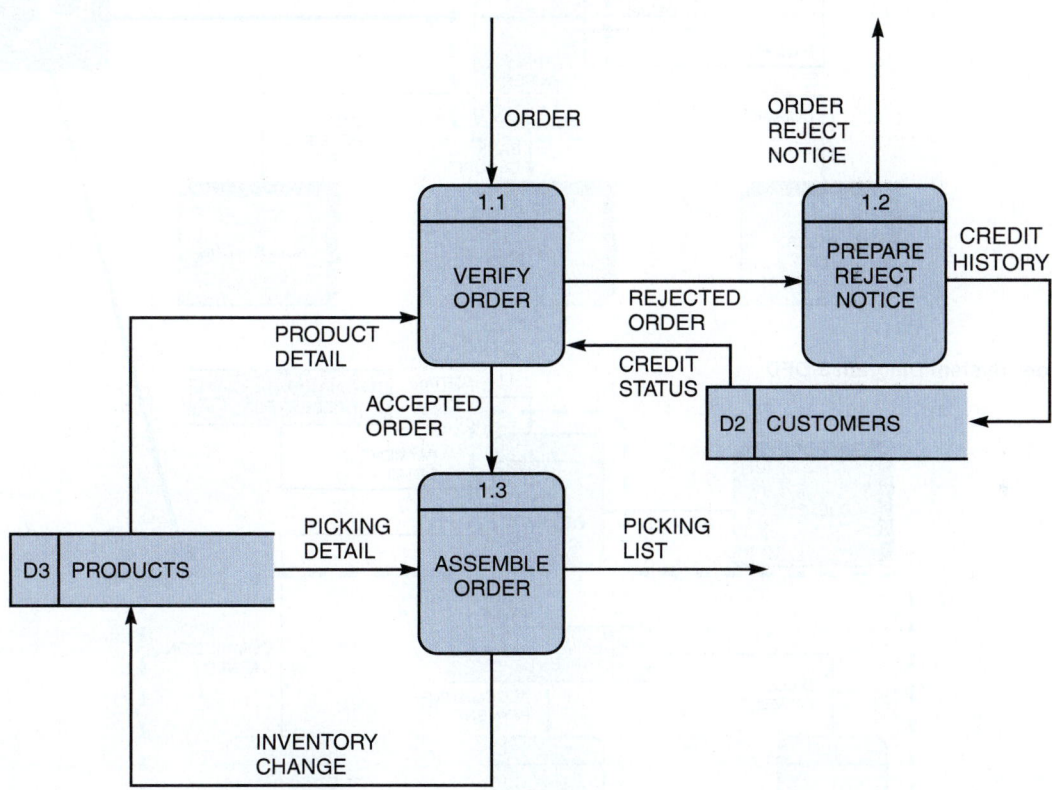

FIGURE 5-15 This diagram does not show the symbols that connect to data flows entering or leaving FILL ORDER on the context diagram.

Balancing examples. Balancing ensures that the input and output data flows of the parent DFD are maintained on the child DFD. For example, Figure 5-16 shows two DFDs: The order system diagram 0 is shown at the top of the figure, and the exploded diagram 3 DFD is shown at the bottom.

The two DFDs are balanced because the child diagram at the bottom has the same input and output flows as the parent process 3 shown at the top. To verify the balancing, notice that the parent process 3, APPLY PAYMENT, has one incoming data flow from an external entity, and three outgoing data flows to external entities. Examine the child DFD, which is diagram 3. Ignore the internal data flows and count the data flows to and from external entities. From the diagram, it is evident that the three processes maintain the same one incoming and three outgoing data flows as the parent process.

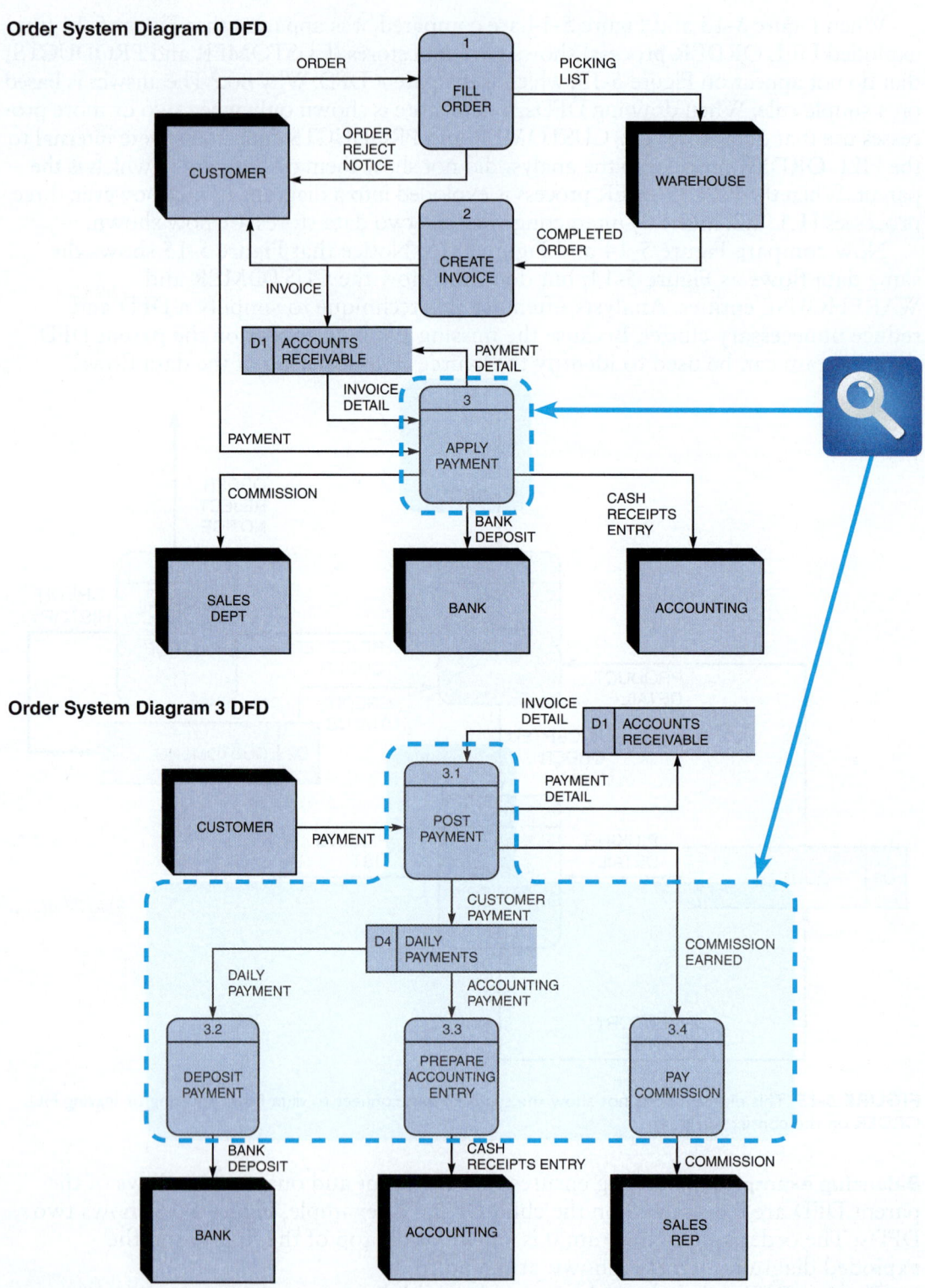

FIGURE 5-16 The order system diagram 0 is shown at the top of the figure, and the exploded diagram 3 DFD (for the APPLY PAYMENT process) is shown at the bottom. The two DFDs are balanced because the child diagram at the bottom has the same input and output flows as the parent process 3 shown at top.

Another example of balancing is shown in Figure 5-17 and Figure 5-18. The DFDs in these figures were created using the Visible Analyst CASE tool.

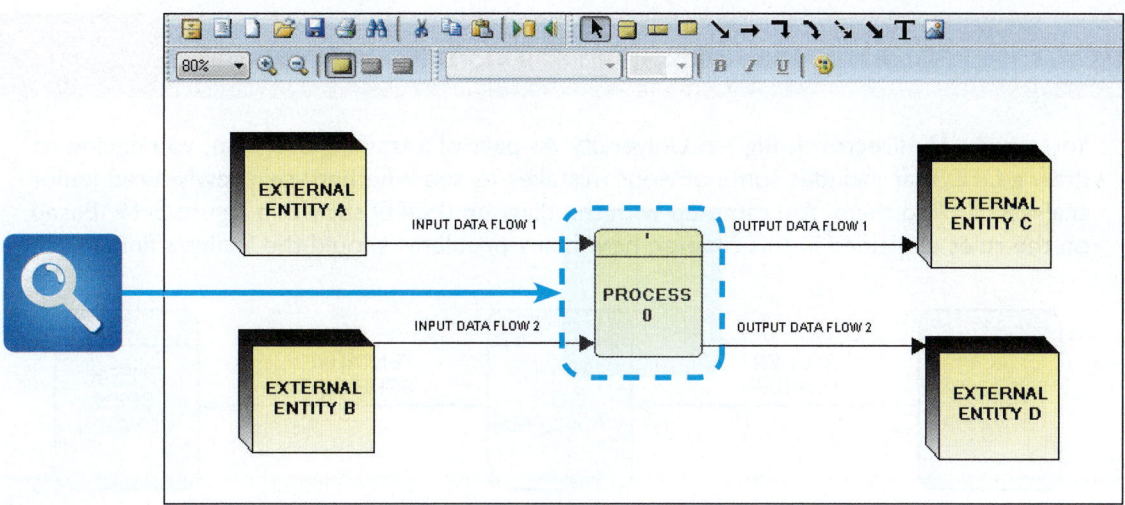

FIGURE 5-17 Examples of a parent DFD diagram, showing process 0 as a black box.

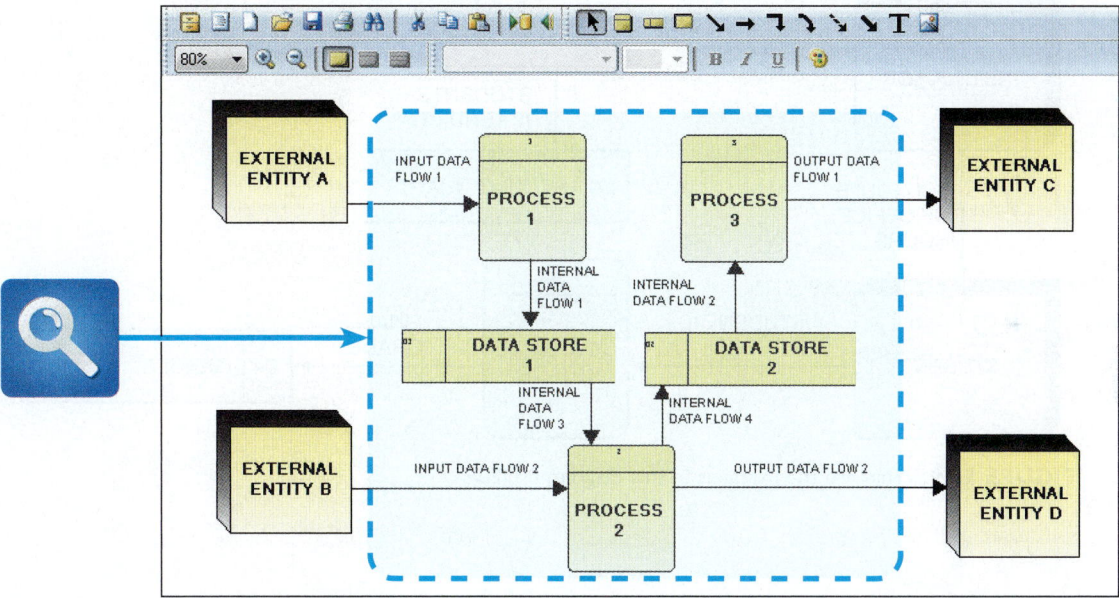

FIGURE 5-18 In the next level of detail, the process 0 black box reveals three processes, two data stores, and four internal data flows — all of which are shown inside the dashed line.

Figure 5-17 shows a sample context diagram. The process 0 symbol has two input flows and two output flows. Notice that process 0 can be considered as a black box, with no internal detail shown. In Figure 5-18, process 0 (the parent DFD) is exploded into the next level of detail. Now three processes, two data stores, and four internal data flows are visible. Notice that the details of process 0 are shown inside a dashed line, just as if the inside of the process was visible.

The DFDs in Figure 5-17 and Figure 5-18 are balanced because the four data flows into and out of process 0 are maintained on the child DFD. The DFDs are also leveled because each internal process is numbered to show that it is a child of the parent process.

CASE IN POINT 5.1:   BIG TEN UNIVERSITY

You are the IT director at Big Ten University. As part of a training program, you decide to draw a DFD that includes some obvious mistakes to see whether your newly hired junior analysts can find them. You came up with the diagram 0 DFD shown in Figure 5-19. Based on the rules explained in this chapter, how many problems should the analysts find?

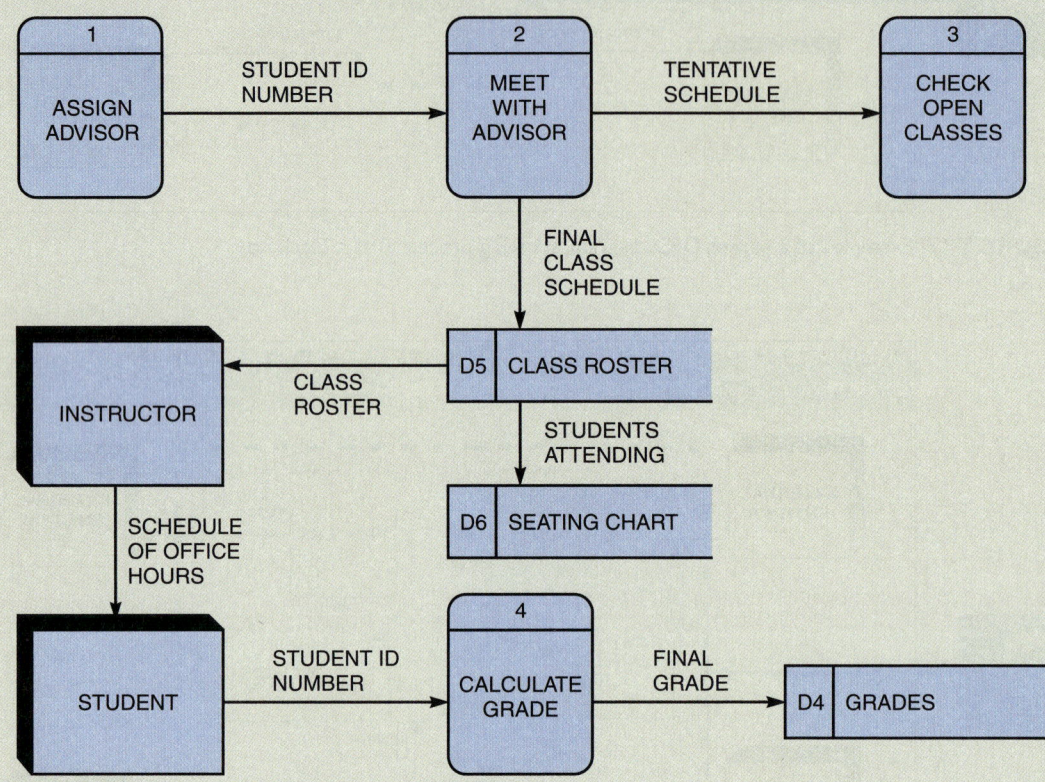

FIGURE 5-19 What are the mistakes in this diagram 0 DFD?

5.6 DATA DICTIONARY

A set of DFDs produces a logical model of the system, but the details within those DFDs are documented separately in a data dictionary, which is the second component of structured analysis.

A **data dictionary**, or **data repository**, is a central storehouse of information about the system's data. An analyst uses the data dictionary to collect, document, and organize specific facts about the system, including the contents of data flows, data stores, entities, and processes. The data dictionary also defines and describes all data elements and meaningful combinations of data elements. A **data element**, also called a **data item** or **field**, is the smallest piece of data that has meaning within an information system. Examples of data elements are student grade, salary, Social Security number, account balance, and company name. Data elements are combined into **records**, also called **data structures**. A record is a meaningful combination of related data elements that is included in a data flow or retained in a data store. For example, an auto parts store inventory record might include part number, description, supplier code, minimum and maximum stock levels, cost, and list price.

Significant relationships exist among the items in a data dictionary. For example, data stores and data flows are based on data structures, which in turn are composed of data elements. Data flows are connected to data stores, entities, and processes. Accurately documenting these relationships is essential so the data dictionary is consistent with the DFDs. CASE tools can be used to help document the design.

5.6.1 Using CASE Tools for Documentation

The more complex the system, the more difficult it is to maintain full and accurate documentation. Fortunately, modern CASE tools simplify the task by flowing documentation automatically from the modeling diagrams into the central repository, along with information entered by the user.

A CASE repository ensures data consistency, which is especially important where multiple systems require the same data. In a large company, for example, the sales, accounting, and shipping systems all might use a data element called CUSTOMER NUMBER. Once the CUSTOMER NUMBER element has been defined in the repository, other processes can access it, data flows, and data stores. The result is that all systems across the enterprise can share data that is up to date and consistent.

5.6.2 Documenting the Data Elements

Every data element in the data dictionary must be documented. Some analysts like to record their notes on online or manual forms. Others prefer to enter the information directly into a CASE tool. Irrespective of the specific CASE tool used, the objective is the same: to provide clear, comprehensive information about the data and processes that make up the system.

Figure 5-20 shows a sample screen that illustrates how a data element representing a SOCIAL SECURITY NUMBER might be recorded in the Visible Analyst data dictionary. Regardless of the terminology or method, the following attributes usually are recorded and described in the data dictionary:

- *Data element name or label.* The data element's standard name, which should be meaningful to users.

- *Alias.* Any name(s) other than the standard data element name; this alternate name is called an **alias**. For example, if there is a data element named CURRENT BALANCE, various users might refer to it by alternate names, such as OUTSTANDING BALANCE, CUSTOMER BALANCE, RECEIVABLE BALANCE, or AMOUNT OWED.

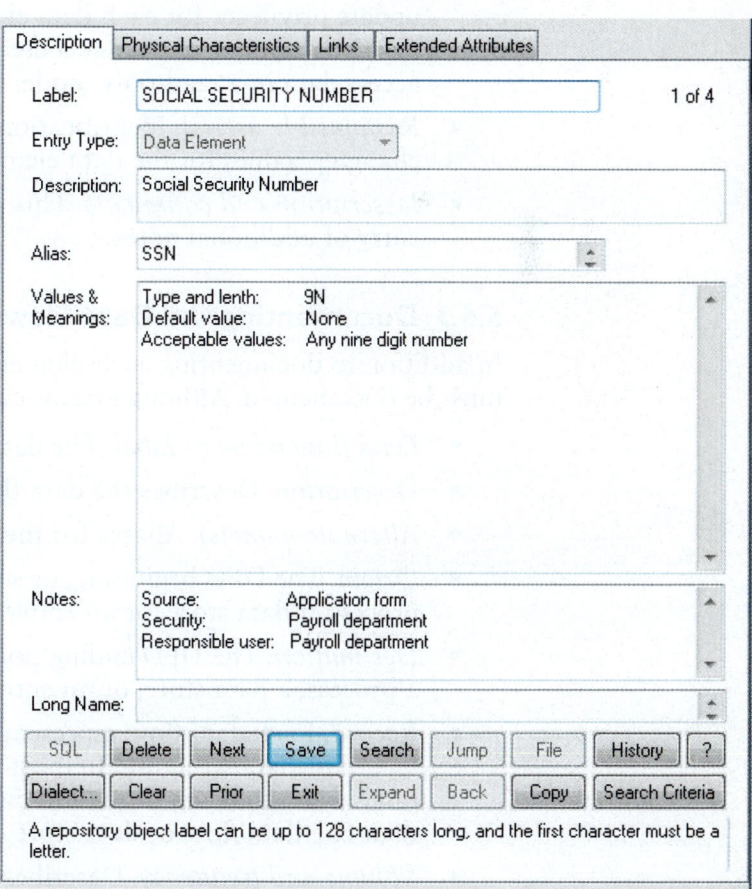

FIGURE 5-20 A Visible Analyst screen describes the data element named SOCIAL SECURITY NUMBER.

Source: Visible Systems Corporation.

- *Type and length.* Type refers to whether the data element contains numeric, alphabetic, or character values. Length is the maximum number of characters for an alphabetic or character data element or the maximum number of digits and number of decimal positions for a numeric data element. In addition to text and numeric data, sounds and images can also be stored in digital form. In some systems, these binary data objects are managed and processed just as traditional data elements are. For example, an employee record might include a digitized photo image of the person.

- *Default value.* The default value is the value for the data element if a value otherwise is not entered for it. For example, all new customers might have a default value of $500 for the CREDIT LIMIT data element.

- *Acceptable values.* Specification of the data element's **domain**, which is the set of values permitted for the data element. These values either can be specifically listed or referenced in a table, or can be selected from a specified range of values. Also indicate if a value for the data element is optional. Some data elements have additional **validity rules**. For example, an employee's salary must be within the range defined for the employee's job classification.

- *Source.* The specification for the origination point for the data element's values. The source could be a specific form, a department or outside organization, another information system, or the result of a calculation.

- *Security.* Identification for the individual or department that has access or update privileges for each data element. For example, only a credit manager has the authority to change a credit limit, while sales reps are authorized to access data in a read-only mode.

- *Responsible user(s).* Identification of the user(s) responsible for entering and changing values for the data element.

- *Description and comments.* This part of the documentation allows permits the entry of additional notes.

5.6.3 Documenting the Data Flows

In addition to documenting each data element, all data flows in the data dictionary must be documented. Although terms can vary, the typical attributes are as follows:

- *Data flow name or label.* The data flow name as it appears on the DFDs.

- *Description.* Describes the data flow and its purpose.

- *Alternate name(s).* Aliases for the DFD data flow name(s).

- *Origin.* The DFD beginning, or source, for the data flow; the origin can be a process, a data store, or an entity.

- *Destination.* The DFD ending point(s) for the data flow; the destination can be a process, a data store, or an entity.

- *Record.* Each data flow represents a group of related data elements called a record or data structure. In most data dictionaries, records are defined separately from the data flows and data stores. When records are defined, more than one data flow or data store can use the same record, if necessary.

- *Volume and frequency.* Describes the expected number of occurrences for the data flow per unit of time. For example, if a company has 300 employees, a TIME CARD data flow would involve 300 transactions and records each week as employees submit their work hour data.

5.6.4 Documenting the Data Stores

Every DFD data store in the data dictionary must be documented. Figure 5-21 shows the definition of a data store named IN STOCK. Typical characteristics of a data store are as follows:

- *Data store name or label*. The data store name as it appears on the DFDs.
- *Description*. Describes the data store and its purpose.
- *Alternate name(s)*. Aliases for the DFD data store name.
- *Attributes*. Standard DFD names that enter or leave the data store.
- *Volume and frequency*. Describes the estimated number of records in the data store and how frequently they are updated.

1. This data store has an alternative name, or alias.
2. For consistency, data flow names are standardized throughout the data dictionary.
3. It is important to document these estimates because they will affect design decisions in subsequent SDLC phases.

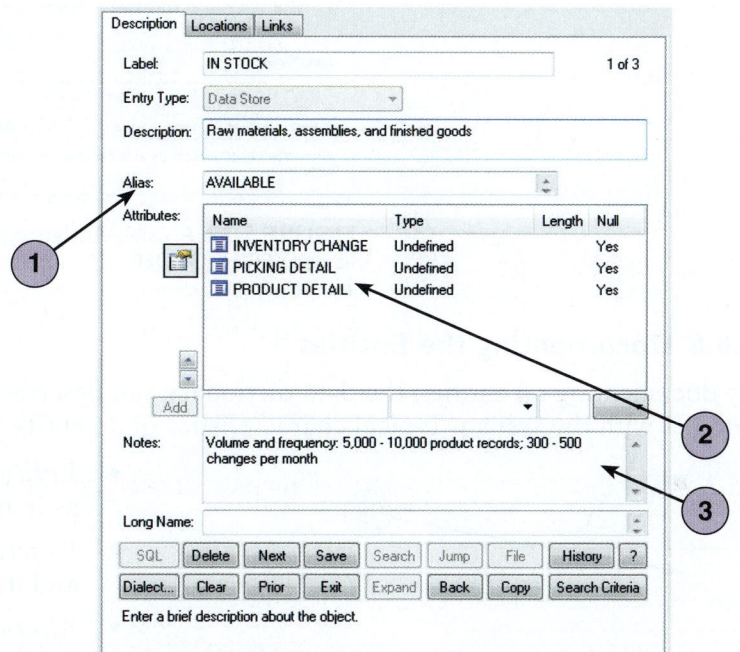

FIGURE 5-21 A Visible Analyst screen that documents a data store named IN STOCK.
Source: Visible Systems Corporation.

5.6.5 Documenting the Processes

Every process must be documented, as shown in Figure 5-22. The documentation includes a description of the process's characteristics and, for functional primitives, a process description, which is a model that documents the processing steps and business logic.

The following are typical characteristics of a process:

- *Process name or label*. The process name as it appears on the DFDs.
- *Description*. A brief statement of the process's purpose.
- *Process number*. A reference number that identifies the process and indicates relationships among various levels in the system.
- *Process description*. This section includes the input and output data flows. For functional primitives, the process description also documents the processing steps and business logic. The next section explains how to write process descriptions.

1. The process number identifies this process. Any subprocesses are numbered 1.1, 1.2, 1.3, and so on.
2. These data flows will be described specifically elsewhere in the data dictionary.

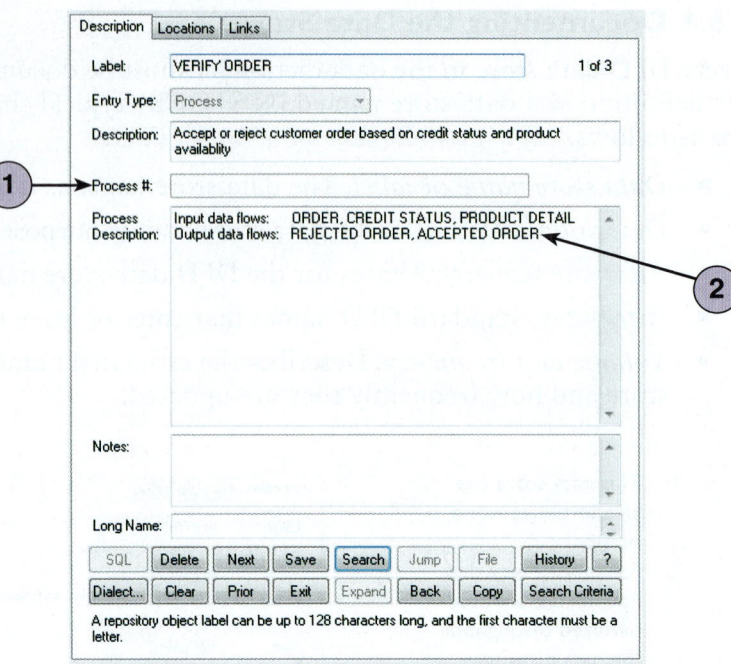

FIGURE 5-22 A Visible Analyst screen that describes a process named VERIFY ORDER

Source: Visible Systems Corporation.

5.6.6 Documenting the Entities

By documenting all entities, the data dictionary can describe all external entities that interact with the system. Typical characteristics of an entity include the following:

- *Entity name.* The entity name as it appears on the DFDs.

- *Description.* Describe the entity and its purpose.

- *Alternate name(s).* Any aliases for the entity name.

- *Input data flows.* The standard DFD names for the input data flows to the entity.

- *Output data flows.* The standard DFD names for the data flows leaving the entity.

5.6.7 Documenting the Records

A record is a data structure that contains a set of related data elements that are stored and processed together. Data flows and data stores consist of records that must be documented in the data dictionary. Characteristics of each record must also be defined, as shown in Figure 5-23.

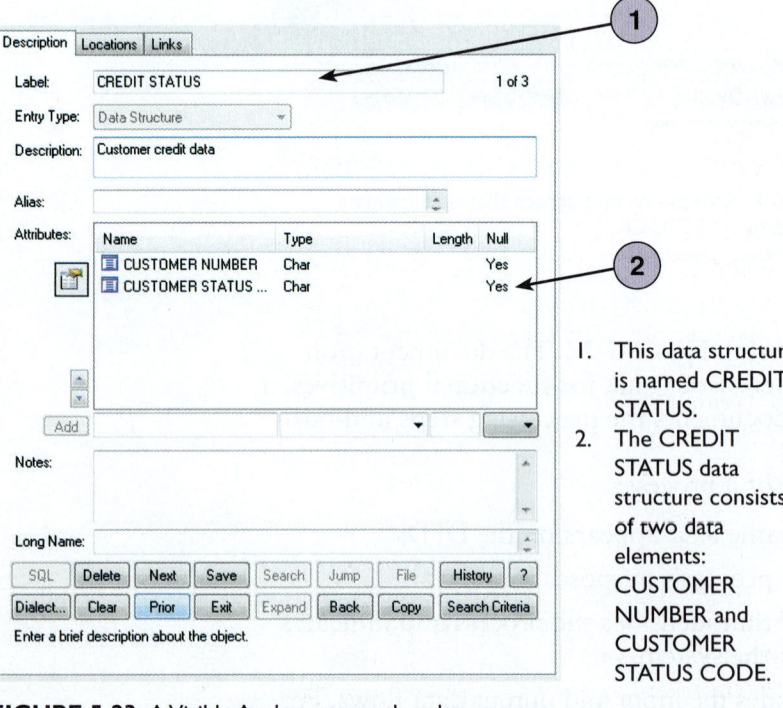

1. This data structure is named CREDIT STATUS.
2. The CREDIT STATUS data structure consists of two data elements: CUSTOMER NUMBER and CUSTOMER STATUS CODE.

FIGURE 5-23 A Visible Analyst screen that documents a record, or data structure, named CREDIT STATUS

Source: Visible Systems Corporation.

Typical characteristics of a record include the following:

- *Record or data structure name.* The record name as it appears in the related data flow and data store entries in the data dictionary.
- *Definition or description.* A brief definition of the record.
- *Alternate name(s).* Any aliases for the record name.
- *Attributes.* A list of all the data elements, or fields, included in the record. The data element names must match exactly those entered in the data dictionary.

5.6.8 Data Dictionary Reports

The data dictionary serves as a central storehouse of documentation for an information system. A data dictionary is created when the system is developed, and is updated constantly as the system is implemented, operated, and maintained. In addition to describing each data element, data flow, data store, record, entity, and process, the data dictionary documents the relationships among these components.

Many valuable reports can be obtained from a data dictionary, including the following:

- An alphabetized list of all data elements by name
- A report describing each data element and indicating the user or department that is responsible for data entry, updating, or deletion
- A report of all data flows and data stores that use a particular data element
- Detailed reports showing all characteristics of data elements, records, data flows, processes, or any other selected item stored in the data dictionary

5.7 PROCESS DESCRIPTION TOOLS

A process description documents the details of a functional primitive and represents a specific set of processing steps and business logic. Using a set of process description tools, a model is created that is accurate, complete, and concise. Typical process description tools include structured English, decision tables, and decision trees. When a functional primitive is analyzed, the processing steps are broken down into smaller units in a process called modular design.

It should be noted that this chapter deals with structured analysis, but the process description tools can also be used in object-oriented development, which is described in Chapter 6. As explained in Chapter 1, O-O analysis combines data and the processes that act on the data into things called objects, and similar objects can be grouped together into classes, and O-O processes are called methods. Although O-O programmers use different terminology, they create the same kind of modular coding structures, except that the processes, or methods, are stored inside the objects, rather than as separate components.

5.7.1 Modular Design

Modular design is based on combinations of three logical structures, sometimes called control structures, which serve as building blocks for the process. Each logical structure must have a single entry and exit point. The three structures are called sequence, selection, and iteration. A rectangle represents a step or process, a diamond shape represents a condition or decision, and the logic follows the lines in the direction indicated by the arrows.

FIGURE 5-24 Sequence structure.

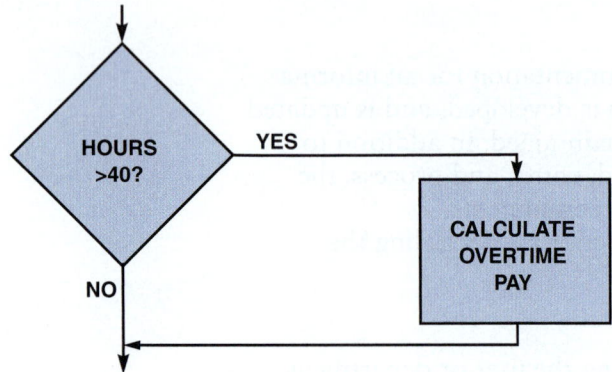

FIGURE 5-25 Selection structure.

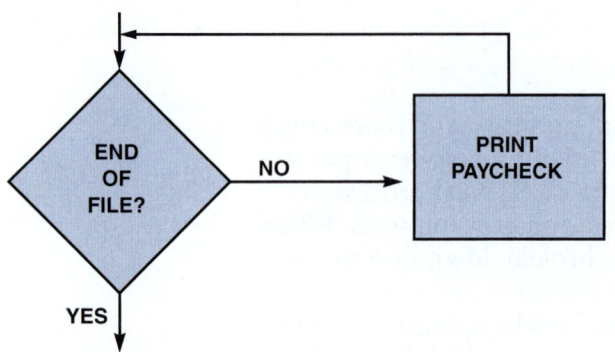

FIGURE 5-26 Iteration structure.

1. **Sequence.** The completion of steps in sequential order, one after another, as shown in Figure 5-24. One or more of the steps might represent a subprocess that contains additional logical structures.

2. **Selection.** The completion of one of two or more process steps based on the results of a test or condition. In the example shown in Figure 5-25, the system tests the input, and if the hours are greater than 40, it performs the CALCULATE OVERTIME PAY process.

3. **Iteration.** The completion of a process step that is repeated until a specific condition changes, as shown in Figure 5-26. An example of iteration is a process that continues to print paychecks until it reaches the end of the payroll file. Iteration also is called **looping.**

Sequence, selection, and iteration structures can be combined in various ways to describe processing logic.

5.7.2 Structured English

Structured English is a subset of standard English that describes logical processes clearly and accurately. When using structured English, be mindful of the following guidelines:

- Use only the three building blocks of sequence, selection, and iteration.

- Use indentation for readability.

- Use a limited vocabulary, including standard terms used in the data dictionary and specific words that describe the processing rules.

An example of structured English appears in Figure 5-27, which shows the VERIFY ORDER process that was illustrated earlier. Notice that the structured English version documents the actual logic that will be coded into the system. Structured English can help process descriptions accurate and understandable to users and system developers.

Structured English might look familiar to programming students because it resembles **pseudocode,** which is used in program design. Although the techniques are similar, the primary purpose of structured English is to describe the underlying business logic, while programmers, who are concerned with coding, mainly use pseudocode as a shorthand notation for the actual code.

Following structured English rules ensures that process descriptions are understandable to users who must confirm that the process is correct, as well as to other analysts and programmers who must design the information system from the descriptions.

5.7.3 Decision Tables

A decision table is a logical structure that shows every combination of conditions and outcomes. Analysts often use decision tables to describe a process and ensure that they have considered all possible situations. Decision tables can be created using tools such as Microsoft PowerPoint, Word, or Excel.

TABLES WITH ONE CONDITION:
If a process has a single condition, there only are two possibilities — *yes* or *no*. Either the condition is present or it is not, so there are only two rules. For example, to trigger an overtime calculation, the process condition might be: *Are the hours greater than 40?* If so, the calculation is made. Otherwise, it is not.

TABLES WITH TWO CONDITIONS:
Suppose there is a need to create a decision table based on the VERIFY

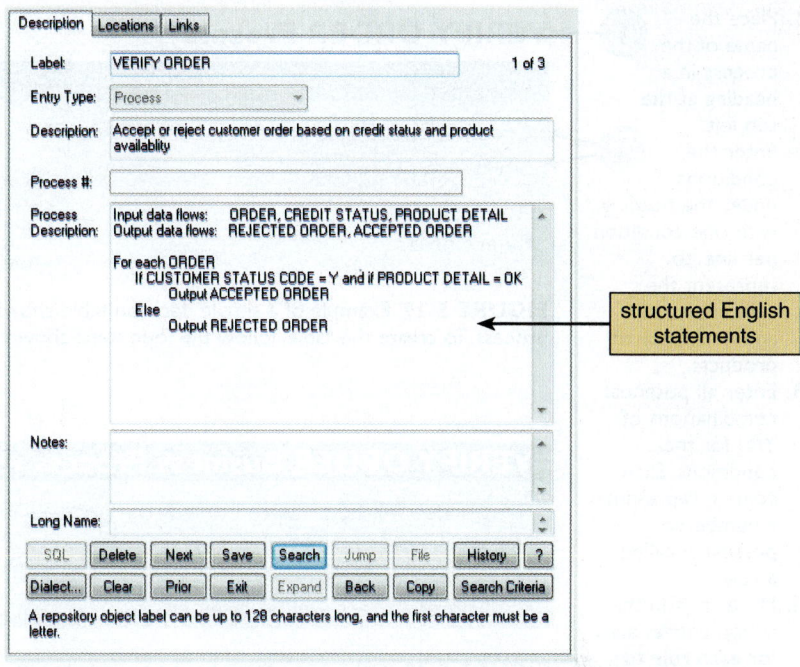

FIGURE 5-27 The VERIFY ORDER process description includes logical rules and a structured English version of the policy. Notice the alignment and indentation of the logic statements.

Source: Visible Systems Corporation.

ORDER business process shown in Figure 5-28. When documenting a process, it is important to ensure that every possibility is listed. In this example, the process description contains two conditions: product stock status and customer credit status. If *both* conditions are met, the order is accepted. Otherwise the order is rejected.

VERIFY ORDER Business Process with Two Conditions

• An order will be accepted only if the product is in stock and the customer's credit status is OK.

• All other orders will be rejected.

FIGURE 5-28 The VERIFY ORDER business process has two conditions. For an order to be accepted, the product must be in stock and the customer must have an acceptable credit status.

After all the conditions and outcomes have been identified, the next step is to create a decision table similar to the one shown in Figure 5-29. Notice that each condition has two possible values, so the number of rules doubles each time another condition is added. For example, one condition creates two rules, two conditions create four rules, three conditions create eight rules, and so on. In the two-condition example in Figure 5-29, four possibilities exist, but Rule 1 is the *only* combination that will accept an order.

TABLES WITH THREE CONDITIONS: Suppose the company now decides that the credit manager can waive the customer credit requirement, as shown in Figure 5-30. That creates a third condition, so there will be eight possible rules. The new decision table might resemble the one shown in Figure 5-31.

1. Place the name of the process in a heading at the top left.
2. Enter the conditions under the heading, with one condition per line, to represent the customer status and availability of products.
3. Enter all potential combinations of Y/N for the conditions. Each column represents a numbered possibility called a rule.
4. Place an X in the action entries area for each rule to indicate whether to accept or reject the order.

VERIFY ORDER Process

	1	2	3	4
Credit status is OK	Y	Y	N	N
Product is in stock	Y	N	Y	N
Accept order	X			
Reject order		X	X	X

FIGURE 5-29 Example of a simple decision table showing the processing logic of the VERIFY ORDER process. To create the table, follow the four steps shown.

VERIFY ORDER Business Process with Three Conditions

- An order will be accepted only if the product is in stock and the customer's credit status is OK.
- The credit manager can waive the credit status requirement.
- All other orders will be rejected.

FIGURE 5-30 A third condition has been added to the VERIFY ORDER business process. For an order to be accepted, the product must be in stock and the customer must have an acceptable credit status. However, the credit manager now has the authority to waive the credit status requirements.

First, the Y-N patterns must be filled in, as shown in Figure 5-31. The best way to assure that all combinations appear is to use patterns like these. The first condition uses a pattern of Y-Y-Y-Y followed by N-N-N-N; the second condition uses a repeating Y-Y-N-N pattern; and the pattern in the third condition is a series of Y-Ns.

VERIFY ORDER Process with Credit Waiver (initial version)

	1	2	3	4	5	6	7	8
Credit status is OK	Y	Y	Y	Y	N	N	N	N
Product is in stock	Y	Y	N	N	Y	Y	N	N
Waiver from credit manager	Y	N	Y	N	Y	N	Y	N
Accept order	X	X			X			
Reject order			X	X		X	X	X

FIGURE 5-31 This decision table is based on the VERIFY ORDER conditions shown in Figure 5-30. With three conditions, there are eight possible combinations, or rules.

The next step is very important, regardless of the number of conditions. Each numbered column, or rule, represents a different set of conditions. The logic must be carefully analyzed and the outcome for each rule shown. Before going further, study the table in Figure 5-31 to be sure the logical outcome for each of the eight rules is understood.

When all the outcomes have been determined, the next step is to simplify the table. In a multicondition table, some rules might be duplicates, redundant, or unrealistic. To simplify the table, follow these steps:

1. Study each combination of conditions and outcomes. When there are rules with three conditions, only one or two of them may control the outcome, and the other conditions simply do not matter.

2. If there are conditions that do not affect the outcome, mark them with dashes (-) as shown in the first table in Figure 5-32.

3. Now combine and renumber the rules, as shown in the second table in Figure 5-32.

After following these steps, Rules 1 and 2 can be combined, because credit status is OK in both rules, so the waiver would not matter. Rules 3, 4, 7, and 8 also can be combined because the product is not in stock, so other conditions do not matter. The result is that instead of eight possibilities, only four logical rules control the Verify Order process.

VERIFY ORDER Process with Credit Waiver (with rules marked for combination)

	1	2	3	4	5	6	7	8
Credit status is OK	Y	Y	-	-	N	N	-	-
Product is in stock	Y	Y	N	N	Y	Y	N	N
Waiver from credit manager	-	-	-	-	Y	N	-	-
Accept order	X	X			X			
Reject order			X	X		X	X	X

1. Because the product is not in stock, the other conditions do not matter.
2. Because the other conditions are met, the waiver does not matter.

VERIFY ORDER Process with Credit Waiver (after rule combination and simplification)

	1 (COMBINES PREVIOUS 1, 2)	2 (PREVIOUS 5)	3 (PREVIOUS 6)	4 (COMBINES PREVIOUS 3, 4, 7, 8)
Credit status is OK	Y	N	N	-
Product is in stock	Y	Y	Y	N
Waiver from credit manager	-	Y	N	-
Accept order	X	X		
Reject order			X	X

FIGURE 5-32 In the first decision table, dashes have been added to indicate that a condition is not relevant. In the second version of the decision table, rules have been combined following the steps shown below. Notice that in the final version, only four rules remain. These rules document the logic and will be transformed into program code when the system is developed.

MULTIPLE OUTCOMES: In addition to multiple conditions, decision tables can have more than two possible outcomes. For example, the sales promotion policy shown in Figure 5-33 includes three conditions: Was the customer a preferred customer, did the customer order $1,000 or more, and did the customer use our company charge card? Based on these conditions, four possible actions can occur, as shown in the decision table in Figure 5-34.

SALES PROMOTION POLICY – Holiday Season

- Preferred customers who order $1,000 or more are entitled to a 5% discount, and an additional 5% discount if they use our charge card.

- Preferred customers who do not order $1,000 or more will receive a $25 bonus coupon.

- All other customers will receive a $5 bonus coupon.

FIGURE 5-33 A sales promotion policy with three conditions. Notice that the first statement contains two separate conditions: one for the 5% discount, and another for the additional discount.

Sales Promotion Policy (initial version)

	1	2	3	4	5	6	7	8
Preferred customer	Y	Y	Y	Y	N	N	N	N
Ordered $1,000 or more	Y	Y	N	N	Y	Y	N	N
Used our charge card	Y	N	Y	N	Y	N	Y	N
5% discount	X	X						
Additional 5% discount	X							
$25 bonus coupon			X	X				
$5 bonus coupon					X	X	X	X

FIGURE 5-34 This decision table is based on the sales promotion policy in Figure 5-33. This is the initial version of the table, before simplification.

As explained in the preceding section, most tables can be simplified, and this one is no exception. After studying the conditions and outcomes, the following becomes apparent:

- In Rule 1, all three conditions are met, so *both* 5% discounts apply.

- In Rule 2, a preferred customer orders $1,000 or more, but does not use our charge card, so only *one* 5% discount applies.

- Rules 3 and 4 can be combined into a single rule. Why? If preferred customers do not order $1,000 or more, it does not matter whether they use our charge card — either way, they earn only a $25 bonus coupon. Therefore, Rules 3 and 4 really are a single rule.

- Rules 5, 6, 7, and 8 also can be combined into a single rule — because if the person is *not* a preferred customer, he or she can *only* receive a $5 bonus coupon, and the other conditions simply do not matter. A dash is inserted if a condition is irrelevant, as shown in Figure 5-35.

If dashes are added for rules that are not relevant, the table should resemble the one shown in Figure 5-35. When the results are combined and simplified, only four rules remain: Rule 1, Rule 2, Rule 3 (a combination of initial Rules 3 and 4), and Rule 4 (a combination of initial Rules 5, 6, 7, and 8).

Decision tables often are the best way to describe a complex set of conditions. Many analysts use decision tables because they are easy to construct and understand, and programmers find it easy to work from a decision table when developing code.

Sales Promotion Policy (final version)

	1	2	3	4	5	6	7	8
Preferred customer	Y	Y	Y	Y	N	N	N	N
Ordered $1,000 or more	Y	Y	N	N	-	-	-	-
Used our charge card	Y	N	-	-	-	-	-	-
5% discount	X	X						
Additional 5% discount	X							
$25 bonus coupon			X	X				
$5 bonus coupon					X	X	X	X

FIGURE 5-35 In this version of the decision table, dashes have been added to indicate that a condition is not relevant. As this point, it appears that several rules can be combined.

CASE IN POINT 5.2:   ROCK SOLID OUTFITTERS (PART 1)

Leah Jones is the IT manager at Rock Solid Outfitters, a medium-sized supplier of outdoor climbing and camping gear. Steve Allen, the marketing director, has asked Leah to develop a special web-based promotion. As Steve described it to Leah, Rock Solid will provide free shipping for any customer who either completes an online survey form or signs up for the Rock Solid online newsletter. Additionally, if a customer completes the survey and signs up for the newsletter, Rock Solid will provide a $10 merchandise credit for orders of $100 or more. Leah has asked you to develop a decision table that will reflect the promotional rules that a programmer will use. She wants you to show all possibilities, and then to simplify the results to eliminate any combinations that would be unrealistic or redundant.

5.7.4 Decision Trees

A **decision tree** is a graphical representation of the conditions, actions, and rules found in a decision table. Decision trees show the logic structure in a horizontal form that resembles a tree with the roots at the left and the branches to the right. Like flowcharts, decision trees are useful ways to present the system to management. Decision trees and decision tables provide the same results, but in different forms. In many situations, a graphic is the most effective means of communication.

Figure 5-36 is based on the sales promotion policy shown in Figure 5-33. A decision tree is read from left to right, with the conditions along the various branches and the actions at the far right. Because the example has two conditions with four resulting sets of actions, the example has four terminating branches at the right side of the tree.

Whether to use a decision table or a decision tree often is a matter of personal preference. A decision table might be a better way to handle complex combinations of conditions. On the other hand, a decision tree is an effective way to describe a relatively simple process.

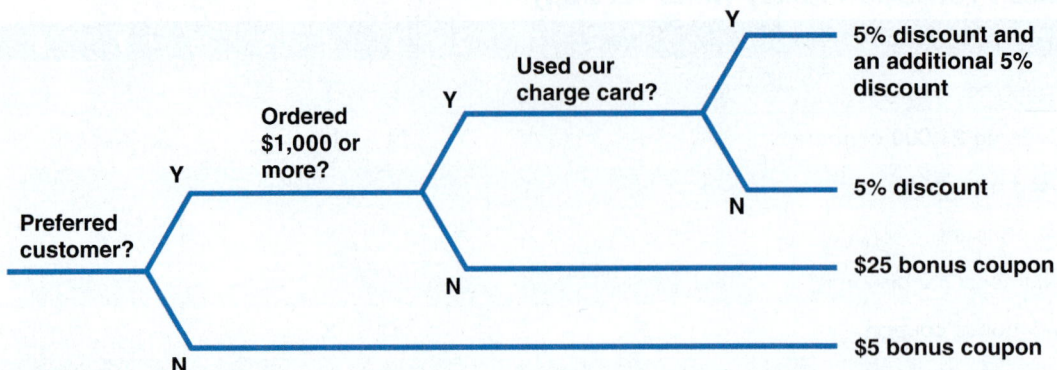

FIGURE 5-36 This decision tree example is based on the same Sales Promotion Policy shown in the decision tables in Figures 5-34 and 5-35. Like a decision table, a decision tree shows all combinations of conditions and outcomes. The main difference is the graphical format, which some viewers may find easier to interpret.

CASE IN POINT 5.3:   ROCK SOLID OUTFITTERS (PART 2)

Leah Jones, the IT manager at Rock Solid Outfitters, thinks you did a good job on the decision table task she assigned to you. Now she wants you to use the same data to develop a decision tree that will show all the possibilities for the web-based promotion described in Part 1 of the case. She also wants you to discuss the pros and cons of decision tables versus decision trees.

5.8 LOGICAL VERSUS PHYSICAL MODELS

While structured analysis tools are used to develop a logical model for a new information system, such tools can also be used to develop physical models of an information system. A physical model shows how the system's requirements are implemented. During the systems design phase, a physical model of the new information system is created that follows from the logical model and involves operational tasks and techniques.

5.8.1 Sequence of Models

To understand the relationship between logical and physical models, think back to the beginning of the systems analysis phase. To understand how the current tasks were carried out the existing system, the physical operations of the existing system were studied before the logical model. Many systems analysts create a physical model of the current system and then develop a logical model of the current system before tackling a logical model of the new system. Performing that extra step allows them to understand the current system better.

5.8.2 Four-Model Approach

Many analysts follow a **four-model approach**, which means that they develop a physical model of the current system, a logical model of the current system, a logical model of the new system, and a physical model of the new system. The major benefit of the four-model approach is that it provides a clear picture of current system functions before any modifications or improvements are made. That is important because mistakes made early in systems development will affect later SDLC phases and can result in unhappy users and additional costs. Taking additional steps to avoid these potentially costly mistakes can prove to be well worth the effort. Another advantage is that the requirements of a new information system often are quite similar to those of the current information system, especially where the proposal is based on new computer technology rather than a large number of new requirements. Adapting the current system logical model to the new system logical model in these cases is a straightforward process.

The only disadvantage of the four-model approach is the added time and cost needed to develop a logical and physical model of the current system. Most projects have very tight schedules that might not allow time to create the current system models. Additionally, users and managers want to see progress on the new system — they are much less concerned about documenting the current system. The systems analyst must stress the importance of careful documentation and resist the pressure to hurry the development process at the risk of creating serious problems later.

CASE IN POINT 5.4:   TIP TOP STAFFING

Tip Top Staffing supplies employees to hundreds of IT firms that require specialized skills for specific projects. Systems analysts Lisa Nuevo and Bill Goodman are working on the logical model of Tip Top's billing and records system, using DFDs, a data dictionary, and process descriptions. At some point while working on the logical model of the system, Lisa felt that some improvements should be made in the data forms that Tip Top uses to obtain information about job applicants. Was the subject of improving the forms a physical implementation issue? Is Lisa going off on a tangent by considering how something will be done, instead of sticking to what will be done?

A QUESTION OF ETHICS

iStockphoto.com/faberfoto_it

This is your first week in your new job at Safety Zone, a leading producer of IT modeling software. Your prior experience with a smaller competitor gave you an edge in landing the job, and you are excited about joining a larger company in the same field.

So far, all is going well and you are getting used to the new routine. However, you are concerned about one issue. In your initial meeting with the IT manager, she seemed very interested in the details of your prior position, and some of her questions made you a little uncomfortable. She did not actually ask you to reveal any proprietary information, but she made it clear that Safety Zone likes to know as much as possible about its competitors.

Thinking about it some more, you try to draw a line between information that is OK to discuss, and topics such as software specifics or strategy that should be considered private. This is the first time you have ever been in a situation like this. How will you handle it?

5.9 CHAPTER SUMMARY

During data and process modeling, a systems analyst develops graphical models to show how the system transforms data into useful information. The end product of data and process modeling is a logical model that will support business operations and meet user needs. Data and process modeling involves three main tools: data flow diagrams, a data dictionary, and process descriptions.

Data flow diagrams (DFDs) graphically show the movement and transformation of data in the information system. DFDs use four symbols: The process symbol transforms data; the data flow symbol shows data movement; the data store symbol shows data at rest; and the external entity symbol represents someone or something connected to the information system. Various rules and techniques are used to name, number, arrange, and annotate the set of DFDs to make them consistent and understandable.

A set of DFDs is like a pyramid with the context diagram at the top. The context diagram represents the information system's scope and its external connections but not its internal workings. Diagram 0 displays the information system's major processes, data stores, and data flows and is the exploded version of the context diagram's process symbol, which represents the entire information system. Lower-level DFDs show additional detail of the information system through the leveling technique of numbering and partitioning. Leveling continues until the functional primitive processes are reached, which are not decomposed further and are documented with process descriptions. All diagrams must be balanced to ensure their consistency and accuracy.

The data dictionary is the central documentation tool for structured analysis. All data elements, data flows, data stores, processes, entities, and records are documented in the data dictionary. Consolidating documentation in one location allows the analyst to verify the information system's accuracy and consistency more easily and generate a variety of useful reports.

Each functional primitive process is documented using structured English, decision tables, and decision trees. Structured English uses a subset of standard English that defines each process with combinations of the basic building blocks of sequence, selection, and iteration. Using decision tables or decision trees can also document the logic.

Structured analysis tools can be used to develop a logical model during one systems analysis phase and a physical model during the systems design phase. Many analysts use a four-model approach, which involves a physical model of the current system, a logical model of the current system, a logical model of the new system, and a physical model of the new system.

Key Terms

alias A term used in various data dictionaries to indicate an alternate name, or a name other than the standard data element name, that is used to describe the same data element.

balancing A process used to maintain consistency among an entire series of diagrams, including input and output data flows, data definition, and process descriptions.

black box A metaphor for a process or action that produces results in a non-transparent or non-observable manner. In data flow diagrams, a process appears as a black box where the inputs, outputs, and general function of the process are known, but the underlying details are not shown.

black hole A process that has no output.

business logic Rules to determine how a system handles data and produces useful information, reflecting the operational requirements of the business. Examples include adding the proper amount of sales tax to invoices, calculating customer balances and finance charges, and determining whether a customer is eligible for a volume-based discount. Also called **business rules**.

business rules *See* **business logic**.

child diagram The lower-level diagram in an exploded data flow diagram.

context diagram A top-level view of an information system that shows the boundaries and scope.

control structure Serve as building blocks for a process. Control structures have one entry and exit point. They may be completed in sequential order, as the result of a test or condition, or repeated until a specific condition changes. Also called **logical structure**.

data dictionary A central storehouse of information about a system's data.

data element A single characteristic or fact about an entity. A data element, field, or attribute is the smallest piece of data that has meaning within an information system. For example, a Social Security number or company name could be examples of a data element. Also called **data item**.

data flow A path for data to move from one part of the information system to another.

data item *See* **data element**.

data repository A symbol used in data flow diagrams to represent a situation in which a system must retain data because one or more processes need to use that stored data at a later time. Used interchangeably with the term **data store**.

data store *See* **data repository**.

data structure A meaningful combination of related data elements that is included in a data flow or retained in a data store. A framework for organizing and storing data.

decision table A table that shows a logical structure, with all possible combinations of conditions and resulting actions.

decision tree A graphical representation of the conditions, actions, and rules found in a decision table.

decomposing Another way of conveying a process or system that has been broken down from a general, top-level view to more detail. The terms exploded and partitioned can also be used.

diagram 0 A diagram depicting the first level of detail below the initial context diagram. Diagram 0 (zero) zooms in on the context diagram and shows major processes, data flows, and data stores, as well as repeating the external entities and data flows that appear in the context diagram.

diverging data flow A data flow in which the same data travels to two or more different locations.

domain The set of values permitted for a data element.

entity A person, place, thing, or event for which data is collected and maintained. For example, an online sales system may include entities named CUSTOMER, ORDER, PRODUCT, and SUPPLIER.

exploding A diagram is said to be exploded if it "drills down" to a more detailed or expanded view.

field A single characteristic or fact about an entity. A field, or attribute, is the smallest piece of data that has meaning within an information system. For example, a Social Security number or company name could be examples of a field. The terms *data element*, *data item*, and *field* are used interchangeably.

four-model approach A physical model of the current system, a logical model of the current system, a logical model of the new system, and a physical model of the new system are all developed.

functional primitive A single function that is not exploded further. The logic for functional primitives is documented in a data dictionary process description.

Gane and Sarson A popular symbol set used in data flow diagrams. Processes, data flows, data stores, and external entities all have a unique symbol.

gray hole A process with an input obviously insufficient to generate the shown output.

iteration The completion of a process step that is repeated until a specific condition changes.

leveling The process of drawing a series of increasingly detailed diagrams to reach the desired level of detail.

logical model Shows what a system must do, regardless of how it will be implemented physically.

logical structure *See* **control structure**.

looping Refers to a process step that is repeated until a specific condition changes. For example, a process that continues to print paychecks until it reaches the end of the payroll file is looping. Also known as repetition.

modular design A design that can be broken down into logical blocks. Also known as partitioning or top-down design.

parent diagram The higher or more top-level diagram in an exploded data flow diagram.

partitioning The breaking down of overall objectives into subsystems and modules.

physical model A model that describes how a system will be constructed.

process 0 In a data flow diagram, process 0 (zero) represents the entire information system, but does not show the internal workings.

process description A documentation of a functional primitive's details, which represents a specific set of processing steps and business logic.

pseudocode A technique for representing program logic.

record A set of related fields that describes one instance, or member of an entity, such as one customer, one order, or one product. A record might have one or dozens of fields, depending on what information is needed. Also called a tuple.

selection A control structure in modular design, it is the completion of two or more process steps based on the results of a test or condition.

sequence The completion of steps in sequential order, one after another.

sink An external entity that receives data from an information system.

source An external entity that supplies data to an information system.

spontaneous generation An unexplained generation of data or information. With respect to data flow diagrams, processes cannot spontaneously generate data flows — they must have an input to have an output.

structured English A subset of standard English that describes logical processes clearly and accurately.

terminator A data flow diagram symbol that indicates a data origin or final destination. Also called an external entity.

validity rule Check that is applied to data elements when data is entered to ensure that the value entered is valid. For example, a validity rule might require that an employee's salary number be within the employer's predefined range for that position.

Yourdon A type of symbol set that is used in data flow diagrams. Processes, data flows, data stores, and external entities each have a unique symbol in the Yourdon symbol set.

Chapter Exercises

Questions

1. Describe data and process modeling concepts and tools.
2. Explain the differences between Gane and Sarson and Yourdon symbols. Provide examples of symbols that represent processes, data flows, data stores, and entities.
3. What is the difference between a context diagram and diagram 0? Which symbol is *not* used in a context diagram?
4. How would you *explode* DFDs?
5. Describe a data dictionary and list the types of information it contains.
6. How would you level DFDs?
7. How would you balance DFDs?
8. What is the purpose of decision tables? How do you create them?
9. Why would a manager prefer a decision tree instead of a decision table?
10. What is structured English?

Discussion Topics

1. Suppose you were assigned to develop a logical model of the registration system at a school or college. Would you be better off using a top-down approach, or would a bottom-up strategy be better? What would influence your decision?
2. Some systems analysts find it better to start with a decision table, and then construct a decision tree. Others believe it is easier to do it in the reverse order. Which do you prefer? Why?
3. What are some of the benefits and shortcomings of using CASE tools for process modeling activities?
4. A systems analyst attended a weeklong workshop on structured analysis. When she returned to her job, she told her boss that structured analysis was not worth the time to learn and use on the job. Her view was that it was too academic and had too much new terminology to be useful. Do you agree? Why or why not?
5. This chapter describes a *black box* concept that allows more detail to be shown as a process is exploded. Can the concept be applied in business management generally, or is it limited to information systems design? Provide some reasons and examples.

Projects

1. Draw a context diagram and a diagram 0 DFD that represents the information system at a typical library.
2. On the Internet, locate at least three firms that offer CASE tools as shareware or free, public domain software. Describe what you found.
3. Explore the use of Structured English to describe processes in fields other than systems analysis.
4. Create a decision table with three conditions. You can make one up, or use a scenario from everyday life. Either way, be sure to show all possible outcomes.
5. The data flow symbols shown in Figure 5-1 were designed by Ed Yourdon, a well-known IT author, lecturer, and consultant. Many IT professionals consider him to be among the most influential men and women in the software field. Learn more about Mr. Yourdon by visiting his website at *www.yourdon.com*, and write a brief review of his work.

CHAPTER 6 Object Modeling

Chapter 6 is the third of four chapters in the systems analysis phase of the SDLC. This chapter discusses object modeling techniques that analysts use to create a logical model. In addition to structured analysis, object-oriented analysis is another way to represent and design an information system.

The chapter includes four "Case in Point" discussion questions to help contextualize the concepts described in the text. A "Question of Ethics" considers the situation where an employee wants to skip a course and just sit the exam, and requests a copy of the training materials from someone else who took the course.

LEARNING OBJECTIVES

When you finish this chapter, you should be able to:

- Explain how object-oriented analysis can be used to describe an information system
- Define object modeling terms and concepts, including objects, attributes, methods, messages, classes, and instances
- Explain relationships among objects and the concept of inheritance
- Draw an object relationship diagram
- Describe Unified Modeling Language (UML) tools and techniques, including use cases, use case diagrams, class diagrams, sequence diagrams, state transition diagrams, and activity diagrams
- Explain the advantages of using CASE tools in developing the object model
- Explain how to organize an object model

CHAPTER CONTENTS

6.1 INTRODUCTION

Chapter 5 explained how to use structured analysis techniques to develop a data and process model of the proposed system. Chapter 6 explains object-oriented analysis, which is another way to view and model system requirements. This chapter illustrates the use of object-oriented techniques to document, analyze, and model the information system. Chapter 7, which concludes the systems analysis phase, describes how to evaluate alternatives, develop the system requirements document, and prepare for the systems design phase of the SDLC.

6.2 OVERVIEW OF OBJECT-ORIENTED ANALYSIS

As stated in Chapter 1, the most popular systems development options are structured analysis, object-oriented (O-O) analysis, and agile methods, also called adaptive methods. The table in Figure 1-17 shows the three alternatives and describes some pros and cons for each approach. As the table indicates, O-O methodology is popular because it integrates easily with O-O programming languages such as Java, Smalltalk, VB.Net, Python, and Perl. Programmers also like O-O code because it is modular, reusable, and easy to maintain.

Object-oriented (O-O) analysis describes an information system by identifying things called objects. An object represents a real person, a place, an event, or a transaction. For example, when a patient makes an appointment to see a doctor, the patient is an object, the doctor is an object, and the appointment itself is an object.

Object-oriented analysis is a popular approach that sees a system from the viewpoint of the objects themselves as they function and interact. The end product of O-O analysis is an **object model**, which represents the information system in terms of objects and O-O concepts.

6.2.1 Object-Oriented Terms and Concepts

Chapter 4 stated that the Unified Modeling Language (UML) is a widely used method of visualizing and documenting an information system. In this chapter, the UML is used to develop object models. The first step is to understand basic O-O terms, including objects, attributes, methods, messages, classes, and instances. This chapter shows how systems analysts use those terms to describe an information system.

An object represents a person, a place, an event, or a transaction that is significant to the information system. In Chapter 5, DFDs were created that treated data and processes separately. An object, however, includes data *and* the processes that affect that data. For example, a customer object has a name, an address, an account number, and a current balance. Customer objects also can perform specific tasks, such as placing an order, paying a bill, and changing their address.

An object has certain **attributes**, which are characteristics that describe the object. For example, a car has attributes such as make, model, and color. An object also has **methods**, which are tasks or functions that the object performs when it receives a **message**, or command, to do so. For example, a car performs a method called OPERATE WIPERS when it is sent a message with the wiper control, and it can APPLY BRAKES when it is sent a message by pressing the brake pedal. Figure 6-1 shows examples of attributes, messages, and methods for a car object.

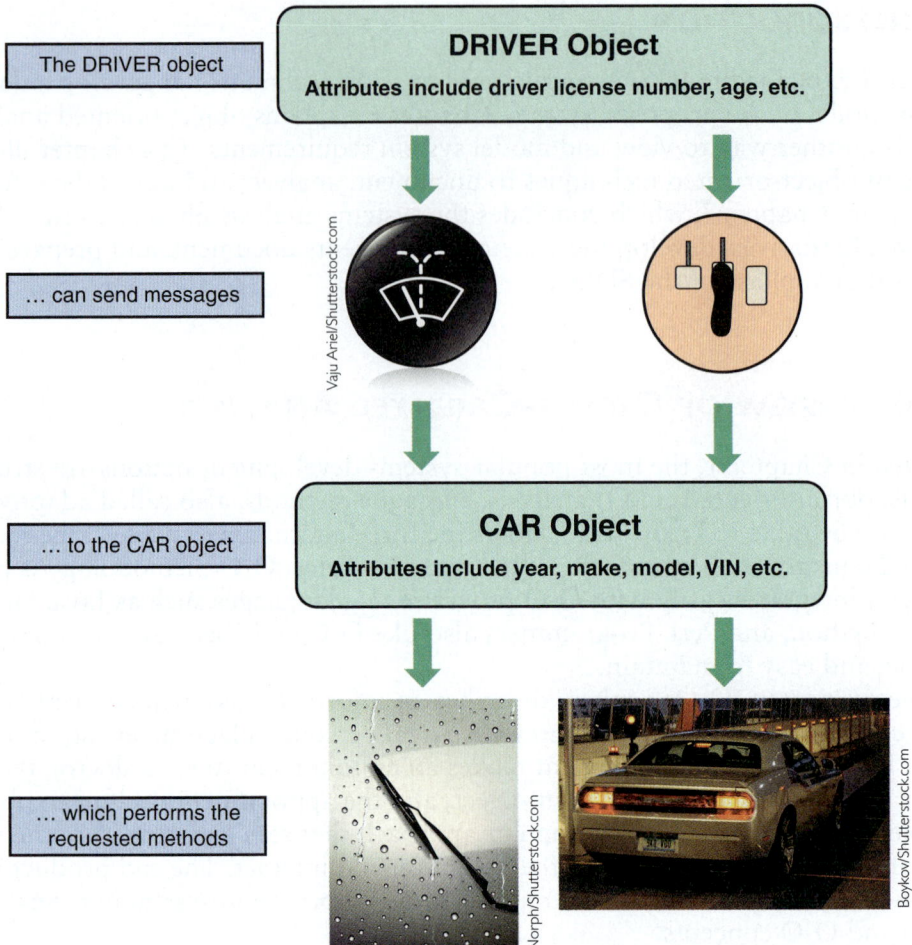

FIGURE 6-1 Objects have attributes, can send and receive messages, and perform actions called methods.

A class is a group of similar objects. For example, Ford Fiestas belong to a class called CAR. An **instance** is a specific member of a class. A Toyota Camry, for example, is an instance of the CAR class. At an auto dealership many instances of the CAR class may be observed: the TRUCK class, the MINIVAN class, and the SPORT UTILITY VEHICLE class, among others. Although the term "object" usually refers to a particular instance, systems analysts sometimes use the term to refer to a class of objects. Usually the meaning is understood from the context and the way the term is used.

6.2.2 Objects

Consider a simplistic example of how the UML might describe a family with parents and children. UML represents an object as a rectangle with the object name at the top, followed by the object's attributes and methods.

Figure 6-2 shows a PARENT object with certain attributes such as name, age, sex, and hair color. If there are two parents, then there are two instances of the PARENT object. The PARENT object can perform methods, such as reading a bedtime story, driving the carpool van, or preparing a school lunch. When a PARENT object receives a message, it performs an action, or method.

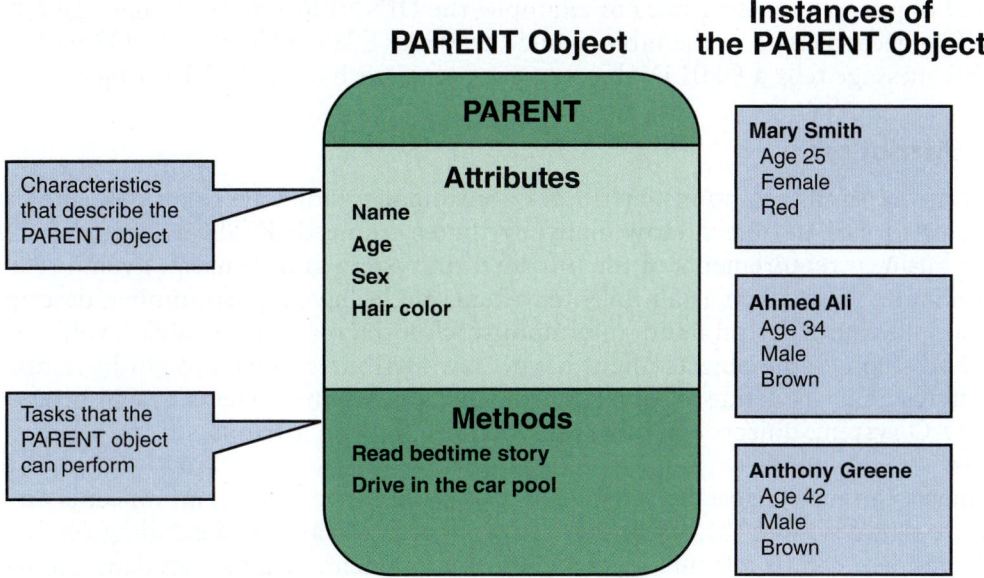

FIGURE 6-2 The PARENT object has four attributes and two methods. Mary Smith, Ahmed Ali, and Anthony Greene are instances of the PARENT object.

For example, the message GOOD NIGHT from a child might tell the PARENT object to read a bedtime story, while the message DRIVE from another parent signals that it is the PARENT object's turn to drive in the car pool.

Continuing with the family example, the CHILD object in Figure 6-3 possesses the same attributes as the PARENT object and an additional attribute that shows the number of siblings. A CHILD object performs certain methods, such as picking up toys, eating dinner, playing, cooperating, and getting ready for bed. To signal the CHILD object to perform those tasks, a parent can send certain messages that the

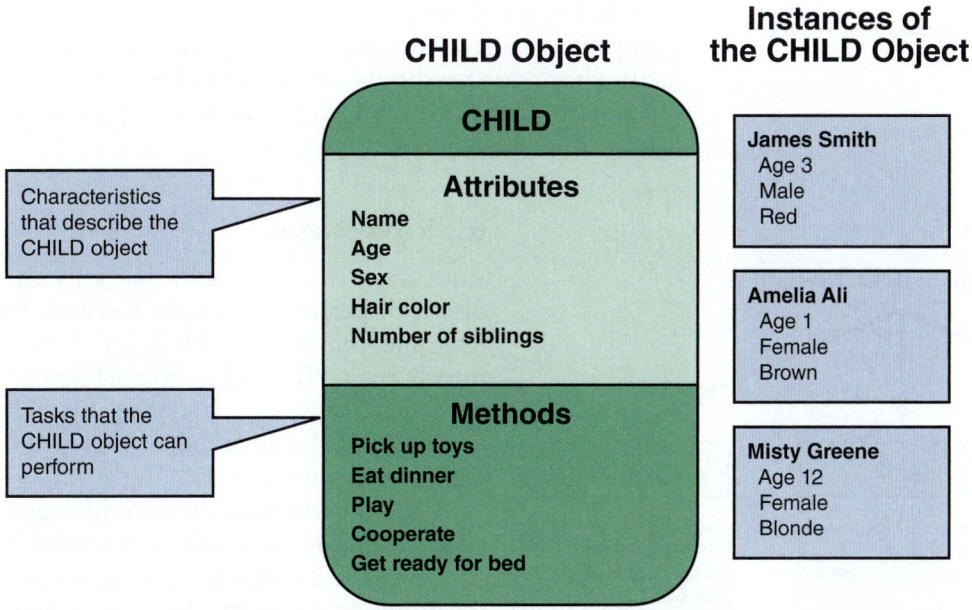

FIGURE 6-3 The CHILD object has five attributes and five methods. James Smith, Amelia Ali, and Misty Greene are instances of the CHILD object.

CHILD object will understand. For example, the DINNER'S READY message tells a CHILD object to come to the table, while the SHARE WITH YOUR BROTHER/ SISTER message tells a CHILD object to cooperate with other CHILD objects.

6.2.3 Attributes

If objects are similar to nouns, attributes are similar to adjectives that describe the characteristics of an object. How many attributes are needed? The answer depends on the business requirements of the information system and its users. Even a relatively simple object, such as an inventory item, might have a part number, description, supplier, quantity on hand, minimum stock level, maximum stock level, reorder time, and so on. Some objects might have a few attributes; others might have dozens.

Systems analysts define an object's attributes during the systems design process. In an O-O system, objects can inherit, or acquire, certain attributes from other objects.

Objects can have a specific attribute called a state. The state of an object is an adjective that describes the object's current status. For example, depending on the state, a student can be a future student, a current student, or a past student. Similarly, a bank account can be active, inactive, closed, or frozen.

Method:	Steps:
MORE FRIES	1. Heat oil
	2. Fill fry basket with frozen potato strips
	3. Lower basket into hot oil
	4. Check for readiness
	5. When ready raise basket and let drain
	6. Pour fries into warming tray
	7. Add salt

FIGURE 6-4 The MORE FRIES method requires the server to perform seven specific steps.

6.2.4 Methods

A method defines specific tasks that an object can perform. Just as objects are similar to nouns and attributes are similar to adjectives, methods resemble verbs that describe *what* and *how* an object does something.

Consider a server who prepares fries in a fast-food restaurant. A systems analyst might describe the operation as a method called MORE FRIES, as shown in Figure 6-4. The MORE FRIES method includes the steps required to heat the oil, fill the fry basket with frozen potato strips, lower it into the hot oil, check for readiness, remove the basket when ready and drain the oil, pour the fries into a warming tray, and add salt.

6.2.5 Messages

A message is a command that tells an object to perform a certain method. For example, the message PICK UP TOYS directs the CHILD class to perform all the necessary steps to pick up the toys. The CHILD class understands the message and executes the method.

The same message to two different objects can produce different results. The concept that a message gives different meanings to different objects is called polymorphism. For example, in Figure 6-5,

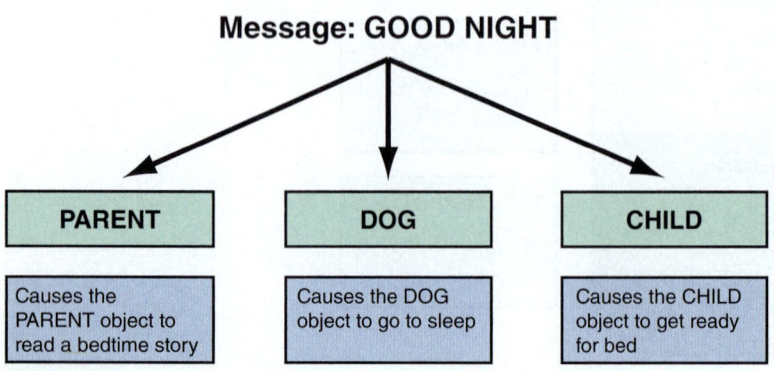

FIGURE 6-5 In an example of polymorphism, the message GOOD NIGHT produces different results, depending on which object receives it.

the message GOOD NIGHT signals the PARENT object to read a bedtime story, but the same message to the CHILD object signals it to get ready for bed. If the family also had a DOG object, the same message would tell the dog to sleep.

An object can be viewed as a black box, because a message to the object triggers changes within the object without specifying how the changes must be carried out. A gas pump is an example of a black box. When the economy grade is selected at a pump, it is not necessary to think about how the pump determines the correct price and selects the right fuel, as long as it does so properly.

The black box concept is an example of **encapsulation**, which means that all data and methods are self-contained. A black box does not want or need outside interference. By limiting access to internal processes, an object prevents its internal code from being altered by another object or process. Encapsulation allows objects to be used as modular components anywhere in the system, because objects send and receive messages but do not alter the internal methods of other objects.

Object-oriented designs typically are implemented with O-O programming languages. The major advantages of O-O designs are that systems analysts can save time and avoid errors by using modular objects, and programmers can translate the designs into code, working with reusable program modules that have been tested and verified. For example, in Figure 6-6, an INSTRUCTOR object sends an ENTER GRADE message to an instance of the STUDENT RECORD class. Notice that the INSTRUCTOR object and STUDENT RECORD class could be reused, with minor modifications, in other school information systems where many of the attributes and methods would be similar.

FIGURE 6-6 In a school information system, an INSTRUCTOR object sends an ENTER GRADE message to an instance of the STUDENT RECORD class.

6.2.6 Classes

An object belongs to a group or category called a class. All objects within a class share common attributes and methods, so a class is like a blueprint, or template for all the objects within the class. Objects within a class can be grouped into **subclasses**, which are more specific categories within a class. For example, TRUCK objects represent a subclass within the VEHICLE class, along with other subclasses called CAR, MINIVAN, and SCHOOL BUS, as shown in Figure 6-7. Notice that all four subclasses share common traits of the VEHICLE class, such as

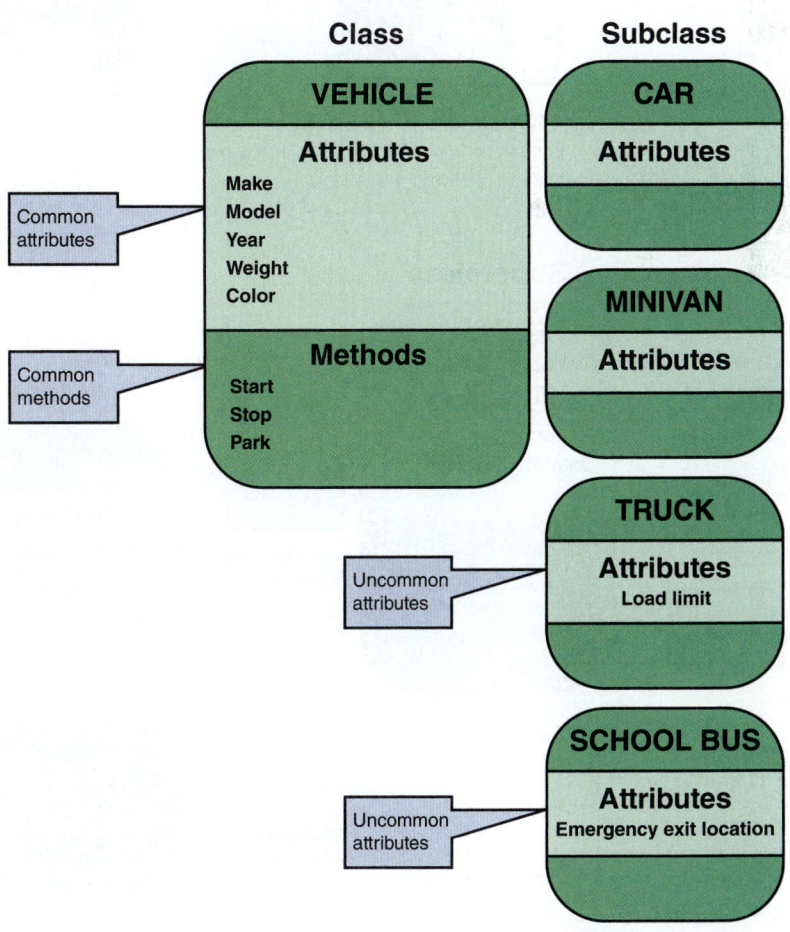

FIGURE 6-7 The VEHICLE class includes common attributes and methods. CAR, TRUCK, MINIVAN, and SCHOOL BUS are instances of the VEHICLE class.

FIGURE 6-8 A typical fitness center might have students, instructors, class schedules, and a registration process.

CandyBox Images/Shutterstock.com

make, model, year, weight, and color. Each subclass also can possess traits that are uncommon, such as a load limit for the TRUCK or an emergency exit location for the SCHOOL BUS.

A class can belong to a more general category called a **superclass**. For example, a NOVEL class belongs to a superclass called BOOK, because all novels are books in this example. The NOVEL class can have subclasses called HARDCOVER, PAPERBACK, and DIGITAL.

Similarly, consider a fitness center illustrated in Figure 6-8 that might have students, instructors, class schedules, and a registration process. As shown in Figure 6-9, the EMPLOYEE class belongs to the PERSON superclass, because every employee is a person, and the INSTRUCTOR class is a subclass of EMPLOYEE.

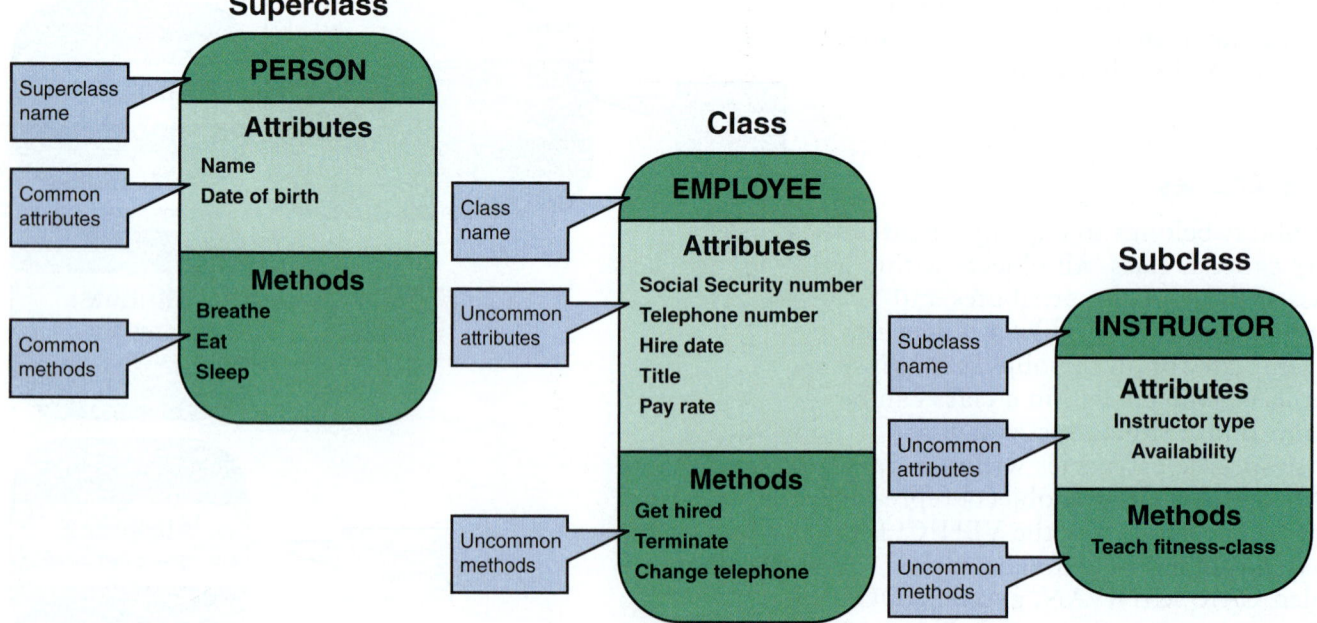

FIGURE 6-9 At the fitness center, the PERSON subclass includes common attributes and methods. EMPLOYEE is a class within the PERSON superclass. INSTRUCTOR is a subclass within the EMPLOYEE class.

6.3 RELATIONSHIPS AMONG OBJECTS AND CLASSES

Relationships enable objects to communicate and interact as they perform business functions and transactions required by the system. Relationships describe what objects need to know about each other, how objects respond to changes in other objects, and the effects of membership in classes, superclasses, and subclasses. Some relationships are stronger than others (just as a relationship between family members is stronger than one between casual acquaintances). The strongest relationship is called inheritance. Inheritance enables an object, called a child, to derive one or more of its attributes from another object, called a parent. In the example in Figure 6-10, the INSTRUCTOR object (child) inherits many traits from the EMPLOYEE object (parent), including Social Security number, Telephone number, and Hire date. The INSTRUCTOR object also can possess additional attributes, such as Type of Instructor. Because all employees share certain attributes, those attributes are assumed through inheritance and do not need to be repeated in the INSTRUCTOR object.

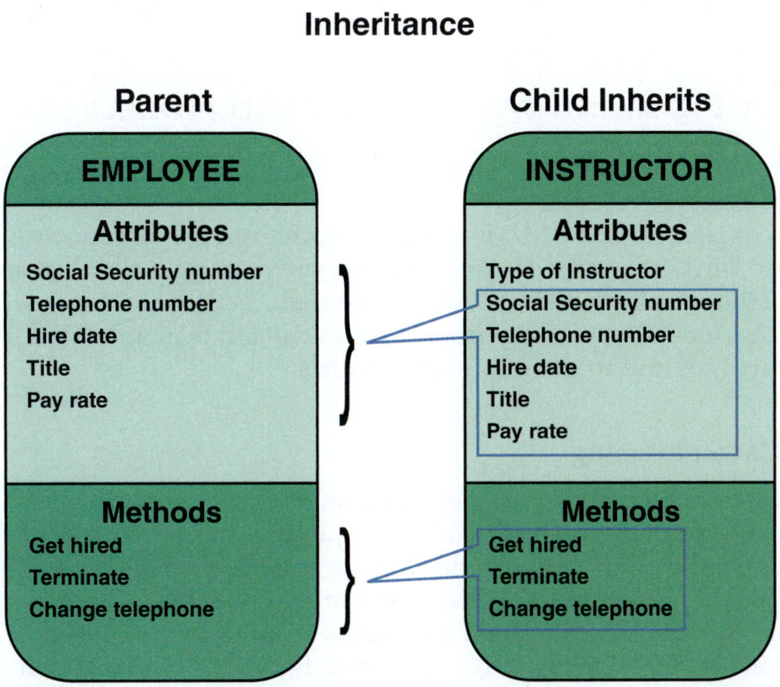

Inheritance

Parent	Child Inherits
EMPLOYEE	**INSTRUCTOR**
Attributes	**Attributes**
Social Security number	Type of Instructor
Telephone number	Social Security number
Hire date	Telephone number
Title	Hire date
Pay rate	Title
	Pay rate
Methods	**Methods**
Get hired	Get hired
Terminate	Terminate
Change telephone	Change telephone

FIGURE 6-10 An inheritance relationship exists between the INSTRUCTOR and EMPLOYEE objects. The INSTRUCTOR (child) object inherits characteristics from the EMPLOYEE (parent) class, and can have additional attributes of its own.

6.3.1 Object Relationship Diagram

After objects, classes, and relationships have been identified, an object relationship diagram can be prepared to provide an overview of the system. That model is used as a guide to continue to develop additional diagrams and documentation. Figure 6-11 shows an object relationship diagram for a fitness center. Notice that the model shows the objects and how they interact to perform business functions and transactions.

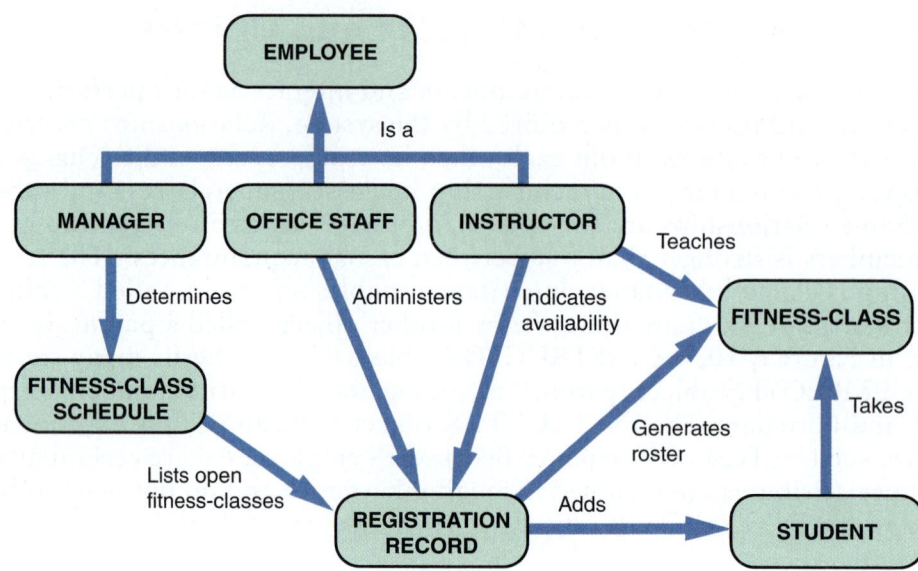

FIGURE 6-11 An object relationship diagram for a fitness center.

6.4 OBJECT MODELING WITH THE UNIFIED MODELING LANGUAGE

Just as structured analysis uses DFDs to model data and processes, systems analysts use UML to describe O-O systems.

Chapter 4 explained that UML is a popular technique for documenting and modeling a system. UML uses a set of symbols to represent graphically the various components and relationships within a system. Although the UML can be used for business process modeling and requirements modeling, it is mainly used to support O-O system analysis and to develop object models.

6.4.1 Use Case Modeling

A **use case** represents the steps in a specific business function or process. An external entity, called an actor, initiates a use case by requesting the system to perform a function or process. For example, in a medical office system, a PATIENT (actor) can MAKE APPOINTMENT (use case), as shown in Figure 6-12.

Notice that the UML symbol for a use case is an oval with a label that describes the action or event. The actor is shown as a stick figure, with a label that identifies the actor's role. The line from the actor to the use case is called an association, because it links a particular actor to a use case.

Use cases also can interact with other use cases. When the outcome of one use case is incorporated by another use case, we say that the second case *uses* the first case. UML indicates the relationship with an arrow that *points at* the use case being used. Figure 6-13 shows an example where a student adds a fitness class, and Produce Fitness-Class Roster *uses* the results of Add Fitness-Class to generate a new fitness-class roster. Similarly, if an instructor changes his or her availability, Update Instructor Information *uses* the Change Availability use case to update the instructor's information.

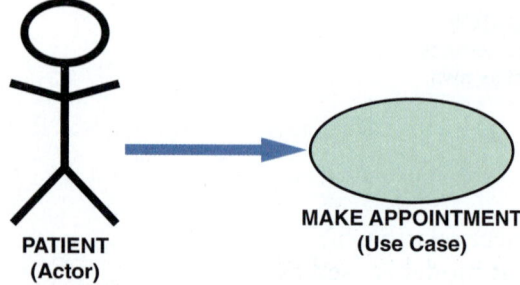

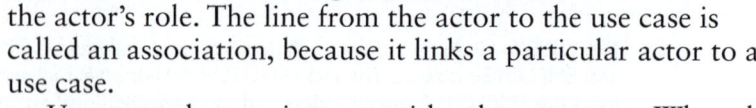
PATIENT
(Actor)

MAKE APPOINTMENT
(Use Case)

FIGURE 6-12 In a medical office system, a PATIENT (actor) can MAKE APPOINTMENT (use case). The UML symbol for a use case is an oval. The actor is shown as a stick figure.

To create use cases, start by reviewing the information that gathered during the requirements modeling phase. The objective is to identify the actors and the functions or transactions they initiate. For each use case, develop a **use case description** in the form of a table. A use case description documents the name of the use case, the actor, a description of the use case, a step-by-step list of the tasks and actions required for successful completion, a description of alternative courses of action, preconditions, postconditions, and assumptions. Figure 6-14 shows an example of the Add New Student use case for the fitness center.

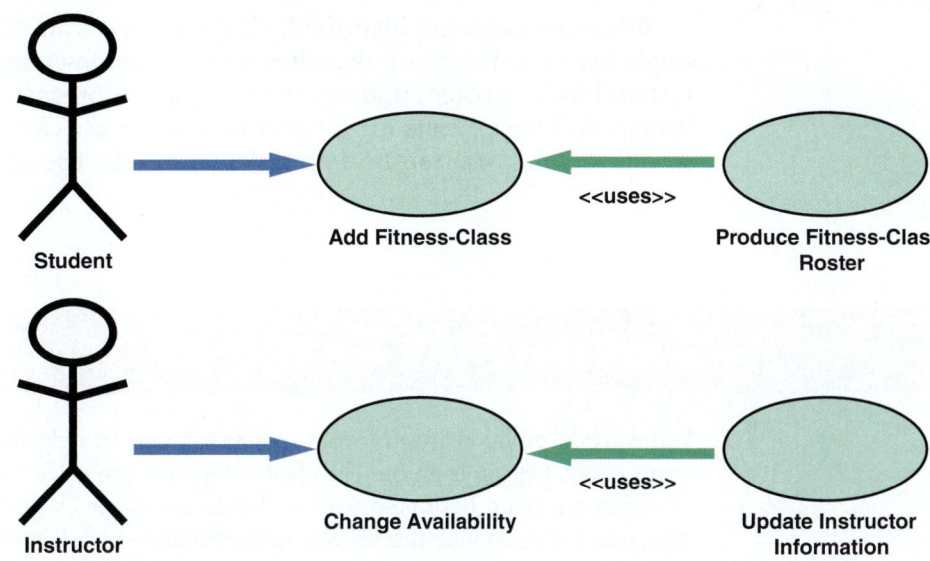

FIGURE 6-13 When a student adds a class, PRODUCE FITNESS-CLASS ROSTER uses the results of ADD FITNESS-CLASS to generate a new roster. When an instructor changes his or her availability, UPDATE INSTRUCTOR INFORMATION uses the CHANGE AVAILABILITY use case to update the instructor's information.

ADD NEW STUDENT Use Case

Add New Student

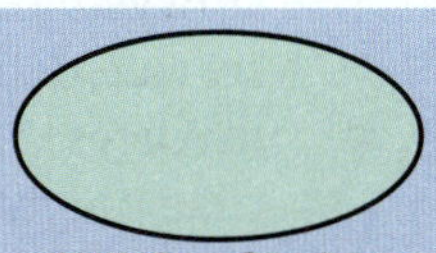

Name:	Add New Student
Actor:	Student/Manager
Description:	Describes the process used to add a student to a fitness-class
Successful completion:	1. Manager checks FITNESS-CLASS SCHEDULE object for availability 2. Manager notifies student 3. Fitness-class is open and student pays fee 4. Manager registers student
Alternative:	1. Manager checks FITNESS-CLASS SCHEDULE object for availability 2. Fitness-class is full 3. Manager notifies student
Precondition:	Student requests fitness-class
Postcondition:	Student is enrolled in fitness-class and fees have been paid
Assumptions:	None

FIGURE 6-14 The ADD NEW STUDENT use case description documents the process used to add a current student into an existing class at the fitness center.

When use cases are identified, all the related transactions should be grouped into a single use case. For example, when a hotel customer reserves a room, the reservation system blocks a room, updates the occupancy forecast, and sends the customer a confirmation. Those events are all part of a single use case called Reserve Room, and the specific actions are step-by-step tasks within the use case.

CASE IN POINT 6.1:   HILLTOP MOTORS

You were hired by Hilltop Motors as a consultant to help the company plan a new information system. Hilltop is an old-line dealership, and the prior owner was slow to change. A new management team has taken over, and they are eager to develop a first-class system. Right now, you are reviewing the service department, which is going through a major expansion. You decide to create a model of the service department in the form of a use case diagram. The main actors in the service operation are customers; service writers, who prepare work orders and invoices; and mechanics, who perform the work. You are meeting with the management team tomorrow morning. Create a draft of the diagram to present to them.

6.4.2 Use Case Diagrams

A use case diagram is a visual summary of several related use cases within a system or subsystem. Consider a typical auto service department, as shown in Figure 6-15. The service department involves customers; service writers, who prepare work orders and invoices; and mechanics, who perform the work. Figure 6-16 shows a possible use case diagram for the auto service department.

FIGURE 6-15 A typical auto service department might involve customers, service writers who prepare work orders and invoices, and mechanics who perform the work.

iStockphoto.com/Sean Locke

Use Case Diagram: Auto Service Department

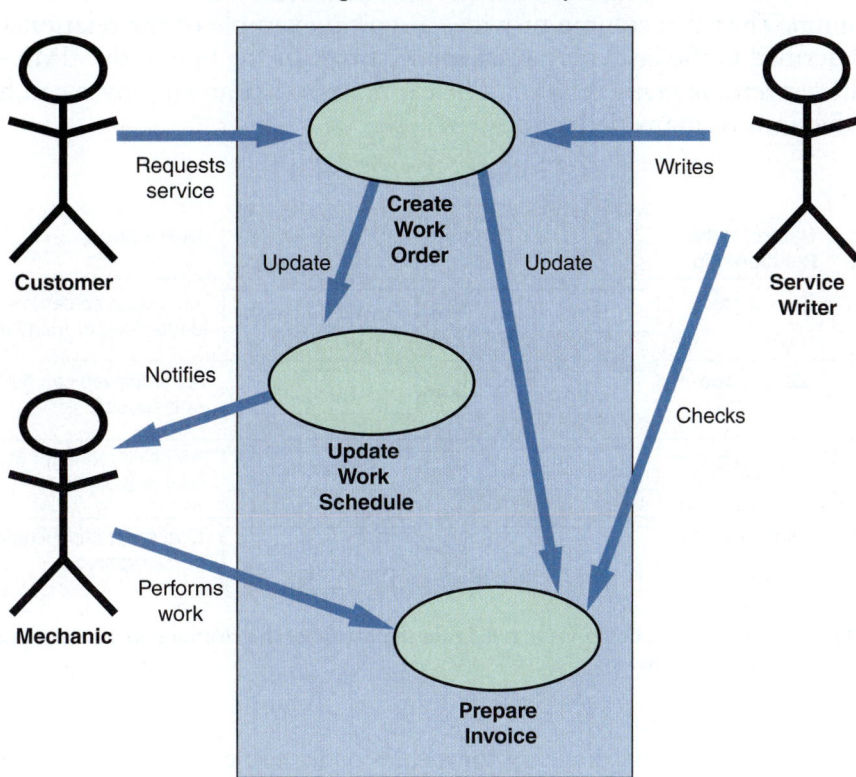

FIGURE 6-16 A use case diagram to handle work at an auto service department.

When a use case diagram is created, the first step is to identify the system boundary, which is represented by a rectangle. The **system boundary** shows what is included in the system (inside the rectangle) and what is not included in the system (outside the rectangle). After the system boundary is identified, use cases are placed on the diagram, the actors are added, and the relationships shown.

6.4.3 Class Diagrams

A **class diagram** shows the object classes and relationships involved in a use case. Like a DFD, a class diagram is a logical model, which evolves into a physical model and finally becomes a functioning information system. In structured analysis, entities, data stores, and processes are transformed into data structures and program code. Similarly, class diagrams evolve into code modules, data objects, and other system components.

In a class diagram, each class appears as a rectangle, with the class name at the top, followed by the class's attributes and methods. Lines show relationships between classes and have labels identifying the action that relates the two classes. To create a class diagram, review the use case and identify the classes that participate in the underlying business process.

The class diagram also includes a concept called **cardinality**, which describes how instances of one class relate to instances of another class. For example, an employee might have earned no vacation days or one vacation day or many vacation days. Similarly, an employee might have no spouse or one spouse. Figure 6-17 shows various UML notations and cardinality examples. Notice that in Figure 6-17, the first column shows a UML notation symbol that identifies the relationship shown in the second column. The third column provides a typical example of the relationship, which is described in the last column. In the first row of the figure, the UML notation *0..* * identifies a *zero or many* relation. The example is that an employee can have no payroll deductions or many deductions.

UML Notation	Nature of the Relationship	Example		Description
0..*	Zero or many	Employee 1	Payroll Deduction 0..*	An employee can have no payroll deductions or many deductions.
0..1	Zero or one	Employee 1	Spouse 0..1	An employee can have no spouse or one spouse.
1	One and only one	Office Manager 1	Sales Office 1	An office manager manages one and only one office.
1..*	One or many	Order 1	Item Ordered 1..*	One order can include one or many items ordered.

FIGURE 6-17 Examples of UML notations that indicate the nature of the relationship between instances of one class and instances of another class.

Figure 6-18 shows a class diagram for a sales order use case. Notice that the sales office has one sales manager who can have anywhere from zero to many sales reps. Each sales rep can have anywhere from zero to many customers, but each customer has only one sales rep.

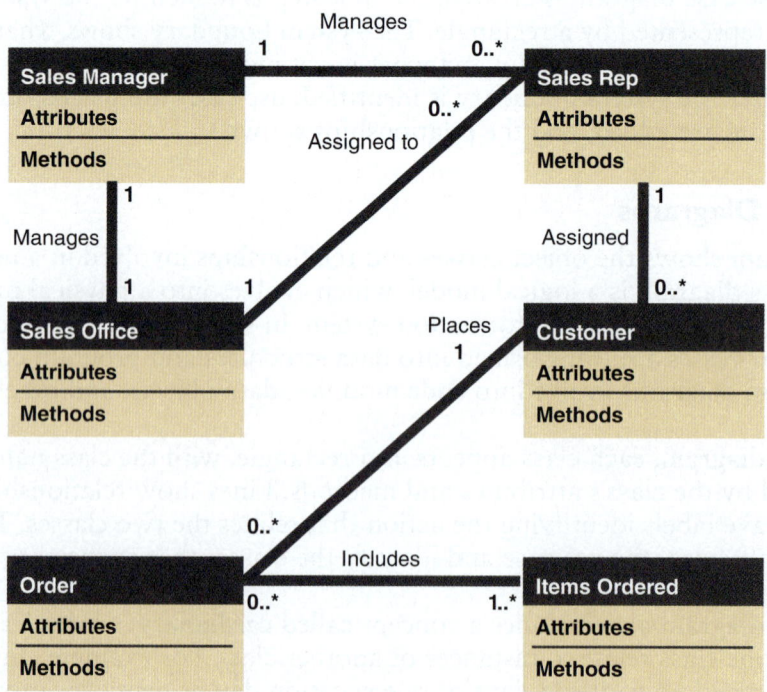

FIGURE 6-18 Class diagram for a sales order use case (attributes and methods omitted for clarity).

CASE IN POINT 6.2: TRAIN THE TRAINERS, INC.

Train the Trainers develops seminars and workshops for corporate training managers, who in turn train their employees. Your job at Train the Trainers is to put together the actual training materials. Right now, you are up against a deadline. The new object modeling seminar has a chapter on cardinality, and the client wants you to come up with at least three more examples for each of the four cardinality categories listed in Figure 6-17. The four categories are *zero or many*, *zero or one*, *one and only one*, and *one or many*. Even though you are under pressure, you are determined to use examples that are realistic and familiar to the students. What examples will you submit?

6.4.4 Sequence Diagrams

A sequence diagram is a dynamic model of a use case, showing the interaction among classes during a specified time period. A sequence diagram graphically documents the use case by showing the classes, the messages, and the timing of the messages. Sequence diagrams include symbols that represent classes, lifelines, messages, and focuses. These symbols are shown in Figure 6-19.

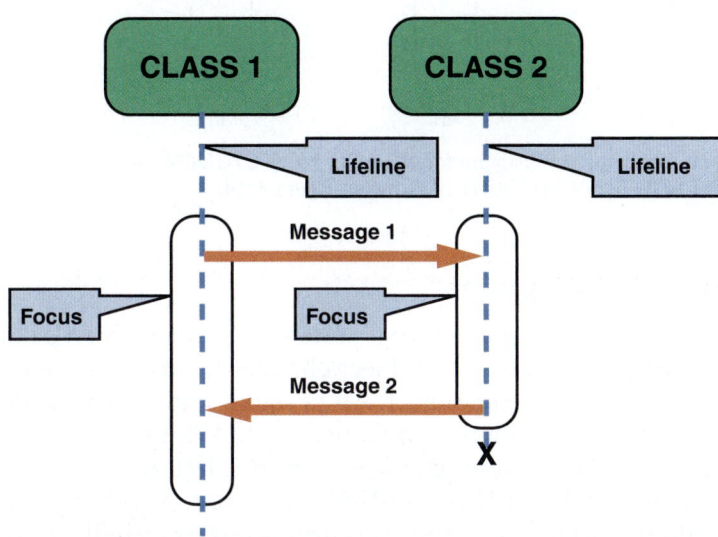

FIGURE 6-19 A sequence diagram with two classes. Notice the X that indicates the end of the CLASS 2 lifeline. Also notice that each message is represented by a line with a label that describes the message, and that each class has a focus that shows the period when messages are sent or received.

CLASSES: A class is identified by a rectangle with the name inside. Classes that send or receive messages are shown at the top of the sequence diagram.

LIFELINES: A lifeline is identified by a dashed line. The lifeline represents the time during which the object above it is able to interact with the other objects in the use case. An *X* marks the end of the lifeline.

MESSAGES: A message is identified by a line showing direction that runs between two objects. The label shows the name of the message and can include additional information about the contents.

FOCUSES: A focus is identified by a narrow vertical shape that covers the lifeline. The focus indicates when an object sends or receives a message.

Figure 6-20 shows a sequence diagram for the ADD NEW STUDENT use case in the fitness center example. Notice that the vertical position of each message indicates the timing of the message.

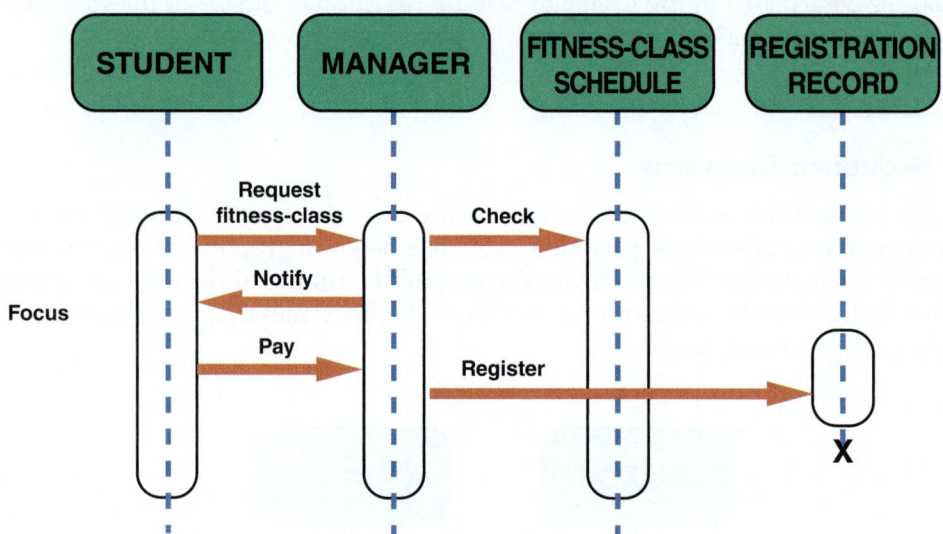

FIGURE 6-20 The sequence diagram for the ADD NEW STUDENT use case. The use case description for ADD NEW STUDENT is shown in Figure 6 14.

6.4.5 State Transition Diagrams

Earlier in this chapter it was explained that state refers to an object's current status. A state transition diagram shows how an object changes from one state to another, depending on events that affect the object. All possible states must be documented in the state transition diagram, as shown in Figure 6-21. A bank account, for example, could be opened as a NEW account, change to an ACTIVE or EXISTING account, and eventually become a CLOSED or FORMER account. Another possible state for a bank account could be FROZEN, if the account's assets are legally attached.

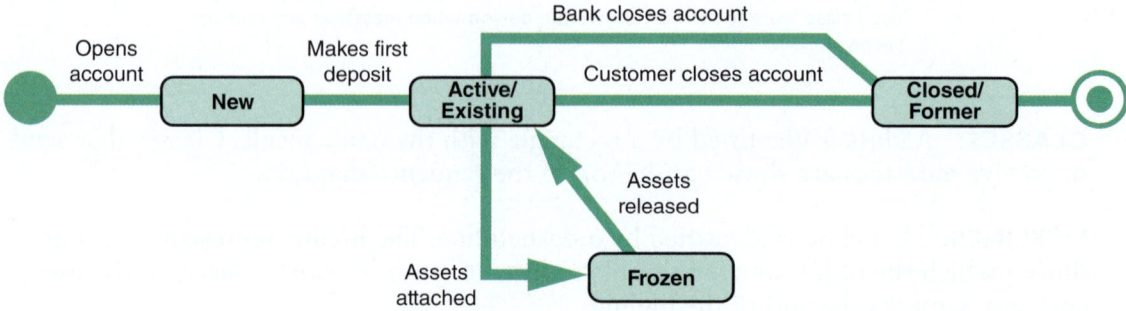

FIGURE 6-21 An example of a state transition diagram for a bank account.

In a state transition diagram, the states appear as rounded rectangles with the state names inside. The small circle to the left is the initial state, or the point where the object first interacts with the system. Reading from left to right, the lines show direction and describe the action or event that causes a transition from one state to another. The circle at the right with a hollow border is the final state.

6.4.6 Activity Diagrams

An activity diagram resembles a horizontal flowchart that shows the actions and events as they occur. Activity diagrams show the order in which the actions take place and identify the outcomes. Figure 6-22 shows an activity diagram for a cash withdrawal at an ATM machine. Notice that the customer initiates the activity by inserting an ATM card and requesting cash. Activity diagrams also can display multiple use cases in the form of a grid, where classes are shown as vertical bars and actions appear as horizontal arrows.

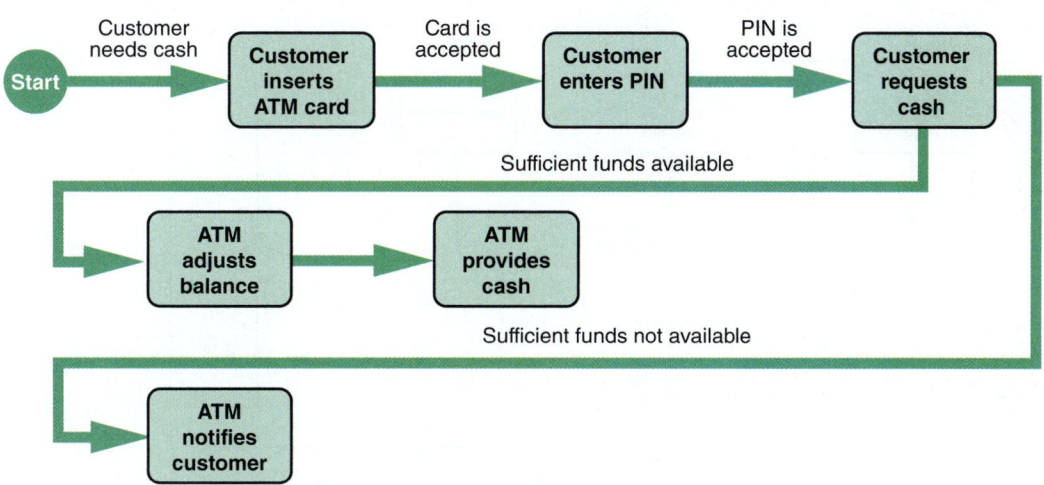

FIGURE 6-22 An activity diagram showing the actions and events involved in withdrawing cash from an ATM.

Sequence diagrams, state transition diagrams, and activity diagrams are dynamic modeling tools that can help a systems analyst understand how objects behave and interact with the system.

CASE IN POINT 6.3: TRAVELBIZ

Jack Forester and Lisa Turner are systems analysts in the IT department of TravelBiz, a nationwide travel agency that specializes in business travel. TravelBiz has decided to expand into the vacation travel market by launching a new business division called TravelFun. The IT director assigned Jack and Lisa to create a flexible, efficient information system for the new division. Jack wants to use traditional analysis and modeling techniques for the project. Lisa, on the other hand, wants to use an O-O methodology. Which approach would you suggest and why?

6.4.7 Business Process Modeling

In addition to sequence diagrams and activity diagrams, business process models (BPM) can be used to represent the people, events, and interaction in a system. BPM initially was discussed in Chapter 4 as a requirements modeling tool, but it can be used anytime during the systems development process. BPM works well with object modeling, because both methods focus on the actors and the way they behave.

Figure 6-23 shows the Bizagi Modeler tool, which supports business process modeling and simulation using the standard BPM notation. This free Windows application includes video tutorials, support forums, and reusable templates.

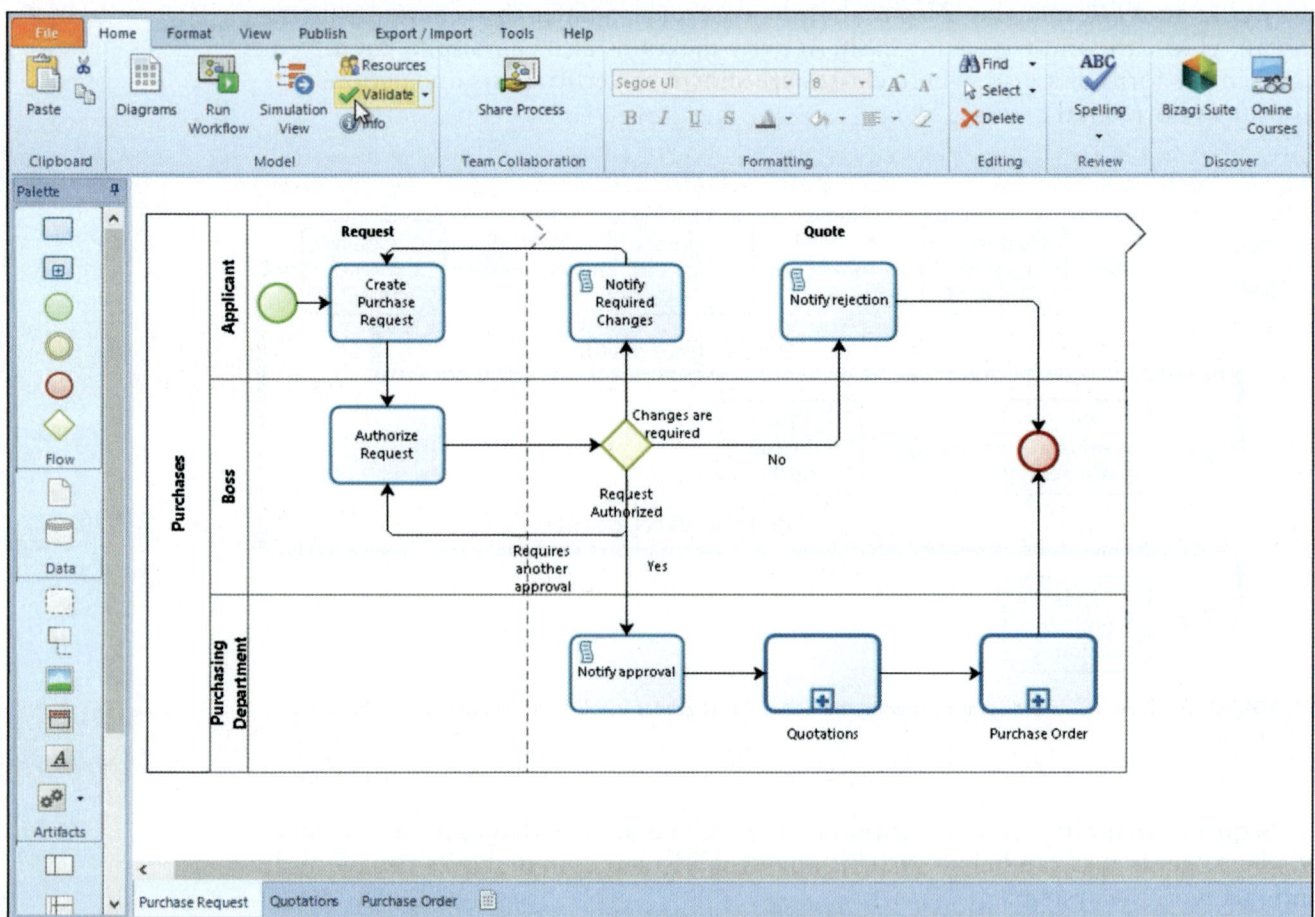

FIGURE 6-23 The Bizagi Modeler tool supports business process modeling and simulation using the standard BPM notation.
Source: bizagi.com

6.4.8 CASE Tools

Object modeling requires many types of diagrams to represent the proposed system. Creating the diagrams by hand is time consuming and tedious, so systems analysts rely on CASE tools to speed up the process and provide an overall framework for documenting the system components. In addition, CASE tools ensure consistency and provide common links so that once objects are described and used in one part of the design, they can be reused multiple times without further effort.

6.5 ORGANIZING THE OBJECT MODEL

The previous section described how to use O-O tools and techniques to build a logical model of the information system. The next step is to organize the diagrams and documentation so the object model is easily read and understood. If a CASE tool is used to develop the design, the CASE software will perform much of this work automatically.

There are many ways to proceed with the task of organizing the object model, and experience is the best teacher. After identifying the system's objects, classes, and relationships, an object relationship diagram should be developed that provides an overview of the system. If a CASE-generated model is not used, each diagram or object definition should be supported by clear, relevant documentation that can be accessed easily by anyone who reviews the object model. For example, use cases and use case diagrams should be organized so they can be linked to the appropriate class, state transition, sequence, and activity diagrams. The diagrams and documentation are the foundation for the system's design, so accuracy is important. Remember that it is much easier to repair a diagram now than to change the software later.

CASE IN POINT 6.4:   CYBER ASSOCIATES

One of your responsibilities at Cyber Associates, an IT consulting firm, is to assign new systems analysts to various tasks and projects. Some of the senior people believe that inexperienced analysts should start with O-O techniques, which are easier to learn and apply. Others think that an analyst should learn structured analysis first, and then proceed to O-O skills. What is your viewpoint, and why?

A QUESTION OF ETHICS

iStockphoto.com/faberfoto_it

Your company sent several staff members for UML training. An outside vendor provided the training. Everyone who attended the training received a copy of the instructor's materials, which included study guides and sample exam questions and solutions.

After completing the training course, you are eligible to sit a certification exam. If you pass the exam, you will be credentialed as a "UML Expert" by an independent agency. You can parlay these credentials into a higher salary and boost your career.

A coworker who did not attend the training asks for a copy of the training materials. He wants to take the exam without "wasting his time in class." Should you give him a copy of the training materials? If you do, how might this diminish your accomplishments? If you don't, would you be hurting the team by not helping another member become more knowledgeable about the UML?

6.6 CHAPTER SUMMARY

This chapter introduced object modeling, which is a popular technique that describes a system in terms of objects. Objects represent real people, places, events, and transactions. Unlike structured analysis, which treats data and processes separately, objects include data and processes that can affect the data. During the implementation process, systems analysts and programmers transform objects into program code modules that can be optimized, tested, and reused as often as necessary.

Object-oriented terms include classes, attributes, instances, messages, and methods. Classes include objects that have similar attributes, or characteristics. Individual members of a class are called object instances. Objects within a class can be grouped into subclasses, which are more specific categories within the class. A class also can belong to a more general category called a superclass.

Objects can send messages, or commands, that require other objects to perform certain methods, or tasks. The concept that a message gives different meanings to different objects is called polymorphism. An object resembles a black box, with encapsulated, or self-contained, data and methods. The strongest relationship between objects is inheritance.

After identifying the objects, classes, and relationships, an object relationship diagram is prepared that shows the objects and how they interact to perform business functions and transactions.

The Unified Modeling Language (UML) is a widely used method of visualizing and documenting an information system. UML techniques include use cases, use case diagrams, class diagrams, sequence diagrams, state transition diagrams, and activity diagrams.

A use case describes a business situation initiated by an actor, who interacts with the information system. Each use case represents a specific transaction, or scenario. A use case diagram is a visual summary of related use cases within a system or subsystem. A class diagram represents a detailed view of a single use case, showing the classes that participate in the underlying business transaction and the relationship among class instances, which is called cardinality. A sequence diagram is a dynamic model of a use case, showing the interaction among classes during a specified time period. Sequence diagrams include lifelines, messages, and focuses. A state transition diagram shows how an object changes from one state to another, depending on events that affect the object. An activity diagram resembles a horizontal flowchart that shows actions and events as they occur in a system.

CASE tools provide an overall framework for system documentation. CASE tools can speed up the development process, ensure consistency, and provide common links that enable objects to be reused.

At the end of the object modeling process, the use cases and use case diagrams are organized and class, sequence, state transition, and activity diagrams are created.

In addition to object models, the business process model (BPM) can be used to represent the people, events, and interaction in a system.

Key Terms

activity diagram   A diagram that resembles a horizontal flowchart that shows the actions and events as they occur. Activity diagrams show the order in which actions take place and identify the outcome.

attribute   A single characteristic or fact about an entity. An attribute, or field, is the smallest piece of data that has meaning within an information system. For example, a Social Security number or company name could be examples of an attribute. In object-oriented analysis, an attribute is part of a class diagram that describes the characteristics of objects in the class. Also known as a data element.

cardinality   A concept that describes how instances of one entity relate to instances of another entity. Described in entity-relationship diagrams by notation that indicates combinations that include zero or one-to-many, one-to-one, and many-to-many.

child   In inheritance, a child is the object that derives one or more attributes from another object, called the parent.

class diagram   A detailed view of a single use case, showing the classes that participate in the use case and documenting the relationship among the classes.

encapsulation   The idea that all data and methods are self-contained, as in a black box.

focus   In a sequence diagram, a focus indicates when an object sends or receives a message. It is indicated by a narrow vertical rectangle that covers the lifeline.

inheritance   A type of object relationship. Inheritance enables an object to derive one or more of its attributes from another object (e.g., an INSTRUCTOR object may inherit many traits from the EMPLOYEE object, such as hire date).

instance   A specific member of a class.

lifeline   In a sequence diagram, a lifeline is used to represent the time during which the object above it is able to interact with the other objects in the use case. An X marks the end of a lifeline.

message   An object-oriented command that tells an object to perform a certain method.

method   Defines specific tasks that an object must perform. Describes what and how an object does something.

object model   Describes objects, which combine data and processes. Object models are the end product of object-oriented analysis.

parent   In inheritance, a parent is the object from which the other object, the child, derives one or more attributes.

polymorphism   The concept that a message gives different meanings to different objects (e.g., a GOOD NIGHT message might produce different results depending on whether it is received by a child or the family dog).

relationships   Enable objects to communicate and interact as they perform the business functions and transactions required by a system. Relationships describe what objects need to know about each other, how objects respond to changes in other objects, and the effects of membership in classes, superclasses, and subclasses.

state   An adjective that describes an object's current status (e.g., a student could be a CURRENT, FUTURE, or PAST student).

state transition diagram   Shows how an object changes from one state to another, depending on the events that affect the object.

subclass   A further division of objects in a class. Subclasses are more specific categories within a class.

superclass   A more generalized category to which objects may belong (e.g., a NOVEL class might belong to a superclass called BOOK).

system boundary Shows what is included and excluded from a system. Depicted by a shaded rectangle in use case diagrams.

use case Represents the steps in a specific business function or process in UML.

use case description A description in UML that documents the name of the use case, the actor, a description of the use case, a step-by-step list of the tasks required for successful completion, and other key descriptions and assumptions.

Chapter Exercises

Questions

1. What is object-oriented analysis, and what are some advantages of this method?
2. Define an object, and provide three examples.
3. Define an attribute, and provide three examples.
4. Define a method, and provide three examples.
5. Define encapsulation, and explain how it is used in object-oriented analysis.
6. Define polymorphism, and provide three examples.
7. Define a class, subclass, and superclass, and provide three examples of each.
8. Define an actor, and provide three examples.
9. Define a use case and a use case diagram, and prepare a sample of each.
10. Define the term "black box," and explain why it is an important concept in object-oriented analysis. Can you think of other black boxes that you use in everyday life?

Discussion Topics

1. The chapter mentioned that systems analysts and programmers transform objects into program code modules. Modular design is a very popular concept in many industries. What other modular design examples can you suggest?
2. You are an IT consultant, and you are asked to create a new system for a small real estate brokerage firm. You have no experience with object-oriented approach, and you decide to try it. How will you begin? How will the tasks differ from structured analysis?
3. The UML is a large and complex modeling language. How can an IT professional tell when a UML diagram is correct and not just visually pleasing?
4. You are creating a system for a bowling alley to manage information about its leagues. During the modeling process, you create a state transition diagram for an object called *League Bowlers*. What are the possible states of a league bowler, and what happens to a bowler who quits the league and rejoins the following season?
5. A debate is raging at the IT consulting firm where you work. Some staff members believe that it is harder for experienced analysts to learn object modeling techniques, because the analysts are accustomed to thinking about data and processes as separate entities. Others believe that solid analytical skills are easily transferable and do not see a problem in crossing over to the newer approach. What do you think, and why?

Projects

1. Write a brief history of the UML, and prepare a presentation on the subject.
2. Contact the IT staff at your school or at a local business to learn they use object-oriented programming languages. If so, determine what languages and versions are used, how long they have been in use, and why they were selected.
3. Perform a web search for the exact phrase "object-oriented systems analysis". How many hits did you get? Provide three examples.
4. Prepare a report on at least three CASE tools that provide UML support.
5. Investigate business process modeling languages, such as BPEL.

CHAPTER 7 Development Strategies

Chapter 7 is the final chapter in the systems analysis phase of the SDLC. This chapter describes software trends, acquisition and development strategies, traditional versus web-based development, outsourcing versus in-house development, the system requirements document, prototyping, and preparing for the transition to the next SDLC phase — systems design.

The chapter includes four "Case in Point" discussion questions to help contextualize the concepts described in the text. The "Question of Ethics" concerns how truthful an answer should be when submitting a response to an RFP. Is a slight exaggeration acceptable if it means the company will win the contract?

LEARNING OBJECTIVES

When you finish this chapter, you should be able to:

- Describe the concept of Software as a Service
- Define Web 2.0 and cloud computing
- Explain software acquisition alternatives, including traditional and web-based software development strategies
- Describe software outsourcing options, including offshore outsourcing and the role of service providers
- Explain advantages and disadvantages of in-house software development
- Discuss cost-benefit analysis and financial analysis tools
- Describe a request for proposal (RFP) and a request for quotation (RFQ)
- Describe the system requirements document
- Explain the transition from systems analysis to systems design

CHAPTER CONTENTS

7.1 INTRODUCTION

The main objective of the systems analysis phase is to build a logical model of the new information system. Chapters 4, 5, and 6 explained requirements modeling, data and process modeling, and object modeling. Chapter 7 describes the remaining activities in the systems analysis phase, which include evaluation of alternative solutions, preparation of the system requirements document, and presentation of the system requirements document to management. The chapter also explains the transition to systems design.

7.2 DEVELOPMENT STRATEGIES OVERVIEW

Just a few years ago, a typical company either developed software itself, purchased a software package (which might need some modification), or hired consultants or outside resources to perform the work. Today, a company has many more choices for software acquisition, including application service providers, web-hosted software options, and firms that offer a variety of enterprise-wide software solutions.

Selecting the best development path is an important decision that requires companies to consider three key topics: the impact of the Internet, software outsourcing options, and in-house software development alternatives. These topics are reviewed in the following sections.

7.3 THE IMPACT OF THE INTERNET

The Internet has triggered enormous changes in business methods and operations, and software acquisition is no exception. This section examines Software as a Service, the changing marketplace for software, and how web-based development compares to traditional methods. The section concludes with a description of Internet-related trends, including Web 2.0, cloud computing, and mobile devices.

7.3.1 Software as a Service

In the traditional model, software vendors develop and sell application packages to customers. Typically, customers purchase licenses that give them the right to use the software under the terms of the license agreement. Although this model still accounts for most software acquisition, a new model, called **Software as a Service (SaaS)**, is changing the picture dramatically.

SaaS is a model of software deployment in which an application is hosted as a service provided to customers over the Internet. SaaS reduces the customer's need for software maintenance, operation, and support.

In a highly competitive marketplace, major vendors constantly strive to deliver new and better solutions. For example, Microsoft claims that its SaaS platform offers the best solution and business value. Figure 7-1 shows Salesforce.com's view that SaaS offers great potential benefits to business.

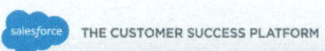

SaaS: Software as a Service

Power Your Business with the Best of the Web

New to SaaS? Welcome!

If you're just starting to explore the concept of SaaS, this is the place to find out what SaaS can do for you, see how SaaS is different, identify questions about SaaS, and learn more about developing SaaS applications.

What is SaaS?

Software as a service (or SaaS) is a way of delivering applications over the Internet—as a service. Instead of installing and maintaining software, you simply access it via the Internet, freeing yourself from complex software and hardware management.

SaaS applications are sometimes called Web-based software, on-demand software, or hosted software. Whatever the name, SaaS applications run on a SaaS provider's servers. The provider manages access to the application, including security, availability, and performance.

SAAS: THE PAYOFF

FIGURE 7-1 Salesforce.com stresses the benefits of SaaS for business.
Source: salesforce.com

7.3.2 Traditional vs. Web-Based Systems Development

A systems analyst must consider whether development will take place in a web-centric framework or in a traditional environment. This section provides an overview of some of the similarities and differences.

In an Internet-based system, the web becomes an integral part of the application, rather than just a communication channel, and systems analysts need new application development tools and solutions to handle the new systems. Two major web-based development environments are Microsoft's .NET and IBM's WebSphere, which are shown in Figure 7-2 and Figure 7-3, respectively. Microsoft regards .NET as a framework for building and running Windows applications and web services. IBM describes WebSphere as a software platform for service-oriented architecture (SOA) environments.

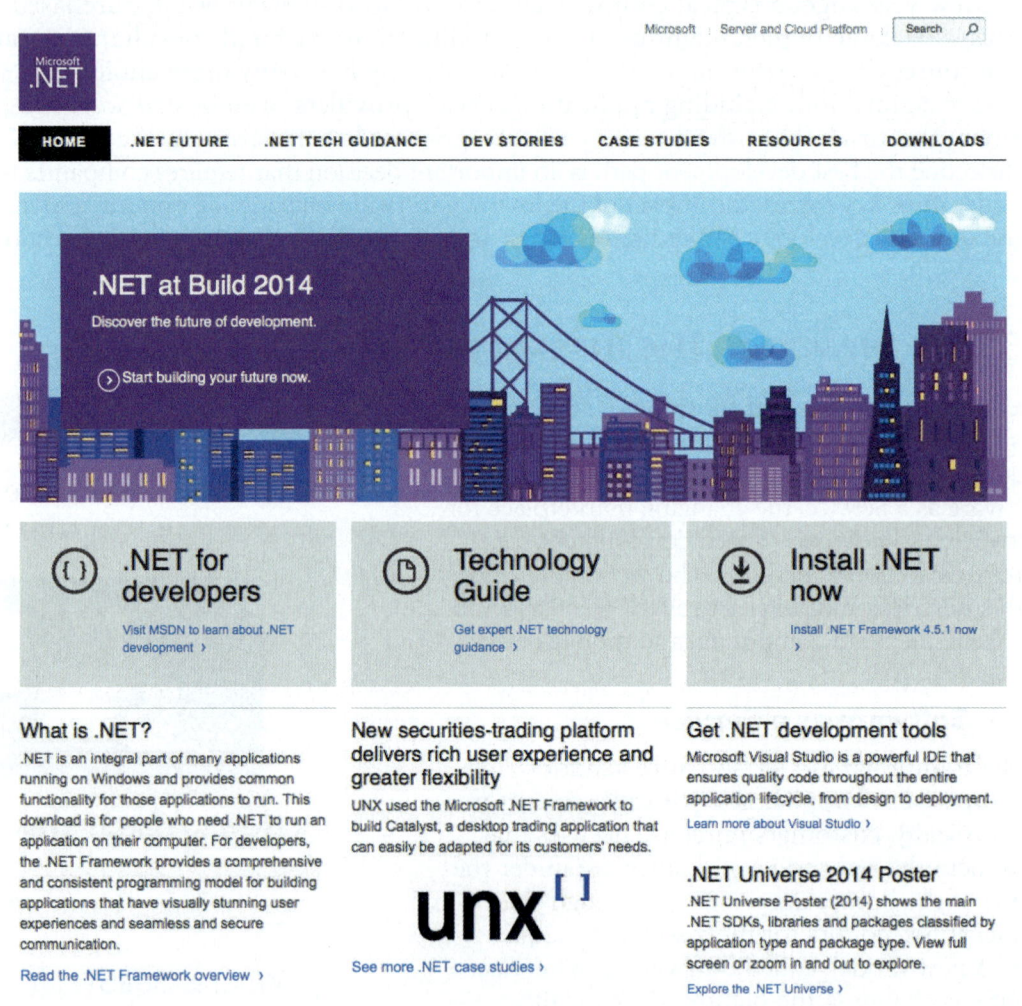

FIGURE 7-2 Microsoft's .NET Framework supports building and running applications and web services.
Source: Microsoft Corporation.

Although there is a major trend toward web-based architecture, many firms rely on traditional systems, either because they are using legacy applications that are not easily replaced or because they do not require a web component to satisfy user needs. To choose between traditional and web-based development, consider some key differences between them. Building the application in a web-based environment can offer greater benefits (and sometimes greater risks) when compared to a traditional environment. The following sections list some characteristics of traditional versus web-based development.

TRADITIONAL DEVELOPMENT: In a traditional systems development environment:

- Compatibility issues, including existing hardware and software platforms and legacy system requirements, influence systems design.

- Systems are designed to run on local and wide-area company networks.

- Systems often utilize Internet links and resources, but web-based features are treated as enhancements rather than core elements of the design.

- Development typically follows one of three main paths: in-house development, purchase of a software package with possible modification, or use of outside consultants.

- Scalability can be affected by network limitations and constraints.

- Many applications require substantial desktop computing power and resources.

- Security issues usually are less complex than with web-based systems, because the system operates on a private company network, rather than the Internet.

WEB-BASED DEVELOPMENT: In a web-based systems development environment:

- Systems are developed and delivered in an Internet-based framework such as .NET or WebSphere.

- Internet-based development treats the web as the platform, rather than just a communication channel.

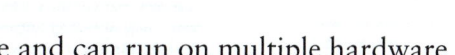

FIGURE 7-3 IBM's WebShere is a software platform for SOA environments.
Source: IBM Corporation

- Web-based systems are easily scalable and can run on multiple hardware environments.

- Large firms tend to deploy web-based systems as enterprise-wide software solutions for applications such as customer relationship management, order processing, and materials management.

- Web-based software treats the software application as a service that is less dependent on desktop computing power and resources.

- When companies acquire web-based software as a *service* rather than a *product* they purchase, they can limit in-house involvement and have the vendor install, configure, and maintain the system by paying agreed-upon fees.

- Web-based software usually requires additional layers, called middleware, to communicate with existing software and legacy systems.

- Web-based solutions open more complex security issues that should be addressed.

7.3.3 Evolving Trends: Web 2.0, Cloud Computing, and Mobile Devices

In the constantly changing world of IT, no area is more dynamic than Internet technology. Three examples of evolving trends are Web 2.0, cloud computing, and mobile devices. Systems analysts should be aware of these trends and consider them as they plan large-scale systems. Web 2.0, cloud computing, and mobile devices are discussed in more detail in Chapter 10.

Many IT professionals use the term **Web 2.0** to describe a second generation of the web that enables people to collaborate, interact, and share information much more effectively. This new environment is based on continuously available user applications rather than static HTML webpages, without limitations regarding the number of users or how they access, modify, and exchange data. The Web 2.0 environment enhances interactive experiences, including wikis and blogs, and social-networking applications such as Twitter, LinkedIn, and Facebook.

As shown in Figure 7-4, the National Institute of Standards and Technology (NIST) defines **cloud computing** as, "a model for enabling ubiquitous, convenient, on-demand network access to a shared pool of configurable computing resources

FIGURE 7-4 NIST definition of cloud computing.

Source: nist.gov

(e.g., networks, servers, storage, applications, and services) that can be rapidly provisioned and released with minimal management effort or service provider interaction." Cloud computing is often represented by a cloud symbol that indicates a network or the Internet. Cloud computing can be viewed as an online SaaS and data environment supported by supercomputer technology.

Mobile devices have become commonplace. Smartphones and tablets are now found in personal use and across the enterprise in most organizations. Developing apps for mobile devices requires new platforms, such as IBM's Bluemix shown in Figure 7-5.

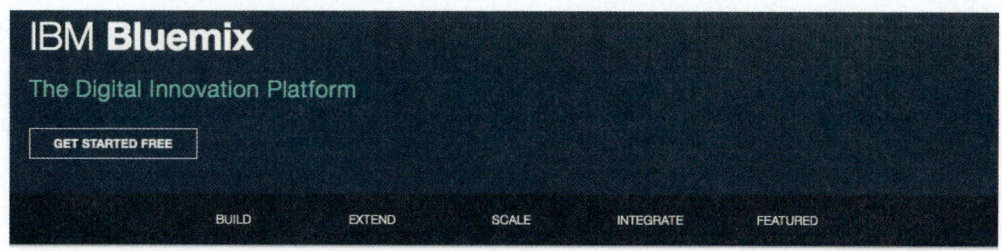

Build your apps, your way.

Use a combination of the most prominent open-source compute technologies to power your apps. Then let Bluemix handle the rest.

Instant Runtimes

App-centric runtime environments based on Cloud Foundry.

CLOUD FOUNDRY

Check out runtimes on Bluemix

Containers

Portable and consistent delivery of your app without having to manage an OS.

docker

Check out containers on Bluemix

Virtual Machines

Get the most flexibility and control over your environment with VMs.

openstack
POWERED

Check out VMs on Bluemix

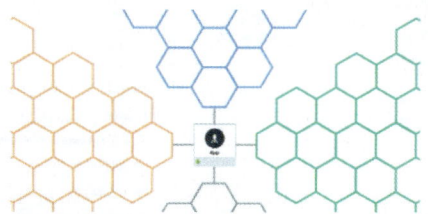

Extend apps with services.

Choose from IBM, third-party, and community services to extend the functionality of your apps. If you have existing infrastructure or APIs, you can securely connect those to Bluemix as well.

BROWSE CATALOG

FIGURE 7-5 IBM Bluemix is the cloud platform that helps developers rapidly build, manage, and run web and mobile applications.

Source: IBM Bluemix

7.4 OUTSOURCING

Outsourcing is the transfer of information systems development, operation, or maintenance to an outside firm that provides these services, for a fee, on a temporary or long-term basis. Outsourcing can refer to relatively minor programming tasks, renting software from a service provider, outsourcing a basic business process, often called **business process outsourcing (BPO)**, or handling a company's entire IT function. Numerous firms and organizations offer information about outsourcing topics and issues. For example, the Outsourcing Center site at *www. outsourcing-center.com* provides free research, case studies, database directories, market intelligence, and updates on trends and best practices in outsourcing as a strategic business solution.

7.4.1 The Growth of Outsourcing

Traditionally, firms outsourced IT tasks as a way of controlling costs and dealing with rapid technological change. While those reasons still are valid, outsourcing has become part of an overall IT strategy for many organizations. The outsourcing trend also has affected software vendors, who have adjusted their marketing accordingly. For example, Oracle Corporation offers a service called Oracle On Demand, which provides hosted or SaaS cloud applications, as shown in Figure 7-6. Oracle also cites data that shows that businesses spend up to 80% of their IT budgets maintaining existing software and systems, which forces IT managers "... to spend time managing tedious upgrades instead of revenue-generating IT projects."

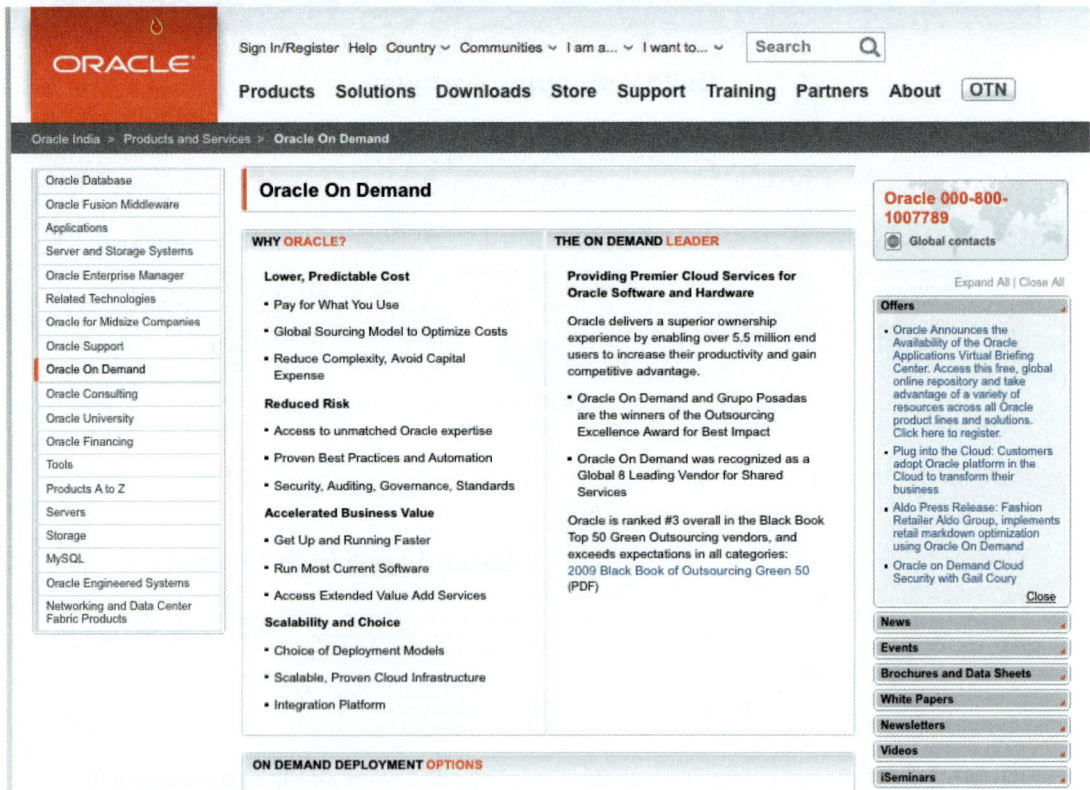

FIGURE 7-6 Oracle On Demand cloud services.
Source: Oracle Corporation

A firm that offers outsourcing solutions is called a **service provider**. Some service providers concentrate on specific software applications; others offer business services such as order processing and customer billing. Still others offer enterprise-wide software solutions that integrate and manage functions such as accounting, manufacturing, and inventory control.

Two popular outsourcing options involve application service providers and firms that offer Internet business services. These terms are explained in the following sections.

APPLICATION SERVICE PROVIDERS: An application service provider (ASP) is a firm that delivers a software application, or access to an application, by charging a usage or subscription fee. An ASP provides more than a license to use the software; it *rents* an operational package to the customer. ASPs typically provide commercially available software such as databases and accounting packages. If a company uses an ASP to supply a data management package, for example, the company does not have to design, develop, implement, or maintain the package. ASPs represent a rapidly growing trend, using the Internet as the primary delivery channel.

INTERNET BUSINESS SERVICES: Some firms offer Internet business services (IBS), which provide powerful web-based support for transactions such as order processing, billing, and customer relationship management. Another term for IBS is managed hosting, because the outside firm (host) manages system operations.

An IBS solution is attractive to customers because it offers online data center support, mainframe computing power for mission-critical functions, and universal access via the Internet. Many firms, such as Rackspace, compete in the managed cloud services market, as shown in Figure 7-7.

FIGURE 7-7 Rackspace managed cloud services.
Source: Rackspace US, Inc.

7.4.2 Outsourcing Fees

Firms that offer SaaS rather than a product, have developed fee structures that are based on how the application is used by customers during a specific time period. Several models exist, including fixed fee, subscription, and usage or transaction.

A fixed fee model uses a set fee based on a specified level of service and user support. An example of a fixed fee model is Oracle's On Demand service. A subscription model has a variable fee based on the number of users or workstations that have access to the application. Finally, a usage model or transaction model charges a variable fee based on the volume of transactions or operations performed by the application.

When a company considers outsourcing, it should estimate usage characteristics to determine which fee structure would be most desirable and then attempt to negotiate a service provider contract based on that model.

7.4.3 Outsourcing Issues and Concerns

When a company decides to outsource IT functions, it takes an important step that can affect the firm's resources, operations, and profitability. Mission-critical IT systems should be outsourced only if the result is a cost-attractive, reliable business solution that fits the company's long-term business strategy and involves an acceptable level of risk. Moving IT work overseas raises even more issues, including potential concerns about control, culture, communication, and security.

In addition to long-term strategic consequences, outsourcing also can raise some concerns. For example, a company must turn over sensitive data to an external service provider and trust the provider to maintain security, confidentiality, and quality. Also, before outsourcing, a company must carefully review issues relating to insurance, potential liability, licensing and information ownership, warranties, and disaster recovery.

Most important, a company considering outsourcing must realize that the solution can be only as good as the outsourcing firm that provides the service. A dynamic economy can give rise to business failures and uncertainty about the future. In this climate, it is especially important to review the history and financial condition of an outsourcing firm before making a commitment.

Mergers and acquisitions also can affect outsourcing clients. Even with large, financially healthy firms, a merger or acquisition can have some impact on clients and customers. If stability is important, an outsourcing client should consider these issues.

Outsourcing can be especially attractive to a company whose volume fluctuates widely, such as a defense contractor. In other situations, a company might decide to outsource application development tasks to an IT consulting firm if the company lacks the time or expertise to handle the work on its own. Outsourcing relieves a company of the responsibility of adding IT staff in busy times and downsizing when the workload lightens. A major disadvantage of outsourcing is that it raises employee concerns about job security. Talented IT people usually prefer positions where the firm is committed to in-house IT development — if they do not feel secure, they might decide to work directly for the service provider.

7.4.4 Offshore Outsourcing

Offshore outsourcing, or global outsourcing, refers to the practice of shifting IT development, support, and operations to other countries. In a trend similar to the outflow of manufacturing jobs over a several-decade period, many firms are sending IT work overseas.

For example, Dartmouth professor Matthew Slaughter has noted that IT work will move offshore even faster than manufacturing, because it is easier to ship work across networks and telephone lines and put consultants on airplanes than it is to ship bulky raw materials, build factories, and deal with tariffs and transportation issues. Several years ago, the IT consulting firm Gartner, Inc., accurately forecasted the steady growth of offshore outsourcing, and predicted that outsourcing would evolve from labor-intensive maintenance and support to higher-level systems development and software design.

In addition to exporting IT jobs, many large multinational firms, including Microsoft and IBM, have opened technical centers in India, China, and other countries. Some observers believe that India might gain as many as 2 million IT jobs in the next decade.

The main reason for offshore outsourcing is the same as domestic outsourcing: lower bottom-line costs. Offshore outsourcing, however, involves some unique risks and concerns. For example, workers, customers, and shareholders in some companies have protested this trend and have raised public awareness of possible economic impact. Even more important, offshore outsourcing involves unique concerns regarding project control, security issues, disparate cultures, and effective communication with critical functions that might be located halfway around the globe.

CASE IN POINT 7.1:   TURNKEY SERVICES

Turnkey Services is an application service provider that offers payroll and tax preparation services for hundreds of businesses in the Midwest. The firm is considering a major expansion into accounting and financial services, and is looking into the possibility of supporting this move by hiring IT subcontractors in several foreign countries. Peter Belmont, Turnkey's president, has asked you to help him reach a decision. Specifically, he wants you to cite the pros and cons of offshore outsourcing. He expects you to perform Internet research on this topic, and he wants you to present your views at a meeting of Turnkey managers next week.

7.5 IN-HOUSE SOFTWARE DEVELOPMENT OPTIONS

In addition to numerous outsourcing options, a company can choose to develop its own systems, or purchase, possibly customize, and implement a software package. These development alternatives are shown in Figure 7-8. Although many factors influence this decision, the most important consideration is the total cost of ownership (TCO), which was explained in Chapter 4. In addition to these options, companies also develop user applications designed around commercial software packages, such as Microsoft Office, to improve user productivity and efficiency.

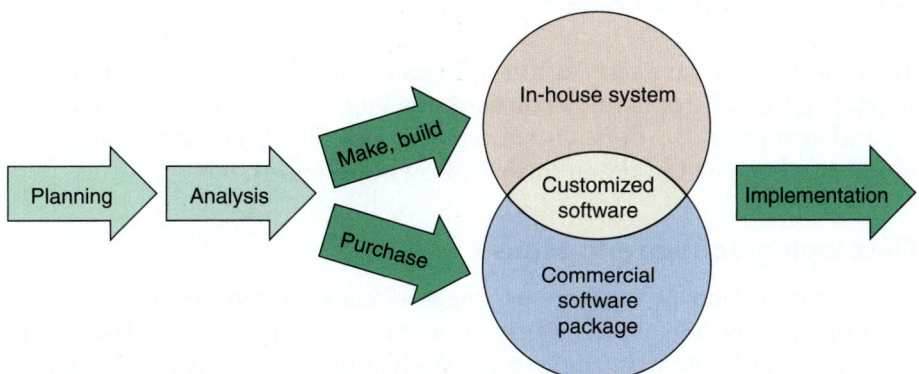

FIGURE 7-8 Instead of outsourcing, a company can choose to develop a system in-house, or purchase and possibly customize a commercial package.

7.5.1 Make or Buy Decision

The choice between developing versus purchasing software often is called a **make or buy**, or **build or buy**, decision. The company's IT department makes, builds, and develops **in-house software**. A **software package** is obtained from a vendor or application service provider.

The package might be a standard commercial program or a customized package designed specifically for the purchaser. Companies that develop software for sale are called **software vendors**. A firm that enhances a commercial package by adding custom features and configuring it for a particular industry is called a **value-added reseller (VAR)**.

Software packages are available for every type of business activity. A software package that can be used by many different types of organizations is called a **horizontal application**. An accounting package is a good example of a horizontal application because many different businesses or separate divisions that exist in large, diversified companies can utilize it.

In contrast, a software package developed to handle information requirements for a specific type of business is called a **vertical application**. For example, organizations with special system requirements include colleges, banks, hospitals, insurance companies, construction companies, real estate firms, and airlines. Figure 7-9 shows a typical restaurant point of sale (POS) system running on various devices. The organizations may need vertical applications to handle their unique business requirements but often use horizontal applications for basic business needs, such as payroll processing and accounts payable.

FIGURE 7-9 Restaurants use vertical applications like point of sale (POS) systems to support their unique business requirements.

Source: http://www.rmpos.com/sliderimages/posthatfits.jpg

Of the in-house software acquisition options — developing a system, buying a software package, or customizing a software package — each has advantages, disadvantages, and cost considerations, as shown in Figure 7-10. These software acquisition options are described in detail in the following sections.

7.5.2 Developing Software In-House

With an enormous variety of software packages available to handle horizontal and vertical business operations, why would a firm choose to develop its own software? Typically, companies choose in-house development to satisfy unique business requirements, to minimize changes in business procedures and policies, to meet constraints of existing systems and existing technology, and to develop internal resources and capabilities.

REASONS FOR IN-HOUSE DEVELOPMENT	REASONS FOR PURCHASING A SOFTWARE PACKAGE
Satisfy unique business requirements	Lower costs
Minimize changes in business procedures and policies	Requires less time to implement
Meet constraints of existing systems	Proven reliability and performance benchmarks
Meet constraints of existing technology	Requires less technical development staff
Develop internal resources and capabilities	Future upgrades provided by the vendor
Satisfy unique security requirements	Obtain input from other companies

FIGURE 7-10 Companies consider various factors when comparing in-house development with the purchase of a software package.

SATISFY UNIQUE BUSINESS REQUIREMENTS: Companies often decide to develop software in-house because no commercially available software package can meet their unique business requirements. A college, for example, needs a course scheduling system based on curriculum requirements, student demand, classroom space, and available instructors. A package delivery company needs a system to identify the best combination of routes and loading patterns for the company's fleet of delivery trucks. If existing software packages cannot handle those requirements, then in-house developed software might be the only choice.

MINIMIZE CHANGES IN BUSINESS PROCEDURES AND POLICIES: A company also might choose to develop its own software if available packages will require changes in current business operations or processes. Installing a new software package almost always requires some degree of change in how a company does business; however, if the installation of a purchased package will be too disruptive, the organization might decide to develop its own software instead.

MEET CONSTRAINTS OF EXISTING SYSTEMS: Any new software installed must work with existing systems. For example, if a new budgeting system must interface with an existing accounting system, finding a software package that works correctly with the existing accounting system might prove difficult. If so, a company could develop its own software to ensure that the new system will interface with the old system.

MEET CONSTRAINTS OF EXISTING TECHNOLOGY: Another reason to develop software in-house is that the new system must work with existing hardware and legacy systems. That could require a custom design, an upgrade to the environment, or in-house software that can operate within those constraints. A systems analyst addresses the issue of technical feasibility during the preliminary investigation. Now, in the systems analysis phase, the analyst must determine whether in-house software development is the best overall solution.

DEVELOP INTERNAL RESOURCES AND CAPABILITIES: By designing a system in-house, companies can develop and train an IT staff that understands the organization's business functions and information support needs. Many firms feel that in-house IT resources and capabilities provide a competitive advantage because an in-house team can respond quickly when business problems or opportunities arise. For example, if a company lacks internal resources, it must depend on an outside firm for vital business support. Also, outsourcing options might be attractive, but a series of short-term solutions would not necessarily translate into lower TCO over the long term. Top managers often feel more comfortable with an internal IT team to provide overall guidance and long-term stability. In-house development also allows a firm to leverage the skill set of the IT team, which is already on board and being compensated.

7.5.3 Purchasing a Software Package

If a company decides not to outsource, a commercially available software package might be an attractive alternative to developing its own software. Advantages of purchasing a software package over developing software in-house include lower costs, less time to implement a system, proven reliability and performance benchmarks, less technical development staff, future upgrades that are provided by the vendor, and the ability to obtain input from other companies who already have implemented the software.

LOWER COSTS: Because many companies use software packages, software vendors spread the development costs over many customers. Compared with software developed in-house, a software package almost always is less expensive, particularly in terms of initial investment. However, even though the initial cost is less, purchased software can involve expenses caused by business disruption, changing business processes, and retraining employees.

REQUIRES LESS TIME TO IMPLEMENT: When a software package is purchased, it already has been designed, programmed, tested, and documented. The in-house time normally spent on those tasks, therefore, is eliminated. Of course, the software must still be installed and integrated into the systems environment, which can take a significant amount of time. Also, even though implementation is quicker, TCO can be higher due to added training expenses and software modifications.

PROVEN RELIABILITY AND PERFORMANCE BENCHMARKS: If the package has been on the market for any length of time, any major problems probably have been detected already and corrected by the vendor. If the product is popular, it almost certainly has been rated and evaluated by independent reviewers.

REQUIRES LESS TECHNICAL DEVELOPMENT STAFF: Companies that use commercial software packages often are able to reduce the number of programmers and systems analysts on the IT staff. Using commercial software also means that the IT staff can concentrate on systems whose requirements cannot be satisfied by software packages.

FUTURE UPGRADES PROVIDED BY THE VENDOR: Software vendors regularly upgrade software packages by adding improvements and enhancements to create a new version or release. A new release of a software package, for example, can include drivers to support a new laser printer or a new type of data storage technology. In many cases, the vendor receives input and suggestions from current users when planning future upgrades.

INPUT FROM OTHER COMPANIES: Using a commercial software package means that users in other companies can be contacted to obtain their input and impressions.

Trying the package or making a site visit to observe the system in operation may be very useful before a final decision is made. Companies can make use of user groups to share experiences with a software package.

7.5.4 Customizing a Software Package

If the standard version of a software product does not satisfy a company's requirements, the firm can consider adapting the package to meet its needs. Three ways to customize a software package are:

1. Purchase a basic package that vendors will customize to suit the project's needs. Many vendors offer basic packages in a standard version with add-on components that are configured individually. A vendor offers options when the standard application will not satisfy all customers. A human resources information system is a typical example, because each company handles employee compensation and benefits differently.

2. Negotiate directly with the software vendor to make enhancements to meet the project's needs by paying for the changes.

3. Purchase the package and make project-specific modifications, if this is permissible under the terms of the software license. A disadvantage of this approach is that systems analysts and programmers might be unfamiliar with the software and will need time to learn the package and make the modifications correctly.

Additionally, some advantages of purchasing a standard package disappear if the product must be customized. If the vendor does the customizing, the modified package probably will cost more and take longer to obtain. Another issue is future support: Although vendors regularly upgrade their standard software packages, they might not upgrade a customized version. In addition, if the modifications are done by the company purchasing the software, when a new release of the package becomes available, the company might have to modify the new version on its own, because the vendor will not support modifications installed by the customer.

7.5.5 Creating User Applications

Business requirements sometimes can be fulfilled by a user application, rather than a formal information system or commercial package. User applications are examples of user productivity systems, which were discussed in Chapter 1.

A **user application** utilizes standard business software, such as Microsoft Word or Microsoft Excel, which has been configured in a specific manner to enhance user productivity. For example, to help a sales rep respond rapidly to customer price requests, an IT support person can set up a form letter with links to a spreadsheet that calculates incentives and discounts. In addition to configuring the software, the IT staff can create a **user interface**, which includes screens, commands, controls, and features that enable users to interact more effectively with the application. User interface design is described in Chapter 8.

In some situations, user applications offer a simple, low-cost solution. Most IT departments have a backlog of projects, and IT solutions for individuals or small groups do not always receive a high priority. At the same time, application software is more powerful, flexible, and user friendly than ever. Companies such as Microsoft and Corel offer software suites and integrated applications that can exchange data with programs that include tutorials, wizards, and Help features to guide less experienced users who know what they need to do but do not know how to make it happen.

Many companies empower lower-level employees by providing more access to data and more powerful data management tools. The main objective is to allow lower-level employees more access to the data they require to perform their jobs, with no intervention from the IT department. This can be accomplished by creating effective user interfaces for company-wide applications such as accounting, inventory, and sales systems. Another technique is to customize standard productivity software, such as Microsoft Word or Microsoft Excel, to create user

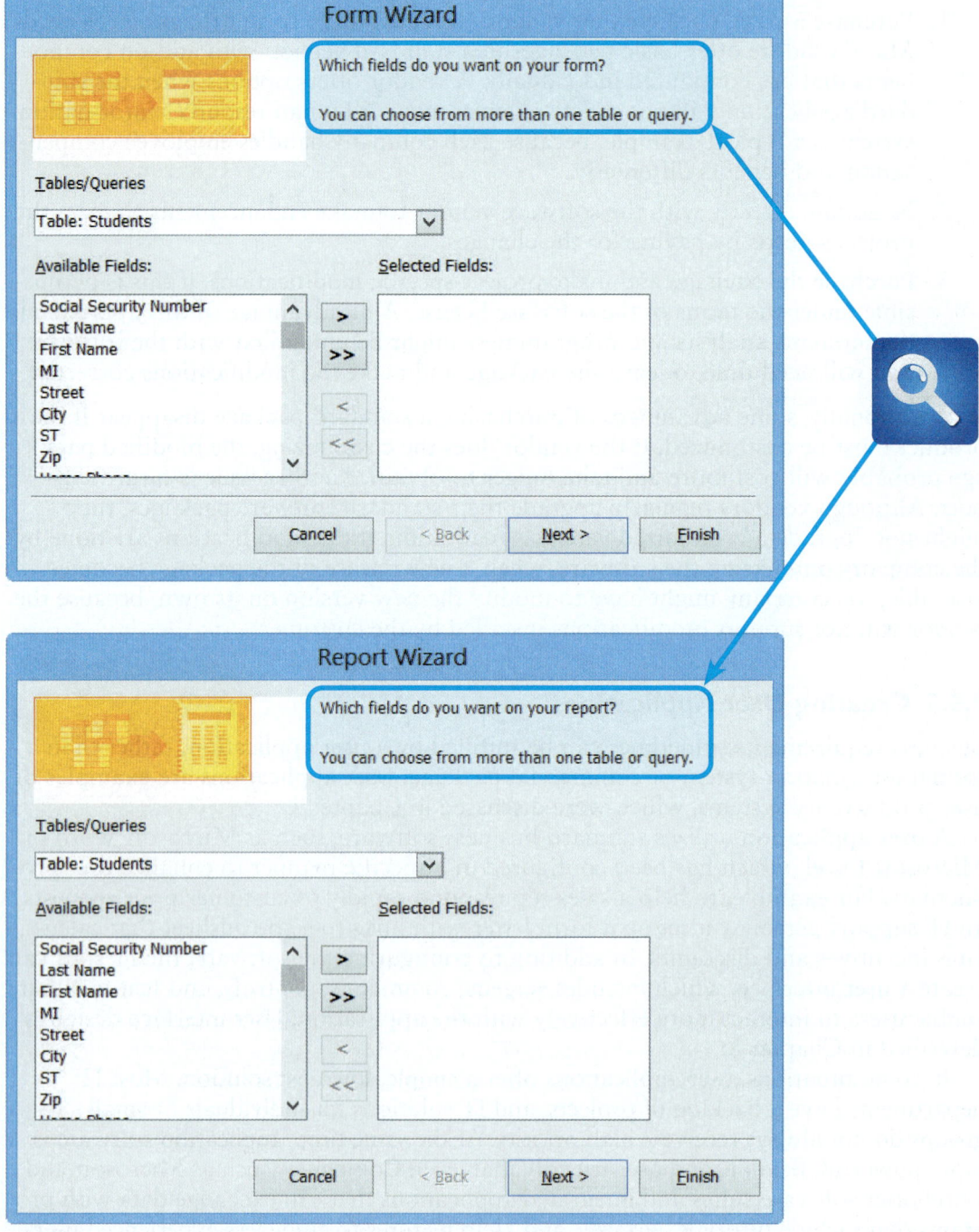

FIGURE 7-11 Microsoft Access includes Form Wizard and a Report Wizard tools that ask a series of questions and then create the form or report.
Source: Microsoft Corporation.

applications. In either case, empowerment makes the IT department more productive because it can spend less time responding to the daily concerns and data needs of users and more time on high-impact systems development projects that support strategic business goals.

Empowerment reduces costs and makes good business sense, but companies that adopt this approach must provide the technical support that empowered users require. In most large and medium-sized companies, a service desk or information center (IC) within the IT department is responsible for providing user support. The service desk offers services such as hotline assistance, training, and guidance to users who need technical help.

Once they learn an application, many users can perform tasks that once required a programmer. Some user applications have powerful screen generators and report generators that allow users to design their own data entry forms and reports. For example, as shown in Figure 7-11, Microsoft Access includes a Form Wizard and a Report Wizard, which are menu-driven tools that can create screen forms and reports. These design tools allow users to design specific input and output views that meet their operational needs — with little or no assistance required from the IT staff.

Users typically require spreadsheets, database management programs, and other software packages to meet their information needs. If user applications access corporate data, appropriate controls must be provided to ensure data security and integrity. For example, some files should be hidden totally from view; others should have read-only properties so users can view, but not change, the data.

7.6 THE SYSTEMS ANALYST'S ROLE

At some point in the systems development process, the company must decide whether to use an outsourcing option, develop software in-house, acquire a software package, develop user applications, or select some combination of these solutions. The decision depends on the company's current and anticipated future needs. It will affect the remaining SDLC phases and the systems analyst's subsequent involvement in the project. The decision to develop software in-house, for example, will require more participation from the systems analyst than outsourcing or choosing a commercial package. Management usually makes a determination after receiving written recommendations from the IT staff and a formal presentation, which is described later in this chapter.

Even a single system can use a mix of software alternatives. For example, a company might purchase a standard software package to process its payroll, and then develop its own software to handle the interface between the payroll package and the company's in-house manufacturing cost analysis system.

The evaluation and selection of alternatives is not a simple process. The objective is to obtain the product with the lowest total cost of ownership, but actual cost and performance can be difficult to forecast. When selecting hardware and software, systems analysts often work as an evaluation and selection team. A team approach ensures that critical factors are not overlooked and that a sound choice is made. The evaluation and selection team also must include users, who will participate in the selection process and feel a sense of ownership in the new system.

The primary objective of the evaluation and selection team is to eliminate system alternatives that will not meet requirements, rank the alternatives that are feasible, and present the viable alternatives to management for a final decision. The process begins with a careful study of the costs and benefits of each alternative, as explained in the following section.

CASE IN POINT 7.2: STERLING ASSOCIATES

Joan Sterling is CEO and principal stockholder of Sterling Associates, which specializes in advising clients on IT projects and information systems development. Joan is creating a brochure for prospective new clients. She wants you to develop a section that describes payback analysis, ROI, and NPV in simple terms, and mentions the pros and cons of each financial analysis tool. She suggested that you start by reviewing the material in Part C of the Systems Analyst's Toolkit.

7.7 ANALYZING COST AND BENEFITS

Financial analysis tools have been around for a long time. From the abacus to the slide rule, people have always sought easier ways to work with numbers. This section describes cost and benefit analysis, and explains popular tools that can help a systems analyst examine an IT project.

Chapter 2 explained that economic feasibility is one of the four feasibility measurements that are made during the preliminary investigation of a systems request. Now, at the end of the systems analysis phase of the SDLC, financial analysis tools and techniques must be applied to evaluate development strategies and decide how the project will move forward. Part C of the Systems Analyst's Toolkit describes three popular tools, which are payback analysis, return on investment (ROI), and net present value (NPV). These tools, and others, can be used to determine TCO, which was described in Chapter 4. At this stage, the analyst will identify specific systems development strategies and choose a course of action. For example, a company might find that its total cost of ownership will be higher if it develops a system in-house, compared with outsourcing the project or using an ASP.

An accurate forecast of TCO is critical, because nearly 80% of total costs occur *after* the purchase of the hardware and software, according to Gartner, Inc. An IT department can develop its own TCO estimates, or use TCO calculation tools offered by vendors. For example, as shown in Figure 7-12, HP offers an online TCO calculator that includes a questionnaire and a graphical display of results. In the example, the HP interactive TCO calculator is used to determine the ROI of migrating to an Infrastructure-as-a-Service (IaaS) environment in the cloud from a traditional server environment.

7.7.1 Financial Analysis Tools

Part C of the Systems Analyst's Toolkit explains how to use three main cost analysis tools: payback analysis, return on investment (ROI), and net present value (NPV). **Payback analysis** determines how long it takes an information system to pay for itself through reduced costs and increased benefits. **Return on investment (ROI)** is a percentage rate that compares the total net benefits (the return) received from a project to the total costs (the investment) of the project. The **net present value (NPV)** of a project is the total value of the benefits minus the total value of the costs, with both costs and benefits adjusted to reflect the point in time at which they occur.

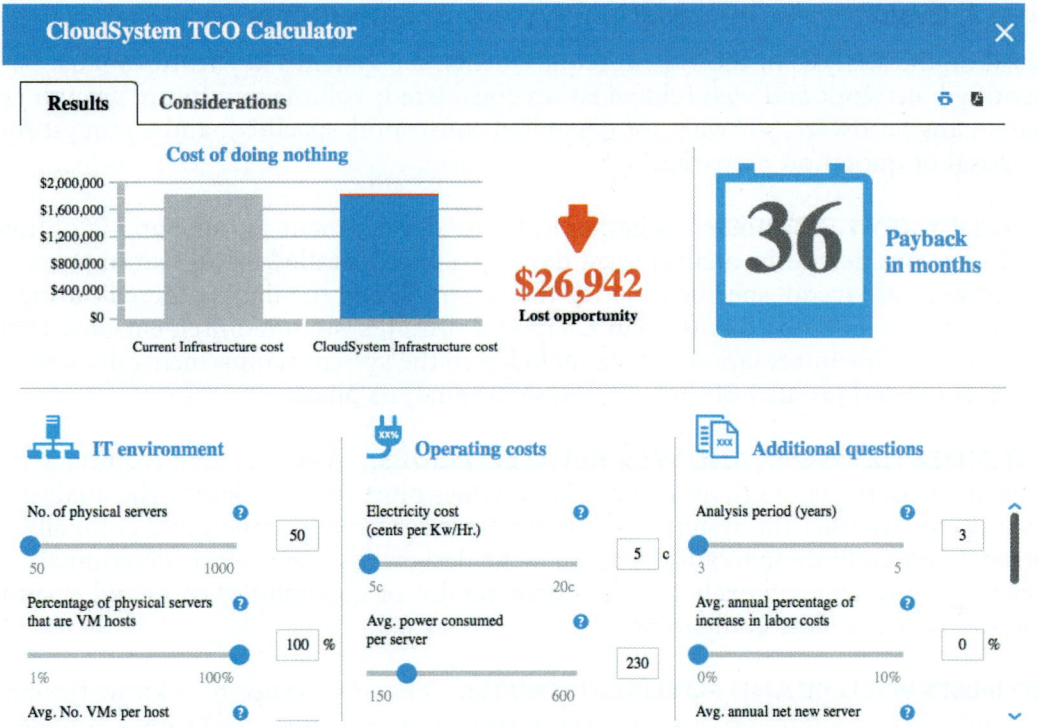

FIGURE 7-12 In this example, the HP interactive TCO calculator is used to determine the ROI of migrating to an Infrastructure-as-a-Service (IaaS) environment in the cloud from a traditional server environment.

Source: Hewlett-Packard Development Company, L.P.

7.7.2 Cost-Benefit Analysis Checklist

Chapter 2 explained how to use the payback analysis tool during the preliminary investigation to help determine whether a project is economically feasible. Now, all the financial analysis tools will be used to evaluate various development strategies. The best way to apply the tools is to develop a cost-benefit checklist with the following steps:

1. List each development strategy being considered.
2. Identify all costs and benefits for each alternative. Be sure to indicate when costs will be incurred and benefits realized.
3. Consider future growth and the need for scalability.
4. Include support costs for hardware and software.
5. Analyze various software licensing options, including fixed fees and formulas based on the number of users or transactions.
6. Apply the financial analysis tools to each alternative.
7. Study the results and prepare a report to management.

7.8 THE SOFTWARE ACQUISITION PROCESS

Although each situation is different, the following section describes a typical example of the issues and tasks involved in software acquisition.

Step 1: Evaluate the Information System Requirements

Based on the analysis of the system requirements, the system's key features must be identified; network and web-related issues considered; volume and future growth estimated; any hardware, software, or personnel constraints specified; and a request for proposal or quotation prepared.

IDENTIFY KEY FEATURES: Whether in-house development or outsourcing options are being considered, the analyst must develop a clear, detailed list of features that can serve as an overall specification for the system. Using the data gathered during fact-finding, which was discussed in Chapter 4, list all system requirements and critical features. This information will be included in the system requirements document, which is the end product of the SDLC systems analysis phase.

CONSIDER NETWORK AND WEB-RELATED ISSUES: As the system requirements are evaluated, the network and web-related issues must be considered. The analyst must decide whether the system will run on a network, the Internet, or a company intranet and build these requirements into the design. Also, it must be determined whether the system will exchange data with vendor or customer systems and ensure that the system will be compatible.

ESTIMATE VOLUME AND FUTURE GROWTH: The analyst needs to know the current volume of transactions and forecast future growth. Figure 7-13 shows volume estimates for an order processing system. In addition to current levels, the figure displays two forecasts; one based on the existing order processing procedures and another that assumes a new website is operational.

Online Order Processing System Estimated Activity During Next 12-Month Period

	CURRENT LEVEL	FUTURE GROWTH (based on existing procedures)	FUTURE GROWTH (assuming new website is operational)
Customers	36,500	40,150	63,875
Daily Orders	1,435	1,579	2,811
Daily Order Lines	7,715	7,893	12,556
Sales Reps	29	32	12
Order Processing Support Staff	2	4	3
Products	600	650	900

FIGURE 7-13 Volume estimates for an order processing system showing current activity levels and two forecasts: one based on the existing order processing procedures and another that assumes a new website is operational.

A comparison of the two forecasts shows that the website will generate more new customers, process almost 80% more orders, and substantially reduce the need for sales reps and support staff. If in-house development is being considered, make sure that the software and hardware can handle future transaction volumes and data storage requirements. Conversely, if outsourcing is being considered, volume and usage data is essential to analyze ASP fee structures and develop cost estimates for outsourcing options.

SPECIFY HARDWARE, SOFTWARE, OR PERSONNEL CONSTRAINTS: The analyst must determine whether existing hardware, software, or personnel issues will affect the acquisition decision. For example, if the firm has a large number of legacy systems or if an enterprise resource planning (ERP) strategy has been adopted, these factors will have an impact on the decision. Also, the company's policy regarding outsourcing IT functions must be investigated, and whether outsourcing is part of a long-term strategy. With regard to personnel issues, in-house staffing requirements must be defined to develop, acquire, implement, and maintain the system — and determine whether the company is willing to commit to those staffing levels versus an outsourcing option.

PREPARE A REQUEST FOR PROPOSAL OR QUOTATION: To obtain the information needed to make a decision, the analyst should prepare a request for proposal or a request for quotation. The two documents are similar but used in different situations, based on whether or not a specific software product has been selected.

A **request for proposal (RFP)** is a document that describes the company, lists the IT services or products needed, and specifies the features required. An RFP helps ensure that the organization's business needs will be met. An RFP also spells out the service and support levels required. Based on the RFP, vendors can decide if they have a product that will meet the company's needs. RFPs vary in size and complexity, just like the systems they describe. An RFP for a large system can contain dozens of pages with unique requirements and features. An RFP can be used to designate some features as essential and others as desirable. An RFP also requests specific pricing and payment terms.

Figure 7-14 shows an example of a website where ready-made RFP templates for selecting software can be obtained. This RFP is part of a suite of RFP templates offered by Infotivity Technologies. Over 100 application area RFP templates are available.

Request for Proposal Tools - RFP Templates

Accurately choose the right software! Prevent expensive do-overs and other time-wasters by using these in-depth RFP and **requirements templates**. Now you can put your project on the fast track to success by using certified software selection questions to elicit better, more precise information from vendors, and by evaluating and selecting software based on your exact needs. The **selection templates** below can be used individually or as an integrated group.

Details...

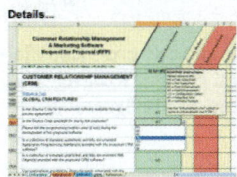

Designed specifically for selecting software, these extremely detailed *Request for Proposals templates* enable the creation of an RFP tailored precisely to your needs. Available for over 100 application areas, each of these highly **customizable RFP Templates** is pre-loaded with thousands of software selection requirements guaranteed to address all industry standard and many "exception case" issues. Organized by business process, these **RFP templates** can be used as detailed user requirements checklists in addition to eliciting proposals from vendors in any software acquisition project.

☑ *RFP Template Toolkit Included* - A comprehensive collection of software selection tools. This included a **matching software evaluation matrix** (scorecard) and a wide collection of supporting checklists addressing all phases of the software selection process. View the Complete Tool List

☑ *Avoid Fatal Omissions* - These specialized Request for Proposal templates contains a highly detailed collection of system requirements and *Cloud/Web-based SaaS* operational & security evaluation questions to investigate all aspects of a proposed solution.

☑ *Prevent False Starts* when evaluating, selecting, and implementing Cloud-based or On-Premise systems. A comprehensive set of ratios, scorecard, and comparison functions for software RFP response evaluation ensures thorough investigation of all vendor system proposals.

FIGURE 7-14 Infotivity Technologies offers a suite of ready-made RFP templates.
Source: Infotivity

When several responses to an RFP are evaluated, it is helpful to use an evaluation model. An **evaluation model** is a technique that uses a common yardstick to measure and compare vendor ratings.

Figure 7-15 shows two evaluation models for a network project. The evaluation model at the top of the figure simply lists the key elements and each vendor's score. The model at the bottom of the figure adds a weight factor. In this example, each element receives a rating based on its relative importance. Although the initial scores are the same in both models, notice that vendor A has the highest point total in the top example, but vendor C emerges as the best in the weighted model.

Unweighted Evaluation Model for a Network Project

Instructions: Rate each vendor on a scale from 1(low) to 10 (high), then add vendor scores to calculate total points.			
	VENDOR A	**VENDOR B**	**VENDOR C**
Price	6	5	9
Completion Date	2	5	8
Layout/Design	8	8	5
References	10	6	3
TOTAL POINTS	26	24	25

Weighted Evaluation Model for a Network Project

Instructions: Rate each vendor on a scale from 1(low) to 10 (high), then multiply the vendor's score by the weight factor. Add vendor scores to calculate total points.			
	WEIGHT FACTOR	**VENDOR A**	**VENDOR B**	**VENDOR C**
Price	25	6 * 25 = 150	5 * 25 = 125	9 * 25 = 225
Completion Date	25	2 * 25 = 50	5 * 25 = 125	8 * 25 = 200
Layout/Design	35	8 * 35 = 280	8 * 35 = 280	5 * 35 = 175
References	15	10 * 15 = 150	6 * 15 = 90	3 * 15 = 45
TOTAL POINTS	100	630	620	645

FIGURE 7-15 The three vendors have the same initial ratings, but the two evaluation models produce different results. In the unweighted model at the top of the figure, vendor A has the highest total points. However, after applying weighting factors, vendor C is the winner, as shown in the model at the bottom of the figure.

No standard method exists for assigning the weight factors. Each firm will have its own approach, which might be tailored to fit a specific situation. An analyst usually obtains as much input as possible, then circulates proposed values for further comment and, hopefully, a consensus.

Evaluation models are valuable tools that can be used throughout the SDLC. A spreadsheet program can be used to build an evaluation model, experiment with different weighting factors, and graph the results.

A **request for quotation (RFQ)** is more specific than an RFP. When an RFQ is used, the specific product or service desired is already known; only price quotations or bids are needed. RFQs can involve outright purchase or a variety of leasing options and can include maintenance or technical support terms. Some vendors even provide convenient RFP or RFQ forms on their websites. RFPs and RFQs have the same objective: to obtain vendor replies that are clear, comparable, and responsive, so that a well-informed selection decision can be made.

Step 2: Identify Potential Vendors or Outsourcing Options

The next step is to identify potential vendors or outsourcing providers. The Internet is a primary marketplace for all IT products and services, and descriptive information can be found on the web about all major products and acquisition alternatives.

If vertical applications for specific industries need to be located, industry trade journals or websites can be used to find reviews for industry-specific software. Industry trade groups can often provide referrals to companies that offer specific software solutions.

Another approach is to work with a consulting firm. Many IT consultants offer specialized services that help companies select software packages. A major advantage of using a consultant is that the analyst can tap into broad experience that is difficult for any one company to acquire. Consultants can be located by contacting professional organizations or industry sources, or simply by searching the Internet. Using a consultant involves additional expense but can prevent even more costly mistakes.

No matter what are the topics of interest, there are sure to be one or more online forums, or newsgroups, where people gather to meet, offer support, and exchange ideas. Forums can be hosted by private or public entities or reside in a larger communities such as Google Groups, or Yahoo Groups, which allow users to join existing groups or start their own. A web search can locate forums of interest, or the websites of specific companies, such as Microsoft, can provide a valuable source of information for IT professionals, including blogs, forums, webcasts, and other resources, as shown in Figure 7-16.

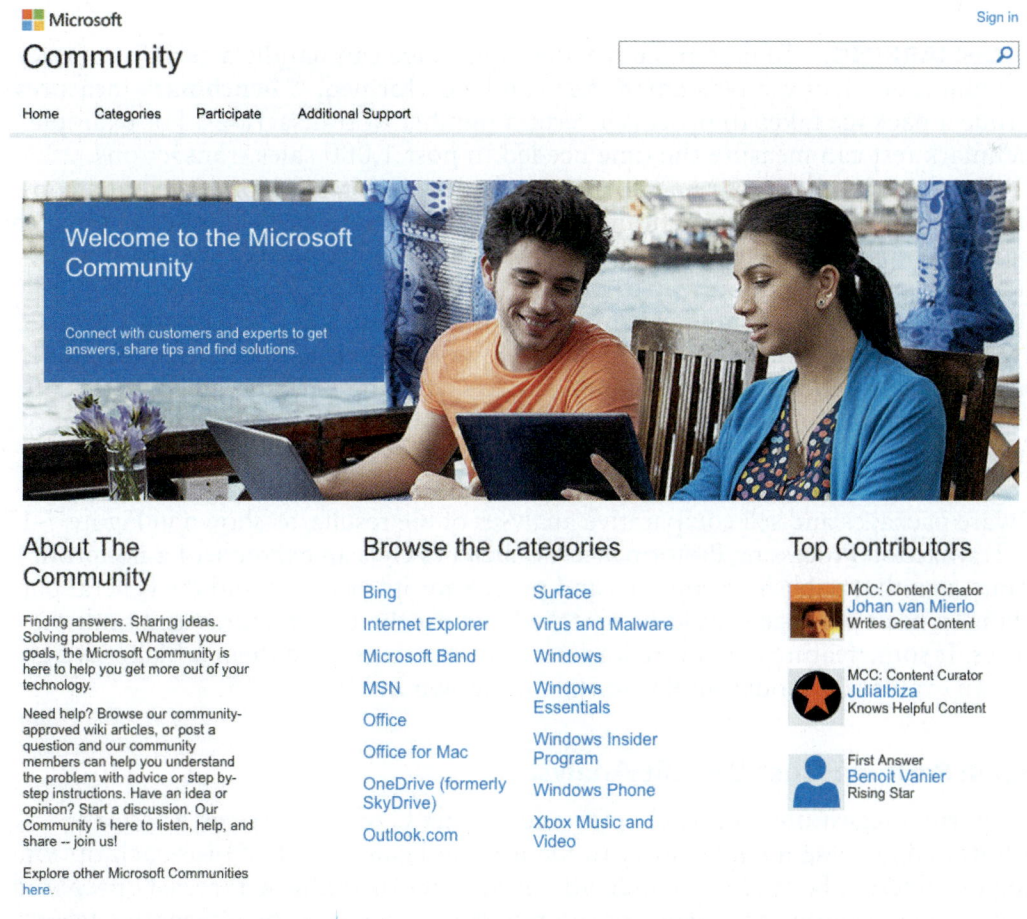

FIGURE 7-16 Microsoft Communities is a valuable resource for IT professionals.
Source: Microsoft Corporation.

Step 3: Evaluate the Alternatives

After identifying the alternatives, the analyst must select the one that best fits the company's needs. Information about the options should be obtained from as many sources as possible, including vendor presentations and literature, product documentation, trade publications, and companies that perform software testing and evaluation. To learn more about particular software packages, search the Internet using keywords that describe the application. Websites maintained by consultants and software publishers often include product references and links to vendors. As part of the evaluation process, try to obtain information from existing users, test the application, and benchmark the package.

EXISTING USERS: Existing users can be contacted to obtain feedback and learn about their experiences. For large-scale software packages, ASPs and vendors typically supply user references. User references are important because it must be known whether the software package has worked well for similar companies. Be aware that some vendors limit their reference lists to satisfied clients, so mostly positive feedback should be expected from those firms.

APPLICATION TESTING: If a software package is one of the options, find out if it is possible for users in the organization to try the product. For horizontal applications or small systems, using a demo copy to enter a few sample transactions could be an acceptable test. For vertical applications or large systems, a team of IT staff and users might need several days or weeks to perform tests.

BENCHMARKING: To determine whether a package can handle a certain transaction volume efficiently, a benchmark test can be performed. A **benchmark** measures the time a package takes to process a certain number of transactions. For example, a benchmark test can measure the time needed to post 1,000 sales transactions.

If benchmarks are used, remember that a benchmark test is conducted in a controlled environment, which might not resemble the actual day-to-day situation at the project's company. Although benchmarking cannot predict project-specific results, benchmark testing is a good way to measure relative performance of two or more competing products in a standard environment.

Many IT publications publish regular reviews of individual packages, including benchmark tests, and often have annual surveys covering various categories of software. Most of the publications now offer online and mobile versions, with additional features, search capability, and IT links.

Information can also be obtained from independent firms that benchmark various software packages and sell comparative analyses of the results, as shown in Figure 7-17. The Transaction Processing Performance Council (TPC) is an example of a nonprofit organization that publishes standards and reports for its members and the general public.

Finally, each package should be matched against the RFP features and rank the choices. If some features are more important than others, give them a higher weight using an evaluation model similar to the one shown in Figure 7-15.

Step 4: Perform Cost-Benefit Analysis

Review the suggestions in this chapter and in Part C of the Systems Analyst's Toolkit, and develop a spreadsheet to identify and calculate TCO for each option being considered. Be sure to include all costs, using the volume forecasts prepared. If outsourcing options are being considered, carefully study the alternative fee

FIGURE 7-17 The Transaction Processing Performance Council (TPC) is a nonprofit organization that publishes standards and reports for its members and the general public.
Source: TPC.org

structure models described earlier. If possible, prepare charts to show the results graphically, and build in what-if capability so the impact of one or more variables changing can be gauged.

If a software package is being considered, be sure to consider acquisition options. When software is purchased, a **software license** is being bought that gives the purchaser the right to use the software under certain terms and conditions. For example, the license could allow the software to be used only on a single computer, a specified number of computers, a network, or an entire site, depending on the terms of the agreement. Other license restrictions could prohibit making the software available to others or modifying the program. For desktop applications, software license terms and conditions usually cannot be modified. For large-scale systems, license agreement terms often can be negotiated.

Also consider user support issues, which can account for a significant part of TCO. If an outsourcing alternative is selected, the arrangement probably will include certain technical support and maintenance. If in-house development is chosen, the cost of providing these services must be considered. If a software package is purchased, consider a supplemental **maintenance agreement**, which offers additional support and assistance from the vendor. The agreement might provide full support for a period of time or list specific charges for particular services. Some software packages provide free technical support for a period of time. Afterward, support is offered with a charge per occurrence, or per minute or hour of technical support time. Some software vendors contact registered owners whenever a new release is available and usually offer the new release at a reduced price.

Step 5: Prepare a Recommendation

The analyst should prepare a recommendation that evaluates and describes the alternatives, together with the costs, benefits, advantages, and disadvantages of each option. At this point, it may be required to submit a formal system requirements document and deliver a presentation. Review the suggestions for presenting written proposals and oral presentations in Part A of the Systems Analyst's Toolkit. Additional suggestions about preparing the system requirements document and the management presentation are contained in the following section.

Step 6: Implement the Solution

Implementation tasks will depend on the solution selected. In-house options will require more time and effort than outsourcing alternatives. For large systems or network installations, the process can require considerable time and effort. The installation strategy should be planned well in advance, especially if any disruption of normal business operations is expected. If the software package is customized, then the task will be more complex and difficult.

Before the new software becomes operational, all implementation steps must be completed, including loading, configuring, and testing the software; training users; and converting data files to the new system's format. Chapter 11 discusses implementation strategies and techniques in more detail.

CASE IN POINT 7.3: Doug's Sporting Goods

Doug's Sporting Goods sells hiking and camping supplies. The company has grown considerably in the last two years. Doug Sawyer, the company's founder and president, wants to develop a customer order entry system and hired your IT consulting firm to advise him about software alternatives. Doug is leaning toward in-house development because he does not want to depend on outside vendors and suppliers for technical support and upgrades. Doug also says that he is not interested in selling on the Web, but that could change in the future.

Doug wants to meet with you tomorrow to make a decision. What will you say to Doug at the meeting?

7.9 COMPLETION OF SYSTEMS ANALYSIS TASKS

To complete the systems analysis phase, the analyst must prepare the system requirements document and the presentation to management.

7.9.1 System Requirements Document

The system requirements document, or **software requirements specification**, contains the requirements for the new system, describes the alternatives that were considered, and makes a specific recommendation to management. This important document is the starting point for measuring the performance, accuracy, and completeness of the finished system before entering the systems design phase.

The system requirements document is like a contract that identifies what the system developers must deliver to users. Recall that system requirements are identified during the fact-finding process, and a system requirements checklist is created at that time. Various examples of system requirements are listed in Chapter 4. The system requirements document should be written in language that users can understand so they can offer input, suggest improvements, and approve the final version.

Because the system requirements document can be lengthy, they should be formatted and organized so it is easy to read and use. The system requirements document should include a cover page and a detailed table of contents. An index and a glossary of terms can be added to make the document easier to use. The content of the system requirements document will depend on the company and the complexity of the system.

7.9.2 Presentation to Management

The presentation to management at the end of the systems analysis phase is one of the most critical milestones in the systems development process. At this point, managers make key decisions that affect the future development of the system.

Prior to a management presentation, two other presentations may be given: one to the principal individuals in the IT department to keep them posted, and another presentation to users to answer their questions and invite feedback. The system requirements document is the basis for all three presentations, and it (or a summary) should be distributed in advance so the recipients can review it.

When preparing the presentation, review the suggestions in Part A of the Systems Analyst's Toolkit, which can help design and deliver a successful presentation. If a slide presentation is planned, review the Toolkit guidelines for effective presentations. In addition to the techniques found in the Toolkit, also keep the following suggestions in mind:

- Begin the presentation with a brief overview of the purpose and primary objectives of the system project, the objectives of this presentation, and what decisions need to be made.

- Summarize the primary viable alternatives. For each alternative, describe the costs, advantages, and disadvantages.

- Explain why the evaluation and selection team chose the recommended alternative.

- Allow time for discussion and for questions and answers.

- Obtain a final decision from management or agree on a timetable for the next step in the process.

The object of the management presentation is to obtain approval for the development of the system and to gain management's full support, including necessary financial resources. Management probably will choose one of five alternatives: develop an in-house system, modify a current system, purchase or customize a software package, perform additional systems analysis work, or stop all further work. Depending on their decision, the next task of the systems analyst will be one of the following:

1. Implement an outsourcing alternative. If outsourcing is selected, the analyst will work with representatives of the service provider to achieve a smooth transition to the new environment.

2. Develop an in-house system. Begin systems design tasks, as described in Chapters 8, 9, and 10.

3. Purchase or customize a software package. Negotiate the purchase terms with the software vendor for management approval. Then, if the package will be used without modification, the analyst can begin planning the systems implementation phase. If modifications must be made to the package, the next step is to start the systems design phase. If the vendor will make the modifications,

then the analyst's next step is to start planning the testing and documentation of the modifications as part of the systems implementation phase, which is described in Chapter 11.

4. Perform additional systems analysis work. Management might want the analyst to investigate certain alternatives further, explore alternatives not examined, develop a prototype, reduce the project scope because of cost constraints, or expand the project scope based on new developments. If necessary, the analyst will perform the additional work and schedule a follow-up presentation.

5. Stop all further work. The decision might be based on the analyst's recommendation, a shift in priorities or costs, or for other reasons. Whatever the reason, if that is management's decision, then there are no additional tasks for the project other than to file all the research in a logical location so it can be retrieved if the project is reopened in the future.

After the presentation and management decision, the project will begin a transition to the systems design phase of the SDLC. If an in-house system is being developed, or a package is being modified, a model of the proposed system will be built, and the analyst will start designing the user interface, output, input, and data structures.

7.10 TRANSITION TO SYSTEMS DESIGN

In a traditional SDLC environment, systems design usually started when the systems analysis phase was done. Using the system requirements specification as a blueprint, developers transformed the logical design into a working model that could be tested, reviewed by users, and implemented. Today, the process is much more dynamic. In general, systems development is faster, more flexible, and more user-oriented. The introduction of adaptive methods such as agile development and extreme programming has changed the landscape significantly. Depending on the project, system developers often blend traditional and cutting-edge development methods, because what works in one situation might not work in another.

This textbook discusses systems analysis in Chapters 4, 5, 6, and 7, and systems design in Chapters 8, 9, and 10. However, in a typical IT workplace, all these tasks — and more — are integrated and managed together.

This section discusses preparation for systems design and the relationship between logical and physical design.

7.10.1 Preparing for Systems Design

Regardless of the development method, systems design requires accurate documentation. Traditionally, a system requirements document provided detailed specifications for output, input, data, processes, and whatever else was needed. Although agile methods do not require a particular form of documentation, a successful development team must understand and record user requirements as they evolve during the project.

7.10.2 Logical and Physical Design

A logical design defines *what* must take place, not *how* it will be accomplished. Logical designs do not address the actual methods of implementation. In contrast, a physical design is like a set of blueprints for the actual construction of a building. Typically, a physical design describes the actual processes of entering, verifying, and storing data; the physical layout of data files and sorting procedures, the format of reports, and so on. Because logical and physical designs are related so closely, good systems design is impossible without careful, accurate systems analysis. For example, the analyst might return to fact-finding if it was discovered that an important issue was overlooked, if users had significant new needs, or if legal or governmental requirements changed.

CASE IN POINT 7.4:   DOWNTOWN!

Downtown! is a rapidly growing web-based retailer with about 100 management and technical support employees at its headquarters office in Florida. Mary Estrada, the firm's IT manager, is planning a new information system that will give users better access to sales and marketing data and trends. She has a concern, however. She knows that users often request reports but use only a small portion of the data. In many offices she sees inboxes filled with printed reports gathering dust. Mary asked for your opinion: What if new system users could design most of their own reports without assistance from the IT staff, by using a powerful, user-friendly report writer program? Do you think they would request as many reports or the same types of reports? What are the pros and cons of giving users total control over output?

A QUESTION OF ETHICS

iStockphoto.com/faberfoto_it

Sally works as a junior analyst for a medium-sized IT consulting firm. Her manager, Bob, has asked her to draft a response to an RFP from a large company that is seeking IT consulting services in connection with a new accounting system.

As Sally worked on the RFP, she noticed a specific question about her firm's recent experience on this type of system. To the best of her knowledge, the firm has only worked on one other accounting project in the last three years. When Bob saw Sally's draft response, he was upset about the way she answered the question. "You don't have to be quite that candid," he said. "Even though we only had one *formal* project, we do have several people who worked on accounting systems before they came here."

"Yes," Sally replied, "But that isn't what the question is asking." As he left her office, Bob's final comment was, "If we want that job, we'll have to come up with a better answer." Thinking about it, Sally isn't comfortable with anything but a straight answer. Is this an ethical question? What are Sally's options?

7.11 CHAPTER SUMMARY

This chapter described system development strategies, and the preparation and presentation of the system requirements document.

An important trend that views Software as a Service (SaaS), rather than a product, has created new software acquisition options. Systems analysts must consider web-based development environments such as .NET, WebSphere, Bluemix, and various outsourcing options, including application service providers and Internet business services. Application service providers (ASPs) charge subscription fees for providing application software packages. Internet business services (IBSs) offer powerful web-based servers, software hosting, and IT support services to customers.

Traditional systems must function in various hardware and software environments, be compatible with legacy systems, and operate within the constraints of company networks and desktop computing capability. Such systems utilize Internet links and resources as enhancements. In contrast, Internet-based systems treat the web as the platform, rather than just a communication channel. Many large companies use web-based systems to handle enterprise-wide applications. Compared to traditional systems, web-based systems are more scalable, less dependent on specific hardware and software, and more adaptable to outsourcing the operation and support of a software application.

The web generation called Web 2.0 is fueling the expansion of information sharing, user collaboration, and social-networking applications such as Twitter, LinkedIn, and Facebook. Another development, called cloud computing because of the commonly used cloud symbol for the Internet, describes an overall online software and data environment, powered by supercomputer technology that is the ultimate form of SaaS.

If a company chooses to handle its own software development needs, it can create in-house systems, or purchase (and possibly customize) commercially available software packages from a software vendor or value-added reseller (VAR).

Compared with developing an in-house system, an existing commercial software package can be an attractive alternative, because a package generally costs less, takes less time to implement, has a proven track record, and is upgraded frequently. In-house development or customizing a software package might be the best choice when a standard software package cannot meet specific business requirements or constraints. In addition to customizing software packages, companies can create user applications based on standard software that has been specially configured to enhance user productivity.

The systems analyst's role in the software development process depends on the specific development strategy. In-house development requires much more involvement than outsourcing or choosing a commercial package.

The most important factor in choosing a development strategy is total cost of ownership (TCO). Financial analysis tools include payback analysis, which determines how long it takes for a system to pay for itself through reduced costs and increased benefits; return on investment (ROI), which compares a project's total return with its total costs; and net present value (NPV), which analyzes the value of a project by adjusting costs and benefits to reflect the time that they occur.

The process of acquiring software involves a series of steps: evaluate the system requirements, consider network and web-related issues, identify potential software vendors or outsourcing options, evaluate the alternatives, perform cost-benefit analysis, prepare a recommendation, and implement the solution. During software acquisition, a company can use a request for proposal (RFP) or a request for quotation (RFQ). An RFP invites vendors to respond to a list of system requirements and features; an RFQ seeks bids for a specific product or service.

The system requirements document is the deliverable, or end product, of the systems analysis phase. The document details all system requirements and constraints, recommends the best solution, and provides cost and time estimates for future development work. The system requirements document is the basis for the management presentation. At this point, the firm might decide to develop an in-house system, modify the current system, purchase or customize a software package, perform additional systems analysis work, or stop all further work.

Key Terms

application service provider (ASP) A firm that delivers a software application, or access to an application, by charging a usage or subscription fee.

benchmark A measure of the time a package takes to process a certain number of transactions.

build or buy A choice between developing in-house software and purchasing software, often called a build or buy, or make or buy, decision.

business process outsourcing (BPO) The outsourcing of a basic business process. *See* also outsourcing.

cloud computing An online software and data environment in which applications and services are accessed and used through an Internet connection rather than on a local computer; refers to the cloud symbol for the Internet.

evaluation and selection team A group of people involved in selecting hardware and software. The group includes systems analysts and users. A team approach ensures that critical factors are not over-looked and that a sound choice is made.

evaluation model A technique that uses a common yardstick to measure and compare vendor ratings.

fixed fee model A service model that charges a set fee based on a specified level of service and user support.

forum An online discussion on a particular topic, where people meet, offer support, and exchange ideas.

global outsourcing The practice of shifting IT development, support, and operations to other countries.

horizontal application A software package that can be used by many different types of organizations.

in-house software An information center or help desk within the IT department responsible for providing user support and offering services such as hotline assistance, training, and guidance to users who need technical help.

information center (IC) A facility that supports users by training them on application software. User support specialists answer questions, troubleshoot problems, and serve as a clearinghouse for user problems and solutions. Also known as service desk or help desk.

Internet business services (IBS) Services that provide powerful web-based support for transactions such as order processing, billing, and customer relationship management.

logical design The definition of an information system's functions and features, and the relationships among its components.

maintenance agreement A specification of the conditions, charges, and time frame for users to contact the vendor for assistance when they have system problems or questions.

make or buy The choice between developing in-house software and purchasing software often is called a make or buy, or build or buy, decision.

managed hosting An operation is managed by the outside firm, or host. Another term for Internet business services (IBS).

middleware Software that connects dissimilar applications and enables them to communicate and exchange data. For example, middleware can link a departmental database to a web server that can be accessed by client computers via the Internet or a company intranet.

mobile device Smartphones, tablets, and other computing devices that are not permanently tethered to a desk. They connect to the network wirelessly.

net present value (NPV) The total value of the benefits minus the total value of the costs, with both the costs and benefits being adjusted to reflect the point in time at which they occur.

newsgroup An online discussion on a particular topic, where people meet, offer support, and exchange ideas. The electronic equivalent of the physical bulletin board. Also called a forum.

offshore outsourcing The practice of shifting IT development, support, and operations to other countries.

outsourcing The transfer of information systems development, operation, or maintenance to an outside firm that provides these services, for a fee, on a temporary or long-term basis.

payback analysis A determination of how long it takes an information system to pay for itself through reduced costs and increased benefits.

physical design A plan for the actual implementation of the system.

report generator A tool for designing formatted reports rapidly. Also called a report writer.

request for proposal (RFP) A written list of features and specifications given to prospective vendors before a specific product or package has been selected.

request for quotation (RFQ) Used to obtain a price quotation or bid on a specific product or package.

return on investment (ROI) A percentage rate that measures profitability by comparing the total net benefits (the return) received from a project to the total costs (the investment) of the project. ROI = (total benefits − total costs) / total costs.

screen generator An interactive tool that helps design a custom interface, create screen forms, and handle data entry format and procedures. Also called a form painter.

service desk A centralized resource staffed by IT professionals that provides users with the support they need to do their jobs. Also called help desk.

service-oriented architecture (SOA) A way of engineering systems in which reusable business functionality is provided by services through well-defined interfaces. Technically, not software architecture but an architectural style.

service provider A firm that offers outsourcing solutions. Two popular outsourcing options involve application service providers and firms that offer Internet business services.

Software as a Service (SaaS) A model of software delivery in which functionality is delivered on-demand as a network-accessible service, rather than as a traditional software application that is downloaded and installed on the customer's computer.

software license A legal agreement that gives users the right to use the software under certain terms and conditions.

software package Software that is purchased or leased from another firm. A commercially produced software product, or family of products.

software requirements specification A document that contains the requirements for the new system, describes the alternatives that were considered, and makes a specific recommendation to management. It is the end product of the systems analysis phase. Sometimes also called a system requirements document.

software vendor Company that develops software for sale.

subscription model A service model that charges a variable fee for an application based on the number of users or workstations that have access to the application.

transaction model A service model that charges a variable fee for an application based on the volume of transactions or operations performed by the application. Also called a usage model.

usage model *See* **transaction model**.

user application Programs that utilize standard business software, such as Microsoft Office, which has been configured in a specific manner to enhance user productivity.

user interface Includes screens, commands, controls, and features that enable users to interact more effectively with an application.

value-added reseller (VAR) A firm that enhances a commercial package by adding custom features and configuring it for a particular industry.

vertical application A software package that has been developed to handle information requirements for a specific type of business.

Web 2.0 A second generation of the web that enables people to collaborate, interact, and share information much more dynamically, based on continuously available user applications rather than static HTML webpages. Interactive experience is a hallmark of Web 2.0.

Chapter Exercises

Questions

1. Describe the concept of software as a service rather than a product. Is this an important trend? Why or why not?
2. Explain the difference between horizontal and vertical application software. Suggest two examples of each type.
3. What are three typical reasons why companies develop their own information systems?
4. What are user applications? Suggest three examples that could boost user productivity.
5. What are main steps in the software acquisition process?
6. What is an RFP, and how does it differ from an RFQ?
7. What is the purpose of a benchmark test? Suggest at least two examples of benchmarks.
8. What is an evaluation model? How would you create a weighted evaluation model?
9. What decisions might management reach at the end of the systems analysis phase, and what would be the next step in each case?
10. Explain the relationship between logical and physical design.

Discussion Topics

1. As more companies outsource systems development, will there be less need for in-house systems analysts? Why or why not?
2. How has the proliferation of mobile devices affected IT professionals?
3. Suppose you tried to explain the concept of weighted evaluation models to a manager, and she responded by asking, "So, how do you set the weight factors? Is it just a subjective guess?" How would you reply?
4. Select a specific vertical application to investigate. Visit local computer stores and use the Internet to determine what software packages are available. Describe the features of two packages.
5. Select a specific horizontal application to investigate. Visit local computer stores and use the Internet to determine what software packages are available. Describe the features of two packages.

Projects

1. Various firms and organizations offer IT benchmarking. Locate an example on the Internet, and describe its services.
2. Investigate the ROI of cloud-based software development environments.
3. Turn to Part C of the Systems Analyst's Toolkit and review the concept of net present value (NPV). Determine the NPV for the following: An information system will cost $95,000 to implement over a one-year period and will produce no savings during that year. When the system goes online, the company will save $30,000 during the first year of operation. For the next four years, the savings will be $20,000 per year. Assuming a 12% discount rate, what is the NPV of the system?
4. Visit the IT department at your school or at a local company and determine whether the systems were developed in-house or purchased. If packages were acquired, find out what customizing was done, if any. Write a brief memo describing the results.
5. To create user applications as described in this chapter, systems analysts often use macros. Learn more about macros by using the Help feature in Microsoft Word, and suggest three tasks that might be performed by macros.

PHASE 3 SYSTEMS DESIGN

© 2013 Scott Adams, Inc./Dist. by UNIVERSAL UCLICK

As the Dilbert cartoon suggests, system requirements change constantly. This is one of the reasons agile methods are so popular: They accommodate changes more easily than traditional approaches. A good systems analyst must budget for change and schedule the project accordingly.

Systems design is the third of five phases in the systems development life cycle. In the previous phase, systems analysis, a logical model of the new system was developed. The output of that phase, the system requirements document, is used as input to the system design phase, where a physical design is created that satisfies the system requirements.

Chapter 8 explains how to design an effective user interface, and how to handle data security and control issues. Chapter 9 focuses on the data design skills that are necessary for a systems analyst to construct the physical model of the information system. Chapter 10 describes system architecture, which translates the logical design of an information system into a physical blueprint.

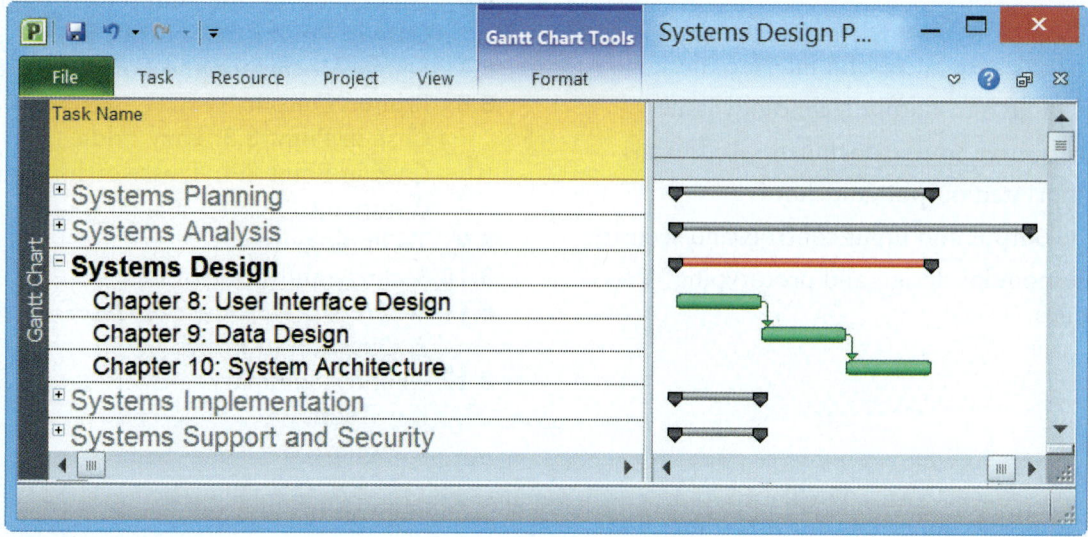

CHAPTER 8

User Interface Design

Chapter 8 is the first of three chapters in the systems design phase of the SDLC. This chapter explains how to design an effective user interface, and how to handle data security and control issues. The chapter stresses the importance of user feedback and involvement in all design decisions.

The chapter includes four "Case in Point" discussion questions to help contextualize the concepts described in the text. The "Question of Ethics" considers the ethical (and possibly legal) constraints on how far the creative work of others can be used without crediting the source, for example, in the design of a company's website.

LEARNING OBJECTIVES

When you finish this chapter, you should be able to:

- Explain the concept of user interface design and human-computer interaction, including basic principles of user-centered design
- Explain how experienced interface designers perform their tasks
- Describe rules for successful interface design
- Discuss input and output technology issues
- Design effective source documents and forms
- Explain printed output guidelines
- Describe output and input controls and security
- Explain modular design and prototyping techniques

CHAPTER CONTENTS

8.1 INTRODUCTION

User interface design is the first task in the systems design phase of the SDLC. Designing the interface is extremely important because everyone wants a system that is easy to learn and use.

After discussing the user interface, human-computer interaction, and interface design rules, the chapter describes output, data security and control issues, prototyping, and the next steps in the systems design process.

8.2 SYSTEMS DESIGN PHASE OVERVIEW

Because the components of a system are interdependent, the design phase is not a series of clearly defined steps. Although work may start in one area, it is possible to be working with several different elements at the same time. For example, a decision to change a report format might require changes in data design or input screens. The design checklist will include the user interface, input and output procedures, data design, and system architecture. At the end of this phase, the analyst prepares a systems design specification and delivers a presentation to management.

The goal of **systems design** is to build a system that is effective, reliable, and maintainable.

- A system is *effective* if it supports business requirements and meets user needs.
- A system is *reliable* if it handles input errors, processing errors, hardware failures, or human mistakes. A good design will anticipate errors, detect them as early as possible, make it easy to correct them, and prevent them from damaging the system itself. Other characteristics of a reliable system include it being available nearly all of the time, and proper backups maintained in case of system failure.
- A system is *maintainable* if it is flexible, scalable, and easily modified. Changes might be needed to correct problems, adapt to user requirements, or take advantage of new technology.

Although each project is different, the following basic principles usually apply.

8.2.1 Will It Succeed?

A system might have advanced technology and powerful features, but the *real* test is whether users like it and feel that it meets their needs. Some suggestions for successful design include thinking like a user, anticipating future needs, providing flexibility, and managing data effectively.

THINK LIKE A USER: Carefully examine any point where users provide input or receive output. The user interface must be easy to learn. Input processes should be easy to follow, intuitive, and forgiving of errors. Predesigned output should be attractive and easy to understand, with an appropriate level of detail.

ANTICIPATE FUTURE NEEDS: Consider a parts inventory database that contains a one-character field for category such as electrical, mechanical, or hydraulic. The design works well, but what if the company decides to break these overall groups down into more specific segments? A better design would anticipate possible expansion to two or more characters. For example, in 1999, there was widespread concern about what was called the *Y2K issue* because many older programs used only two characters to store the year and might not recognize the start of a new century.

PROVIDE FLEXIBILITY: Suppose that a user wants a screen display of all customer balances that exceed $5,000 in an accounts receivable system. How should that feature be designed? The program could be coded to check customer balances against a fixed value of 5,000, which is a simple solution for both the programmer and the user because no extra keystrokes are required to produce the display. However, that approach is inflexible. A better approach would be to let the user enter the amount, or start with a **default value** that displays automatically. Users can press the Enter key to accept the value or type in another value. Often the best design strategy is to offer several alternatives, so users can decide what will work best for them.

MANAGE DATA EFFECTIVELY: In addition to its effect on users, data management impacts company efficiency, productivity, and security. To reduce input errors, the system should enter and verify data as soon as possible, and each data item should have a specific type, such as alphabetic, numeric, or alphanumeric, and a range of acceptable values.

It is important to collect input data as close to its source as possible. For instance, using barcode scanners rather than manual forms on a warehouse freight dock, or having salespeople use tablets to record orders rather than filling in source documents. The easiest, most accurate, and least expensive data input strategy is automated data capture, such as the radio frequency identification (RFID) scanner shown in Figure 8-1.

FIGURE 8-1 Automated data entry methods, such as the RFID scanner shown in this figure, reduce input errors and improve employee productivity.

Courtesy of Intermec Technologies

In an efficient design, data is entered only once. For example, if input data for a payroll system also is needed for a human resources system, the analyst could design an interface to transfer data automatically, or a central data storage area could be created that both systems can access. Chapter 9 describes normalization, which is a set of rules that can help avoid data design problems. A secure system also includes **audit trails** that can log every instance of data entry and changes. For example, the system should record when a customer's credit limit was set, by whom, and any other information necessary to construct the history of a transaction.

8.3 CHAPTER OVERVIEW

Traditionally, a chapter on user interface design started with a discussion of output because output is what users touched, viewed, and needed to do their jobs. Today, the situation is different, for several important reasons:

- Users can design their own output. System designers are more aware of user needs and desires. A system can maintain data integrity and still allow users to view, sort, filter, and examine data in any way that helps them do their jobs. There was a time when the MIS department made those choices and users had little or no say in the matter. Today, successful applications are designed quite differently — the system developer identifies user needs, and then creates a design that will satisfy users *and* meet corporate requirements.

- Centralized IT departments no longer produce reams of printed reports. Those reports, called greenbar reports because of their appearance, often gathered dust while sitting on top of file cabinets. While a few examples might persist, the overwhelming trend has been customer-designed output. The customer might be an individual user or a community of users, such as a department. As Chapter 4 pointed out, the IT team must understand user requirements before creating a solution.

- The user interface itself has evolved into a two-way channel, with powerful output capability, and most user information needs can be met with screen-generated data, which a user can print, view, or save. Well into the 1980s and beyond, a user interface was a blank character-based screen, which might or might not offer menu choices. If a user entered a command improperly, the system responded with an error message, which frustrated users and stifled productivity. Many hardware-centric vendors did not understand the importance of the user interface and its implications.

Apple was a pioneer in user interface development, introducing the **graphical user interface (GUI)**, complete with mouse and screen icons, in the early 1980s. At that point, not many companies were ready for this concept. When software giant Microsoft finally jumped on the GUI bandwagon with its Windows® operating system, the corporate doors swung open, and everyone from managers on down said, "How did we ever do without this?"

The user interface continues to evolve. The widespread use of mobile devices such as the iPad and other tablets, coupled with the ubiquity of the iPhone and other smartphones, has greatly influenced user interface design. Indeed, key user experience lessons from these devices have been reflected back into the user interface for mainstream operating systems such as Mac OS X and Microsoft Windows 10.

It is difficult to predict the future, but the introduction of the Apple Watch, Android Wear, and other wearable devices promises to further shake up user interface design principles. Advanced technology will support the evolution, but the *real* driving force will be user empowerment, which results in customer satisfaction, increased productivity, and bottom-line savings.

8.4 WHAT IS A USER INTERFACE?

A user interface (UI) describes how users interact with a computer system, and consists of all the hardware, software, screens, menus, functions, output, and features that affect two-way communications between the user and the computer. The UI is the key to **usability**, which includes user satisfaction, support for business functions, and system effectiveness.

Many industry leaders believe that the best interfaces are the ones that users do not even notice — they make sense because they do what users expect them to do. For example, as shown in Figure 8-2, Apple believes

Designing Great Apps

Exceptional user experience is a hallmark of Apple products, and a distinguishing feature of the most successful apps built for iOS and OS X. Use the resources below to learn how to build the polished, engaging, and intuitive apps that Apple customers expect.

FIGURE 8-2 Apple has long been a leader in creating elegant user interfaces for its products.
Source: © 2015 Apple Inc

that designing an exceptional user interface is essential to a successful app. Apple has long distinguished itself from its competitors by the intuitiveness of its products. Apple's command of the market suggests that consumers are willing to pay a premium for products that "just work."

When developing older systems, analysts typically designed all the printed and screen output first, then worked on the inputs necessary to produce the results. Often, the user interface mainly consisted of process-control screens that allowed the user to send commands to the system. That approach worked well with traditional systems that simply transformed input data into structured output.

As information management evolved from centralized data processing to dynamic, enterprise-wide systems, the primary focus also shifted — from the IT department to the users themselves. The IT group became a supplier of information technology, rather than a supplier of information. Today, the main focus is on users within and outside the company, how they communicate with the information system, and how the system supports the firm's business operations.

In a **user-centered** system, the distinction blurs between input, output, and the interface itself. Most users work with a varied mix of input, screen output, and data queries as they perform their day-to-day job functions. Because all those tasks require interaction with the computer system, the user interface is a vital element in the systems design phase.

User interface design requires an understanding of human-computer interaction and user-centered design principles, which are discussed in the next section.

8.4.1 Human-Computer Interaction

A user interface is based on basic principles of human-computer interaction. **Human-computer interaction (HCI)** describes the relationship between computers and the people who use them to perform their jobs, like the worker shown in Figure 8-3. HCI concepts

FIGURE 8-3 HCI is essential to employee productivity, whether the work is done in a traditional office setting or on a construction site like the one shown in this figure.

apply to everything from smartphones to global networks. In its broadest sense, a user interface includes all the communications and instructions necessary to enter input to the system and to obtain output in the form of screen displays or printed reports.

Early user interfaces involved users typing complex commands on a keyboard, which displayed as green text on a black screen. Then came the graphical user interface (GUI), which was a huge improvement because it used icons, graphical objects, and pointing devices. Today, designers strive to translate user behavior, needs, and desires into an interface that users don't really notice. IBM has stated that the best user interfaces are "*almost transparent — you can see right through the interface to your own work.*" In other words, a transparent interface does not distract the user and calls no attention to itself.

A systems analyst designs user interfaces for in-house–developed software and customize interfaces for various commercial packages and user productivity applications. The main objective is to create a user-friendly design that is easy to learn and use.

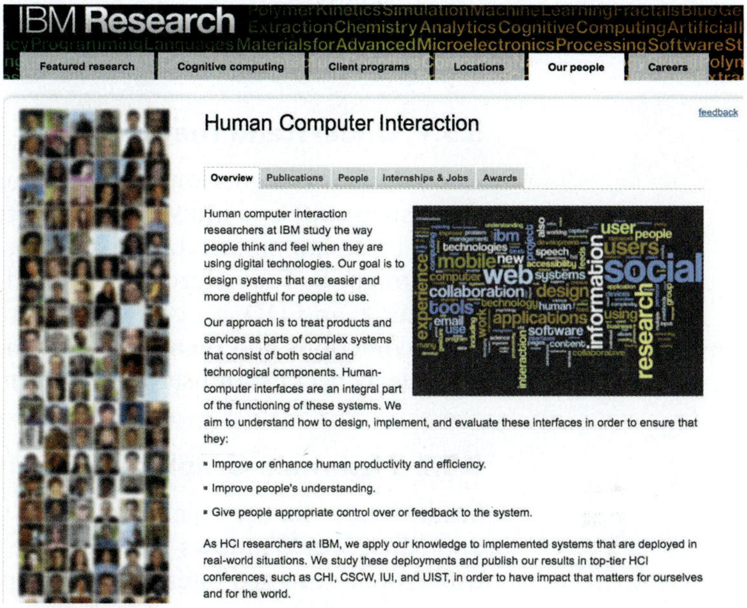

Industry leaders Microsoft and IBM both devote considerable resources to user interface research. Figure 8-4 describes IBM Research's work on human-computer interaction. Their stated goal is to "design systems that are easier and more delightful for people to use."

FIGURE 8-4 IBM's research division is a leader in exploring human-computer interaction (HCI).

Source: IBM Research Division

Because HCI has a major impact on user productivity, it gets lots of attention — especially where multimillion-dollar issues are concerned. For example, in the article "User Unfriendly" by Elizabeth Gardner from the February 2012 issue of *Health Data Management,* the author describes how software usability has a major impact on the medical profession, and not everyone is happy about it — particularly physicians who often struggle with electronic health records (EHRs) systems that are poorly designed. In her article, Ms. Gardner points out that physicians often multi-task, answering a question about one patient while writing a prescription for another, and EHR software was not designed around that type of workflow.

CASE IN POINT 8.1:   CASUAL OBSERVER SOFTWARE

Casual Observer Software's main product is a program that monitors and analyzes user keystrokes and mouse clicks to learn more about the way employees use their computer systems. The problem is that some users feel this is an unwarranted intrusion into their privacy, and they prefer not to be observed. Some even fear that the data would be used for other reasons, including performance appraisal. You are a consultant who has been hired by a client firm that is trying to decide whether or not to use this software.

Before you advise the client, go back to Chapter 4 and consider the Hawthorne Effect, which suggests that employees might behave differently when they know they are being observed. Finally, think about the ethical issues that might be involved in this situation. What will you advise your client, and why?

8.5 SEVEN HABITS OF SUCCESSFUL INTERFACE DESIGNERS

Although IT professionals have different views about interface design, most would agree that good design depends on seven basic principles. Successful interface designers use these basic principles as a matter of course — they become habits. These desirable habits are described in the following sections.

8.5.1 Understand the Business

The interface designer must understand the underlying business functions and how the system supports individual, departmental, and enterprise goals. The overall objective is to design an interface that helps users to perform their jobs. A good starting point might be to analyze a functional decomposition diagram (FDD). As described in Chapter 4, an FDD is a graphical representation of business functions that starts with major functions and then breaks them down into several levels of detail. An FDD can provide a checklist of user tasks that must be included in the interface design.

8.5.2 Maximize Graphical Effectiveness

Studies show that people learn better visually. The immense popularity of Apple's iOS and Microsoft Windows is largely the result of their GUIs that are easy to learn and use. A well-designed interface can help users learn a new system rapidly and be more productive. Also, in a graphical environment, a user can display and work with multiple windows on a single screen and transfer data between programs. If the interface supports data entry, it must follow the guidelines for data entry screen design that are discussed later in this chapter.

8.5.3 Think Like a User

A systems analyst should understand user experience, knowledge, and skill levels. If a wide range of capability exists, the interface should be flexible enough to accommodate novices as well as experienced users.

To develop a user-centered interface, the designer must learn to think like a user and see the system through a user's eyes. The interface should use terms and metaphors that are familiar to users. Users are likely to have real-world experience with many other machines and devices that provide feedback, such as automobiles, ATMs, and microwave ovens. Based on that experience, users will expect useful, understandable feedback from a computer system.

8.5.4 Use Models and Prototypes

From a user's viewpoint, the interface is the most critical part of the system design because it is where he or she interacts with the system — perhaps for many hours each day. It is essential to construct models and prototypes for user approval. An interface designer should obtain as much feedback as possible, as early as possible. Initial screen designs can be presented to users in the form of a storyboard, which is a sketch that shows the general screen layout and design. The storyboard can be created with software or drawn freehand. Users must test all aspects of the interface design and provide feedback to the designers. User input can be obtained in interviews, via questionnaires, and by observation. Interface designers also can obtain data, called usability metrics, by using software that can record and measure user interaction with the system.

8.5.5 Focus on Usability

The user interface should include all tasks, commands, and communications between users and the information system. The opening screen should show the main options (Figure 8-5 is an illustration). Each screen option leads to another screen, with more options. The objective is to offer a reasonable number of choices that a user easily can comprehend. Too many options on one screen can confuse a user — but too few options increase the number of submenu levels and complicate the navigation process. Often, an effective strategy is to present the most common choice as a default but allow the user to select other options.

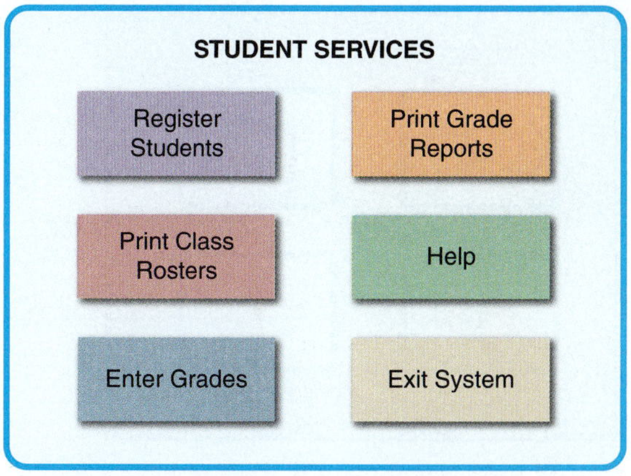

8.5.6 Invite Feedback

Even after the system is operational, it is important to monitor system usage and solicit user suggestions. The analyst can determine if system features are being used as intended by observing and surveying users. Sometimes, full-scale operations highlight problems that were not apparent when the prototype was tested. Based on user feedback, Help screens might need revision and design changes to allow the system to reach its full potential.

8.5.7 Document Everything

All screen designs should be documented for later use by programmers. If a CASE tool or screen generator is being used, the screen designs should be numbered and saved in a hierarchy similar to a menu tree. User-approved sketches and storyboards also can be used to document the user interface.

By applying basic user-centered design principles, a systems analyst can plan, design, and deliver a successful user interface.

FIGURE 8-5 The opening screen displays the main options for a student registration system. A user can click an option to see lower-level actions and menu choices.

8.6 GUIDELINES FOR USER INTERFACE DESIGN

What follows is a set of general guidelines for user interface design. These guidelines are distilled from years of best practices in the industry. There is some overlap because many of the main guidelines share common elements.

Although there is no standard approach to interface design, these guidelines are a starting point suitable for traditional systems development. User interface development for web applications or for mobile apps has its own unique considerations, above and beyond these general guidelines. Perhaps the *most* important guideline is that not all of these recommendations must be followed — the best interface is the one that works best for the users.

8.6.1 Create an Interface That Is Easy to Learn and Use

1. Focus on system design objectives, rather than calling attention to the interface.
2. Create a design that is easy to understand and remember. Maintain a common design in all modules of the interface, including the use of color, screen placements, fonts, and the overall "look and feel."

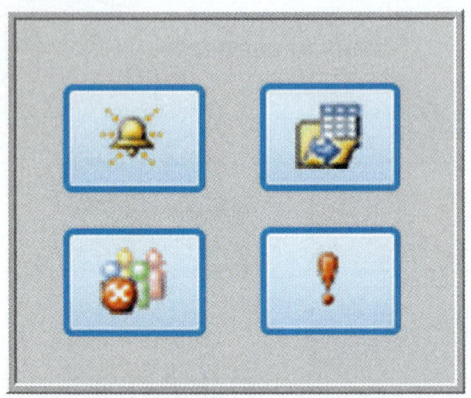

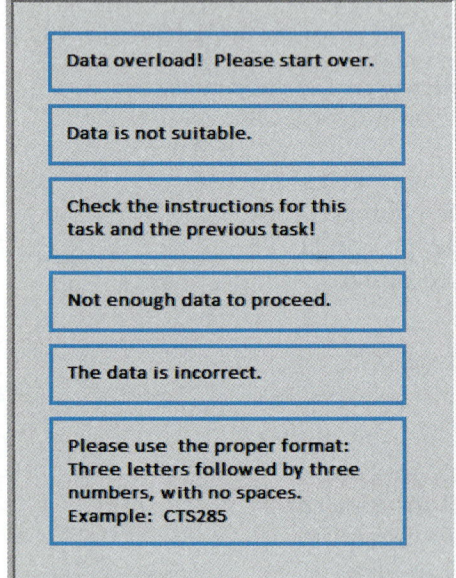

FIGURE 8-6 In the example at the top, the icons do not have a clear message. In the Help text examples at the bottom, only one message is understandable. The others would frustrate and annoy most users.

3. Provide commands, actions, and system responses that are consistent and predictable.

4. Allow users to correct errors easily.

5. Clearly label all controls, buttons, and icons.

6. Select familiar images that users can understand, and provide on-screen instructions that are logical, concise, and clear. For example, the top screen in Figure 8-6 shows four control buttons, but none of them has an obvious meaning. In the bottom screen, the first five messages provide little or no information. The last message is the only one that is easy to understand.

7. Show all commands in a list of menu items, but dim any commands that are not available to the user.

8. Make it easy to navigate or return to any level in the menu structure.

8.6.2 Enhance User Productivity

The interface is where a user interacts with the system, so it can have a dramatic effect on productivity. If the interface empowers a user and enables him or her to handle more complex tasks, the user becomes more productive. Conversely, if the interface is difficult to work with, productivity declines.

1. Organize tasks, commands, and functions in groups that resemble actual business operations. Group functions and submenu items in a multilevel menu hierarchy, or tree, that is logical and reflects how users typically perform the tasks. Figure 8-7 shows an example of a menu hierarchy for an order tracking system.

2. Create alphabetical menu lists or place the selections used frequently at the top of the menu list. No universally accepted approach to menu item placement exists. The best strategy is to design a prototype and obtain feedback from users. Some applications even allow menus to show recently used commands first. Some users like that feature, but others find it distracting. The best approach is to offer a choice, and let users decide.

3. Provide shortcuts for experienced users so they can avoid multiple menu levels. Shortcuts can be created using hot keys that allow a user to press the Alt key + the underlined letter of a command.

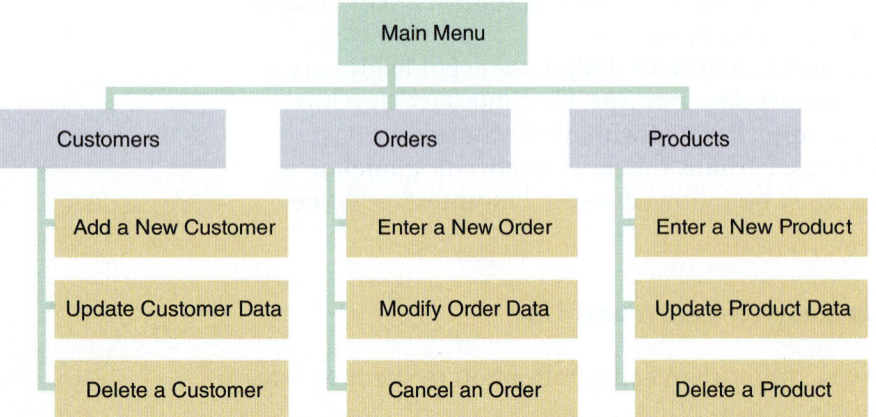

FIGURE 8-7 This menu hierarchy shows tasks, commands, and functions organized into logical groups and sequences. The structure resembles a functional decomposition diagram (FDD), which is a model of business functions and processes.

4. Use default values if the majority of values in a field are the same. For example, if 90% of the firm's customers live in Albuquerque, use *Albuquerque* as the default value in the City field.

5. Use a duplicate value function that enables users to insert the value from the same field in the previous record, but allow users to turn this feature on or off as they prefer.

6. Provide a fast-find feature that displays a list of possible values as soon as users enter the first few letters.

7. If available, consider a **natural language** feature that allows users to type commands or requests in normal text phrases. For example, many applications allow users to request Help by typing a question into a dialog box. The software then uses natural language technology to retrieve a list of topics that match the request. Natural language technology is used in speech recognition systems, text-to-speech synthesizers, automated voice response systems, web search engines, text editors, and language instruction materials.

8.6.3 Provide Users with Help and Feedback

This is one of the most important guidelines because it has a high impact on users. Never allow Help to slow a user down. Instead, make Help easy to find, but not around when users don't need it.

1. Ensure that help is always available on demand. Help screens should provide information about menu choices, procedures, shortcuts, and errors.

2. Provide user-selected help and context-sensitive help. User-selected help displays information when the user requests it. By making appropriate choices through the menus and submenus, the user eventually reaches a screen with the desired information. Figure 8-8 shows the main Help screen for the student registration system. **Context-sensitive** help offers assistance for the task in progress.

3. Provide a direct route for users to return to the point from where help was requested. Title every help screen to identify the topic, and keep help text simple and concise. Insert blank lines between paragraphs to make Help easier to read, and provide examples where appropriate.

4. Include contact information, such as a telephone extension or email address, if a department or help desk is responsible for assisting users.

5. Require user confirmation before data deletion *(Are you sure?)* and provide a method of recovering data that is deleted inadvertently. Build in safeguards that prevent critical data from being changed or erased.

6. Provide an "Undo" key or a menu choice that allows the user to undo the results of the most recent command or action.

7. When a user-entered command contains an error, highlight the erroneous part and allow the user to make the correction without retyping the entire command.

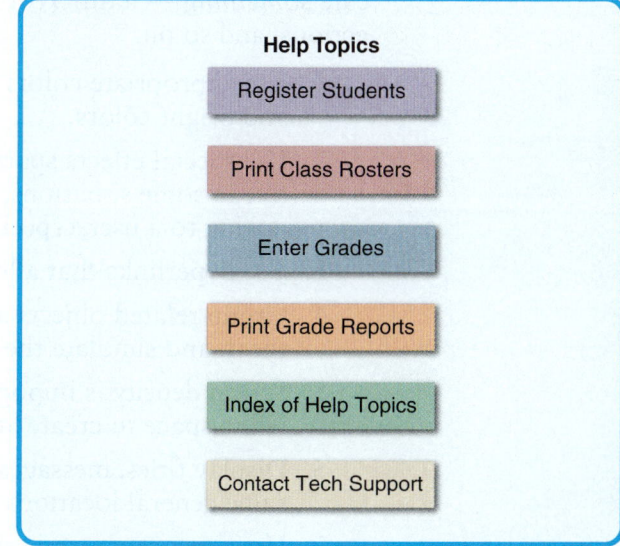

FIGURE 8-8 The main Help screen for a student registration system.

8. Use hypertext links to assist users as they navigate help topics.

9. Display messages at a logical place on the screen, and be consistent.

10. Alert users to lengthy processing times or delays. Give users an on-screen progress report, especially if the delay is lengthy.

11. Allow messages to remain on the screen long enough for users to read them. In some cases, the screen should display messages until the user takes some action.

12. Let the user know whether the task or operation was successful or not. For example, use messages such as *Update completed, All transactions have been posted,* or *The ID Number was not found.*

13. Provide a text explanation if an icon or image is used on a control button. This can be accomplished using a "mouse hover" to display a pop-up box with explanation when the mouse is moved over an icon or image.

14. Use messages that are specific, understandable, and professional. Avoid messages that are cute, cryptic, or vague, such as *ERROR — You have entered an unacceptable value,* or *Error DE-4-16.* Better examples are:

   - *Enter a number from 1 (low) to 5 (high)*
   - *Customer number must be numeric*
   - *Please re-enter a numeric value*
   - *Call the Accounting Department, Ext. 239 for assistance*

8.6.4 Create an Attractive Layout and Design

This is a subjective area because reasonable people can differ on what is attractive. The analyst should consider color, layout, and ease of use. Screen mock-ups and menu trees can be created and tried on users to get their input. If in doubt, err on the side of doing a bit less. For example, blinking messages initially may seem like a good idea, they might not be the best choice for the interface design. Also try to avoid too many fonts, styles, and sizes, which can be distracting. Each separate style should communicate *something* — a different level of detail, another topic, mandatory versus optional actions, and so on.

1. Use appropriate colors to highlight different areas of the screen; avoid gaudy and bright colors.

2. Use special effects sparingly. For example, animation and sound might be effective in some situations, but too many special effects can be distracting and annoying to a user, especially if he or she must view them repeatedly.

3. Use hyperlinks that allow users to navigate to related topics.

4. Group related objects and information. Visualize the screen the way a user will see it, and simulate the tasks that the user will perform.

5. Screen density is important. Keep screen displays uncluttered, with enough white space to create an attractive, readable design.

6. Display titles, messages, and instructions in a consistent manner and in the same general locations on all screens.

7. Use consistent terminology. For example, do not use the terms *delete, cancel,* and *erase* to indicate the same action. Similarly, the same sound always should signal the same event.

8. Ensure that commands always will have the same effect. For example, if the BACK control button returns a user to the prior screen, the BACK command always should perform that function throughout the application.

9. Ensure that similar mouse actions will produce the same results throughout the application. The results of pointing, clicking, and double-clicking should be consistent and predictable.

10. When the user enters data that completely fills the field, do not move automatically to the next field. Instead, require the user to confirm the entry by pressing the Enter key or Tab key at the end of every fill-in field.

11. Remember that users are accustomed to a pattern of red = stop, yellow = caution, and green = go. Stick to that pattern and use it when appropriate to reinforce on-screen instructions.

12. Provide a keystroke alternative for each menu command, with easy-to-remember letters, such as File, Exit, and Help.

13. Use familiar commands if possible, such as Cut, Copy, and Paste.

14. Provide a Windows look and feel in the interface design if users are familiar with Windows-based applications.

15. Avoid complex terms and technical jargon; instead, select terms that come from everyday business processes and the vocabulary of a typical user.

8.6.5 Enhance the Interface

A designer can include many features, such as menu bars, toolbars, dialog boxes, text boxes, toggle buttons, list boxes, scroll bars, drop-down list boxes, option buttons, check boxes, command buttons, and calendar controls, among others. Screen design requires a sense of aesthetics as well as technical skills. User feedback should be obtained early and often as the design process continues.

1. The opening screen is especially important because it introduces the application and allows users to view the primary options. The starting point can be a **switchboard** with well-placed command buttons that allow users to navigate the system. Figure 8-9 shows the switchboard of TurboTax, introducing a tax preparation program. The main options are clearly displayed on an uncluttered screen. The addition of the picture showing tax professionals ready to help provides a sense of calm and confidence to the user — something particularly important for users who are likely to be confused and/or nervous when beginning the tax preparation process.

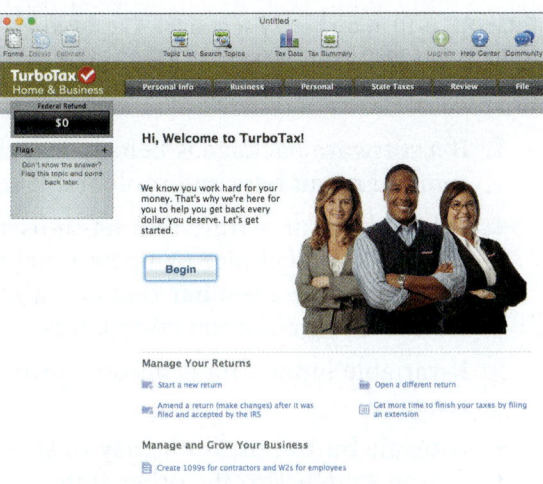

FIGURE 8-9 An example of a switchboard introducing TurboTax. The main options are clearly displayed on an uncluttered screen — something particularly important for users who are likely to be confused and/or nervous when beginning the tax preparation process.
© Intuit Canada ULC, 2014

2. Use a **command button** to initiate an action such as printing a form or requesting help. For example, when a user clicks the Find Student command button in Figure 8-10, a dialog box opens with instructions.

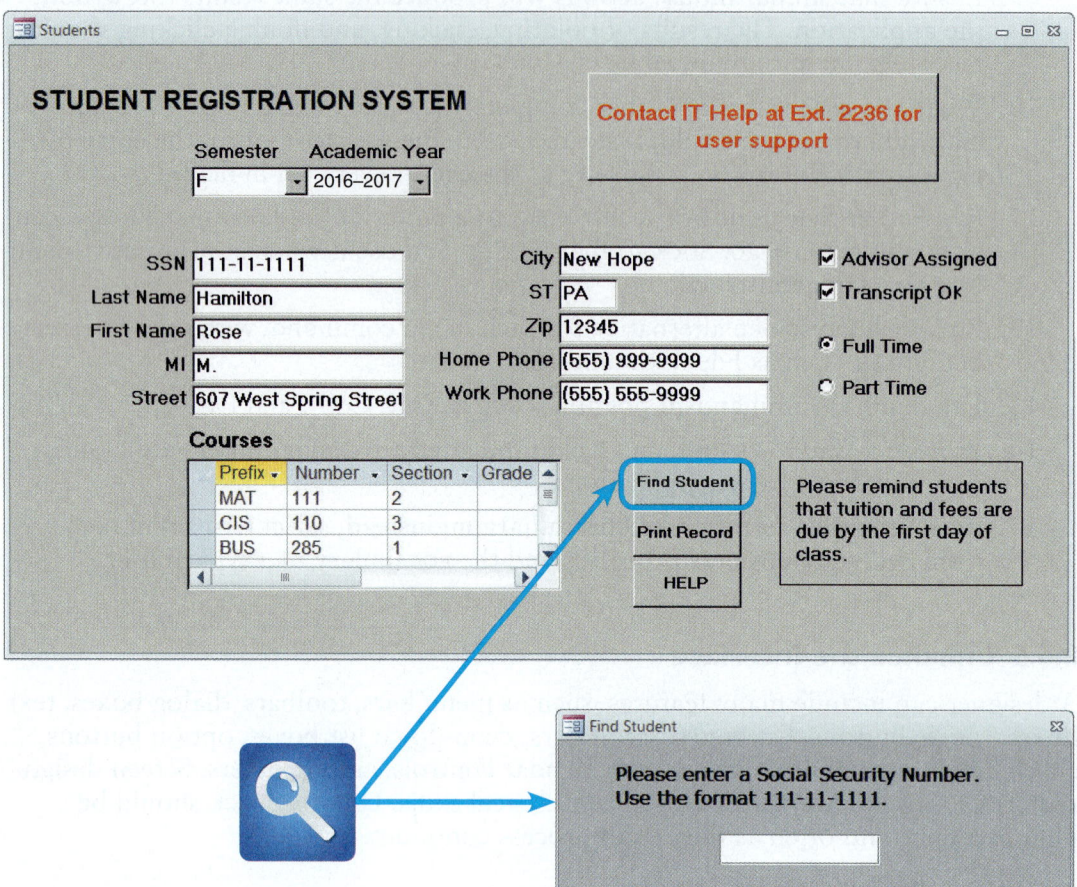

FIGURE 8-10 A data entry screen for a student registration system. This screen uses several design features that are described in the text. When a user clicks the Find Student command button, a dialog box is displayed with instructions.

3. If a software package is being used, check to see if it allows the creation of customized **menu bars** and toolbars. If so, consider these options.

4. Add a shortcut feature that lets a user select a menu command either by clicking the desired choice or by pressing the Alt key + the underlined letter. Some forms also use a **toolbar** that contains icons or buttons that represent shortcuts for executing common commands.

5. If variable input data is needed, provide a **dialog box** that explains what is required.

6. A **toggle button** makes it easy to show on or off status — clicking the toggle button switches to the other state.

7. Use **list boxes** that display the available choices. If the list does not fit in the box, a **scroll bar** allows the user to move through the available choices. Also, be sure to provide another way to enter data that does not align with a specific list choice.

8. Use an **option button**, sometimes called a **radio button**, to control user choices. For example, if the user can select only one option, display a suitable message

(Choose one item), but if there is no restriction, display a different message *(Choose all that apply)*. Use a black dot to show selected options.

9. If check boxes are used to select one or more choices from a group, show the choices with a checkmark or an X.

10. When dates must be entered, use a calendar control that allows the user to select a date that the system will use as a field value.

8.6.6 Focus on Data Entry Screens

Data entry is especially important because it is in the job description of so many users.

1. Whenever possible, use a data entry method called form filling, where a blank form that duplicates or resembles the source document is completed on the screen.

2. Restrict user access to screen locations where data is entered. For example, in the Eventbrite event management data entry when the screen in Figure 8-11 appears, the system should position the insertion point in the first data entry location. After the operator enters an event title, the insertion point should move automatically to the entry location for the next field (Location). A user should be able to position the insertion point only in places where data is entered on the form.

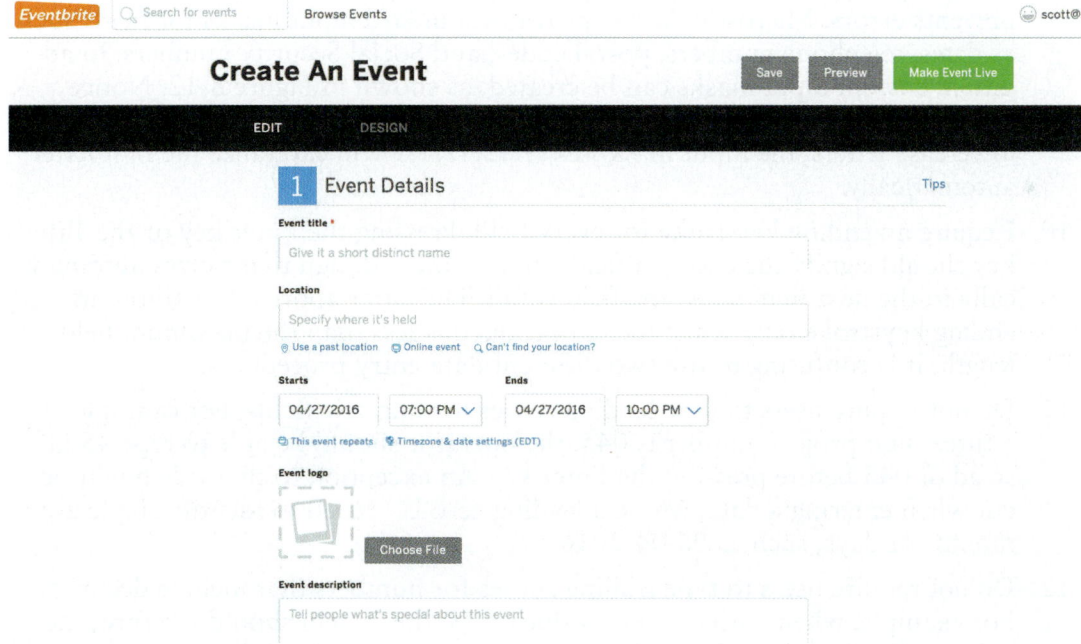

FIGURE 8-11 In this data entry screen for creating events, the system generates start and end dates and times automatically, but these can be changed by the user at any time. A red asterisk, as shown beside Event Title, indicates required fields. Gray text within the data entry field lets the user know what information to provide. This text is replaced with user input.
Source: © 2015 Eventbrite

3. Provide a way to leave the data entry screen at any time without entering the current record, such as a "Cancel" button. Since the application shown in Figure 8-11 is web-based, this can be accomplished by selecting the "Back" button of the browser (not shown).

4. Provide a descriptive caption for every field, and show the user where to enter the data and the required or maximum field size. Typically, white boxes show the location and length of each field. Other methods used to indicate field locations are video highlighting, underscores, special symbols, or a combination of these features.

5. Provide a means for users to move among fields on the form in a standard order or in any order they choose. In a GUI, the user can override the standard field order and select field locations using the mouse or arrow keys.

6. Allow users to add, change, delete, and view records. Messages such as *Apply these changes? (Y/N)* or *Delete this record? (Y/N)* should require users to confirm the actions. Highlighting the letter N as a default response will avoid problems if the user presses the Enter key by mistake.

7. Design the screen form layout to match the layout of the source document. If the source document fields start at the top of the form and run down in a column, the input screen should use the same design.

8. Display a sample format if a user must enter values in a field in a specific format. For example, provide an on-screen instruction to let users know that the date format is MMDDYY, and provide an example if the user must enter separators, such as slashes.

9. In addition to the sample format in the preceding rule, it might be better to use an **input mask**, which is a template or pattern that restricts data entry and prevents errors. Microsoft Access provides standard input masks for fields such as dates, telephone numbers, postal codes, and Social Security numbers. In addition, custom input masks can be created, as shown in Figure 8-12. Notice that a mask can have a specific format. For example, if a user enters text in lowercase letters, the input mask >L<??????????? will capitalize the first letter automatically.

10. Require an ending keystroke for every field. Pressing the Enter key or the Tab key should signify the end of a field entry. Avoid a design that moves automatically to the next item when the field is full. The latter approach requires an ending keystroke only when the data entered is less than the maximum field length. It is confusing to use two different data entry procedures.

11. Do not require users to type leading zeroes for numeric fields. For example, if a three-digit project number is 045, the operator should be able to type 45 instead of 045 before pressing the Enter key. An exception to that rule might occur when entering a date, where a leading zero is needed to identify single-digit months or days, such as 06-04-2016.

12. Do not require users to type trailing zeroes for numbers that include decimals. For example, when a user types a value of 98, the system should interpret the value as 98.00 if the field has been formatted to include numbers with two decimal places. The decimal point is needed only to indicate nonzero decimal places, such as 98.76.

13. Display default values so operators can press the Enter key to accept the suggested value. If the default value is not appropriate, the operator can change it.

14. Use a default value when a field value will be constant for successive records or throughout the data entry session. For example, if records are input in order by date, the date used in the first transaction should be used as the default date until a new date is entered, at which time the new date becomes the default value.

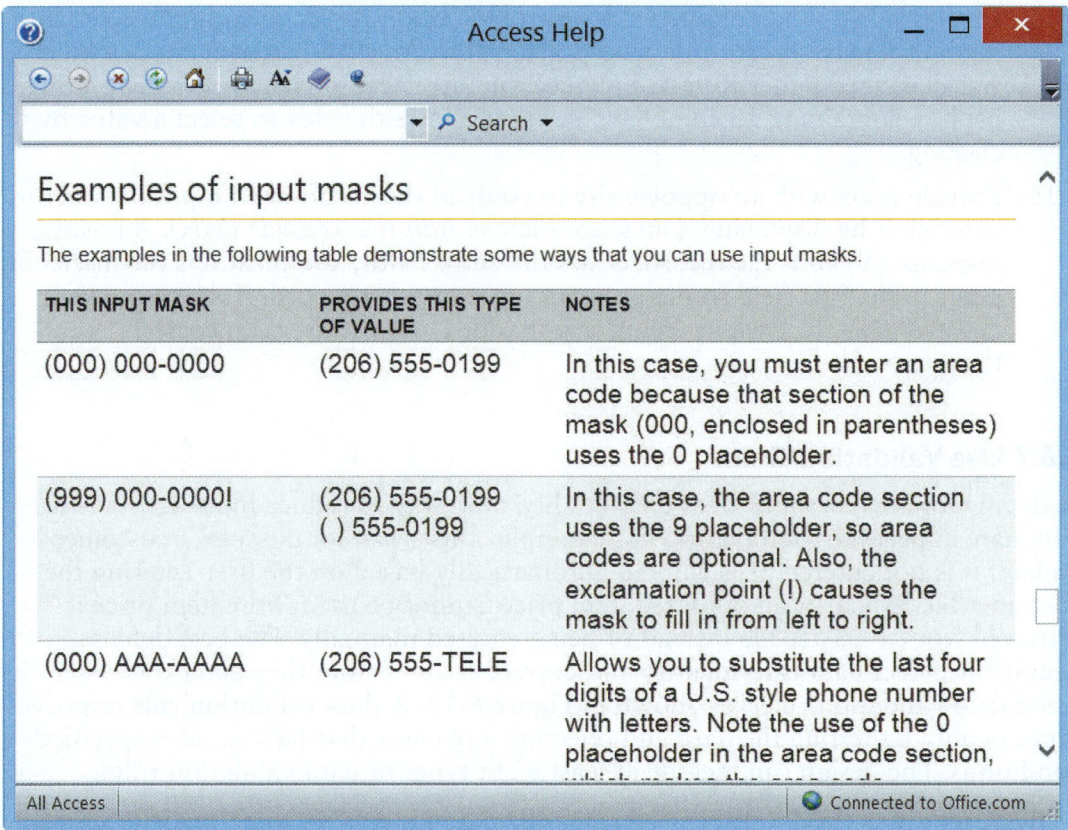

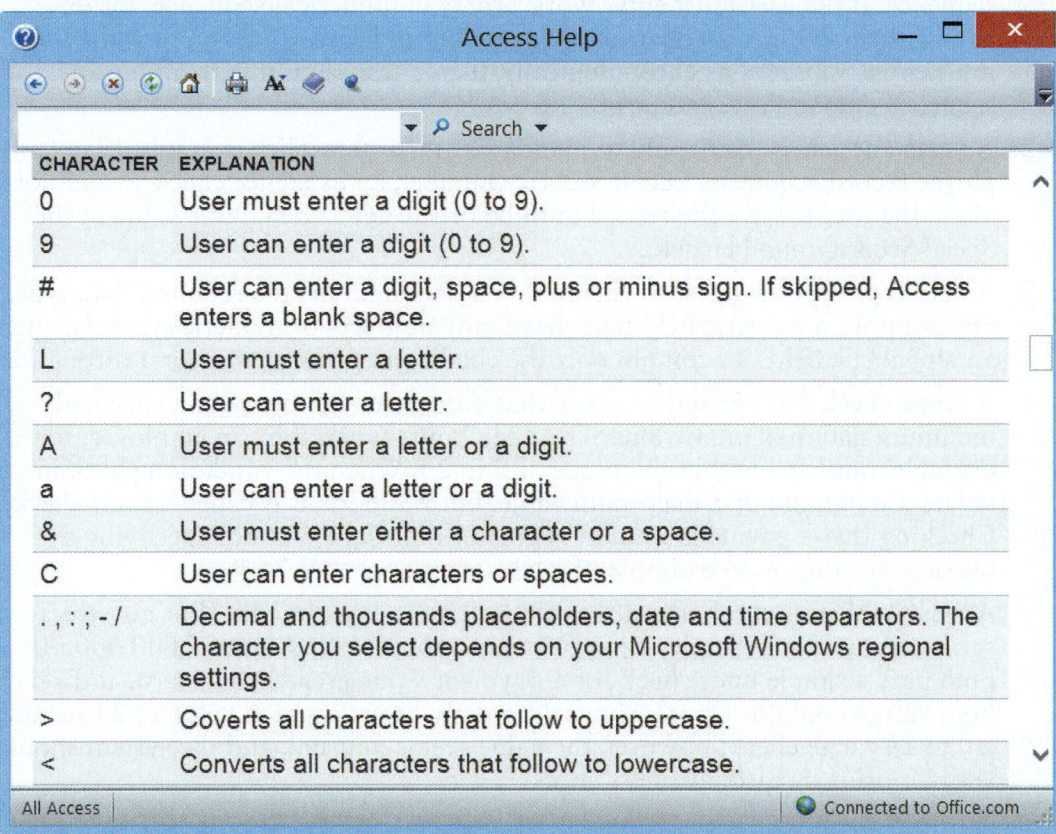

FIGURE 8-12 Microsoft Access provides various input masks for dates, phone numbers, and postcodes, among others. In addition, it is easy to create a custom mask using the characters shown here.

15. Display a list of acceptable values for fields, and provide meaningful error messages if the user enters an unacceptable value. An even better method, which was described under Rule 5: Enhance the Interface, is to provide a drop-down list box containing acceptable values that allows the user to select a value by clicking.

16. Provide users with an opportunity to confirm the accuracy of input data before entering it by displaying a message such as *Add this record? (Y/N)*. A positive response (Y) adds the record, clears the entry fields, and positions the insertion point in the first field so the user can input another record. If the response is negative (N), the current record is not added and the user can correct the errors.

8.6.7 Use Validation Rules

Reducing input errors improves data quality. One way to reduce input errors is to eliminate unnecessary data entry. For example, a user cannot misspell a customer name if it is not entered or is entered automatically based on the user entering the customer ID. Similarly, an outdated item price cannot be used if the item price is retrieved from a master file instead of being entered manually. The best defense against incorrect data is to identify and correct errors before they enter the system by using data validation rules, as shown in Figure 8-13. A data validation rule improves input quality by testing the data and rejecting any entry that fails to meet specified conditions. The design can include at least eight types of data validation rules.

1. A sequence check can be used when the data must be in some predetermined sequence. If the user must enter work orders in numerical sequence, for example, then an out-of-sequence order number indicates an error, or if the user must enter transactions chronologically, then a transaction with an out-of-sequence date indicates an error.

2. An existence check can apply to mandatory data items. For example, if an employee record requires a Social Security number, an existence check would not allow the user to save the record until he or she enters a suitable value in the Social Security number field.

3. A data type check can test to ensure that a data item fits the required data type. For example, a numeric field must have only numbers or numeric symbols, and an alphabetic field can contain only the characters A through Z (or a through z).

4. A range check can be used to verify that data items fall between a specified minimum and maximum value. The daily hours worked by an employee, for example, must fall within the range of 0 to 24. When the validation check involves a minimum or a maximum value, but not both, it is called a limit check. Checking that a payment amount is greater than zero, but not specifying a maximum value, is an example of a limit check.

5. A reasonableness check identifies values that are questionable, but not *necessarily* wrong. For example, input payment values of $.05 and $5,000,000.00 both pass a simple limit check for a payment value greater than zero, and yet both values could be errors. Similarly, a daily-hours-worked value of 24 passes a 0 to 24 range check; however, the value seems unusual, and the system should verify it using a reasonableness check.

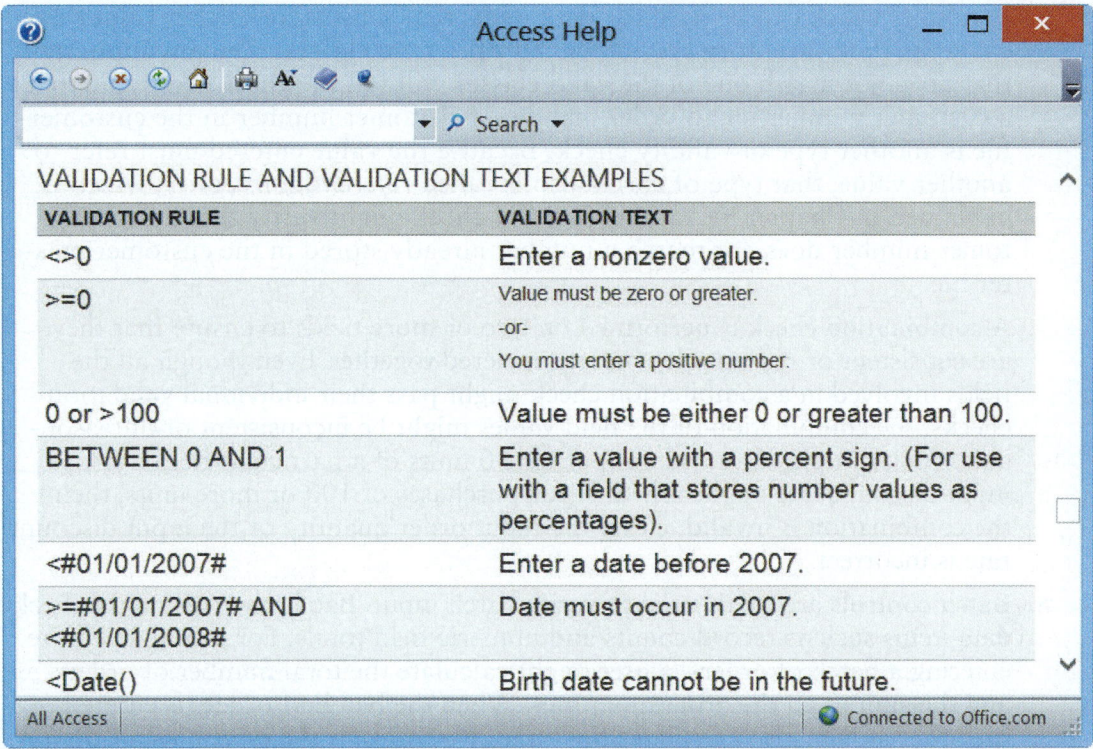

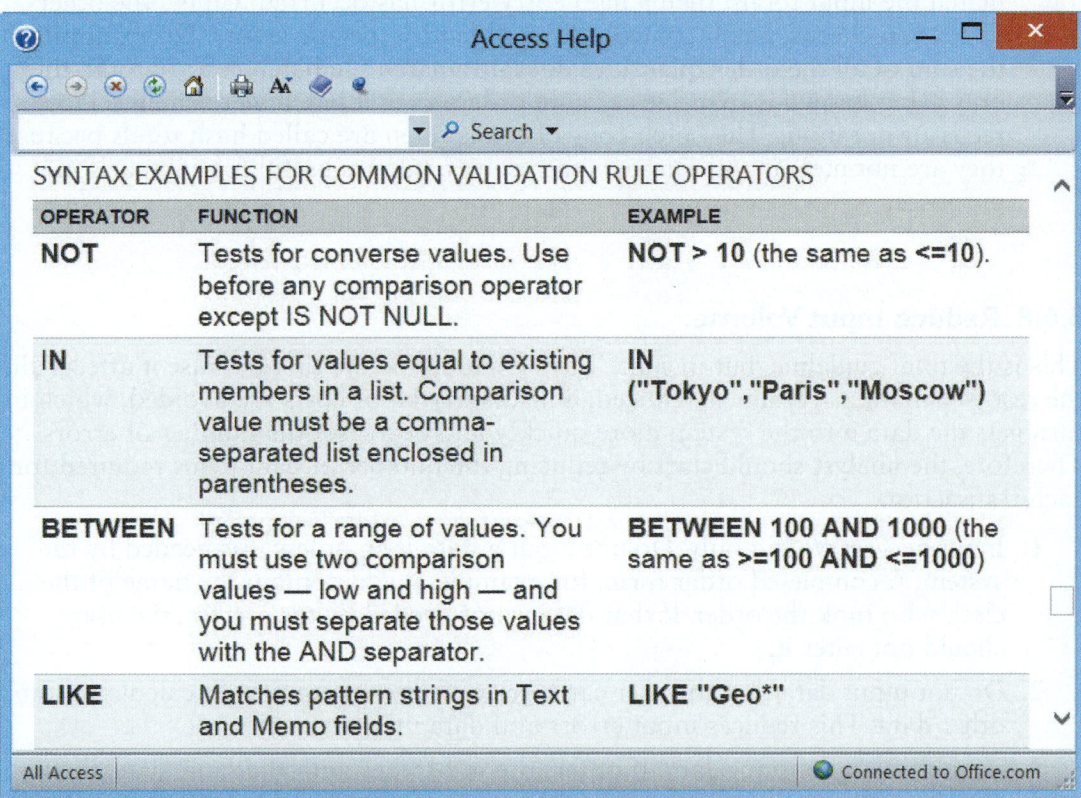

FIGURE 8-13 Microsoft Access provides validation rules that can improve data quality by requiring the input to meet specific requirements or conditions.

6. A validity check can be used for data items that must have certain values. For example, if an inventory system has 20 valid item classes, then any input item that does not match one of the valid classes will fail the check. Verifying that a customer number on an order matches a customer number in the customer file is another type of validity check. Because the value entered must refer to another value, that type of check also is called *referential integrity*, which is explained in Chapter 9. Another validity check might verify that a new customer number does not match a number already stored in the customer master file.

7. A combination check is performed on two or more fields to ensure that they are consistent or reasonable when considered together. Even though all the fields involved in a combination check might pass their individual validation checks, the combination of the field values might be inconsistent or unreasonable. For example, if an order input for 30 units of a particular item has an input discount rate applicable only for purchases of 100 or more units, then the combination is invalid; either the input order quantity or the input discount rate is incorrect.

8. Batch controls are totals used to verify batch input. Batch controls might check data items such as record counts and numeric field totals. For example, before entering a batch of orders, a user might calculate the total number of orders and the sum of all the order quantities. When the batch of orders is entered, the order system also calculates the same two totals. If the system totals do not match the input totals, then a data entry error has occurred. Unlike the other validation checks, batch controls do not identify specific errors. For example, if the sum of all the order quantities does not match the batch control total, the only thing known is that one or more orders in that batch were entered incorrectly or not input. The batch control totals often are called hash totals because they are not meaningful numbers themselves, but are useful for comparison purposes.

8.6.8 Reduce Input Volume

This is the final guideline, but in some ways it should be the first because it affects all the rest. When input volume is reduced, unnecessary labor costs are avoided, which in turn gets the data into the system more quickly and decreases the number of errors. Therefore, the analyst should start by reducing the number of data items required for each transaction.

1. Input necessary data only. Do not input a data item unless it is needed by the system. A completed order form, for example, might contain the name of the clerk who took the order. If that data is not needed by the system, the user should not enter it.

2. Do not input data that the user can retrieve from system files or calculate from other data. This reduces input errors and data inconsistencies.

3. Do not input constant data. If orders are in batches with the same date, then a user should enter the order date only once for the first order in the batch. If orders are entered online, then the user can retrieve the order date automatically using the current system date.

4. Use codes. Codes are shorter than the data they represent, and coded input can reduce data entry time. Codes are discussed in Chapter 9.

CASE IN POINT 8.2:   BOOLEAN TOYS

When should a systems analyst decide a design issue, and when should users be allowed to select what works best for them? The field of ergonomics is concerned with improving the work environment and studying how users interact with their environment.

Suppose you are a systems analyst studying the order processing system at Boolean Toys, a fast-growing developer of software for preschool children. You know that many data entry users have complained about the input screens. Some users would prefer to rearrange the order of the fields; others would like to change the background color on their screens; still others want shortcuts that would allow them to avoid a series of introductory screens.

What if Boolean's users could customize their own data entry screens without assistance from the IT staff by using a menu-driven utility program? What would be the pros and cons of such an approach?

8.7 SOURCE DOCUMENT AND FORM DESIGN

No matter how data enters an information system, the quality of the output is only as good as the quality of the input. The term **garbage in, garbage out (GIGO)** is familiar to IT professionals, who know that the best time to avoid problems is when the data is entered. The main objective is to ensure the quality, accuracy, and timeliness of input data. Unfortunately, the dream of a "paperless office" has never been realized. Even with RFID technology and automated data capture, we still enter data on source documents and forms, and instead of a human-computer interface, systems analysts must deal with the challenge of a human-paper interface.

A **source document** collects input data, triggers or authorizes an input action, and provides a record of the original transaction. During the input design stage, the analyst develops source documents that are easy to complete and use for data entry. Source documents generally are paper-based, but also can be provided online. Either way, the design considerations are the same.

Consider a time when it was a struggle to complete a poorly designed form. There might have been insufficient space, confusing instructions, or poor organization — all symptoms of incorrect **form layout**.

Good form layout makes the form easy to complete and provides enough space, both vertically and horizontally, for users to enter the data. A form should indicate data entry positions clearly using blank lines or boxes and descriptive captions. Also consider using check boxes whenever possible, so users can select choices easily. However, be sure to include an option for any input that does not match a specific check box.

The placement of information on a form also is important. Source documents typically include most of the zones shown in Figure 8-14. The heading zone usually contains the company name or logo and the title and number of the form. The control zone contains codes, identification

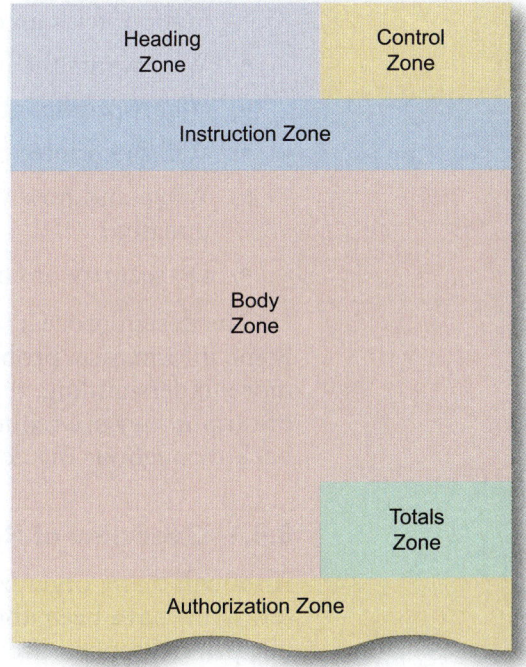

FIGURE 8-14 Source document zones.

information, numbers, and dates that are used for storing completed forms. The instruction zone contains instructions for completing the form. The main part of the form, called the body zone, usually takes up at least half of the space on the form and contains captions and areas for entering variable data. If totals are included on the form, they appear in the totals zone. Finally, the authorization zone contains any required signatures.

Information should flow on a form from left to right and top to bottom to match the way users read documents naturally. That layout makes the form easy to use for the individual who completes the form and for users who enter data into the system using the completed form.

The same user-friendly design principles also apply to printed forms such as invoices and monthly statements, except that heading information usually is pre-printed. Column headings should be short but descriptive, avoiding nonstandard abbreviations, with reasonable spacing between columns for better readability.

The order and placement of printed fields should be logical, and totals should be identified clearly. When designing a preprinted form, contact the form's vendor for advice on paper sizes, type styles and sizes, paper and ink colors, field placement, and other important form details. The goal is to design a form that is attractive, readable, and effective.

Layout and design also are important on web-based forms. There are many resources that will help with designing efficient, user-friendly forms. These include websites that must conform to the U.S. federal government's accessibility guidelines, which can be found online at *http://www.section508.gov*.

8.8 PRINTED OUTPUT

Before designing printed output, there are several questions to consider:

- Why is this being delivered as printed output, rather than screen-based information, with an option for users to view, print, or save as needed?
- Who wants the information, why is it needed, and how will it be used?
- What specific information will be included?
- Will the printed output be designed for a specific device?
- When and how will the information be delivered, and how often must it be updated?
- Do security or confidentiality issues exist? How will they be managed?

The design process should not begin until these questions have been answered. Some information probably was gathered during the systems analysis phase. To gain more understanding, the analyst should meet with users to find out exactly what kind of output *they* are requesting. Prototypes and mock-ups can be used to obtain feedback throughout the design process.

8.8.1 Overview of Report Design

Although many organizations strive to reduce the flow of paper and printed reports, few firms have been able to eliminate printed output totally. Because they are portable, printed reports are convenient, and even necessary in some situations. Many users find it handy to view screen output, then print the information they need for a discussion or business meeting. Printed output also is used in turnaround documents, which are output documents that are later entered back into the same or another information system. In some areas, the telephone or utility bill, for example, might be a turnaround document printed by the company's billing system. When the required portion of the bill is returned with payment, the bill is scanned into the company's accounts receivable system to record the payment accurately.

Designers use a variety of styles, fonts, and images to produce reports that are attractive and user friendly. Whether printed or viewed on-screen, reports must be easy to read and well organized. Rightly or wrongly, some managers judge an entire project by the quality of the reports they receive.

Database programs such as Microsoft Access include a variety of report design tools, including a Report Wizard, which is a menu-driven feature that designers can use to create reports quickly and easily. Many online web-based database systems also provide similar report design guidelines.

Although the vast majority of reports are designed graphically, some systems still produce one or more **character-based reports** that use a character set with fixed spacing. Printing character-based reports on high-speed impact printers is a fast, inexpensive method for producing large-scale reports, such as payroll or inventory reports, or registration rosters at a school. This is especially true if multiple copies are required.

8.8.2 Types of Reports

To be useful, a report must include the information that a user needs. From a user's point of view, a report with too little information is of no value. Too much information, however, can make a report confusing and difficult to understand. When designing reports, the essential goal is to match the report to the user's specific information needs. Depending on their job functions, users might need one or more of the reports described in the following sections.

DETAIL REPORTS: A **detail report** produces one or more lines of output for each record processed. Because it contains one or more lines for each record, a detail report can be quite lengthy. Consider, for example, a large auto parts business. If the firm stocks 3,000 parts, then the detail report would include 3,000 detail lines on approximately 50 printed pages. A user who wants to locate any part in short supply has to examine 3,000 detail lines to find the critical items. A better alternative might be an exception report.

EXCEPTION REPORTS: An **exception report** displays only those records that meet a specific condition or conditions. Exception reports are useful when the user wants information only on records that might require action, but does not need to know the details. For example, a credit manager might use an exception report to identify only those customers with past-due accounts, or a customer service manager might want a report on all packages that were not delivered within a specified time period.

SUMMARY REPORTS: Upper-level managers often want to see total figures and do not need supporting details. A sales manager, for example, might want to know total sales for each sales representative but not want a detail report listing every sale made by them. In that case, a **summary report** is appropriate. Similarly, a personnel manager might need to know the total regular and overtime hours worked by employees in each store but might not be interested in the number of hours worked by each employee.

8.8.3 User Involvement

Users should approve all report designs in advance. The best approach is to prepare a sample report, called a mock-up, or prototype, for users to review. The sample should include typical field values and contain enough records to show all the design features. Depending on the type of printed output, a Microsoft Word document can be created or a report generator used to create mock-up reports.

8.8.4 Report Design Principles

Printed reports must be attractive, professional, and easy to read. For example, a well-designed report should provide totals and subtotals for numeric fields. In the report shown in Figure 8-15, notice that when the value of a control field, such as Store Number, changes, a control break occurs. A control break usually causes specific actions, such as printing subtotals for a group of records. That type of detail report is called a control break report. To produce a control break report, the records must be arranged, or sorted, in control field order.

   Good report design requires effort and attention to detail. To produce a well-designed report, the analyst must consider design features such as report headers and footers, page headers and footers, column headings and alignment, column spacing, field order, and grouping of detail lines.

REPORT HEADERS AND FOOTERS: Every report should have a report header and a report footer. The report header, which appears at the beginning of the report, identifies the report and contains the report title, date, and other necessary information. The report footer, which appears at the end of the report, can include grand totals for numeric fields and other end-of-report information, as shown in Figure 8-15.

PAGE HEADERS AND FOOTERS: Every page should include a page header, which appears at the top of the page and includes the column headings that identify the data. The headings should be short but descriptive. Avoid abbreviations unless the users will understand them clearly. Either a page header or a page footer, which appears at the bottom of the page, is used to display the report title and the page number.

   Database programs such as Microsoft Access make it easy to create groups and subgroups based on particular fields. The report can also calculate and display totals, averages, record counts, and other data for any group or subgroup. For example, a large company might want to see total sales and number of sales broken down by product within each of the 50 states. The information shown in Figure 8-16 is part of Access' online help that refers to a step-by-step process for creating multilevel grouping.

REPEATING FIELDS: Report design is an art, not a science. User involvement is essential, but users often don't know what they want without seeing samples. For example, consider the issue of repeating fields. The sample report in Figure 8-15 repeats the store number on every row. Is that a good thing? The best advice is to ask users what they think and be guided accordingly. A similar issue exists with regard to the overtime hours column. Is it better to print the zero overtime data or only print actual hours, so the data stands out clearly? Again, the best answer is usually the one that works best for users.

CONSISTENT DESIGN: Look and feel are important to users, so reports should be uniform and consistent. When a system produces multiple reports, each report should

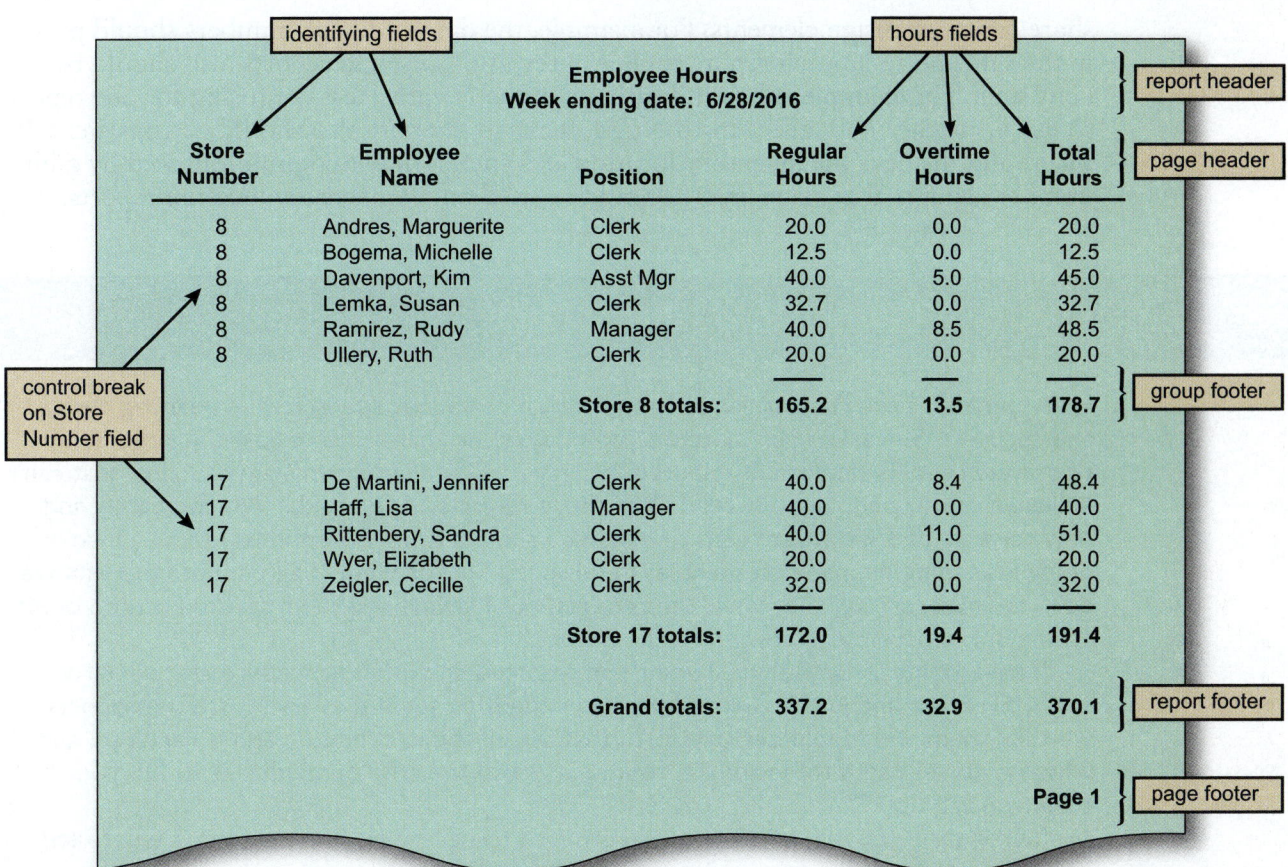

FIGURE 8-15 The Employee Hours report is a detailed report with control breaks, subtotals, and grand totals. Notice that a report header identifies the report, a page header contains column headings, a group footer contains subtotals for each store, a report footer contains grand totals, and a page footer identifies the page number.

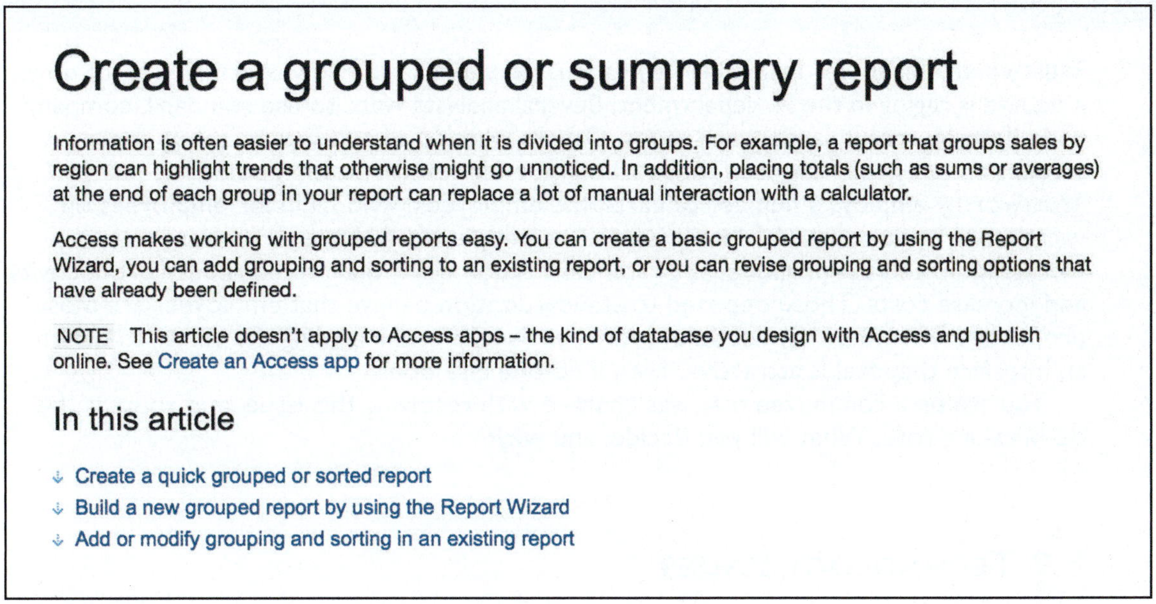

Create a grouped or summary report

Information is often easier to understand when it is divided into groups. For example, a report that groups sales by region can highlight trends that otherwise might go unnoticed. In addition, placing totals (such as sums or averages) at the end of each group in your report can replace a lot of manual interaction with a calculator.

Access makes working with grouped reports easy. You can create a basic grouped report by using the Report Wizard, you can add grouping and sorting to an existing report, or you can revise grouping and sorting options that have already been defined.

NOTE   This article doesn't apply to Access apps – the kind of database you design with Access and publish online. See Create an Access app for more information.

In this article

⇣ Create a quick grouped or sorted report

⇣ Build a new grouped report by using the Report Wizard

⇣ Add or modify grouping and sorting in an existing report

FIGURE 8-16 Microsoft Access includes an easy-to-use tool for grouping data.

Source: © 2015 Microsoft

share common design elements. For example, the date and page numbers should print in the same place on each report page. Abbreviations used in reports also should be consistent. For example, when indicating a numeric value, it is confusing for one report to use #, another *NO*, and a third *NUM*. Items in a report also should be consistent. If one report displays the inventory location as a shelf number column followed by a bin number column, that same layout should be used on all inventory location reports.

CASE IN POINT 8.3:   LAZY EDDIE

Lynn Jennings is the IT manager at Lazy Eddie, a chain that specializes in beanbag chairs and recliners. She asked Jan Lauten, a senior systems analyst, to review the large number of printed reports that are distributed to Lazy Eddie's 35 store managers. "Jan, I just can't believe that our people really read all of those reports," Lynn said. "We constantly add new reports, and we never seem to eliminate the old ones. Sometimes I think all we're doing is keeping the paper companies in business!" Jan replied, "I agree, but what can we do? The managers say they want the reports, but I always see them stacked on top of file cabinets. I've never seen anyone read a report."

"I have an idea," Lynn said. "I want you to come up with a procedure that requires users to review and justify their information needs to see if they really use the reports we send them. You could design a form that asks if the information still is required, and why. Try to get users to decide if a report is worth the cost of producing it. Do you think you can do it?"

"Sure I can," Jan replied. When Jan returned to her office, she wondered where to begin. What advice would you give to Jan?

CASE IN POINT 8.4:   TRUSTWORTHY INSURANCE COMPANY

Trustworthy Insurance maintains its headquarters in a large Midwestern city. Right now, a debate is raging in the IT department. Several analysts want to use standard, company-wide desktop screen layouts and icons. Others want to allow users to set up their screens any way they choose. Those who argue for standardization point out that Trustworthy employs a number of part-time employees, who fill in for employees on vacation. Without a standard interface, these people would have to reorient to every workstation, and the proponents of standardization claim that would reduce productivity and increase costs. Those opposed to standardization believe that employees are most productive when they have control over their workplace, including the ability to design an interface they feel is attractive, even if no one else does.

You are on a committee that was charged with resolving this issue, and yours is the tie-breaking vote. What will you decide, and why?

8.9 TECHNOLOGY ISSUES

Unlike early innovations such as the mouse and the inkjet printer, most technology advances today affect both output and input. In a very real sense, output *and* input have become interdependent, as they are in a user interface, and it is difficult to cite examples of changes in one that would not cause, or at least encourage, changes in the other. For example, new touch-screen input technology generates output that must be properly designed and sized for a particular device, which might be a smartphone, a tablet, or a 23-inch desktop monitor.

The following sections discuss output and input technology separately, but interface designers should always be alert to the possible opportunities, or potential problems, of input/output linkage.

8.9.1 Output Technology

Although business information systems still provide most output as screen displays and printed matter, technology is having an enormous impact on how people communicate and obtain information. This trend is especially important to firms that use information technology to lower their costs, improve employee productivity, and communicate effectively with their customers.

In addition to screen output and printed matter, output can be delivered in many ways. The system requirements document probably identified user output needs. Now, in the systems design phase, the analyst creates the actual forms, reports, documents, and other types of output that might be accessed from workstations, notebooks, tablets, smartphones, and other devices. How the information will be used, stored, and retrieved must also be considered. The following subsections explain various output types and technologies.

INTERNET-BASED INFORMATION DELIVERY: Millions of firms use the Internet to reach new customers and markets around the world. To support the explosive growth in ecommerce, web designers must provide user-friendly screen interfaces that display output and accept input from customers. For example, a business can link its inventory system to its website so the output from the inventory system is displayed as an online catalog. Customers visiting the website can review the items, obtain current prices, and check product availability.

Another example of web-based output is a system that provides customized responses to product or technical questions. When a user enters a product inquiry or requests technical support, the system responds with appropriate information from an on-site knowledge base. Web-based delivery allows users to download a universe of files and documents to support their information needs. For example, the web provides consumers with instant access to brochures, product manuals, and parts lists, while prospective homebuyers can obtain instant quotes on mortgages, insurance, and other financial services.

To reach prospective customers and investors, companies also use a live or prerecorded webcast, which is an audio or video media file distributed over the Internet. Radio and TV stations also use this technique to broadcast program material to their audiences.

EMAIL: Email is an essential means of internal and external business communication. Employees send and receive email on local or wide area networks, including the Internet. Companies send new product information to customers via email, and financial services companies use email messages to confirm online stock trades. Employees use email to exchange documents, data, and schedules and to share business-related information they need to perform their jobs. In many firms, email has virtually replaced traditional memos and printed correspondence.

BLOGS: Web-based logs, called blogs, are another form of web-based output. Because blogs are journals written from a particular point of view, they not only deliver facts to web readers but also provide opinions. Blogs are useful for posting news, reviewing current events, and promoting products.

INSTANT MESSAGING: This popular form of communication is another way for individuals and companies to communicate effectively over the Internet. Although some users feel that it can be a distraction, others like the constant flow of communication, especially as a team member in a collaborative situation.

WIRELESS DEVICES: Messages and data can be transmitted to a wide array of mobile devices, including tablet computers, smartphones, and similar wireless products that combine portable computing power, multimedia capability, and Internet access.

DIGITAL AUDIO, IMAGES, AND VIDEO: Sounds, images, and video clips can be captured, stored in digital format, and transmitted as output to users who can reproduce the content.

Audio or video output can be attached to an email message or inserted as a clip in a Microsoft Word document. Businesses also use automated systems to handle voice transactions and provide information to customers. For example, using a telephone keypad, a customer can confirm an airline seat assignment, check a credit card balance, or determine the current price of a mutual fund.

If a picture is worth a thousand words, then digital images and video clips certainly are high-value output types that offer a whole new dimension. For example, an insurance adjuster with a digital camera phone can take a picture, submit the image via a wireless device, and receive immediate authorization to pay a claim on the spot. If images are a valuable form of output, video clips are even better in some situations. For example, video clips provide online virtual tours that allow realtors to show off the best features of homes they are marketing. The user can zoom in or out and rotate the image in any direction.

PODCASTS: A podcast is a specially formatted digital audio file that can be downloaded by Internet users from a variety of content providers. Many firms use podcasts as sales and marketing tools, and to communicate with their own employees. Using software such as iTunes, users can receive a podcast, launch the file on their computer, and store it on their portable player. Podcasts can include images, sounds, and video.

AUTOMATED FAX SYSTEMS: An automated fax or faxback system allows a customer to request a fax using email, via the company website or by telephone. The response is transmitted in a matter of seconds back to the user's fax machine. Although most users prefer to download documents from the web, many established organizations still offer an automated faxback service as another way to provide immediate response 24 hours a day to a certain set of customers.

COMPUTER OUTPUT TO MICROFILM (COM): Computer output to microfilm (COM) is often used by large firms to scan and store images of original documents to provide high-quality records management and archiving. With the advent of digital storage media, microfilm is not used as much as it used to be, but it still has its place for certain archival situations. For example, COM systems are especially important for legal reasons, or where it is necessary to display a signature, date stamp, or other visual features of a document.

COMPUTER OUTPUT TO DIGITAL MEDIA: This process is used when many paper documents must be scanned, stored in digital format, and retrieved quickly. For example, if an insurance company stores thousands of paper application forms, special software can treat the documents as data and extract information from a particular column or area on the form. Digital storage media can include magnetic tape, CDs, DVDs, and high-density laser disks.

SPECIALIZED FORMS OF OUTPUT: An incredibly diverse marketplace requires many forms of specialized output and devices. For example:

- Portable, web-connected devices that can run multiple apps, handle multimedia output, and provide powerful, multipurpose communication for users

- Retail point-of-sale terminals that handle computer-based credit card transactions, print receipts, and update inventory records

- Automatic teller machines (ATMs) that can process bank transactions and print deposit and withdrawal slips

- Special-purpose printers that can produce labels, employee ID cards, driver's licenses, gasoline pump receipts, and, in some states, lottery tickets

- Plotters that can produce high-quality images such as blueprints, maps, and electronic circuit diagrams

- Electronic detection of data embedded in credit cards, bank cards, and employee identification cards

8.9.2 Input Technology

Input technology has changed dramatically in recent years. In addition to traditional devices and methods, there has been a rapid expansion of new hardware and ways to capture and enter data into a system, some of which are shown in Figure 8-17. Businesses are using the new technology to speed up the input process, reduce costs, and capture data in new forms, such as the digital signature shown in Figure 8-18.

Input methods should be cost-efficient, timely, and as simple as possible. Systems analysts study transactions and business operations to determine how and when data should enter the system. Usually, the first decision is whether to use batch or online input methods. Each method has advantages and disadvantages, and the systems analyst must consider the following factors.

INPUT TECHNOLOGY		
Traditional	**Evolving**	**Emerging**
Keyboard	Body motion detection	Brain-Computer Interface (BCI)
Mouse	Advanced voice recognition	Neural networks
Pointing devices	Biological feedback	Artificial intelligence (AI)
Microphone	Embedded magnetic data	Advanced motion sensors
OCR (optical character recognition)	RFID	Two-way satellite interface
MICR (magnetic ink character recognition)	Advanced optical recognition	Virtual environments
Graphic input devices	Physical adaptation devices	3-D technology

FIGURE 8-17 Input devices can be very traditional, or based on the latest technology.

FIGURE 8-18 When a customer's signature is stored in digital form, it becomes input to the information system.

iStockphoto/tirc83

BATCH INPUT: Using batch input, data entry usually is performed on a specified time schedule, such as daily, weekly, monthly, or longer. For example, batch input occurs when a payroll department collects time cards at the end of the week and enters the data as a batch. Another example is a school that enters all grades for the academic term in a batch.

ONLINE INPUT: Although batch input is used in specific situations, most business activity requires online data entry. The online method offers major advantages, including the immediate validation and availability of data. A popular online input method is source data automation, which combines online data entry and automated data capture using input devices such as RFID tags, magnetic data strips, or even smartphones. Source data automation is fast and accurate, and minimizes human involvement in the translation process.

Many large companies use a combination of source data automation and a powerful communication network to manage global operations instantly. Some common examples of source data automation are:

- Businesses that use point-of-sale (POS) terminals equipped with bar code scanners and magnetic swipe scanners to input credit card data
- ATMs that read data strips on bank cards
- Factory employees who use magnetic ID cards to clock on and off specific jobs so the company can track production costs accurately
- Hospitals that imprint bar codes on patient identification bracelets and use portable scanners when gathering data on patient treatment and medication
- Retail stores that use portable bar code scanners to log new shipments and update inventory data
- Libraries that use handheld scanners to read optical strips on books

TRADE-OFFS: Although online input offers many advantages, it does have some disadvantages. For example, unless source data automation is used, manual data entry is slower and more expensive than batch input because it is performed at the time the transaction occurs and often done when computer demand is at its highest.

The decision to use batch or online input depends on business requirements. For example, hotel reservations must be entered and processed immediately, but hotels can enter their monthly performance figures in a batch. In fact, some input occurs naturally in batches. A cable TV provider, for example, receives customer payments in batches when the mail arrives.

8.10 SECURITY AND CONTROL ISSUES

A company must do everything in its power to protect its data. This includes not only the firm's own information but that of its customers, employees, and suppliers. Most assets have a value, but corporate data is priceless because without safe, secure, accurate data, a company cannot function.

The following sections discuss output and input data security and control.

8.10.1 Output Security and Control

Output must be accurate, complete, current, and secure. Companies use various output control methods to maintain output integrity and security. For example, every report should include an appropriate title, report number or code, printing date, and time period covered. Reports should have pages that are numbered consecutively, identified as *Page nn of nn*, and the end of the report should be labeled clearly. Control totals and record counts should be reconciled against input totals and counts. Reports should be selected at random for a thorough check of correctness and completeness. All processing errors or interruptions must be logged so they can be analyzed.

Output security protects privacy rights and shields the organization's proprietary data from theft or unauthorized access. To ensure output security, several important tasks must be performed. First, limit the number of printed copies and use a tracking procedure to account for each copy. When printed output is distributed from a central location, specific procedures should be used to ensure that the output is delivered to authorized recipients only. That is especially true when reports contain sensitive information, such as payroll data. All sensitive reports should be stored in secure areas. All pages of confidential reports should be labeled appropriately.

As shown in Figure 8-19, it is important to shred sensitive reports, out-of-date reports, and output from aborted print runs. Blank check forms must be stored in a secure location and be inventoried regularly to verify that no forms are missing. If signature stamps are used, they must be stored in a secure location away from the forms storage location.

In most organizations, the IT department is responsible for coordinating output control and security measures. Systems analysts must be concerned with security issues as they design, implement, and support information systems. Whenever possible, security should be designed into the system by using passwords, shielding sensitive data, and controlling user access. Physical security always will be necessary, especially in the case of printed output that is tangible and can be viewed and handled easily.

FIGURE 8-19 To maintain output security, it is important to shred sensitive material.

Cupertino/Shutterstock.com

Enterprise-wide data access creates a whole new set of security and control issues. Many firms have responded to those concerns by installing diskless workstations. A diskless workstation is a network terminal that supports a full-featured user interface but limits the printing or copying of data, except to certain network resources that can be monitored and controlled. This concept worked well with terminals that had limited hardware and software features.

However, over time, the number of removable media devices has expanded greatly, along with a wide variety of physical interfaces such as USB, FireWire, and PCMCIA, as well as wireless interfaces such as Wi-Fi and Bluetooth. A popular security solution is the use of a network-based application, often called a port protector, which controls access to and from workstation interfaces.

8.10.2 Input Security and Control

Input control includes the necessary measures to ensure that input data is correct, complete, and secure. Input control must be the focus during every phase of input design, starting with source documents that promote data accuracy and quality. When a batch input method is used, the computer can produce an input log file that identifies and documents the data entered.

Every piece of information should be traceable back to the input data that produced it. That means the analyst must provide an audit trail that records the source of each data item and when it entered the system. In addition to recording the original source, an audit trail must show how and when data is accessed or changed, and by whom. All those actions must be logged in an audit trail file and monitored carefully.

A company must have procedures for handling source documents to ensure that data is not lost before it enters the system. All source documents that originate from outside the organization should be logged when they are received. Whenever source documents pass between departments, the transfer should be recorded.

Data security policies and procedures protect data from loss or damage, which is a vital goal in every organization. If the safeguards are not 100% effective, data recovery utilities should be able to restore lost or damaged data. Once data is entered, the company should store source documents in a safe location for some specified length of time. The company should have a **records retention policy** that meets all legal requirements and business needs.

Audit trail files and reports should be stored and saved. Then, if a data file is damaged, the information can be used to reconstruct the lost data. Data security also involves protecting data from unauthorized access. System sign-on procedures should prevent unauthorized individuals from entering the system, and users should change their passwords regularly. Having several levels of access also is advisable. For example, a data entry person might be allowed to *view* a credit limit, but not *change* it. Sensitive data can be encrypted, or coded, in a process called encryption, so only users with decoding software can read it.

8.11 WHERE DO WE GO FROM HERE?

The systems design phase begins with user interface design, followed by chapters on data design and system architecture. At this point, keep in mind that the deeper a project is into the systems design process, the more expensive it will be to make changes and correct mistakes. The analyst must be alert for any changes or modifications that would affect the project's timetable or development costs. Two strategies that will help avoid major problems are a modular design approach and the use of prototyping. The following sections discuss these topics.

8.11.1 Modular Design

In a modular design, individual components, called **modules**, are created that connect to a higher-level program or process. In a structured design, each module represents a specific process, which is shown on a data flow diagram (DFD) and documented in a process description. If an object-oriented design is being used, as described in Chapter 6, code modules represent classes. Modular design is explained in more detail in Chapter 11, which describes systems implementation.

Modules should be designed to perform a single function. Independent modules provide greater flexibility because they can be developed and tested individually, and then combined or reused later in the development process. Modular design is especially important in designing large-scale systems because separate teams of analysts and programmers can work on different areas and then integrate the results.

8.11.2 Prototyping

Prototyping produces an early, rapidly constructed working version of the proposed information system, called a prototype. Prototyping, which involves a repetitive sequence of analysis, design, modeling, and testing, is a common technique that can be used to design anything from a new home to a computer network. For example, engineers use a prototype to evaluate an aircraft design before production begins, as shown in the wind tunnel testing in Figure 8-20.

User input and feedback is essential at every stage of the systems development process. Prototyping allows users to examine a model that accurately represents system outputs, inputs, interfaces, and processes. Users can "test-drive" the model in a risk-

FIGURE 8-20 Wind tunnel testing is a typical example of prototyping.
Courtesy of NASA

free environment and either approve it or request changes. In some situations, the prototype evolves into the final version of the information system. In other cases, the prototype is intended only to validate user requirements and is discarded afterward.

Perhaps the most intense form of prototyping occurs when agile methods are used. As described in Chapter 1, agile methods build a system by creating a series of prototypes and constantly adjusting them to user requirements. As the agile process continues, developers revise, extend, and merge earlier versions into the final product. An agile approach emphasizes continuous feedback, and each incremental step is affected by what was learned in the prior steps.

Systems analysts generally use two prototyping methods, system prototyping and design prototyping.

SYSTEM PROTOTYPING: **System prototyping** produces a full-featured, working model of the information system. A system prototype that meets all requirements is ready for implementation, as shown in Figure 8-21. Because the model is "on track" for implementation, it is especially important to obtain user feedback, and to be sure that the prototype meets all requirements of users and management.

DESIGN PROTOTYPING: Systems analysts also use prototyping to verify user requirements, after which the prototype is discarded and implementation continues. The approach is called **design prototyping**, or **throwaway prototyping**. In this case, the prototyping objectives are more limited, but no less important. The end product of design prototyping is a user-approved model that documents and benchmarks the features of

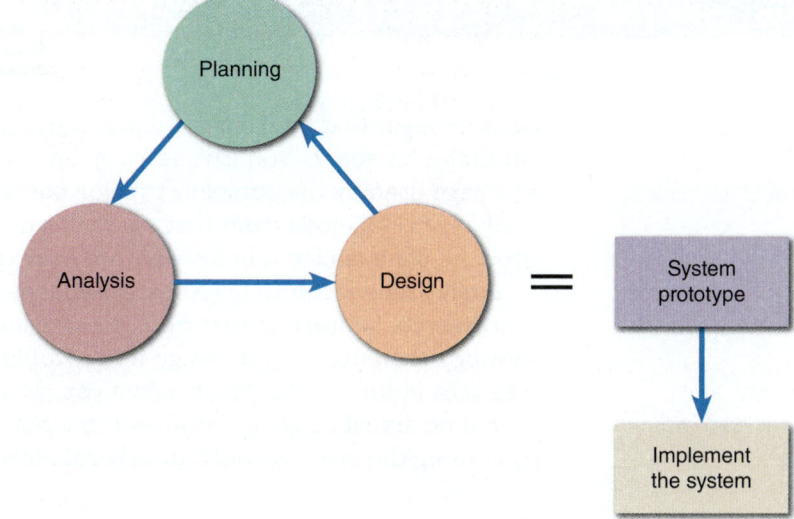

FIGURE 8-21 The end product of system prototyping is a working model of the information system, ready for proper implementation.

the finished system. Design prototyping makes it possible to capture user input and approval while continuing to develop the system within the framework of the SDLC. Systems analysts typically use design prototyping as they construct outputs, inputs, and user interfaces.

TRADE-OFFS: Prototyping offers many benefits, including the following:

- Users and systems developers can avoid misunderstandings.
- System developers can create accurate specifications for the finished system based on the prototype.
- Managers can evaluate a working model more effectively than a paper specification.
- Systems analysts can use a prototype to develop testing and training procedures before the finished system is available.
- Prototyping reduces the risk and potential financial exposure that occur when a finished system fails to support business needs.

Although most systems analysts believe that the advantages of prototyping far out-weigh any disadvantages, the following potential problems should be considered:

- The rapid pace of development can create quality problems, which are not dis-covered until the finished system is operational.
- Other system requirements, such as reliability and maintainability, cannot be tested adequately using a prototype.
- In very complex systems, the prototype can become unwieldy and difficult to manage.
- A client or user might want to adopt the prototype with few to no changes, mistakenly thinking that the prototype will meet their needs though it may need further customization, leading to increased maintenance costs later in the SDLC.

A QUESTION OF ETHICS

iStockphoto.com/faberfoto_it

Jacob thought that he did a good job of designing the company's tech support webpage, but Emily, his supervisor, isn't so sure. She is concerned that Jacob's design is very similar to a page used by the company's major competitor, and she asked him whether he had used any HTML code from that site in his design. Although Jacob didn't copy any of the code, he did examine it in his web browser to see how they handled some design issues.

Emily asked Jacob to investigate webpage copyright issues and report back to her. In his research, he learned that outright copying would be a copyright violation, but merely viewing other sites to get design ideas would be permissible. What is not so clear is the gray area in the middle. Jacob asked you, as a friend, for your opinion on this question: Even if no actual copying is involved, are there ethical constraints on how far you should go in using the creative work of others? How would you answer Jacob?

8.12 CHAPTER SUMMARY

The purpose of systems design is to create a physical model of the system that satisfies the design requirements that were defined during the systems analysis phase. The chapter began with a discussion of user interface design and human-computer interaction (HCI) concepts. A graphical user interface (GUI) uses visual objects and techniques that allow users to communicate effectively with the system. User-centered design principles include understanding the business, maximizing graphic effectiveness, thinking like a user, using models and prototypes, focusing on usability, inviting feedback, and documenting everything.

When designing the user interface, it should be transparent; create an interface that is easy to learn and use; enhance user productivity; make it easy to obtain help or correct errors; minimize input data problems; provide feedback; create an attractive layout and design; and use familiar terms and images. Control features, such as menu bars, toolbars, drop-down list boxes, dialog boxes, toggle buttons, list boxes, option buttons, check boxes, and command buttons, can also be added. Controls are placed on a main switchboard, which is like a graphical version of a main menu.

The chapter described various types of printed reports, including detail, exception, and summary reports. The features and sections of reports, including control fields, control breaks, report headers and footers, page headers and footers, and group headers and footers, were explained. Other types of output such as web-based information delivery, audio output, instant messaging, podcasts, email, and other specialized forms of output were also discussed.

The discussion of input design began with a description of source documents and the various zones in a document, including the heading zone, the control zone, the instruction zone, the body zone, the totals zone, and the authorization zone. The discussion of data entry screen design explained the use of input masks and validation rules to reduce data errors. Input masks are like templates that only permit certain combinations of characters, and data validation rules can provide checks to ensure that inappropriate data is prevented from entering the system. These checks can include data sequence, existence, range and limit, reasonableness, and validity, among others.

Batch and online input methods were also described, as were input media and procedures, and input volume. Input methods include data capture and data entry. Data capture, which may be automated, involves identifying and recording source data. Data entry involves converting source data into a computer-readable form and entering it into the system. New technology offers optical and voice recognition systems, biological feedback devices, motion sensors, and a variety of graphical input devices.

Finally, security and control was discussed. Output control includes physical protection of data and reports, and control of unauthorized ports or devices that can extract data from the system. Input controls include audit trails, encryption, password security, data security, and the creation of access levels to limit persons authorized to view or use data.

Key Terms

audit trail A record of the source of each data item and when it entered a system. In addition to recording the original source, an audit trail must show how and when data is accessed or changed, and by whom. All these actions must be logged in an audit trail file and monitored carefully.

authorization zone Part of a form that contains any required signatures.

automated fax A system that allows a customer to request a fax using email, the company website, or a telephone. The response is transmitted in a matter of seconds back to the user's fax machine.

batch A group of data, usually inputted into an information system at the same time.

batch control A total used to verify batch input. Batch controls might check data items such as record counts and numeric field totals. For example, before entering a batch of orders, a user might calculate the total number of orders and the sum of all the order quantities. When the batch of orders is entered, the order system also calculates the same two totals. If the system totals do not match the input totals, then a data entry error has occurred.

batch input A process where data entry is performed on a specified time schedule, such as daily, weekly, monthly, or longer. For example, batch input occurs when a payroll department collects time cards at the end of the week and enters the data as a batch.

blog An online journal. The term is a contraction of "web log."

calendar control A calendar control allows the user to select a date that the system will display and store as a field value.

character-based report A report created using a single mono-spaced character set.

check box Used to select one or more choices from a group. A check mark, or an X, represents selected options.

combination check A type of data validation check that is performed on two or more fields to ensure that they are consistent or reasonable when considered together. Even though all the fields involved in a combination check might pass their individual validation checks, the combination of the field values might be inconsistent or unreasonable.

command button Onscreen button that initiates an action such as printing a form or requesting Help.

computer output to microfilm (COM) Scanning and storing images of paper documents. Often used by large firms to provide high-quality records management and archiving.

context-sensitive A feature that is sensitive to the current conditions when it is invoked. For example, context-sensitive help offers assistance for a task in progress.

control break A control break usually causes specific actions to occur, such as printing subtotals for a group of records.

control break report A detail report that focuses on control breaks.

control field order In a control break report, the records are arranged or sorted in the same order as the control fields.

data security Protection of data from loss or damage and recovers data when it is lost or damaged.

data type check A type of data validation check that is used to ensure that a data item fits the required data type. For example, a numeric field must have only numbers or numeric symbols, and an alphabetic field can contain only the characters A through Z or the characters a through z.

data validation rule A mechanism to improve input quality by testing the data and rejecting any entry that fails to meet specified conditions.

default value A value that a system displays automatically.

design prototyping Creating a prototype of user requirements, after which the prototype is discarded and implementation continues. Also called throwaway prototyping.

detail report A detail report produces one or more lines of output for each record processed.

dialog box Allows a user to enter information about a task that a system will perform.

diskless workstation A network terminal that supports a full-featured user interface, but limits the printing or copying of data, except to certain network resources that can be monitored and controlled more easily.

electronic health record (EHR) An electronic record of a patient's health information generated as the patient encounters various health care providers and shared among multiple facilities and agencies.

exception report A document displaying only those records that meet a specific condition or conditions. Exception reports are useful when the user wants information only on records that might require action, but does not need to know the details.

existence check A type of data validation check that is used for mandatory data items. For example, if an employee record requires a Social Security number, an existence check would not allow the user to save the record until he or she enters a suitable value in the SSN field.

faxback A system that allows a customer to request a fax using email, the company website, or a telephone. The response is transmitted in a matter of seconds back to the user's fax machine.

form filling A very effective method of online data entry where a blank form that duplicates or resembles the source document is completed on the screen. The user enters the data and then moves to the next field.

form layout The physical appearance and placement of data on a form. Form layout makes the form easy to complete and provides enough space, both vertically and horizontally, for users to enter the data.

garbage in, garbage out (GIGO) The concept that the quality of the output is only as good as the quality of the input.

graphical user interface (GUI) The use of graphical objects and techniques allowing users to communicate with a system. A well-designed GUI can help users learn a new system rapidly and work with the system effectively.

hash total Not meaningful numbers themselves, but are useful for comparison purposes. Also known as batch control totals.

human-computer interaction (HCI) A description of the relationship between computers and the people who use them to perform business-related tasks. HCI concepts apply to everything from a PC desktop to the main menu for a global network.

input control The necessary measures to ensure that input data is correct, complete, and secure. A systems analyst must focus on input control during every phase of input design, starting with source documents that promote data accuracy and quality.

input mask Template or pattern that makes it easier for users to enter data. Often used in automated forms to guide an unfamiliar user.

limit check Occurs when a validation check involves a minimum or a maximum value, but not both. Checking that a payment amount is greater than zero, but not specifying a maximum value, is an example of a limit check.

list box An output mechanism that displays a list of choices that the user can select.

menu bar A set of user-selectable software application options, usually located across the top of the screen.

mock-up When designing a report, a sample report is prepared, which is a mock-up, or prototype, for users to review. The sample should include typical field values and contain enough records to show all the design features.

module Related program code organized into small units that are easy to understand and maintain. A complex program could have hundreds or even thousands of modules.

natural language A software feature that allows users to type commands or requests in normal English (or other language) phrases.

online data entry A data entry method used for most business activity. The online method offers major advantages, including the immediate validation and availability of data.

option button Radio buttons that represent groups of options. The user can select only one option at a time; a selected option contains a black dot. *See also* **radio button**.

output control Methods to maintain output integrity and security. For example, every report should include an appropriate title, report number or code, printing date, and time period covered. Reports should have pages that are numbered consecutively, identified as Page xx of xx, and the end of the report should be labeled clearly.

output security Output security protects privacy rights and shields the organization's proprietary data from theft or unauthorized access.

page footer Appears at the bottom of the page and is used to display the name of the report and the page number.

page header Appears at the top of the page and includes the column headings that identify the data.

podcast A web-based broadcast that allows a user to receive audio or multimedia files using music player software such as iTunes, and listen to them on a PC or download them to a portable MP3 player or smartphone.

port protector Network-based security application that controls access to and from workstation interfaces.

prototyping The method by which a prototype is developed. It involves a repetitive sequence of analysis, design, modeling, and testing. It is a common technique that can be used to design anything from a new home to a computer network.

radio button See **option button**.

range check A type of data validation check that tests data items to verify that they fall between a specified minimum and maximum value. The daily hours worked by an employee, for example, must fall within the range of 0 to 24.

reasonableness check A type of data validation check that identifies values that are questionable, but not necessarily wrong. For example, input payment values of $0.05 and $5,000,000.00 both pass a simple limit check for a payment value greater than zero, and yet both values could be errors.

records retention policy Rules designed to meet all legal requirements and business needs for keeping records.

report footer Appears at the end of the report, can include grand totals for numeric fields and other end-of-report information.

report header Appears at the beginning of a report and identifies the report as well as the report title, date, and other necessary information.

RFID tag An input device used in source data automation.

scroll bar In user interface design, a scroll bar allows the user to move through the available choices for an input field.

sequence check A type of data validation check that is used when the data must be in some predetermined sequence. If the user must enter work orders in numerical sequence, for example, then an out-of-sequence order number indicates an error. If the user must enter transactions chronologically, then a transaction with an out-of-sequence date indicates an error.

source data automation A popular online input method that combines online data entry and automated data capture using input devices such as magnetic data strips, or swipe scanners.

source document A form used to request and collect input data, trigger or authorize an input action, and provide a record of the original transaction. During the input design stage, you develop source documents that are easy to complete and inexpensive.

storyboard Sketches used during prototyping to show the general screen layout and design.

summary report A report used by individuals at higher levels in the organization that includes less detail than reports used by lower-level employees.

switchboard The use of command buttons in a user interface to enable users to navigate a system and select from groups of related tasks.

system prototyping Producing a full-featured, working model of the information system being developed.

systems design The goal of systems design is to build a system that is effective, reliable, and maintainable.

throwaway prototyping *See* **design prototyping**.

toggle button A GUI element used to represent on or off status. Clicking the toggle button switches to the other status.

toolbar A GUI element that contains icons or buttons that represent shortcuts for executing common commands.

totals zone If a form has data totals, they will appear in this section of the form.

transparent interface A user interface that users don't really notice — a user-friendly interface that does not distract the user and calls no attention to itself.

turnaround document Output document that is later entered back into the same or another information system. A telephone or utility bill, for example, might be a turnaround document printed by the company's billing system. When the bill is returned with payment, it is scanned into the company's accounts receivable system to record the payment accurately.

usability User interface design includes user satisfaction, support for business functions, and system effectiveness.

usability metrics Data that interface designers can obtain by using software that can record and measure user interactions with the system.

user-centered A term that indicates the primary focus is upon the user. In a user-centered system, the distinction blurs between input, output, and the interface itself.

validity check A type of data validation check that is used for data items that must have certain values. For example, if an inventory system has 20 valid item classes, then any input item that does not match one of the valid classes will fail the check.

webcast A one-way transmission of information or training materials, such as a Webinar session, available on demand or for a specific period to online participants.

Chapter Exercises

Questions

1. Provide an overview of the systems design phase.
2. Explain Apple's view of user interface design, especially for apps.
3. Describe the habits of successful interface designers.
4. List the eight main guidelines for user interface design. How would you rank them in order of importance? Explain your answer.
5. How has input technology changed in recent years? Provide examples of traditional, evolving, and emerging input technology.
6. What are input masks? What are validation rules? Why are they important?
7. What is the difference between a detail report, a summary report, and an exception report?
8. What are the main principles of source document design?
9. Provide suggestions for reducing input volume.
10. Describe modular design, and explain the two main prototyping methods.

Discussion Topics

1. Some systems analysts maintain that source documents are unnecessary. They say that all input can be entered directly into the system, without wasting time in an intermediate step. Do you agree? Can you think of any situations where source documents are essential?
2. Some systems analysts argue, "Give users what they ask for. If they want lots of reports and reams of data, then that is what you should provide. Otherwise, they will feel that you are trying to tell them how to do their jobs." Others say, "Systems analysts should let users know what information can be obtained from the system. If you listen to users, you'll never get anywhere because they really don't know what they want and don't understand information systems." What do you think of these arguments?
3. Suppose your network support company employs 75 technicians who travel constantly and work at customer sites. Your task is to design an information system that provides technical data and information to the field team. What types of output and information delivery would you suggest for the system?
4. A user interface can be quite restrictive. For example, the interface design might not allow a user to exit to a Windows desktop or to log on to the Internet. Should a user interface include such restrictions? Why or why not?
5. How is the increased use of smartphones and tablets, with their smaller screen size, affecting user interface design practices?

Projects

1. Visit the administrative office at your school or a local company. Ask to see examples of input screens. Analyze the design and appearance of each screen, and try to identify at least one possible improvement.

2. Search the web to find an especially good example of a user interface that includes guidelines in this chapter. Document your research and discuss it with your class.

3. Review Section 8.4.1 and the accompanying text about EHR usability. Research the current status of EHR usability, and describe all noteworthy developments.

4. Suggest at least two good examples and two bad examples of source document design.

5. Explore the emerging area of wearable computing, such as the Apple Watch and Android Wear, and comment on the impact of these devices on user interface design.

CHAPTER 9

Data Design

Chapter 9 is the second of three chapters in the systems design phase of the SDLC. This chapter focuses on the data design skills that are necessary for a systems analyst to construct the physical model of the information system.

The chapter includes four "Case in Point" discussion questions to help contextualize the concepts described in the text. The "Question of Ethics" raises the important and timely issue of sharing customers' data without their explicit consent.

LEARNING OBJECTIVES

When you finish this chapter, you should be able to:

- Explain file-oriented systems and how they differ from database management systems
- Explain data design terminology, including entities, fields, common fields, records, files, tables, and key fields
- Describe data relationships, draw an entity-relationship diagram, define cardinality, and use cardinality notation
- Explain the concept of normalization
- Explain the importance of codes and describe various coding schemes
- Explain data warehousing and data mining
- Differentiate between logical and physical storage and records
- Explain data control measures

CHAPTER CONTENTS

9.1 INTRODUCTION

During the systems analysis phase, a logical model of the system was created. Now, it must be decided how data will be organized, stored, and managed. These are important issues that affect data quality and consistency.

This chapter begins with a review of data design concepts and terminology, then discusses file-based systems and database systems, including web-based databases. How to create entity-relationship diagrams that show the relationships among data elements is explained, along with how to use normalization concepts. How to use codes to represent data items is also discussed. The chapter concludes with a discussion of data storage and access issues, including data warehousing and data mining, physical design, logical and physical records, data storage formats, and data control.

9.2 DATA DESIGN CONCEPTS

Systems analysts must understand basic data design concepts, including data structures and the evolution of the relational database model.

9.2.1 Data Structures

A data structure is a framework for organizing, storing, and managing data. Data structures consist of files or tables that interact in various ways. Each file or table contains data about people, places, things, or events. For example, one file or table might contain data about customers, and other files or tables might store data about products, orders, suppliers, or employees. Many older, legacy systems were called file-oriented. Over time, the modern relational database became a standard model for systems developers. The following example of an auto service shop will compare the two concepts.

9.2.2 Mario and Danica: A Data Design Example

Figure 9-1 shows an auto shop mechanic at work. Imagine two shops that are very similar but use two different information system designs. Let's call them Mario's Auto Shop and Danica's Auto Shop. Mario uses two file-oriented systems, while Danica uses a database management system.

MARIO'S AUTO SHOP: Mario relies on two file-oriented systems, sometimes called file processing systems, to manage his business. The two systems store data in separate files that are not connected or linked. Figure 9-2 shows Mario's file-oriented systems:

FIGURE 9-1 In the example shown here, data about the mechanic, the customer, and the brake job might be stored in a file-oriented system or in a database system.

Lisa F. Young/Shutterstock.com

- The MECHANIC SYSTEM uses the MECHANIC file to store data about shop employees

- The JOB SYSTEM uses the JOB file to store data about work performed at the shop.

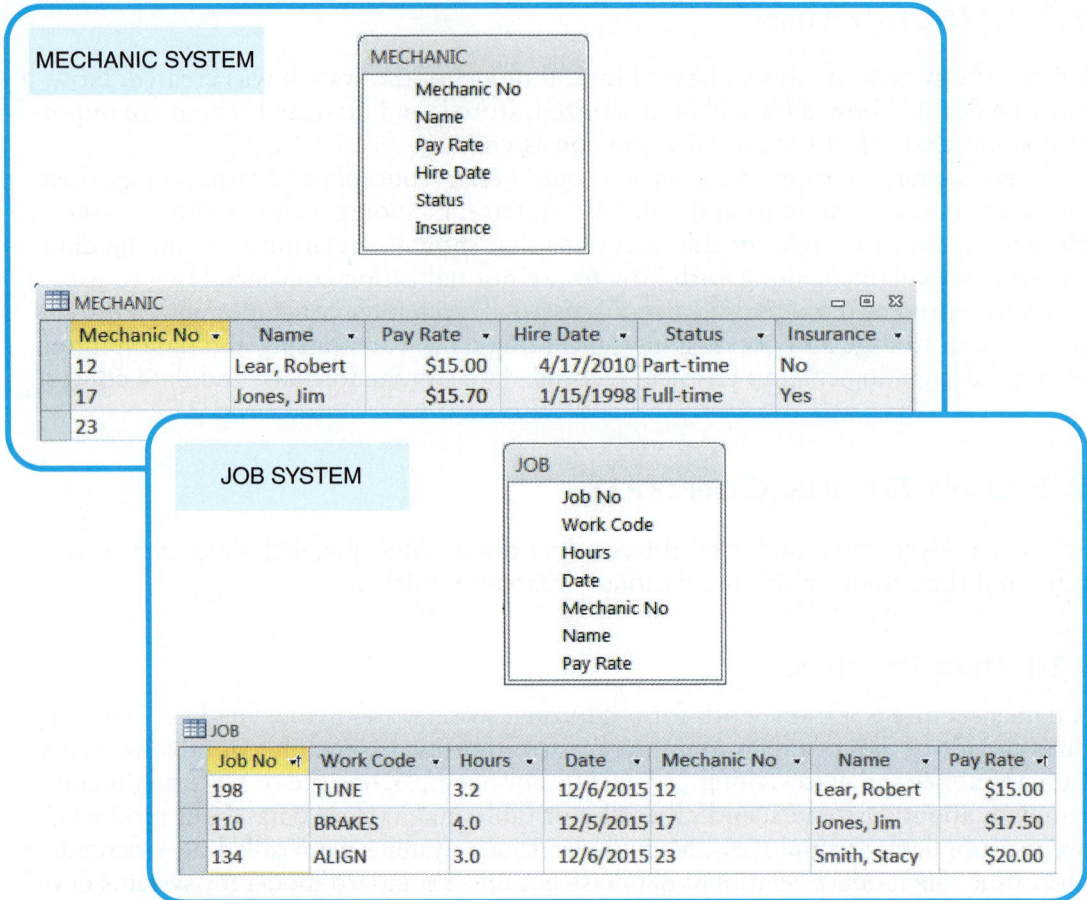

FIGURE 9-2 Mario's shop uses two separate systems, so certain data must be entered twice. This redundancy is inefficient and can produce errors.

Unfortunately, using two separate systems means that some data is stored in two different places, and the data might or might not be consistent. For example, three data items (Mechanic No, Name, and Pay Rate) are stored in both files. This redundancy is a major disadvantage of file-oriented systems because it threatens data quality and integrity. In fact, Figure 9-2 includes a typical discrepancy: Jim Jones' pay rate is shown as $15.70 in the MECHANIC SYSTEM file and $17.50 in the JOB SYSTEM file.

DANICA'S AUTO SHOP: Danica uses a database management system (DBMS) with two separate tables that are joined, so they act like one large table, as shown in Figure 9-3. In Danica's SHOP OPERATIONS SYSTEM, the tables are linked by the Mechanic No field, which is called a *common field* because it connects the tables. Notice that except for the common field, no other data items are duplicated. The DBMS design, also called a **relational database** or **relational model**, was introduced in the 1970s and continues to be the dominant approach for organizing, storing, and managing business data.

Mario's file-oriented systems show two different pay rates for Jim Jones, most likely because of a data entry error in one of them. That type of error could not occur in Danica's relational database, because an employee's pay rate is stored in only one place. However, DBMSs are not immune to data entry problems, which are discussed in detail later in this chapter.

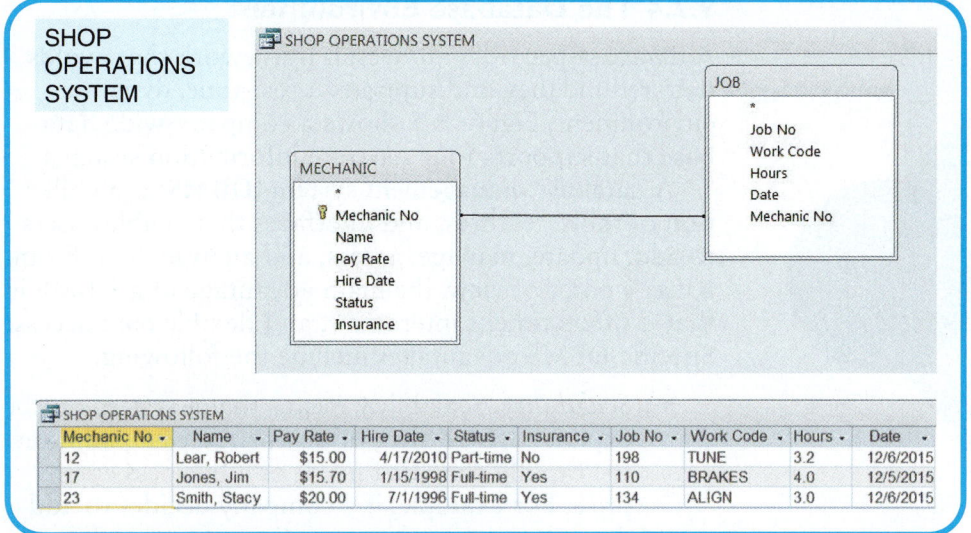

FIGURE 9-3 Danica's SHOP OPERATIONS SYSTEM uses a database design, which avoids duplication. The data can be viewed as if it were one large table, regardless of where the data is physically stored.

9.2.3 Is File Processing Still Important?

Although file processing is an older approach, some companies still use this method to handle large volumes of structured data on a regular basis. Many older legacy systems utilized file processing because it worked well with mainframe hardware and batch input. Although it has very limited use today, file processing can be cost-effective in certain situations. For example, consider a credit card company that posts thousands of daily transactions from a TRANSACTIONS file to account balances stored in a CUSTOMERS file, as shown in Figure 9-4. For that relatively simple process, file processing might be an option.

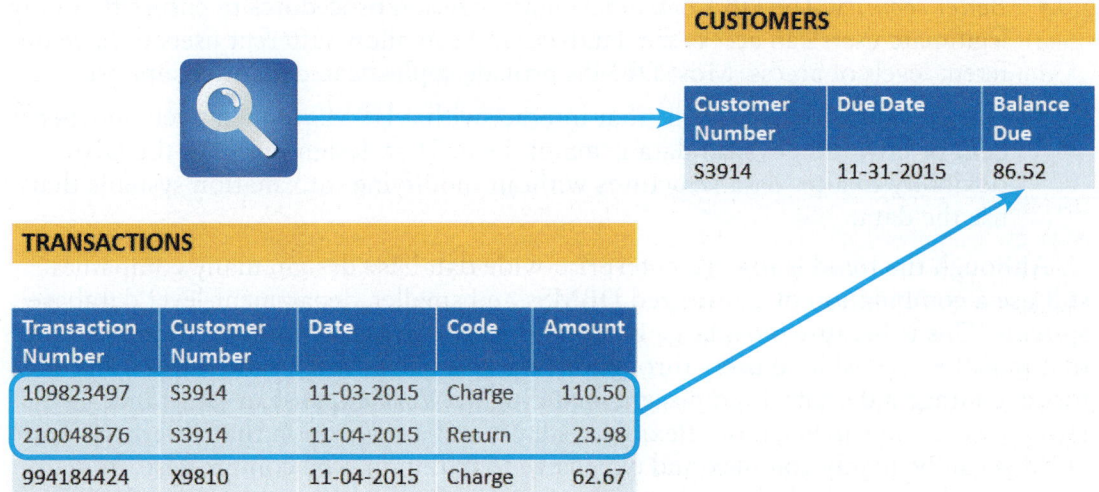

FIGURE 9-4 A credit card company that posts thousands of daily transactions might consider a file processing option.

FIGURE 9-5 In this example, a sales database can support four separate business systems.

9.2.4 The Database Environment

A database provides an overall framework that avoids data redundancy and supports a real-time, dynamic environment. Figure 9-5 shows a company-wide database that supports four separate information systems.

A **database management system (DBMS)** is a collection of tools, features, and interfaces that enables users to add, update, manage, access, and analyze data. From a user's point of view, the main advantage of a DBMS is that it offers timely, interactive, and flexible data access. Specific DBMS advantages include the following:

- *Scalability.* Scalability means that a system can be expanded, modified, or downsized easily to meet the rapidly changing needs of a business enterprise. For example, if a company decides to add data about secondary suppliers of material it uses, a new table can be added to the relational database and linked with a common field.

- *Economy of scale.* Database design allows better utilization of hardware. If a company maintains an enterprise-wide database, processing is less expensive using powerful servers and communication networks. The inherent efficiency of high-volume processing on larger computers is called **economy of scale**.

- *Enterprise-wide application.* A DBMS is typically managed by a person called a **database administrator (DBA)**. The DBA assesses overall requirements and maintains the database for the benefit of the entire organization rather than a single department or user. Database systems can support enterprise-wide applications more effectively than file processing systems.

- *Stronger standards.* Effective database administration helps ensure that standards for data names, formats, and documentation are followed uniformly throughout the organization.

- *Better security.* The DBA can define authorization procedures to ensure that only legitimate users can access the database and can allow different users to have different levels of access. Most DBMSs provide sophisticated security support.

- *Data independence.* Systems that interact with a DBMS are relatively independent of how the physical data is maintained. That design provides the DBA flexibility to alter data structures without modifying information systems that use the data.

Although the trend is toward enterprise-wide database design, many companies still use a combination of centralized DBMSs and smaller, department-level database systems. This is because most large businesses view data as a company-wide resource that must be accessible to users throughout the company. At the same time, other factors encourage a decentralized design, including network expense; a reluctance to move away from smaller, more flexible systems; and a realization that enterprise-wide DBMSs can be highly complex and expensive to maintain. The compromise, in many cases, is a client/server design, where processing is shared among several computers. Client/server systems are described in detail in Chapter 10. As with many design decisions, the best solution depends on the organization's needs and particular circumstances.

9.3 DBMS Components

A DBMS provides an interface between a database and users who need to access the data. Although users are concerned primarily with an easy-to-use interface and support for their business requirements, a system analyst must understand all of the components of a DBMS. In addition to interfaces for users, database administrators, and related systems, a DBMS also has a data manipulation language, a schema and subschemas, and a physical data repository, as shown in Figure 9-6.

9.3.1 Interfaces for Users, Database Administrators, and Related Systems

When users, database administrators, and related information systems request data and services, the DBMS processes the request, manipulates the data, and provides a response.

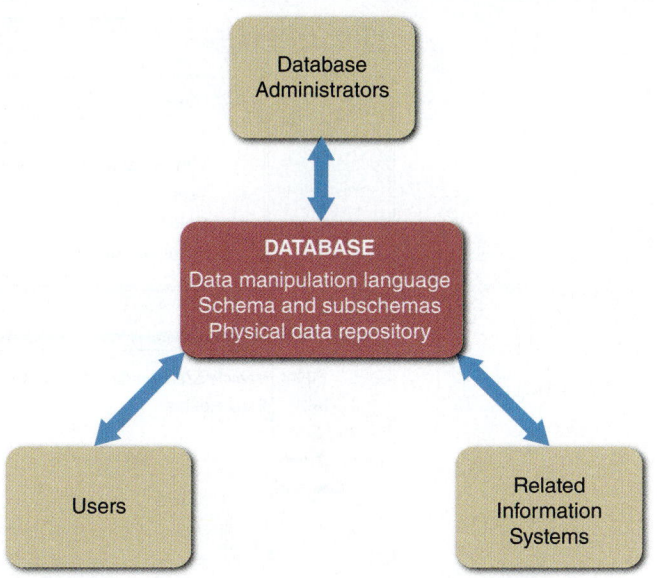

FIGURE 9-6 In addition to interfaces for users, database administrators, and related information systems, a DBMS also has a data manipulation language, a schema and subschemas, and a physical data repository.

USERS: Users typically work with predefined queries and switchboard commands but also use query languages to access stored data. A **query language** allows a user to specify a task without specifying how the task will be accomplished. Some query languages use natural language commands that resemble ordinary English sentences. With a **query by example (QBE)** language, the user provides an example of the data requested. Many database programs also generate **SQL (Structured Query Language)**, which is a language that allows client workstations to communicate with servers and mainframe computers. Figure 9-7 shows a QBE request for all Lime Squeeze or Blue Candy 2013 Ford Fiestas with a power moonroof. The QBE request generates the SQL commands shown at the bottom of Figure 9-7.

DATABASE ADMINISTRATORS: A DBA is responsible for DBMS management and support. DBAs are concerned with data security and integrity, preventing unauthorized access, providing backup and recovery, audit trails, maintaining the database, and supporting user needs. Most DBMSs provide utility programs to assist the DBA in creating and updating data structures, collecting and reporting patterns of database usage, and detecting and reporting database irregularities.

RELATED INFORMATION SYSTEMS: A DBMS can support several related information systems that provide input to, and require specific data from, the DBMS. Unlike a user interface, no human intervention is required for two-way communication between the DBMS and the related systems.

9.3.2 Data Manipulation Language

A **data manipulation language (DML)** controls database operations, including storing, retrieving, updating, and deleting data. Most commercial DBMSs, such as Oracle and IBM's DB2, use a DML. Some database products, such as Microsoft Access, also provide an easy-to-use graphical environment that enables users to control operations with menu-driven commands.

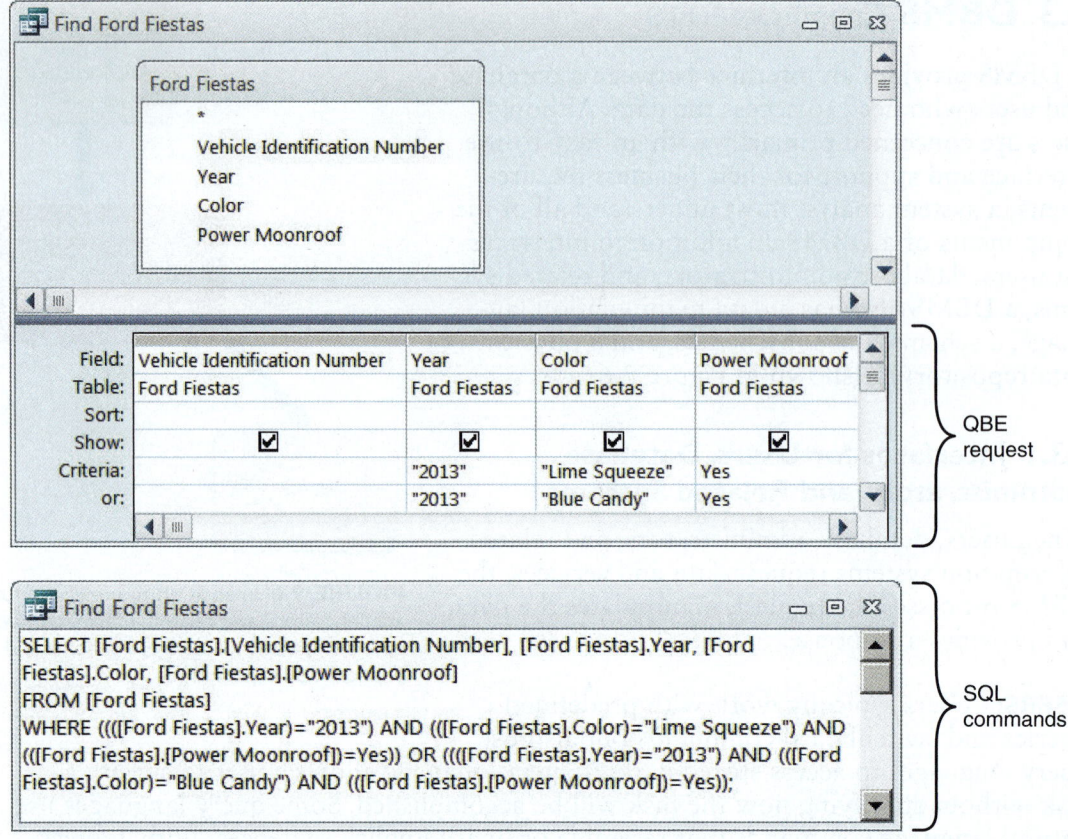

FIGURE 9-7 Using QBE, a user can display all 2013 Ford Fiestas that have a power moonroof and are either Lime Squeeze or Blue Candy color.

9.3.3 Schema

The complete definition of a database, including descriptions of all fields, tables, and relationships, is called a **schema**. One or more subschemas can also be defined. A **subschema** is a view of the database used by one or more systems or users. A subschema defines only those portions of the database that a particular system or user needs or is allowed to access. For example, to protect individual privacy, the project management system should not be permitted to retrieve employee pay rates. In that case, the project management system subschema would not include the pay rate field. Database designers also use subschemas to restrict the level of access permitted. For example, specific users, systems, or locations might be permitted to create, retrieve, update, or delete data, depending on their needs and the company's security policies.

9.3.4 Physical Data Repository

Chapter 5 discussed a data dictionary, which describes all data elements included in the logical design. At this stage of the systems development process, the data dictionary is transformed into a physical data repository, which also contains the schema and subschemas. The physical repository might be centralized, or it might be distributed at several locations. In addition, the stored data might be managed by a single DBMS or several systems. To resolve potential database connectivity and access problems, companies use ODBC-compliant software that enables communication among various systems and DBMSs. **ODBC**, which stands for **open database connectivity**, is an industry-standard protocol that makes it possible for software from different vendors to interact and exchange data. ODBC uses SQL statements that the DBMS understands and can execute, similar to the ones shown in Figure 9-7. Another common standard is called **JDBC**, or **Java database connectivity**. JDBC enables Java applications to exchange data with any database that uses SQL statements and is JDBC-compliant.

Physical design issues are described in Chapter 10, which discusses system architecture, and in Chapter 11, which discusses system implementation and data conversion.

9.4 WEB-BASED DESIGN

Figure 9-8 lists some major characteristics of web-based design. In a web-based design, the Internet serves as the front end, or interface, for the database management system. Internet technology provides enormous power and flexibility because the related information system is not tied to any specific combination of hardware and software. Access to the database requires only a web browser and an Internet connection. Web-based systems are popular because they offer ease of access, cost-effectiveness, and worldwide connectivity — all of which are vital to companies that must compete in a global economy.

CHARACTERISTIC	EXPLANATION
Global access	The Internet enables worldwide access, using existing infrastructure and standard telecommunications protocols.
Ease of use	Web browsers provide a familiar interface that is user-friendly and easily learned.
Multiple platforms	Web-based design is not dependent on a specific combination of hardware or software. All that is required is a browser and an Internet connection.
Cost effectiveness	Initial investment is relatively low because the Internet serves as the communication network. Users require only a browser, and web-based systems do not require powerful workstations. Flexibility is high because numerous outsourcing options exist for development, hosting, maintenance, and system support.
Security issues	Security is a universal issue, but Internet connectivity raises special concerns. These can be addressed with a combination of good design, software that can protect the system and detect intrusion, stringent rules for passwords and user identification, and vigilant users and managers.
Adaptability issues	The Internet offers many advantages in terms of access, connectivity, and flexibility. Migrating a traditional database design to the web, however, can require design modification, additional software, and some added expense.

FIGURE 9-8 Web-based design characteristics include global access, ease of use, multiple platforms, cost effectiveness, security issues, and adaptability issues. In a web-based design, the Internet serves as the front end, or interface, to the database management system. Access to the database requires only a web browser and an Internet connection.

9.4.1 Connecting to the Web

To access data in a web-based system, the database must be connected to the Internet or intranet. The database and the Internet speak two different languages, however. Databases are created and managed by using various languages and commands that have nothing to do with HTML, which is the language of the web. The objective is to connect the database to the web and enable data to be viewed and updated.

To bridge the gap, it is necessary to use middleware, which is software that integrates different applications and allows them to exchange data. Middleware can interpret client requests in HTML form and translate the requests into commands that the database can execute. When the database responds to the commands, middleware translates the results into HTML pages that can be displayed by the user's browser, as shown in Figure 9-9. Notice that the four steps in the process can take place using the Internet or a company intranet as the communications channel. Middleware is discussed in more detail in Chapter 10.

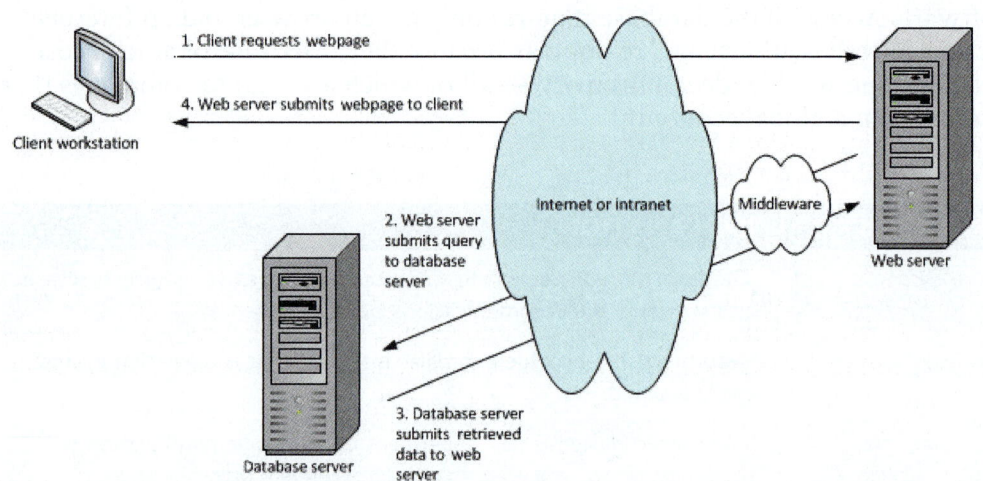

FIGURE 9-9 When a client workstation requests a webpage (1), the web server uses middleware to generate a data query to the database server (2). The database server responds (3), and the middleware translates the retrieved data into an HTML page that can be sent by the web server and displayed by the user's browser (4).

9.4.2 Data Security

Web-based data must be secure yet easily accessible to authorized users. To achieve this goal, well-designed systems provide security at three levels: the database itself, the web server, and the telecommunication links that connect the components of the system.

Data security is discussed in Section 9.11 and in Chapter 12.

9.5 DATA DESIGN TERMS

Using the concepts discussed in the previous sections, a systems analyst can select a design approach and begin to construct the system. The first step is to understand data design terminology.

9.5.1 Definitions

Data design terms include *entity, table, file, field, record, tuple,* and *key field.* These terms are explained in the following sections.

ENTITY: An entity is a person, place, thing, or event for which data is collected and maintained. For example, an online sales system may include entities named CUSTOMER, ORDER, PRODUCT, and SUPPLIER. When DFDs were prepared during the systems analysis phase, various entities and data stores were identified. Now the relationships among the entities will be considered.

TABLE OR FILE: Data is organized into tables or files. A table, or file, contains a set of related records that store data about a specific entity. Tables and files are shown as two-dimensional structures that consist of vertical columns and horizontal rows. Each column represents a field, or characteristic of the entity, and each row represents a record, which is an individual instance, or occurrence of the entity. For example, if a company has 10,000 customers, the CUSTOMER table will include 10,000 records, each representing a specific customer.

 Although they can have different meanings in a specific context, the terms *table* and *file* often can be used interchangeably.

FIELD: A field, also called an attribute, is a single characteristic or fact about an entity. For example, a CUSTOMER entity might include the Customer ID, First Name, Last Name, Address, City, State, Postal Code, and Email Address.

 A common field is an attribute that appears in more than one entity. Common fields can be used to link entities in various types of relationships.

RECORD: A record, also called a tuple (rhymes with couple), is a set of related fields that describes one instance, or occurrence, of an entity, such as one customer, one order, or one product. A record might have one or dozens of fields, depending on what information is needed.

9.5.2 Key Fields

During the systems design phase, key fields are used to organize, access, and maintain data structures. The four types of keys are primary keys, candidate keys, foreign keys, and secondary keys.

PRIMARY KEY: A primary key is a field or combination of fields that uniquely and minimally identifies a particular member of an entity. For example, in a customer table the customer number is a unique primary key because no two customers can have the same customer number. That key is also minimal because it contains no information beyond what is needed to identify the customer. In a CUSTOMER table, a Customer ID might be used as a unique primary key. Customer ID is an example of a primary key based on a single field.

 A primary key can also be composed of two or more fields. For example, if a student registers for three courses, his or her student number will appear in three records in the registration system. If one of those courses has 20 students, 20 separate records will exist for that course number — one record for each student who registered.

 In the registration file, neither the student number nor the course ID is unique, so neither field can be a primary key. To identify a specific student in a specific course, the primary key must be a combination of student number and course ID. In that case, the primary key is called a combination key. A combination key can also be called a composite key, a concatenated key, or a multivalued key.

Figure 9-10 shows four different tables: STUDENT, ADVISOR, COURSE, and GRADE. Three of these tables have single-field primary keys. Notice that in the GRADE table, however, the primary key is a combination of two fields: STUDENT NUMBER and COURSE NUMBER.

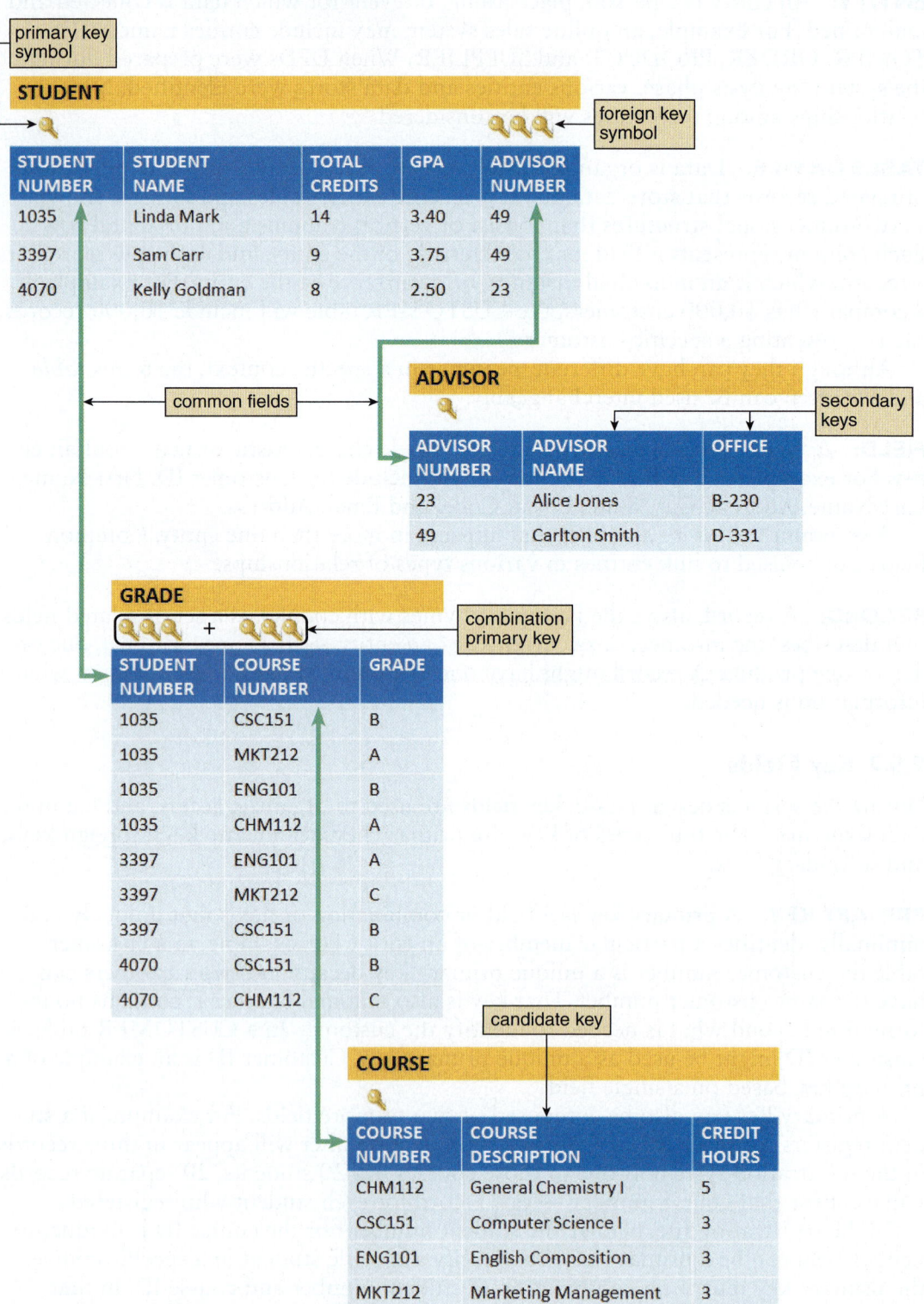

FIGURE 9-10 Examples of common fields, primary keys, candidate keys, foreign keys, and secondary keys.

CANDIDATE KEY: Sometimes there is a choice of fields or field combinations to use as the primary key. Any field that can serve as a primary key is called a **candidate key**. For example, if every employee has a unique employee number, then it could be used as a primary key. Note that an employee's Social Security number would not be a good choice for a candidate key: contrary to popular belief, Social Security numbers are not unique. Because only one field can be designated as a primary key, the field that contains the least amount of data and is the easiest to use should be selected. Any field that is not a primary key or a candidate key is called a **nonkey field**.

The primary keys shown in Figure 9-10 are also candidate keys. Another candidate key is the COURSE DESCRIPTION field in the COURSE table. What about the OFFICE field in the ADVISOR table? It could not be a candidate key because more than one advisor might share the same office.

FOREIGN KEY: Recall that a common field exists in more than one table and can be used to form a relationship, or link, between the tables. For example, in Figure 9-10, the ADVISOR NUMBER field appears in both the STUDENT table and the ADVISOR table and joins the tables together. Notice that ADVISOR NUMBER is a primary key in the ADVISOR table, where it uniquely identifies each advisor, and is a foreign key in the STUDENT table. A **foreign key** is a field in one table that must match a primary key value in another table in order to establish the relationship between the two tables.

Unlike a primary key, a foreign key need not be unique. For example, Carlton Smith has advisor number 49. The value 49 must be a unique value in the ADVISOR table because it is the primary key, but 49 can appear any number of times in the STUDENT table, where the advisor number serves as a foreign key.

Figure 9-10 also shows how two foreign keys can serve as a composite primary key in another table. Consider the GRADE table at the bottom of the figure. The two fields that form the primary key for the GRADE table are both foreign keys: the STUDENT NUMBER field, which must match a student number in the STUDENT table, and the COURSE NUMBER field, which must match one of the course IDs in the COURSE table.

How can these two foreign keys serve as a primary key in the GRADE table? Notice that student numbers and course IDs can appear any number of times in the table, but the *combination* of a specific student and a specific course occurs only once. For example, student 1035 appears four times and course CSC151 appears three times — but there is only *one* combined instance of student 1035 *and* course CSC151. Because the combination of the specific student (1035) and the specific course (CSC151) is unique, it ensures that the grade (B) will be assigned to the proper student in the proper course.

SECONDARY KEY: A **secondary key** is a field or combination of fields that can be used to access or retrieve records. Secondary key values are not unique. For example, to access records for only those customers in a specific postal code, the postal code field would be used as a secondary key. Secondary keys can also be used to sort or display records in a certain order. For example, the GPA field in a STUDENT file could be used to display records for all students in grade point order.

The need for a secondary key arises because a table can have only one primary key. In a CUSTOMER file, the CUSTOMER NUMBER is the primary key, so it must be unique. The customer's name might be known but not the customer's number. For example, to access a customer named James Morgan without knowing his customer number, the table is searched using the CUSTOMER NAME field as a secondary key. The records for all customers named James Morgan are retrieved and then the correct record is selected.

In Figure 9-10, student name and advisor names are identified as secondary keys, but other fields could also be used. For example, to find all students who have a particular advisor, the ADVISOR NUMBER field in the STUDENT table could be used as a secondary key.

9.5.3 Referential Integrity

Validity checks can help avoid data input errors. One type of validity check, called referential integrity, is a set of rules that avoids data inconsistency and quality problems. In a relational database, referential integrity means that a foreign key value cannot be entered in one table unless it matches an existing primary key in another table. For example, referential integrity would prevent a customer order from being entered in an order table unless that customer already exists in the customer table. Without referential integrity, there might be an order called an orphan, because it had no related customer.

In the example shown in Figure 9-10, referential integrity will not allow a user to enter an advisor number (foreign key value) in the STUDENT table unless a valid advisor number (primary key value) already exists in the ADVISOR table.

Referential integrity can also prevent the deletion of a record if the record has a primary key that matches foreign keys in another table. For example, suppose that an advisor resigns to accept a position at another school. The advisor cannot be deleted from the ADVISOR table while records in the STUDENT table still refer to that advisor number. Otherwise, the STUDENT records would be orphans. To avoid the problem, students must be reassigned to other advisors by changing the value in the ADVISOR NUMBER field; then the advisor record can be deleted.

When creating a relational database, referential integrity can be built into the design. Figure 9-11 shows a Microsoft Access screen that identifies a common field and allows the user to enforce referential integrity rules.

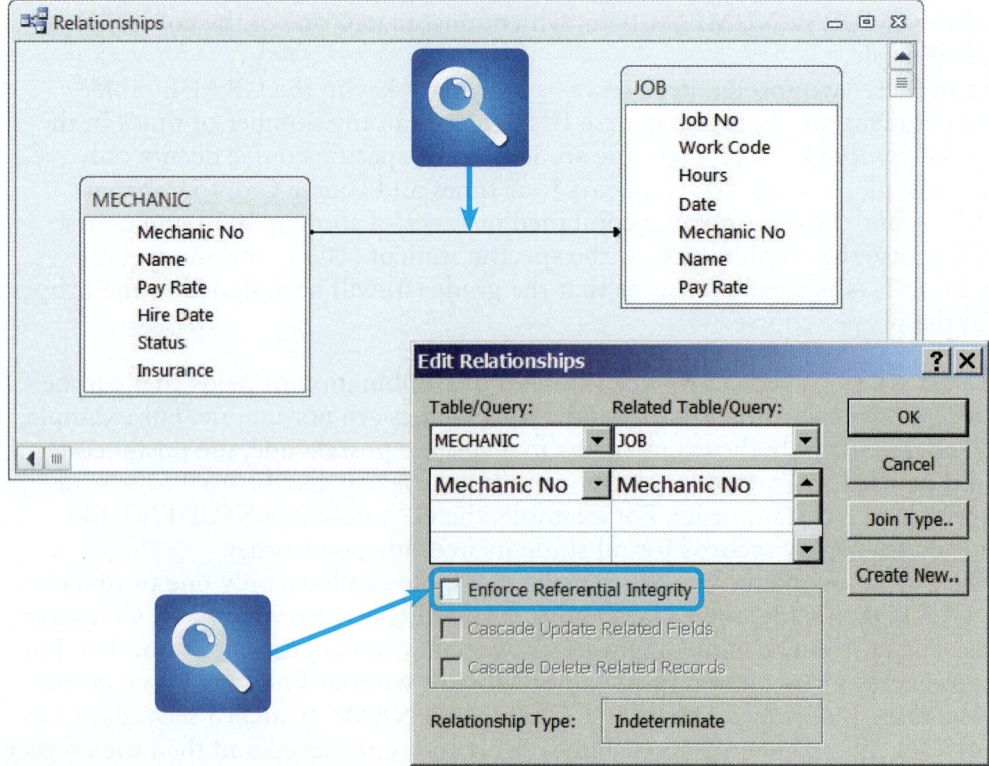

FIGURE 9-11 Microsoft Access allows a user to specify that referential integrity rules will be enforced in a relational database design.

9.6 ENTITY-RELATIONSHIP DIAGRAMS

Recall that an entity is a person, place, thing, or event for which data is collected and maintained. For example, entities might be customers, sales regions, products, or orders. An information system must recognize the relationships among entities. For example, a CUSTOMER entity can have several instances of an ORDER entity, and an EMPLOYEE entity can have one instance, or none, of a SPOUSE entity.

An **entity-relationship diagram (ERD)** is a model that shows the logical relationships and interaction among system entities. An ERD provides an overall view of the system and a blueprint for creating the physical data structures.

9.6.1 Drawing an ERD

The first step is to list the entities that were identified during the systems analysis phase and to consider the nature of the relationships that link them. At this stage, a simplified method can be used to show the relationships between entities.

Although there are different ways to draw ERDs, a popular method is to represent entities as rectangles and relationships as diamond shapes. The entity rectangles are labeled with singular nouns, and the relationship diamonds are labeled with verbs, usually in a top-to-bottom and left-to-right fashion. For example, in Figure 9-12, a DOCTOR entity *treats* a PATIENT entity. Unlike data flow diagrams, entity-relationship diagrams depict relationships, not data or information flows.

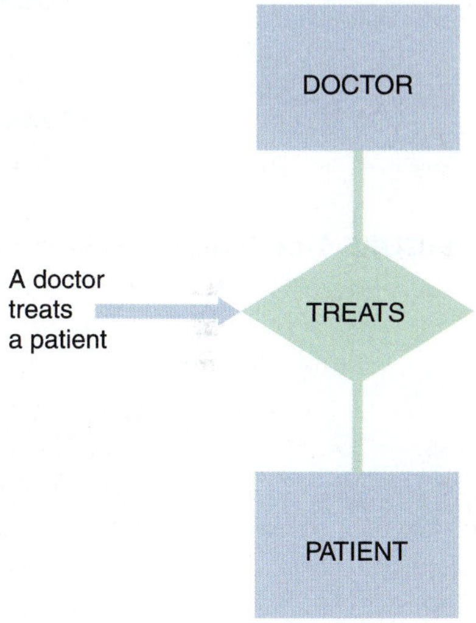

FIGURE 9-12 In an entity-relationship diagram, entities are labeled with singular nouns and relationships are labeled with verbs. The relationship is interpreted as a simple English sentence.

9.6.2 Types of Relationships

Three types of relationships can exist between entities: one-to-one, one-to-many, and many-to-many.

A **one-to-one relationship**, abbreviated **1:1**, exists when exactly one of the second entity occurs for each instance of the first entity. Figure 9-13 shows examples of several 1:1 relationships. A number 1 is placed alongside each of the two connecting lines to indicate the 1:1 relationship.

A **one-to-many relationship**, abbreviated **1:M**, exists when one occurrence of the first entity can relate to many instances of the second entity, but each instance of the second entity can associate with only one instance of the first entity. For example, the relationship between DEPARTMENT and EMPLOYEE is one-to-many: One department can have many employees, but each employee works in only one department at a time. Figure 9-14 shows several 1:M relationships. The line connecting the *many* entity is labeled with the letter M, and the number 1 labels the other connecting line. How many is *many*?

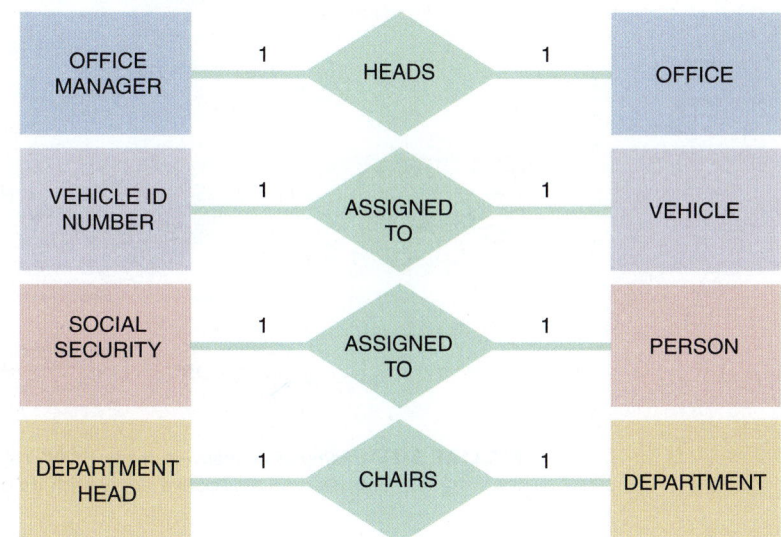

FIGURE 9-13 Examples of one-to-one (1:1) relationships.

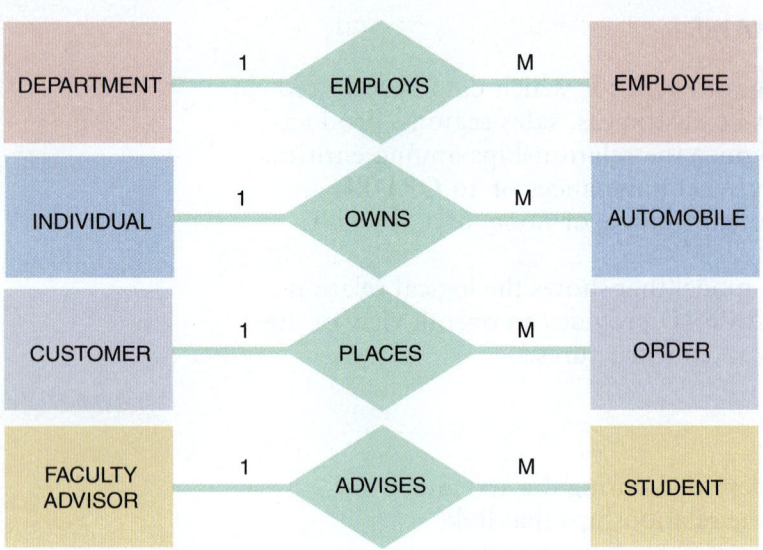

FIGURE 9-14 Examples of one-to-many (1:M) relationships.

The first 1:M relationship shown in Figure 9-14 shows the entities INDIVIDUAL and AUTOMOBILE. One individual might own five automobiles, or one, or none. Thus, *many* can mean any number, including zero.

A **many-to-many relationship**, abbreviated **M:N**, exists when one instance of the first entity can relate to many instances of the second entity, and one instance of the second entity can relate to many instances of the first entity. The relationship between STUDENT and CLASS, for example, is many-to-many — one student can take many classes, and one class can have many students enrolled. Figure 9-15 shows several M:N

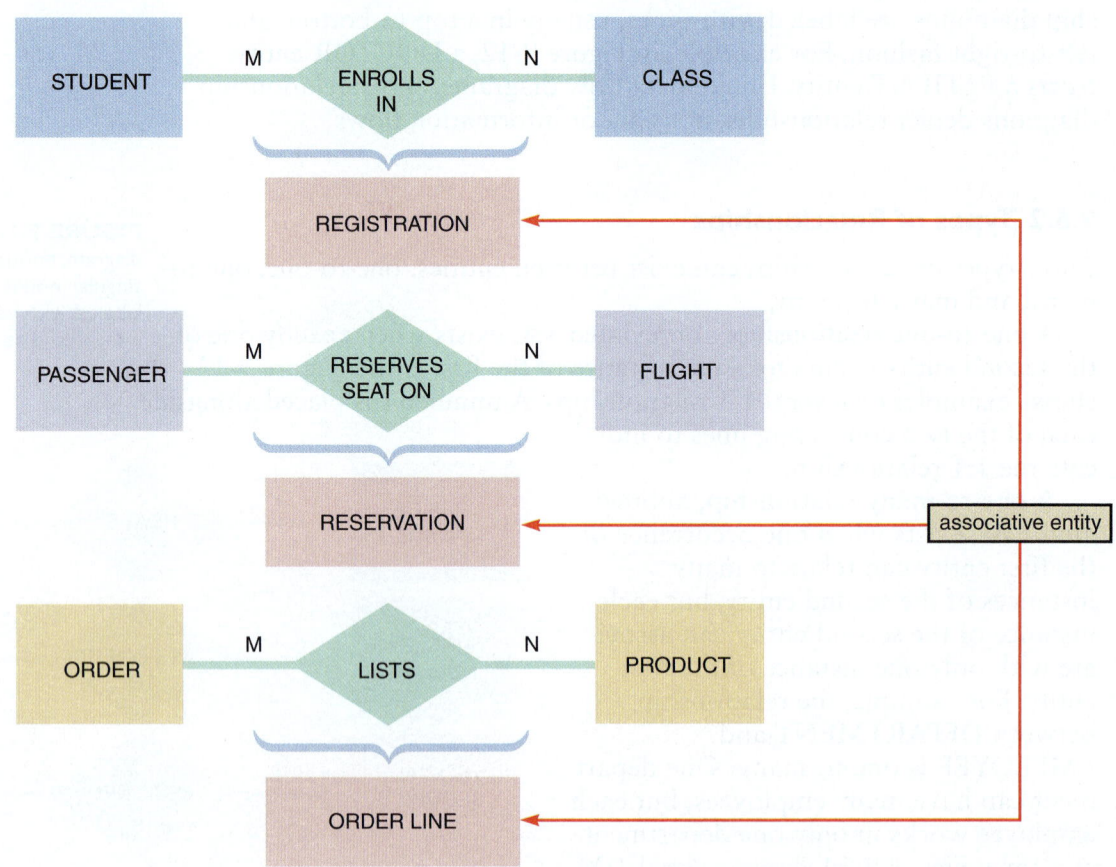

FIGURE 9-15 Examples of many-to-many (M:N) relationships. Notice that the event or transaction that links the two entities is an associative entry with its own set of attributes and characteristics.

entity relationships. One of the connecting lines is labeled with the letter M, and the letter N labels the other connection.

Notice that an M:N relationship is different from 1:1 or 1:M relationships because the event or transaction that links the two entities is actually a third entity, called an **associative entity**, that has its own characteristics. In the first example in Figure 9-15, the ENROLLS IN symbol represents a REGISTRATION entity that records each instance of a specific student enrolling in a specific course. Similarly, the RESERVES SEAT ON symbol represents a RESERVATION entity that records each instance of a specific passenger reserving a seat on a specific flight. In the third example, the LISTS symbol represents an ORDER LINE entity that records each instance of a specific product listed in a specific customer order.

Figure 9-16 shows an ERD for a sales system. Notice the various entities and relationships shown in the figure, including the associative entity named ORDER LINE. The detailed nature of these relationships is called cardinality. An analyst must understand cardinality in order to create a data design that accurately reflects all relationships among system entities.

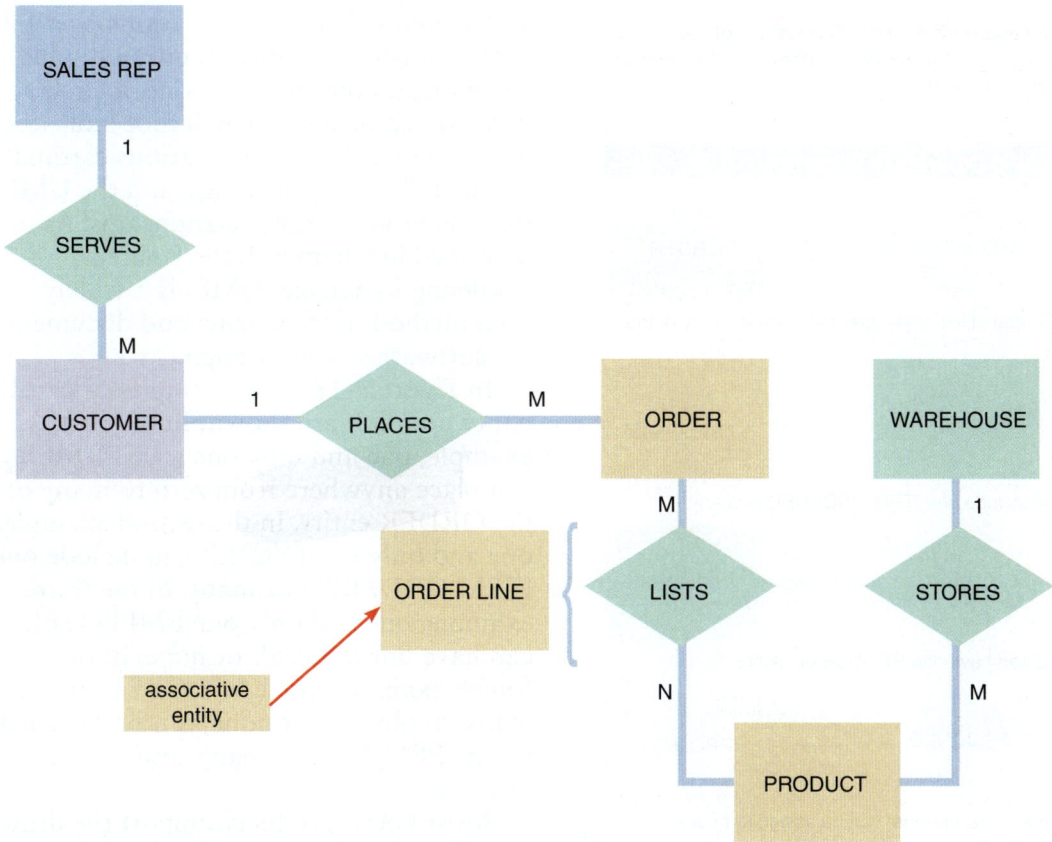

FIGURE 9-16 An entity-relationship diagram for SALES REP, CUSTOMER, ORDER, PRODUCT, and WAREHOUSE. Notice that the ORDER and PRODUCT entities are joined by an associative entity named ORDER LINE.

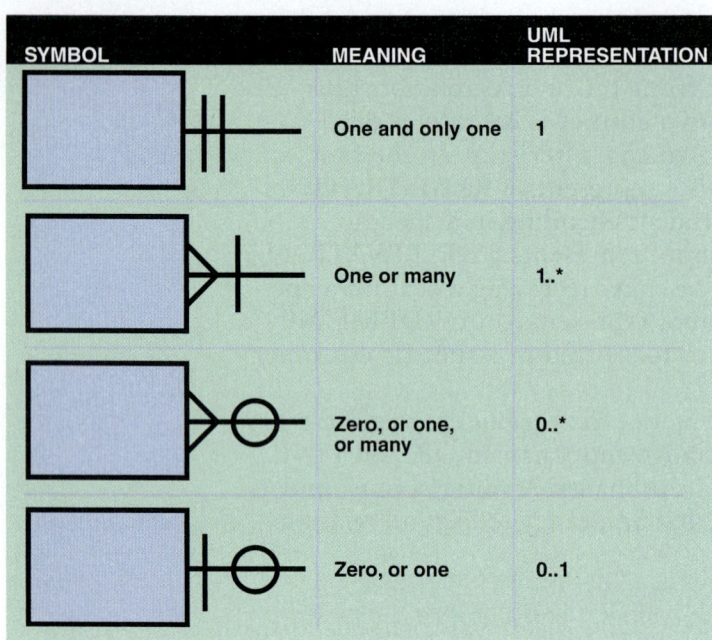

FIGURE 9-17 Crow's foot notation is a common method of indicating cardinality. The four examples show how various symbols can be used to describe the relationships between entities.

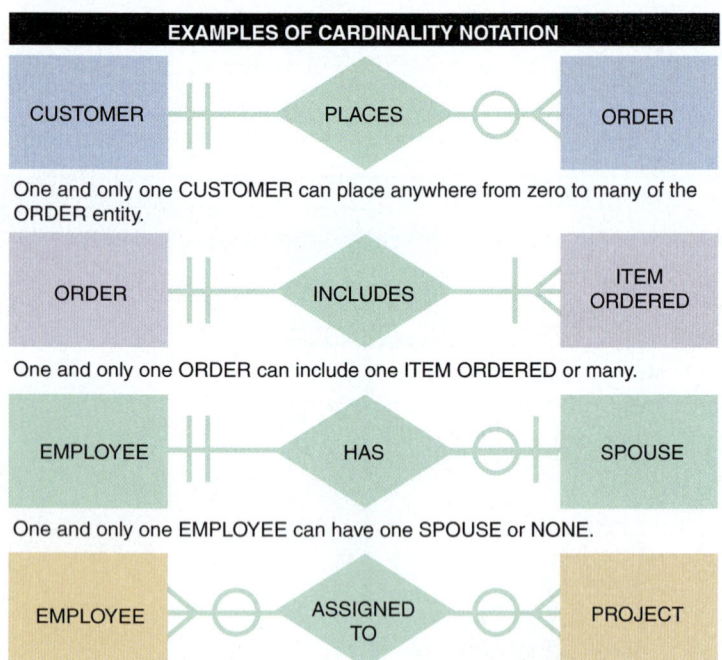

FIGURE 9-18 In the first example of cardinality notation, one and only one CUSTOMER can place anywhere from zero to many of the ORDER entity. In the second example, one and only one ORDER can include one ITEM ORDERED or many. In the third example, one and only one EMPLOYEE can have one SPOUSE or none. In the fourth example, one EMPLOYEE, or many employees, or none, can be assigned to one PROJECT, or many projects, or none.

9.6.3 Cardinality

After an analyst draws an initial ERD, he or she must define the relationships in more detail by using a technique called cardinality. Cardinality describes the numeric relationship between two entities and shows how instances of one entity relate to instances of another entity. For example, consider the relationship between two entities: CUSTOMER and ORDER. One customer can have one order, many orders, or none, but each order must have one and only one customer. An analyst can model this interaction by adding **cardinality notation**, which uses special symbols to represent the relationship.

A common method of cardinality notation is called **crow's foot notation** because of the shapes, which include circles, bars, and symbols that indicate various possibilities. A single bar indicates one, a double bar indicates one and only one, a circle indicates zero, and a crow's foot indicates many. Figure 9-17 shows various cardinality symbols, their meanings, and the UML representations of the relationships. As described in Chapter 4, the Unified Modeling Language (UML) is a widely used method of visualizing and documenting software systems design.

In Figure 9-18, four examples of cardinality notation are shown. In the first example, one and only one CUSTOMER can place anywhere from zero to many of the ORDER entity. In the second example, one and only one ORDER can include one ITEM ORDERED or many. In the third example, one and only one EMPLOYEE can have one SPOUSE or none. In the fourth example, one EMPLOYEE, or many employees, or none, can be assigned to one PROJECT, or many projects, or none.

Most CASE products support the drawing of ERDs from entities in the data repository. Figure 9-19 shows part of a library system ERD drawn using the Visible Analyst CASE tool. Notice that crow's foot notation is used to show the nature of the relationships, which are described in both directions.

Library System Data Model

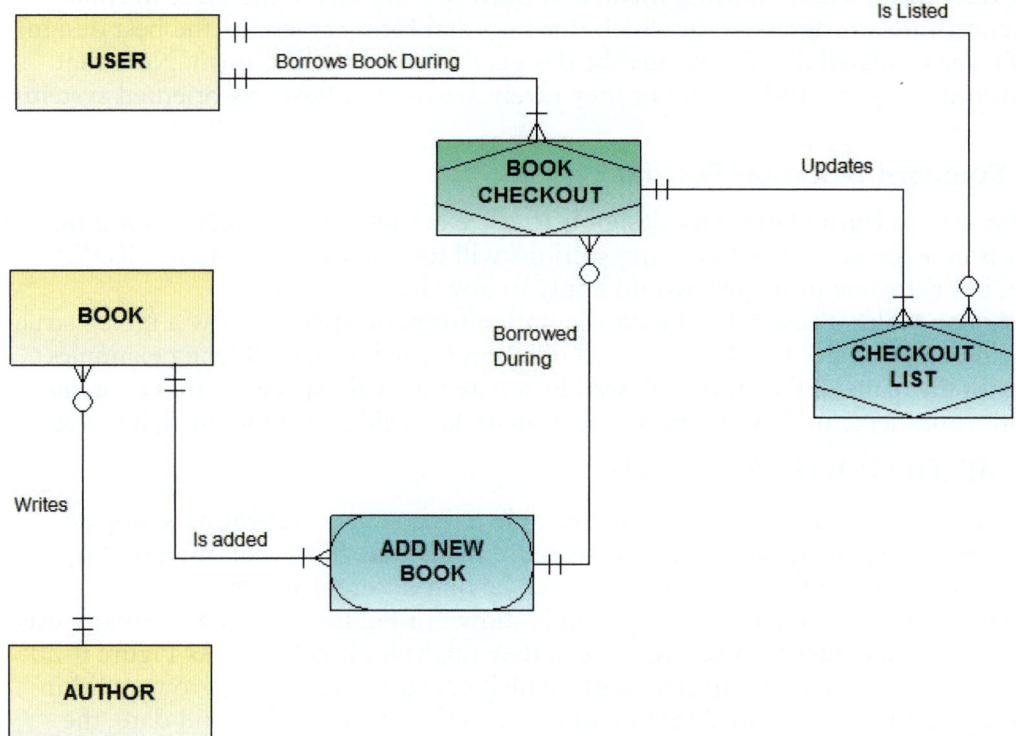

FIGURE 9-19 An ERD for a library system drawn with Visible Analyst. Notice that crow's foot notation has been used and relationships are described in both directions.

CASE IN POINT 9.1:   TOPTEXT PUBLISHING

TopText Publishing is a textbook publishing company with a headquarters location, a warehouse, and three sales offices that each have a sales manager and sales reps. TopText sells to schools, colleges, and individual customers. Many authors write more than one book for TopText, and more than one author writes some books. TopText maintains an active list of more than 100 books, each identified by a universal code called an ISBN. You have been asked to draw an ERD for the TopText information system and to include cardinality notation in your diagram.

9.7 DATA NORMALIZATION

Normalization is the process of creating table designs by assigning specific fields or attributes to each table in the database. A **table design** specifies the fields and identifies the primary key in a particular table or file. Working with a set of initial table designs, normalization is used to develop an overall database design that is simple, flexible, and free of data redundancy. Normalization involves applying a set of rules that can help identify and correct inherent problems and complexities in table designs. The concept of normalization is based on the work of Edgar Codd, a British computer scientist who formulated the basic principles of relational database design.

The normalization process typically involves four stages: unnormalized design, first normal form, second normal form, and third normal form. The three normal forms constitute a progression in which third normal form represents the best design. Most business-related databases must be designed in third normal form. Note that normal forms beyond 3NF exist, but they rarely are used in business-oriented systems.

9.7.1 Standard Notation Format

The best way to learn about data design is to use examples, and standard notation format is no exception. The following sections will use the example of an ORDER system, but the same principles would apply to any situation.

Designing tables is easier if a **standard notation format** is used to show a table's structure, fields, and primary key. The standard notation format in the following examples starts with the name of the table, followed by a parenthetical expression that contains the field names separated by commas. The primary key field(s) is underlined, like this:

NAME (<u>FIELD 1</u>, FIELD 2, FIELD 3)

During data design, the analyst must be able to recognize a repeating group of fields. A **repeating group** is a set of one or more fields that can occur any number of times in a single record, with each occurrence having different values.

A typical example of a repeating group is shown in Figure 9-20. If a company used written source documents to record orders, they might look like this. As Figure 9-20 shows, two orders contain multiple items, which constitute repeating groups within the same order number. Notice that in addition to the order number and date, the records with multiple products contain repetitions of the product number, description, number ordered, supplier number, supplier name, and ISO status. A repeating group can be thought of as a set of child (subsidiary) records contained within the parent (main) record.

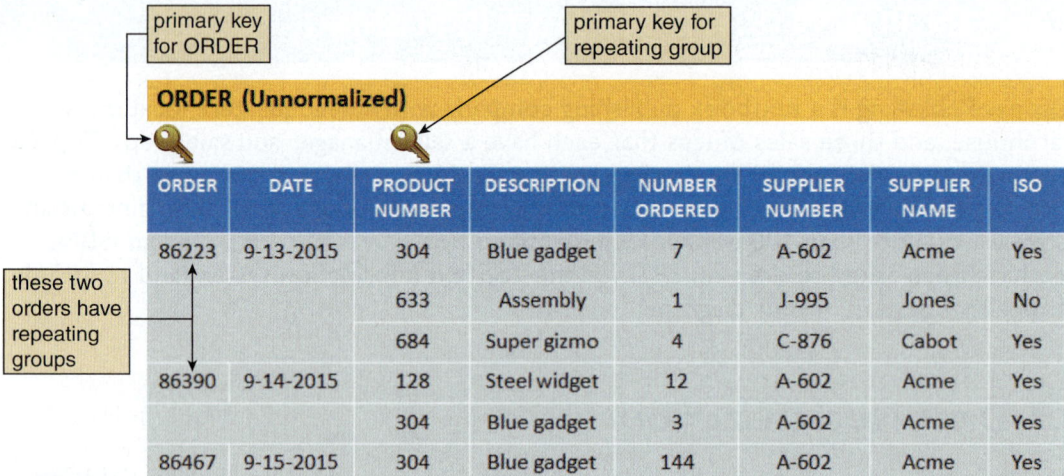

FIGURE 9-20 In the ORDER table design, two orders have repeating groups that contain several products. ORDER is the primary key for the ORDER table, and PRODUCT NUMBER serves as a primary key for the repeating group. Because it contains repeating groups, the ORDER table is unnormalized.

A table design that contains a repeating group is called **unnormalized**. The standard notation method for representing an unnormalized design is to enclose the repeating group of fields within a second set of parentheses. An example of an unnormalized table looks like this:

NAME (<u>FIELD 1</u>, FIELD 2, FIELD 3, (REPEATING FIELD 1, REPEATING FIELD 2))

Now review the unnormalized ORDER table design shown in Figure 9-20. Following the notation guidelines, the design can be described as follows:

ORDER (<u>ORDER</u>, DATE, (<u>PRODUCT NUMBER</u>, DESCRIPTION, NUMBER ORDERED, SUPPLIER NUMBER, SUPPLIER NAME, ISO))

The notation indicates that the ORDER table design contains eight fields, which are listed within the outer parentheses. The ORDER field is underlined to show that it is the primary key. The PRODUCT NUMBER, DESCRIPTION, NUMBER ORDERED, SUPPLIER NUMBER, SUPPLIER NAME, and ISO and NUMBER ORDERED fields are enclosed within an inner set of parentheses to indicate that they are fields within a repeating group. Notice that PRODUCT NUMBER is also underlined because it acts as the primary key of the repeating group. If a customer orders three different products in one order, then six fields must be repeated for each product, as shown in Figure 9-20.

9.7.2 First Normal Form

A table is in **first normal form (1NF)** if it does not contain a repeating group. To convert an unnormalized design to 1NF, the table's primary key must be expanded to include the primary key of the repeating group.

For example, in the ORDER table shown in Figure 9-20, the repeating group consists of six fields: PRODUCT NUMBER, DESCRIPTION, NUMBER ORDERED, SUPPLIER NUMBER, SUPPLIER NAME, and ISO. Of the three fields, only PRODUCT NUMBER can be a primary key because it uniquely identifies each instance of the repeating group. The DESCRIPTION cannot be a primary key because it might or might not be unique. For example, a company might sell a large number of parts with the same descriptive name, such as *washer*, relying on a coded part number to identify uniquely each washer size.

When the primary key of the ORDER table is expanded to include PRODUCT NUMBER, the repeating group is eliminated and the ORDER table is now in 1NF, as shown:

ORDER (<u>ORDER</u>, DATE, <u>PRODUCT NUMBER</u>, DESCRIPTION, NUMBER ORDERED, SUPPLIER NUMBER, SUPPLIER NAME, ISO)

Figure 9-21 shows the ORDER table in 1NF. Notice that when the repeating group is eliminated, additional records emerge — one for each combination of a specific order and a specific product. The result is more records but a greatly simplified design. In the new version, the repeating group for order number 86223 has become three separate records, and the repeating group for order number 86390 has become two separate records. Therefore, when a table is in 1NF, each record stores data about a single instance of a specific order and a specific product.

Also notice that the 1NF design shown in Figure 9-21 has a combination primary key. The primary key of the 1NF design cannot be the ORDER field alone, because the order number does not uniquely identify each product in a multiple-item order. Similarly, PRODUCT NUMBER cannot be the primary key, because it appears more than once if several orders include the same product. Because each record must reflect a specific product in a specific order, *both* fields are needed, ORDER and PRODUCT NUMBER, to identify a single record uniquely. Therefore, the primary key is the *combination* of two fields: ORDER and PRODUCT NUMBER.

> in 1NF, the primary key is a **unique** combination of a specific ORDER and a specific PRODUCT NUMBER

ORDER in 1NF

ORDER	DATE	PRODUCT NUMBER	DESCRIPTION	NUMBER ORDERED	SUPPLIER NUMBER	SUPPLIER NAME	ISO
86223	9-13-2015	304	Blue gadget	7	A-602	Acme	Yes
86223	9-13-2015	633	Assembly	1	J-995	Jones	No
86223	9-13-2015	684	Super gizmo	4	C-876	Cabot	Yes
86390	9-14-2015	128	Steel widget	12	A-602	Acme	Yes
86390	9-14-2015	304	Blue gadget	3	A-602	Acme	Yes
86467	9-15-2015	304	Blue gadget	144	A-602	Acme	Yes

in 1NF
- There are no repeating groups
- The primary key is a **unique** combination of two foreign key values: ORDER and PRODUCT NUMBER
- All fields depend on the primary key, but some fields do not depend on the **whole** key — only part of it

FIGURE 9-21 The ORDER table as it appears in 1NF. The repeating groups have been eliminated. Notice that the repeating group for order 86223 has become three separate records, and the repeating group for order 86390 has become two separate records. The 1NF primary key is a combination of ORDER and PRODUCT NUMBER, which uniquely identifies each record.

9.7.3 Second Normal Form

To understand second normal form (2NF), the concept of functional dependence must be understood. For example, *Field A* is **functionally dependent** on *Field B* if the value of *Field A* depends on *Field B*. For example, in Figure 9-21, the DATE value is functionally dependent on the ORDER, because for a specific order number, there can be only one date. In contrast, a product description is *not* dependent on the order number. For a particular order number, there might be several product descriptions — one for each item ordered.

A table design is in **second normal form (2NF)** if it is in 1NF *and* if all fields that are not part of the primary key are functionally dependent on the *entire* primary key. If any field in a 1NF table depends on only one of the fields in a combination primary key, then the table is not in 2NF.

Notice that if a 1NF design has a primary key that consists of only one field, the problem of partial dependence does not arise — because the entire primary key is a single field. Therefore, a 1NF table with a single-field primary key is automatically in 2NF.

Now reexamine the 1NF design for the ORDER table shown in Figure 9-21:

ORDER (ORDER, DATE, PRODUCT NUMBER, DESCRIPTION, NUMBER ORDERED, SUPPLIER NUMBER, SUPPLIER NAME, ISO)

Recall that the primary key is the combination of the order number and the product number. The NUMBER ORDERED field depends on the *entire* primary key because NUMBER ORDERED refers to a specific product number *and* a specific order number. In contrast, the DATE field depends on the order number, which is only a part of the primary key. Similarly, the DESCRIPTION field depends on the product number, which is also only a part of the primary key. Because some fields are not dependent on the *entire* primary key, the design is not in 2NF.

A standard process exists for converting a table from 1NF to 2NF. The objective is to break the original table into two or more new tables and reassign the fields so that each nonkey field will depend on the entire primary key in its table. To accomplish this, the following steps should be followed:

1. Create and name a separate table for each field in the existing primary key. For example, in Figure 9-21, the ORDER table's primary key has two fields, ORDER and PRODUCT NUMBER, so two tables must be created. The ellipsis (. . .) indicates that fields will be assigned later. The result is:

    ORDER (<u>ORDER</u>, . . .)
    PRODUCT (<u>PRODUCT NUMBER</u>, . . .)

2. Create a new table for each possible combination of the original primary key fields. In the Figure 9-21 example, a new table would be created with a combination primary key of ORDER and PRODUCT NUMBER. This table describes individual lines in an order, so it is named ORDER LINE, as shown:

    ORDER LINE (<u>ORDER</u>, <u>PRODUCT NUMBER</u>)

3. Study the three tables and place each field with its appropriate primary key, which is the minimal key on which it functionally depends. When all the fields have been placed, remove any table that did not have any additional fields assigned to it. The remaining tables are the 2NF version of the original table. The three tables can be shown as:

    ORDER (<u>ORDER</u>, DATE)
    PRODUCT (<u>PRODUCT NUMBER</u>, DESCRIPTION, SUPPLIER NUMBER, SUPPLIER NAME, ISO)
    ORDER LINE (<u>ORDER</u>, <u>PRODUCT NUMBER</u>)

Figure 9-22 shows the 2NF table designs. By following the steps, the original 1NF table has been converted into three 2NF tables.

Why is it important to move from 1NF to 2NF? Four kinds of problems are found with 1NF designs that do not exist in 2NF:

1. Consider the work necessary to change a particular product's description. Suppose 500 current orders exist for product number 304. Changing the product description involves modifying 500 records for product number 304. Updating all 500 records would be cumbersome and expensive.

2. 1NF tables can contain inconsistent data. Because someone must enter the product description in each record, nothing prevents product number 304 from having different product descriptions in different records. In fact, if product number 304 appears in a large number of order records, some of the matching product descriptions might be inaccurate or improperly spelled. Even the presence or absence of a hyphen in the orders for *All-purpose gadget* would create consistency problems. If a data entry person must enter a term such as *IO1 Queue Controller* numerous times, it certainly is possible that some inconsistency will result.

3. Adding a new product is a problem. Because the primary key must include an order number and a product number, values are needed for both fields in order to add a record. What value should be used for the order number when no

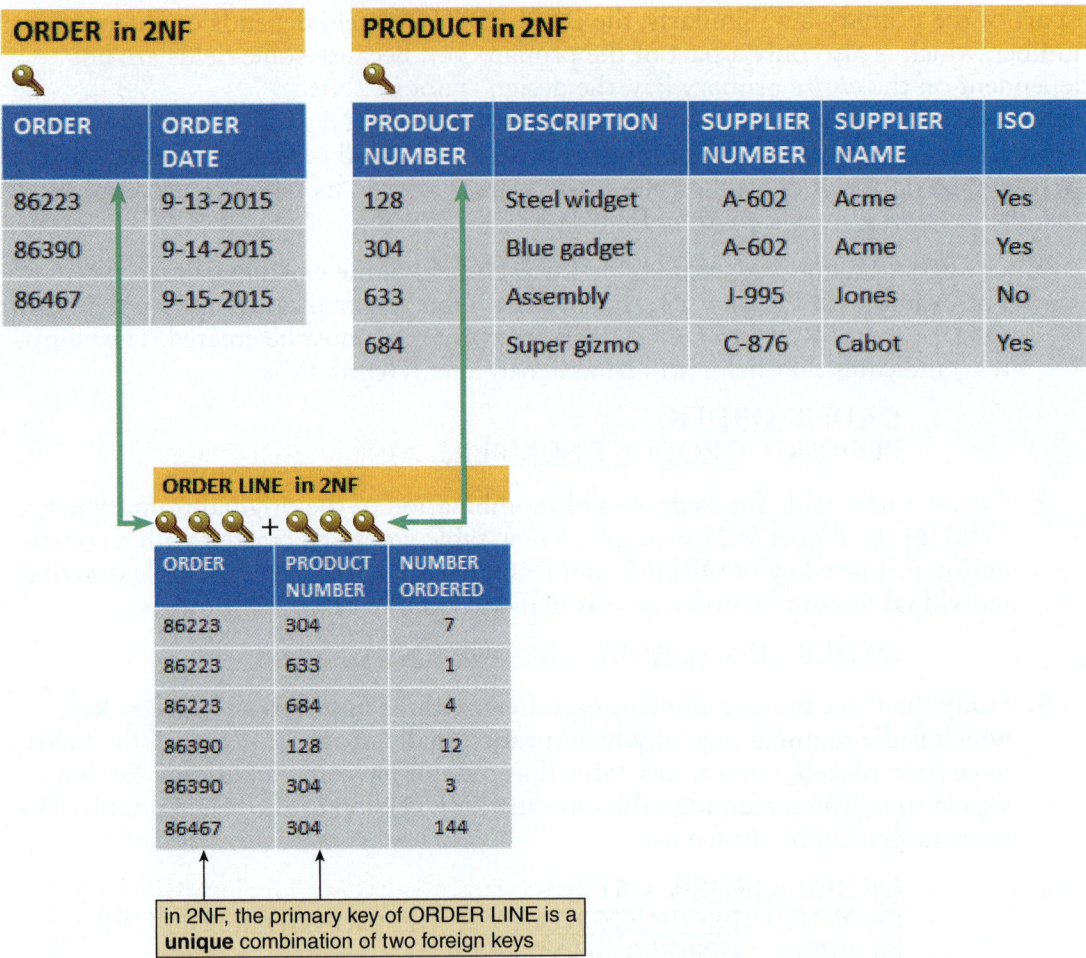

FIGURE 9-22 ORDER, PRODUCT, and ORDER LINE tables in 2NF. All fields are functionally dependent on the primary key.

customer has ordered the product? A dummy order number could be used, and later replaced with a real order number when the product is ordered to solve the problem, but that solution also creates difficulties.

4. Deleting a product is a problem. If all the related records are deleted once an order is filled and paid for, what happens if the only record that contains product number 633 is deleted? The information about that product number and its description is lost.

Has the 2NF design eliminated all potential problems? To change a product description, now just one PRODUCT record needs to be changed. Multiple, inconsistent values for the product description are impossible because the description appears in only one location. To add a new product, a new PRODUCT record is created, instead of creating a dummy order record. When the last ORDER LINE record for a particular product number is removed, that product number and its description is not lost because the PRODUCT record still exists. The four potential problems are eliminated, and the three 2NF designs are superior to both the original unnormalized table and the 1NF design.

9.7.4 Third Normal Form

A popular rule of thumb is that a design is in 3NF if every nonkey field depends on *the key, the whole key, and nothing but the key*. A 3NF design avoids redundancy and data integrity problems that still can exist in 2NF designs.

Continuing the ORDER example, now review the PRODUCT table design in Figure 9-23:

PRODUCT (<u>PRODUCT NUMBER,</u> DESCRIPTION, SUPPLIER NUMBER, SUPPLIER NAME, ISO)

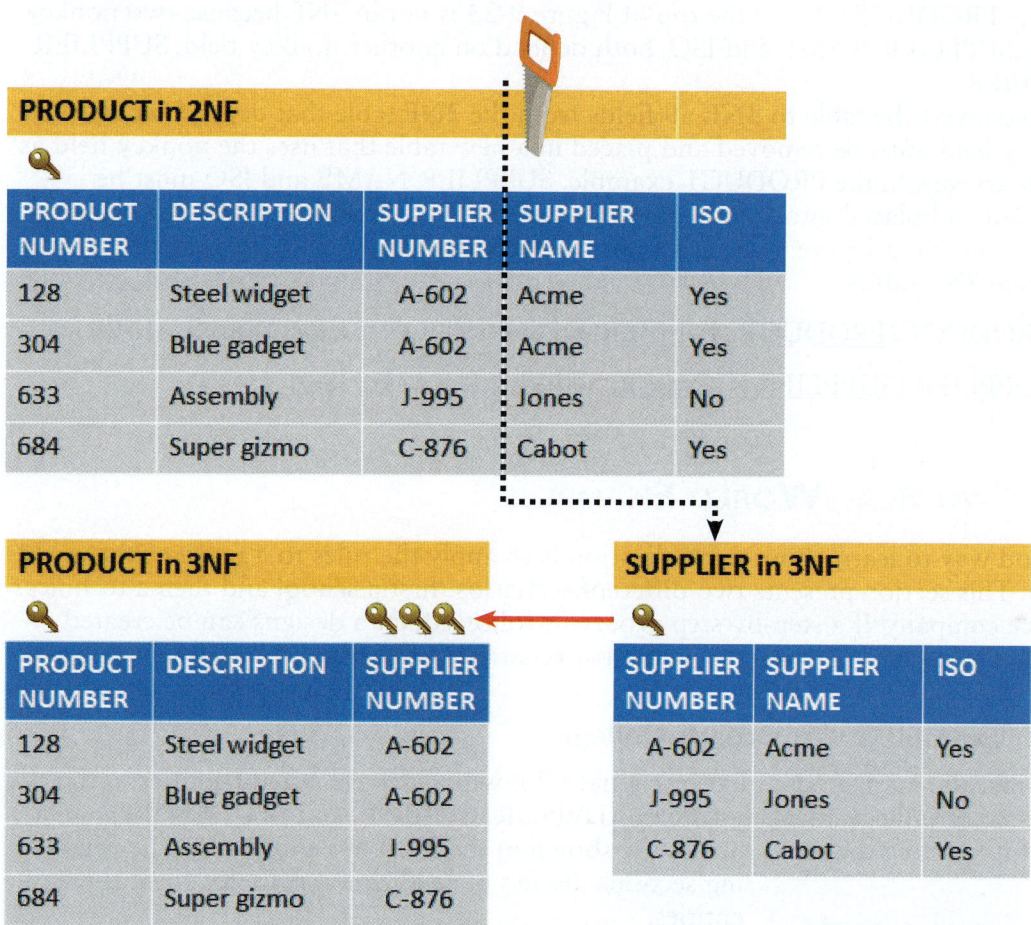

FIGURE 9-23 When the PRODUCT table is transformed from 2NF to 3NF, the result is two separate tables: PRODUCT and SUPPLIER. Note that in 3NF, all fields depend on the key alone.

The PRODUCT table is in 1NF because it has no repeating groups. The table is also in 2NF because the primary key is a single field. But the table still has four potential problems:

1. To change a supplier name, every record in which that name appears must be changed. With hundreds, or even thousands of records, the process would be slow, expensive, and subject to input errors.

2. The 2NF design allows a supplier to have a different name or ISO status in different records.

3. Because the supplier name is included in the ORDER table, a dummy ORDER record must be created to add a new supplier who has not yet been received any orders.

4. If all the orders for a supplier are deleted, that supplier's number and name will be lost.

Those potential problems are caused because the design is not in 3NF. A table design is in **third normal form (3NF)** if it is in 2NF and if no nonkey field is dependent on another nonkey field. Remember that a nonkey field is a field that is not a candidate key for the primary key.

The PRODUCT table at the top of Figure 9-23 is not in 3NF because two nonkey fields, SUPPLIER NAME and ISO, both depend on another nonkey field, SUPPLIER NUMBER.

To convert the table to 3NF, all fields from the 2NF table that depend on another nonkey field must be removed and placed in a new table that uses the nonkey field as a primary key. In the PRODUCT example, SUPPLIER NAME and ISO must be removed and placed into a new table that uses SUPPLIER NUMBER as the primary key. As shown in Figure 9-23, third normal form divides the 2NF version into two separate 3NF tables:

PRODUCT (<u>PRODUCT NUMBER</u>, DESCRIPTION, SUPPLIER NUMBER)

SUPPLIER (<u>SUPPLIER NUMBER</u>, SUPPLIER NAME, ISO)

9.8 Two Real-World Examples

A good way to learn about normalization is to apply the rules to a representative situation. This section presents two different scenarios: first a school and then a technical service company. If a step-by-step process is followed, data designs can be created that are efficient, maintainable, and error-resistant.

9.8.1 Example 1: Crossroads College

Consider the familiar situation in Figure 9-24, which depicts several entities in the Crossroads College advising system: ADVISOR, COURSE, and STUDENT. The relationships among the three entities are shown in the ERD in Figure 9-25. The following sections discuss normalization rules for these three entities.

Before the normalization process is started, it is noted that the STUDENT table contains fields that relate to the ADVISOR and COURSE entities, so a decision is made to begin with the initial design for the STUDENT table, which is shown in Figure 9-26. Notice that the table design includes the student number, student name, total credits taken, grade point average (GPA), advisor number, advisor name, and, for every course the student has taken, the course number, course description, number of credits, and grade received.

The STUDENT table in Figure 9-26 is unnormalized because it has a repeating group. The STUDENT table design can be written as:

FIGURE 9-24 A faculty advisor, who represents an entity, can advise many students, each of whom can register for one or many courses.

STUDENT (<u>STUDENT NUMBER</u>, STUDENT NAME, TOTAL CREDITS, GPA, ADVISOR NUMBER, ADVISOR NAME, OFFICE, (<u>COURSE NUMBER</u>, CREDIT HOURS, GRADE))

To convert the STUDENT record to 1NF, the primary key must be expanded to include the key of the repeating group, producing:

STUDENT (<u>STUDENT NUMBER</u>, STUDENT NAME, TOTAL CREDITS, GPA, ADVISOR NUMBER, ADVISOR NAME, OFFICE, <u>COURSE NUMBER</u>, CREDIT HOURS, GRADE)

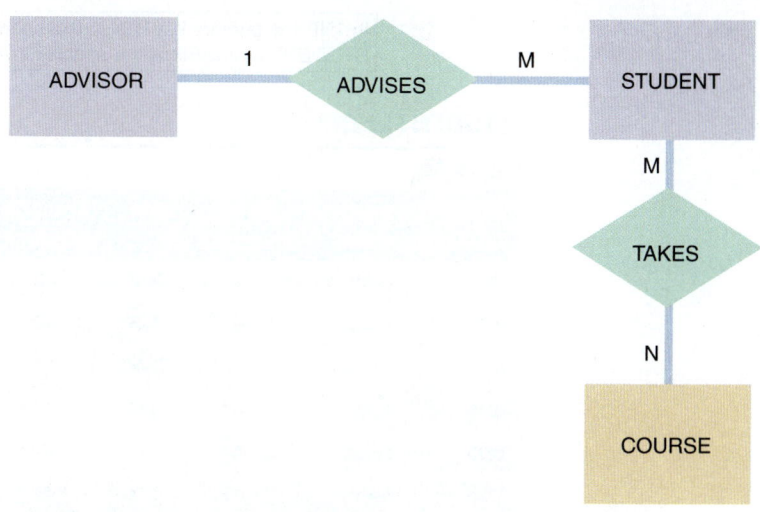

FIGURE 9-25 An initial entity-relationship diagram for ADVISOR, STUDENT, and COURSE.

STUDENT (Unnormalized)

STUDENT NUMBER	STUDENT NAME	TOTAL CREDITS	GPA	ADVISOR NUMBER	ADVISOR NAME	OFFICE	COURSE NUMBER	CREDIT HOURS	GRADE
1035	Linda	47	3.60	49	Smith	B212	CSC151	4	B
							MKT212	3	A
							ENG101	3	B
							CHM112	4	A
							BUS105	2	A
3397	Sam	29	3.00	49	Smith	B212	ENG101	3	A
							MKT212	3	C
							CSC151	4	B
4070	Kelly	14	2.90	23	Jones	C333	CSC151	4	B
							CHM112	4	C
							ENG101	3	C
							BUS105	2	C

FIGURE 9-26 The STUDENT table is unnormalized because it contains a repeating group that represents the course each student has taken.

Figure 9-27 shows the 1NF version of the sample STUDENT data. Do any of the fields in the 1NF STUDENT table depend on only a portion of the primary key? The student name, total credits, GPA, advisor number, and advisor name all relate only to the student number and have no relationship to the course number. The course description depends on the course number but not on the student number. Only the GRADE field depends on the entire primary key.

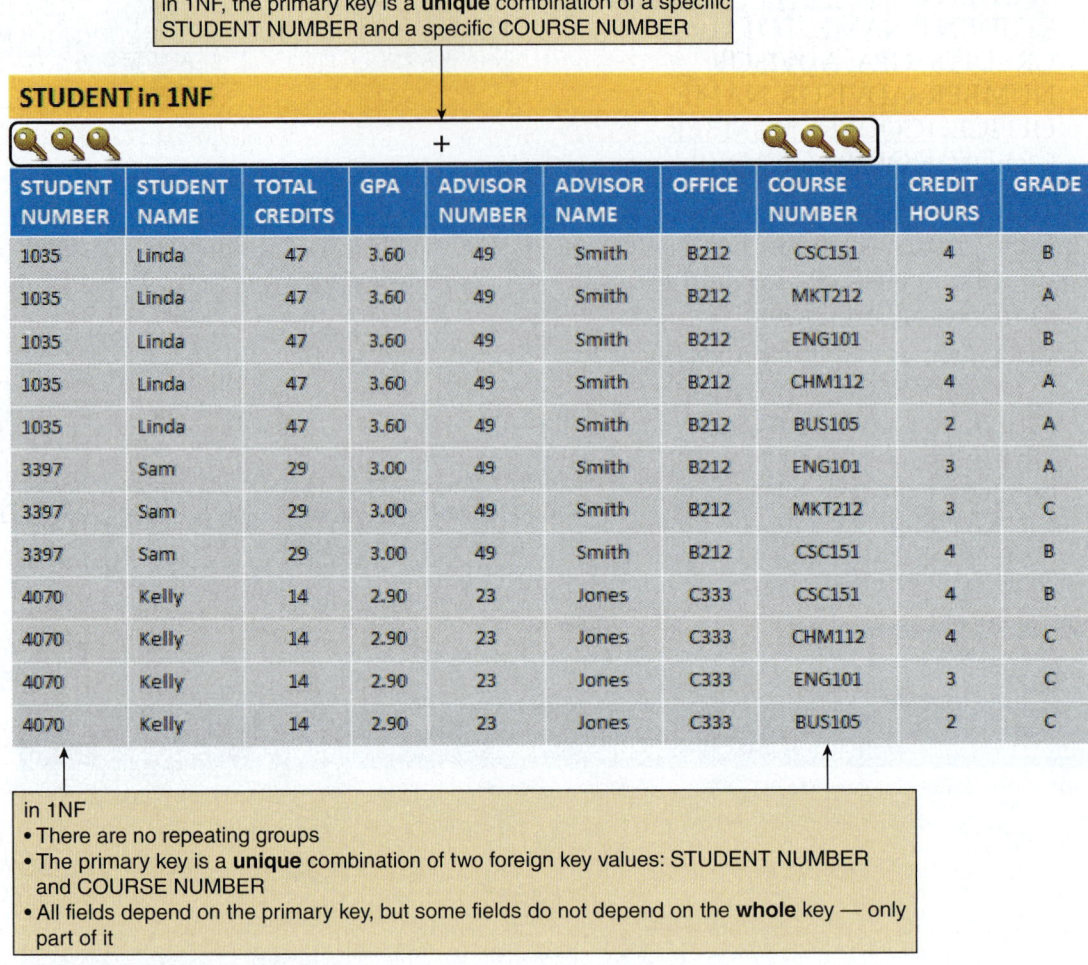

in 1NF, the primary key is a **unique** combination of a specific STUDENT NUMBER and a specific COURSE NUMBER

STUDENT in 1NF

STUDENT NUMBER	STUDENT NAME	TOTAL CREDITS	GPA	ADVISOR NUMBER	ADVISOR NAME	OFFICE	COURSE NUMBER	CREDIT HOURS	GRADE
1035	Linda	47	3.60	49	Smith	B212	CSC151	4	B
1035	Linda	47	3.60	49	Smith	B212	MKT212	3	A
1035	Linda	47	3.60	49	Smith	B212	ENG101	3	B
1035	Linda	47	3.60	49	Smith	B212	CHM112	4	A
1035	Linda	47	3.60	49	Smith	B212	BUS105	2	A
3397	Sam	29	3.00	49	Smith	B212	ENG101	3	A
3397	Sam	29	3.00	49	Smith	B212	MKT212	3	C
3397	Sam	29	3.00	49	Smith	B212	CSC151	4	B
4070	Kelly	14	2.90	23	Jones	C333	CSC151	4	B
4070	Kelly	14	2.90	23	Jones	C333	CHM112	4	C
4070	Kelly	14	2.90	23	Jones	C333	ENG101	3	C
4070	Kelly	14	2.90	23	Jones	C333	BUS105	2	C

in 1NF
- There are no repeating groups
- The primary key is a **unique** combination of two foreign key values: STUDENT NUMBER and COURSE NUMBER
- All fields depend on the primary key, but some fields do not depend on the **whole** key — only part of it

FIGURE 9-27 The student table in 1NF. Notice that the primary key has been expanded to include STUDENT NUMBER and COURSE NUMBER.

Following the 1NF – 2NF conversion process described earlier, a new table would be created for each field and combination of fields in the primary key, and the other fields would be placed with their appropriate key. The result is:

STUDENT (<u>STUDENT NUMBER</u>, STUDENT NAME, TOTAL CREDITS, GPA, ADVISOR NUMBER, ADVISOR NAME, OFFICE)
COURSE (<u>COURSE NUMBER</u>, CREDIT HOURS)
GRADE (<u>STUDENT NUMBER</u>, COURSE NUMBER, GRADE)

The original 1NF STUDENT table has now been converted into three tables, all in 2NF. In each table, every nonkey field depends on the entire primary key.

Figure 9-28 shows the 2NF STUDENT, COURSE, and GRADE designs and sample data. Are all three tables STUDENT in 3NF? The COURSE and GRADE tables are in 3NF. STUDENT is not in 3NF, however, because the ADVISOR NAME and OFFICE fields depend on the ADVISOR NUMBER field, which is not part of the STUDENT primary key. To convert STUDENT to 3NF, the ADVISOR NAME and OFFICE fields are removed from the STUDENT table and placed into a table with ADVISOR NUMBER as the primary key.

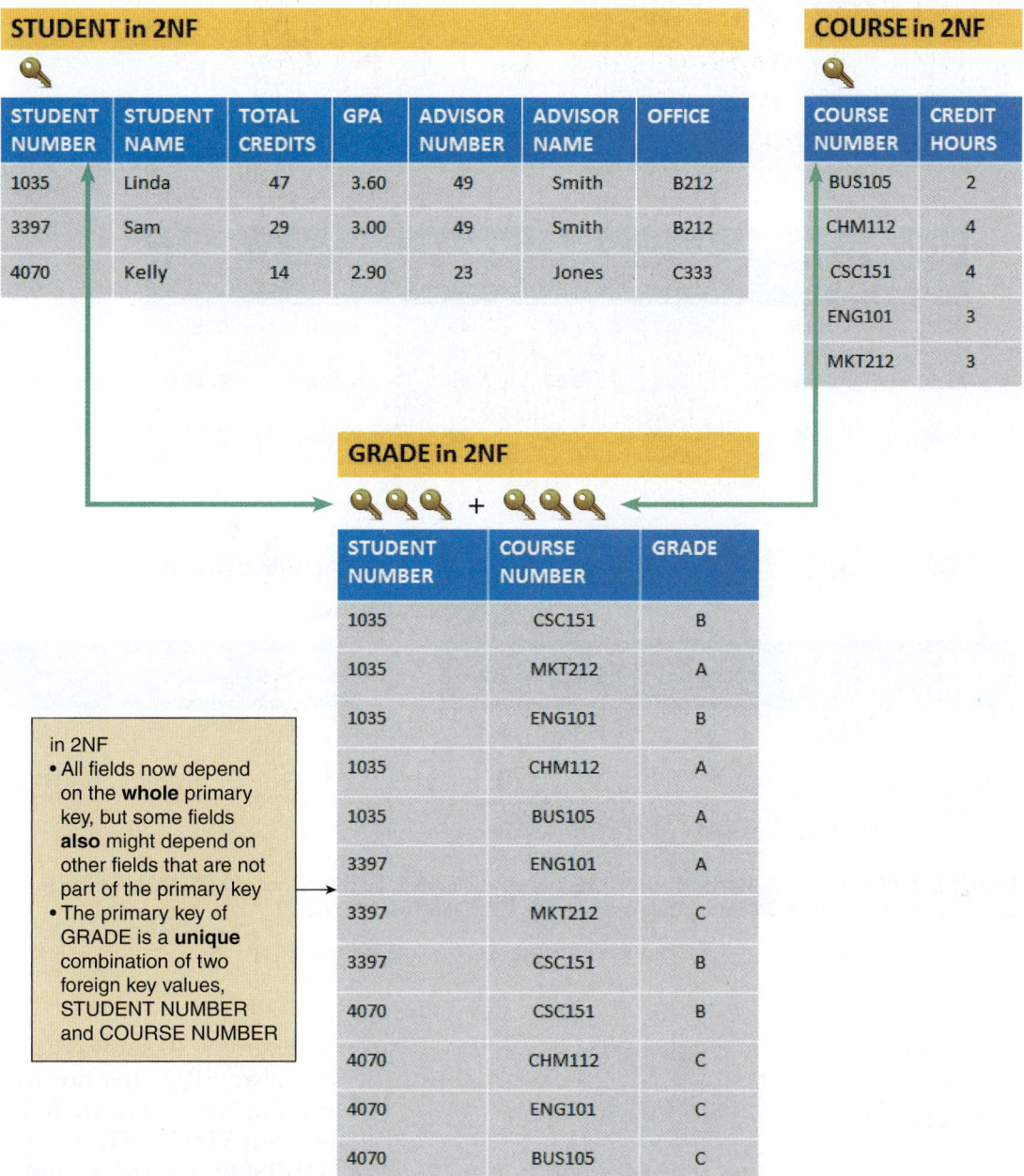

FIGURE 9-28 The STUDENT, COURSE, and GRADE tables in 2NF. Notice that all fields are functionally dependent on the entire primary key of their respective tables.

Figure 9-29 shows the 3NF versions of the sample data for STUDENT, ADVISOR, COURSE, and GRADE. The final 3NF design is:

STUDENT (<u>STUDENT NUMBER</u>, STUDENT NAME, TOTAL CREDITS, GPA, ADVISOR NUMBER)

ADVISOR (<u>ADVISOR NUMBER</u>, ADVISOR NAME, OFFICE)

COURSE (<u>COURSE NUMBER</u>, CREDIT HOURS)

GRADE (<u>STUDENT NUMBER</u>, <u>COURSE NUMBER</u>, GRADE)

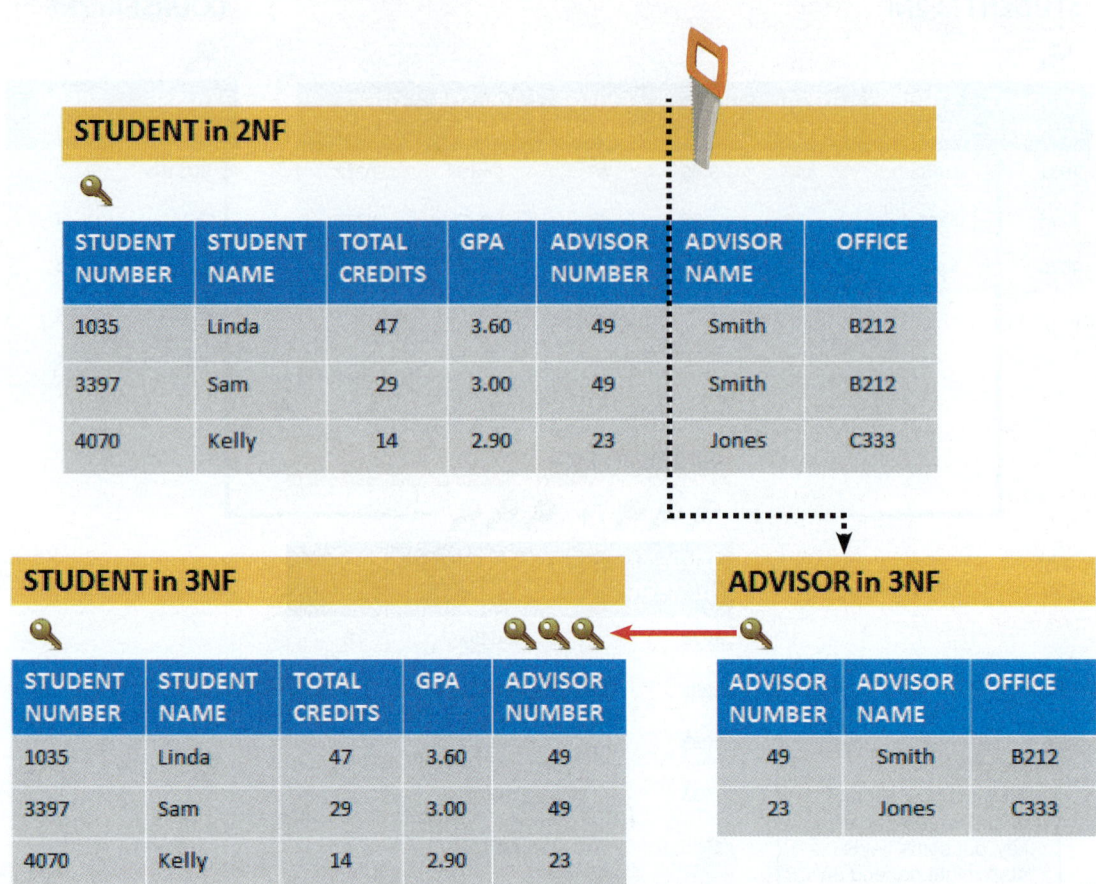

FIGURE 9-29 STUDENT, ADVISOR, COURSE, and GRADE tables in 3NF. When the STUDENT table is transformed from 2NF to 3NF, the result is two tables: STUDENT and ADVISOR.

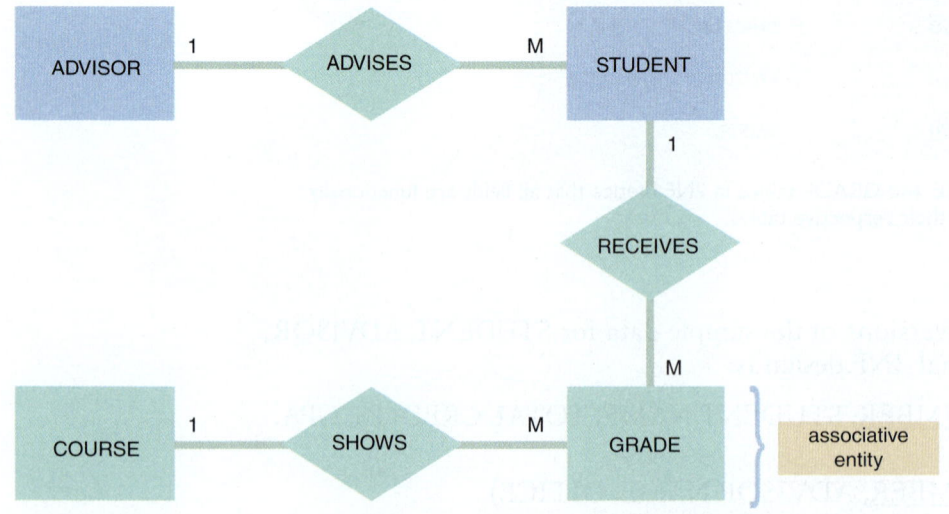

FIGURE 9-30 The entity-relationship diagram for STUDENT, ADVISOR, and COURSE after normalization. The GRADE entry was identified during the normalization process. GRADE is an associative entity that links the STUDENT and COURSE tables.

Figure 9-30 shows the complete ERD after normalization. Now there are four entities: STUDENT, ADVISOR, COURSE, and GRADE (which is an associative entity). Note how Figure 9-25, which was drawn before GRADE was identified as an entity, shows that the M:N relationship between STUDENT and COURSE has been converted into two 1:M relationships: one relationship between STUDENT and GRADE and the other relationship between COURSE and GRADE.

To create 3NF designs, the nature of first, second, and third normal forms must be understood. A systems analyst will encounter designs that are much more complex than the examples in this chapter.

CASE IN POINT 9.2:   CYBERTOYS

You handle administrative support for CyberToys, a small chain that sells computer hardware and software and specializes in personal service. The company has four stores located at malls and is planning more. Each store has a manager, a technician, and between one and four sales reps.

Bruce and Marcia Berns, the owners, want to create a personnel records database, and they asked you to review a table that Marcia designed. She suggested fields for store number, location, store telephone, manager name, and manager home telephone. She also wants fields for technician name and technician home telephone and fields for up to four sales rep names and sales rep home telephones.

Draw Marcia's suggested design and analyze it using the normalization concepts you learned in the chapter. What do you think of Marcia's design and why? What would you propose?

9.8.2 Example 2: Magic Maintenance

Magic Maintenance provides on-site service for electronic equipment. Figure 9-31 shows the overall database design that such a firm might use. The figure contains

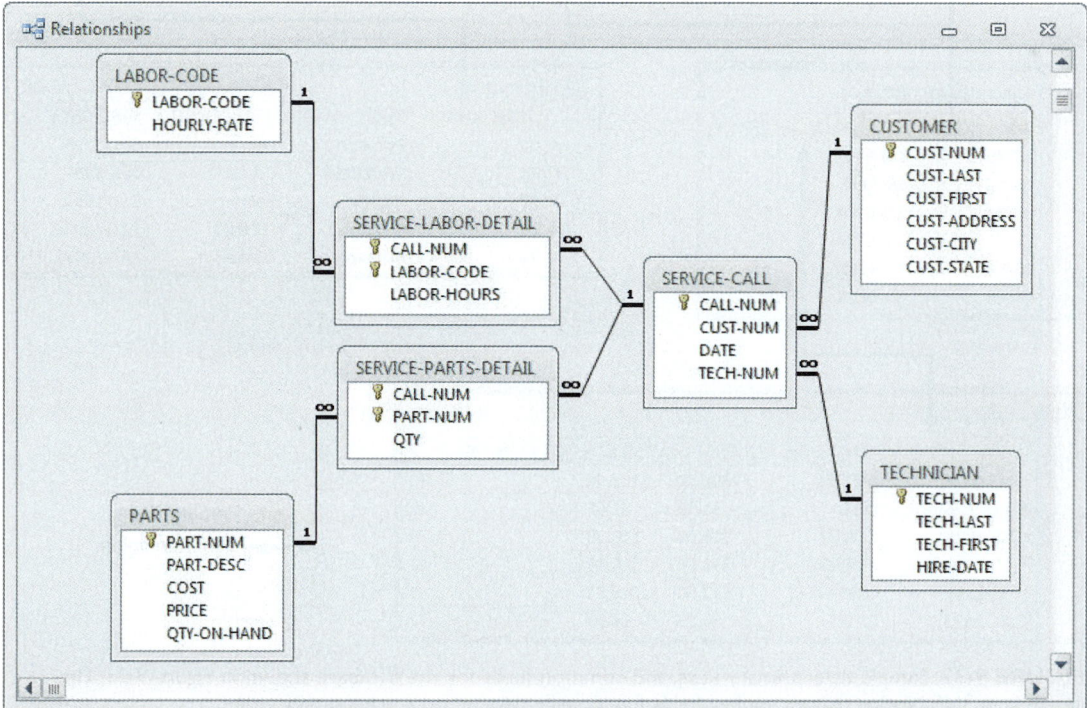

FIGURE 9-31 A relational database design for a computer service company uses common fields to link the tables and form an overall data structure. Notice the one-to-many notation symbols, and the primary keys, which are indicated with gold-colored key symbols.

examples of many concepts described earlier. The database consists of seven separate tables, all joined by common fields so they form an integral data structure.

Figure 9-32 shows even more detail, including sample data, primary keys, and common fields. Notice that the entities include customers, technicians, service calls, and parts. Other tables store data about labor and parts that are used on specific service calls. Also notice that all tables use a single field as a primary key, except the SERVICE-LABOR-DETAIL and SERVICE-PARTS-DETAIL tables, where the primary key requires a combination of two fields to uniquely identify each record.

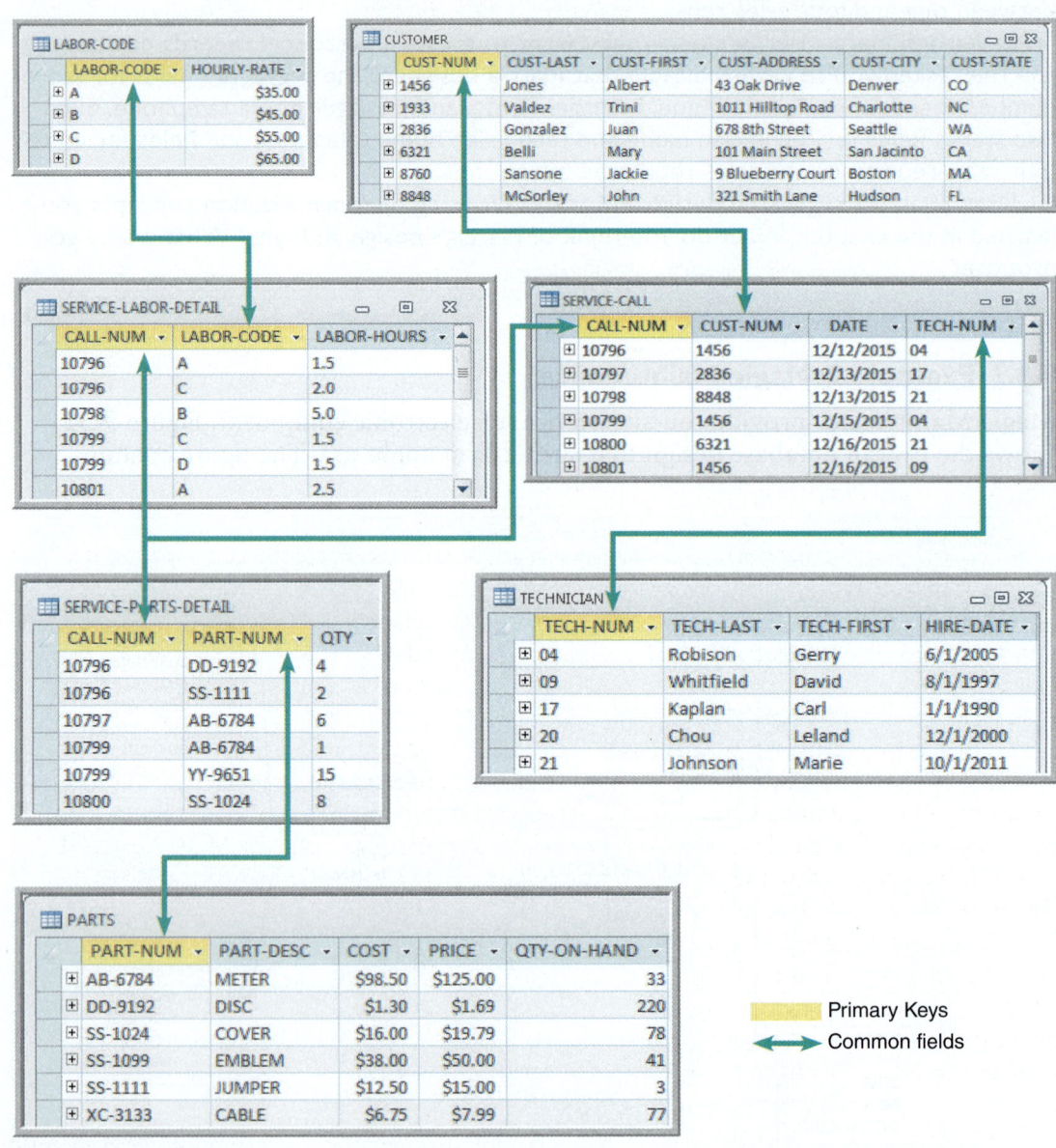

FIGURE 9-32 Sample data, primary keys, and common fields for the database shown in Figure 9-31. The design is in 3NF. Notice that all nonkey fields functionally depend on a primary key alone.

CASE IN POINT 9.3:   DotCom Tools

DotCom Tools operates a small business that specializes in hard-to-find woodworking tools. The firm advertises in various woodworking magazines, and currently accepts mail and telephone orders. DotCom is planning a website that will be the firm's primary sales channel. The site will feature an online catalog, powerful search capabilities, and links to woodworking information and resources.

DotCom has asked you, an IT consultant, whether a set of codes would be advantageous and, if so, what codes you would suggest. Provide at least two choices for a customer code and at least two choices for a product code. Be sure to describe your choices and provide some specific examples. Also include an explanation of why you selected these particular codes and what advantages they might offer.

9.9 USING CODES

A code is a set of letters or numbers that represents a data item. Codes can be used to simplify output, input, and data formats.

9.9.1 Overview of Codes

Because codes can represent data, they are encountered constantly in everyday life. Student numbers, for example, are unique codes to identify students in a school registration system. Three students with the name John Turner might be enrolled at the same school, but *only* one is student number 268960.

A postal code is another common example. A nine-digit postal code contains a lot of information. For example, the first digit identifies one of 10 main geographical areas in the United States. The combination of the next three digits identifies a major city or major distribution point. The fifth digit identifies an individual post office, an area within a city, or a specific delivery unit. The last four digits identify a post office box or a specific street address.

For example, consider the zip code 32901-6975 shown in Figure 9-33. This is called the "5+4" zip code format. The first digit, 3, indicates a broad geographical area in the southeastern United States. The next two digits, 29, indicate the area east of Orlando in Florida. The next two digits, 01, represent the city of Melbourne, FL. The last four digits represent the specific location of the Florida Institute of Technology: 150 W. University Blvd.

Codes can be used in many ways. Because codes are shorter than the data they represent, they save storage space and costs, reduce data transmission time, and decrease data entry time. Codes can also be used to reveal or conceal information. The last two digits of a seven-digit part number, for example, might represent the supplier number or the maximum discount that a salesperson can offer.

Broad geographical location in southeastern US	FL Orlando East	Melbourne	Florida Tech 150 W. University Blvd.
3	29	01	6975

FIGURE 9-33 A zip code is an example of a significant digit code that uses groups and subgroups to store data. This example is for the zip code 32901-6975, which is the location of the Florida Institute of Technology in Melbourne, FL.

Finally, codes can reduce data input errors in situations when the coded data is easier to remember and enter than the original source data, when only certain valid codes are allowed, and when something within the code itself can provide immediate verification that the entry is correct.

9.9.2 Types of Codes

Companies use many different coding methods. Because information system users must work with coded data, the codes should be easy to learn and apply. If it is planned to create new codes or change existing ones, comments and feedback from users should be obtained. The following section describes seven common coding methods.

1. **Sequence codes** are numbers or letters assigned in a specific order. Sequence codes contain no additional information other than an indication of order of entry into the system. For example, a human resource system issues consecutive employee numbers to identify employees. Because the codes are assigned in the order in which employees are hired, the code can be used to see that employee number 584 was hired after employee number 433. The code, however, does not indicate the starting date of either person's employment.

2. **Block sequence codes** use blocks of numbers for different classifications. College course numbers usually are assigned using a block sequence code. 100-level courses, such as Chemistry 110 and Mathematics 125, are freshman-level courses, whereas course numbers in the 200s indicate sophomore-level courses. Within a particular block, the sequence of numbers can have some additional meaning, such as when English 151 is the prerequisite for English 152.

3. **Alphabetic codes** use alphabet letters to distinguish one item from another based on a category, an abbreviation, or an easy-to-remember value, called a mnemonic code. Many classification codes fit more than one of the following definitions:

   a. **Category codes** identify a group of related items. For example, a local department store uses a two-character category code to identify the department in which a product is sold: GN for gardening supplies, HW for hardware, and EL for electronics.

   b. **Abbreviation codes** are alphabetic abbreviations. For example, standard state codes include NY for New York, ME for Maine, and MN for Minnesota. Some abbreviation codes are called **mnemonic codes** because they use a specific combination of letters that are easy to remember. Many three-character airport codes such as those pictured in Figure 9-34 are mnemonic codes, such as ATL for Atlanta and MIA for Miami. However, some airport codes are not mnemonic, such as ORD (Chicago O'Hare) or MCO (Orlando).

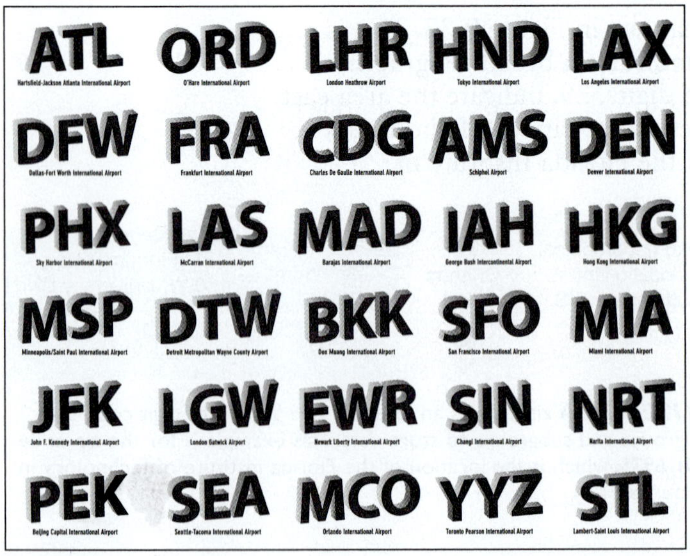

FIGURE 9-34 Abbreviations for some of the world's busiest airports.
BLANKartist/Shutterstock.com

4. **Significant digit codes** distinguish items by using a series of subgroups of digits. Postal codes, for example, are significant digit codes. Other such codes include inventory location codes that consist of a two-digit warehouse code, followed by a one-digit floor number code, a two-digit section code, a one-digit aisle number, and a two-digit bin number code. Figure 9-35 illustrates the inventory location code 11205327. What looks like a large eight-digit number is actually five separate numbers, each of which has significance.

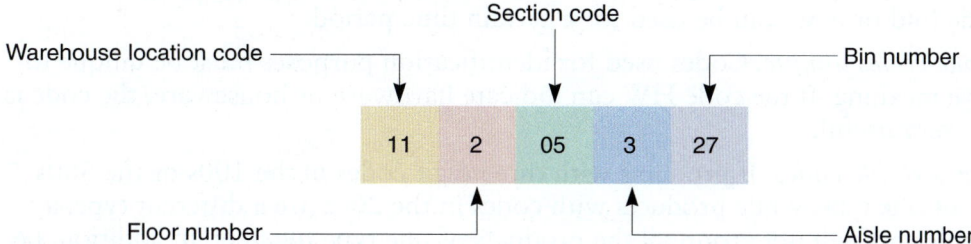

FIGURE 9-35 Sample of a code that uses significant digits to pinpoint the location of an inventory item.

5. **Derivation codes** combine data from different item attributes, or characteristics. Most magazine subscription codes are derivation codes. For example, one popular magazine uses a subscriber's five-digit postal code, followed by the first, third, and fourth letters of the subscriber's last name, the last two digits of the subscriber's house number, and the first, third, and fourth letters of the subscriber's street name. A sample is shown in Figure 9-36.

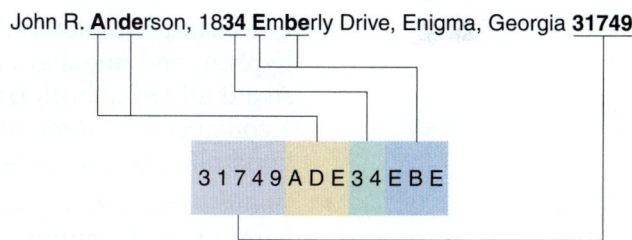

FIGURE 9-36 A magazine subscriber code is derived from various parts of the name and address.

6. **Cipher codes** use a keyword to encode a number. A retail store, for example, might use a 10-letter word, such as CAMPGROUND, to code wholesale prices, where the letter C represents 1, A represents 2, and so on. Thus, the code, GRAND, indicates that the store paid $562.90 for the item.

7. **Action codes** indicate what action is to be taken with an associated item. For example, a student records program might prompt a user to enter or click an action code such as D (to display a record), A (to add a record), and X (to exit the program).

9.9.3 Designing Codes

Here are some code design suggestions:

- *Keep codes concise.* Do not create codes that are longer than necessary. For example, if a code is needed to identify each of 250 customers, a six-digit code is not needed.

- *Allow for expansion.* A coding scheme must allow for reasonable growth in the number of assigned codes. For example, if the company currently has eight warehouses, do not use a one-digit code for the warehouse number. If two more warehouses are added, the code must be increased to two digits or changed to a character code in order to identify each location. The rule also applies to using a single letter as a character code because more than 26 data items might be needed in the future. Of course, more characters can be added, which is just what the airline industry has done. Most airlines now use six-character codes that allow millions of combinations.

- *Keep codes stable.* Changes in codes can cause consistency problems and require data updates. During the changeover period, all the stored occurrences of a particular code and all documents containing the old code will have to change as users switch to the new code. Usually, both the old and new codes are used for an interim period, and special procedures are required to handle the two codes. For example, when telephone area codes change, either area code (old or new) can be used for a certain time period.

- *Make codes unique.* Codes used for identification purposes must be unique to have meaning. If the code HW can indicate hardware or houseware, the code is not very useful.

- *Use sortable codes.* If products with three-digit codes in the 100s or the 300s are of one type, while products with codes in the 200s are a different type, a simple sort will not group all the products of one type together. In addition, be careful that single-digit character codes will sort properly with double-digit codes — in some cases a leading zero must be added (01, 02, 03, and so on) to ensure that codes sort correctly.

- *Use a simple structure.* Do not code some part numbers with two letters, a hyphen, and one digit, and others with one letter, a hyphen, and two digits. Avoid allowing both letters and numbers to occupy the same positions within a code because some of those are easily confused. This situation might be a good place to use an input mask to assure that the correct data type is entered.

- *Avoid confusion.* It is easy to confuse the number zero (0) and the uppercase letter O, or the number one (1) with the lowercase letter L (l) or uppercase letter I. For example, the five-character code 5Z081 easily can be misread as 5ZO8I, or 52081.

- *Make codes meaningful.* Codes should be easy to remember, user-friendly, convenient, and easy to interpret. Using SW as a code for the southwest sales region, for example, has far more meaning than the code 14. Using ENG as the code for the English department is easier to interpret and remember than either XVA or 132.

- *Use a code for a single purpose.* Do not use a code to classify unrelated attributes. For example, if a single code is used to identify the combination of an employee's department *and* the employee's insurance plan type, users will have difficulty identifying all the subscribers of a particular plan, or all the workers in a particular department, or both. A separate code for each separate characteristic makes much more sense.

- *Keep codes consistent.* For example, if the payroll system already is using two-digit codes for departments, do not create a new, different coding scheme for the personnel system. If the two systems already are using different coding schemes, try to establish a consistent coding scheme.

9.10 DATA STORAGE AND ACCESS

Data storage and access involve strategic business tools, such as data warehousing and data mining software, as well as logical and physical storage issues, selection of data storage formats, and special considerations regarding storage of date fields.

9.10.1 Tools and Techniques

Companies use data warehousing and data mining as strategic tools to help manage the huge quantities of data they need for business operations and decisions. A large number of software vendors compete for business in this fast-growing IT sector.

DATA WAREHOUSING: Large firms maintain many databases, which might or might not be linked together into an overall structure. To provide rapid access to this information, companies use software packages that organize and store data in special configurations called data warehouses. A **data warehouse** is an integrated collection of data that can include seemingly unrelated information, no matter where it is stored in the company. Because it can link various information systems and databases, a data warehouse provides an enterprise-wide view to support management analysis and decision making.

A data warehouse allows users to specify certain dimensions, or characteristics. By selecting values for each characteristic, a user can obtain multidimensional information from the stored data. For example, in a typical company, most data is generated by transaction-based systems, such as order processing systems, inventory systems, and payroll systems. If a user wants to identify the customer on sales order 34071, he or she can retrieve the data easily from the order processing system by entering an order number.

On the other hand, suppose that a user wants to see June 2015 sales results for Sally Brown, the sales rep assigned to Jo-Mar Industries. The data is stored in two different systems with different databases: the sales information system and the human resources information system, as shown in Figure 9-37. Without a data warehouse, it would be difficult for a user to extract data that spans several information systems and time frames. Rather than accessing separate systems, a data warehouse stores transaction data in a format that allows users to retrieve and analyze the data easily.

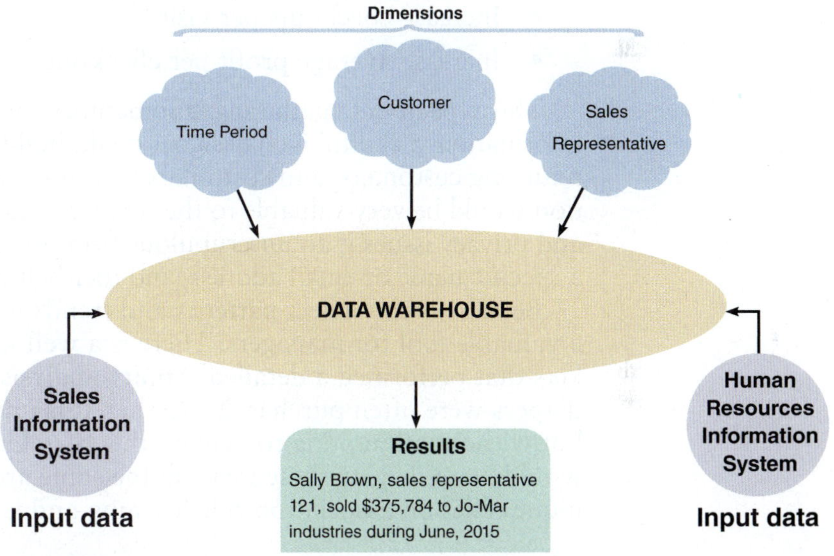

While a data warehouse typically spans the entire enterprise,

FIGURE 9-37 A data warehouse stores data from several systems. By selecting data dimensions, a user can retrieve specific information without having to know how or where the data is stored.

many firms prefer to use a **data mart**, which is designed to serve the needs of a specific department, such as sales, marketing, or finance. Each data mart includes only the data that users in that department require to perform their jobs. There are pros and cons to both approaches, and the best solution usually depends on the specific situation.

Regardless of the overall approach, storing large quantities of data is like building a house — it doesn't just happen. A well-constructed data warehouse needs an architecture that includes detailed planning and specifications.

DATA MINING: **Data mining** software looks for meaningful data patterns and relationships. For example, data mining software could help a consumer products firm identify potential customers based on their prior purchases. Information about customer behavior is valuable, but data mining also raises serious ethical and privacy issues, such as the example in the Question of Ethics feature in this chapter.

The enormous growth in ecommerce has focused attention on data mining as a marketing tool. In an article called "Data Mining on the Web" that appeared in the January 2000 issue of *New Architect*, a web-based magazine, Dan R. Greening noted that web hosts typically possess a lot of information about visitors, but most of it is of little value. His article mentions that smart marketers and business analysts are using data mining techniques, which he describes as "machine learning algorithms that find buried patterns in databases, and report or act on those findings." He concludes by saying that "The great advantage of web marketing is that you can measure visitor interactions more effectively than in brick-and-mortar stores or direct mail. Data mining works best when you have clear, measurable goals." Some of the goals he suggests are:

- Increase the number of pages viewed per session
- Increase the number of referred customers
- Reduce **clicks to close**, which means average page views to accomplish a purchase or obtain desired information
- Increase checkouts per visit
- Increase average profit per checkout

This type of data gathering is sometimes called **clickstream storage**. Armed with this information, a skillful web designer could build a profile of typical new customers, returning customers, and customers who browse but do not buy. Although this information would be very valuable to the retailer, clickstream storage could raise serious legal and privacy issues if an unscrupulous firm sought to link a customer's web behavior to a specific name or email address, and then sell or otherwise misuse the information.

Because it can detect patterns and trends in large amounts of data, data mining is a valuable tool for managers. There is a well-known story about a chain of supermarkets that performed a detailed affinity analysis of purchases, and found that beer and diapers were often purchased together. It is unclear whether or not this story is true, but without attempting to explain this correlation, the obvious tactic for a retailer would be to display these items in the same area of the store. This data mining technique relies on association rule learning and is often called **market basket analysis**.

9.10.2 Logical versus Physical Storage

It is important to understand the difference between logical storage and physical storage. **Logical storage** refers to data that a user can view, understand, and access, regardless of how or where that information actually is organized or stored. In contrast, **physical storage** is strictly hardware-related because it involves the process of reading and writing binary data to physical media, such as a hard drive, CD/DVD, or network-based storage device. For example, portions of a document might be stored in different physical locations on a hard drive, but the user sees the document as a single logical entity on the computer screen.

Logical storage consists of alphabetic and numeric **characters**, such as the letter *A* or the number 9. As described earlier in this chapter, a set of related characters forms a field, which describes a single characteristic, or attribute, of a person, place, thing, or event. A field also is called a data element or a data item.

When designing fields, space should be provided for the largest values that can be anticipated, without allocating unnecessarily large storage capacities that will not be used. For example, suppose a customer order entry system is being designed for a firm with 800 customers. It would be a mistake to limit the customer number field to three, or even four characters. Instead, a five-character field with leading zeros that could store customer numbers from *00001* to *99999* should be considered.

A mix of alphabetic and numeric characters can also be considered, which many people find easier to view and use. Alphabetic characters expand the storage capacity because there are 26 possible values for each character position. Most airlines now use six alphabetic characters as a record locator, which has over 300 million possible values.

A logical record is a set of field values that describes a single person, place, thing, or event. For example, a logical customer record contains specific field values for a single customer, including the customer number, name, address, telephone number, credit limit, and so on. Application programs see a logical record as a group of related fields, regardless of how or where the data is stored physically.

The term *record* usually refers to a logical record. Whenever an application program issues a read or write command, the operating system supplies one logical record to the program or accepts one logical record from the program. The physical data might be stored on one or more servers, in the same building or thousands of miles away, but all the application program sees is the logical record — the physical storage location is irrelevant.

9.10.3 Data Coding

Computers represent data as bits, (short for *binary digits*), that have only two possible values: 1 and 0. A computer understands a group of bits as a digital code that can be transmitted, received, and stored. Computers use various data coding and storage schemes, such as EBCDIC, ASCII, and binary. A more recent coding standard called Unicode is also popular. Also, the storage of dates raises some design issues that must be considered.

EBCDIC, ASCII, AND BINARY: EBCDIC (pronounced EB-see-dik), which stands for Extended Binary Coded Decimal Interchange Code, is a coding method used on mainframe computers and high-capacity servers. ASCII (pronounced ASK-ee), which stands for American Standard Code for Information Interchange, is a coding method used on most personal computers. EBCDIC and ASCII both require eight bits, or one byte, for each character. For example, the name Ann requires three bytes of storage, the number *12,345* requires five bytes of storage, and the number *1,234,567,890* requires ten bytes of storage.

Compared with character-based formats, a binary storage format offers a more efficient storage method because it represents numbers as actual binary values, rather than as coded numeric digits. For example, an integer format uses only 16 bits, or two bytes, to represent the number *12,345* in binary form. A long integer format uses 32 bits, or four bytes, to represent the number *1,234,567,890* in binary form.

UNICODE: Unicode is a more recent coding standard that uses two bytes per character, rather than one. This expanded scheme enables Unicode to represent more than 65,000 unique, multilingual characters. Why is this important? Consider the challenge of running a multinational information system, or developing a program that will be sold in Asia, Europe, and North America. Because it supports virtually all languages, Unicode has become a global standard.

Traditionally, domestic software firms developed a product in English, then translated the program into one or more languages. This process was expensive, slow, and error-prone. In contrast, Unicode creates translatable content right from the start.

Today, most popular operating systems support Unicode, and the Unicode Consortium maintains standards and support, as shown in Figure 9-38.

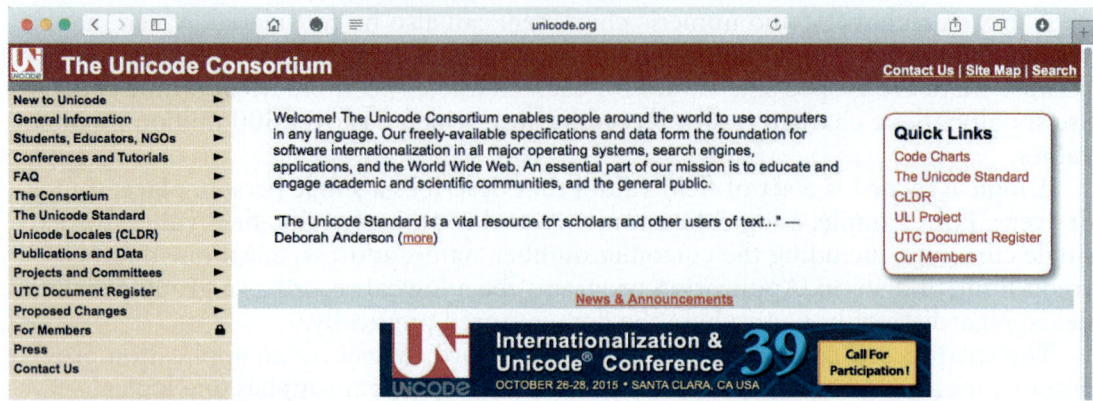

FIGURE 9-38 Unicode is an international coding format that represents characters as integers, using 16 bits (two bytes) per character. The Unicode Consortium maintains standards and support for Unicode.
Source: 1991–2015 Unicode, Inc.

STORING DATES: What is the best way to store dates? The answer depends on how the dates will be displayed and whether they will be used in calculations.

At the beginning of the twenty-first century, many firms that used only two digits to represent the year were faced with a major problem called the **Y2K issue**. Based on that experience, most date formats now are based on the model established by the **International Organization for Standardization (ISO)**, which requires a format of four digits for the year, two for the month, and two for the day (YYYYMMDD). A date stored in that format can be sorted easily and used in comparisons. If a date in ISO form is larger than another date in the same form, then the first date is later. For example, 20150504 (May 4, 2015) is later than 20130927 (September 27, 2013).

But, what if dates must be used in calculations? For example, if a manufacturing order placed on June 23 takes three weeks to complete, when will the order be ready?

If a payment due on August 13 is not paid until April 27 of the following year, exactly how late is the payment and how much interest is owed? In these situations, it is easier to use absolute dates.

An **absolute date** is the total number of days from some specific base date. To calculate the number of days between two absolute dates, one date is subtracted from the other. For example, if the base date is January 1, 1900, then May 4, 2015 has an absolute date of 42128. Similarly, September 27, 2013, has an absolute date value of 41544. If the earlier date value is subtracted from the later one, the result is 584 days. A spreadsheet can be used to determine and display absolute dates easily, as shown in Figure 9-39.

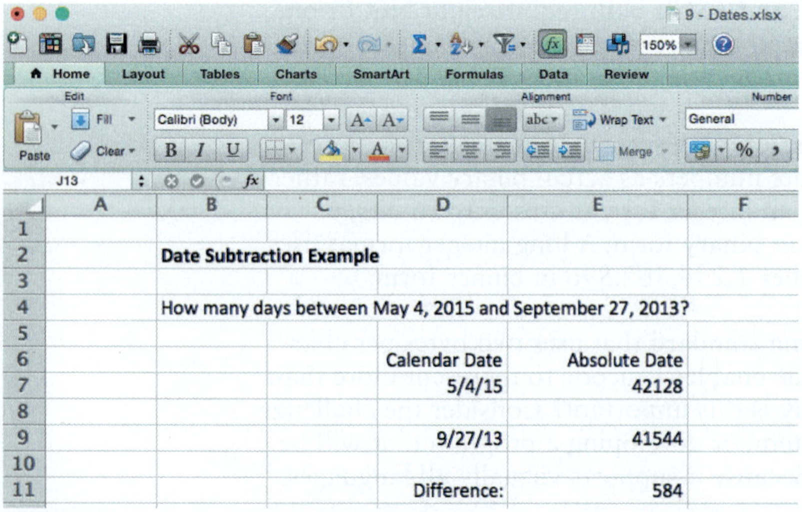

FIGURE 9-39 Microsoft Excel uses absolute dates in calculations. In this example, May 4, 2015, is displayed as 42128, and September 27, 2013, is displayed as 41544. The difference between the dates is 584 days.

9.11 DATA CONTROL

Just as it is important to secure the physical part of the system, as shown in Figure 9-40, file and database control must include all measures necessary to ensure that data storage is correct, complete, and secure. File and database control is also related to input and output techniques discussed earlier.

FIGURE 9-40 In addition to network monitoring, system security includes access codes, data encryption, passwords, and audit trails.

iStockphoto/DenGuy

A well-designed DBMS must provide built-in control and security features, including subschemas, passwords, encryption, audit trail files, and backup and recovery procedures to maintain data. The analyst's main responsibility is to ensure that the DBMS features are used properly.

Earlier in this chapter, it was explained that a subschema can be used to provide a limited view of the database to a specific user, or level of users. Limiting access to files and databases is the most common way of protecting stored data. Users must furnish a proper user ID and password to access a file or database. Different privileges, also called **permissions**, can be associated with different users, so some employees can be limited to read-only access, while other users might be allowed to update or delete data. For highly sensitive data, additional access codes can be established that restrict specific records or fields within records. Stored data can also be encrypted to prevent unauthorized access. Encryption is the process of converting readable data into unreadable characters to prevent unauthorized access to the data.

All system files and databases must be backed up regularly and a series of **backup** copies must be retained for a specified period of time. In the event of a file catastrophe, **recovery procedures** can be used to restore the file or database to its current state at the time of the last backup. **Audit log files**, which record details of all accesses and changes to the file or database, can be used to recover changes made since the last backup. **Audit fields**, which are special fields within data records to provide additional control or security information, can also be included. Typical audit fields include the date the record was created or modified, the name of the user who performed the action, and the number of times the record has been accessed.

CASE IN POINT 9.4:   SOCCERMOM

SoccerMom Company sells a patented seat that spectators can take to youth soccer games. The seat folds so it is small enough to fit in the glove box of most vehicles. The company operates a factory in Kansas and also contracts its manufacturing projects to small firms in Canada and Mexico.

An unusual problem has occurred for this small multinational company: People are getting confused about dates in internal memos, purchase orders, and email. Towson Hopkins handles all IT functions for SoccerMom. When he designed the company's database, he was not aware that the format for dates in Canada and Mexico was different from the format used in the United States. For example, in Canada and Mexico, the notation 7/1/15 indicates January 7, 2015, whereas in the United States the same notation indicates July 1, 2015. Although it seems like a small point, the date confusion has resulted in several order cancellations.

Towson has asked for your advice. You could suggest writing a simple program to convert the dates automatically or designing a switchboard command that would allow users to select a date format as data is entered. You realize, however, that SoccerMom might want to do business in other countries in the future. What would be the best course of action? Should SoccerMom adapt to the standard of each country, or should it maintain a single international format? What are the arguments for each option?

A QUESTION OF ETHICS

iStockphoto.com/faberfoto_it

Olivia is the database manager at Tip Top Toys, a relatively small division of Worldwide Enterprises. Worldwide has nine other divisions, which include insurance, healthcare products, and financial planning services, to name a few.

Riccardo, corporate marketing director for Worldwide, has requested Tip Top's customer shopping data to target people who might be likely to purchase items or services from other Worldwide divisions. Olivia is not totally comfortable with this, and pointed out Tip Top's web privacy policy, which states "Tip Top Toys, a division of Worldwide Enterprises, will not share personal data with other companies without a customer's consent."

Riccardo replied that the statement only applies to outside companies — not other Worldwide divisions. He said he checked with the corporate legal department, and they agreed. Emily responded, "Even if it is legally OK, it's not the *right* thing to do. Many people take our statement to mean that their data does not leave Tip Top. At the very least, we should give customers a choice, and share the data only with their consent."

Do you agree with Olivia? Why or why not?

9.12 CHAPTER SUMMARY

This chapter continued the study of the systems design phase of the SDLC. It was explained that files and tables contain data about people, places, things, or events that affect the information system. File-oriented systems, also called file processing systems, manage data stored in separate.

A database consists of linked tables that form an overall data structure. A database management system (DBMS) is a collection of tools, features, and interfaces that enable users to add, update, manage, access, and analyze data in a database.

DBMS designs are more powerful and flexible than traditional file-oriented systems. A database environment offers scalability, support for organization-wide access, economy of scale, data sharing among user groups, balancing of conflicting user requirements, enforcement of standards, controlled redundancy, effective security, flexibility, better programmer productivity, and data independence. Large-scale databases are complex and require extensive security and backup/recovery features.

DBMS components include interfaces for users, database administrators, and related systems; a data manipulation language; a schema; and a physical data repository. Other data management techniques include data warehousing, which stores data in an easily accessible form for user access, and data mining, which looks for meaningful patterns and relationships among data. Data mining also includes clickstream storage, which records how users interact with a site, and market basket analysis, which can identify product relationships and consumer buying patterns.

In an information system, an entity is a person, place, thing, or event for which data is collected and maintained. A field, or attribute, is a single characteristic of an entity. A record, or tuple, is a set of related fields that describes one instance of an entity. Data is stored in files (in a file-oriented system) and tables (in a database environment).

A primary key is the field or field combination that uniquely and minimally identifies a specific record; a candidate key is any field that could serve as a primary key. A foreign key is a field or field combination that must match the primary key of another file or table. A secondary key is a field or field combination used as the basis for sorting or retrieving records.

An entity-relationship diagram (ERD) is a graphic representation of all system entities and the relationships among them. The ERD is based on entities and data stores in DFDs prepared during the systems analysis phase. The three basic relationships represented in an ERD are one-to-one (1:1), one-to-many (1:M), and many-to-many (M:N). In an M:N relationship, the two entities are linked by an associative entity.

The relationship between two entities is also referred to as cardinality. A common form of cardinality notation is called crow's foot notation, which uses various symbols to describe the characteristics of the relationship.

Normalization is a process for avoiding problems in data design. A first normal form (1NF) record has no repeating groups. A record is in second normal form (2NF) if it is in 1NF and all nonkey fields depend on the entire primary key. A record is in third normal form (3NF) if it is in 2NF and if no field depends on a nonkey field.

Data design tasks include creating an initial ERD; assigning data elements to an entity; normalizing all table designs; and completing the data dictionary entries for files, records, and data elements.

A code is a set of letters or numbers used to represent data in a system. Using codes can speed up data entry, reduce data storage space, and reduce transmission time. Codes can also be used to reveal or to conceal information. The main types of codes are sequence codes, block sequence codes, classification codes, alphabetic codes (including category codes, abbreviation codes, and mnemonic codes), significant digit codes, derivation codes, cipher codes, and action codes.

Logical storage is information seen through a user's eyes, regardless of how or where that information actually is organized or stored. Physical storage is hardware-related and involves reading and writing binary data to physical media. A logical record is a related set of field values that describes a single person, place, thing, or event. Data storage formats include EBCDIC, ASCII, binary, and Unicode. Dates can be stored in several formats, including ISO and absolute format.

File and database control measures include limiting access to the data, data encryption, backup/recovery procedures, audit-trail files, and internal audit fields.

Key Terms

1:1 A type of entity relationship. A one-to-one relationship, abbreviated 1:1, exists when exactly one of the second entity occurs for each instance of the first entity.

1:M A type of entity relationship. A one-to-many relationship, abbreviated 1:M, exists when one occurrence of the first entity can be related to many occurrences of the second entity, but each occurrence of the second entity can be associated with only one occurrence of the first entity.

abbreviation code Alphabetic abbreviation. For example, standard state codes include NY for New York, ME for Maine, and MN for Minnesota.

absolute date The total number of days from some specific base date. To calculate the number of days between two absolute dates, subtract one date from the other. For example, using a base date of January 1, 1900, September 27, 2012, has an absolute date value of 41179 and July 13, 2011, has an absolute date of 40737. If the earlier date value is subtracted from the later one, the result is 442 days.

action code Indicates what action is to be taken with an associated item. For example, a student records program might prompt a user to enter or click an action code such as D (to display the student's record), A (to add a record), and X (to exit the program).

alphabetic code Uses alphabet letters to distinguish one item from another based on a category, an abbreviation, or an easy-to-remember value, called a mnemonic code.

ASCII Stands for American Standard Code for Information Interchange, a data storage coding method used on most personal computers and workstations.

associative entity An entity that has its own set of attributes and characteristics. Associative entities are used to link between many-to-many (M:N) relationships.

audit fields Special fields within data records to provide additional control or security information. Typical audit fields include the date the record was created or modified, the name of the user who performed the action, and the number of times the record has been accessed.

audit log files Record details of all accesses and changes to a file or database and can be used to recover changes made since the last backup.

backup The process of saving a series of file or data copies to be retained for a specified period of time. Data can be backed up continuously, or at prescribed intervals.

binary storage format A format that offers efficient storage of numeric data. For example, when numeric data types are specified using Microsoft Access, there are a variety of storage formats choices, including integer and long integer, among others.

bit The smallest unit of data is one binary digit.

block sequence code Cipher that uses blocks of numbers for different classifications.

byte A group of eight bits is called a byte, or a character. A set of bytes forms a field, which is an individual fact about a person, place, thing, or event.

candidate key Sometimes it is possible to have a choice of fields or field combinations to use as the primary key. Any field that could serve as a primary key is called a candidate key.

cardinality notation Code that shows relationships between entities.

category code Cipher that identifies a group of related items. For example, a local department store may use a two-character category code to identify the department in which a product is sold.

character A group of eight bits is called a character, or a byte. A set of bytes forms a field, which is an individual fact about a person, place, thing, or event.

cipher code Use of a keyword to encode a number. A retail store, for example, may use a 10-letter word, such as CAMPGROUND, to code wholesale prices, where the letter C represents 1, A represents 2, and so on. Thus, the code, GRAND, would indicate that the store paid $562.90 for the item.

clicks to close The average number of page views to accomplish a purchase or obtain desired information.

clickstream storage Recording web visitor behavior and traffic trends for later data mining use.

code A set of letters or numbers that represents a data item. Codes can be used to simplify output, input, and data formats.

combination key A type of data validation check that is performed on two or more fields to ensure that they are consistent or reasonable when considered together. Even though all the fields involved in a combination check might pass their individual validation checks, the combination of the field values might be inconsistent or unreasonable.

common field An attribute that appears in more than one entity. Common fields can be used to link entities in various types of relationships.

composite key Sometimes it is necessary for a primary key to consist of a combination of fields. In that case, the primary key is called a combination key, composite key, concatenated key, or multi-valued key.

concatenated key *See* **composite key.**

crow's foot notation A type of cardinality notation. It is called crow's foot notation because of the shapes, which include circles, bars, and symbols, that indicate various possibilities. A single bar indicates one, a double bar indicates one and only one, a circle indicates zero, and a crow's foot indicates many.

data manipulation language (DML) A data manipulation language controls database operations, including storing, retrieving, updating, and deleting data. Most commercial DBMSs, such as Oracle and IBM's DB2, use a DML.

data mart A specialized database designed to serve the needs of a specific department, such as sales, marketing, or finance. Each data mart includes only the data that users in that department require to perform their jobs.

data mining Looking for meaningful patterns and relationships among data. For example, data mining software could help a consumer products firm identify potential customers based on their prior purchases.

data warehouse An integrated collection of data that can support management analysis and decision making.

database administrator (DBA) Someone who manages a database management system (DBMS). The DBA assesses overall requirements and maintains the database for the benefit of the entire organization rather than a single department or user.

database management system (DBMS) A collection of tools, features, and interfaces that enables users to add, update, manage, access, and analyze data in a database.

derivation code Combining data from different item attributes, or characteristics, to build the code. Most magazine subscription codes are derivation codes.

EBCDIC Stands for Extended Binary Coded Decimal Interchange Code, a coding method used on mainframe computers and some high-capacity servers.

economy of scale The inherent efficiency of high-volume processing on larger computers. Database design allows better utilization of hardware. If a company maintains an enterprise-wide database, processing is less expensive using a powerful mainframe server instead of using several smaller computers.

entity-relationship diagram (ERD) A graphical model of the information system that depicts the relationships among system entities.

file Each file or table contains data about people, places, things, or events that interact with the information system.

file-oriented system A file-oriented system, also called a file processing system, stores and manages data in one or more separate files.

first normal form (1NF) A record is said to be in first normal form (1NF) if it does not contain a repeating group (a set of data items that can occur any number of times in a single record).

foreign key A field in one table that must match a primary key value in another table in order to establish the relationship between the two tables.

functionally dependent Functional dependence is an important concept for understanding the second normal form (2NF). The field X is said to be functionally dependent on the field Y if the value of X depends on the value of Y. For example, an order date is dependent on an order number; for a particular order number, there is only one value for the order date. In contrast, the product description is not dependent on the order number. For a particular order number, there might be several product descriptions, one for each item ordered.

International Organization for Standardization (ISO) A network of national standards institutes from 140 countries working in partnership with international organizations, governments, industry, business, and consumer representatives. The ISO acts as a bridge between public and private sectors.

JDBC (Java database connectivity) A standard that enables Java applications to exchange data with any database that uses SQL statements and is ODBC-compliant.

key fields Used during the systems design phase to organize, access, and maintain data structures. The four types of key fields are primary keys, candidate keys, foreign keys, and secondary keys.

logical record A logical record contains field values that describe a single person, place, thing, or event. Application programs *see* a logical record as a set of fields, regardless of how or where the data is stored physically.

logical storage Refers to information as seen through a user's eyes, regardless of how or where that information is organized or stored.

M:N A type of entity relationship. A many-to-many relationship, abbreviated M:N, exists when one instance of the first entity can be related to many instances of the second entity, and one instance of the second entity can be related to many instances of the first entity.

many-to-many relationship *See* **M:N.**

market basket analysis A type of analysis that can detect patterns and trends in large amounts of data.

mnemonic code Ciphers using a specific combination of letters that are easy to remember. Many three-character airport codes are mnemonic codes. For example, LAX represents Los Angeles.

multivalued key Sometimes it is necessary for a primary key to consist of a combination of fields. In that case, the primary key is called a combination key, composite key, concatenated key, or multivalued key.

nonkey field Any field that is not a primary key or a candidate key is called a nonkey field.

normalization A process by which analysts identify and correct inherent problems and complexities in their record designs.

ODBC (open database connectivity) An industry-standard protocol that makes it possible for software from different vendors to interact and exchange data.

one-to-many relationship *See* **1:M.**

one-to-one relationship *See* **1:1.**

orphan An unassociated or unrelated record or field. An orphan could be created if a customer order was entered in an order table where that customer did not already exist in the customer table. Referential integrity would prevent the creation of this orphan.

permissions User-specific privileges that determine the type of access a user has to a database, file, or directory. Also called user rights.

physical storage Information storage mechanism that is strictly hardware-related, because it involves the process of reading and writing binary data to physical media, such as a hard drive, flash drive, or DVD.

primary key A field or combination of fields that uniquely and minimally identifies a particular member of an entity. For example, in a customer table the customer number is a unique primary key because no two customers can have the same customer number. That key is also minimal because it contains no information beyond what is needed to identify the customer.

query by example (QBE) A language allows the user to provide an example of the data requested.

query language Allows a user to specify a task without specifying how the task will be accomplished. Some query languages use natural language commands that resemble ordinary English sentences

recovery procedure Process for restoring data and restarting a system after an interruption. Recovery procedures can be used to restore a file or database to its current state at the time of the last backup.

referential integrity A type of validity check. Referential integrity is a set of rules that avoids data inconsistency and quality problems.

relational database A database in which tables are related by common fields, creating a unified data structure that provides improved data quality and access.

relational model A model used in relational databases. The relational model was introduced during the 1970s and became popular because it was flexible and powerful.

repeating group A set of one or more fields that can occur any number of times in a single record, with each occurrence having different values.

schema The complete definition of a database, including descriptions of all fields, records, and relationships.

second normal form (2NF) A record design is in second normal form (2NF) if it is in 1NF and if all fields that are not part of the primary key are dependent on the entire primary key. If any field in a 1NF record depends on only one of the fields in a combination primary key, then the record is not in 2NF. A 1NF record with a primary key that is a single field is automatically in 2NF.

secondary key A field or combination of fields that can be used to access or retrieve records. Secondary key values are not unique. For example, to access records for only those customers in a specific postal code, the postal code field could be used as a secondary key.

sequence code Numbers or letters assigned in a specific order. Sequence codes contain no additional information other than an indication of order of entry into a system.

significant digit code Cipher that distinguishes items by using a series of subgroups of digits. U.S. Postal Service zip codes, for example, are significant digit codes.

SQL (Structured Query Language) A query language that allows PC users to communicate with servers and mainframe computers.

standard notation format A representation that makes designing tables easier as it clearly shows a table's structure, fields, and primary key.

subschema A view of the database used by one or more systems or users. A subschema defines only those portions of the database that a particular system or user needs or is allowed to access.

table Each file or table contains data about people, places, things, or events that interact with the information system.

table design Specifies the fields and identifies the primary key in a particular table or file.

third normal form (3NF) A record design is in third normal form (3NF) if it is in 2NF and if no nonkey field is dependent on another nonkey field. A nonkey field is a field that is not a candidate key for the primary key.

tuple A tuple (rhymes with couple), or record, is a set of related fields that describes one instance, or member of an entity, such as one customer, one order, or one product. A tuple might have one or dozens of fields, depending on what information is needed.

Unicode A relatively recent coding method that represents characters as integers. Unlike EBCDIC and ASCII, which use eight bits for each character, Unicode requires 16 bits per character, which allows it to represent more than 65,000 unique characters.

unnormalized A record that contains a repeating group, which means that a single record has multiple occurrences of a particular field, with each occurrence having different values.

Y2K issue A problem faced by many firms in the year 2000 because their computer systems used only two digits to represent the year; most dates now use a four-digit format for the year (YYYYMMDD).

Chapter Exercises

Questions

1. In the auto shop examples in Section 9.2.2, what are some problems that might arise in Mario's system? Why won't Danica run into the same problems? Provide specific examples in your answer.
2. What is a DBMS? Briefly describe the components of a DBMS.
3. Describe a primary key, candidate key, secondary key, foreign key, and a combination key. Use your imagination to provide an example of each key that is *not* in the textbook.
4. What are entity-relationship diagrams and how are they used? What symbol is used for a relationship? What is an associative entity? Provide an example.
5. What is cardinality, and what symbols do you use in the crow's foot notation method?
6. What are data warehousing and data mining? How do businesses use these tools?
7. What is an unnormalized design, and how do you convert an unnormalized design to 1NF? In your answer, refer to specific pages and figures in this chapter.
8. How would you define second normal form? How do you convert a 1NF design to 2NF? In your answer, refer to specific pages and figures in this chapter.
9. How would you define third normal form? How do you convert a 2NF design to 3NF? In your answer, refer to specific pages and figures in this chapter.
10. How would a specific date, such as April 27, 2015, be represented as an absolute date?

Discussion Topics

1. Are there ethical issues to consider when planning a database? For example, should sensitive personal data (such as medical information) be stored in the same DBMS that manages employee salary and benefits data? Why or why not?
2. Suggest three typical business situations where referential integrity avoids data problems.
3. Consider an automobile dealership with three locations. Data fields exist for stock number, vehicle identification number, make, model, year, color, and invoice cost. Identify the possible candidate keys, the likely primary key, a probable foreign key, and potential secondary keys.
4. We use lots of codes in our personal and business lives. How many can your class name?
5. Many large organizations have had their database system hacked and customer data stolen. How should the security for the database be different than security for the rest of the system? Does it make a difference for web-based data designs? If so, how?

Projects

1. Search the Internet to find information about date formats. Determine whether the date format used in the United States is the most common format.
2. Visit the IT department at your school or at a local business and determine how the organization uses database management systems. Describe your findings in a memo.

3. Use Microsoft Access or similar database software to create a DBMS for the imaginary company called TopText Publishing, which is described in Case in Point 9.1. Add several sample records to each table and report to the class on your progress.

4. Suppose you work in IT, and the sales team needs answers to three specific questions. The data might be stored physically in seven tables. You know how to create Microsoft Access queries, but to learn more about database logic and design, you decide to study Figure 9-32, and then pretend to tell the database how to find the answers, step by step:

   a. Did any customers receive service after 5/4/2015? If so who were they?

   b. Did technician Marie Johnson put in more than six hours of labor on any service calls? If so, which ones?

   c. Were any parts used on service calls in Washington? If so, what were the part numbers, descriptions, and quantities?

5. Visit the bookstore at your school or in your area. Interview the manager or store employees to learn more about the business and the entities that are involved in bookstore operations. Remember that an entity is a person, place, thing, or event that affects an information system. Draw an ERD, including cardinality, which describes the bookstore's operations.

CHAPTER 10

System Architecture

Chapter 10 is the final chapter in the systems design phase of the SDLC. This chapter describes system architecture, which translates the logical design of an information system into a physical blueprint. Designing the system architecture requires consideration of servers, clients, processing methods, networks, and related issues.

The chapter includes four "Case in Point" discussion questions to help contextualize the concepts described in the text. The "Question of Ethics" explores the trade-offs between the potential benefits of installing tracking software on users' computers to improve the system's response to common usage patterns versus the ethical issues related to invasion of privacy by constant monitoring of employees' online activity.

LEARNING OBJECTIVES

When you finish this chapter, you should be able to:

- Provide a checklist of issues to consider when selecting a system architecture
- Trace the evolution of system architecture from mainframes to current designs
- Explain client/server architecture, including tiers, cost-benefit issues, and performance
- Compare in-house ecommerce development with packaged solutions and service providers
- Discuss the impact of cloud computing and Web 2.0
- Define network topology, including hierarchical, bus, ring, star, and mesh models
- Describe wireless networking, including wireless standards, topologies, and trends
- Describe the system design specification

CHAPTER CONTENTS

10.1 INTRODUCTION

At this point in the SDLC, the objective is to determine an overall architecture to implement the information system. Chapter 1 explained that an information system requires hardware, software, data, procedures, and people to accomplish a specific set of functions. An effective system combines those elements into an architecture, or design, that is flexible, cost-effective, technically sound, and able to support the information needs of the business. This chapter covers a wide range of topics that support the overall system design, just as a plan for a new home would include a foundation plan, building methods, wiring and plumbing diagrams, traffic flows, and costs.

System architecture translates the logical design of an information system into a physical structure that includes hardware, software, network support, processing methods, and security. The end product of the systems design phase is the system design specification. If this document is approved, the next step is systems implementation.

10.2 ARCHITECTURE CHECKLIST

Just as an architect begins a project with a list of the owner's requirements, a systems analyst must approach system architecture with an overall checklist. Before making a decision, the analyst must consider several issues that will affect the architecture choice:

- Corporate organization and culture
- Enterprise resource planning (ERP)
- Initial and total cost of ownership (TCO)
- Scalability
- Web integration
- Legacy system interface requirements
- Processing options
- Security issues
- Corporate portals

10.2.1 Corporate Organization and Culture

To be successful, an information system must perform well in a company's organization and culture. For example, consider two large bicycle brands, Green Bikes and Blue Bikes. Each firm has three operating divisions: an Asian subsidiary that manufactures the bicycles, a factory in Los Angeles that produces bike accessories and clothing, and a plant in Canada that makes bike carriers, racks, and custom trailers.

On the surface, the two firms are similar, but they have very different organizations and corporate cultures. Green Bikes is highly centralized and oversees day-to-day operations from its Los Angeles office. Blue Bikes also has a Los Angeles executive office but allows its three business units to operate separately, with minimal corporate oversight. Both firms are successful, and it is unlikely that their managerial styles will change anytime soon.

Suppose both firms asked a consultant to suggest an IT architecture that would boost productivity and reduce costs. How might corporate organization and culture issues affect the consultant's recommendation? There is no easy answer to that question. The best approach probably would be to study day-to-day business functions, talk to users at all levels, and focus on operational feasibility issues, just as was done earlier in the development process.

10.2.2 Enterprise Resource Planning (ERP)

Many companies use enterprise resource planning (ERP) software, which was described in Chapter 1. The objective of ERP is to establish a company-wide strategy for using IT that includes a specific architecture, standards for data, processing, network, and user interface design. A main advantage of ERP is that it describes a specific hardware and software environment, also called a platform, which ensures connectivity and easy integration of future systems, including in-house software and commercial packages.

Many companies are extending internal ERP systems to their suppliers and customers, using a concept called supply chain management (SCM). For example, in a totally integrated supply chain system, a customer order could cause a manufacturing system to schedule a work order, which in turn triggers a call for more parts from one or more suppliers. In a dynamic, highly competitive economy, SCM can help companies achieve faster response, better customer service, and lower operating costs.

Oracle is an example of a company offering ERP solutions. As shown in Figure 10-1, Oracle's ERP products are cloud-based services that support employee collaboration, provide access to information from mobile devices, and deliver data analytics capabilities to gain insight into business processes.

FIGURE 10-1 Oracle offers ERP solutions as a cloud-based service.
Source: Oracle

CASE IN POINT 10.1:   ABC SYSTEMS

You are a systems analyst at ABC Systems, a fast-growing IT consulting firm that provides a wide range of services to companies that want to establish ecommerce operations. During the last 18 months, ABC acquired two smaller firms and set up a new division that specializes in supply chain management. Aligning ABC's internal systems was quite a challenge, and top management was not especially happy with the integration cost or the timetable. To avoid future problems, you have decided to suggest an ERP strategy, and you plan to present your views at the staff meeting tomorrow. ABC's management team is very informal and prefers a loose, flexible style of management. How will you persuade them that ERP is the way to go?

10.2.3 Initial Cost and TCO

The importance of considering economic feasibility and TCO during systems planning and analysis was discussed earlier. TCO includes tangible purchases, fees, and contracts called *hard* costs. However, additional *soft* costs of management, support, training, and downtime are just as important but more difficult to measure.

A TCO analysis should include the following questions.

- If in-house development was selected as the best alternative initially, is it still the best choice? Is the necessary technical expertise available, and does the original cost estimate appear realistic?

- If a specific package was chosen initially, is it still the best choice? Are newer versions or competitive products available? Have any changes occurred in pricing or support?

- Have any new types of outsourcing become available?

- Have any economic, governmental, or regulatory events occurred that could affect the proposed project?

- Have any significant technical developments occurred that could affect the proposed project?

- Have any major assumptions changed since the company made the build versus buy decision?

- Are there any merger or acquisition issues to consider, whereby the company might require compatibility with a specific environment?

- Have any new trends occurred in the marketplace? Are new products or technologies on the verge of being introduced?

- Have the original TCO estimates been updated? If so, are there any significant differences?

The answers to these questions might affect the initial cost and TCO for the proposed system. The system requirements and alternatives should be reviewed now, before proceeding to design the system architecture.

10.2.4 Scalability

A network is composed of individual nodes. A node represents a physical device, wired or wireless, that can send, receive, or manage network data. For example, nodes can be servers, computers, shared printers, mass storage devices, wireless access points, or tablets.

As described in Chapter 4, scalability, sometimes also called extensibility, refers to a system's ability to expand, change, or downsize easily to meet the changing needs of a business enterprise. Scalability is especially important in implementing systems that are volume-related, such as transaction processing systems. A scalable system is necessary to support a dynamic, growing business. For example, a scalable network could handle anywhere from a few dozen nodes to thousands of nodes, and a scalable DBMS could support the acquisition of an entire new sales division. When investing large amounts of money in a project, management is especially concerned about scalability issues that could affect the system's life expectancy.

10.2.5 Web Integration

An information system includes applications, which are programs that handle the input, manage the processing logic, and provide the required output. The systems analyst must know if a new application will be part of an ecommerce strategy and the degree of integration with other web-based components. As mentioned earlier, a **web-centric** architecture follows Internet design protocols and enables a company to integrate the new application into its ecommerce strategy. Even where ecommerce is not involved, a web-centric application can run on the Internet or a company intranet or extranet. A web-based application avoids many of the connectivity and compatibility problems that typically arise when different hardware environments are involved. In a web-based environment, a firm's external business partners can use standard web browsers to import and export data.

10.2.6 Legacy Systems

A new system might have to interface with one or more legacy systems, which are older systems that use outdated technology but still are functional. For example, a new marketing information system might need to report sales data to a server-based accounting system and obtain product cost data from a legacy manufacturing system.

Interfacing a new system with a legacy system involves analysis of data formats and compatibility. In some cases, a company will need to convert legacy file data, which can be an expensive and time-consuming process. Middleware, which is discussed later in this chapter, might be needed to pass data between new systems and legacy systems. Finally, to select the best architecture, the analyst must know if the new application eventually will replace the legacy system or will co-exist with it.

10.2.7 Processing Options

In planning the architecture, designers must also consider how the system will process data — online or in batches. For example, a high-capacity transaction processing system, such as an order entry system, requires more network, processing, and data storage resources than a monthly billing system that handles data in batches. Also, if the system must operate online, 24 hours a day and seven days a week (24/7), provision must be made for backup and speedy recovery in the event of system failure.

The characteristics of online and batch processing methods are described later in this chapter, with examples of each type.

10.2.8 Security Issues

From the simple password protection shown in Figure 10-2 to complex intrusion detection systems, security threats and defenses are a major concern to a systems analyst. As the physical design is translated into specific hardware and software, the analyst must consider security issues and determine how the company will address them. Security is especially important when data or processing is performed at remote locations, rather than at a centralized facility. In mission-critical systems, security issues will have a major impact on system architecture and design.

Web-based systems introduce additional security concerns, as critical data must be protected in the Internet environment. Also, firms that use ecommerce applications must assure customers that their personal data is safe and secure. The lamentable number of high-profile security breaches in large corporations in recent years suggests that security issues should play an even larger role in system architecture considerations. System security concepts and strategies are discussed in detail in Chapter 12.

FIGURE 10-2 User IDs and passwords are traditional elements of system security.
JMiks/Shutterstock.com

10.2.9 Corporate Portals

Depending on the system, the planned architecture might include a corporate portal. A **portal** is an entrance to a multifunction website. After entering a portal, a user can navigate to a destination using various tools and features provided by the portal designer. A **corporate portal** can provide access for customers, employees, suppliers, and the public. A well-designed portal can integrate with various other systems and provide a consistent look and feel across multiple organizational divisions.

10.3 System Architecture: Then and Now

Every business information system must carry out three main functions:

- Manage applications that perform the processing logic
- Handle data storage and access
- Provide an interface that allows users to interact with the system

Depending on the architecture, the three functions are performed on a server, on a client, or are divided between the server and the client. During system design, the analyst must determine where the functions will be carried out and ascertain the advantages and disadvantages of each design approach.

10.3.1 Mainframe Architecture

A **server** is a computer that supplies data, processing services, or other support to one or more computers, called **clients**. The earliest servers were mainframe computers, and a system design where the server performs *all* the processing sometimes is described as **mainframe architecture**. Although the actual server does not have to be a mainframe, the term *mainframe architecture* typically describes a multiuser environment, where the server is significantly more powerful than the clients. A systems analyst should know the history of mainframe architecture to understand the server's role in modern system design.

In the 1960s, mainframe architecture was the *only* choice. In addition to centralized data processing, the earliest systems performed all data input and output at a central location, often called a **data processing center**. Physical data was delivered or transmitted in some manner to the data processing center, where it was entered into the system. Users in the organization had no input or output capability, except for printed reports that were distributed by a corporate IT department.

As network technology advanced, companies installed terminals at remote locations, so that users could enter and access data from anywhere in the organization, regardless of where the centralized computer was located. A terminal included a keyboard and display screen to handle input and output but lacked independent processing capability. In a centralized design, as shown in Figure 10-3, the remote user's keystrokes are transmitted from his or her terminal to the mainframe, which responds by sending screen output back to the user's screen.

Today, mainframe architecture still is used in industries that require large amounts of processing that can be done at a central location. For example, a bank might use mainframe servers to update customer balances each night. In a blend of old and new technology, many organizations are moving some of their data processing off their mainframes and into the cloud, as discussed in Section 10.5.1. Indeed, a mainframe can be used to implement part of a cloud computing infrastructure.

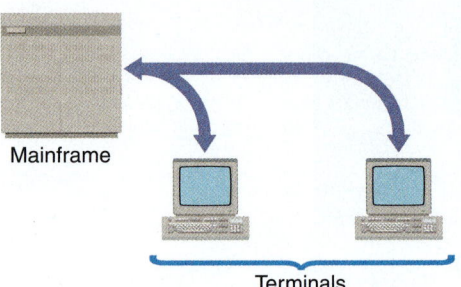

FIGURE 10-3 In a centralized design, the remote user's keystrokes are transmitted to the mainframe, which responds by sending screen output back to the user's screen.

10.3.2 Impact of the Personal Computer

When PC technology exploded in the 1990s, powerful microcomputers quickly appeared on corporate desktops. Users found that they could run their own word processing, spreadsheet, and database applications, without assistance from the IT group, in a mode called **stand-alone** computing. Before long, companies linked the stand-alone computers into networks that enabled the user clients to exchange data and perform local processing.

When an individual user works in stand-alone mode, the workstation performs all the functions of a server by storing, accessing, and processing data, as well as providing a user interface. Although stand-alone PCs improved employee productivity and allowed users to perform tasks that previously required IT department assistance, stand-alone computing could be inefficient and expensive. Even worse, maintaining data on individual workstations raised major concerns about data security, integrity, and consistency. Without a central storage location, it was impossible to protect and back up valuable business data, and companies were exposed to enormous risks. In some cases, users who were frustrated by a lack of support and services from the IT department created and managed their own databases. In addition to security concerns, this led to data inconsistency and unreliability.

10.3.3 Network Evolution

As technology became available, companies resolved the problems of stand-alone computing by joining clients into a **local area network (LAN)** that allows sharing of data and hardware resources, as shown in Figure 10-4. One or more LANs, in turn, can connect to a centralized server. Further advances in technology made it possible to create powerful networks that could use satellite links, high-speed fiber-optic lines, or the Internet to share data.

A **wide area network (WAN)** spans long distances and can connect LANs that are continents apart, as shown in Figure 10-5. When a user accesses data on a LAN or WAN, the network is **transparent** because users see the data as if it were stored on their own workstation. Company-wide systems that connect one or more LANs or WANs are called **distributed systems**. The capabilities of a distributed system depend on the power and capacity of the underlying data communication network. Compared to mainframe architecture, distributed systems increase concerns about data security and integrity because many individual clients require access to perform processing.

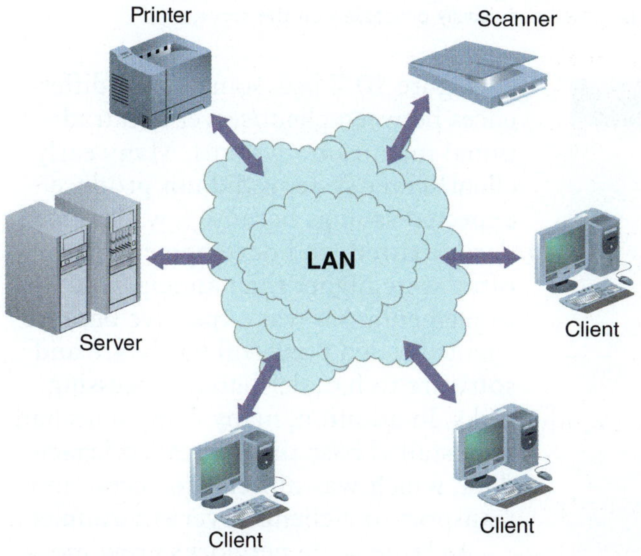

FIGURE 10-4 A LAN allows sharing of data and hardware, such as printers and scanners.

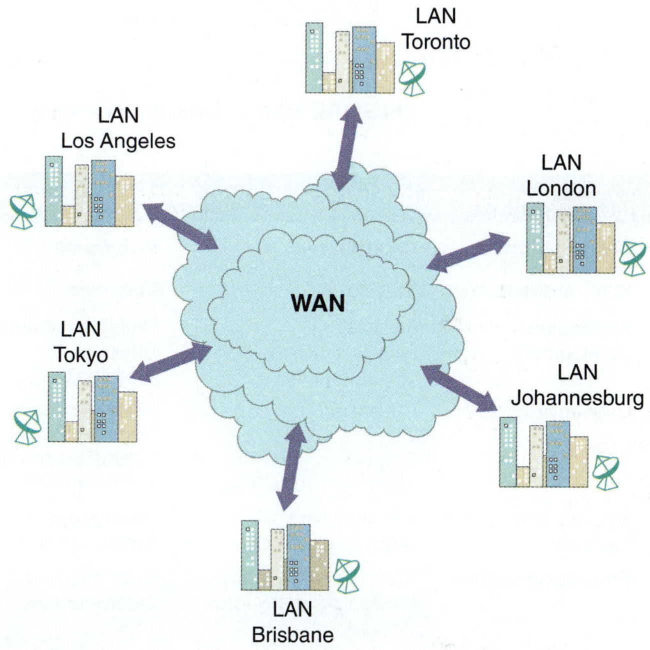

FIGURE 10-5 A WAN can connect many LANs and link users who are continents apart.

10.4 CLIENT/SERVER DESIGNS

Today's interconnected world requires an information architecture that spans the entire enterprise. Whether it's a departmental network or a multinational corporation, a systems analyst works with a distributed computing strategy called **client/server architecture**.

10.4.1 Overview

The term *client/server* generally refers to systems that divide processing between one or more networked clients and a central server. In a typical client/server system, the client handles the entire user interface, including data entry, data query, and screen presentation logic. The server stores the data and provides data access and database management functions. Application logic is divided in some manner between the server and the clients.

In a client/server interaction, the client submits a request for information from the server, which carries out the operation and responds to the client. As shown in Figure 10-6, the data file is not transferred from the server to the client — only the request and the result are transmitted across the network. To fulfill a request from a client, the server might contact other servers for data or processing support, but that process is transparent to the client.

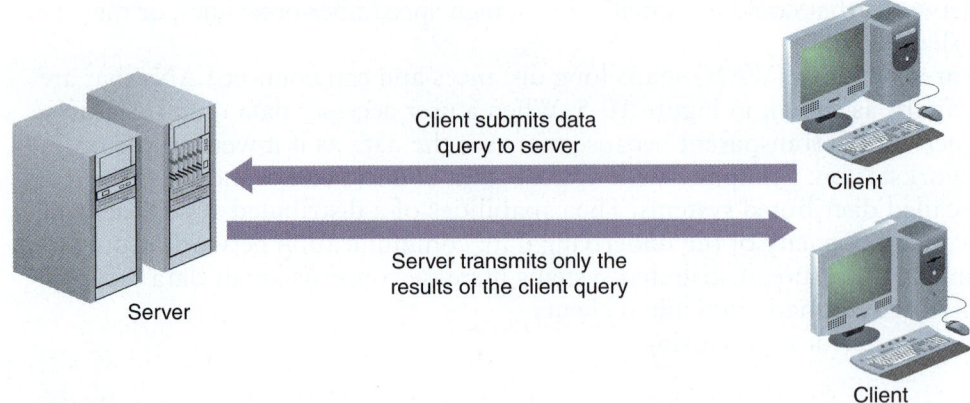

Client submits data query to server

Client

Server transmits only the results of the client query

Server

Client

FIGURE 10-6 In a client/server design, data is stored and usually processed on the server.

Comparison of Client/Server and Mainframe Systems		
Characteristics	**Client/Server**	**Mainframe**
Basic architecture	Very flexible	Very rigid
Application development	Flexible Fast Object-oriented	Highly structured Slow Traditional
User environment	PC-based GUI Empowers the user Improves productivity	Uses terminals Text interface Constrains the user Limited options
Security and control features	Decentralized Difficult to control	Centralized Easier to control
Processing options	Can be shared and configured in any form desired	Extensive and programmable
Data storage options	Can be distributed to place data closer to users	All data is stored centrally
Hardware/software integration	Very flexible Multivendor model	Very rigid Single proprietary vendor

FIGURE 10-7 Comparison of the characteristics of client/server and mainframe systems.

Figure 10-7 lists some major differences between client/server and traditional mainframe systems. Many early client/server systems did not produce expected savings because few clear standards existed, and development costs often were higher than anticipated. Implementation was expensive because clients needed powerful hardware and software to handle shared processing tasks. In addition, many companies had an installed base of data, called **legacy data**, which was difficult to access and transport to a client/server environment.

As large-scale networks grew more powerful, client/server systems became more cost-effective. Many companies invested in client/server systems to achieve a unique combination of computing power, flexibility, and support for changing business operations. Today, client/server architecture remains a popular form of systems design, using Internet protocols and network models, such as the ones described later in this chapter. As businesses form new alliances with customers and suppliers, the client/server concept continues to expand to include clients and servers outside the organization. Service-Oriented Architecture (SOA, described in Chapter 7) is an example of a networked system where a service can be a client and a server simultaneously, and it can exist outside of corporate boundaries.

Cloud computing, which is discussed in Section 10.5.1, is seen by some observers as an entirely new concept. Others see it as the ultimate form of client/server architecture, where Internet-based computing becomes the *server* part of client/server and handles processing tasks, while the Internet itself becomes the platform that replaces traditional networks. The bottom line is that it doesn't matter whether cloud computing is part of a client/server evolution or a whole new way of thinking about computing. Either way, successful systems must support business requirements, and system architecture is an important step in the systems development process.

10.4.2 The Client's Role

The client/server relationship must specify how the processing will be divided between the client and the server. A **fat client**, also called a **thick client**, design locates all or most of the application processing logic at the client. A **thin client** design locates all or most of the processing logic at the server.

In the late 1990s, Sun Microsystems (now part of Oracle) was a strong advocate of thin-client computing, which was also referred to as **net-centric computing**. The thin client was a Java-powered terminal, which communicated using standard Internet protocols with powerful servers. Thin clients were expected to provide lower TCO, since maintenance was centralized. However, many users rebelled at the limited functionality provided by thin clients (e.g., no Microsoft Office) and the latency problems inherent in network access to remote applications and data. In the end, fat clients (e.g., regular PCs) remained popular, even with all their management issues and higher TCO.

Today's laptop computers, tablets, and smartphones are so powerful that the allure of thin clients has mostly passed, with the exception of access to the cloud for large datasets and specialized processing needs. The app ecosystem has also changed the TCO equation in favor of powerful computing for clients at the edge of the system architecture.

10.4.3 Client/Server Tiers

Early client/server designs were called two-tier designs. In a **two-tier design**, the user interface resides on the client, all data resides on the server, and the application logic can run either on the server or on the client, or be divided between the client and the server.

More recently, another form of client/server design, called a three-tier design, has become popular. In a **three-tier design**, the user interface runs on the client and the data is stored on the server, just as with a two-tier design. A three-tier design also has a middle layer between the client and server that processes the client requests and translates them into data access commands that can be understood and carried out by the server, as shown in Figure 10-8. The middle layer can be considered an **application server**, because it provides the **application logic**, or business logic, required by the system. Three-tier designs also are called *n*-tier designs, to indicate that some designs use more than one intermediate layer.

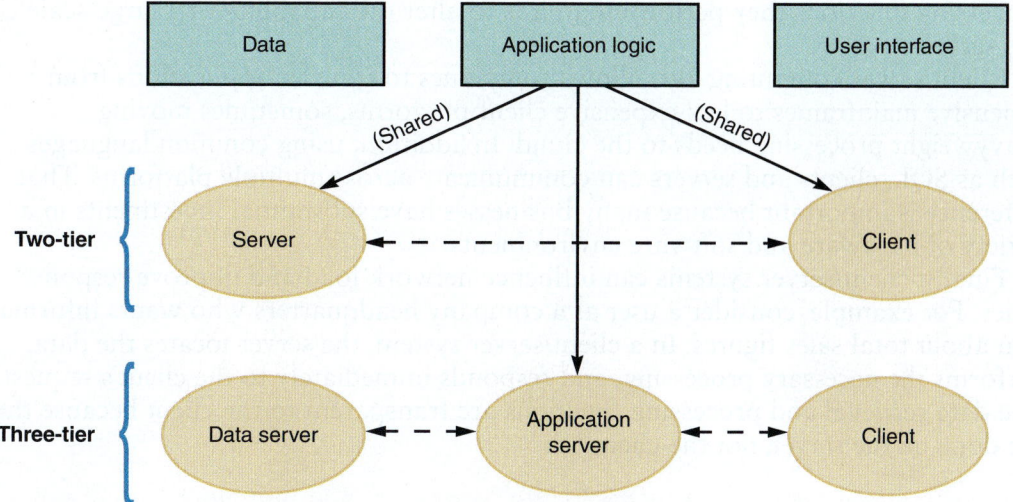

FIGURE 10-8 Characteristics of two-tier versus three-tier client/server design.

Architecture		Data	Application Logic	User Interface
Central data processing center	Server	X	X	X
	Client			
Central server with remote terminals	Server	X	X	
	Client			X
Stand-alone client	Server			
	Client	X	X	X
Two-tier client/server	Server	X	X	
	Client		X	X
Three-tier client/server	Data server	X		
	Application server		X	
	Client			X

FIGURE 10-9 The location of the data, the application logic, and the user interface depend on the type of architecture.

The advantage of the application logic layer is that a three-tier design may enhance overall performance by reducing the data server's workload. The separate application logic layer also relieves clients of complex processing tasks. Because it can run on a server that is much more powerful than the typical client workstations, the middle layer is more efficient and cost-effective in large-scale systems. Figure 10-9 shows where the data, the application logic, and the user interface are located on various architectures. In a client/server system, the tiers communicate using software called middleware, as described in the following section.

10.4.4 Middleware

In a multi-tier system, special software called middleware (described in Chapter 7) enables the tiers to communicate and pass data back and forth. Middleware is sometimes called glueware because it is used to connect two or more software components in a federated system architecture. Middleware plays an important role in integrating legacy systems and web-based and/or cloud-based applications. Middleware can also be seen as representing the slash in the term *client/server*.

10.4.5 Cost-Benefit Issues

To support business requirements, information systems need to be scalable, powerful, and flexible. For most companies, client/server systems offer the best combination of features to meet those needs. Whether a business is expanding or downsizing, client/server systems enable the firm to scale the system in a rapidly changing environment. As the size of the business changes, it is easier to adjust the number of clients and the processing functions they perform than it is to alter the capability of a large-scale central server.

Client/server computing also allows companies to transfer applications from expensive mainframes to less-expensive client platforms, sometimes moving heavyweight processing needs to the cloud. In addition, using common languages such as SQL, clients and servers can communicate across multiple platforms. That difference is important because many businesses have substantial investments in a variety of hardware and software environments.

Finally, client/server systems can influence network load and improve response times. For example, consider a user at a company headquarters who wants information about total sales figures. In a client/server system, the server locates the data, performs the necessary processing, and responds immediately to the client's request. The data retrieval and processing functions are transparent to the client because they are done on the server, not the client.

10.4.6 Performance Issues

While it provides many advantages, client/server architecture does involve performance issues that relate to the separation of server-based data and networked clients that must access the data.

Consider the difference between client/server design and a centralized environment, where a server-based program issues a command that is executed by the server's own CPU. Processing speed is enhanced because program instructions and data both travel on an internal system bus, which moves data more efficiently than an external network.

In contrast to the centralized system, a client/server design separates applications and data. Networked clients submit data requests to the server, which responds by sending data back to the clients. When the number of clients and the demand for services increases beyond a certain level, network capacity becomes a constraint, and system performance declines dramatically.

The performance characteristics of a client/server system are not the same as a centralized processing environment. Client/server response times increase gradually as more requests are made but then rise dramatically when the system nears its capacity. This point is called the knee of the curve, because it marks a sharp decline in the system's speed and efficiency. To deliver and maintain acceptable performance, system developers must anticipate the number of users, network traffic, server size and location, and design a client/server architecture that can support current and future business needs.

To enhance performance, client/server systems must be designed so the client contacts the server only when necessary and makes as few trips as possible. This is one of the goals of the HTTP/2 protocol used between a server and a web browser.

Another issue that affects client/server performance is data storage. Just as processing can be done at various places, data can be stored in more than one location using a distributed database management system (DDBMS).

Using a DDBMS offers several advantages: Data stored closer to users can reduce network traffic; the system is scalable, so new data sites can be added without reworking the system design; with data stored in various locations, the system is less likely to experience a catastrophic failure. A potential disadvantage of distributed data storage involves data security: It can be more difficult to maintain controls and standards when data is stored in various locations. In addition, the architecture of a DDBMS is more complex and difficult to manage. From a system design standpoint, the challenge is that companies often want it both ways — they want the control that comes with centralization *and* the flexibility associated with decentralization.

10.5 THE IMPACT OF THE INTERNET

The Internet has had an enormous impact on system architecture. The Internet has become more than a communication channel — many IT observers see it as a fundamentally different environment for system development.

Recall that in a traditional client/server system, the client handles the user interface, as shown in Figure 10-9, and the server (or servers in a multi-tier system) handles the data and application logic. In a sense, part of the system runs on the client, part on the server. In contrast, in an Internet-based architecture, in addition to data and application logic, the entire user interface is provided by the web server in the form of HTML documents that are displayed by the client's browser. Shifting the responsibility for the interface from the client to the server simplifies data transmission and results in lower hardware cost and complexity.

The advantages of Internet-based architecture have changed fundamental ideas about how computer systems should be designed, and we are moving rapidly to a total online environment. At the same time, millions of people are using web-based collaboration and social networking applications to accomplish tasks that used to be done in person, over the phone, or by more traditional Internet channels. The following sections examine cloud computing and Web 2.0. It is important to understand these trends, which are shaping the IT industry's future.

10.5.1 Cloud Computing

Cloud computing refers to the cloud symbol that often is used to represent the Internet. The cloud computing concept envisions a *cloud* of remote computers that provide a total online software and data environment that is hosted by third parties. For example, a user's computer does not perform all the processing or computing tasks — the cloud does some or all of it. This concept is in contrast to today's computing model, which is based on networks that strategically distribute processing and data across the enterprise. In a sense, the cloud of computers acts as one giant computer that performs tasks for users.

Figure 10-10 shows users connected to the cloud, which performs the computing work. Instead of requiring specific hardware and software on the user's computer, cloud computing spreads the workload to powerful remote systems that are part of the cloud. The user appears to be working on a local system, but all computing is actually performed in the cloud. No software updates or system maintenance are required of the user.

Cloud computing effectively eliminates compatibility issues, because the Internet itself is the platform. This architecture also provides **scaling on demand**, which matches resources to needs at any given time. For example, during peak loads, additional cloud servers might come online automatically to support the workload.

Cloud computing is an ideal platform for powerful Software as a Service (SaaS) applications. As described in Chapter 7, SaaS is a popular deployment method where software is not purchased but is paid for as a service, much like one pays for electricity or cable TV each month. In this architecture, service providers can easily make updates and changes to services without involving the users.

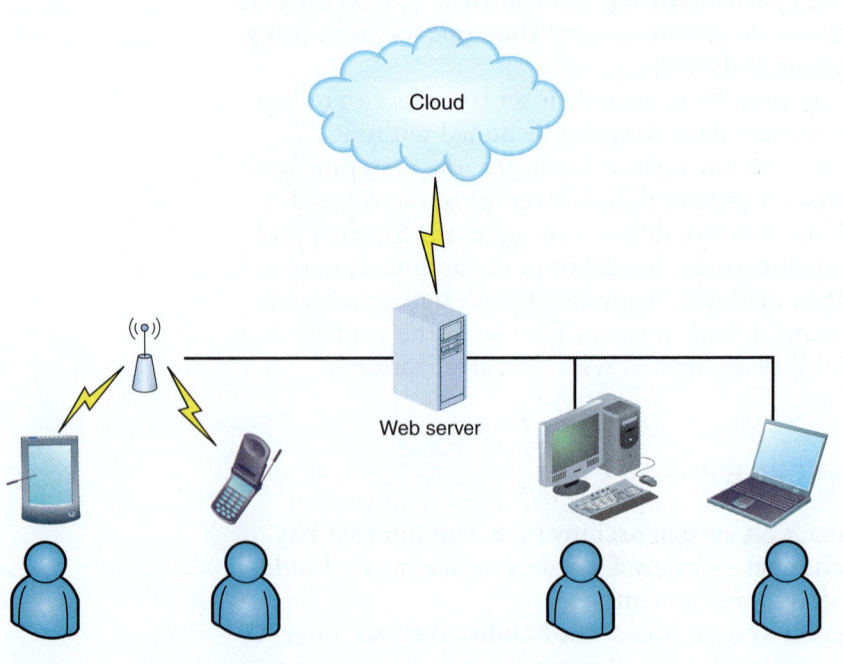

FIGURE 10-10 Cloud computing.

Even though cloud computing has tremendous advantages, some concerns exist. First, cloud computing may require more **bandwidth** (the amount of data that can be transferred in a fixed time period) than traditional client/server networks. Second, because cloud computing is

Internet-based, if a user's Internet connection becomes unavailable, the user will be unable to access any cloud-based services. In addition, there are security concerns associated with sending large amounts of data over the Internet, as well as concerns about storing it securely. Finally, there is the issue of control. Because a service provider hosts the resources and manages data storage and access, the provider has complete control of the system. Many firms are wary of handing over control of mission-critical data and systems to a third-party provider. This is particularly true when the cloud provider's servers are physically located in another jurisdiction or country.

Future technology advances will make cloud computing even more feasible, desirable, and secure. As the IT industry moves toward a web-based architecture, cloud computing is being marketed aggressively and growing rapidly. It has become a cornerstone of enterprise system architecture and will continue to be for the foreseeable future.

10.5.2 Web 2.0

As described in Chapter 7, the shift to Internet-based collaboration has been so powerful and compelling that it has been named Web 2.0. Web 2.0 is not a reference to a more technically advanced version of the current web. Rather, Web 2.0 envisions a second generation of the web that will enable people to collaborate, interact, and share information more dynamically. Some view Web 2.0 as a stepping stone toward the semantic web, called Web 3.0 by some, where the documents shared on the Internet have semantics (meaning) and not just syntax (HTML markup).

Social networking sites, such as Facebook, Twitter, and LinkedIn are seeing explosive growth in the Web 2.0 environment. Another form of social collaboration is called a wiki. A wiki is a web-based repository of information that anyone can access, contribute to, or modify. In a sense, a wiki represents the collective knowledge of a group of people. One of the best-known wikis is *Wikipedia.org*, but smaller-scale wikis are growing rapidly at businesses, schools, and other organizations that want to compile and share information.

One of the goals of Web 2.0 is to enhance creativity, interaction, and shared ideas. In this regard, the Web 2.0 concept resembles the agile development process and the open-source software movement. Web 2.0 communities and services are based on a body of data created by users. As users collaborate, new layers of information are added in an overall environment known as the Internet operating system. These layers can contain text, sound bytes, images, and video clips that are shared with the user community.

10.6 ECOMMERCE ARCHITECTURE

The huge expansion of online commerce is reshaping the IT landscape. Internet business solutions must be efficient, reliable, and cost-effective. When planning an ecommerce architecture, analysts can examine in-house development, packaged solutions, and service providers. The following sections discuss these options.

10.6.1 In-House Solutions

Chapter 7 described how to analyze advantages and disadvantages of in-house development versus purchasing a software package. The same basic principles apply to system design.

If a decision is made to proceed with an in-house solution, there must be an overall plan to help achieve the project's goals. Figure 10-11 offers guidelines for companies developing ecommerce strategies. An in-house solution usually requires a

Guidelines for In-house Ecommerce Site Development
Analyze the company's business needs and develop a clear statement of your goals. Consider the experience of other companies with similar projects.
Obtain input from users who understand the business and technology issues involved in the project. Plan for future growth, but aim for ease of use.
Determine whether the IT staff has the necessary skills and experience to implement the project. Consider training, additional resources, and the use of consultants if necessary.
Consider integration requirements for existing legacy systems or enterprise resource planning. Select a physical infrastructure carefully, so it will support the application, now and later.
Develop the project in modular form so users can test and approve the functional elements as you go along.
Connect the application to existing in-house systems and verify interactivity.
Test every aspect of the site exhaustively. Consider a preliminary rollout to a pilot group to obtain feedback before a full launch.

FIGURE 10-11 Guidelines for companies developing ecommerce strategies.

greater initial investment but provides more flexibility for a company that must adapt quickly in a dynamic ecommerce environment. By working in-house, a company has more freedom to integrate with customers and suppliers and is less dependent on vendor-specific solutions.

For smaller companies, the decision about in-house web development is even more critical, because this approach will require financial resources and management attention that many small companies might be unable or unwilling to commit. An in-house strategy, however, can provide valuable benefits, including the following:

- A unique website, with a look and feel consistent with the company's other marketing efforts

- Complete control over the organization of the site, the number of pages, and the size of the files

- A scalable structure to handle increases in sales and product offerings in the future

- More flexibility to modify and manage the site as the company changes

- The opportunity to integrate the firm's web-based business systems with its other information systems, creating the potential for more savings and better customer service

Whether a firm uses an in-house or a packaged design, the decision about web hosting is a separate issue. Although internal hosting has some advantages, such as greater control and security, the expense would be much greater, especially for a small- to medium-sized firm.

CASE IN POINT 10.2: SMALL POTATOES, INC.

Small Potatoes is a family-operated seed business that has grown rapidly. Small Potatoes specializes in supplying home gardeners with the finest seeds and gardening supplies. Until now, the firm has done all its business by placing ads in gardening and health magazines, and taking orders using a toll-free telephone number.

Now, the family has decided to establish a website and sell online, but there is some disagreement about the best way to proceed. Some say it would be better to develop the site on their own, and Betty Lou Jones, a recent computer science graduate, believes she can handle the task. Others, including Sam Jones, Betty's grandfather, feel it would be better to outsource the site and focus on the business itself. Suppose the family asked for your opinion. What would you say? What additional questions would you ask?

10.6.2 Packaged Solutions

If a small company is reluctant to take on the challenge and complexity of developing an Internet commerce site in-house, an alternative can be a packaged solution. This is true even for medium- to large-sized firms. Many vendors, including IBM and Microsoft, offer turnkey systems for companies that want to get an e-business up and running quickly, as shown in Figure 10-12. For large-scale systems that must integrate with existing applications, packaged solutions might be less attractive.

E-commerce platform for seamless, omni-channel shopping experiences

IBM Omnichannel Commerce Virtual Tour
Experience IBM's leading eCommerce and fulfillment platform.

→ Learn more

IBM® WebSphere® Commerce provides an e-commerce platform that can deliver seamless and consistent omni-channel shopping experiences, including mobile, social and in-store. WebSphere Commerce helps engage your customers with immersive brand experiences through contextually relevant content, marketing and promotions, while extending your brand across customer touch points.

Features and capabilities of WebSphere Commerce

| **Storefronts:** Achieve faster time-to-market and simplify your web or mobile store creation | **B2B e-Commerce:** Make it easier for partners, customers and resellers to do business with you | **B2C e-Commerce:** Provide consistent shopping experiences across channels | **Customer Experience:** Create and manage engaging and compelling customer experiences |

FIGURE 10-12 IBM WebSphere Commerce offers software solutions for companies that want to get an e-business up and running quickly.
Source: IBM

10.6.3 Service Providers

Another alternative is to use an application service provider (ASP). As explained in Chapter 7, an ASP provides applications, or access to applications, by charging a usage or subscription fee. Today, many ASPs offer full-scale Internet business services for companies that decide to outsource those functions.

A systems analyst confronts a bewildering array of products and strategies when implementing Internet-based systems. A good starting point might be to consider the experience of other companies in the same industry. Many firms offer the names of clients and customers, along with their success stories. Although this information might or might not be reliable, it can provide valuable knowledge regarding a vendor's products and services.

10.7 PROCESSING METHODS

In selecting an architecture, the systems analyst must determine which transactions will be handled online, and what functions, if any, can be carried out using a batch processing method.

10.7.1 Online Processing

Early computer systems were designed to handle data records as a group, or *batch*. Fewer systems use that model today. However, even the most advanced online systems must perform maintenance, post large quantities of data during off-hours when network traffic is low, and carry out housekeeping tasks just as their legacy computer ancestors did. This section discusses the online processing capability that is at the core of powerful, modern systems, and the following section describes the evolution of batch processing.

An **online system** handles transactions when and where they occur and provides output directly to users. Because it is interactive, online processing avoids delays and allows a constant dialog between the user and the system.

An airline reservations system is a familiar example of online processing. When online customers visit the airline's website, they can enter their origin, destination, travel dates, and travel times. The system searches a database and responds by displaying available flights, times, and prices. The customer can make a reservation, enter a name, address, credit card information, and other required data and the system creates the reservation, assigns a seat, and updates the flight database immediately.

ATM QUERY PROCESS

Step 1:   Customer enters his or her account number and requests an account balance

Step 2:   Retrieves current account balance

Step 3:   Verifies bank account number and displays balance on ATM screen

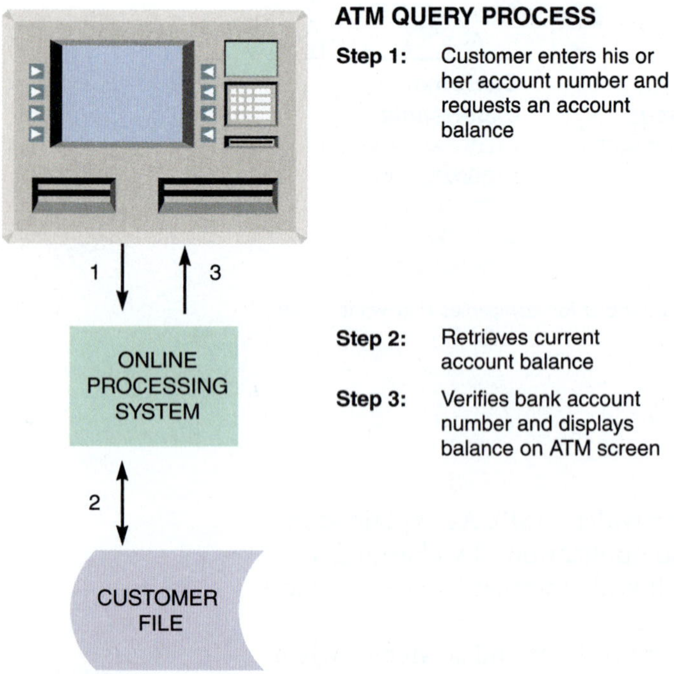

FIGURE 10-13 When a customer requests a balance, the ATM system verifies the account number, submits the query, retrieves the current balance, and displays the balance on the ATM screen.

Online processing can also be used with file-oriented systems. Figure 10-13 shows what happens when a customer uses an ATM to inquire about an account balance. After the ATM verifies the customer's card and password, the customer enters the request (Step 1). Then, the system accesses the account master file using the account number as the primary key and retrieves the customer's record (Step 2). The system verifies the account number and displays the balance (Step 3). Data is retrieved and the system transmits the current balance to the ATM, which prints it for the customer.

Online processing systems have four typical characteristics:

1. The system processes transactions completely when and where they occur.

2. Users interact directly with the information system.

3. Users can access data randomly.

4. The information system must be available whenever necessary to support business functions.

10.7.2 Batch Processing: Still with Us After All These Years

Batch processing means that data is managed in groups, or batches. That was an acceptable choice in the 1960s, and for most firms, it was the *only* choice. Today, all businesses need real-time information to operate, and batch processing is not always desirable. However, batch methods can be efficient and convenient in some situations.

For example, batch processing can be used for large amounts of data that must be processed on a routine schedule, such as weekly paychecks, daily credit card transaction updates, or closing stock data that must be calculated and published in the following day's news media. The advantages of batch methods include:

- Tasks can be planned and run on a predetermined schedule, without user involvement.

- Batch programs that require major network resources can run at times when costs, and impact on other traffic, will be lowest.

- A batch method is well-suited to address security, audit, and privacy concerns, because it runs in a relatively controlled environment.

10.7.3 Real-World Examples

The diagram in Figure 10-14 shows how a **point-of-sale (POS)** terminal, such as that used in a supermarket, might trigger a series of online and batch processing events. Notice that the system uses online processing to handle data entry and inventory updates, while reports and accounting entries are performed in a batch. A company would choose a mix of online and batch processing when it makes good business sense. Consider the following scenario in a typical retail store:

- During business hours, a salesperson enters a sale on a POS terminal, which is part of an online system that handles daily sales transactions and maintains an up-to-date inventory file.

- When the salesperson enters the transaction, online processing occurs. The system performs calculations, updates the inventory file, and produces output on the POS terminal in the form of a screen display and a printed receipt. At the same time, each sales transaction creates input data for day-end batch processing.

POINT OF SALE (POS) PROCESSING

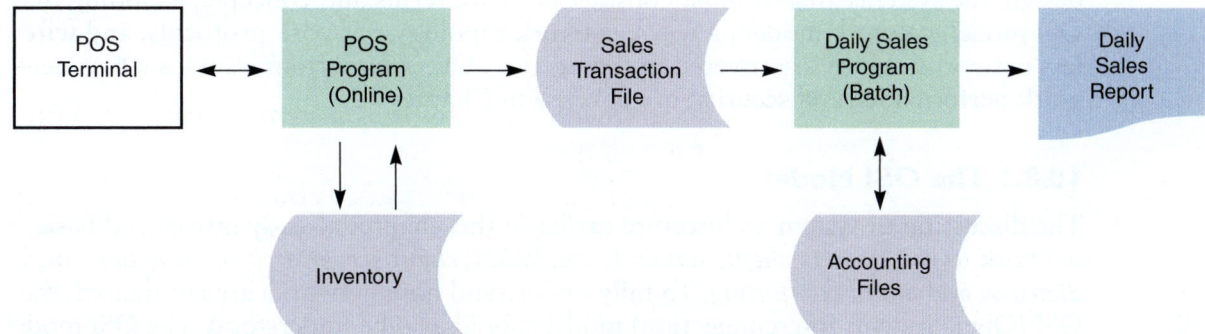

FIGURE 10-14 Many retailers use a combination of online and batch processing. When a salesperson enters the sale on the POS terminal, the online system retrieves data from the item file, updates the quantity in stock, and produces a sales transaction record. At the end of the day, a batch processing program produces a daily sales report and updates the accounting system.

- When the store closes, the system uses the sales transactions to produce the daily sales report, perform the related accounting entries, and analyze the data to identify slow or fast-moving items, sales trends, and related issues — such as store discounts for the next day.

Online or batch processing are totally different but can work well together. In this scenario, an online system handles point-of-sale processing, which must be done as it occurs, while a batch method provides routine, overnight processing and marketing analysis. Online processing allows the data to be entered and validated immediately, so the information always is up to date. However, a heavy volume of online transactions can be expensive for smaller firms, and data backup and recovery also adds to IT costs. In contrast, when used properly, batch processing can be cost-effective and less vulnerable to system disruption.

CASE IN POINT 10.3:   R/WAY TRUCKING COMPANY

You are the new IT manager at R/Way, a small but rapidly growing trucking company headquartered in Cleveland, Ohio. The company slogan is "Ship It R/Way — State-of-the-Art in Trucking and Customer Service." R/Way's information system currently consists of a file server and three workstations where freight clerks enter data, track shipments, and prepare freight bills. To perform their work, the clerks obtain data from the server and use database and spreadsheet programs stored on their PCs to process the data.

Unfortunately, your predecessor did not design a relational database. Instead, data is stored in several files, including one for shippers, one for customers, and one for shipments. The system worked well for several years but cannot handle current volume or support online links for R/Way shippers and customers. The company president is willing to make changes, but he is reluctant to spend money on major IT improvements unless you can convince him that they are necessary.

What would you recommend and why?

10.8 NETWORK MODELS

A network allows the sharing of hardware, software, and data resources in order to reduce expenses and provide more capability to users. When planning a network design, the systems analyst must consider network terms and concepts, including the OSI model, network modeling tools, network topology, network protocols, and wireless networks, which are covered in this section. Other important issues, such as network performance and security, are covered in Chapter 12.

10.8.1 The OSI Model

The discussion of system architecture earlier in this chapter already introduced basic network terms, such as *client, server, LAN, WAN, client/server architecture, tiers, middleware,* and *cloud computing.* To fully understand how networks are configured, the OSI (Open Systems Interconnection) model should also be understood. The OSI model describes how data moves from an application on one computer to an application on another networked computer. The OSI model consists of seven layers, and each layer performs a specific function. The OSI model provides physical design standards that assure seamless network connectivity, regardless of the specific hardware environment.

10.8.2 Network Topology

The way a network is configured is called the network topology. Topology can refer to a physical or a logical view of the network. For example, physical topology describes the actual network cabling and connections, while logical topology describes the way the components interact. It is important to understand the distinction, because a specific physical topology might be able to support more than one logical topology. For example, it is not uncommon to run cabling in a certain pattern because of physical installation and cost issues, but to use a different pattern for the logical topology.

Computers may be physically arranged in a circular shape, such as those shown in Figure 10-15, but that might or might not reflect the network topology. The examples shown in Figure 10-16 to Figure 10-20 represent a logical topology, as seen by network users, who may not know or care about the physical cabling pattern.

FIGURE 10-15 Although these computers form a physical circle, the physical layout has no bearing on the network topology, which might be a bus, ring, star, or other logical design.

LAN and WAN networks typically are arranged in four patterns: hierarchical, bus, ring, and star. The concepts are the same regardless of the size of the network, but the physical implementation is different for a large-scale WAN that spans an entire business enterprise compared with a small LAN in a single department. These four common topologies are described in the following sections.

HIERARCHICAL NETWORK: In a hierarchical network, as shown in Figure 10-16, one or more powerful servers control the entire network. Departmental servers control lower levels of processing and network devices. An example of a hierarchical network might be a retail clothing chain, with a central computer that stores data about sales activity and inventory levels, and local computers that handle store-level operations. The stores transmit data to the central computer, which analyzes sales trends, determines optimum stock levels, and coordinates a supply chain management system. In this situation, a hierarchical network might be used, because it mirrors the actual operational flow in the organization.

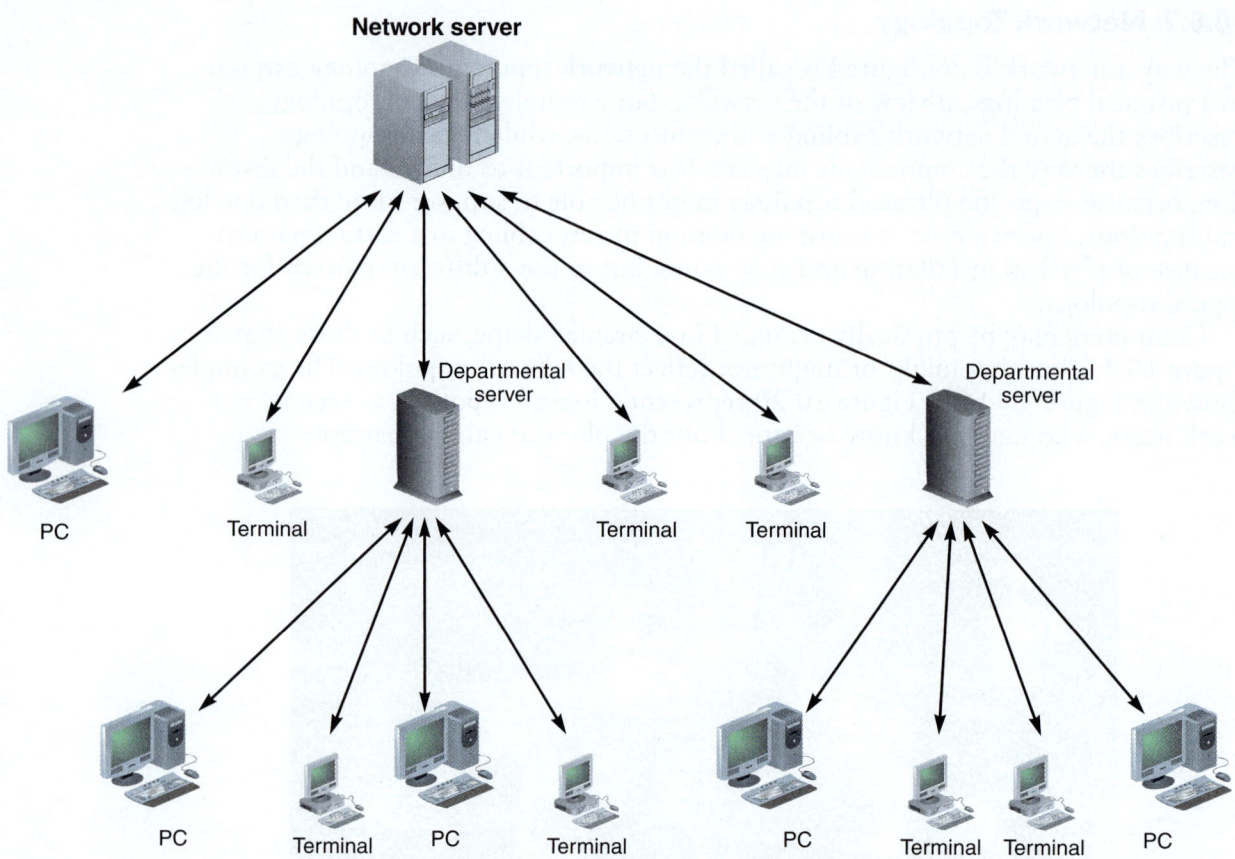

FIGURE 10-16 A hierarchical network with a single server that controls the network.

One disadvantage of a hierarchical network is that if a business adds additional processing levels, the network becomes more complex and expensive to operate and maintain. Hierarchical networks were often used in traditional mainframe-based systems but are less common today.

BUS NETWORK: In a **bus network**, as shown in Figure 10-17, a single communication path connects the central server, departmental servers, workstations, and peripheral devices. Information is transmitted in either direction between networked devices, and all messages travel over the same central bus. Bus networks require less cabling than other topologies, because only a single cable is used. Devices can also be attached or detached from the network at any point without disturbing the rest of the network. In addition, a failure in one workstation on the network does not necessarily affect other workstations on the network.

One major disadvantage of a bus network is that if the central bus becomes damaged or defective, the entire network shuts down. Another disadvantage is that overall performance declines as more users and devices are added, because all message traffic must flow along the central bus. This does not occur in the treelike structure of a hierarchical network or the hub-and-spoke design of a star network, where network paths are more isolated and independent.

The bus network is one of the oldest LAN topologies, and is a simple way to connect multiple workstations. Before the proliferation of star networks, bus networks were very common. They share characteristics of hardware bus networks. Today, the bus design is less popular, but some firms have retained bus networks to avoid the expense of new wiring and hardware.

RING NETWORK: Although ring networks are still around, they are somewhat outdated. IBM was a leader in ring network technology when they introduced their token ring LAN, and large companies who use IBM mainframe equipment still deploy the ring network design. A ring network, as shown in Figure 10-18, resembles a circle where the data flows in only one direction from one device to the next. In function, a ring network can be thought of as a bus network with the ends connected. One disadvantage of a ring network is that if a network device (such as a PC or a server) fails, the devices downstream from the failed device cannot communicate with the network.

STAR NETWORK: Because of its speed and versatility, the star network is a popular LAN topology. A star network has a central networking device called a switch, which manages the network and acts as a communications conduit for all network traffic. In the past, a device known as a hub was used to connect star networks, but a switch offers advanced technology and much better performance. A hub or switch functions like a familiar multi-socket power strip, but with network devices such as servers, workstations, and printers plugged in rather than electrical appliances. The hub broadcasts network traffic, called data frames, to all connected devices. In contrast, a switch enhances network performance by sending traffic only to specific network devices that need to receive the data.

A star configuration, as shown in Figure 10-19, provides a high degree of network control, because all traffic flows into and out of the switch. An inherent disadvantage of the star design is that the entire network is dependent on the switch. However, in most large star networks, backup switches are available immediately in case of hardware failure.

MESH NETWORK: In the mesh network shown in Figure 10-20, each node connects to every other node. While this design is extremely reliable, it is also very expensive to install and maintain. A mesh network resembles the Internet in that a message can travel on more than one path. Originally developed for military applications, the primary advantage of a mesh network is redundancy,

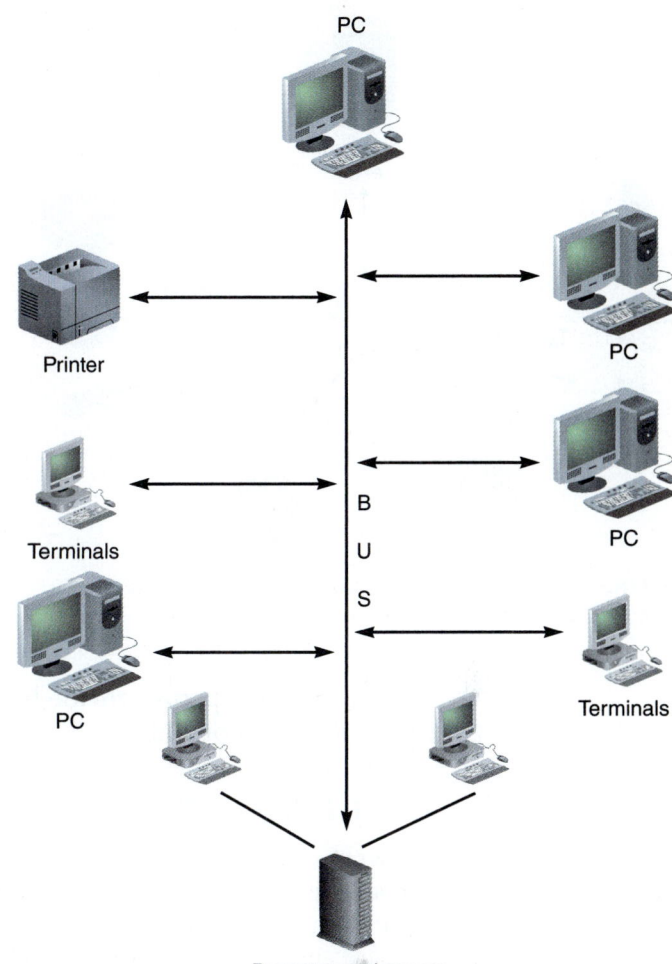

FIGURE 10-17 A bus network with all the devices connected to a single communication path.

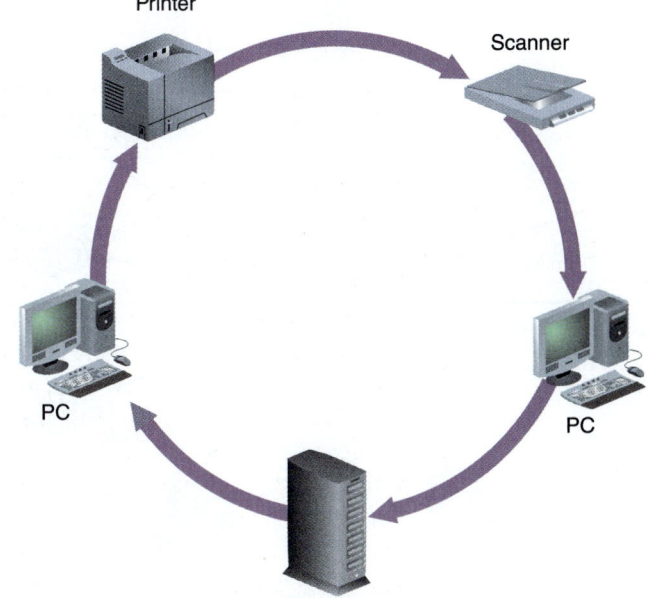

FIGURE 10-18 A ring network with a set of computers that sends and receives data flowing in one direction.

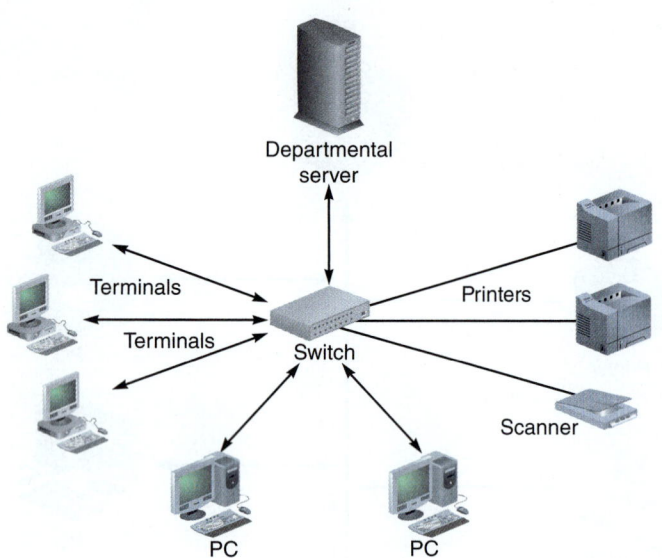

FIGURE 10-19 A star network with a switch, departmental server, and connected computers and devices.

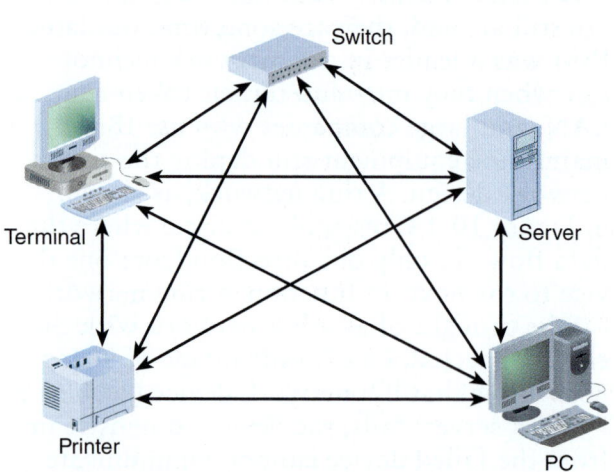

FIGURE 10-20 A mesh network is used in situations where a high degree of redundancy is needed, such as military applications. The redundant design provides alternate data paths but is expensive to install and maintain.

because multiple paths provide backup if communication problems arise or some nodes become inoperable.

10.8.3 Network Devices

Networks such as LANs or WANs can be interconnected using devices called routers. A **router** is a device that connects network segments, determines the most efficient data path, and guides the flow of data.

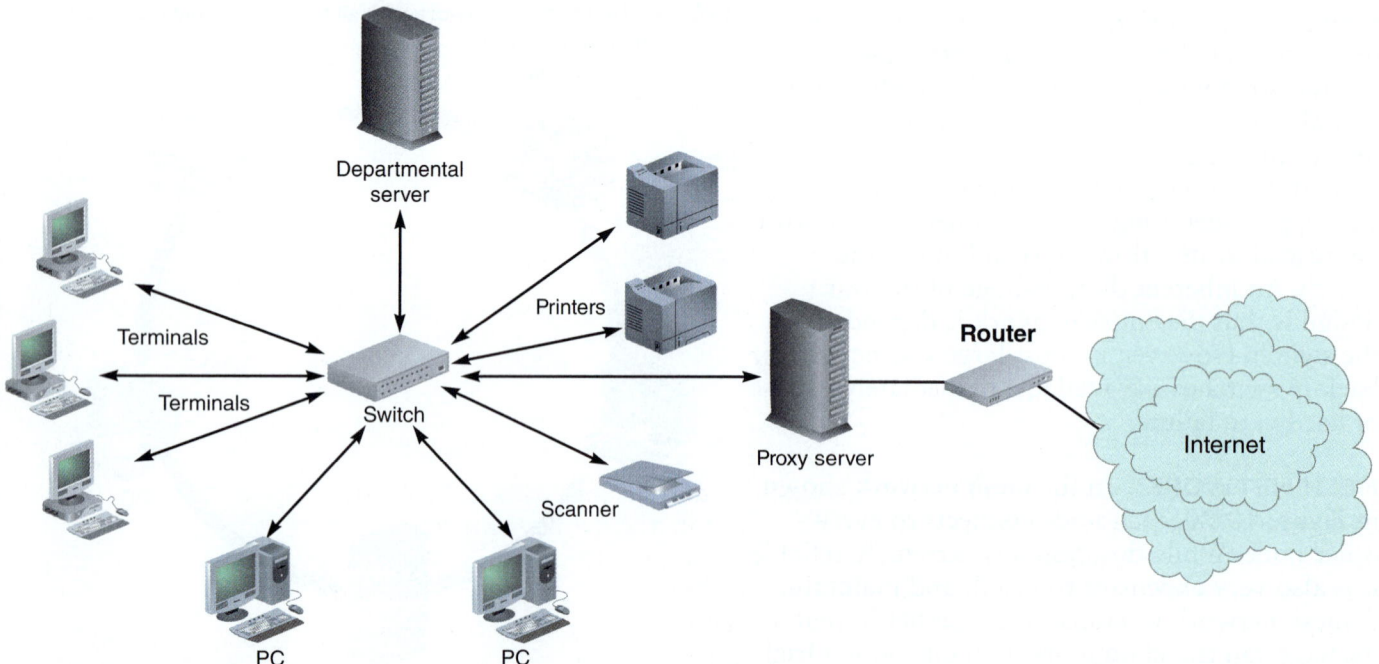

FIGURE 10-21 Routers can be used to create gateways between different network topologies and large, dissimilar networks such as the Internet.

Using a router, any network topology can connect to a larger, dissimilar network, such as the Internet. This connection is called a gateway. The example in Figure 10-21 shows a star topology, where a switch connects nodes in the LAN and the router links the network to the Internet. A device called a **proxy server** provides Internet connectivity for internal LAN users. The vast majority of business networks use routers to integrate the overall network architecture.

10.8.4 Modeling Tools

As a network model is translated into a physical version of the system, traditional software tools, such as Microsoft Visio (a multipurpose drawing tool), can be used to represent the physical structure and network components. Newer applications, such as Creatly.com, offer network diagram drawing capabilities that are completely web-based, as shown in Figure 10-22.

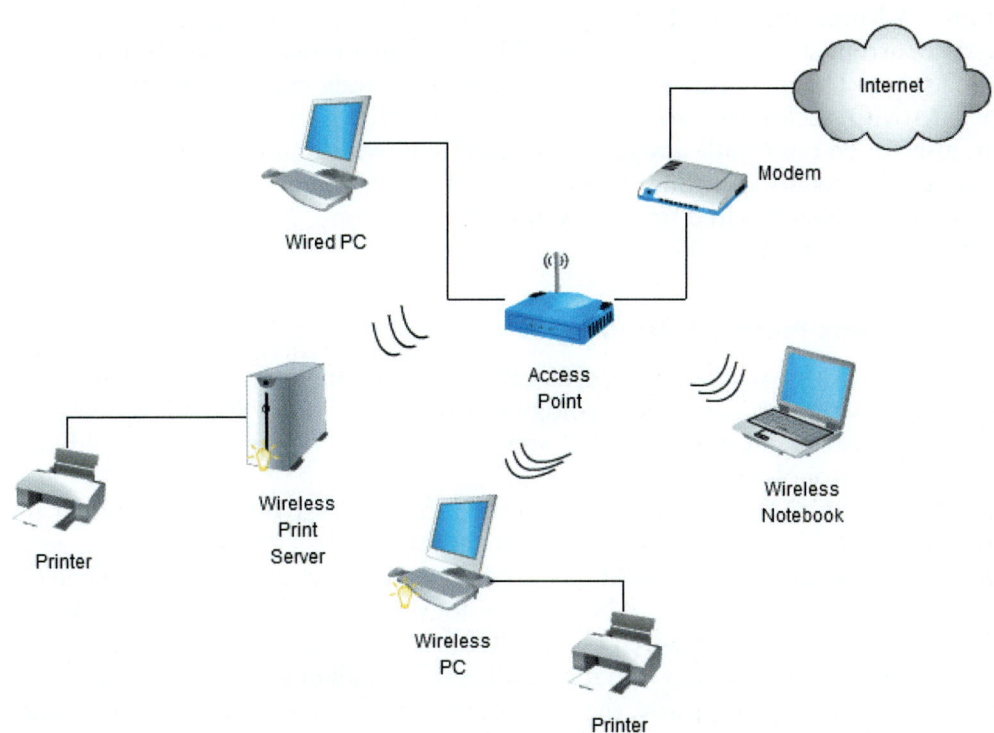

FIGURE 10-22 Creatly is a web-based software application for creating network diagrams.
Source: © 2008-2015 Cinergix Pty. Ltd.

10.9 WIRELESS NETWORKS

Although a wired LAN provides enormous flexibility, the cabling cost can be substantial, as well as the inevitable wiring changes that occur in a dynamic organization. Many companies find wireless technology to be an attractive alternative. A **wireless local area network**, or **WLAN**, is relatively inexpensive to install and is well-suited to workgroups and users who are not anchored to a specific desk or location. Most notebook computers and other mobile devices are equipped with built-in wireless capability, and it is relatively simple to add this feature to existing desktop computers and workstations in order to set up a wireless network.

Like their wired counterparts, wireless networks have certain standards and topologies, which are discussed in the following sections.

10.9.1 Wireless Network Standards

Wireless networks are based on various standards and protocols that still are evolving. The most popular of these is called IEEE 802.11, which is a family of standards developed by the Institute of Electrical and Electronics Engineers (IEEE) for wireless LANs.

Current wireless networks are based on variations of the original 802.11 standard. Several versions, or amendments, were intended to improve bandwidth, range, and security. The IEEE 802.11 set of standards changes very rapidly, in large part due to pressure from consumer groups and industry leaders moving toward ever-faster wireless networks. Wireless network speed is measured in Mbps (megabits per second) or Gbps (gigabits per second).

For example, when the 802.11b standard was introduced in 1999, the average speed was 11 Mbps. Later versions, such as 802.11g and 802.11n, increased bandwidth to 54 Mbps and 450 Mbps, respectively, and were widely accepted by the IT industry. Current standards, such as 802.11ac, can theoretically reach speeds of nearly 7 Gbps. The increased speed is accomplished using multiple input/multiple output (MIMO) technology to boost performance. MIMO relies on multiple data paths, also called multipath design, to increase bandwidth and range.

If wireless capacity continues to expand and security issues can be overcome, WLANs could replace wired networks in many situations. Wireless security is discussed in detail in Chapter 12.

10.9.2 Wireless Network Topologies

Like wired networks, wireless networks can also be arranged in different topologies. The two most common network topologies available for IEEE 802.11 WLANs are the Basic Service Set and the Extended Service Set Figure 10-23 shows simplified models of these topologies.

The Basic Service Set (BSS), also called the infrastructure mode, is shown at the top of Figure 10-23. In this configuration, a central wireless device, called an access point or wireless access point (WAP), is used to serve all wireless clients. The access point is similar to a hub in the LAN star topology, except it provides network services to wireless clients instead of wired clients. Because access points use a single communications medium, the air, they broadcast all traffic to all clients, just as a hub would do in a wired network. Typically, the access point itself is connected to a wired network, so wireless clients can access the wired network.

The second wireless topology is the Extended Service Set (ESS), as shown at the bottom of Figure 10-23. An Extended Service Set is made up of two or more Basic Service Set networks. Thus, using an ESS topology, wireless access can be expanded over a larger area. Each access point provides wireless services over a limited range. As a client moves away from one access point and closer to another, a process called roaming automatically allows the client to associate with the stronger access point, allowing for undisrupted service.

10.9.3 Wireless Trends

Wireless technology has brought explosive change to the IT industry, and will continue to affect businesses, individuals, and society. Even in the ever-changing world of IT, it would be difficult to find a more dynamic area than wireless technology.

Basic Service Set

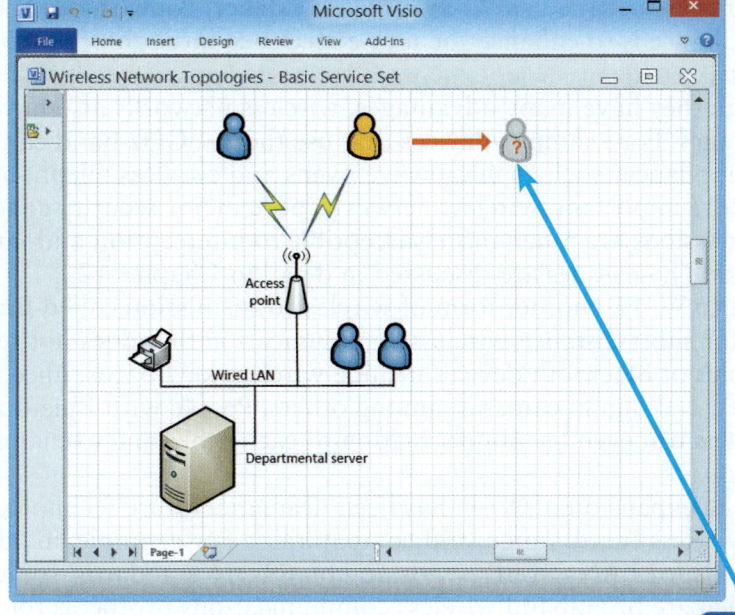

Extended Service Set

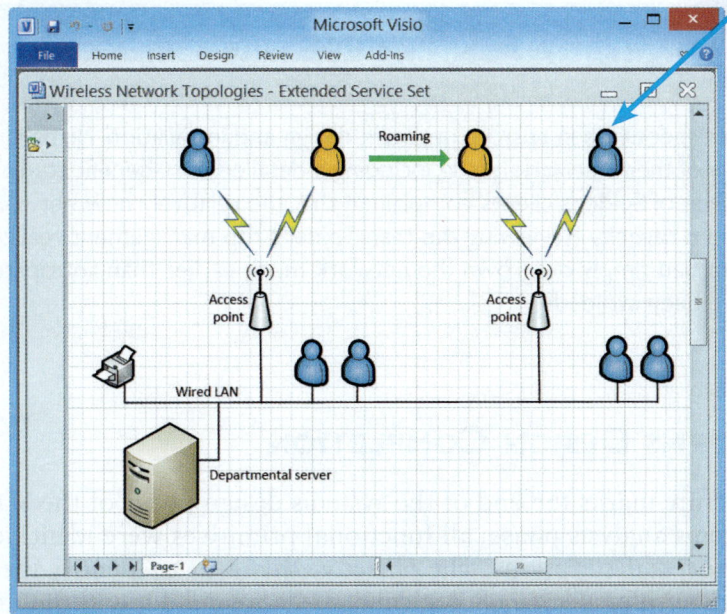

FIGURE 10-23 The user in the upper screen has moved out of the BSS coverage area and cannot communicate. In the lower screen, the user roams into another ESS coverage area and the transition is seamless.

With the growing popularity of 802.11, many firms offer networking products, services, and information. One of the most significant groups is the Wi-Fi Alliance, which maintains a website at *www.wi-fi.org*. According to the site, the Alliance is a nonprofit international association formed in 1999 to certify interoperability of wireless network products based on IEEE 802.11 specifications. Products that meet the requirements are certified as **Wi-Fi (wireless fidelity)** compatible. The stated goal of the Wi-Fi Alliance is to enhance the user experience through product interoperability.

Even though they have many advantages, wireless networks also have limitations and disadvantages. For example, devices that use the 2.4 GHz band can pick up interference from appliances such as microwave ovens and cordless telephones that use the same band. More important, wireless networks pose major security concerns because wireless transmissions are much more susceptible to interception and intrusion than wired networks. These issues are discussed in detail in Chapter 12.

In addition to Wi-Fi, another form of wireless transmission called **Bluetooth** is very popular for short-distance wireless communication that does not require high power. Examples of Bluetooth devices include wireless keyboards, mice, printers, cell phone headsets, and digital cameras, among others. People with Bluetooth-equipped phones or tablets can even beam information to each other and exchange digital notes.

Although the expansion of Wi-Fi has been dramatic, future technology promises even greater wireless speed, range, and compatibility. For example, in addition to 802.11 protocols for LANs, IEEE is working on **802.16** standards, sometimes called **Wi-MAX**, which are broadband wireless communications protocols for **MANs (metropolitan area networks)**.

CASE IN POINT 10.4:   SPIDER IT SERVICES

Spider IT Services specializes in custom network design and installation. Firms hire Spider to do an overall analysis of their network needs, including a detailed cost-benefit study. Recently, a problem arose. One of Spider's clients complained that the relatively new network was too slow and lacked sufficient capacity. Reviewing the case, Spider's top management realized that the rapidly growing client had simply outgrown the network much earlier than anticipated. How could this problem have been avoided?

10.10 SYSTEMS DESIGN COMPLETION

System architecture marks the end of the systems design phase of the SDLC. Recall that in the systems analysis phase, all functional primitives were identified and documented with process descriptions. The objective then was to identify the system's functions and determine *what* each logical module would do, without attempting to determine *how* that function would be carried out. Moving from analysis to design tasks, the development process continued with consideration of output and user interface design, data design, and system architecture issues. Now, based on a clear definition of system requirements and design, software applications can be developed, documented, and tested as part of the systems implementation phase of the SDLC, which is described in Chapter 11.

Developers must also consider system management and support tools that can monitor system performance, deal with fault management, handle backup, and provide for disaster recovery. These topics are covered in detail in Chapter 12.

The final activities in the systems design phase are preparing a system design specification, obtaining user approval, and delivering a presentation to management.

10.10.1 System Design Specification

The system design specification is a document that presents the complete design for the new information system, along with detailed costs, staffing, and scheduling for completing the next SDLC phase — systems implementation.

The system design specification is the baseline against which the operational system will be measured. Unlike the system requirements document, which is written for users to understand, the system design specification is oriented toward the programmers who will use it to create the necessary programs. Some sections of the system requirements document are repeated in the system design specification, such as process descriptions, data dictionary entries, and data flow diagrams.

The system design specification varies in length, so it should be organized carefully. One typically includes a cover page, a detailed table of contents, and an index. The contents of the system design specification depend on company standards and the complexity of the system. A typical system design specification includes the following sections.

1. *Management Summary.* This is a brief overview of the project for company managers and executives. It outlines the development efforts to date, provides a current status report, summarizes project costs, reviews the benefits of the new system, presents the systems implementation schedule, and highlights any issues that management will need to address.

2. *System Components.* This section contains the complete design for the new system, including the user interface, outputs, inputs, files, databases, and network specifications. Source documents, report and screen layouts, DFDs, and all other relevant documentation should be included. In addition, the requirements for all support processing, such as backup and recovery, start-up processing, and file retention should be included. If the purchase of a software package is part of the strategy, include any interface information required between the package and the system being developed. If a CASE design tool is used, design diagrams and most other documentation can be produced directly from the tool.

3. *System Environment.* This section describes the constraints, or conditions, affecting the system, including any requirements that involve operations, hardware, systems software, or security. Examples of operational constraints include transaction volumes that must be supported, data storage requirements, processing schedules, reporting deadlines, and online response times.

4. *Implementation Requirements.* In this section, start-up processing, initial data entry or acquisition, user training requirements, and software test plans are specified.

5. *Time and Cost Estimates.* This section provides detailed schedules, cost estimates, and staffing requirements for the systems development phase and revised projections for the remainder of the SDLC. Total costs-to-date for the project and a comparison of those costs with prior estimates are also presented.

6. *Additional Material.* Other material can be included at the end of the system design specification. In this section, documents from earlier phases can be inserted if they would be helpful to readers.

10.10.2 User Approval

Users must review and approve the interface design, report and menu designs, data entry screens, source documents, and other areas of the system that affect them. The review and approval process continues throughout the systems design phase. When the design for a report is complete, the systems analyst should meet with users to review the prototype, adjust the design if necessary, and obtain written approval. Chapter 8 contains guidelines and suggestions about report design.

Securing approvals from users throughout the design phase is very important. That approach ensures that a major task of obtaining approvals is not left to the end, it keeps the users involved with the system's development, and it provides feedback about whether or not the project is on target. Some sections of the system design specification might not interest users, but anything that does affect them should be approved as early as possible.

Other IT department members also need to review the system design specification. IT management will be concerned with staffing, costs, hardware and systems software requirements, network impact, and the effect on the operating environment when the new system is added. The programming team will want to get ready for its role, and the operations group will be interested in processing support, report distribution, network loads, integration with other systems, and any hardware or software issues for which they need to prepare. As always, a systems analyst must be a good communicator to keep people up to date, obtain their input and suggestions, and obtain necessary approvals.

When the system design specification is complete, the document is distributed to a target group of users, IT department personnel, and company management. It should be distributed at least one week before a presentation to allow the recipients enough time to review the material.

10.10.3 Presentations

Usually, the systems analyst will give several presentations at the end of the systems design phase. The presentations offer an opportunity to explain the system, answer questions, consider comments, and secure final approval. Part A of the Systems Analyst's Toolkit provides valuable guidelines and tips about oral presentations.

The first presentation is to the other systems analysts, programmers, and technical support staff members who will be involved in future project phases or operational support for the system. Because of the audience, the presentation is technically oriented.

The next presentation is to department managers and users from departments affected by the system. As in the first presentation, the primary objective is to obtain support and approval for the systems design. This is not a technical presentation; it is aimed at user interaction with the system and management's interest in budgets, schedules, staffing, and impact on the production environment.

The final presentation is delivered to management. By the time this presentation is delivered, all necessary approvals should have been obtained from prior presentations, and the users and IT department should be onboard. Just like the management presentation at the end of the systems analysis phase, this presentation has a key objective: to obtain management's approval and support for the next development step — systems implementation — including a solid commitment for financial and other resources needed.

Based on the presentation and the data submitted, management might reach one of three decisions: proceed with systems development, perform additional work on the systems design phase, or terminate the project.

A QUESTION OF ETHICS

iStockphoto.com/faberfoto_it

The new accounting system is operational, but feedback from users has been negative. The most common complaint is that the system is not user-friendly. Some people in the IT department think that more user training would solve the problem. However, Sam, the IT manager, is opposed to a fresh round of training. "Let's just set up the network to monitor the users' keystrokes and mouse clicks, and see what the patterns are," he suggested. "We can analyze the data and come up with tips and suggestions that would make the system easier to use."

Your initial reaction is that Sam is wrong, for two reasons. First, you believe that monitoring would not be an effective method to learn what users really want. In your view, that should have been done in the system requirements phase. Second, you are bothered by an ethical question: Even though the proposed monitoring would involve company business, the company network, and company time, you feel that many users would resent the unannounced monitoring and might feel that their performance or other computing activities were being appraised without their knowledge.

Sam has asked to you to write up a recommendation. What will you say about the ethical question that troubles you?

10.11   CHAPTER SUMMARY

An information system combines hardware, software, data, procedures, and people into a system architecture. The architecture translates the system's logical design into a physical structure that includes hardware, software, and processing methods. The software consists of application programs, also called applications, which handle the input, manage the processing logic, and provide the required output.

Before selecting a system architecture, the analyst must consider enterprise resource planning, initial cost and TCO, scalability, web integration, legacy interface requirements, processing options, security issues, and corporate portals.

Enterprise resource planning (ERP) establishes an enterprise-wide strategy for IT resources and specific standards for data, processing, network, and user interface design. Companies can extend ERP systems to suppliers and customers in a process called supply chain management. A systems analyst must assess initial cost and TCO and ensure that the design is scalable. Scalability means that a system can be expanded, modified, or downsized easily to meet business needs. The analyst must also consider if the system will be web-centric and follow Internet design protocols, and if it must interface with existing systems, called legacy systems. System security is an important concern throughout the design process, especially for ecommerce applications that involve credit card and personal data. Processing options affect system design and resources required. The planned architecture can include a corporate portal that is an entrance to a multifunction website. Corporate portals can provide access for customers, employees, suppliers, and others.

A system architecture requires servers and clients. Servers are computers that supply data, processing services, or other support to one or more computers called clients. In mainframe architecture, the server performs all processing, and terminals communicate with the centralized system. Clients can be connected in distributed systems to form LANs or WANs.

Client/server architecture divides processing between one or more clients and a central server. In a typical client/server system, the client handles the entire user interface, including data entry, data query, and screen presentation logic. The server stores the data and provides data access and database management functions. Application logic is divided in some manner between the server and the clients. In a typical client/server interaction, the client submits a request for information from the server, which carries out the operation and responds to the client. Compared to file server designs, client/server systems are more scalable and flexible.

A fat, or thick, client design places all or most of the application processing logic at the client. A thin client design places all or most of the processing logic at the server. Compared with maintaining a central server, fat client TCO can be is higher than thin clients, because of initial hardware and software requirements and the ongoing expense of maintaining and updating remote client computers. However, the fat client design may be simpler to develop, because the architecture resembles traditional file server designs where all processing is performed at the client.

Client/server designs can be two-tier or three-tier (also called *n*-tier). In a two-tier design, the user interface resides on the client, all data resides on the server, and the application logic can run either on the server or on the client, or be divided between the client and the server. In a three-tier design, the user interface runs on the client and the data is stored on the server, just as with a two-tier design. A three-tier design also has a middle layer between the client and server that processes the client requests and translates them into data access commands that can be understood and carried out by the server. The middle layer is called an application server because it provides the application logic, or business logic. Middleware is software that connects dissimilar applications and enables them to communicate and pass data. In planning the system design, a systems analyst must also consider cost-benefit and performance issues.

The Internet has had an enormous impact on system architecture. In implementing a design, an analyst should consider ecommerce architecture, the availability of packaged solutions, and service providers. The analyst should also understand the concepts of cloud computing and Web 2.0, which are shaping the future of Internet computing. Cloud computing uses a cloud symbol to represent the Internet. The cloud, which is transparent to users, provides a hardware-independent environment where remote servers handle all processing and computing functions, and the Internet itself replaces traditional networks. Web 2.0 refers to a new generation of the web that encourages people to collaborate, interact, and share information more dynamically. Web 2.0 is fueling the explosive growth of social networking and group-based communications.

The most prevalent processing method today is online processing. Users interact directly with online systems that continuously process their transactions when and where they occur and continuously update files and databases. In contrast, batch systems process transactions in groups and execute them on a predetermined schedule. Many online systems also use batch processing to perform routine tasks, such as handling reports and accounting entries.

Networks allow the sharing of hardware, software, and data resources in order to reduce expenses and provide more capability to users. The network is represented by a seven-layer model called the OSI model.

The way a network is configured is called the network topology. Networks typically are arranged in five patterns: hierarchical, bus, ring, star, and mesh. A single mainframe computer usually controls a hierarchical network, a bus network connects workstations in a single-line communication path, a ring network connects workstations in a circular communication path, a star network connects workstations to a central computer or networking device called a switch, and a mesh network connects every network node to every other node. Wireless networks, or WLANs, based on IEEE 802.11 standards, have seen explosive growth, especially in situations where the flexibility of wireless is important. The IEEE 802.11ac standard uses MIMO, or multipath technology, which has increased wireless network speed and range. WLANs have two major topologies: BSS and ESS. Although wireless networks are very popular, they do have some limitations and disadvantages, including interference and security concerns.

The system design specification presents the complete systems design for an information system and is the basis for the presentations that complete the systems design phase. Following the presentations, the project either progresses to the systems development phase, requires additional systems design work, or is terminated.

Key Terms

802.11 A family of wireless network specifications developed by the IEEE.

802.11ac An IEEE wireless network specification, approved in 2014, that uses expanded multiple input/multiple output (MIMO) technology to achieve theoretical speeds of nearly 7 Gbps while increasing the wireless range, and is backward-compatible with 802.11 a, b, g, and n.

802.11b An IEEE wireless network specification introduced in 1999, based on a frequency of 2.4 GHz, and maximum bandwidth of 11 Mbps. Replaced by 802.11g.

802.11g An IEEE wireless network specification introduced in 2003 based on a frequency of 2.4 GHz and maximum bandwidth of 54 Mbps; compatible with and replaced 802.11b, and has been superseded by the 802.11n standard.

802.11n An IEEE wireless network specification adopted in 2009 that uses multiple input/multiple output (MIMO) technology to achieve speeds of 200+ Mbps while increasing the wireless range, and is backward-compatible with 802.11 a, b, and g.

802.16 Specifications developed by the IEEE for broadband wireless communications over MANs (metropolitan area networks). *See also* Wi-Max.

access point A central wireless device that provides network services to wireless clients.

application Part of the information system, an application handles the input, manages the processing logic, and provides the required output.

application logic The underlying business rules or logic for an application.

application server A computer acting as "middlemen" between customers and an organization's databases and applications. Often used to facilitate complex business transactions.

bandwidth The amount of data that the system can handle in a fixed time period. Bandwidth requirements are expressed in bits per second (bps).

Basic Service Set (BSS) A wireless network configuration in which a central wireless device called an access point is used to serve all wireless clients; also called infrastructure mode.

Bluetooth A form of wireless transmission very popular for short-distance wireless communication that does not require high power.

bus network A computer network where a single communication path connects the mainframe computer, server, workstations, and peripheral devices. Information is transmitted in either direction from any workstation to another workstation, and any message can be directed to a specific device.

client/server architecture Generally refers to systems that divide processing between one or more networked clients and a central server. In a typical client/ server system, the client handles the entire user interface, including data entry, data query, and screen presentation logic. The server stores the data and provides data access and database management functions. Application logic is divided in some manner between the server and the clients.

client Workstation that users interact with in a client/server design. These workstations, or computers, are supplied data, processing services, or other support from other computers, called servers.

corporate portal A website that provides various tools and features for an organization's customers, employees, suppliers, and the public.

data frames Traffic on a computer network.

data processing center A central location where physical data was delivered or transmitted in some manner and entered into the system. Users in the organization had no input or output capability, except for printed reports that were distributed by a corporate IT department.

distributed database management system (DDBMS) A system for managing data stored at more than one location. Using a DDBMS offers several advantages: Data stored closer to users can reduce network traffic; the system is scalable, so new data sites can be added without reworking the system design; and with data stored in various locations, the system is less likely to experience a catastrophic failure. A potential disadvantage of distributed data storage involves data security. It can be more difficult to maintain controls and standards when data is stored in various locations.

distributed system Company-wide systems that are connected by one or more LANs or WANs. The capabilities of a distributed system depend on the power and capacity of the underlying data communication network.

Extended Service Set (ESS) A wireless network configuration made up of two or more Basic Service Set (BSS) networks, which allows wireless clients to roam from BSS to BSS.

extensibility Refers to a system's ability to expand, change, or downsize easily to meet the changing needs of a business enterprise. Also known as scalability.

fat client A network design that locates all or most of the application processing logic at the client. Also called a thick client design.

glueware Software that connects dissimilar applications and enables them to communicate and exchange data. For example, middleware can link a departmental database to a web server that can be accessed by client computers via the Internet or a company intranet. Also called middleware.

Gbps (gigabits per second) A bandwidth or throughput measurement.

hierarchical network A network design where one computer (typically a mainframe) controls the entire network. Satellite computers or servers control lower levels of processing and network devices.

HTTP/2 The second major version of the network protocol used by the web. Released as a standard in 2015.

hub The center of a star network. Switches in modern networks have largely replaced hubs.

infrastructure mode A wireless network configuration in which a central wireless device called an access point is used to serve all wireless clients; also called Basic Service Set (BSS).

Institute of Electrical and Electronics Engineers (IEEE) A professional organization that establishes standards for telecommunications.

Internet operating system Part of the Web 2.0 model, an online computing environment created by online communities and services, based on layers of shared information that can contain text, sound bytes, images, and video clips.

knee of the curve A performance characteristic of a client/server computing environment. Client/server response times tend to increase gradually and then rise dramatically as the system nears its capacity. The point where response times increase dramatically.

legacy data The data associated with an older, less technologically advanced legacy system.

local area network (LAN) A network design that allows the sharing of data and hardware, such as printers and scanners. Advances in data communication technology have made it possible to create powerful networks that use satellite links, high-speed fiber-optic lines, or the Internet to share data.

logical topology A view of a network that describes the way the components interact, rather than the actual network cabling and connections.

mainframe architecture A system design where the server performs all the processing.

MAN (metropolitan area network) A network that uses 802.16 standards, which are broadband wireless communications protocols.

Mbps (megabits per second) A bandwidth or throughput measurement.

mesh network A network design in which each node connects to every other node. While this design is very reliable, it is also expensive to install and maintain.

multipath design A network design that relies on multiple data paths to increase bandwidth and range, using MIMO (multiple input/multiple output) technology.

multiple input/multiple output (MIMO) A wireless networking technology incorporated in the IEEE 802.11n and 802.11ac standards that uses multiple data streams and multiple antennas to achieve higher transmission speeds and substantially increase wireless range over earlier standards.

net-centric computing A distributed environment where applications and data are downloaded from servers and exchanged with peers across a network on an as-needed basis.

network topology The way a network is configured. LAN and WAN networks typically are arranged in one of four common patterns: hierarchical, bus, star, and ring.

node A physical device, wired or wireless, that can send, receive, or manage network data.

***n*-tier design** A multilevel design or architecture. For example, three-tier designs are also called n-tier designs, to indicate that some designs use more than one intermediate layer.

online system Handling transactions when and where they occur and providing output directly to users. Because it is interactive, online processing avoids delays and allows a constant dialog between the user and the system.

OSI (Open Systems Interconnection) model Describes how data actually moves from an application on one computer to an application on another networked computer. The OSI consists of seven layers, and each layer performs a specific function.

physical topology The connection structure of an actual network's cabling.

platform A specific hardware and software configuration that supports IT business goals, such as hardware connectivity and easy integration of future applications. Also called an environment.

point-of-sale (POS) The part of an information system that handles daily sales transactions and maintains the online inventory file.

portal An entrance to a multifunction website. After entering a portal, a user can navigate to a destination, using various tools and features provided by the portal designer.

proxy server A networking device that provides Internet connectivity for internal LAN users.

ring network A network resembling a circle of computers that communicate with each other. A ring network often is used when processing is performed at local sites rather than at a central location.

roaming A process that allows wireless clients to move from one access point to another, automatically associating with the stronger access point and allowing for uninterrupted service.

router A device that connects network segments, determines the most efficient data path, and guides the flow of data.

scaling on demand The ability to match network resources to needs at any given time; a feature of cloud computing. For example, during peak loads, additional cloud servers might come on line automatically to support increased workloads.

semantic web An evolution of the web where the documents shared on the Internet have semantics (meaning) and not just syntax (HTML markup). Sometimes called Web 3.0.

server Computer in a client/server design that supplies data, processing, and services to client workstations.

stand-alone When personal computers first appeared in large numbers in the 1990, users found that they could run their own word processing, spreadsheet, and database applications, without assistance from the IT group, in a mode called stand-alone computing.

star network A network design with a central device and one or more workstations connected to it in a way that forms a star pattern.

supply chain management (SCM) The coordination, integration, and management of materials, information, and finances as they move from suppliers to customers, both within and between companies. In a totally integrated supply chain, a customer order could cause a production planning system to schedule a work order, which in turn could trigger a call for certain parts from one or more suppliers.

switch Central networking device in a star network, which manages the network and acts as a conduit for all network traffic.

system architecture A translation of the logical design of an information system into a physical structure that includes hardware, software, network support, and processing methods.

thick client A system design that locates most or all of the application processing logic at the client. Also called a fat client design.

thin client A system design that locates most or all of the processing logic at the server.

three-tier design In a three-tier design, the user interface runs on the client and the data is stored on the server, just as in a two-tier design. A three-tier design also has a middle layer between the client and server that processes the client requests and translates them into data access commands that can be understood and carried out by the server.

transparent A network is transparent if a user sees the data as if it were stored on his or her own workstation.

two-tier design A network design where the user interface resides on the client, all data resides on the server, and the application logic can run either on the server or on the client, or be divided between the client and the server.

web-centric A strategy or approach that emphasizes a high degree of integration with other web-based components. A web-centric architecture follows Internet design protocols and enables a company to integrate the new application into its ecommerce strategy.

Wi-Fi (wireless fidelity) Family of popular IEEE local area network wireless networking standards, also known as 802.11, including 802.11a, b, g, and n. 802.11n is the most recent standard. 802.11ac and 802.11ad are proposed new standards.

Wi-Fi Alliance A nonprofit international association formed in 1999 to certify interoperability of wireless network products based on IEEE 802.11 specifications.

wide area network (WAN) A network spanning long distances that can link users who are continents apart.

wiki A web-based repository of information that anyone can access, contribute to, or modify.

wireless access point (WAP) A central wireless device that provides network services to wireless clients. Also called an access point.

wireless local area network (WLAN) A wireless network that is relatively inexpensive to install and is well-suited to workgroups and users who are not anchored to a specific desk or location.

Wi-Max IEEE 802.16 specifications, which are expected to enable wireless multimedia applications with a range of up to 30 miles. *See also* 802.16.

Chapter Exercises

Questions

1. This chapter begins with an architecture checklist. If you had to rank the items, from most important to least important, what would your list look like?
2. What is enterprise resource planning (ERP)? What is supply chain management (SCM)?
3. Suppose you had a client who never used a network. Explain, in everyday terms, the role of network servers and clients.
4. Describe client/server architecture, including fat and thin clients, client/server tiers, and middleware.
5. Trace the history of system architecture, with particular emphasis on the impact of the personal computer and the Internet. Be sure to include examples.
6. Is batch processing still relevant? Why or why not?
7. Explain the difference between a LAN and a WAN.
8. Define the term *topology*, and draw a sketch of each wired and wireless network topology.
9. Explain the main difference between the BSS and ESS wireless topologies. To what kind of wireless topology do the 802.16 standards apply?
10. List the sections of a system design specification, and describe the contents.

Discussion Topics

1. Information technology has advanced dramatically in recent years. At the same time, enormous changes in the business world have occurred as companies reflect global competition and more pressure for quality, speed, and customer service. Did the new technology inspire the business changes, or was it the other way around?
2. Ecommerce has seen explosive growth in recent years. What are the most important reasons for this trend? Will it continue? Why or why not?
3. This chapter describes guidelines that an analyst can use when considering a system architecture. In your view, are all the items of equal weight and importance, or should some be ranked higher? Justify your position.
4. One manager states, "When a new system is proposed, I want a written report, not an oral presentation, which is like a sales pitch. I only want to see the facts about costs, benefits, and schedules." Do you agree with that point of view?
5. How is the proliferation of mobile devices that are locally powerful, use apps instead of full-fledged applications, and rely on wireless network connectivity changing system architecture design considerations?

Projects

1. Visit the IT department at your school or a local company to learn about the network they use. Describe the network and draw a sketch of the configuration.
2. Prepare a 10-minute talk explaining Web 2.0 and cloud computing to a college class. Using the text and your own Internet research, briefly describe the five most important points you will include in your presentation.
3. Perform research on the Internet to identify a service provider that offers web-based business solutions, and write a report describing the firm and its services.
4. Perform research on the Internet to learn about emerging trends in wireless networking, and typical costs involved in the installation of a wireless LAN.
5. Examine the role wireless networks are having in the developing world. Why are some places bypassing LANs and physical cabling altogether and moving to a wireless system architecture? What are the advantages and disadvantages of this?

PHASE **4** SYSTEMS IMPLEMENTATION

© 2015 Scott Adams, Inc./Dist. by UNIVERSAL UCLICK

As the Dilbert cartoon suggests, successful systems implementation requires considerable effort. After all, without a working system delivered to the customer, all other phases of the SDLC have little meaning. In software engineering, the construction phase is often jokingly referred to as "a small matter of programming" — but of course it's no small matter at all.

Systems implementation is the fourth of five phases in the systems development life cycle. In the previous phase, systems design, a physical model of the system was developed. The output of that phase, the system design specification, is used as input to the systems implementation phase, where a completely functioning information system is created.

Chapter 11 describes application development, documentation, testing, training, data conversion, and system changeover.

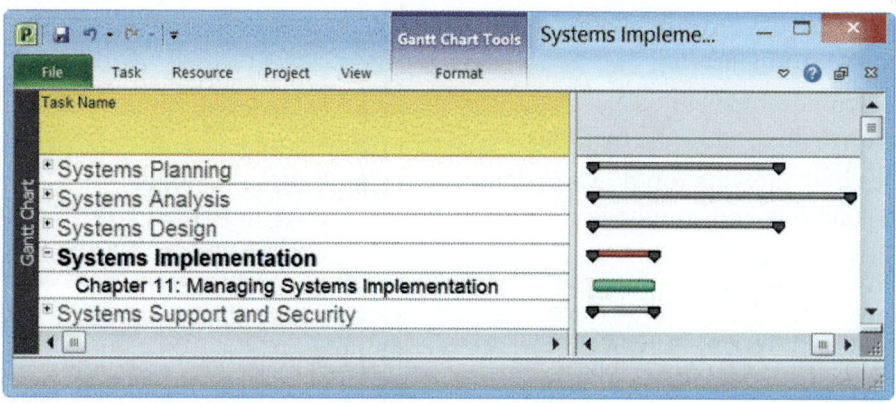

CHAPTER 11 | Managing Systems Implementation

Chapter 11 describes the systems implementation phase of the SDLC. This chapter describes application development, installation, and evaluation.

The chapter includes four "Case in Point" discussion questions to help contextualize the concepts described in the text. The "Question of Ethics" concerns an issue that all testers have to deal with: when to stop testing. In the example, there is an ethical question raised about whether or not a 90% pass rate is sufficient to ship the product, assuming the remaining bugs will be fixed once the system is operational.

LEARNING OBJECTIVES

When you finish this chapter, you should be able to:

- Explain the importance of software quality assurance and software engineering
- Describe application development using structured, object-oriented, and agile methods
- Draw a structure chart showing top-down design, modular design, cohesion, and coupling
- Explain the coding process
- Explain unit, integration, and system testing
- Differentiate between program, system, operations, and user documentation
- List the main steps in system installation and evaluation
- Develop training plans for various user groups, compare in-house and vendor training options, and describe effective training techniques
- Describe data conversion and changeover methods
- Explain post-implementation evaluation and the final report to management

CHAPTER CONTENTS

11.1 INTRODUCTION

Managing systems implementation involves application development, testing, documentation, training, data conversion, system changeover, and post-implementation evaluation of the results.

During systems implementation, the system design specification serves as a blueprint for constructing the new system. The initial task is application development, which requires systems analysts and programmers to work together to construct the necessary programs and code modules. Before a changeover, the system must be tested and documented carefully, users must be trained, and existing data must be converted. After the new system is operational, a formal evaluation of the results takes place as part of a final report to management.

11.2 SOFTWARE QUALITY ASSURANCE

In today's competitive business environment, companies are intensely concerned with the quality of their products and services. A successful organization must improve quality in every area, including its information systems. Top management must provide the leadership, encouragement, and support needed for high-quality IT resources.

No matter how carefully a system is designed and implemented, problems can occur. Rigorous testing can detect errors during implementation, but it is much less expensive to correct mistakes earlier in the development process. The main objective of **quality assurance** is to avoid problems or to identify them as soon as possible. Poor quality can result from inaccurate requirements, design problems, coding errors, faulty documentation, and ineffective testing.

To improve the finished product, software systems developers should consider software engineering and internationally recognized quality standards.

11.2.1 Software Engineering

Software engineering is the disciplined application of engineering principles to the creation of complex, long-lived applications. It is an amalgam of people, process, and technology. Software engineering is broader that just development. It includes five technical activity areas: requirements, design, construction, testing, and maintenance and evolution. It is support by non-technical activities, such as cost and effort estimation, project management, and **process improvement**.

The website for the Software Engineering Institute (SEI) at Carnegie Mellon University is shown in Figure 11-1. SEI is a leader in software engineering and provides quality standards and suggested procedures for software developers and systems analysts. SEI's primary objective is to find better, faster, and less-expensive methods of software development. To achieve that goal, SEI designed an influential set of software development standards called the **Capability Maturity Model (CMM)**, which has been used successfully by thousands of organizations around the globe. The purpose of the model is to improve software quality, reduce development time, and cut costs. The five maturity levels of the software CMM are shown in Figure 11-2.

After the original software CMM was released and updated, other capability maturity models were introduced. Eventually the SEI established a new model, called **Capability Maturity Model Integration (CMMI)**, that integrates software and systems development into a much larger framework. The CMMI tracks an organization's processes, using five maturity levels, from Level 1, which is referred to as unpredictable, poorly controlled, and reactive, to Level 5, in which the optimal result is process improvement.

FIGURE 11-1 The Software Engineering Institute at Carnegie Mellon University has had profound influence on software engineering research and practice.

Source: Software Engineering Institute

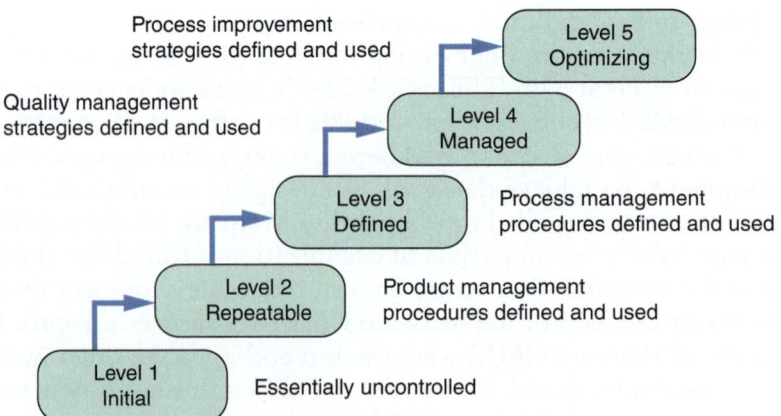

FIGURE 11-2 The CMM has five maturity levels, from Level 1 (Initial), which is essentially uncontrolled development, to Level 5 (Optimizing), in which process improvement strategies are defined and used.

Source: Scott Tilley

11.2.2 International Organization for Standardization (ISO)

What do automobiles, water, and software have in common? Along with thousands of other products and services, they are all covered by standards from the International Organization for Standardization (ISO), which was discussed in Chapter 9.

ISO standards include everything from internationally recognized symbols, such as those shown in Figure 11-3, to the ISBN numbering system that identifies this textbook. In addition, ISO seeks to offer a global consensus of what constitutes good management practices that can help firms deliver consistently high-quality products and services — including software.

Because software is so important to a company's success, many firms seek assurance that software systems, either purchased or developed in-house, will meet rigid quality standards. In 2014, ISO updated a set of guidelines, called **ISO 9000-3:2014**, which provided a quality assurance framework for developing and maintaining software.

A company can specify ISO standards when it purchases software from a supplier or use ISO guidelines for in-house software development to ensure that the final result measures up to ISO standards. ISO requires a specific development plan, which outlines a step-by-step process for transforming user requirements into a finished product. ISO standards can be quite detailed. For example, ISO requires that a software supplier document all testing and maintain records of test results. If problems are found, they must be resolved, and any modules affected must be retested. Additionally, software and hardware specifications of all test equipment must be documented and included in the test records.

FIGURE 11-3 ISO symbols include internationally recognized symbols.

bytedust/Shutterstock.com

11.3 OVERVIEW OF APPLICATION DEVELOPMENT

Application development is the process of constructing the programs and code modules that serve as the building blocks of the information system. In Chapter 1, it was explained that structured analysis, object-oriented (O-O) analysis, and agile methods are three popular development options. Regardless of the method, the objective is to translate the design into program and code modules that will function properly. Because systems implementation usually is very labor-intensive, developers often use project management tools and techniques to control schedules and budgets.

11.3.1 Review the System Design

At this point, it is helpful to review the tasks involved in the creation of the system design:

- Chapter 4 focused on requirements modeling and how to use functional decomposition diagrams (FDDs) to break complex business operations down into smaller units, or functions.

- Chapter 5 focused on structured data and process modeling, and data flow diagrams (DFDs). The development of process descriptions for functional primitive processes that documented the business logic and processing requirements was also discussed.

- Chapter 6 focused on an object-oriented model of the new system that included use case diagrams, class diagrams, sequence diagrams, state transition diagrams, and activity diagrams.
- Chapter 7 focused on selecting a development strategy.
- Chapter 8 focused on designing the user interface.
- Chapter 9 focused on data design issues, analyzing relationships between system entities, and constructing entity-relationship diagrams (ERDs).
- Chapter 10 focused on overall system architecture considerations.

Taken together, this set of tasks produced an overall design and a plan for physical implementation.

11.3.2 Application Development Tasks

If traditional structured or object-oriented (O-O) methods were used during system design, the process of translating the design into a functioning application can begin. If an agile development method was selected, development begins with planning the project, followed by laying the groundwork, assembling the team, and preparing to interact with the customers.

TRADITIONAL METHODS: Building a new system requires careful planning. After an overall strategy is established, individual modules must be designed, coded, tested, and documented. A module consists of related program code organized into small units that are easy to understand and maintain. After the modules are developed and tested individually, more testing takes place, along with thorough documentation of the entire system, as shown in Figure 11-4.

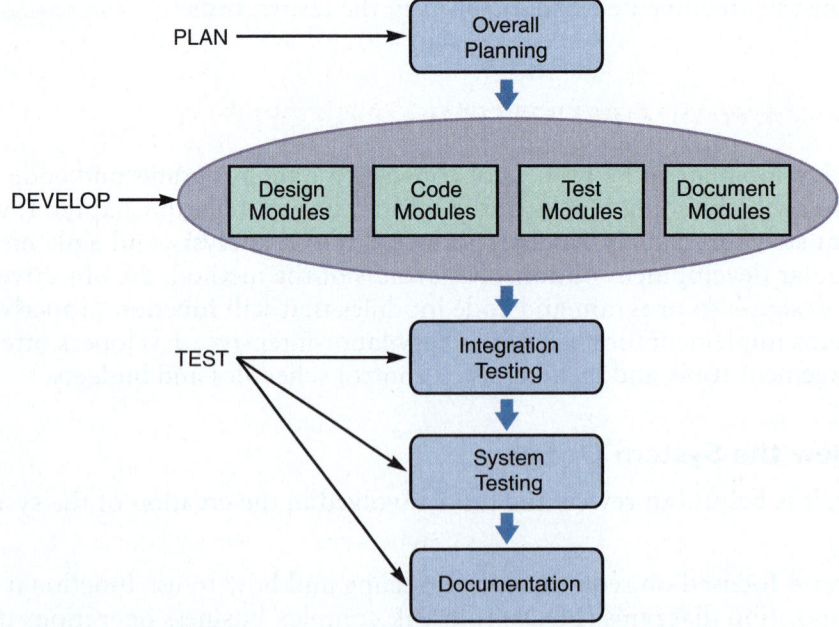

FIGURE 11-4 The main steps in traditional application development.

When program modules are created using structured or object-oriented methods, the process starts by reviewing requirements documentation from prior SDLC phases and creating a set of program designs. If a documentation file was built early in the development process and updated regularly, there is a valuable repository of information. The documentation centerpiece is the system design specification, accompanied by diagrams, source documents, screen layouts, report designs, data dictionary entries, and user comments. If a CASE tool was used during the systems analysis and design process, the analyst's job will be much easier. At this point, coding and testing tasks begin. Although programmers typically perform the actual coding, IT managers usually assign systems analysts to work with them as a team.

AGILE METHODS: If an agile approach is decided upon, intense communication and collaboration will now begin between the IT team and the users or customers. The objective is to create the system through an iterative process of planning, designing, coding, and testing. Agile projects use various iterative and incremental models, including Extreme Programming (XP) as shown in Figure 11-5. Agile development and XP are discussed in detail later in this chapter.

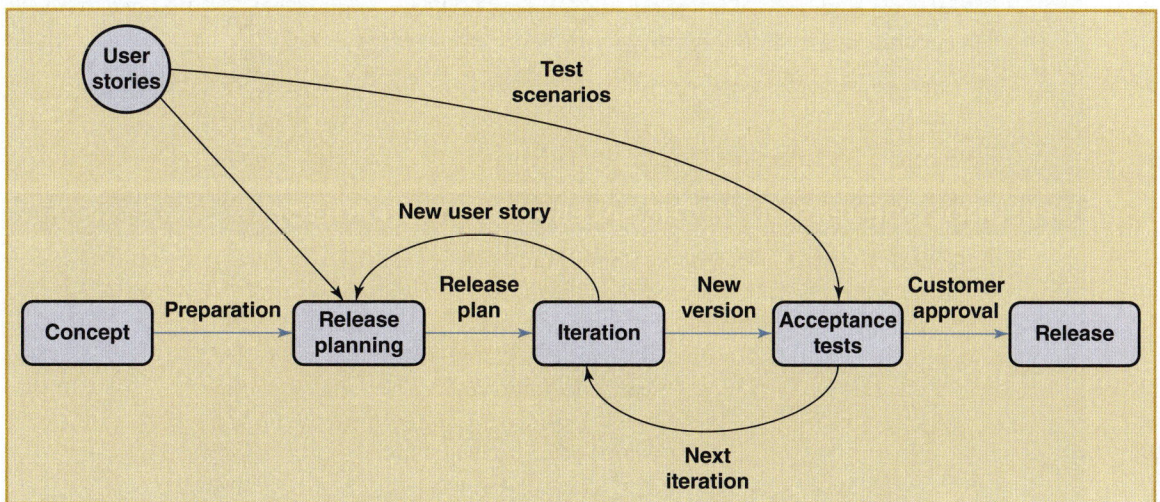

FIGURE 11-5 Simplified model of an Extreme Programming (XP) project. Note the emphasis on iteration and testing.

11.3.3 Systems Development Tools

Each systems development approach has its own set of tools that has worked well for that method. For example, structured development relies heavily on DFDs and structure charts; object-oriented methods use a variety of Unified Modeling Language (UML) diagrams, including use case, class, sequence, and transition state diagrams; and agile methods tend to use spiral or other iterative models such as the example shown in Figure 11-5.

   System developers can also use multipurpose tools to help them translate the system logic into properly functioning program modules. These generic tools include entity-relationship diagrams, flowcharts, pseudocode, decision tables, and decision trees.

ENTITY-RELATIONSHIP DIAGRAMS: Chapter 9 described the use of entity-relationship diagrams to show the interaction among system entities and objects. An ERD is a useful tool regardless of the methodology used because the various relationships (one-to-one, one-to-many, and many-to-many) must be understood and implemented in the application development process.

FLOWCHARTS: As described in Chapter 5, flowcharts can be used to represent program logic and are very useful in visualizing a modular design. A flowchart represents logical rules and interaction graphically, using a series of symbols connected by arrows. Using flowcharts, programmers can break large systems into subsystems and modules that are easier to understand and code.

PSEUDOCODE: Pseudocode is a technique for representing program logic. Pseudocode is similar to structured English, which was explained in Chapter 5. Pseudocode is not language-specific, so it can be used to describe a software module in plain English without requiring strict syntax rules. Using pseudocode, a systems analyst or a programmer can describe program actions that can be implemented in any programming language. Figure 11-6 illustrates an example of pseudocode that documents a sales promotion policy.

SAMPLE OF A SALES PROMOTION POLICY
• Preferred customers who order more than $1,000 are entitled to a 5% discount, and an additional 5% discount if they used our charge card.
• Preferred customers who do not order more than $1,000 receive a $25 bonus coupon.
• All other customers receive a $5 bonus coupon.

PSEUDOCODE VERSION OF THE SALES PROMOTION POLICY
IF customer is a preferred customer, and
IF customer orders more than $1,000 then
Apply a 5% discount, and
IF customer uses our charge card, then
Apply an additional 5% discount
ELSE
Award a $25 bonus coupon
ELSE
Award a $5 bonus coupon

FIGURE 11-6 Sample of a sales promotion policy with logical rules (top) and a pseudocode version of the same policy (bottom). Notice the alignment and indentation of the logic statements in the pseudocode.

DECISION TABLES AND DECISION TREES: As explained in Chapter 5, decision tables and decision trees can be used to model business logic for an information system. In addition to being used as modeling tools, analysts and programmers can use decision tables and decision trees during system development, as code modules that implement the logical rules are developed. Figure 11-7 shows an example of a decision tree that documents the sales promotion policy shown in Figure 11-6. Notice that the decision tree accurately reflects the sales promotion policy, which has three separate conditions and four possible outcomes.

11.3.4 Project Management

Regardless of whether structured analysis, object-oriented design, or agile methods are used, even a modest-sized project might have hundreds or even thousands of modules. For this reason, application development can become quite complex and difficult to manage. At this stage, project management is especially important.

Users and managers are looking forward to the new system, and it is very important to set realistic schedules, meet project deadlines, control costs, and maintain

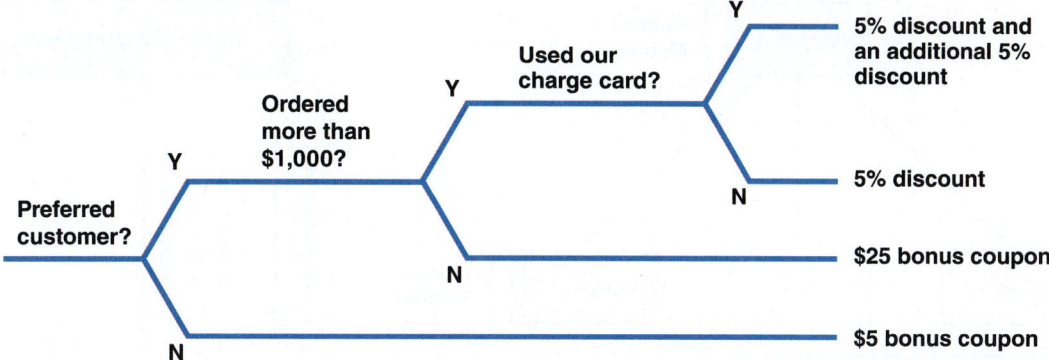

FIGURE 11-7 Sample decision tree that reflects the sales promotion policy in Figure 11-6. Like a decision table, a decision tree shows the action to be taken based on certain properties.

quality. To achieve these goals, the systems analyst or project manager should use project management tools and techniques similar to those described in Chapter 3 to monitor and control the development effort.

The following sections describe the application development process. Structured development techniques and tools are discussed first, followed by object-oriented and agile development methods.

11.4 STRUCTURED APPLICATION DEVELOPMENT

Structured application development usually involves a **top-down approach**, which proceeds from a general design to a detailed structure. After a systems analyst documents the system's requirements, he or she breaks the system down into subsystems and modules in a process called **partitioning**. This approach is also called modular design, and is similar to constructing a leveled set of DFDs. By assigning modules to different programmers, several development areas can proceed at the same time. As explained in Chapter 3, project management software can be used to monitor work on each module, forecast overall development time, estimate required human and technical resources, and calculate a critical path for the project.

Because all the modules must work together properly, an analyst must proceed carefully, with constant input from programmers and IT management to achieve a sound, well-integrated structure. The analyst must also ensure that integration capability is built into each design and thoroughly tested.

11.4.1 Structure Charts

Structure charts show the program modules and the relationships among them. A structure chart consists of rectangles that represent the program modules, with arrows and other symbols that provide additional information. Typically, a higher-level module, called a **control module**, directs lower-level modules, called **subordinate modules**. In a structure chart, symbols represent various actions or conditions. Structure chart symbols represent modules, data couples, control couples, conditions, and loops.

MODULE: A rectangle represents a module, as shown in Figure 11-8. In the figure, double vertical lines at the edges of a rectangle indicate that module 1.3 is a library module. A **library module** is reusable code and can be invoked from more than one point in the chart.

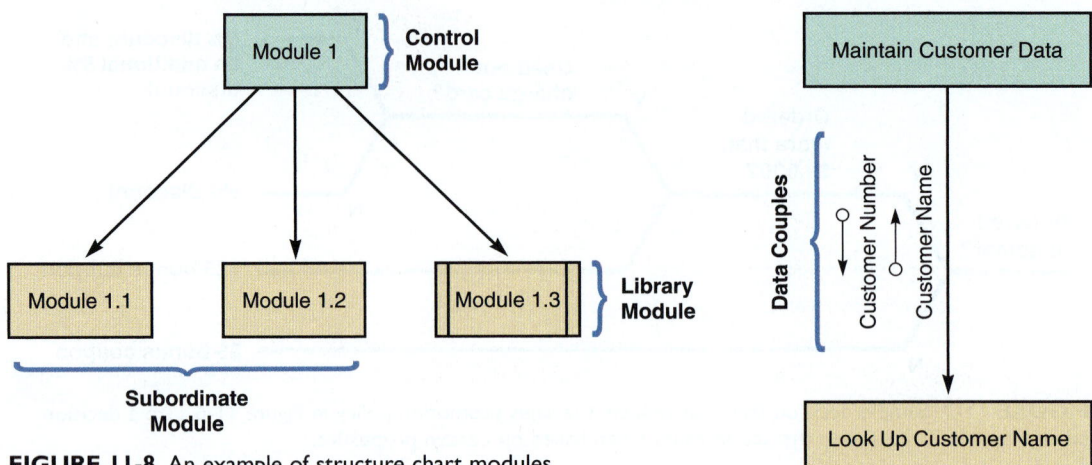

FIGURE 11-8 An example of structure chart modules.

FIGURE 11-9 An example of a structure chart data couple.

DATA COUPLE: An arrow with an empty circle represents a data couple. A data couple shows data that one module passes to another. In the data couple example shown in Figure 11-9, the Look Up Customer Name module exchanges data with the Maintain Customer Data module.

CONTROL COUPLE: An arrow with a filled circle represents a control couple. A control couple shows a message, also called a status flag, which one module sends to another. In the example shown in Figure 11-10, the Update Customer File module sends an Account Overdue flag back to the Maintain Customer Data module. A module uses a flag to signal a specific condition or action to another module.

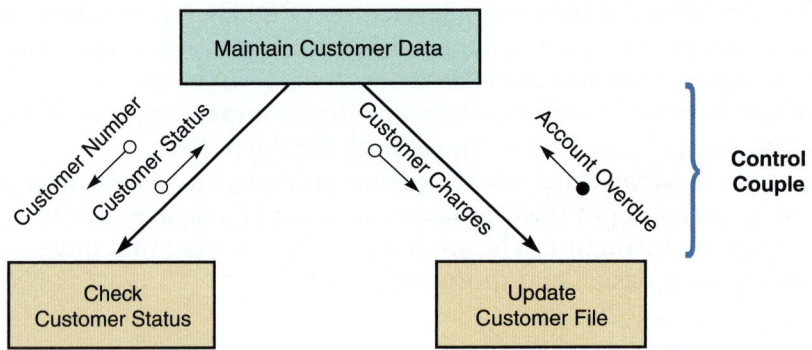

FIGURE 11-10 An example of a structure chart control couple.

CONDITION: A line with a diamond on one end represents a condition. A condition line indicates that a control module determines which subordinate modules will be invoked, depending on a specific condition. In the example shown in Figure 11-11, Sort Inventory Parts is a control module with a condition line that triggers one of the three subordinate modules.

LOOP: A curved arrow represents a loop. A loop indicates that one or more modules are repeated. In the example shown in Figure 11-12, the Get Student Grades and Calculate GPA modules are repeated.

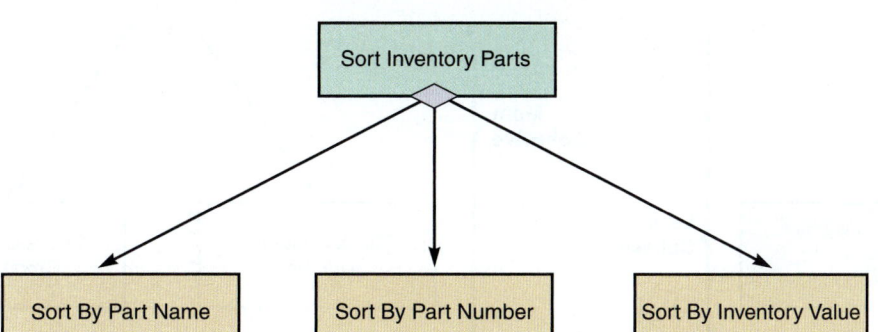

FIGURE 11-11 The diagram shows a control module that triggers three subordinate modules.

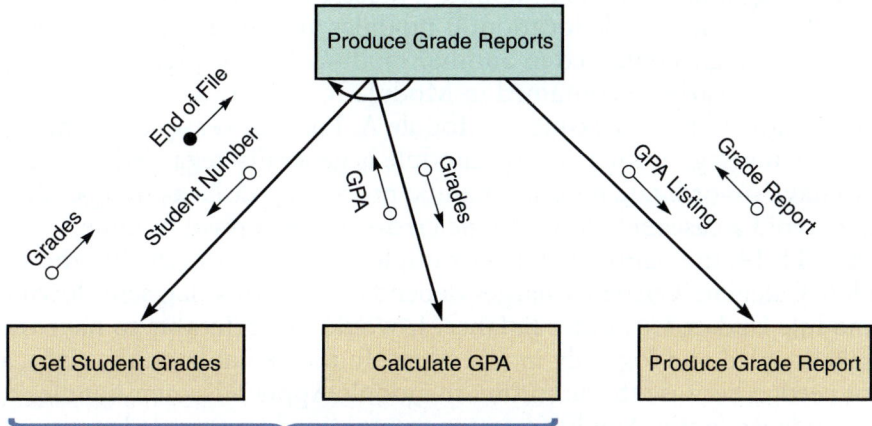

The curved arrow indicates that these modules are repeated.

FIGURE 11-12 The diagram shows a structure chart loop with two repeating modules.

11.4.2 Cohesion and Coupling

Cohesion and coupling are important tools for evaluating the overall design. As explained in the following sections, it is desirable to have modules that are highly cohesive and loosely coupled. Otherwise, system maintenance becomes more costly due to difficulties in making changes to the system's structure.

Cohesion measures a module's scope and processing characteristics. A module that performs a single function or task has a high degree of cohesion, which is desirable. Because it focuses on a single task, a cohesive module is much easier to code and reuse. For example, a module named Verify Customer Number is more cohesive than a module named Calculate and Print Statements. If the word *and* is found in a module name, this implies that more than one task is involved.

If a module must perform multiple tasks, more complex coding is required and the module will be more difficult to create and maintain. To make a module more cohesive, split it into separate units, each with a single function. For example, by splitting the module Check Customer Number and Credit Limit in Figure 11-13 into two separate modules, Check Customer Number and Check Customer Credit Limit, cohesion is greatly improved.

Coupling describes the degree of interdependence among modules. Modules that are independent are loosely coupled, which is desirable. Loosely coupled modules are easier to maintain and modify because the logic in one module does not affect other

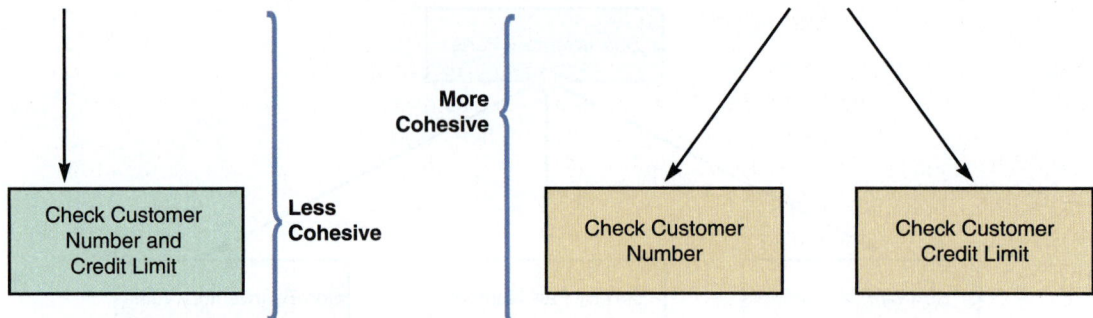

FIGURE 11-13 Two examples of cohesion. Notice that the single module on the left is less cohesive than the two modules on the right.

modules. If a programmer needs to update a loosely coupled module, he or she can accomplish the task in a single location. If modules are **tightly coupled**, one module is linked to internal logic contained in another module. For example, Module A might refer to an internal variable contained in Module B. In that case, a logic error in the Module B will affect the processing in Module A. For that reason, passing a status flag down as a message from a control module is generally regarded as poor design. It is better to have subordinate modules handle processing tasks as independently as possible, to avoid a cascade effect of logic errors in the control module.

In Figure 11-14, the tightly coupled example on the left shows that the subordinate module Calculate Current Charges depends on a status flag sent down from the control module Update Customer Balance. It would be preferable to have the modules loosely coupled and logically independent. In the example on the right, a status flag is not needed because the subordinate module Apply Discount handles discount processing independently. Any logic errors are confined to a single location: the Apply Discount module.

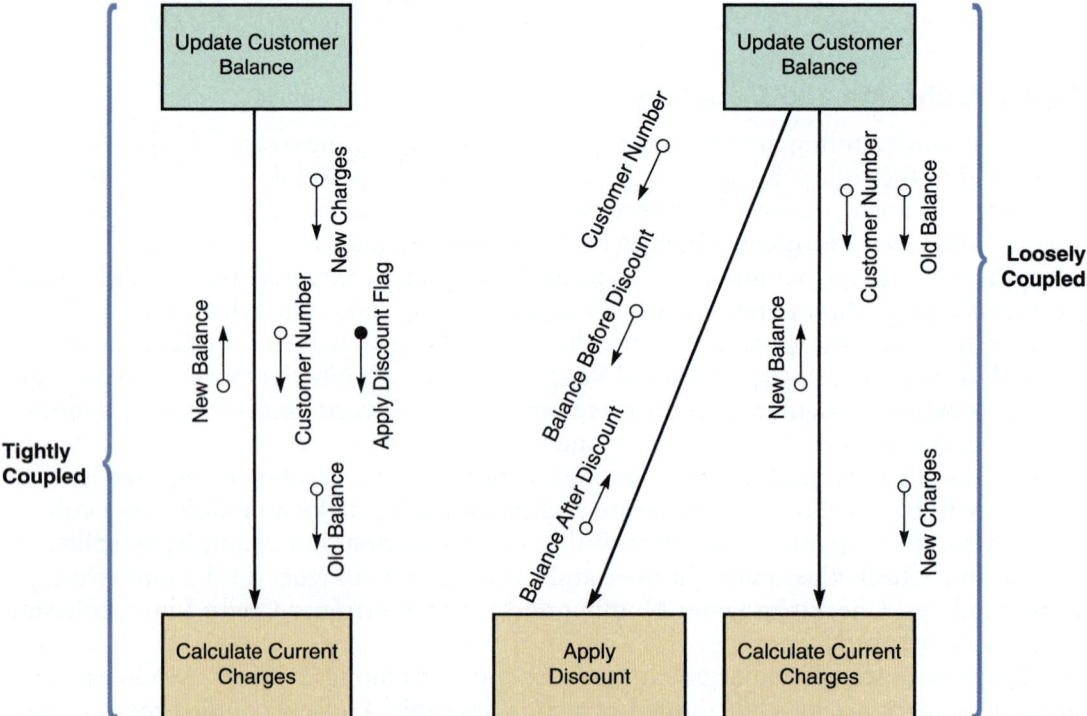

FIGURE 11-14 An example of tightly coupled and loosely coupled structure charts.

11.4.3 Drawing a Structure Chart

If a structured analysis method was used during system design, the structure charts will be based on the DFDs created during data and process modeling.

Typically, four steps are followed when creating a structure chart. DFDs are reviewed to identify the processes and methods, identify the program modules and determine control-subordinate relationships, add symbols for couples and loops, and analyze the structure chart to ensure that it is consistent with the system documentation.

STEP 1. REVIEW THE DFDS: The first step is to review all DFDs for accuracy and completeness, especially if changes have occurred since the systems analysis phase. If object models were also developed, they should be analyzed to identify the objects, the methods that each object must perform, and the relationships among the objects. A method is similar to a functional primitive and requires code to implement the necessary actions.

STEP 2. IDENTIFY MODULES AND RELATIONSHIPS: Working from the logical model, functional primitives or object methods are transformed into program modules. When analyzing a set of DFDs, remember that each DFD level represents a processing level. If DFDs are being used, one works way down from the context diagram to the lower-level diagrams, identifying control modules and subordinate modules, until the functional primitives are reached. If more cohesion is desired, processes can be divided into smaller modules that handle a single task. Figure 11-15 shows a structure chart based on the order system from Chapter 5. Notice how the three-level structure chart relates to the three DFD levels.

STEP 3. ADD COUPLES, LOOPS, AND CONDITIONS: Next, couples, loops, and conditions are added to the structure chart. If DFDs are being used, the data flows and the data dictionary can be reviewed to identify the data elements that pass from one module to another. In addition to adding the data couples, control couples are added where a module is sending a control parameter, or flag, to another module. Loops and condition lines that indicate repetitive or alternative processing steps are also added, as shown in Figure 11-15. If an object model was developed, the class diagrams and object relationship diagrams can be reviewed to be sure that the interaction among the objects is fully understood.

STEP 4. ANALYZE THE STRUCTURE CHART AND THE DATA DICTIONARY: At this point, the structure chart is ready for careful analysis. Each process, data element, or object method should be checked to ensure that the chart reflects all previous documentation and that the logic is correct. All modules should be strongly cohesive and loosely coupled. Often, several versions of the chart must be drawn. Some CASE tools can help analyze the chart and identify problem areas.

11.5 OBJECT-ORIENTED APPLICATION DEVELOPMENT

Object-oriented methods were described in Chapter 6. O-O analysis makes it easier to translate an object model directly into an object-oriented programming language. This process is called object-oriented development, or OOD. Although many structured design concepts also apply to object-oriented methodology, there are some differences.

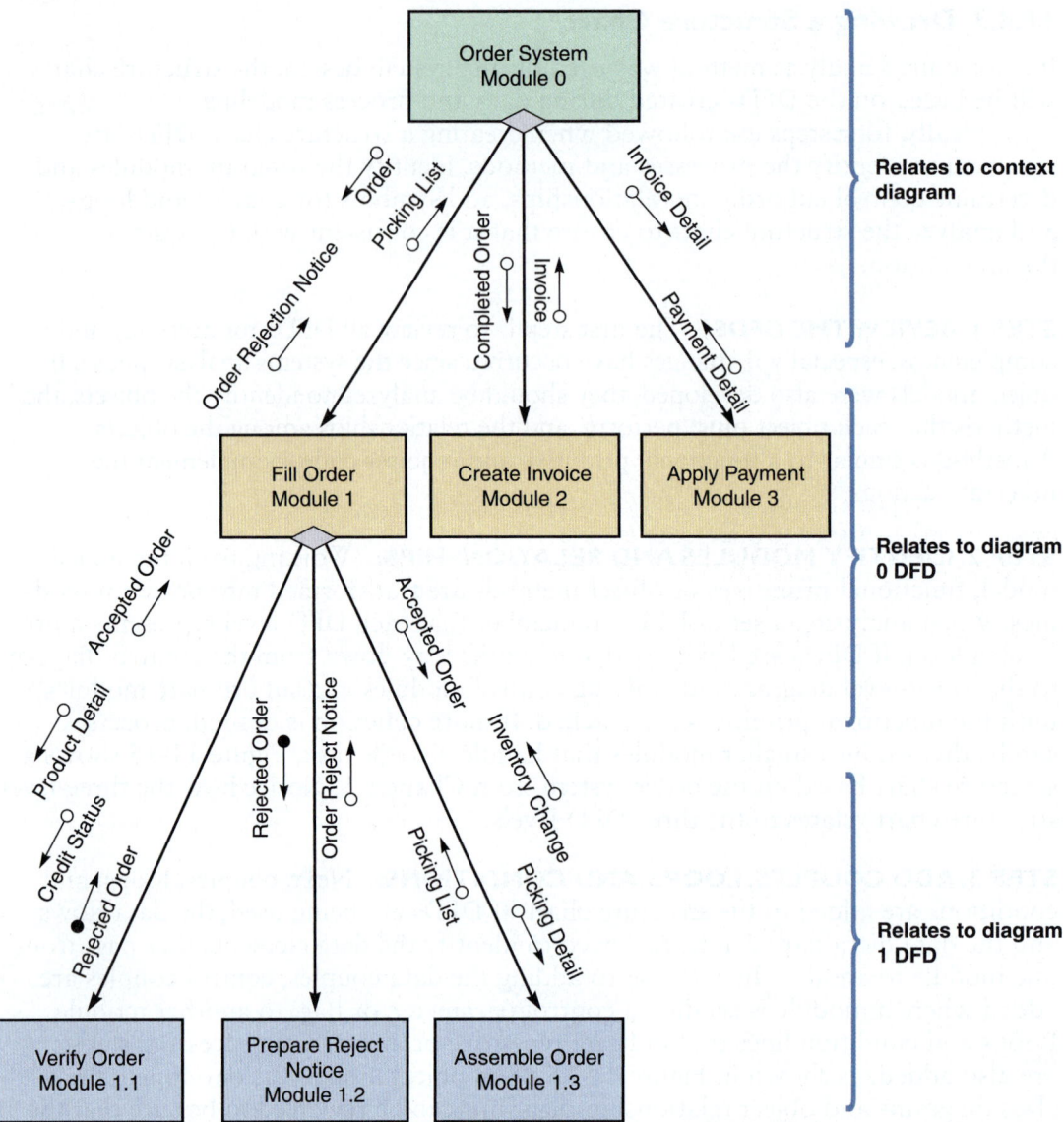

FIGURE 11-15 A structure chart based on the order system DFDs in Chapter 5. The three-level structure chart relates to the three DFD levels.

11.5.1 Characteristics of Object-Oriented Application Development

When implementing a structured design, a structure chart is used to describe the interaction between program modules, as explained earlier. In contrast, when implementing an object-oriented design, relationships between objects already exist. Because object interaction is defined during the O-O analysis process, the object model itself represents the application's structure.

As explained in Chapter 6, objects contain both data and program logic, called **methods**. Individual object instances belong to classes of objects with similar characteristics. The relationship and interaction among classes are described using a class diagram, such as the one shown in Figure 11-16. A class diagram includes the class *attributes*, which describe the characteristics of objects in the class, and *methods*, which represent program logic. For example, the Customer class describes customer objects. Customer attributes include Number, Name, Address, and so on. Methods for the Customer class include Place order, Modify order, and Pay invoice, among others. The Customer class can exchange messages with the Order class.

In addition to class diagrams, programmers get an overview of object interaction by using object relationship diagrams that were developed during the O-O analysis process. For example, Figure 11-17 shows an object relationship diagram for a fitness center. Notice that the model shows the objects and how they interact to perform business functions and transactions.

Properly implemented, object-oriented development can speed up projects, reduce costs, and improve overall quality. However, these results are not always achieved. Organizations sometimes have unrealistic expectations and do not spend enough time learning about, preparing for, and implementing the OOD process. For example, no one would build a bridge without an analysis of needs, supporting data, and a detailed blueprint — and the bridge would not be opened for traffic until it had been carefully inspected and checked to ensure that all specifications were met. O-O software developers sometimes forget that the basic rules of architecture also apply to their projects.

In summary, to secure the potential benefits of object-oriented development, systems analysts must carefully analyze, design, implement, test, and document their O-O projects.

11.5.2 Implementation of Object-Oriented Designs

When a programmer translates an object-oriented design into an application, he or she analyzes the classes, attributes, methods, and messages that are documented in the object model. During this process, the programmer makes necessary revisions and updates to class diagrams, sequence diagrams, state transition diagrams, and activity diagrams.

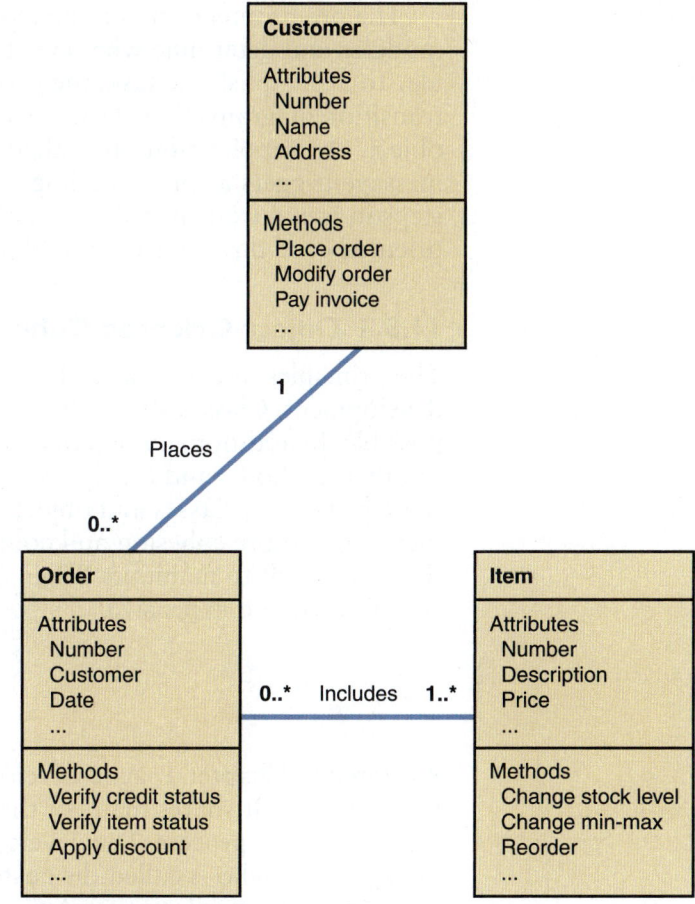

FIGURE 11-16 A simplified class diagram for a customer order processing system.

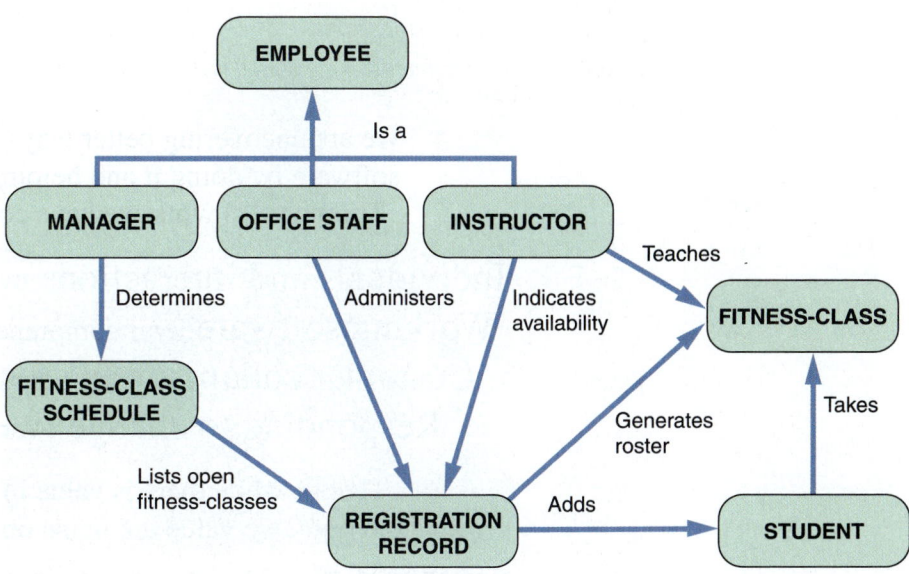

FIGURE 11-17 An object-relationship diagram for a fitness center.

The programmer's main objective is to translate object methods into program code modules and determine what event or message will trigger the execution of each module. To accomplish the task, the programmer analyzes sequence diagrams and state transition diagrams that show the events and messages that trigger changes to an object. O-O applications are called event-driven because each event, transaction, or message triggers a corresponding action. The programmer can represent the program steps in pseudocode initially, or use CASE tools and code generators to create object-oriented code directly from the object model.

11.5.3 Object-Oriented Cohesion and Coupling

The principles of cohesion and coupling also apply to object-oriented application development. Classes should be as loosely coupled (independent of other classes) as possible. In addition, an object's methods should also be loosely coupled (independent of other methods) and highly cohesive (perform closely related actions). By following these principles, classes and objects are easier to understand and edit. O-O programmers who ignore cohesion and coupling concepts may end up creating a web of code that is difficult to maintain. When code is scattered in various places, editing becomes complicated and expensive.

11.6 AGILE APPLICATION DEVELOPMENT

As stated in Chapter 1, agile development is a distinctly different systems development method. It shares many of the steps found in traditional development but uses a highly iterative process. The development team is in constant communication with the primary user, who is called the customer, shaping and forming the system to match the customer's specifications. Agile development is aptly named because it is based on a quick and nimble development process that easily adapts to change. Agile development focuses on small teams, intense communication, and rapid development iterations. The four key values of agile software development are shown in Figure 11-18.

Manifesto for Agile Software Development

We are uncovering better ways of developing software by doing it and helping others do it. Through this work we have come to value:

Individuals and interactions over processes and tools
Working software over comprehensive documentation
Customer collaboration over contract negotiation
Responding to change over following a plan

That is, while there is value in the items on the right, we value the items on the left more.

FIGURE 11-18 The manifesto for agile software development.
Source: Agile Software Development

Programmers can use popular agile-friendly languages, such as Python, Ruby, and Perl. However, agile methods do not require a specific programming language, and programmers also use various object-oriented languages, such as Java, C++, C#, and others.

11.6.1 Extreme Programming (XP)

Extreme Programming (XP) is an agile development method. It is an iterative approach, as shown in Figure 11-19, where a team of users and developers immerse themselves in systems development. XP supporters emphasize values such as simplicity, communication, feedback, respect, and courage. Success requires strong commitment to the process, corporate support, and dedicated team members.

The Values of Extreme Programming

Extreme Programming (XP) is based on values. The rules we just examined are the natural extension and consequence of maximizing our values. XP isn't really a set of rules but rather a way to work in harmony with your personal and corporate values. Start with XP's values listed here then add your own by reflecting them in the changes you make to the rules.

Simplicity: We will do what is needed and asked for, but no more. This will maximize the value created for the investment made to date. We will take small simple steps to our goal and mitigate failures as they happen. We will create something we are proud of and maintain it long term for reasonable costs.

Communication: Everyone is part of the team and we communicate face to face daily. We will work together on everything from requirements to code. We will create the best solution to our problem that we can together.

Feedback: We will take every iteration commitment seriously by delivering working software. We demonstrate our software early and often then listen carefully and make any changes needed. We will talk about the project and adapt our process to it, not the other way around.

Respect: Everyone gives and feels the respect they deserve as a valued team member. Everyone contributes value even if it's simply enthusiasm. Developers respect the expertise of the customers and vice versa. Management respects our right to accept responsibility and receive authority over our own work.

Courage: We will tell the truth about progress and estimates. We don't document excuses for failure because we plan to succeed. We don't fear anything because no one ever works alone. We will adapt to changes when ever they happen.

FIGURE 11-19 The five core values of extreme programming (XP).
Source: ©2009, Don Wells

Extreme Programming uses a concept called **pair programming**. In pair programming, two programmers work on the same task on the same computer; one drives (programs) while the other navigates (watches). The onlooker examines the code strategically to see the *forest* while the driver is concerned with the individual *trees* immediately in front of him or her. The two discuss their ideas continuously throughout the process.

Another important concept in XP is that unit tests are designed *before* code is written. This **test-driven development (TDD)** focuses on end results from the beginning and prevents programmers from straying from their goals. Because of the magnitude and intensity of the multicycle process, agile testing relies heavily on automated testing methods.

11.6.2 User Stories

Suppose that a customer has requested a sales tracking system. The first step in an agile process, like any other development method, would be to define the system requirements. The customer begins by meeting with programmers and providing user stories. A user story is a short, simple requirements definition. Programmers review user stories to determine the project's requirements, priorities, and scope. Here are three user story examples:

- *As the sales manager, I want to identify fast or slow moving items so I can manage our inventory more effectively.*

- *As a store manager, I need enough lead time to replenish my stock so I don't run out of hot items.*

- *As a sales representative, I want to offer the best selection of fast selling items and clear out the old stock that is not moving.*

User stories do not deal with technical details and are so short that they are often written on index cards. Each user story is given a priority by the customer, so the requirements can be ranked. In addition, programmers assign a score to each user story that indicates the estimated difficulty of implementation. This information helps the team form a plan and assign its resources. Projects are often composed of many user stories, which taken together form *epics*, from which programmers can estimate the scope, time requirements, and difficulty of the project. In addition to the user stories, frequent face-to-face meetings with customers provide a higher level of detail as the project progresses.

11.6.3 Iterations and Releases

The team must also develop a release plan, which specifies when user stories will be implemented and the timing of the releases. Releases are relatively frequent, and each system release is like a prototype that can be tested and modified as needed.

User stories are implemented in a series of iteration cycles. An iteration cycle includes planning, designing, coding, and testing of one or more features based on user stories. At the beginning of each iteration cycle, which is often two weeks long, the team holds an iteration planning meeting to break down the user stories into specific tasks that are assigned to team members. As new user stories or features are added, the team reviews and modifies the release plan.

As with any development process, success is determined by the customer's approval. The programming team regularly meets with the customer, who tests prototype releases as they become available. This process usually results in additional user stories, and changes are implemented in the next iteration cycle. As the project's code changes during each iteration, obsolete code is removed and remaining code is restructured to keep the system up to date. The iteration cycles continue until all user stories have been implemented, tested, and accepted.

11.6.4 The Future of Agile Development

Agile methodology is very popular for software projects. Its supporters boast that it speeds up software development and delivers precisely what the customer wants, when the customer wants it, while fostering teamwork and empowering employees. However, there are drawbacks to this adaptive rather than predictive method. Critics of agile development often claim that because it focuses on quick iterations and fast releases, it lacks discipline and produces systems of questionable quality. In addition, agile methodology generally does not work as well for larger projects because of their complexity and the lack of focus on a well-defined end product.

Before implementing agile development, the proposed system and development methods should be examined carefully. As experienced IT professionals know, a one-size-fits-all solution does not exist. For more information on agile methods, refer to the discussion of systems development methods in Chapter 1 and agile methods such as Scrum in Chapter 4.

11.7 CODING

Coding is the process of turning program logic into specific instructions that the computer system can execute. Working from a specific design, a programmer uses a programming language to transform program logic into code statements. An individual programmer might create a small program, while larger programs typically are divided into modules that several individuals or groups can work on simultaneously.

11.7.1 Programming Environments

Each IT department has its favorite programming environment and standards. Visual Basic, Java, and Python are examples of commonly used programming languages, and many commercial packages use a proprietary set of commands. As the trend toward Internet-based and mobile applications continues, HTML/XML, Java, Swift, and other web-centric languages will be used extensively.

To simplify the integration of system components and reduce code development time, many programmers use an integrated development environment (IDE). IDEs can make it easier to program interactive software products by providing built-in tools and advanced features, such as real-time error detection, syntax hints, highlighted code, class browsers, and version control. As discussed in Chapter 7, IBM WebSphere and Microsoft .NET are popular IDEs. In addition to these commercial packages, programmers can use open-source IDEs, such as Eclipse. IDEs are discussed in more detail in Part B of the Systems Analyst's Toolkit.

11.7.2 Generating Code

Earlier chapters explained that systems analysts use application generators, report writers, screen generators, fourth-generation languages, and other CASE tools that produce code directly from program design specifications. Some commercial applications can generate editable program code directly from macros, keystrokes, or mouse actions. For example, IBM's Rational toolset can generate code fragments based on UML design documents.

11.8 TESTING THE SYSTEM

After coding, a programmer must test each program to make sure it functions correctly. Later, programs are tested in groups, and finally the development team must test the entire system. The first step is to compile the program using a CASE tool or a language compiler. This process detects syntax errors, which are language grammar errors. The programmer corrects the errors until the program executes properly.

Next, the programmer desk checks the program. **Desk checking** is the process of reviewing the program code to spot **logic errors**, which produce incorrect results. This process can be performed by the person who wrote the program or by other programmers. Many organizations require a more formal type of desk checking called a **structured walkthrough**, or **code review**.

Typically, a group of three to five IT staff members participate in code review. The group usually consists of project team members and might include other programmers and analysts who did not work on the project. The objective is to have a peer group identify errors, apply quality standards, and verify that the program meets the requirements of the system design specification. Errors found during a structured walkthrough are easier to fix while coding is still in the developmental stages.

In addition to analyzing logic and program code, the project team usually holds a session with users called a **design walkthrough**, to review the interface with a cross-section of people who will work with the new system and ensure that all necessary features have been included. This is a continuation of the modeling and prototyping effort that began early in the systems development process.

The next step in application development is to initiate a sequence of unit testing, integration testing, and system testing, as shown in Figure 11-20.

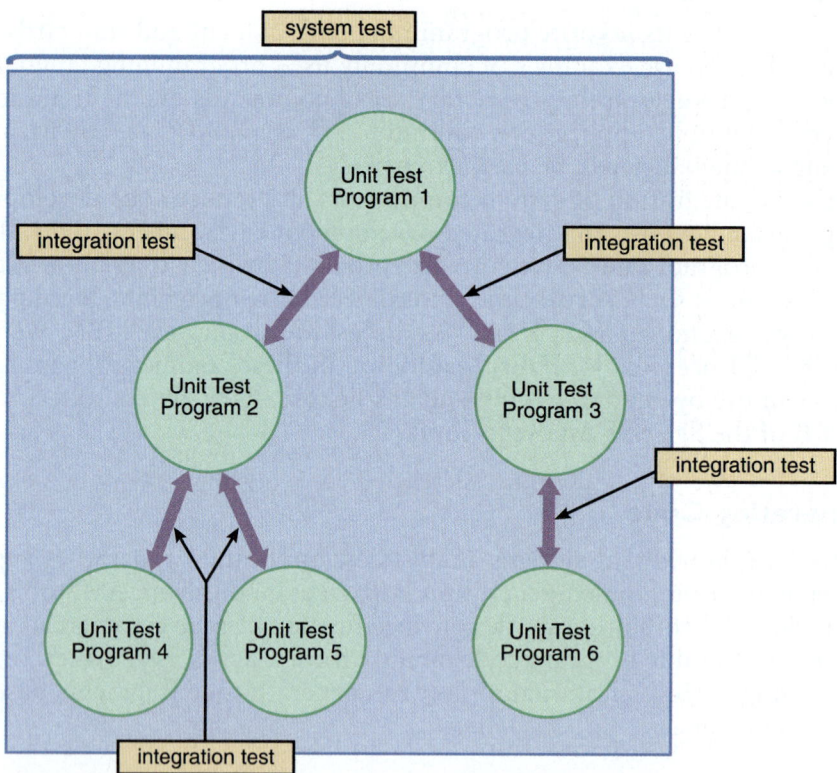

FIGURE 11-20 The first step in testing is unit testing, followed by integration testing and then system testing.

11.8.1 Unit Testing

The testing of an individual program or module is called **unit testing**. The objective is to identify and eliminate execution errors that could cause the program to terminate abnormally, and logic errors that could have been missed during desk checking.

CASE IN POINT 11.1:   YOUR MOVE, INC.

You work for April Olivia, the IT manager at Your Move, Inc., a large retailer specializing in games of all kinds. The company is in the final stages of developing a new inventory management system, and April wants you to handle the testing.

"Be sure you put lots of errors into the test data," she said. "Users are bound to make mistakes, and we need to design built-in safeguards that will catch the mistakes, and either fix them automatically, or alert the user to the problem."

Of course, April's comment makes a lot of sense, but you've never done this before and you wonder how to proceed. Should you try to invent every possible data error? How will you know that you've thought of every situation that could occur? Consider the problem, develop an approach, and write up your plan in a brief memo.

Test data should contain both correct data and erroneous data and should test all possible situations that could occur. For example, for a field that allows a range of numeric values, the test data should contain minimum values, maximum values, values outside the acceptable range, and alphanumeric characters. During testing, programmers can use software tools to determine the location and potential causes of program errors.

During unit testing, programmers must test programs that interact with other programs and files individually before they are integrated into the system. This requires a technique called stub testing. In **stub testing**, the programmer simulates each program outcome or result and displays a message to indicate whether or not the program executed successfully. Each stub represents an entry or exit point that will be linked later to another program or data file.

To obtain an independent analysis, someone other than the programmer who wrote the program usually creates the test data and reviews the results. Systems analysts frequently create test data during the systems design phase as part of an overall test plan. A **test plan** consists of detailed procedures that specify how and when the testing will be performed, who will participate, and what test data will be used. A comprehensive test plan should include scenarios for every possible situation the program could encounter.

Regardless of who creates the test plan, the project manager or a designated analyst also reviews the final test results. Some organizations also require users to approve final unit test results.

11.8.2 Integration Testing

Testing two or more programs that depend on each other is called **integration testing**. For example, consider an information system with a program that checks and validates customer credit status, and a separate program that updates data in the customer master file. The output from the validation program becomes input to the master file update program. Testing the programs independently does not guarantee that the data passed between them is correct. Only by performing integration testing for this pair of programs can one ensure that the programs work together properly. Figure 11-20 shows integration testing for several groups of programs. Notice that a program can have membership in two or more groups.

Systems analysts usually develop the data they use in integration testing. As is the case with all forms of testing, integration test data must consider both normal and unusual situations. For example, integration testing might include passing typical records between two programs, followed by blank records, to simulate an unusual event or an operational problem. Test data that simulates actual conditions should be used because the interface that links the programs is being tested. A testing sequence should not move to the integration test stage unless it has performed properly in all unit tests.

11.8.3 System Testing

After completing integration testing, system testing is performed, which involves the entire information system, as shown in Figure 11-20. A system test includes all likely processing situations and is intended to assure users, developers, and managers that the program meets all specifications and that all necessary features have been included.

During a system test, users enter data, including samples of actual, or live, data, perform queries, and produce reports to simulate actual operating conditions. All processing options and outputs are verified by users and the IT project development team to ensure that the system functions correctly. Commercial software packages must undergo system testing similar to that of in-house developed systems, although unit and integration testing usually are not performed. Regardless of how the system was developed, system testing has the following major objectives:

- Perform a final test of all programs

- Verify that the system will handle all input data properly, both valid and invalid

- Ensure that the IT staff has the documentation and instructions needed to operate the system properly and that backup and restart capabilities of the system are adequate (the details of creating this sort of documentation are discussed later in this chapter)

- Demonstrate that users can interact with the system successfully

- Verify that all system components are integrated properly and that actual processing situations will be handled correctly

- Confirm that the information system can handle predicted volumes of data in a timely and efficient manner

Successful completion of system testing is the key to user and management approval, which is why system tests sometimes are called acceptance tests. Final acceptance tests, however, are performed during systems installation and evaluation with actual user data, as described later in this chapter.

How much testing is necessary depends on the situation and requires good judgment and input from other IT staff members, users, and management. Unfortunately, IT project managers often are pressured to finish testing quickly and hand the system over to users. Common reasons for premature or rushed testing are demands from users, tight systems development budgets, and demands from top management to finish projects early. Those pressures hinder the testing process and often have detrimental effects on the final product's quality.

Testing can be a cost-effective means of providing a quality product. Every error caught during testing eliminates potential expenses and operational problems. No system, however, is 100% error-free. Often, errors go undetected until the system becomes operational. Errors that affect the integrity or accuracy of data must be corrected immediately. Minor errors, such as typographical errors in the user interface, can be corrected later.

Some users want a system that is a completely finished product, while others realize that minor changes can be treated as maintenance items after the system is operational. In the final analysis, a decision must be made whether or not to postpone system installation if problems are discovered. If conflicting views exist, management will decide whether or not to install the system after a full discussion of the options.

CASE IN POINT 11.2: WEBTEST, INC.

As a new systems analyst, you suspect that testing web-based systems probably involves a different set of tools and techniques, compared to testing traditional LAN-based systems. Because you've always wanted to run your own IT company, you have decided to launch a start-up firm called WebTest, Inc., that would offer consulting services specifically aimed at testing the performance, integrity, efficiency, and security of Internet-based systems.

Your idea is to identify and purchase various website testing tools that currently are available, then use these tools as a website testing consultant. No one in your area offers this type of consulting service, so you have high hopes.

Now, you need to perform Internet research to learn more about web testing software that is available. Review the Internet Resources Tools section, which is Part D of the Systems Analyst's Toolkit, and use a search engine to develop a list of at least four products that you might want to use. For each product, write up a brief description of its overall purpose, its features and benefits, its cost, and how it would fit.

11.9 DOCUMENTATION

Documentation describes an information system and helps the users, managers, and IT staff who must interact with it. Accurate documentation can reduce system downtime, cut costs, and speed up maintenance tasks. Figure 11-21 shows an example of the Rigi research environment that can automate the documentation process and help software developers generate accurate, comprehensive reference material through detailed source code analysis.

Documentation is essential for successful system operation and maintenance. In addition to supporting a system's users, accurate documentation is essential for IT staff members who must modify the system, add a new feature, or perform maintenance. Documentation includes program documentation, system documentation, operations documentation, and user documentation.

11.9.1 Program Documentation

Program documentation describes the inputs, outputs, and processing logic for all program modules. The program documentation process starts in the systems analysis phase and continues during systems implementation. Analysts prepare overall documentation, such as process descriptions and report layouts, early in the SDLC. This documentation guides programmers, who construct modules that are well supported by internal and external comments and descriptions that can be understood and maintained easily. A systems analyst usually verifies that program documentation is complete and accurate.

Science of Computer Programming 75 (2010) 247–263

Contents lists available at ScienceDirect

Science of Computer Programming

journal homepage: www.elsevier.com/locate/scico

Rigi—An environment for software reverse engineering, exploration, visualization, and redocumentation

Holger M. Kienle, Hausi A. Müller*

University of Victoria, Canada

ARTICLE INFO

Article history:
Received 30 November 2008
Received in revised form 15 October 2009
Accepted 30 October 2009
Available online 10 November 2009

Keywords:
Reverse engineering
Program comprehension
Tool-building
Tool requirements

ABSTRACT

The Rigi environment is a mature research tool that provides functionality to reverse engineer software systems. With Rigi large systems can be analyzed, interactively explored, summarized, and documented. This is supported with parsers to extract information from source code, an exchange format to store extracted information, analyses to transform and abstract information, a scripting language and library to automate the process, and a visualization engine to interactively explore and manipulate information in the form of typed, directed, hierarchical graphs. In this paper we describe Rigi's main components and functionalities, and assess its impact on reverse engineering research. Furthermore, we discuss Rigi's architecture and design decisions that led to a decoupling of major functionalities, and enable tool extensibility, interoperability and end-user programmability.

FIGURE 11-21 Rigi is a research environment that uses reverse engineering technology to provide software redocumentation capabilities to support program understanding.
Source: ©2009, Elsevier

System developers also use **defect tracking software**, sometimes called **bug tracking software**, to document and track program defects, code changes, and replacement code, called **patches**.

11.9.2 System Documentation

System documentation describes the system's functions and how they are implemented. System documentation includes data dictionary entries, data flow diagrams, object models, screen layouts, source documents, and the systems request that initiated the project. System documentation is necessary reference material for the programmers and analysts who must support and maintain the system.

Most of the system documentation is prepared during the systems analysis and systems design phases. During the systems implementation phase, an analyst must review prior documentation to verify that it is complete, accurate, and up to date, including any changes made during the implementation process. For example, if a screen or report has been modified, the analyst must update the documentation. Updates to the system documentation should be made in a timely manner to prevent oversights.

11.9.3 Operations Documentation

If the information system environment involves a mainframe or centralized servers, the analyst must prepare documentation for the IT group that supports centralized operations. A mainframe installation might require the scheduling of batch jobs and the distribution of printed reports. In this type of environment, the IT operations staff serves as the first point of contact when users experience problems with the system.

Operations documentation contains all the information needed for processing and distributing online and printed output. Typical operations documentation includes the following information:

- Program, systems analyst, programmer, and system identification
- Scheduling information for printed output, such as report run frequency and deadlines
- Input files and where they originate; and output files and destinations
- Email and report distribution lists
- Special forms required, including online forms
- Error and informational messages to operators and restart procedures
- Special instructions, such as security requirements

Operations documentation should be clear, concise, and available online if possible. If the IT department has an operations group, the documentation should be reviewed with them, early and often, to identify any problems. By keeping the operations group informed at every phase of the SDLC, operations documentation can be developed as the project progresses.

11.9.4 User Documentation

User documentation consists of instructions and information to users who will interact with the system and includes user manuals, help screens, and online tutorials. Programmers or systems analysts usually create program documentation and system documentation. To produce effective and clear user documentation — and hence have a successful project — someone with expert skills in this area doing the development is needed, just as someone with expert skills developing the software is needed. The skill set required to develop documentation usually is not the same as that to develop a system. This is particularly true in the world of online documentation, which needs to coordinate with print documentation and intranet and Internet information. Technical writing requires specialized skills, and competent technical writers are valuable members of the IT team.

Just as a system cannot be thrown together in several days, documentation cannot be added at the end of the project. While this has always been true of traditional user documentation, this is an even more critical issue now that online help and context-sensitive help are often used. Context-sensitive help is part of the program and it has to be tested too.

Systems analysts usually are responsible for preparing documentation to help users learn the system. In larger companies, a technical support team that includes technical writers might assist in the preparation of user documentation and training materials. Regardless of the delivery method, user documentation must be clear, understandable, and readily accessible to users at all levels.

User documentation includes the following:

- A system overview that clearly describes all major system features, capabilities, and limitations
- Description of source document content, preparation, processing, and samples
- Overview of menu and data entry screen options, contents, and processing instructions
- Examples of reports that are produced regularly or available at the user's request, including samples

- Security and audit trail information
- Explanation of responsibility for specific input, output, or processing requirements
- Procedures for requesting changes and reporting problems
- Examples of exceptions and error situations
- Frequently asked questions (FAQs)
- Explanation of how to get help and procedures for updating the user manual

11.9.5 Online Documentation

Most users now prefer online documentation, which provides immediate help when they have questions or encounter problems. Many users are accustomed to context-sensitive help screens, hints and tips, hypertext, on-screen demos, and other user-friendly features commonly found in popular software packages; they expect the same kind of support for in-house developed software.

If the system will include online documentation, that fact needs to be identified as one of the system requirements. If someone other than the analysts who are developing the system will create the documentation, that person or group needs to be involved as early as possible to become familiar with the software and begin developing the required documentation and support material. In addition, system developers must determine whether the documentation will be available from within the program, or as a separate entity in the form of a tutorial, slide presentation, reference manual, or website. If necessary, links should be created within the program that will take the user to the appropriate documentation.

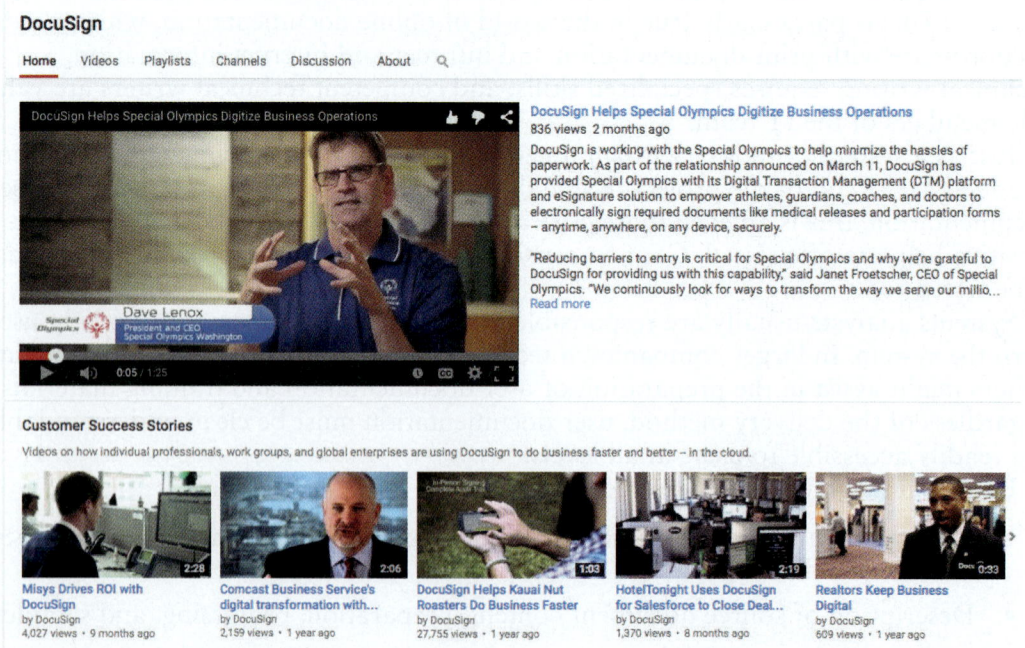

FIGURE 11-22 DocuSign provides electronic document signing services. This example from their YouTube channel documents how the Special Olympics have benefited from digitizing their business operations using DocuSign's products.

Source: YouTube

Effective online documentation is an important productivity tool because it empowers users and reduces the time that IT staff members must spend in providing telephone, email, or face-to-face assistance. Interactive tutorials are especially popular with users who like to learn by doing, and visual impact is very important. The use of YouTube as a host for tutorial videos has become commonplace. For example, DocuSign is a company that provides electronic document signing services. They have a YouTube channel, shown in Figure 11-22, with success stories documenting how customers have benefited from using DocuSign's products.

In addition to program-based assistance, the Internet offers an entirely new level of comprehensive, immediate support. Many programs include links to websites, intranet sites, and Internet-based technical support. For example, the Cisco Systems website shown in Figure 11-23 offers a wide range of support services and social media links that allow Cisco users to collaborate and share their knowledge.

FIGURE 11-23 The Cisco Support Community invites users to contribute valuable experience and documentation using social media.

Source: Cisco Support Community

Although online documentation is essential, written documentation material is also valuable, especially in training users and for reference purposes. A sample page from a user manual is shown in Figure 11-24. Systems analysts or technical writers usually prepare the manual, but many companies invite users to review the material and participate in the development process.

No matter what form of user documentation the system requires, keep in mind that it can take a good deal of time to develop. The time between finishing software coding and the time when a complete package — including documentation — can be released to users is entirely dependent on how well the documentation is planned in advance. If the completion of the project includes providing user documentation, this issue needs to be addressed from the very beginning of the project. Determining what the user documentation requirements are and ascertaining who will complete the documents is critical to a timely release of the project.

Neglecting user documentation issues until after all the program is complete often leads to one of two things: (1) The documentation will be thrown together quickly just to get it out the door on time, and it more than likely will be inadequate; or (2) it will be done correctly, and the product release will be delayed considerably.

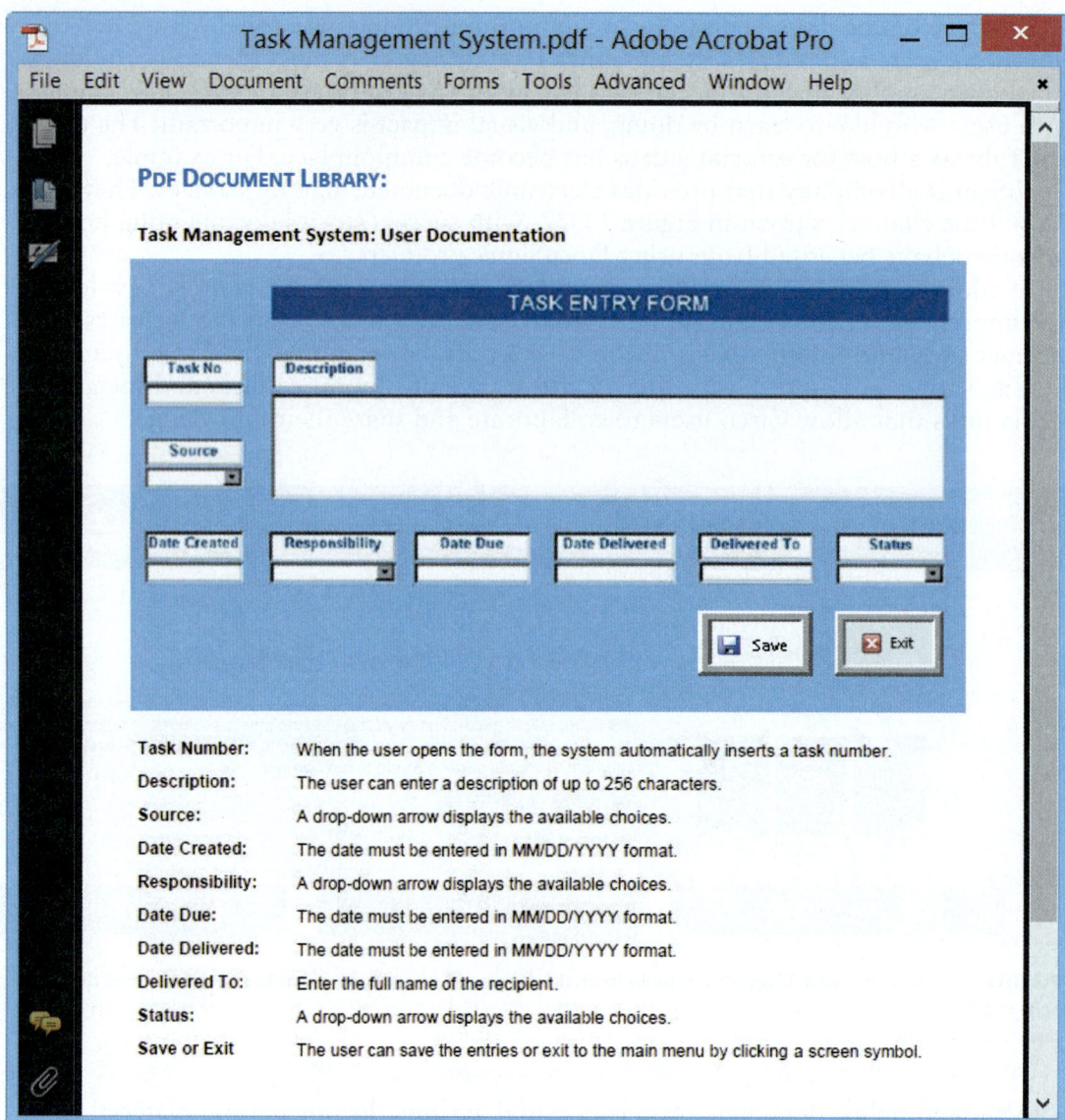

FIGURE 11-24 A sample page from a user manual. The instructions explain how to add a new task to the system.

User training typically is scheduled when the system is installed. The training sessions offer an ideal opportunity to distribute the user manual and explain the procedures for updating it in the future. Training for users, managers, and IT staff is described later in this chapter.

11.10 MANAGEMENT APPROVAL

After system testing is complete, the results are presented to management. The test results should be described, the status of all required documentation updated, and input from users who participated in system testing summarized. Detailed time schedules, cost estimates, and staffing requirements for making the system fully operational should also be provided. If system testing produced no technical, economical, or operational problems, management determines a schedule for system installation and evaluation.

11.11 SYSTEM INSTALLATION AND EVALUATION

The following sections describe system installation and evaluation tasks that are performed for every information systems project, whether the application is developed in-house or purchased as a commercial package.

At this stage of the SDLC, the earlier design activities produced the overall architecture and processing strategy. Users should have been consulted at every stage of development. The programs have been developed and tested individually, in groups, and as a complete system. The necessary documentation has been prepared and checked for accuracy, including support material for IT staff and users. What remains is to carry out the following steps in systems implementation:

- Prepare a separate operational and test environment
- Provide training for users, managers, and IT staff
- Perform data conversion and system changeover
- Carry out a post-implementation evaluation of the system
- Present a final report to management

11.12 OPERATIONAL AND TEST ENVIRONMENTS

Recall that an environment, or platform, is a specific combination of hardware and software. The environment for the actual system operation is called the **operational environment** or **production environment**. The environment that analysts and programmers use to develop and maintain programs is called the **test environment**. A separate test environment is necessary to maintain system security and integrity and protect the operational environment. Typically, the test environment resides on a limited-access workstation or server located in the IT department.

Access to the operational environment is limited to users and must strictly be controlled. Systems analysts and programmers should not have access to the operational environment except to correct a system problem or to make authorized modifications or enhancements. Otherwise, IT department members have no reason to access the day-to-day operational system.

The test environment for an information system contains copies of all programs, procedures, and test data files. Before making any changes to an operational system, the analyst must verify them in the test environment and obtain user approval. Figure 11-25 shows the differences between test environments and operational environments.

An effective testing process is essential to ensure product quality. Every experienced systems analyst can tell a story about an apparently innocent program change that was introduced without being tested properly. In those stories, the innocent change invariably ends up causing some unexpected and unwanted changes to the program. After any modification, the same acceptance tests that were run when the system was developed should be repeated. By restricting access to the operational area and performing all tests in a separate environment, the system can be protected and problems that could damage data or interrupt operations avoided.

The operational environment includes hardware and software configurations and settings, system utilities, telecommunications resources, and any other components that might affect system performance. Because network capability is critically important in a client/server environment, connectivity, specifications, and performance must be verified before installing any applications. All communications features in the test environment should be checked carefully and then checked again after loading the

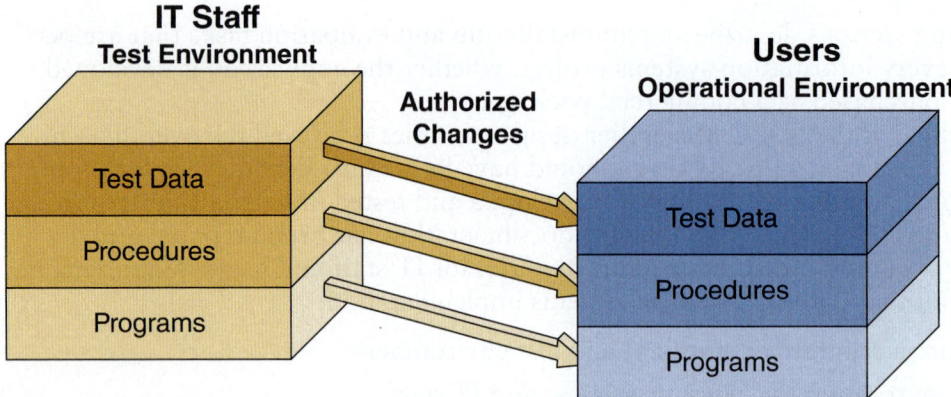

FIGURE 11-25 The test environment versus the operational environment. Notice that access to the test environment is limited to IT staff, while the operational environment is restricted to users.

applications into the operational environment. The documentation should identify all network specifications and settings, including technical and operational requirements for communications hardware and software. If network resources must be built or upgraded to support the new system, the platform must be tested rigorously before system installation begins.

11.13 TRAINING

No system can be successful without proper training, whether it involves software, hardware, or manufacturing. A successful information system requires training for users, managers, and IT staff members. The entire systems development effort can depend on whether or not people understand the system and know how to use it effectively.

11.13.1 Training Plan

A training plan should be considered early in the systems development process. As documentation is created, consider how to use the material in future training sessions. When the system is implemented, it is essential to provide the right training for the right people at the right time. The first step is to identify who should receive training and what training is needed. The organization should be carefully examined to determine how the system will support business operations, and who will be involved or affected. Figure 11-26 shows specific training topics for users, managers, and IT staff. Notice that each group needs a mix of general background and detailed information to understand and use the system.

As shown in Figure 11-26, the three main groups for training are users, managers, and IT staff. A manager does not need to understand every submenu or feature, but he or she does need a system overview to ensure that users are being trained properly and are using the system correctly. Similarly, users need to know how to perform their day-to-day job functions, but they do not need to know how the company allocates system operational charges among user departments. IT staff people probably need the most information. To support the new system, they must have a clear understanding of how the system functions, how it supports business requirements, and the skills that users need to operate the system and perform their tasks.

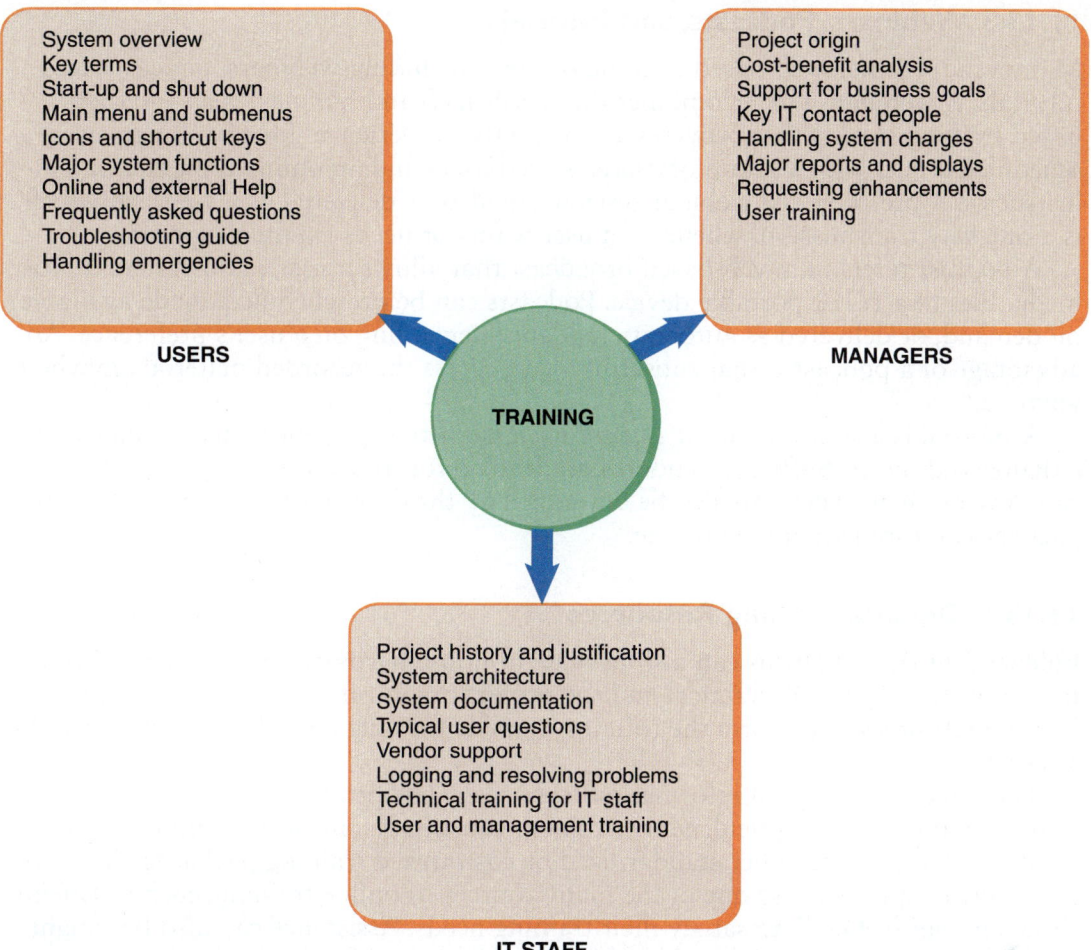

FIGURE 11-26 Examples of training topics for three different groups. Users, managers, and IT staff members have different training needs.

After the objectives are identified, how the company will provide training must be determined. The main choices are to obtain training from vendors, outside training firms, or use IT staff and other in-house resources.

11.13.2 Vendor Training

If the system includes the purchase of software or hardware, then vendor-supplied training is one of the features that should be included in the RFPs (requests for proposal) and RFQs (requests for quotation) that are sent to potential vendors.

Many hardware and software vendors offer training programs free or at a nominal cost for the products they sell. In other cases, the company might negotiate the price for training, depending on their relationship with the vendor and the prospect of future purchases. The training usually is conducted at the vendor's site by experienced trainers who provide valuable hands-on experience. If a large number of people need training, classes may be held at the company's location.

Vendor training often gives the best return on training dollars because it is focused on products that the vendor developed. The scope of vendor training, however, usually is limited to a standard version of the vendor's software or hardware. The vendor's training may have to be supplemented with in-house training, especially if the IT staff customized the vendor's package.

11.13.3 Webinars, Podcasts, and Tutorials

Many vendors offer web-based training options, including webinars, podcasts, and tutorials. A **webinar**, which combines the words *web* and *seminar*, is an Internet-based training session that provides an interactive experience. Most webinars are scheduled events with a group of preregistered users and an online presenter or instructor. A pre-recorded webinar session can also be delivered as a webcast, which is a one-way transmission, whenever a user wants or needs training support.

A *podcast* refers to a web-based broadcast that allows a user to download multi-media files to a PC or portable device. Podcasts can be prescheduled, made available on demand, or delivered as automatic updates, depending on a user's preference. An advantage of a podcast is that subscribers can access the recorded material anywhere, anytime.

A **tutorial** is a series of online interactive lessons that present material and provide a dialog with users. Software vendors can develop tutorials, or a company's IT team can develop them. They can also be developed by third parties for popular software packages and sold separately online.

11.13.4 Outside Training Resources

Independent training firms can also provide in-house hardware or software training. If vendor training is not practical and the project organization does not have the internal resources to perform the training, outside training consultants can be a viable alternative.

The rapid expansion of information technology has produced tremendous growth in the computer-training field. Many training consultants, institutes, and firms are available that provide either standardized or customized training packages. For example, many people now use one of the many sources of online training, such as Udemy shown in Figure 11-27, to satisfy their training needs. Assistance can also be sought from nonprofit sources with an interest in training, including universities, industry associations, and information management organizations.

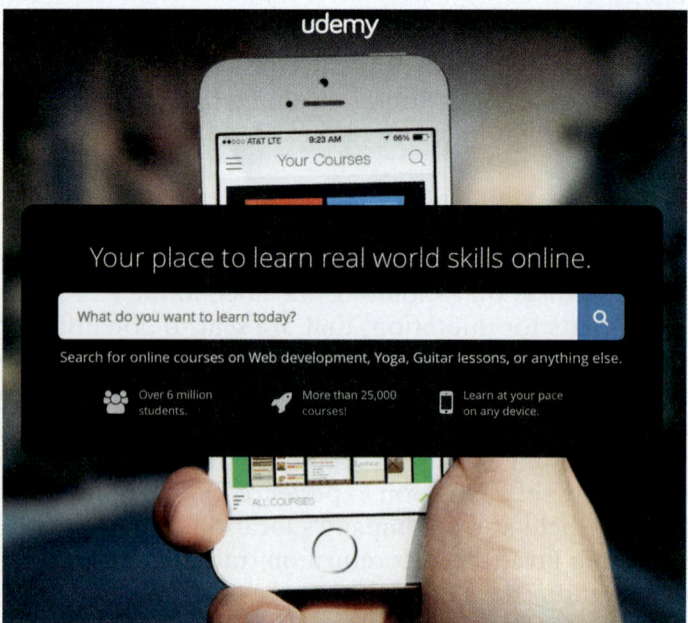

FIGURE 11-27 Udemy is one of many sources of online training.

Source: Udemy.com

11.13.5 Training Tips

The IT staff and user departments often share responsibility for developing and conducting training programs for internally developed software. If the organization has a service desk, their staff might be able to handle user training.

Multimedia is an effective training method. Presentation software, such as Microsoft PowerPoint or Apple Keynote, can be used to design training sessions that combine slides, animation, and sound. Programs that capture actual keystrokes and mouse actions, such as Camtasia and Panopto (shown in Figure 11-28), can be used to replay the screens as a demonstration for users. If a media or graphic arts group is available, they can help prepare training aids, such as videos, charts, and other instructional materials.

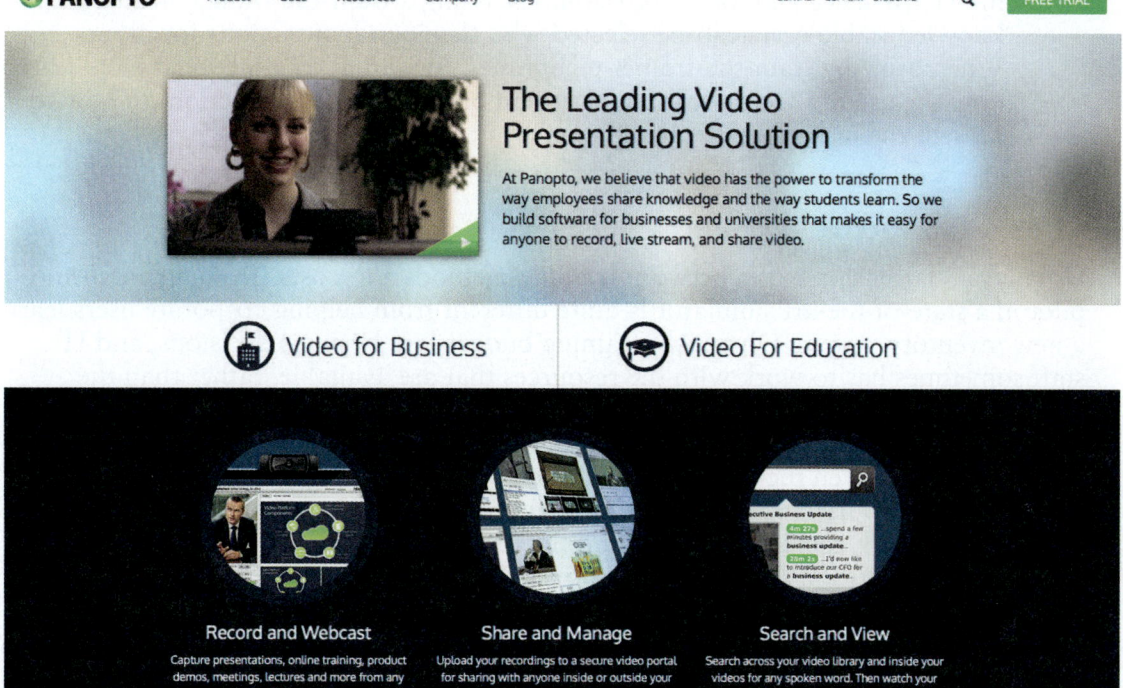

FIGURE 11-28 Panopto is a screen capture and video presentation program that can be used to prepare webcasts and online learning materials.
Source: Panopto.com

Keep the following guidelines in mind when developing a training program:

- *Train people in groups, with separate training programs for distinct groups.* Group training makes the most efficient use of time and training facilities. In addition, if the group is small, trainees can learn from the questions and problems of others. A training program must address the job interests and skills of a wide range of participants. For example, IT staff personnel and users require very different information. Problems often arise when some participants have technical backgrounds and others do not. A single program will not meet everyone's needs.

- *Select the most effective place to conduct the training.* Training employees at the company's location offers several advantages. Employees incur no travel expense, they can respond to local emergencies that require immediate attention, and training can take place in the actual environment where the system will operate. There can be some disadvantages, however. Employees who are distracted by telephone calls and other duties will not get the full benefit of the training. In addition, using the organization's computer facilities for training can disrupt normal operations and limit the amount of actual hands-on training.

- *Provide for learning by hearing, seeing, and doing.* Some people learn best from lectures, discussions, and question-and-answer sessions. Others learn best from viewing demonstrations or from reading documentation and other material. Most people learn best from hands-on experience. Training that supports each type of learning should be provided.

- *Rely on previous trainees.* After one group of users has been trained, they can assist others. Users often learn more quickly from coworkers who share common experience and job responsibilities. Using a train-the-trainer strategy, knowledgeable users can be selected who then conduct sessions for others. When utilizing train-the-trainer techniques, the initial training must include not only the use of the application or system but also some instruction on how to present the materials effectively.

11.13.6 Interactive Training

Usually, a relationship exists between training methods and costs. Training an airline pilot in a state-of-the-art simulator is quite different from helping corporate users learn a new inventory system. Obviously, training budgets are business decisions, and IT staff sometimes has to work with the resources that are available, rather than the resources they wish they had. Most people prefer hands-on training. However, other less-expensive methods can be used, including training manuals, printed handouts, and online materials. Even the user documentation such as that shown in Figure 11-24 can be valuable, if users know how to find and use it.

If a new system is being launched and the resources to develop formal training materials are lacking, a series of dialog boxes that respond with help information and suggestions whenever users select various menu topics can still be designed. A good user interface also includes helpful error messages and hints, as discussed in Chapter 8. However, the most effective training is interactive, self-paced, and multimedia-based. Online training and video tutorials are discussed in the following sections.

ONLINE TRAINING: Regardless of the instructional method, training lessons should include step-by-step instructions for using the features of the information system. Training materials should resemble actual screens, and tasks should be typical of a user's daily work — the more realistic, the better. Video lessons are particularly popular online. For example, Figure 11-29 shows a sample lesson on Android app development in an online tutorial from lynda.com.

Sophisticated online training systems may offer interactive sessions where users can perform practice tasks and view feedback. Online training materials should also include a reference section that summarizes all options and commands, lists all possible error messages, and what actions the user should take when a problem arises.

When training is complete, many organizations conduct a full-scale test, or simulation, which is a dress rehearsal for users and IT support staff. Organizations include all procedures, such as those that they execute only at the end of a month, quarter, or year, in the simulation. As questions or problems arise, the participants consult the system documentation, help screens, or each other to determine appropriate answers or actions. This full-scale test provides valuable experience and builds confidence for everyone involved with the new system.

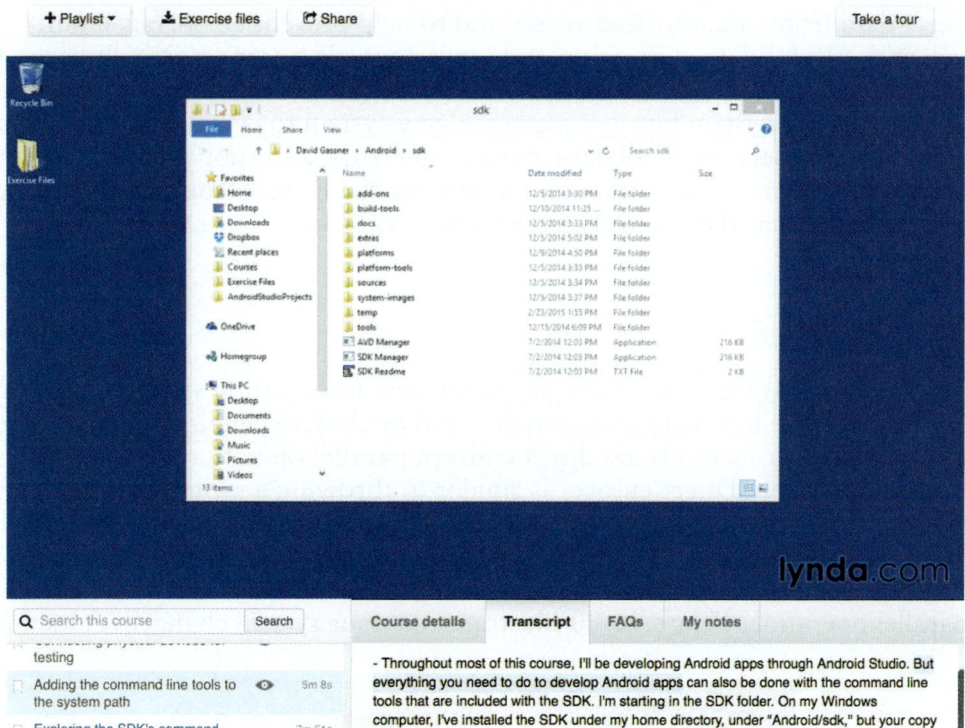

Watching: **Adding the command line tools to the system path**
From: Developing Android Apps Essential Training with David Gassner

FIGURE 11-29 A sample lesson on Android app development in an online tutorial from lynda.com.

Source: lynda.com, Inc.

11.14 DATA CONVERSION

Data conversion is an important part of the system installation process. During **data conversion**, existing data is loaded into the new system. Depending on the system, data conversion can be done before, during, or after the operational environment is complete. A data conversion plan should be developed as early as possible, and the conversion process should be tested when the test environment is developed.

11.14.1 Data Conversion Strategies

When a new system replaces an existing system, the data conversion process should be automated, if possible. The old system might be capable of exporting data in an acceptable format for the new system or in a standard format, such as ASCII or ODBC. ODBC (open database connectivity) is an industry-standard protocol that allows DBMSs from various vendors to interact and exchange data. Most database vendors provide ODBC drivers, which are a form of middleware. As discussed in Chapter 10, middleware connects dissimilar applications and enables them to communicate.

If a standard format is not available, a program to extract the data and convert it to an acceptable format must be developed. Data conversion is more difficult when the new system replaces a manual system, because all data must be entered manually unless it can be scanned. Even when the data conversion is automated, a new system often requires additional data items, which might require manual entry.

11.14.2 Data Conversion Security and Controls

Strict input controls should be maintained during the conversion process, when data is extremely vulnerable. System control measures should be in place and operational to protect data from unauthorized access and to help prevent erroneous input.

Even with careful data conversion and input controls, some errors will occur. For example, duplicate customer records or inconsistent part numbers might have been tolerated by the old system but will cause the new system to crash. Most organizations require that users verify all data, correct all errors, and supply every missing data item during conversion. Although the process can be time-consuming and expensive, it is essential that the new system be loaded with accurate, error-free data.

11.15 SYSTEM CHANGEOVER

System changeover is the process of putting the new information system online and retiring the old system. Changeover can be rapid or slow, depending on the method. The four changeover methods are direct cutover, parallel operation, pilot operation, and phased operation. Direct cutover is similar to throwing a switch that instantly changes over from the old system to the new. Parallel operation requires that both systems run simultaneously for a specified period, which is the slowest method. The other methods, pilot and phased operation, fall somewhere between direct cutover and parallel operation. Figure 11-30 illustrates the four system changeover methods.

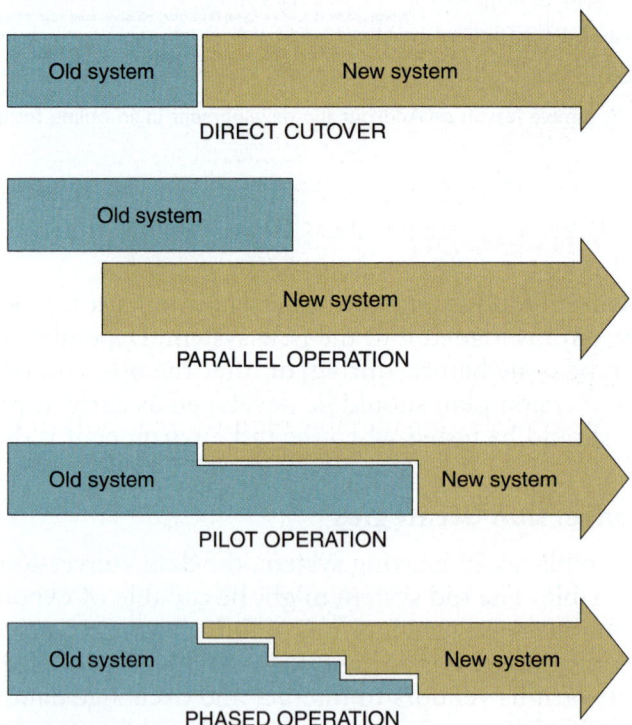

FIGURE 11-30 The four system changeover methods.

11.15.1 Direct Cutover

The direct cutover approach causes the changeover from the old system to the new system to occur immediately when the new system becomes operational. Direct cutover usually is the least expensive changeover method because the IT group has to operate and maintain only one system at a time.

Direct cutover, however, involves more risk than other changeover methods. Regardless of how thoroughly and carefully testing and training is conducted, some difficulties can arise when the system goes into operation. Problems can result from data situations that were not tested or anticipated or from errors caused by users or operators. A system can also encounter difficulties because live data typically occurs in much larger volumes than test data.

Although initial implementation problems are a concern with all four changeover methods, they are most significant when the direct cutover approach is used. Detecting minor errors is also more difficult with direct cutover because users cannot verify current output by comparing it to output from the old system. Major errors can cause a system process to terminate abnormally, and with the direct cutover method, reverting to the old system as a backup option is not possible.

Companies often choose the direct cutover method for implementing commercial software packages because they feel that commercial packages involve less risk of total system failure. Commercial software is certainly not risk-free, but the software vendor usually maintains an extensive knowledge base and can supply reliable, prompt fixes for most problems.

For systems developed in-house, most organizations use direct cutover only for noncritical situations. Direct cutover might be the only choice, however, if the operating environment cannot support both the old and new systems or if the old and new systems are incompatible.

Timing is very important when using a direct cutover strategy. Most systems operate on weekly, monthly, quarterly, and yearly cycles. For example, consider a payroll system that produces output on a weekly basis. Some employees are paid twice a month, however, so the system also operates semimonthly. Monthly, quarterly, and annual reports also require the system to produce output at the end of every month, quarter, and year. When a cyclical information system is implemented in the middle of any cycle, complete processing for the full cycle requires information from both the old and the new systems. To minimize the need to require information from two different systems, cyclical information systems usually are converted using the direct cutover method at the beginning of a quarter, calendar year, or fiscal year.

11.15.2 Parallel Operation

The **parallel operation** changeover method requires that both the old and the new information systems operate fully for a specified period. Data is input into both systems, and output generated by the new system is compared with the equivalent output from the old system. When users, management, and the IT group are satisfied that the new system operates correctly, the old system is terminated.

The most obvious advantage of parallel operation is lower risk. If the new system does not work correctly, the company can use the old system as a backup until appropriate changes are made. It is much easier to verify that the new system is working properly under parallel operation than under direct cutover, because the output from both systems is compared and verified during parallel operation.

Parallel operation, however, does have some disadvantages. First, it is the most costly changeover method. Because both the old and the new systems are in full operation, the company pays for both systems during the parallel period. Users must work in both systems and the company might need temporary employees to handle the extra workload. In addition, running both systems might place a burden on the operating environment and cause processing delays.

Parallel operation is not practical if the old and new systems are incompatible technically, or if the operating environment cannot support both systems. Parallel operation is also inappropriate when the two systems perform different functions or if the new system involves a new method of business operations.

11.15.3 Pilot Operation

The **pilot operation** changeover method involves implementing the complete new system at a selected location of the company. A new sales reporting system, for instance, might be implemented in only one branch office, or a new payroll system might be installed in only one department. In these examples, the group that uses the new system first is called the **pilot site**. During pilot operation, the old system continues to operate for the entire organization, including the pilot site. After the system proves successful at the pilot site, it is implemented in the rest of the organization, usually using the direct cutover method. Therefore, pilot operation is a combination of parallel operation and direct cutover methods.

Restricting the implementation to a pilot site reduces the risk of system failure, compared with a direct cutover method. Operating both systems for only the pilot site is less expensive than a parallel operation for the entire company. In addition, if a parallel approach to complete the implementation is used later on, the changeover period can be much shorter if the system proves successful at the pilot site.

11.15.4 Phased Operation

The **phased operation** changeover method allows the new system to be implemented in stages, or modules. For example, instead of implementing a new manufacturing system all at once, the materials management subsystem is installed first, then the production control subsystem, then the job cost subsystem, and so on. Each subsystem can be implemented by using any of the other three changeover methods.

Analysts sometimes confuse phased and pilot operation methods. Both methods combine direct cutover and parallel operation to reduce risks and costs. With phased operation, however, only a part of the system is given to all users, while pilot operation provides the entire system, but to only some users.

One advantage of a phased approach is that the risk of errors or failures is limited to the implemented module only. For instance, if a new production control subsystem fails to operate properly, that failure might not affect the new purchasing subsystem or the existing shop floor control subsystem.

Phased operation is less expensive than full parallel operation because the analyst has to work with only one part of the system at a time. A phased approach is not possible, however, if the system cannot be separated easily into logical modules or segments. In addition, if the system involves a large number of separate phases, phased operation can cost more than a pilot approach.

Figure 11-31 shows that each changeover method has risk and cost factors. A systems analyst must weigh the advantages and disadvantages of each method and recommend the best choice in a given situation. The final changeover decision will be based on input from the IT staff, users, and management — and the choice must reflect the nature of the business and the degree of acceptable risk.

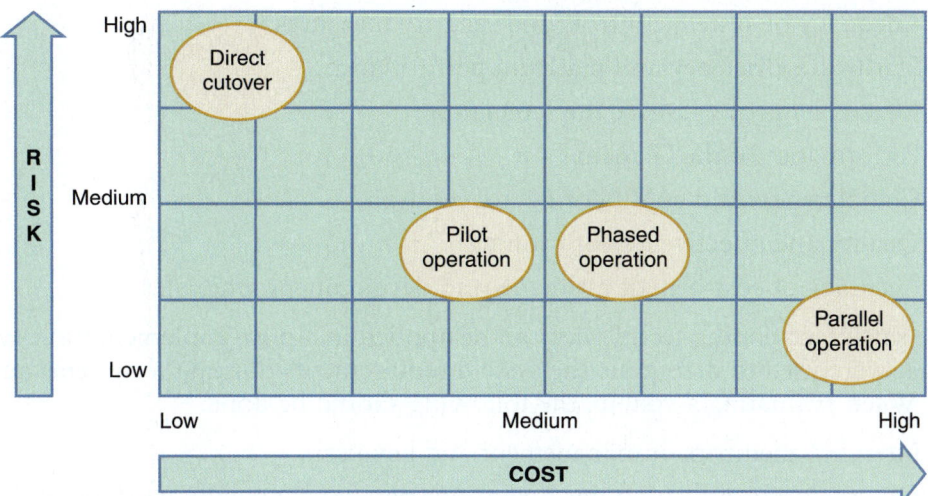

FIGURE 11-31 Relative risk and cost characteristics of the four changeover methods.

CASE IN POINT 11.3:   GLOBAL COOLING

You are a systems analyst at Global Cooling, a leading manufacturer of air conditioning units. You are leading a team that is developing a new production scheduling system. The project is now in the application development stage. Unit testing has been completed, and you are in the final stages of integration testing. Your supervisor, Ella Pham, is eager to implement the new application ahead of schedule and asked if you could trim system testing from two weeks to three days, and use a direct cutover method instead of the parallel changeover method that originally was planned. Write a brief memo expressing your views.

11.16 POST-IMPLEMENTATION TASKS

Once the new system is operational, two additional tasks must be performed: (1) Prepare a post-implementation evaluation, and (2) deliver a final report to management.

11.16.1 Post-Implementation Evaluation

A post-implementation evaluation assesses the overall quality of the information system. The evaluation verifies that the new system meets specified requirements, complies with user objectives, and produces the anticipated benefits. In addition, by providing feedback to the development team, the evaluation also helps improve IT development practices for future projects.

A post-implementation evaluation should examine all aspects of the development effort and the end product — the developed information system. A typical evaluation includes feedback for the following areas:

- Accuracy, completeness, and timeliness of information system output
- User satisfaction
- System reliability and maintainability

- Adequacy of system controls and security measures
- Hardware efficiency and platform performance
- Effectiveness of database implementation
- Performance of the IT team
- Completeness and quality of documentation
- Quality and effectiveness of training
- Accuracy of cost-benefit estimates and development schedules

The same fact-finding techniques can be applied in a post-implementation evaluation that were used to determine the system requirements during the systems analysis phase. When evaluating a system, the following should be done:

- Interview members of management and key users
- Observe users and computer operations personnel actually working with the new information system
- Read all documentation and training materials
- Examine all source documents, output reports, and screen displays
- Use questionnaires to gather information and opinions from a large number of users
- Analyze maintenance and help desk logs

Figure 11-32 shows the first page of a sample user evaluation form for the new information system where users evaluate 18 separate elements on a numerical scale, so the results can be tabulated easily. Following that section, the form provides space for open-ended comments and suggestions.

Whenever possible, people who were not directly involved in developing the system should conduct the post-implementation evaluation. IT staff and users usually perform the evaluation, although some firms use an internal audit group or independent auditors to ensure the accuracy and completeness of the evaluation.

When to perform a post-implementation evaluation for a new system is not always clear. Users can forget details of the developmental effort if too much time elapses before the evaluation. After several months or a year, for instance, users might not remember whether they learned a procedure through training, from user documentation, or by experimenting with the system on their own.

Users also might forget their impressions of IT team members over time. An important purpose of the post-implementation evaluation is to improve the quality of IT department functions, including interaction with users, training, and documentation. Consequently, the evaluation team should perform the assessment while users are able to recall specific incidents, successes, and problems so they can offer suggestions for improvement.

On the other hand, if the evaluation is done too soon, the users may not be able to provide sufficient feedback due to lack of experience with the new system. Post-implementation evaluation is primarily concerned with assessing the quality of the new system. If the team performs the evaluation too soon after implementation, users will not have enough time to learn the new system and appreciate its strengths and weaknesses. Although many IT professionals recommend conducting the evaluation after at least six months of system operation, pressure to finish the project sooner usually results in an earlier evaluation in order to allow the IT department to move on to other tasks.

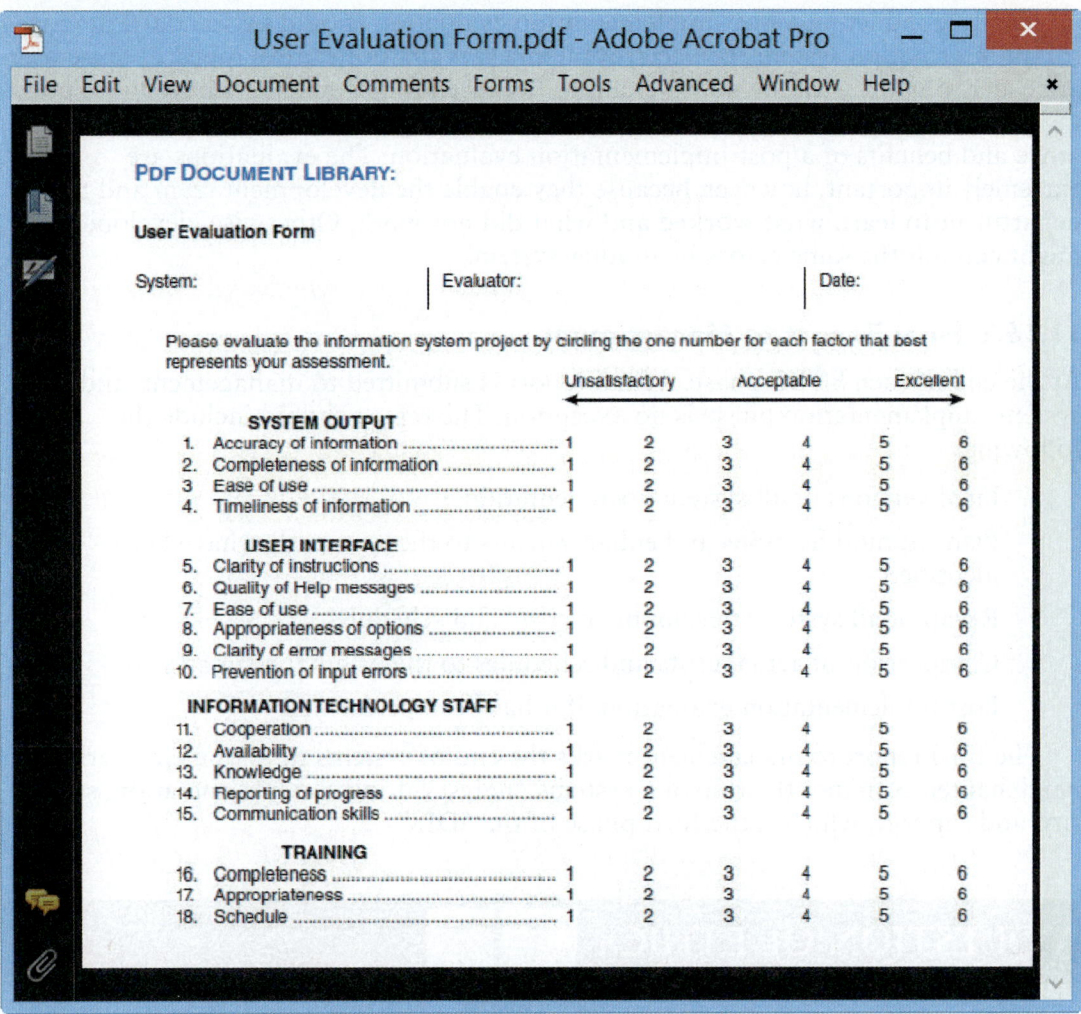

FIGURE 11-32 Sample user evaluation form. The numerical scale allows easy tabulation of results. Following this section, the form provides space for open-ended comments and suggestions.

CASE IN POINT 11.4:   YORKTOWN INDUSTRIES

Cindy Winslow liked her new job as lead systems analyst at Yorktown Industries. She was pleased that her development team completed the new human resources system ahead of schedule and under budget. Cindy looked forward to receiving the post-implementation evaluation because she was confident that both the system and the development team would receive high marks from users and managers.

After the system operated for one month, Cindy received a call from her supervisor, Ted Haines. Ted told her that she would have to handle the evaluation, even though she headed the development effort. Cindy told Ted that she did not feel comfortable evaluating her own team's work. She explained that someone who was not involved in its development should do an independent evaluation. Ted responded that he had full confidence in Cindy's ability to be objective. He explained that no one else was available and he needed the evaluation quickly so he could move forward with the next stage in the corporate development plan.

Cindy was troubled about the situation and she called you, a professional acquaintance, for your advice. What would you tell her and why?

Ideally, conducting a post-implementation evaluation should be standard practice for all information systems projects. Sometimes, evaluations are skipped because users are eager to work with the new system, or because IT staff members have more pressing priorities. In some organizations, management might not recognize the importance and benefits of a post-implementation evaluation. The evaluations are extremely important, however, because they enable the development team and the IT department to learn what worked and what did not work. Otherwise, developers might commit the same errors in another system.

11.16.2 Final Report to Management

At the end of each SDLC phase, a final report is submitted to management, and the systems implementation phase is no exception. The report should include the following:

- Final versions of all system documentation
- Planned modifications and enhancements to the system that have been identified
- Recap of all systems development costs and schedules
- Comparison of actual costs and schedules to the original estimates
- Post-implementation evaluation, if it has been performed

The final report to management marks the end of systems development work. The next chapter examines the role of a systems analyst during systems operation, security, and support, which is the final phase of the SDLC.

A QUESTION OF ETHICS

iStockphoto.com/faberfoto_it

Your friend Jill is handling the testing for the new accounting system, and right now she is very upset about the most recent results. "It seems like every time we fix one thing, another issue pops up! After ten days of testing and adjusting, we are meeting over 90% of the goals and benchmarks. If we're looking for perfection, we'll never make the implementation deadline for the new system, and the users will be all over us. Not to mention top management's reaction to a delay. I'm sure we can resolve some of these issues after the system becomes operational."

How would you respond to Jill? Are ethical issues involved? What are your responsibilities, as an employee, as an IT professional, and as a friend?

11.17 CHAPTER SUMMARY

The systems implementation phase consists of application development, testing, installation, and evaluation of the new system. During application development, analysts determine the overall design strategy and work with programmers to complete design, coding, testing, and documentation. Quality assurance is essential during the implementation phase. Many companies utilize software engineering concepts and quality standards established by the International Organization for Standardization (ISO).

Each systems development approach has its own set of tools. For example, structured development relies heavily on data flow diagrams (DFDs) and structure charts. A structure chart consists of symbols that represent program modules, data couples, control couples, conditions, and loops. Object-oriented methods use a variety of UML diagrams, including use case, class, sequence, and transition state diagrams. Agile methods tend to use iterative and incremental models.

System developers can also use more generic tools to help them translate the system logic into properly functioning program modules. These tools include entity-relationship diagrams, flowcharts, pseudocode, decision tables, and decision trees.

If an agile development approach is used, then the customer creates user stories that describe required features and priority levels. In agile methodology, new system releases are made after many iterations and each is test-driven carefully by the customer.

Cohesion measures a module's scope and processing characteristics. A module that performs a single function or task has a high degree of cohesion, which is desirable. Coupling measures relationships and interdependence among modules. Modules that are relatively independent are loosely coupled, which is desirable. Cohesion and coupling concepts are used in structured development but are also applicable to object-oriented development.

Typically, four steps are followed when creating a structure chart. DFDs and object models are reviewed to identify the processes and methods, identify the program modules and determine control-subordinate relationships, add symbols for couples and loops, and analyze the structure chart to ensure that it is consistent with the system documentation.

Programmers perform desk checking, code review, and unit testing tasks during application development. Systems analysts design the initial test plans, which include test steps and test data for integration testing and system testing. Integration testing is necessary for programs that interact. The final step is system testing for the completed system. System testing includes users in the testing process.

In addition to system documentation, analysts and technical writers also prepare operations documentation and user documentation. Operations documentation provides instructions and information to the IT operations group. User documentation consists of instructions and information for users who interact with the system and includes user manuals, help screens, and tutorials.

During the installation process, an operational, or production, environment is established for the new information system that is completely separate from the test environment. The operational environment contains live data and is accessible only by authorized users. All future changes to the system must be verified in the test environment before they are applied to the operational environment.

Everyone who interacts with the new information system should receive training appropriate to his or her role and skills. The IT department usually is responsible for training. Software or hardware vendors or professional training organizations can also provide training. When a training program is developed, remember the following guidelines: Train people in groups; utilize people already trained to help train others; develop separate programs for distinct employee groups; and provide for learning by using discussions, demonstrations, documentation, training manuals, tutorials, webinars, and podcasts. Users learn better with interactive, self-paced training methods.

Data conversion often is necessary when installing a new information system. When a new system replaces a computerized system, the data conversion process should be automated if possible. The old system might be capable of exporting data in a format that the new system can use, or the data might have to be extracted and converted to an acceptable format. Data conversion from a manual system often requires labor-intensive data entry or scanning. Even when data conversion can be automated, a new system often requires additional data items, which might require manual entry. Strict input controls are important during the conversion process to protect data integrity and quality. Typically, data is verified, corrected, and updated during the conversion process.

System changeover is the process of putting the new system into operation. Four changeover methods exist: direct cutover, parallel operation, pilot operation, and phased operation. With direct cutover, the old system stops and the new system starts simultaneously; direct cutover is the least expensive, but the riskiest changeover method. With parallel operation, users operate both the old and new information systems for some period of time; parallel operation is the most expensive and least risky of the changeover methods. Pilot operation and phased operation represent compromises between direct cutover and parallel operation; both methods are less risky than direct cutover and less costly than parallel operation. With pilot operation, a specified group within the organization uses the new system for a period of time, while the old system continues to operate for the rest of the users. After the system proves successful at the pilot site, it is implemented throughout the organization. With phased operation, the system is implemented in the entire organization, but only one module at a time, until the entire system is operational.

A post-implementation evaluation assesses and reports on the quality of the new system and the work done by the project team. Although it is best if people who were not involved in the systems development effort perform the evaluation, that is not always possible. The evaluation should be conducted early so users have a fresh recollection of the development effort, but not before users have experience using the new system.

The final report to management includes the final system documentation, describes any future system enhancements that already have been identified, and details the project costs. The report represents the end of the development effort and the beginning of the new system's operational life.

Key Terms

acceptance test Testing involves the entire information system, including all typical processing situations. During an acceptance test, users enter data, including samples of actual, or live data, perform queries, and produce reports to simulate actual operating conditions. All processing options and outputs are verified by users and the IT project development team to ensure that the system functions correctly. Sometimes known as a system test.

application development The process of constructing the programs and code modules that are the building blocks of an information system. Application development is handled by an application development group within a traditional IT department that is composed of systems analysts and programmers who handle information system design, development, and implementation.

bug tracking software System developers use defect tracking software, sometimes called bug tracking software, to document and track program defects, code changes, and replacement code, called patches.

Capability Maturity Model (CMM) A model developed by SEI that integrates software and systems development into a process improvement framework.

Capability Maturity Model Integration (CMMI) An SEI-developed process to improve quality, reduce development time, and cut costs. A CMM tracks an organization's software development goals and practices, using five maturity levels, from Level 1 (relatively unstable, ineffective software) to Level 5 (software that is refined, efficient, and reliable).

code review A review of a project team member's work by other members of the team to spot logic errors. Generally, systems analysts review the work of other systems analysts, and programmers review the work of other programmers, as a form of peer review. Structured walkthroughs should take place throughout the SDLC and are called requirements reviews, design reviews, code reviews, or testing reviews, depending on the phase in which they occur. Also known as a structured walkthrough.

coding The process of turning program logic into specific instructions that a computer system can execute.

cohesion A measure of a module's scope and processing characteristics. A module that performs a single function or task has a high degree of cohesion, which is desirable.

condition A specified action or state in a structure chart.

control couple In a structure chart, a control couple shows a message, also called a flag, which one module sends to another.

control module In a structure chart, a control module is a higher-level module that directs lower-level modules, called subordinate modules.

coupling Measures relationships and interdependence among modules. The opposite of cohesion.

customer Primary user of a system, service, or product.

data conversion Existing data is loaded into the new system, transformed as needed. Depending on the system, data conversion can be done before, during, or after the operational environment is complete.

data couple In a structure chart, a data couple shows data that one module passes to another.

defect tracking software System developers use defect tracking software, sometimes called bug tracking software, to document and track program defects, code changes, and replacement code, called patches.

design walkthrough A session with users to review the interface with a cross-section of people who will work with the new system. This is a continuation of the modeling and prototyping effort that began early in the systems development process.

desk checking The process of reviewing the program code to spot logic errors, which produce incorrect results.

direct cutover The direct cutover approach causes the changeover from the old system to the new system to occur immediately when the new system becomes operational.

documentation Material that explains a system, helps people interact with it, and includes program documentation, system documentation, operations documentation, and user documentation.

flowchart A diagram used to describe program logic that represents logical rules and interaction graphically using a series of symbols connected by arrows. Flowcharts can be useful in visualizing modular program designs.

integrated development environment (IDE) A suite of integrated tools to make it easier to plan, construct, and maintain a specific software product. An IDE is designed to allow the easy integration of system components with less time being spent on developing code for interactive modules.

integration testing The testing of two or more programs that depend on each other.

ISO 9000-3:2014 A set of guidelines established and updated by the International Organization for Standardization (ISO) to provide a quality assurance framework for developing and maintaining software.

iteration cycle An agile development cycle that includes planning, designing, coding, and testing one or more features based on user stories.

iteration planning meeting In agile development, a meeting held at the beginning of each iteration cycle to break down user stories into specific tasks that are assigned to team members.

library module In a structure chart, a library module is a module that is reusable and can be invoked from more than one point in the chart.

logic error Mistakes in the underlying logic that produce incorrect results.

loop In a structure chart, a loop indicates that one or more modules are repeated.

loosely coupled Modules that are relatively independent. Loosely coupled modules are easier to maintain and modify because the logic in one module does not affect other modules.

methods In a class diagram, methods represent program logic.

object-oriented development (OOD) The process of translating an object model directly into an object-oriented programming language.

online documentation Provides immediate help when users have questions or encounter problems.

operational environment The environment for the actual system operation. It includes hardware and software configurations, system utilities, and communications resources. Also called the production environment.

operations documentation Contains all the information needed for processing and distributing online and printed output.

parallel operation The parallel operation changeover method requires that both the old and the new information systems operate fully for a specified period. Data is input into both systems, and output generated by the new system is compared with the equivalent output from the old system.

pair programming A practice in Extreme Programming in which two programmers work on the same task on the same computer; one drives (programs) while the other navigates (watches).

partitioning The breaking down of overall objectives into subsystems and modules.

patch Replacement code that is applied to fix bugs or security holes in software.

phased operation The phased operation method allows a new system to be implemented in stages, or modules.

pilot operation The pilot operation changeover method involves implementing the complete new system at a selected location of the company.

pilot site In a pilot operation, the group that uses the new system first is called the pilot site.

post-implementation evaluation An assessment of the overall quality of the information system. The evaluation verifies that the new system meets specified requirements, complies with user objectives, and achieves the anticipated benefits. In addition, by providing feedback to the development team, the evaluation also helps improve IT development practices for future projects.

process improvement   The framework used to integrate software and systems development by a new SEI model, Capability Maturity Model Integration (CMMI).

production environment   The environment for the actual system operation. It includes hardware and software configurations, system utilities, and communications resources. Also called the operational environment.

program documentation   Preparation of program documentation starts in the systems analysis phase and continues during systems implementation. Systems analysts prepare overall documentation, such as process descriptions and report layouts, early in the SDLC. Programmers provide documentation by constructing modules that are well supported by internal and external comments and descriptions that can be understood and maintained easily.

quality assurance (QA)   A process or procedure for minimizing errors and ensuring quality in products. Poor quality can result from inaccurate requirements, design problems, coding errors, faulty documentation, and ineffective testing. A quality assurance (QA) team reviews and tests all applications and systems changes to verify specifications and software quality standards.

release plan   In agile development, a plan that specifies when user stories will be implemented and the timing of the releases. Releases are relatively frequent, and each release is treated as a system prototype that can be tested and modified as needed.

simulation   A dress rehearsal for users and IT support staff. Organizations typically include all procedures, such as those that they execute only at the end of a month, quarter, or year, in their simulations.

software engineering   A software development process that stresses solid design, effective structure, accurate documentation, and careful testing.

status flag   In structured application development, an indicator that allows one module to send a message to another module.

structured walkthrough   A review of a project team member's work by other members of the team. Generally, systems analysts review the work of other systems analysts, and programmers review the work of other programmers, as a form of peer review. Structured walkthroughs should take place throughout the SDLC and are called requirements reviews, design reviews, code reviews, or testing reviews, depending on the phase in which they occur.

stub testing   A form of testing where the programmer simulates each program outcome or result and displays a message to indicate whether or not the program is executed successfully. Each stub represents an entry or exit point that will be linked later to another program or data file.

subordinate module   A lower-level module in a structure chart.

syntax error   Programming language grammar error.

system changeover   The process of putting the new information system online and retiring the old system. Changeover can be rapid or slow, depending on the method.

system documentation   A description of a system's functions and how they are implemented. The analyst prepares most of the system documentation during the systems analysis and systems design phases. System documentation includes data dictionary entries, data flow diagrams, object models, screen layouts, source documents, and the systems request that initiated the project.

system testing   A form of testing involving an entire information system and includes all typical processing situations. During a system test, users enter data, including samples of actual, or live data, perform queries, and produce reports to simulate actual operating conditions. All processing options and outputs are verified by users and the IT project development team to ensure that the system functions correctly.

test data   The data used in unit testing. Test data should contain both correct data and erroneous data and should test all possible situations that could occur.

test-driven development (TDD) An Extreme Programming (XP) concept that unit tests are designed before code is written, focusing on end results and preventing programmers from straying from their goals.

test environment The environment that analysts and programmers use to develop and maintain programs.

test plan A plan designed by a systems analyst that includes test steps and test data for integration testing and system testing.

tightly coupled If modules are tightly coupled, one module refers to internal logic contained in another module.

top-down approach A design approach, also called modular design, where the systems analyst defines the overall objectives of the system, and then breaks them down into subsystems and modules. This breaking-down process is also called partitioning.

training plan A successful information system requires training for users, managers, and IT staff members. The entire systems development effort can depend on whether or not people understand the system and know how to use it effectively. The training plan is a document that details these requirements.

train-the-trainer A strategy where one group of users has been trained and can assist others. Users often learn more quickly from coworkers who share common experience and job responsibilities.

tutorial A series of online interactive lessons that present material and provide a dialog with users.

unit testing The testing of an individual program or module. The objective is to identify and eliminate execution errors that could cause the program to terminate abnormally, and logic errors that could have been missed during desk checking.

user documentation Instructions and information to users who will interact with the system. Includes user manuals, help screens, and tutorials.

user story In agile development, a short, simple requirements definition provided by the customer. Programmers use user stories to determine a project's requirements, priorities, and scope.

webinar An Internet-based training session that provides an interactive experience. The word *webinar* combines the words *web* and *seminar*.

Chapter Exercises

Questions

1. List and describe the main tasks that are performed during systems implementation.
2. What is ISO, and why is it important to a systems developer?
3. What are the most significant differences among structured, object-oriented, and agile methods? What do they have in common?
4. Define a structure chart in language that a non-IT person would understand easily. Also provide a step-by-step description of how to create a structure chart.
5. What is cohesion? What is the difference between close coupling and loose coupling?
6. Describe three main types of testing and the order in which they are performed.
7. What is Panopto and why would you use it?
8. What is the difference between an operational environment and a test environment?
9. List and describe the four main system changeover methods. Which one generally is the least expensive? Which is the safest? Explain your answers.
10. Why is a post-implementation evaluation important? Who should conduct it, and why?

Discussion Topics

1. Your supervisor said, "Integration testing is a waste of time. If each program is tested adequately, integration testing isn't needed. Instead, we should move on to system testing as soon as possible. If modules don't interact properly, we'll handle it then." Do you agree or disagree with this comment? Explain your answer.
2. Suppose you are a systems analyst developing a detailed test plan. Explain the testing strategies you will use in your plan. Will you use live or simulated data?
3. Use the Internet to locate an example of training for a software or hardware product. Write a brief summary of the training, the product, the type of training offered, and the cost of training (if available). Discuss your findings with the class.
4. Suppose that you designed a tutorial to train a person in the use of specific software or hardware, such as a web browser. What specific information would you want to know about the recipient of the training? How would that information affect the design of the training material?
5. Which system changeover method would you recommend for an air traffic control system upgrade? Explain your answer.

Projects

1. In this chapter, you learned about the importance of testing. Design a generic test plan that describes the testing for an imaginary system.
2. Design a generic post-implementation evaluation form. The form should consist of questions that you could use to evaluate any information system. The form should evaluate the training received and any problems associated with the program.
3. Create a one-page questionnaire to distribute to users in a post-implementation evaluation of a recent information system project. Include at least 10 questions that cover the important information you want to obtain.
4. Using the material in this chapter and your own Internet research, prepare a presentation on the pros and cons of agile development methods.
5. Create an online training module using one of the systems discussed in this chapter, such as Udemy or lynda.com, on the topic of managing systems implementations.

PHASE 5 — SYSTEMS SUPPORT AND SECURITY

DELIVERABLE
An operational system that is properly maintained, supported, and secured.

TOOLKIT SUPPORT
Communications, CASE, and financial analysis tools.

As the Dilbert cartoon suggests, security concerns have become a matter of national importance. Major security breaches at large corporations are unfortunately quite commonplace. Sadly, system security is rarely solved by a simple app — it requires a disciplined approach that affects virtually all tasks in the SDLC.

Systems support and security is the final phase in the systems development life cycle. In the previous phase, systems implementation, a functioning system was delivered. The system now moves into the support phase, where the analyst maintains the system, handles security issues, protects the integrity of the system and its data, and is alert to any signs of obsolescence.

Chapter 12 describes systems support and security tasks that continue throughout the useful life of the system, including maintenance, security, backup and disaster recovery, performance measurement, and system obsolescence.

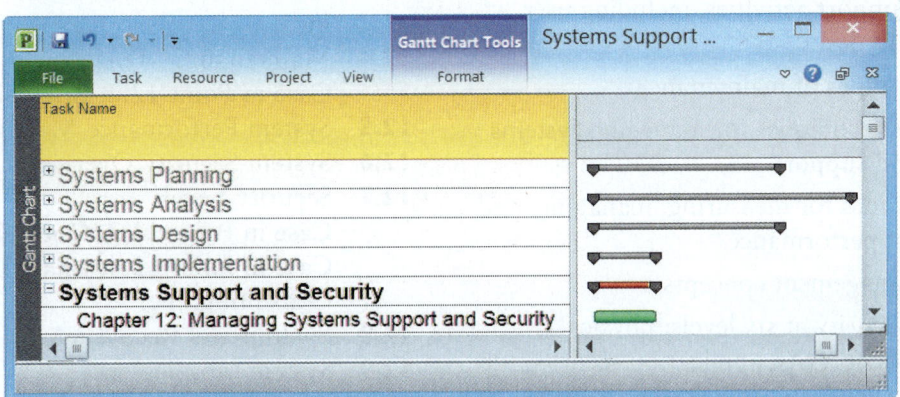

CHAPTER 12 Managing Systems Support and Security

Chapter 12 describes systems support and security tasks that continue throughout the useful life of the system. In addition to user support, this chapter discusses maintenance, security, backup and disaster recovery, performance measurement, and system obsolescence.

The chapter includes four "Case in Point" discussion questions to help contextualize the concepts described in the text. There are two "Question of Ethics" scenarios in this chapter. The first scenario concerns known security vulnerabilities in a system and what should be done about them. The second scenario is about divulging personal information, social media, and free speech.

LEARNING OBJECTIVES

When you finish this chapter, you should be able to:

- Explain the systems support and security phase
- Describe user support activities, including user training and help desks
- Define the four types of maintenance
- Explain various techniques for managing systems maintenance and support
- Describe techniques for measuring, managing, and planning system performance
- Explain risk management concepts
- Assess system security at six levels: physical security, network security, application security, file security, user security, and procedural security
- Describe backup and disaster recovery
- List factors indicating that a system has reached the end of its useful life
- Assess future challenges and opportunities for IT professionals
- Develop a strategic plan for career advancement and strong IT credentials

CHAPTER CONTENTS

12.1 INTRODUCTION

The systems support and security phase begins when a system becomes operational and continues until the system reaches the end of its useful life. Throughout the development process, the objective has been to create an information system that is efficient, easy to use, and affordable. After delivering the system, the IT team focuses on support and maintenance tasks. Managing systems support and security involves three main concerns: user expectations, system performance, and security requirements.

A systems analyst is like an internal consultant who provides guidance, support, and training. Successful systems often need the most support because users want to learn the features, try all the capabilities, and discover how the system can help them perform their tasks. In most organizations, more than half of all IT department effort goes into supporting existing systems.

This chapter begins with a discussion of systems support, including user training and help desks. The four main types of maintenance are discussed: corrective, adaptive, perfective, and preventive. How the IT group uses maintenance teams, configuration management, and maintenance releases is also examined, including the use of system performance issues and maintenance tools. The security system at each of the six security levels is analyzed: physical security, network security, application security, file security, user security, and procedural security. The importance of data backup and recovery issues is also considered. The keys to recognizing system obsolescence are presented. Lastly, some of the possible challenges and opportunities facing systems analysts in the coming years are discussed.

12.2 USER SUPPORT

Companies provide user support in many forms, including user training and a help desk to provide technical support and assistance.

12.2.1 User Training

Chapter 11 described the initial training that is performed when a new system is introduced. Additionally, new employees must be trained on the company's information systems. If significant changes take place in the existing system or if a new version is released, the IT department might develop a **user training package**. Depending on the nature of the changes, the package could include online support via email, a special website, a revision to the user guide, a training manual supplement, or formal training sessions. Training users about system changes is similar to initial training. The main objective is to show users how the system can help them perform their jobs.

12.2.2 Help Desks

As systems and data structures become more complex, users need constant support and guidance. To make data more accessible and to empower users, many IT departments create help desks. A **help desk**, also called a **service desk**, is a centralized resource staffed by IT professionals who provide users with the support they need to do their jobs. A help desk has three main objectives: (1) show people how to use system resources more effectively, (2) provide answers to technical or operational

FIGURE 12-1 Remote access software, such as GoToMyPC shown here, let users access their PCs from anywhere – even with their smartphones or tablets.

Source: gotomypc.com

questions, and (3) make users more productive by teaching them how to meet their own information needs. A help desk is the first place users turn when they need information or assistance.

A help desk does not replace traditional IT maintenance and support activities. Instead, help desks enhance productivity and improve utilization of a company's information resources.

Help desk representatives need strong interpersonal and technical skills plus a solid understanding of the business because they interact with users in many departments. A help desk should document carefully all inquiries, support tasks, and activity levels. The information can identify trends and common problems and can help build a technical support knowledge base.

A help desk can boost its productivity by using **remote control software**, which allows IT staff to take over a user's workstation and provide support and troubleshooting. Popular examples of remote control software include GoToMyPC by Citrix (shown in Figure 12-1), LogMeIn Pro by LogMeIn, and PC Now by WebEx, among many others.

During a typical day, the help desk staff members shown in Figure 12-2 might have to perform the following tasks:

- Show a user how to create a data query or report that displays specific business information

- Resolve network access or password problems

- Demonstrate an advanced feature of a system or a commercial package

- Help a user recover damaged data

- Offer tips for better operation

- Explain an undocumented software feature

- Show a user how to use web conferencing

- Explain how to access the company's intranet or the Internet

- Assist a user in developing a simple database to track time spent on various projects

- Answer questions about software licensing and upgrades

- Provide information about system specifications and the cost of new hardware or software

- Recommend a system solution that integrates data from different locations to solve a business problem

- Provide hardware support by installing or reconfiguring devices such as scanners, printers, network cards, wireless devices, optical drives, backup devices, and multimedia systems

- Show users how to maintain data consistency and integrity among a desktop computer, a notebook computer, and a handheld computer or smartphone

- Troubleshoot software issues via remote control utilities

In addition to functioning as a valuable link between IT staff and users, the help desk is a central contact point for all IT maintenance activities. The help desk is where users report system problems, ask for maintenance, or submit new systems requests. A help desk can utilize many types of automated support, just as outside vendors do, including email responses, on-demand fax capability, an online knowledge base, frequently asked questions (FAQs), discussion groups, bulletin boards, and automated voice mail. Many vendors now provide a live chat feature for online visitors.

FIGURE 12-2 A help desk, also called a service desk, provides support to system users.

Mark Bowden/Getty Images

12.2.3 Outsourcing Issues

As discussed in Chapter 7, many firms outsource various aspects of application development. This trend also includes outsourcing IT support and help desks. As with most business decisions, outsourcing has pros and cons. Typically, the main reason for outsourcing is cost reduction. Offshore call centers can trim expenses and free up valuable human resources for product development.

However, firms have learned that if tech support quality goes down, customers are likely to notice and might shop elsewhere. Critical factors might include phone wait times, support staff performance, and online support tools. The real question is whether a company can achieve the desired savings without endangering its reputation and customer base. Risks can be limited, but only if a firm takes an active role in managing and monitoring support quality and consistency.

12.3 MAINTENANCE TASKS

The systems support and security phase is an important component of TCO (total cost of ownership) because ongoing maintenance expenses can determine the economic life of a system.

Figure 12-3 shows a typical pattern of operational and maintenance expenses during the useful life of a system. **Operational costs** include items such as supplies, equipment rental, and software leases. Notice that the lower area shown in Figure 12-3 represents fixed operational expenses, while the upper area represents maintenance expenses.

Maintenance expenses vary significantly during the system's operational life and include spending to support maintenance activities. **Maintenance activities** include changing programs, procedures, or documentation to ensure correct system

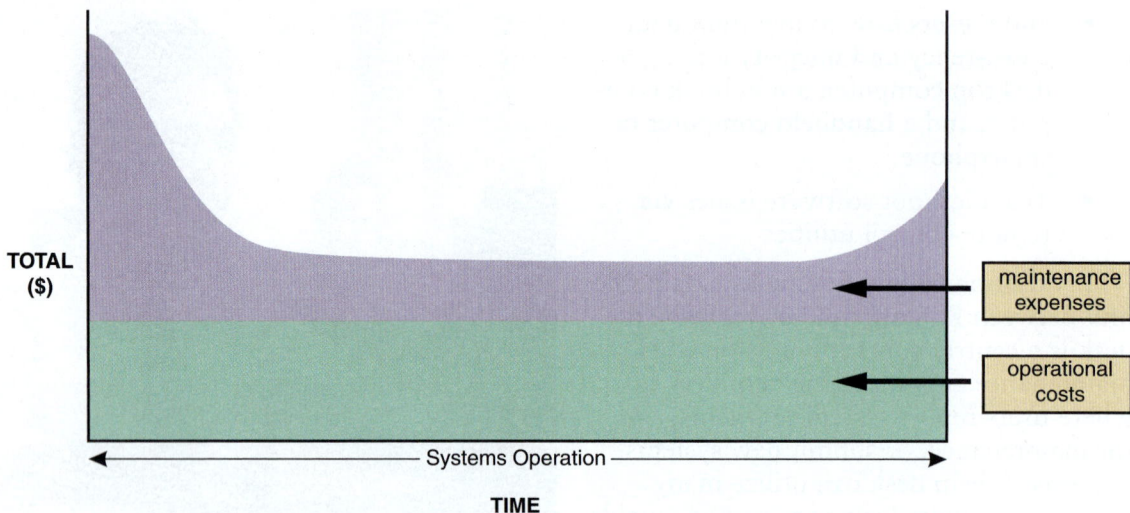

FIGURE 12-3 The total cost of operating an information system includes operational and maintenance costs. Operational costs (green) are relatively constant, while maintenance costs (purple) vary over time.

Examples of Maintenance Tasks

Corrective Maintenance
- Diagnose and fix logic errors
- Replace defective network cabling
- Restore proper configuration settings
- Debug program code
- Update drivers
- Utilize remote control software for problem diagnosis and resolution

Adaptive Maintenance
- Add online capability
- Add support for mobile devices
- Add new data entry field to input screen
- Install links to website
- Create employee portal

Perfective Maintenance
- Upgrade or replace outdated hardware
- Write macros to handle repetitive tasks
- Compress system files
- Optimize user desktop settings
- Upgrade wireless network capability
- Install more powerful network server

Preventive Maintenance
- Install new antivirus software
- Develop standard backup schedule, including off-site and cloud-based strategies
- Implement regular defragmentation process
- Analyze problem report for patterns
- Tighten all cable connections
- Develop user guide covering confidentiality rules and unauthorized use of company IT resources

FIGURE 12-4 Corrective maintenance fixes errors and problems. Adaptive maintenance provides enhancements to a system. Perfective maintenance improves a system's efficiency, reliability, or maintainability. Preventive maintenance avoids future problems.

performance; adapting the system to changing requirements; and making the system operate more efficiently. Those needs are met by corrective, adaptive, perfective, and preventive maintenance.

Although some overlap exists, four types of maintenance tasks can be identified, as shown by the examples in Figure 12-4. **Corrective maintenance** is performed to fix errors, **adaptive maintenance** adds new capability and enhancements, **perfective maintenance** improves efficiency, and **preventive maintenance** reduces the possibility of future system failure. Some analysts use the term *maintenance* to describe only corrective maintenance that fixes problems. It is helpful, however, to view the maintenance concept more broadly and identify the different types of tasks.

Maintenance expenses usually are high when a system is implemented because problems must be detected, investigated, and resolved by corrective maintenance. Once the system becomes stable, costs usually remain low and involve minor adaptive maintenance. Eventually, both adaptive and perfective maintenance activities increase in a dynamic business environment.

Near the end of a system's useful life, adaptive and corrective maintenance expenses increase rapidly, but perfective maintenance typically decreases when it becomes clear that the company plans to replace the system. Figure 12-5 shows the typical patterns for each of the four classifications of maintenance activities over a system's life span.

	Immediately After Implementation	Early Operational Life	Middle Operational Life	Later Operational Life
Corrective Maintenance	High	Low	Low	High
Adaptive Maintenance (Minor Enhancements)	None	Medium	Medium	Medium
Adaptive Maintenance (Major Enhancements)	None	None	Medium to High	Medium to High
Perfective Maintenance	Low	Low to Medium	Medium	Low
Preventive Maintenance	Low	Medium	Medium	Low

FIGURE 12-5 Information systems maintenance depends on the type of maintenance and the age of the system.

12.3.1 Corrective Maintenance

Corrective maintenance diagnoses and corrects errors in an operational system. To avoid introducing new problems, all maintenance work requires careful analysis before making changes. The best maintenance approach is a scaled-down version of the SDLC itself, where investigation, analysis, design, and testing are performed before implementing any solution. Recall from Chapter 11 the differences between a test environment and an operational environment. Any maintenance work that could affect the system must be performed first in the test environment, and then migrated to the operational system.

IT support staff respond to errors in various ways, depending on the nature and severity of the problem. Most organizations have standard procedures for minor errors, such as an incorrect report title or an improper format for a data element. In a typical procedure, a user submits a systems request that is evaluated, prioritized, and scheduled by the system administrator or the systems review committee. If the request is approved, the maintenance team designs, tests, documents, and implements a solution.

As stated in Chapter 2, many organizations use a standard online form for systems requests. In smaller firms, the process might be an informal email message. For more serious situations, such as incorrect report totals or inconsistent data, a user submits a systems request with supporting evidence. Those requests receive a high priority and a maintenance team begins work on the problem immediately.

The worst-case situation is a system failure. If an emergency occurs, the maintenance team bypasses the initial steps and tries to correct the problem immediately. This often requires a *patch*, which is a specially written software module that provides temporary repairs so operations can resume. Meanwhile, a written systems request is prepared by a user or a member of the IT department and added to the maintenance log. When the system is operational again, the maintenance team determines the cause, analyzes the problem, and designs a permanent solution. The IT response team updates the test data files, thoroughly tests the system, and prepares full documentation. Regardless of how the priorities are set, a standard ranking method can be helpful. For example, Figure 12-6 shows a three-level framework for IT support potential impact.

PRIORITY	IMPACT	TIME FRAME
Level 1	Significant impact on IT operations, security, or business activity that requires immediate attention.	Implement patch as soon as possible.
Level 2	Some impact on IT operations, security, or business activity. Requires prompt attention, but operations can continue.	Patch as necessary and begin implementation prior to next release.
Level 3	Little or no impact on current IT operations, security, or business activity	Implement in the next release.

FIGURE 12-6 This three-level ranking framework for IT support considers potential impact and response urgency.

The process of managing system support is described in more detail in Section 12.4, including an overview of maintenance tasks and a procedural flowchart.

12.3.2 Adaptive Maintenance

Adaptive maintenance adds enhancements to an operational system and makes the system easier to use. An **enhancement** is a new feature or capability. The need for adaptive maintenance usually arises from business environment changes such as new products or services, new manufacturing technology, or support for a new web-based operation.

The procedure for minor adaptive maintenance is similar to routine corrective maintenance. A user submits a systems request that is evaluated and prioritized by the systems review committee. A maintenance team then analyzes, designs, tests, and implements the enhancement. Although the procedures for the two types of maintenance are alike, adaptive maintenance requires more IT department resources than minor corrective maintenance.

A major adaptive maintenance project is like a small-scale SDLC project because the development procedure is similar. Adaptive maintenance can be more difficult than new systems development because the enhancements must work within the constraints of an existing system.

12.3.3 Perfective Maintenance

Perfective maintenance involves changing an operational system to make it more efficient, reliable, or maintainable. Requests for corrective and adaptive maintenance normally come from users, while the IT department usually initiates perfective maintenance.

During system operation, changes in user activity or data patterns can cause a decline in efficiency, and perfective maintenance might be needed to restore performance. When users are concerned about performance, it should be determined if a perfective maintenance project could improve response time and system efficiency.

Perfective maintenance can also improve system reliability. For example, input problems might cause a program to terminate abnormally. By modifying the data entry process, errors can be highlighted and users notified that they must enter proper data. When a system is easier to maintain, support is less costly and less risky. In many cases, a complex program can be simplified to improve maintainability.

In many organizations, perfective maintenance is not performed frequently enough. Companies with limited resources often consider new systems development, adaptive maintenance, and corrective maintenance more important than perfective maintenance. Managers and users constantly request new projects, so few resources are available for perfective maintenance work. As a practical matter, perfective maintenance can be performed as part of another project. For example, if a new function must be added to a program, perfective maintenance can be included in the adaptive maintenance project.

Perfective maintenance usually is cost effective during the middle of the system's operational life. Early in systems operation, perfective maintenance usually is not needed. Later, perfective maintenance might be necessary but have a high cost. Perfective maintenance is less important if the company plans to discontinue the system.

When performing perfective maintenance, analysts often use a technique called software reengineering. **Software reengineering** uses analytical techniques to identify potential quality and performance improvements in an information system. In that sense, software reengineering is similar to business process reengineering, which seeks to simplify operations, reduce costs, and improve quality.

Programs that need a large number of maintenance changes usually are good candidates for reengineering. The more a program changes, the more likely it is to become inefficient and difficult to maintain. Detailed records of maintenance work can identify systems with a history of frequent corrective, adaptive, or perfective maintenance.

12.3.4 Preventive Maintenance

To avoid problems, preventive maintenance requires analysis of areas where trouble is likely to occur. Like perfective maintenance, the IT department normally initiates preventive maintenance. Preventive maintenance often results in increased user satisfaction, decreased downtime, and reduced TCO. Preventive maintenance competes for IT resources along with other projects and sometimes does not receive the high priority that it deserves.

Regardless of the type of maintenance, trained professionals must support computer systems, just as skilled technicians must service the particle detector at CERN shown in Figure 12-7. In both cases, the quality of the maintenance will directly affect the organization's success.

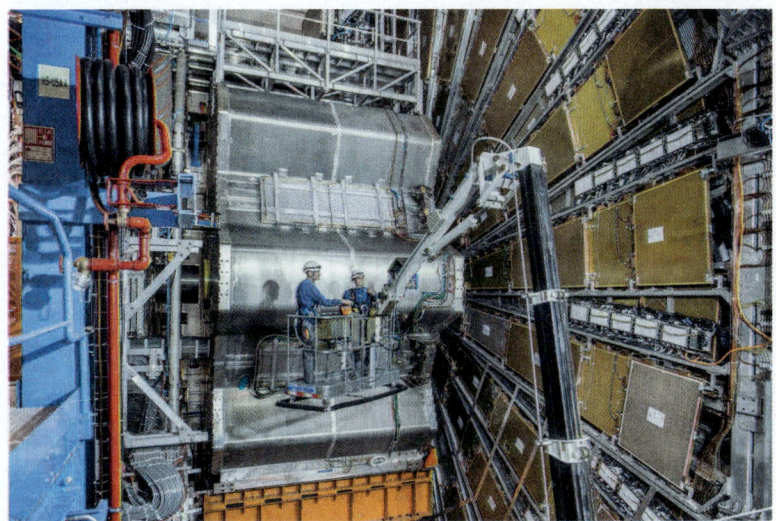

FIGURE 12-7 Technicians use a motorized lift to get into position by the ATLAS particle detector at CERN. Regardless of the type of system, high-quality maintenance must be performed by trained professionals.
Source: Anna Pantelia/CERN

CASE IN POINT 12.1:   OUTBACK OUTSOURCING, INC.

You are a systems analyst at Outback Outsourcing, a firm that handles payroll processing for many large companies. Outback Outsourcing uses a combination of payroll package programs and in-house developed software to deliver custom-made payroll solutions for its clients. Lately, users have flooded you with requests for more new features and web-based capability to meet customer expectations. Your boss, the IT manager, comes to you with a question. She wants to know when to stop trying to enhance the old software and develop a totally new version better suited to the new marketplace. How would you answer her?

12.4 MAINTENANCE MANAGEMENT

System maintenance requires effective management, quality assurance, and cost control. To achieve these goals, companies use various strategies, such as a maintenance team, a maintenance management program, a configuration management process, and a maintenance release procedure. In addition, firms use version control and baselines to track system releases and analyze the system's life cycle. These concepts are described in the following sections.

12.4.1 The Maintenance Team

A maintenance team includes a system administrator and one or more systems analysts and programmers. The system administrator should have solid technical expertise, and experience in troubleshooting and configuring operating systems and hardware. Successful analysts need a strong IT background, solid analytical abilities, good communication skills, and an overall understanding of business operations.

SYSTEM ADMINISTRATOR: A system administrator manages computer and network systems. A system administrator must work well under pressure, have good organizational and communication skills, and be able to understand and resolve complex issues in a limited time frame. In most organizations, a system administrator has primary responsibility for the operation, configuration, and security of one or more systems. The system administrator is responsible for routine maintenance, and usually is authorized to take preventive action to avoid an immediate emergency, such as a server crash, network outage, security incident, or hardware failure.

Systems administration is a vital function. One of the largest professional associations that provide collaboration and support is LISA (Large Installation

FIGURE 12-8 LISA is the USENIX special interest group for system administrators.
Source: USENIX

System Administration), shown in Figure 12-8, which is the USENIX special interest group for system administrators. Notice that LISA members subscribe to a code of ethics, shown in Figure 12-9, which includes professionalism, integrity, privacy, and social responsibility, among other topics.

The System Administrators'
Code of Ethics

We as professional System Administrators do hereby commit ourselves to the highest standards of ethical and professional conduct, and agree to be guided by this code of ethics, and encourage every System Administrator to do the same.

Professionalism I will maintain professional conduct in the workplace and will not allow personal feelings or beliefs to cause me to treat people unfairly or unprofessionally.

Personal Integrity I will be honest in my professional dealings and forthcoming about my competence and the impact of my mistakes. I will seek assistance from others when required.

I will avoid conflicts of interest and biases whenever possible. When my advice is sought, if I have a conflict of interest or bias, I will declare it if appropriate, and recuse myself if necessary.

Privacy I will access private information on computer systems only when it is necessary in the course of my technical duties. I will maintain and protect the confidentiality of any information to which I may have access, regardless of the method by which I came into knowledge of it.

Laws and Policies I will educate myself and others on relevant laws, regulations, and policies regarding the performance of my duties.

Communication I will communicate with management, users, and colleagues about computer matters of mutual interest. I will strive to listen to and understand the needs of all parties.

System Integrity I will strive to ensure the necessary integrity, reliability, and availability of the systems for which I am responsible.

I will design and maintain each system in a manner to support the purpose of the system to the organization.

Education I will continue to update and enhance my technical knowledge and other work-related skills. I will share my knowledge and experience with others.

Responsibility to Computing Community I will cooperate with the larger computing community to maintain the integrity of network and computing resources.

Social Responsibility As an informed professional, I will encourage the writing and adoption of relevant policies and laws consistent with these ethical principles.

Ethical Responsibility I will strive to build and maintain a safe, healthy, and productive workplace.

I will do my best to make decisions consistent with the safety, privacy, and well-being of my community and the public, and to disclose promptly factors that might pose unexamined risks or dangers.

I will accept and offer honest criticism of technical work as appropriate and will credit properly the contributions of others.

I will lead by example, maintaining a high ethical standard and degree of professionalism in the performance of all my duties. I will support colleagues and co-workers in following this code of ethics.

FIGURE 12-9 LISA seeks to establish standards of professional conduct for its members.
Source: ©2014 The USENIX Association

SYSTEMS ANALYSTS: Systems analysts assigned to a maintenance team are like skilled detectives who investigate and rapidly locate the source of a problem by using analysis and synthesis skills. *Analysis* means examining the whole in order to learn about the individual elements, while *synthesis* involves studying the parts to understand the overall system. In addition to strong technical skills, an analyst must have a solid grasp of business operations and functions. Analysts also need effective interpersonal and communications skills, and they must be creative, energetic, and eager for new knowledge.

PROGRAMMERS: In a small organization, a programmer might be expected to handle a wide variety of tasks, but in larger firms, programming work tends to be more specialized. For example, typical job titles include an **applications programmer**, who works on new systems development and maintenance; a systems programmer, who concentrates on operating system software and utilities; and a database programmer, who focuses on creating and supporting large-scale database systems. Many IT departments also use a job title of programmer/analyst to designate positions that require a combination of systems analysis and programming skills.

ORGANIZATIONAL ISSUES: IT managers often divide systems analysts and programmers into two groups: One group performs new system development, and the other group handles maintenance. Some organizations use a more flexible approach and assign IT staff members to various projects as they occur. By integrating development and support work, the people developing the system assume responsibility for maintaining it. Because the team is familiar with the project, additional training or expense is unnecessary, and members are likely to have a sense of ownership from the onset.

Unfortunately, many analysts feel that maintenance is less interesting and less creative than developing new systems. In addition, an analyst might find it challenging to troubleshoot and support someone else's work that might have been poorly documented and organized.

Some organizations that have separate maintenance and new systems groups rotate people from one assignment to the other. When analysts learn different skills, the organization is more versatile and people can shift to meet changing business needs. For instance, systems analysts working on maintenance projects learn why it is important to design easily maintainable systems. Similarly, analysts working on new systems get a better appreciation of the development process and the design compromises necessary to meet business objectives.

One disadvantage of rotation is that it increases overhead because time is lost when people move from one job to another. When systems analysts constantly shift between maintenance and new development, they have less opportunity to become highly skilled at any one job.

Newly hired and recently promoted IT staff members often are assigned to maintenance projects because their managers believe that the opportunity to study existing systems and documentation is a valuable experience. In addition, the mini-SDLC used in many adaptive maintenance projects is good training for the full-scale systems development life cycle. For a new systems analyst, however, maintenance work might be more difficult than systems development, and it might make sense to assign a new person to a development team where experienced analysts are available to provide training and guidance.

CASE IN POINT 12.2: Brightside Insurance, Inc.

As IT manager at Brightside Insurance Company, you organized your IT staff into two separate groups — one team for maintenance projects and the other team for new systems work. That arrangement worked well in your last position at another company. Brightside, however, previously made systems assignments with no particular pattern.

At first, the systems analysts in your group did not comment about the team approach. Now, several of your best analysts have indicated that they enjoyed the mix of work and would not want to be assigned to a maintenance team. Before a problem develops, you have decided to rethink your organizational strategy. Should you go back to the way things were done previously at Brightside? Why or why not? Do other options exist? What are they?

12.4.2 Maintenance Requests

Typically, maintenance requests involve a series of steps, as shown in Figure 12-10. After a user submits a request, a system administrator determines whether immediate action is needed and whether the request is under a prescribed cost limit. In nonemergency requests that exceed the cost limit, a systems review committee assesses the request and either approves it, with a priority, or rejects it. The system administrator notifies affected users of the outcome.

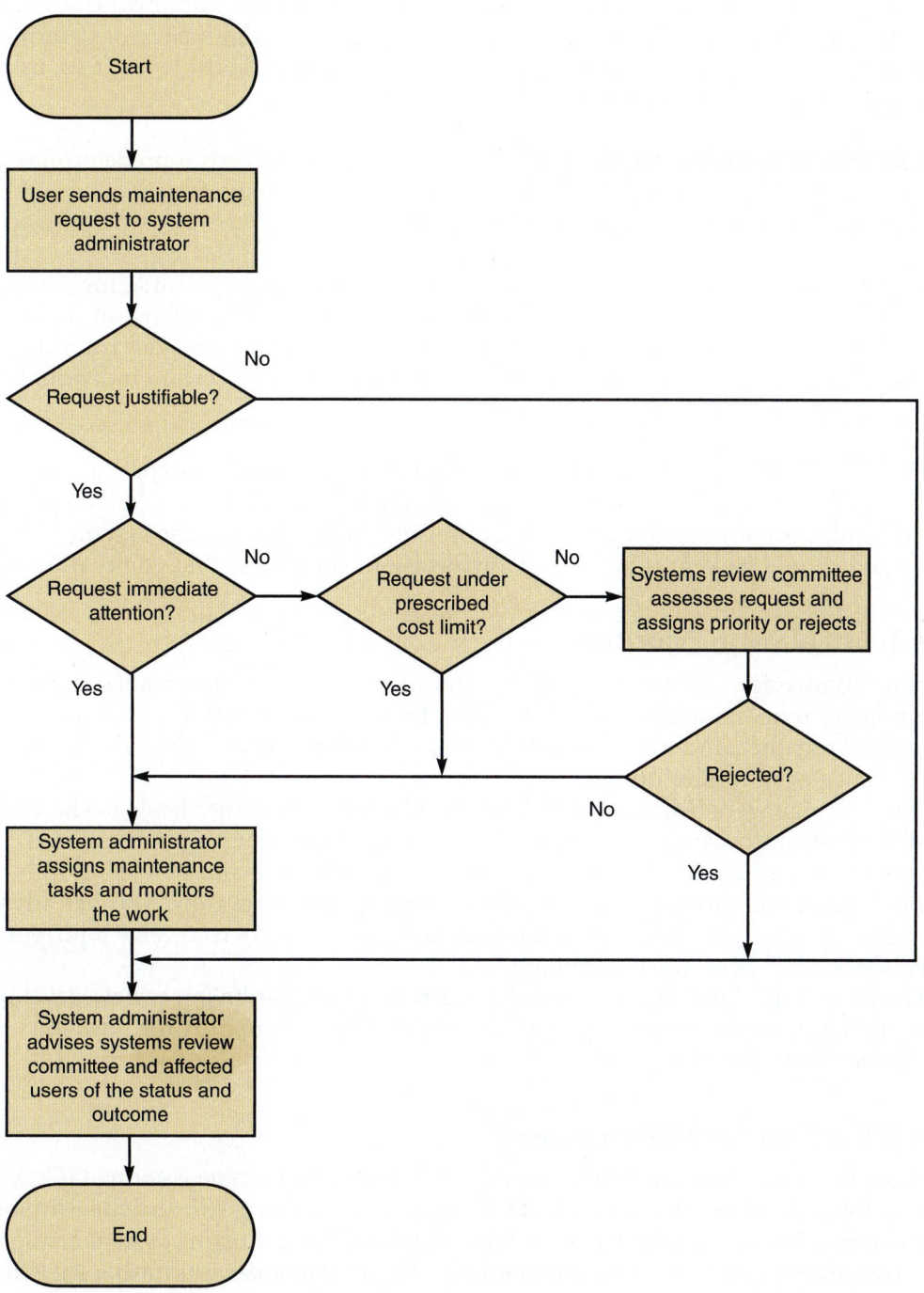

FIGURE 12-10 Although the procedure varies from company to company, the chart shows a typical process for handling maintenance requests.

Users submit most requests for corrective and adaptive maintenance when the system is not performing properly, or if they want new features. IT staff members usually initiate requests for perfective and preventive maintenance. To keep a complete maintenance log, all work must be covered by a specific request that users submit in writing or by email.

INITIAL DETERMINATION: When a user submits a maintenance request, the system administrator makes an initial determination. If the request is justifiable and involves a severe problem that requires immediate attention, the system administrator takes action at once. In justifiable, but noncritical, situations, the administrator determines whether the request can be performed within a preauthorized cost level. If so, he or she assigns the maintenance tasks and monitors the work.

THE SYSTEMS REVIEW COMMITTEE: When a request exceeds a predetermined cost level or involves a major configuration change, the systems review committee either approves it and assigns a priority, or rejects it.

TASK COMPLETION: The system administrator usually is responsible for assigning maintenance tasks to individuals or to a maintenance team. Depending on the situation and the company's policy, the system administrator might consider rotating assignments among the IT staff or limiting maintenance tasks to certain individuals or teams, as explained in the previous section.

USER NOTIFICATION: Users who initiate maintenance requests expect a prompt response, especially if the situation directly affects their work. Even when corrective action cannot occur immediately, users appreciate feedback from the system administrator and should be kept informed of any decisions or actions that could affect them.

12.4.3 Establishing Priorities

In many companies, the systems review committee separates maintenance and new development requests when setting priorities. In other organizations, all requests are considered together, and the most important project gets top priority, whether it is maintenance or new development.

Some IT managers believe that evaluating all projects together leads to the best possible decisions because maintenance and new development require similar IT department resources. In IT departments where maintenance and new development are not integrated, it might be better to evaluate requests separately. Another advantage of a separate approach is that maintenance is more likely to receive a proportional share of IT department resources.

The most important objective is to have a procedure that balances new development and necessary maintenance work to provide the best support for business requirements and priorities.

12.4.4 Configuration Management

Configuration management (CM), sometimes referred to as **change control (CC)**, is a process for controlling changes in system requirements during software development. Configuration management is also an important tool for managing system changes and costs after a system becomes operational. Most companies establish a specific process that describes how system changes must be requested and documented.

As enterprise-wide information systems grow more complex, configuration management becomes critical. Industry standards have emerged, such as the IEEE's Standard 828-2012 for configuration management in systems and software engineering, as shown in Figure 12-11.

CM is especially important if a system has multiple versions that run in different hardware and software environments. Configuration management also helps to organize and handle documentation. An operational system has extensive documentation that covers development, modification, and maintenance for all versions of the installed system. Most documentation material, including the initial systems request, project management data, end-of-phase reports, data dictionary, and the IT operations and user manuals, is stored in the IT department.

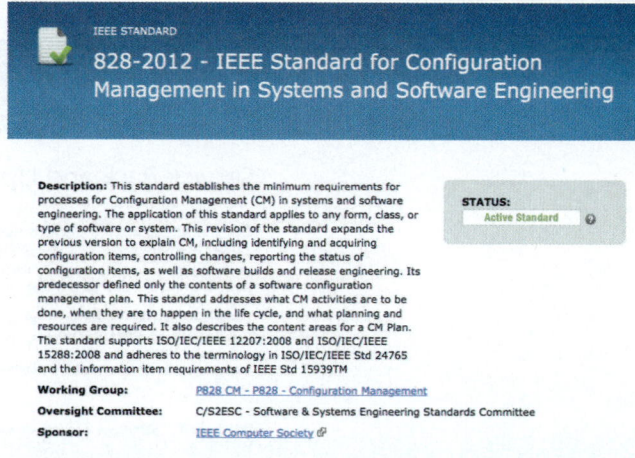

FIGURE 12-11 IEEE Standard 828-2012 for configuration management in systems and software engineering.
Source: IEEE

Keeping track of all documentation and ensuring that updates are distributed properly are important aspects of configuration management.

12.4.5 Maintenance Releases

Keeping track of maintenance changes and updates can be difficult, especially for a complex system. When a **maintenance release methodology** is used, all noncritical changes are held until they can be implemented at the same time. Each change is documented and installed as a new version of the system called a **maintenance release**.

For an in-house developed system, the time between releases usually depends on the level of maintenance activity. A new release to correct a critical error, however, might be implemented immediately rather than saved for the next scheduled release.

When a release method is used, a numbering pattern distinguishes the different releases. In a typical system, the initial version of the system is 1.0, and the release that includes the first set of maintenance changes is version 1.1. A change, for example, from version 1.4 to 1.5 indicates relatively minor enhancements, while whole number changes, such as from version 1.0 to 2.0 or from version 3.4 to 4.0, indicate a significant upgrade.

The release methodology offers several advantages, especially if two teams perform maintenance work on the same system. When a release methodology is used, all changes are tested together before a new system version is released. This approach results in fewer versions, less expense, and less interruption for users. Using a release methodology also reduces the documentation burden because all changes are coordinated and become effective simultaneously.

A release methodology also has some potential disadvantages. Users expect a rapid response to their problems and requests, but with a release methodology, new features or upgrades are available less often. Even when changes would improve system efficiency or user productivity, the potential savings must wait until the next release, which might increase operational costs.

Commercial software suppliers also provide maintenance releases, often called **service packs**, as shown in Figure 12-12. As Microsoft explains, a service pack contains all the fixes and enhancements that have been made available since the last program version or service pack.

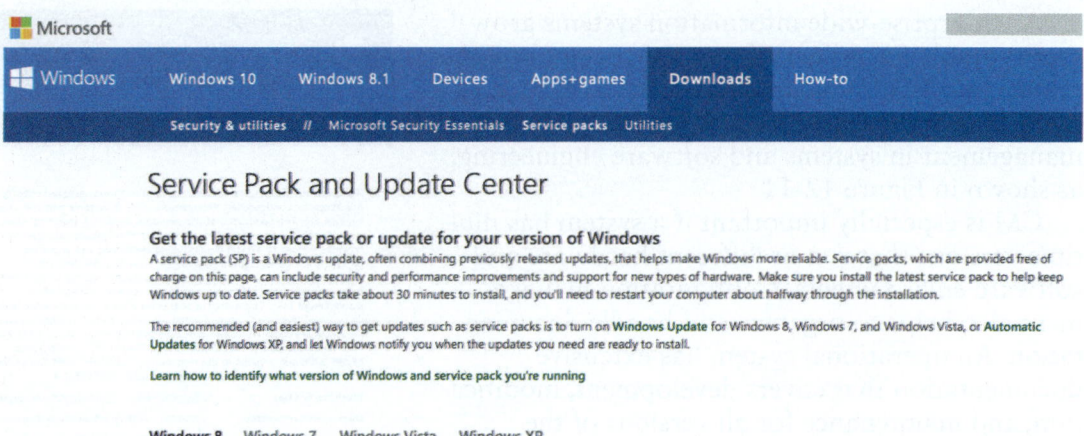

FIGURE 12-12 A Microsoft service pack provides access to updated drivers, tools, security patches, and customer-requested product changes.
Source: Microsoft

12.4.6 Version Control

Version control is the process of tracking system releases, or versions. When a new version of a system is installed, the prior release is **archived**, or stored. If a new version causes a system to fail, a company can reinstall the prior version to restore operations. In addition to tracking system versions, the IT staff is responsible for configuring systems that have several modules at various release stages. For example, an accounting system might have a one-year-old accounts receivable module that must interface with a brand-new payroll module.

Many firms use commercial applications to handle version control for complex systems. There are also numerous free and open-source alternatives. For example, one of the most popular version control systems is git, which is shown in Figure 12-13. Git is a free and open-source program designed for distributed systems. It is relatively easy to use, is available across most major platforms, and is supported by the developer community.

FIGURE 12-13 Git is a popular free version control system.
Source: git-scm.com

12.4.7 Baselines

A **baseline** is a formal reference point that measures system characteristics at a specific time. Systems analysts use baselines as yardsticks to document features and performance during the systems development process. The three types of baselines are functional, allocated, and product.

The **functional baseline** is the configuration of the system documented at the beginning of the project. It consists of all the necessary system requirements and design constraints.

The **allocated baseline** documents the system at the end of the design phase and identifies any changes since the functional baseline. The allocated baseline includes testing and verification of all system requirements and features.

The **product baseline** describes the system at the beginning of system operation. The product baseline incorporates any changes made since the allocated baseline and includes the results of performance and acceptance tests for the operational system.

12.5 SYSTEM PERFORMANCE MANAGEMENT

Years ago, when most firms used a central computer for processing data, it was relatively simple to manage a system and measure its efficiency. Today, companies use complex networks, client/server systems, and cloud computing environments to support business needs. A user at a client workstation often interacts with an information system that depends on other clients, servers, networks, and data located throughout the company. Rather than a single computer, it is the integration of all those components that determines the system's capability and performance. In many situations, IT managers use automated software and CASE tools to manage complex systems.

To ensure satisfactory support for business operations, the IT department must manage system faults and interruptions, measure system performance and workload, and anticipate future needs. The following sections discuss these topics.

12.5.1 Fault Management

No matter how well it is designed, every system will experience some problems, such as hardware failures, software errors, user mistakes, and power outages. A system administrator must detect and resolve operational problems as quickly as possible. That task, often called **fault management**, includes monitoring the system for signs of trouble, logging all system failures, diagnosing the problem, and applying corrective action.

The more complex the system, the more difficult it can be to analyze symptoms and isolate a cause. In addition to addressing the immediate problem, it is important to evaluate performance patterns and trends. For example, the Activity Monitor application shown in Figure 12-14 runs on Apple's Mac OS X to display CPU, memory, energy, disk, and network activity of all running applications in real time. Similar programs, such as the Resource Monitor, are available on Windows. Fault management software can help identify underlying causes, speed up response time, and reduce service outages.

Although system administrators must deal with system faults and interruptions as they arise, the best strategy is to prevent problems by monitoring system performance and workload.

12.5.2 Performance and Workload Measurement

In e-business, slow performance can be as devastating as no performance at all. Network delays and application bottlenecks affect customer satisfaction,

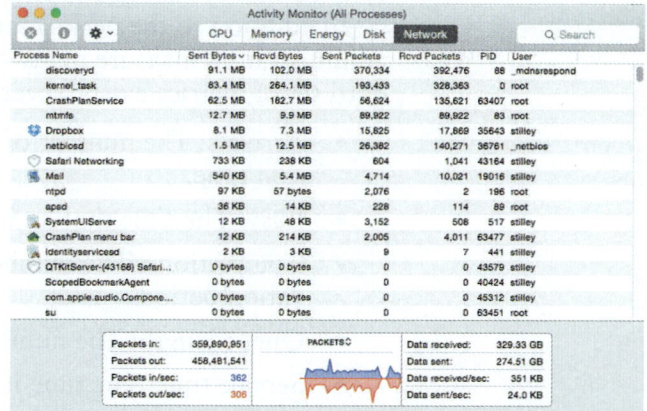

FIGURE 12-14 The Activity Monitor application on Apple's Mac OS X displays CPU, memory, energy, disk, and network activity of all running applications in real time.
Source: Apple

user productivity, and business results. In fact, many IT managers believe that network delays do more damage than actual stoppages because they occur more frequently and are difficult to predict, detect, and prevent. Customers expect reliable, fast response 24 hours a day, seven days a week. To support that level of service, companies use performance management software.

To measure system performance, many firms use **benchmark testing**, which uses a set of standard tests to evaluate system performance and capacity. In addition to benchmark testing, performance measurements, called **metrics**, can monitor the number of transactions processed in a given time period, the number of records accessed, and the volume of online data. Network performance metrics include response time, bandwidth, throughput, and turnaround time, among others.

RESPONSE TIME: **Response time** is the overall time between a request for system activity and the delivery of the response. In the typical online environment, response time is measured from the instant the user presses the Enter key or clicks a mouse button until the requested screen display appears or printed output is ready. Response time is affected by the system design, capabilities, and processing methods. If the request involves network or Internet access, response time is affected by data communication factors.

Online users expect an immediate response, and they are frustrated by any apparent lag or delay. Of all performance measurements, response time is the one that users notice and complain about most.

BANDWIDTH AND THROUGHPUT: *Bandwidth* and *throughput* are closely related terms, and many analysts use them interchangeably. Recall from Chapter 10 that bandwidth describes the amount of data that the system can transfer in a fixed time period. Bandwidth requirements are expressed in bits per second. Depending on the system, bandwidth can be measured in Kbps (kilobits per second), Mbps (megabits per second), or Gbps (gigabits per second). Analyzing bandwidth is similar to forecasting the hourly number of vehicles that will use a highway in order to determine the number of lanes required.

Throughput measures actual system performance under specific circumstances and is affected by network loads and hardware efficiency. Like bandwidth, throughput is expressed as a data transfer rate, such as Kbps, Mbps, or Gbps. Just as traffic jams delay highway traffic, throughput limitations can slow system performance and response time. That is especially true with graphics-intensive systems and web-based systems that are subject to Internet-related conditions.

In addition to the performance metrics explained in the previous section, system administrators measure many other performance characteristics. Although no standard set of metrics exists, several typical examples are:

- Arrivals: The number of items that appear on a device during a given observation time.
- Busy: The time that a given resource is unavailable.
- Completions: The number of arrivals that are processed during a given observation period.
- Queue length: The number of requests pending for a service.
- Service time: The time it takes to process a given task once it reaches the front of the queue.
- Think time: The time it takes an application user to issue another request.
- Utilization: How much of a given resource was required to complete a task.
- Wait time: The time that requests must wait for a resource to become available.

The Computer Measurement Group (CMG) maintains a website, shown in Figure 12-15, that provides support and assistance for IT professionals concerned with performance evaluation and capacity planning.

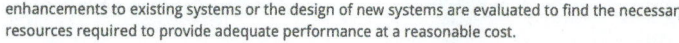

About CMG   Conferences   Contact   Publications   Calendar   Forum   Members

Overview

The Computer Measurement Group is a not-for-profit, worldwide organization of IT professionals committed to sharing information and best practices focused on ensuring the efficiency and scalability of IT service delivery to the enterprise through measurement, quantitative analysis and forecasting.

CMG members are primarily concerned with performance evaluation of existing systems to maximize performance (eg. response time, throughput, etc.) and with capacity management where planned enhancements to existing systems or the design of new systems are evaluated to find the necessary resources required to provide adequate performance at a reasonable cost.

FIGURE 12-15 The Computer Measurement Group is a not-for-profit organization that primarily is concerned with performance evaluation and capacity management.
Source: Computer Measurement Group, Inc

TURNAROUND TIME: Turnaround time applies to centralized batch processing operations, such as customer billing or credit card statement processing. Turnaround time measures the time between submitting a request for information and the fulfillment of the request. Turnaround time can also be used to measure the quality of IT support or services by measuring the time from a user request for help to the resolution of the problem.

The IT department often measures response time, bandwidth, throughput, and turnaround time to evaluate system performance both before and after changes to the system or business information requirements. Performance data is also used for cost-benefit analyses of proposed maintenance and to evaluate systems that are nearing the end of their economically useful lives.

Finally, management uses current performance and workload data as input for the capacity planning process.

12.5.3 Capacity Planning

Capacity planning is a process that monitors current activity and performance levels, anticipates future activity, and forecasts the resources needed to provide desired levels of service.

The first step in capacity planning is to develop a current model based on the system's present workload and performance specifications. Then future demand and user requirements are projected over a one- to three-year time period. The model is analyzed to see what is needed to maintain satisfactory performance and meet requirements. To assist in the process, a technique called what-if analysis can be used.

What-if analysis varies one or more elements in a model in order to measure the effect on other elements. For example, what-if analysis might be used to answer questions such as: How will response time be affected if more client workstations were added to the network? Will the client/server system be able to handle the growth in sales from the new website? What will be the effect on server throughput if more memory is added?

Powerful spreadsheet tools can also assist in performing what-if analysis. For example, Microsoft Excel contains a feature called Goal Seek that determines what changes are necessary in one value to produce a specific result for another value. In the example shown in Figure 12-16, a capacity planning worksheet indicates that the system can handle 3,840 web-based orders per day, at 22.5 seconds each. Excel calculates this automatically using the simple formula =86400/B4 for cell B5. (There are

86,400 seconds in a 24-hour day.) The user wants to know the effect on processing time if the number of transactions increases to 9,000. As the Goal Seek solution in the bottom figure shows, order processing will have to be performed in 9.6 seconds to achieve that goal.

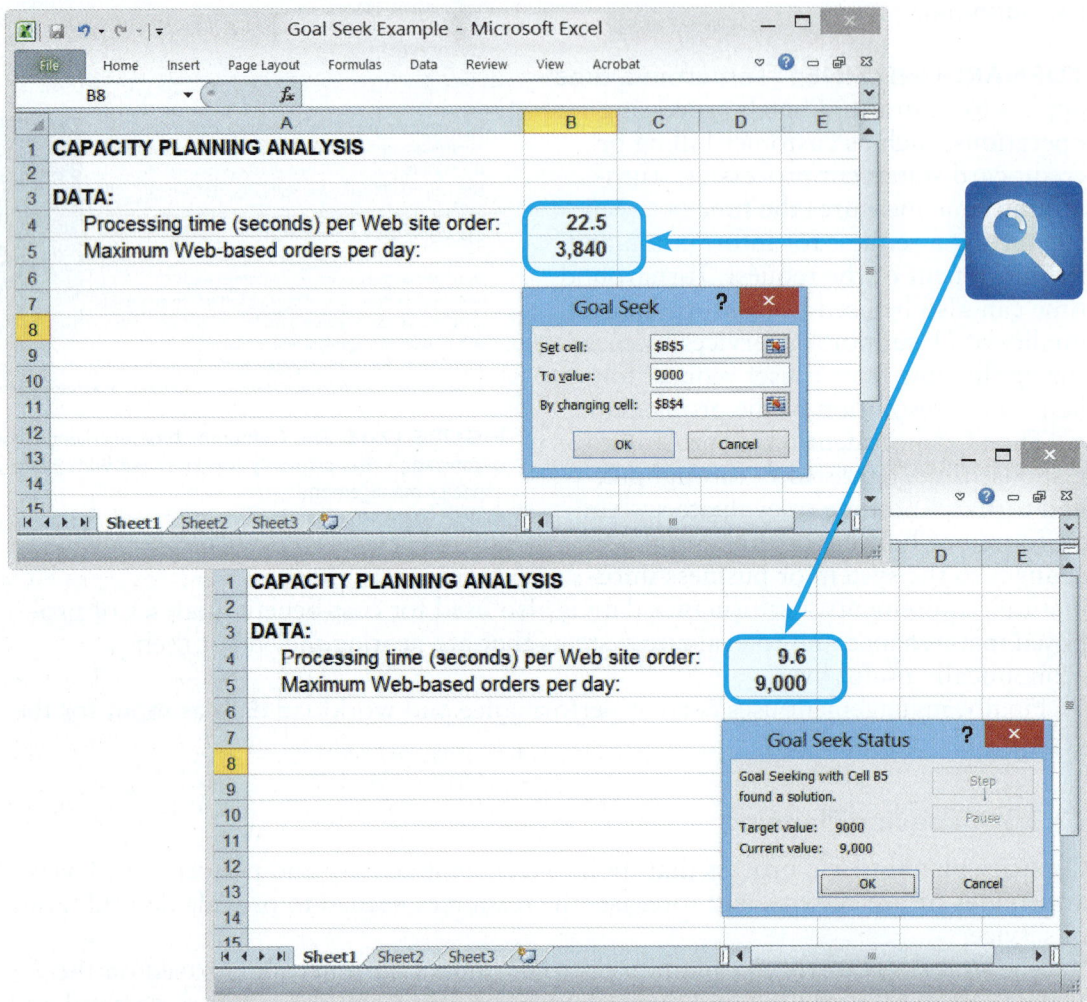

FIGURE 12-16 In this Goal Seek example, the user wants to know the effect on processing time if the number of daily transactions increases from 3,840 to 9,000.

During plan capacity, detailed information is needed about the number of transactions; the daily, weekly, or monthly transaction patterns; the number of queries; and the number, type, and size of all generated reports. If the system involves a LAN, network traffic levels must be estimated to determine whether or not the existing hardware and software can handle the load. If the system uses a client/server design, performance and connectivity specifications must be examined for each platform.

Most important, an accurate forecast of future business activities is needed. If new business functions or requirements are predicted, contingency plans should be developed based on input from users and management. The main objective is to ensure that the system meets all future demands and provides effective support for business operations. Some firms handle their own capacity planning, while others purchase software such as Idera's up.time, shown in Figure 12-17.

12.5.4 System Maintenance Tools

Automated tools can provide valuable assistance during the operation and support phases. Many CASE tools include system evaluation and maintenance features, such as:

- Performance monitors that provide data on program execution times

- Program analyzers that scan source code, provide data element cross-reference information, and help evaluate the impact of a program change

- Interactive debugging analyzers that locate the source of a programming error

- Reengineering tools

- Automated documentation capabilities

- Network activity monitors

- Workload forecasting tools

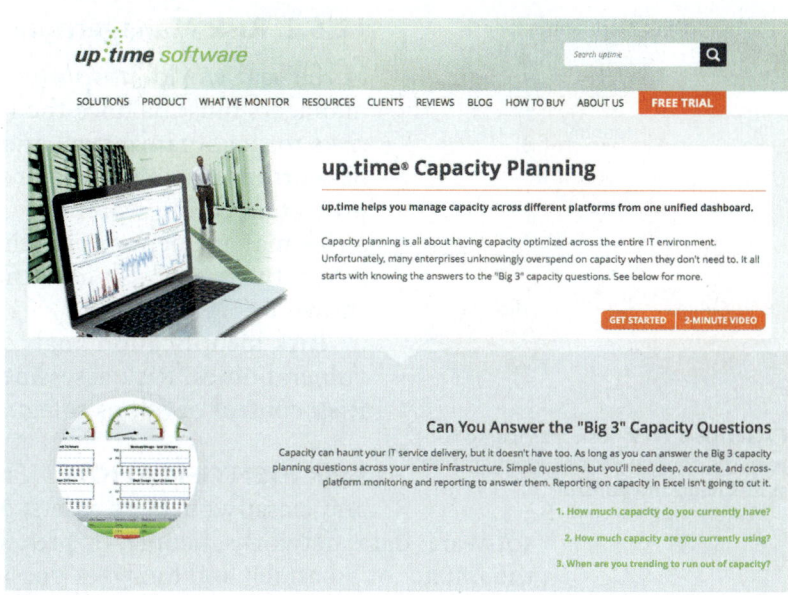

FIGURE 12-17 Idera's up.time is an example of capacity planning software and services.
Source: up.time software

In addition to CASE tools, spreadsheet and presentation software can be used to calculate trends, perform what-if analyses, and create attractive charts and graphs to display the results. Information technology planning is an essential part of the business planning process, and often part of the presentations made to management. Part A of the Systems Analyst's Toolkit has more information on using spreadsheet and presentation software to help communicate effectively.

12.6 SYSTEM SECURITY OVERVIEW

Security is a vital part of every information system. Security protects the system, and keeps it safe, free from danger, and reliable. In a global environment that includes many types of threats and attacks, security is more important than ever. This section includes a discussion of system security concepts, risk management, and common attacks against the system.

12.6.1 System Security Concepts

The **CIA triangle** in Figure 12-18 shows the three main elements of system security: confidentiality, integrity, and availability. **Confidentiality** protects information from unauthorized disclosure and safeguards privacy. **Integrity** prevents unauthorized users from creating, modifying, or deleting information. **Availability** ensures that authorized users have timely and reliable access to necessary information. The first step in managing IT security is to develop a **security policy** based on these three elements.

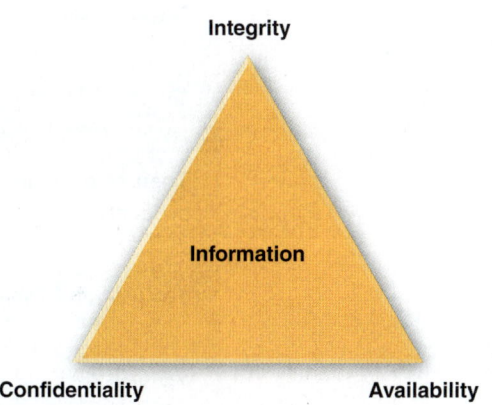

FIGURE 12-18 System security must provide information confidentiality, integrity, and availability (CIA).

Risk Management

FIGURE 12-19 Risk management requires continuous risk identification, assessment, and control.

12.6.2 Risk Management

In the real world, *absolute* security is not a realistic goal. Instead, managers must balance the value of the assets being protected, potential risks to the organization, and security costs. For example, it might not be worth installing an expensive video camera monitoring system to protect an empty warehouse. To achieve the best results, most firms use a risk management approach that involves constant attention to three interactive tasks: risk identification, risk assessment, and risk control, as shown in Figure 12-19.

Risk identification analyzes the organization's assets, threats, and vulnerabilities. Risk assessment measures risk likelihood and impact. Risk control develops safeguards that reduce risks and their impact.

RISK IDENTIFICATION: The first step in risk identification is to list and classify business assets. An asset might include company hardware, software, data, networks, people, or procedures. For each asset, a risk manager rates the impact of an attack and analyzes possible threats. A threat is an internal or external entity that could endanger an asset. For example, threat categories might include natural disasters, software attacks, or theft, as shown in Figure 12-20.

Threat Categories and Examples

THREAT CATEGORY	EXAMPLE
Extortion	Hacker steals trade secrets and threatens to release them if not paid.
Hardware and software failures	Router stops functioning, or software causes the application server to crash.
Human error or failure	Employee accidentally deletes a file.
Natural disasters	Flood destroys company building and networked systems.
Service failure	Electricity is disrupted and brings the entire system down for hours.
Software attack	A group plants destructive software, a virus, or a worm into a company network.
Technical obsolescence	Outdated software is slow, difficult to use, and vulnerable to attacks.
Theft of physical or intellectual property	Physical server is stolen, intellectual property is stolen or used without permission; may be physical or electronic.
Trespass and espionage	Employee enters unlocked server room and views the payroll data on a forbidden system.
Vandalism	Attacker defaces website logo, or destroys CEO's hard drive physically or electronically.

FIGURE 12-20 System threats can be grouped into several broad categories.

Next, the risk manager identifies vulnerabilities and how they might be exploited. A **vulnerability** is a security weakness or soft spot, and an **exploit** is an attack that takes advantage of a vulnerability. To identify vulnerabilities, a risk manager might ask questions like these: *Could hackers break through the proxy server? Could employees retrieve sensitive files without proper authorization? Could people enter the computer room and sabotage our servers?* Each vulnerability is rated and assigned a value. The output of risk identification is a list of assets, vulnerabilities, and ratings.

RISK ASSESSMENT: In IT security terms, a **risk** is the impact of an attack multiplied by the likelihood of a vulnerability being exploited. For example, an impact value of 2 and a vulnerability rating of 10 would produce a risk of 20. On the other hand, an impact value of 5 and a vulnerability rating of 5 would produce a risk of 25. When risks are calculated and prioritized, **critical risks** will head the list. Although ratings can be subjective, the overall process provides a consistent approach and framework.

RISK CONTROL: After risks are identified and assessed, they must be controlled. Control measures might include the following examples: *We could place a firewall on the proxy server. We could assign permissions to sensitive files. We could install biometric devices to guard the computer room.* Typically, management chooses one of four risk control strategies: avoidance, mitigation, transference, or acceptance. **Avoidance** eliminates the risk by adding protective safeguards. For example, to prevent unauthorized access to LAN computers, a secure firewall might be installed. **Mitigation** reduces the impact of a risk by careful planning and preparation. For example, a company can prepare a disaster recovery plan in case a natural disaster occurs. **Transference** shifts the risk to another asset or party, such as an insurance company. **Acceptance** means that nothing is done. Companies usually accept a risk only when the protection clearly is not worth the expense.

The risk management process is iterative — risks are constantly identified, assessed, and controlled. To be effective, risk managers need a combination of business knowledge, IT skills, and experience with security tools and techniques.

12.6.3 Attacker Profiles and Attacks

An **attack** is a hostile act that targets the system, or the company itself. Thus, a disgruntled employee, or a hacker who is 6,000 miles away, might launch an attack. Attackers break into a system to cause damage, steal information, or gain recognition, among other reasons. Attackers can be grouped into categories, as shown in Figure 12-21, while Figure 12-22 describes some common types of attacks. Companies combat security threats and challenges by using a multilevel strategy.

Attacker Characteristics

ATTACKER	DESCRIPTION	SKILL SET
Cyberterrorist	Attacks to advance political, social, or ideological goals.	High
Employee	Uses unauthorized information or privileges to break into computer systems, steal information, or cause damage.	Varies
Hacker	Uses advanced skills to attack computer systems with malicious intent (black hat) or to expose flaws and improve security (white hat).	High
Hacktivist	Attacks to further a social or political cause; often involves shutting down or defacing websites.	Varies
Script kiddie	Inexperienced or juvenile hacker who uses readily available malicious software to disrupt or damage computer systems, and gain recognition.	Low
Spy	Non-employee who breaks into computer systems to steal information and sell it.	High

FIGURE 12-21 IT security professionals have names for various types of attackers.

Types of Attacks and Examples

ATTACK	EXAMPLES
Back door	Attacker finds vulnerability in software package and exploits it.
Denial of service or distributed denial of service	One or more computers send a stream of connection requests to disable a Web server.
Dumpster diving	Attacker scours the trash for valuable information that can be used to compromise the system.
Mail bombing	Enormous volumes of email are sent to a target address.
Malicious code	Attacker sends infected email to the target system. Attackers may use viruses, worms, Trojan horses, keystroke loggers, spyware, or scripts to destroy data, bog down systems, spy on users, or assume control of infected systems.
Man in the middle	The attacker intercepts traffic and poses as the recipient, sending the data to the legitimate recipient but only after reading the traffic or modifying it.
Password cracking	Hacker attempts to discover a password to gain entry into a secured system. This can be a dictionary attack, where numerous words are tried, or a brute force attack, where every combination of characters is attempted.
Phishing	False DNS (Domain Name Server) information steers the user to the attacker's website. Attackers trick users into thinking they are visiting a legitimate site, such as a bank site, then attempt to obtain bank account numbers, usernames, and passwords.
Privilege escalation	Employee tricks a computer into raising his or her account to the administrator level.

(continues)

ATTACK	EXAMPLES
Sniffing	Network traffic is intercepted and scanned for valuable information.
Social engineering	An attacker calls the service desk posing as a legitimate user and requests that his or her password be changed.
Spam	Unwanted, useless email is sent continuously to business email accounts, wasting time and decreasing productivity.
Spoofing	IP address is forged to match a trusted host, and similar content may be displayed to simulate the real site for unlawful purposes.

FIGURE 12-22 Attacks can take many forms, as this table shows. IT security managers must be able to detect these attacks and respond with suitable countermeasures.

12.7 SECURITY LEVELS

To provide system security, six separate but interrelated levels must be considered: physical security, network security, application security, file security, user security, and procedural security. Like the chain shown in Figure 12-23, system security is only as strong as the weakest link. The following sections describe these security levels, and the issues that must be addressed. Top management often makes the final strategic and budget decisions regarding security, but systems analysts should understand the overall picture in order to make informed recommendations.

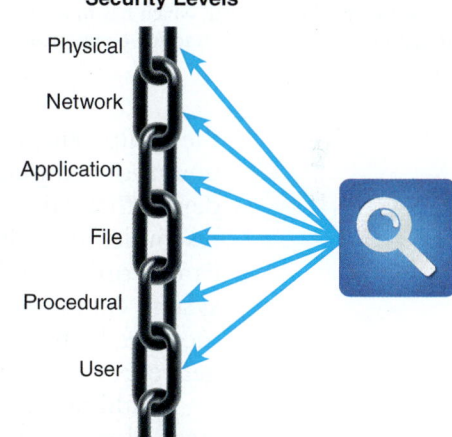

FIGURE 12-23 Each security link has a specific focus, and the overall chain is only as strong as the weakest link.

12.7.1 Physical Security

The first level of system security concerns the physical environment, including IT resources and people throughout the company. Special attention must be paid to critical equipment located in operations centers, where servers, network hardware, and related equipment operate. Large companies usually have a dedicated room built specifically for IT operations. Smaller firms might use an office or storage area. Regardless of its size and shape, an operations center requires special protection from unwanted intrusion. In addition to centrally located equipment, all computers on the network must be secure because each server or workstation can be a potential access point. Physical access to a computer represents an entry point into the system and must be controlled and protected.

OPERATIONS CENTER SECURITY: Perimeter security is essential in any room or area where computer equipment is operated or maintained. Physical access must be controlled tightly, and each entrance must be equipped with a suitable security device. All access doors should have internal hinges and electromagnetic locks that are equipped with a battery backup system to provide standby power in the event of a power outage. When the battery power is exhausted, the doors should fail in a closed position, but it should be possible for someone locked inside the room to open the door with an emergency release.

To enhance security, many companies are installing biometric scanning systems, which map an individual's facial features, fingerprints, handprint, or eye characteristics, as shown in Figure 12-24. These high-tech authentication systems replace magnetic identification badges, which can be lost, stolen, or altered. Apple's Touch ID system, described in Chapter 2, is an example of a biometric security system for smartphones and mobile devices, as discussed in the section on portable computers that follows.

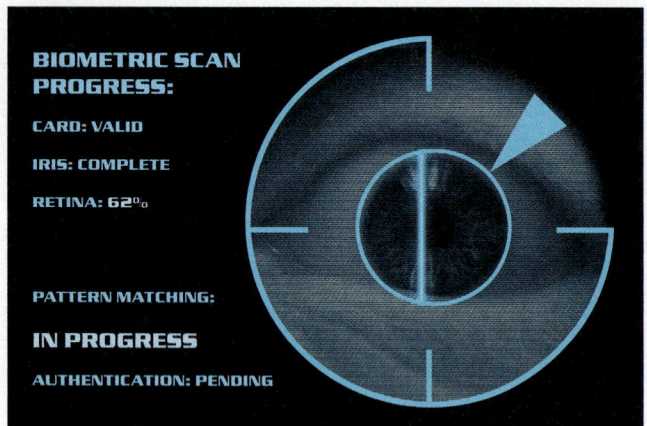

BIOMETRIC SCAN PROGRESS:

CARD: VALID

IRIS: COMPLETE

RETINA: 62%

PATTERN MATCHING:

IN PROGRESS

AUTHENTICATION: PENDING

FIGURE 12-24 Companies use biometric scanning to analyze the features of the eye's iris, which has more than 200 points that can be measured and used for comparison.

Andy Piatt/Shutterstock.com

Video cameras and motion sensors can be used to monitor computer room security and provide documentation of all physical activity in the area. A motion sensor uses infrared technology to detect movement, and can be configured to provide audible or silent alarms, and to send email messages when one is triggered. Other types of sensors can monitor temperature and humidity in the computer room. Motion sensor alarms can be activated at times when there is no expected activity in the computer room, and authorized technicians should have codes to enable or disable the alarms.

SERVERS AND DESKTOP COMPUTERS: If possible, server and desktop computer cases should be equipped with locks. This simple, but important, precaution might prevent an intruder from modifying the hardware configuration of a server, damaging the equipment, or removing a disk drive. Server racks should be locked to avoid the unauthorized placement and retrieval of keystroke loggers. A **keystroke logger** is a device that can be inserted between a keyboard and a computer. Typically, the device resembles an ordinary cable plug, so it does not call attention to itself. The device can record everything that is typed into the keyboard, including passwords, while the system continues to function normally. Keystroke loggers can be used legitimately to monitor, back up, and restore a system, but if placed by an intruder, a keystroke logger represents a serious security threat.

In addition to hardware devices, keystroke logging software also exists. A keystroke logging program can be disguised as legitimate software and downloaded from the Internet or a company network. The program remains invisible to the user as it records keystrokes and uploads the information to whoever installed the program. Such malicious software can be removed by antivirus and antispyware software, discussed later in the Application Security section.

Tamper-evident cases should be used where possible. A tamper-evident case is designed to show any attempt to open or unlock the case. In the event that a computer case has been opened, an indicator LED remains lit until it is cleared with a password. Tamper-evident cases do not prevent intrusion, but a security breach is more likely to be noticed. Many servers now are offered with tamper-evident cases as part of their standard configuration.

Monitor screen savers that hide the screen and require special passwords to clear should be used on any server or workstation that is left unattended. Locking the screen after a period of inactivity is another safeguard. A **BIOS-level password**, also called a **boot-level password** or a **power-on password**, can also be used. This password must be entered before the computer can be started. A boot-level password can prevent an unauthorized person from booting a computer by using a CD-ROM or USB device.

Finally, companies must consider electric power issues. In mission-critical systems, large-scale backup power sources are essential to continue business operations. In other cases, computer systems and network devices should be plugged into an **uninterruptible power supply (UPS)** that includes battery backup with suitable capacity. The UPS should be able to handle short-term operations in order to permit an orderly backup and system shutdown.

PORTABLE COMPUTERS: When assessing physical security issues, be sure to consider additional security provisions for notebook, laptop, and tablet computers. Because of their small size and high value, these computers are tempting targets for thieves and industrial spies. Although the following suggestions are intended as a checklist for note-book computer security, many of them also apply to desktop workstations.

- Select an operating system that allows secure logons, BIOS-level passwords, and strong firewall protection. Log on and work with a user account that has limited privileges rather than an administrator account, and mask the administrator account by giving it a different name that would be hard for a casual intruder to guess.

- Mark or engrave the computer's case with the company name and address, or attach a tamper-proof asset ID tag. Many hardware vendors allow corporate customers to add an asset ID tag in the BIOS. For example, after powering up, the following message may appear: *Property of SCR Associates — Company Use Only.* These measures might not discourage a professional thief, but might deter a casual thief, or at least make the computer relatively less desirable because it would be more difficult to use or resell. Security experts also recommend using a generic carrying case, such as an attaché case, rather than a custom carrying case that calls attention to itself and its contents.

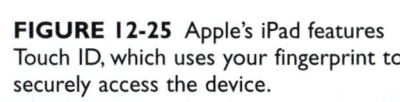

FIGURE 12-25 Apple's iPad features Touch ID, which uses your fingerprint to securely access the device.
Source: Apple

- Consider devices that have a built-in fingerprint reader, such as the iPad with Apple's Touch ID shown in Figure 12-25.

FIGURE 12-26 Absolute LoJack provides data protection and theft recovery for laptops and mobile devices.
Source: Absolute Software Corporation

••ooo Verizon 🤝   1:16 PM   🡕 ⚹ ▬▶

Find My iPhone

Apple ID	stilley@

Password	required

Forgot your Apple ID or password?

Setup Instructions
Version 4.0 (4A86)

FIGURE 12-27 Apple's Find My iPhone app
helps customers locate lost devices, and perform
remote data wipes and factory resets if needed.
Source: Scott Tilley/Apple

- Many notebook computers have a **Universal Security Slot (USS)** that can be fastened to a cable lock or laptop alarm. Again, while these precautions might not deter professional thieves, they might discourage and deter casual thieves.

- Back up all vital data before using the notebook computer outside the office. Save and transport highly sensitive data on removable media, such as a flash memory device, instead of the computer's hard drive.

- Use tracking software that directs the laptop to periodically contact a security tracking center. If the notebook is stolen, the call-in identifies the computer and its physical location. Armed with this information, the security tracking center can alert law enforcement agencies and communications providers. As shown in Figure 12-26, Absolute Software sells a product called LoJack that provides data protection and theft recovery for laptops and mobile devices.

- Apple, Google, and Microsoft offer services to locate lost customer smartphones. The services also permit remote data wipe and factory reset of the devices. For example, Apple's Find My iPhone app is shown in Figure 12-27. Apple also provides a similar cloud-based service.

- While traveling, try to be alert to potential high-risk situations, where a thief, or thieves, might create a distraction and attempt to snatch the computer. These situations often occur in crowded, noisy places like airport baggage claim areas, rental car counters, and security checkpoints. Also, when traveling by car, store the computer in a trunk or lockable compartment where it will not be visible.

- Establish stringent password protection policies that require minimum length and complexity, and set a limit on how many times an invalid password can be entered before the system locks itself down. In some situations, consider establishing file encryption policies to protect extremely sensitive files.

CASE IN POINT 12.3: OUTER BANKS COUNTY

Outer Banks County is a 200-square-mile area in coastal North Carolina, and you are the IT manager. The county has about a hundred office employees who perform clerical tasks in various departments. A recent budget crisis has resulted in a wage and hiring freeze, and morale has declined. The county manager has asked you to install some type of keystroke logger to monitor employees and determine whether they are fully productive. After your conversation, you wonder whether there might be some potential privacy and security issues involved.

For example, does an employer have a duty to notify its employees that it is monitoring them? Should the employer notify them even if not required to do so? From a human resources viewpoint, what would be the best way to approach this issue? Also, does a potential security issue exist? If an unauthorized person gained possession of the keystroke log, he or she might be able to uncover passwords and other sensitive data.

What are your conclusions? Are these issues important, and how would you respond to the county manager's recommendation? Before you answer, you should go on the Internet and learn more about keystroke loggers generally, and specific products that currently are available.

12.7.2 Network Security

A **network** is defined as two or more devices that are connected for the purpose of sending, receiving, and sharing data, which is called network traffic. In order to connect to a network, a computer must have a **network interface**, which is a combination of hardware and software that allows the computer to interact with the network. To provide security for network traffic, data can be encrypted, which refers to a process of encoding the data so it cannot be accessed without authorization.

ENCRYPTING NETWORK TRAFFIC: Network traffic can be intercepted and possibly altered, redirected, or recorded. For example, if an **unencrypted**, or **plain text**, password or credit card number is transmitted over a network connection, it can be stolen. When the traffic is encrypted, it still is visible, but its content and purpose are masked.

Figure 12-28 shows an example of encrypted traffic compared to plain text traffic. In the upper screen, the user has logged on using a password of *sad11e*. Notice that anyone who gains access to this data easily could learn the user's password. In the lower screen, the user has logged on to a secure site, such as an online bank account, and used a password, but the encryption process has made it impossible to decipher the keystrokes.

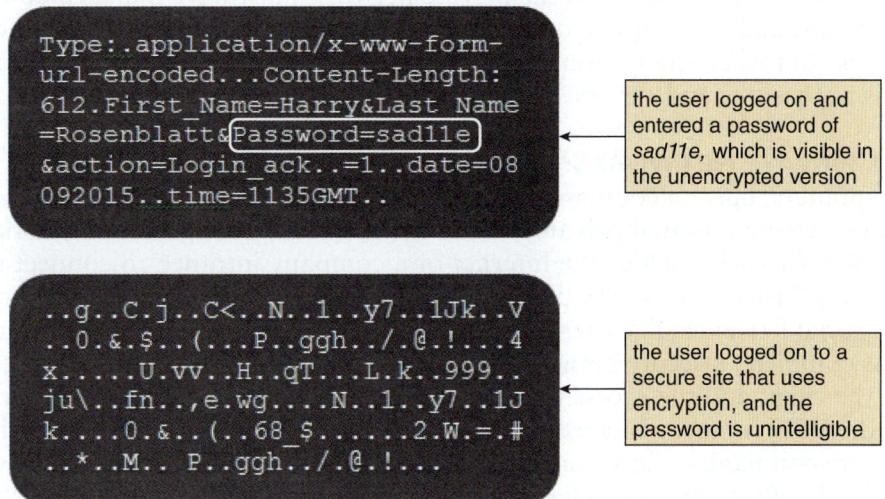

the user logged on and entered a password of *sad11e,* which is visible in the unencrypted version

the user logged on to a secure site that uses encryption, and the password is unintelligible

FIGURE 12-28 The upper screen shows an example of unencrypted text, which contains a visible password. In the lower screen, the encrypted text cannot be read.

Two commonly used encryption techniques are private key encryption and public key encryption. **Private key encryption** is symmetric because a single key is used to encrypt and decrypt information. While this method is simple and fast, it poses a fundamental problem. To use symmetric encryption, both the sender and receiver must possess the same key beforehand, or it must be sent along with the message, which increases the risk of interception and disclosure.

In contrast, **public key encryption (PKE)** is asymmetric, because each user has a pair of keys: a public key and a private key. Public keys are used to encrypt messages. Users can share their public keys freely, while keeping their private keys tightly guarded. Any message encrypted with a user's public key can only be decrypted with that user's private key. This method is commonly used in secure online e-commerce systems.

WIRELESS NETWORKS: As discussed in Chapter 10, wireless network security is a vital concern because wireless transmission is much more vulnerable than traffic on a wired network. However, if wireless traffic is encrypted, any data that is intercepted by an unintended recipient will be useless to the intruder.

The earliest form of wireless security, called **Wired Equivalent Privacy (WEP)**, required each wireless client to use a special, pre-shared key. Although many home and small office networks used this method, it provided relatively weak protection.

WEP was replaced by **Wi-Fi Protected Access (WPA)**, which offered major security improvements based on protocols created by the Wi-Fi Alliance. The most recent wireless security enhancement, called **WPA2**, further strengthens the level of wireless protection. WPA2 is an extension of WPA based on a full implementation of the **IEEE 802.11i** standard. According to the Wi-Fi Alliance, the WPA2 standard became mandatory for all new devices seeking Wi-Fi certification after 2006. WPA2 is compatible with WPA, so companies easily can migrate to the new security standard.

PRIVATE NETWORKS: It is not always practical to secure all network traffic. Unfortunately, encrypting traffic increases the burden on a network, and can decrease network performance significantly. In situations where network speed is essential, such as a web server linked to a database server, many firms use a private network to connect the computers. A **private network** is a dedicated connection, similar to a leased telephone line. Each computer on the private network must have a dedicated interface to the network, and no interface on the network should connect to any point outside the network. In this configuration, unencrypted traffic safely can be transmitted because it is not visible, and cannot be intercepted from outside the network.

VIRTUAL PRIVATE NETWORKS: Private networks work well with a limited number of computers, but if a company wants to establish secure connections for a larger group, it can create a virtual private network (VPN). A **virtual private network (VPN)** uses a public network, such as the Internet or a company intranet, to connect remote users securely. Instead of using a dedicated connection, a VPN allows remote clients to use a special key exchange that must be authenticated by the VPN. Once authentication is complete, a secure network connection, called a **tunnel**, is established between the client and the access point of the local intranet. All traffic is encrypted through the VPN tunnel, which provides an additional level of encryption and security. As more companies allow employees to work from home, a VPN can provide acceptable levels of security and reliability.

PORTS AND SERVICES: A **port**, which is identified by a number, is used to route incoming traffic to the correct application on a computer. In TCP/IP networks, such as the Internet, all traffic received by a computer contains a destination port. Because the destination port determines where the traffic will be routed, the computer sorts the traffic by port number, which is included in the transmitted data. An analogy might be a large apartment building with multiple mailboxes. Each mailbox has the same street address, but a different box number. Port security is critically important because an attacker could use an open port to gain access to the system.

A **service** is an application that monitors, or listens on, a particular port. For example, a typical email application listens on port 25. Any traffic received by that port is routed to the email application. Services play an important role in computer security, and they can be affected by port scans and denial of service attacks.

- Port scans. **Port scans** attempt to detect the services running on a computer by trying to connect to various ports and recording the ports on which a connection was accepted. For example, the result of an open port 25 would indicate that a mail server is running. Port scans can be used to draw an accurate map of a network, and pinpoint possible weaknesses.

- Denial of service. A **denial of service (DoS)** attack occurs when an attacking computer makes repeated requests to a service or services running on certain ports. Because the target computer has to respond to each request, it can become bogged down and fail to respond to legitimate requests. A much more devastating attack based on this method is called a **distributed denial of service (DDoS)** attack. This attack involves multiple attacking computers that can synchronize DOS attacks and immobilize a server, as shown in Figure 12-29. A DDoS attack is an example of the type of serious cyberattacks that United States Computer Emergency Readiness Team (US-CERT), shown in Figure 12-30, was created to address.

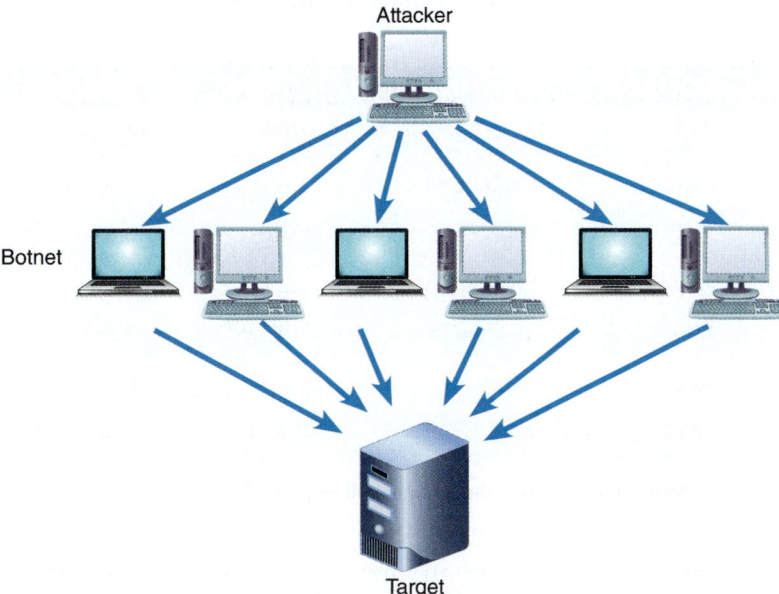

FIGURE 12-29 In a denial of service (DOS) attack, an attacker sends numerous authentication requests with false return addresses. The server tries unsuccessfully to send out authentication approval, and is eventually disabled by the floor of requests. More sophisticated DOS attacks are distributed (DDOS), as shown in this figure. Instead of a single computer, the attacker uses an army of botnets (computers unknowingly infected with malware that are difficult to trace) to attack the target.

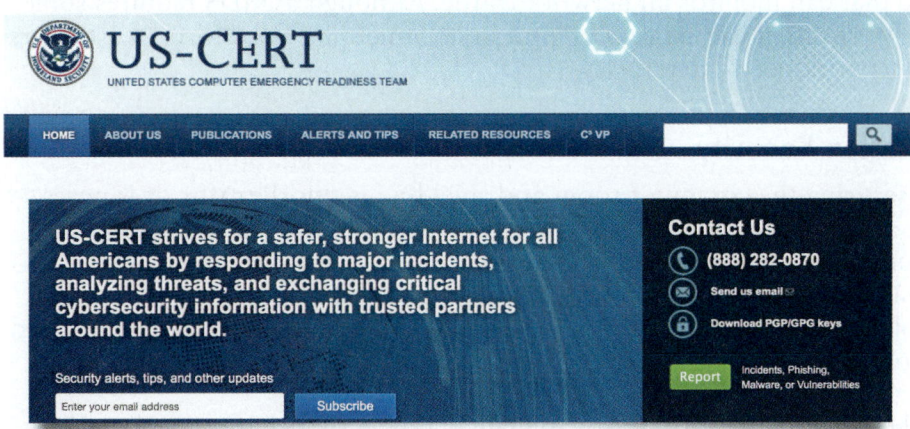

FIGURE 12-30 The United States Computer Emergency Readiness Team (US-CERT) is a key player in the battle against cybersecurity threats.

Source: US-CERT

FIREWALLS: A firewall is the main line of defense between a local network, or intranet, and the Internet. A firewall must have at least one network interface with the Internet, and at least one network interface with a local network or intranet. Firewall software examines all network traffic sent to and from each network interface. Preset rules establish certain conditions that determine whether the firewall will allow the traffic to pass. When a matching rule is found, the firewall automatically accepts, rejects, or drops the traffic. When a firewall rejects traffic, it sends a reply indicating that the traffic is not permissible. When a firewall drops traffic, no reply is sent. Firewalls can be configured to detect and respond to denial of service attacks, port scans, and other suspicious activity.

Figure 12-31 shows a basic set of firewall rules for a company that has a web server and a mail server. In this example, the firewall would accept public web server traffic only on ports 80 and 443, and public mail server traffic only on port 25. The firewall would allow private LAN traffic to any destination and port.

RULE	INTERFACE	SOURCE	DESTINATION	PORT	ACTION
1	Public	Any	Web Server	80	Accept
2	Public	Any	Web Server	443	Accept
3	Public	Any	Web Server	Any	Reject
4	Public	Any	Mail Server	25	Accept
5	Public	Any	Mail Server	Any	Reject
6	Public	Any	Any	Any	Drop
7	Private	LAN	Any	Any	Accept

FIGURE 12-31 Examples of rules that determine whether the firewall will allow traffic to pass.

NETWORK INTRUSION DETECTION: Suppose an intruder attempts to gain access to the system. Obviously, an intrusion alarm should be sounded when certain activity or known attack patterns are detected. A network intrusion detection system (NIDS) is like a burglar alarm that goes off when it detects a configuration violation. The NIDS can also alert the administrator when it detects suspicious network traffic patterns. A NIDS requires fine-tuning to detect the difference between legitimate network traffic and an attack. It is also important that a NIDS be placed on a switch or other network device that can monitor all network traffic. Although a NIDS requires some administrative overhead, it can be very helpful in documenting the efforts of attackers and analyzing network performance.

12.7.3 Application Security

In addition to securing the computer room and shielding network traffic, it is necessary to protect all server-based applications. To do so, the analyst must analyze the application's functions, identify possible security concerns, and carefully study all available documentation. Application security requires an understanding of services, hardening, application permissions, input validation techniques, software patches and updates, and software logs.

SERVICES: The network security section explained how a service is an application that monitors, or listens, on a particular port. Which services are running can be determined by using a port scan utility. If a particular application is not needed, it should be disabled. This will improve system security, performance, and reliability. An unnecessary or improperly configured service could create a vulnerability called a security hole. For example, if a loosely configured FTP (File Transfer Protocol) service is available to a hacker, he or she might be able to upload destructive code to the server.

HARDENING: The hardening process makes a system more secure by removing unnecessary accounts, services, and features. Hardening is necessary because the default configuration of some software packages might create vulnerability. For example, initial software settings often include relatively weak account permissions or file sharing controls. Hardening can be done manually or by using a configuration template, which speeds up the process in a large organization.

Hardening also includes additional protection, such as antivirus and antispyware software. These programs can detect and remove malware, which is hostile software designed to infiltrate, damage, or deny service to a computer system. Malware includes worms, Trojan horses, keystroke loggers, and spyware, among others.

APPLICATION PERMISSIONS: Typically, an application is configured to be run only by users who have specific rights. For example, an administrator account, or superuser account, allows essentially unrestricted access. Other users might be allowed to enter data but not to modify or delete existing data. To prevent unauthorized or destructive changes, the application should be configured so that non-privileged users can access the program but cannot make changes to built-in functions or configurations. User rights, also called permissions, are discussed in more detail in the file security section.

INPUT VALIDATION: As discussed in Chapter 8, when designing the user interface, input validation can safeguard data integrity and security. For example, if an application requires a number from *1* to *10*, what happens if an alphabetic character or the number *31* is entered? If the application is designed properly, it will respond with an appropriate error message. Chapter 8 also explained data entry and validation checks, which are important techniques that can improve data integrity and quality. Failure to validate input data can result in output errors, increased maintenance expense, and erratic system behavior.

PATCHES AND UPDATES: In an operational system, security holes or vulnerabilities might be discovered at any time. Patches can be used to repair these holes, reduce vulnerability, and update the system. Like any other new software, patches must be tested carefully. Before applying a patch, an effort should be made to determine the risks of *not* applying the patch, and the possibility that the patch might affect other areas of the system.

Many firms purchase software packages called third-party software. Patches released by third-party software vendors usually are safe, but any patch must be reviewed carefully before it is applied. Because researching and applying patches is time consuming and expensive, many software vendors offer an automatic update service that enables an application to contact the vendor's server and check for a needed patch or update. Depending on the configuration, available patches can be downloaded and installed without human intervention, or might require approval by IT managers. Although it is convenient, automatic updating carries substantial risks and should be used only if changes can readily be undone if unexpected results or problems develop.

SOFTWARE LOGS: Operating systems and applications typically maintain a log that documents all events, including dates, times, and other specific information. Logs can be important in understanding past attacks and preventing future intrusions. For example, a pattern of login errors might reveal the details of an intrusion attempt.

A log can also include system error messages, login histories, file manipulation, and other information that could help track down unauthorized use. Software logs should be monitored constantly to determine if misuse or wrongdoing has occurred. As explained in the network security section, a network intrusion detection system (NIDS) can alert a system administrator whenever suspicious events occur.

12.7.4 File Security

Computer configuration settings, users' personal information, and other sensitive data are stored in files. The safety and protection of these files is a vital element in any computer security program, and a systems analyst needs to consider the importance of encryption, or encoding files to make them unreadable by unauthorized users, and permissions, which can be assigned to individual users or to user groups.

ENCRYPTION: As explained in the section on network security, encryption scrambles the contents of a file or document to protect it from unauthorized access. All corporate data must be protected, but encryption is especially important for sensitive material, such as personnel or financial records. User data can be encrypted using features built-in to most modern operating systems.

PERMISSIONS: File security is based on establishing a set of permissions, which describe the rights a user has to a particular file or directory on a server. The most common permissions are read, write, and execute. Typical examples of permissions include the following:

- Read a file: The user can read the contents of the file.
- Write a file: The user can change the contents of the file.
- Execute a file: The user can run the file, if it is a program.
- Read a directory: The user can list the contents of the directory.
- Write a directory: The user can add and remove files in the directory.

When assigning file permissions, a system administrator should ensure that each user has only the minimum permissions necessary to perform his or her work — not more. In some firms, the system administrator has broad discretion in assigning these levels; in other companies, an appropriate level of management approval is required for any permissions above a standard user level. In any case, a well-documented and enforced permissions policy is necessary to promote file security and reduce system vulnerability.

USER GROUPS: Individual users who need to collaborate and share files often request a higher level of permissions that would enable any of them to change file content. A better approach, from a system administrator's viewpoint, might be to create a user group, add specific users, and assign file permissions to the group, rather than to the individuals. Many firms use this approach because it allows a user's rights to be determined by his or her work responsibilities, rather than by job title or rank. If a person is transferred, he or she leaves certain groups and joins others that reflect current job duties.

12.7.5 User Security

User security involves the identification of system users and consideration of user-related security issues. Regardless of other security precautions and features, security ultimately depends on system users and their habits, practices, and willingness to support security goals. Unfortunately, many system break-ins begin with a user account that is compromised in some way. Typically, an intruder accesses the system using the compromised account, and may attempt a **privilege escalation attack**, which is an unauthorized attempt to increase permission levels.

User security requires identity management, comprehensive password protection, defenses against social engineering, an effective means of overcoming user resistance, and consideration of new technologies. These topics are discussed in the following sections.

IDENTITY MANAGEMENT: **Identity management** refers to controls and procedures necessary to identify legitimate users and system components. An identity management strategy must balance technology, security, privacy, cost, and user productivity. Identity management is an evolving technology that is being pursued intensively by corporations, IT associations, and governments.

Gartner has described identity management as a "set of electronic records that represent ... people, machines, devices, applications, and services." This definition suggests that not just users, but also each component in a system, must have a verifiable identity that is based on unique characteristics. For example, user authentication might be based on a combination of a password, a Social Security number, an employee number, a job title, and a physical location.

Because of the devastating consequences of intrusion, IT managers should give top priority to identity management strategies and solutions.

PASSWORD PROTECTION: As the section on physical security points out, a secure system must have a password policy that requires minimum length, complexity, and a limit on invalid login attempts. Although passwords are a key element in any security program, users often choose passwords that are easy to recall, and they sometimes resent having to remember complex passwords. For example, for several years in a row, the most common computer password has been "123456," an unfortunate choice that is trivially easy to crack.

As long as passwords are used, IT managers should insist on passwords that have a minimum length, require a combination of case-sensitive letters and numbers, and must be changed periodically. Unfortunately, any password can be compromised if a user writes it down and stores it in an easily accessible location, such as a desk, a bulletin board, or under the keyboard.

Several years ago, a hacker made headlines by gaining access to the email account of a political candidate. The intruder signed on as the candidate, requested a new password, guessed the answers to the security questions, and was able to enter the account. These actions were totally illegal and constituted a serious felony under federal law.

SOCIAL ENGINEERING: Even if users are protecting and securing their passwords, an intruder might attempt to gain unauthorized access to a system using a tactic called **social engineering**. In a social engineering attack, an intruder uses social interaction to gain access to a computer system. For example, the intruder might pretend to be a new employee, an outside technician, or a journalist. Through a series of questions, the intruder tries to obtain the information that he or she needs to compromise the system. A common ploy is for the attacker to contact several people in the same organization, and use some information from one source to gain credibility and entry to another source.

An intruder also might contact the help desk and say: "Hi. This is Anna Dressler from accounting. I seem to have forgotten my password. Could you give me a new one?" Although this request might be legitimate, it also might be an attacker trying to access the system. A password never should be given based solely on this telephone call. The

FEDERAL TRADE COMMISSION
IdentityTheft.gov

What To Do Right Away | What To Do Next | Other Steps

en español

Recovering from identity theft is easier with a plan.

Did you get a data breach notice? Start here >

What To Do Right Away

print checklist

Did someone steal and use your personal information? Act quickly to limit the damage.

Step 1: Call the companies where you know fraud occurred.

Step 2: Place a fraud alert and get your credit report.

Step 3: Report identity theft to the FTC.

Step 4: File a report with your local police department.

FIGURE 12-32 Sample user evaluation form. The numerical scale allows easy tabulation of results. Following this section, the form provides space for open-ended comments and suggestions.
Source: IdentityTheft.gov

user should be required to provide further information to validate his or her identity, such as a unique employee ID, a telephone extension, and a company email address.

One highly publicized form of social engineering is called **pretexting**, which is a method of obtaining personal information under false pretenses. Pretexting is commonly used as part of **identity theft**, wherein personal information or online credentials are stolen and used for illegal purposes. The Federal Trade Commission has a website, shown in Figure 12-32, dedicated to helping consumers battle identity theft. The best way to combat social engineering attacks is with employee education, more training, and a high level of awareness during day-to-day operations.

USER RESISTANCE: Many users, including some senior managers, dislike tight security measures because the measures can be inconvenient and time consuming. Systems analysts should remind users that the company owes the best possible security to its customers, who have entrusted personal information to the firm; to its employees, who also have personal information stored in company files; and to its shareholders, who expect the company to have a suitable, effective, and comprehensive security program that will safeguard company assets and resources. When users understand this overall commitment to security and feel that they are part of it, they are more likely to choose better passwords, be more alert to security issues, and contribute to the overall success of the company's security program.

NEW TECHNOLOGIES: In addition to traditional measures and biometric devices, technology can enhance security and prevent unauthorized access. For example, the security token shown in Figure 12-33 is a physical device that authenticates a legitimate user. Some firms provide employees with security tokens that generate a numeric validation code, which the employee enters in addition to his or her normal password.

Unfortunately, new technology sometimes creates new risks. For example, a powerful search application can scan all the files, documents, emails, chats, and stored webpages on a user's computer. Although this might provide a convenient way for users to locate and retrieve their data, it also can make it easier for an intruder to obtain private information, especially in a multiuser environment, because the program can recall and display almost anything stored on the computer. Also, if an intruder uses the term *password* in a search,

FIGURE 12-33 Security tokens, which come in various forms, can provide an additional level of security.
Lim Yong Hian/Shutterstock.com

the program might be able to find password reminders that are stored anywhere on the computer. To increase privacy for multiuser computers, each user should have a separate account, with individual usernames and passwords.

Business and personal users also should use caution when they consider cloud-based storage and services. In this environment, where the technology changes rapidly, the best bet may be to work with well-established vendors, who can provide significant cloud security experience and safeguards.

12.7.6 Procedural Security

Procedural security, also called operational security, is concerned with managerial policies and controls that ensure secure operations. In fact, many IT professionals believe that security depends more on managerial issues than technology. Management must work to establish a corporate culture that stresses the importance of security to the firm and its people. Procedural security defines how particular tasks are to be performed, from large-scale data backups to everyday tasks, such as storing emails or forms. Other procedures might spell out how to update firewall software or how security personnel should treat suspected attackers.

All employees should understand that they have a personal responsibility for security. For example, an employee handbook might require that users log out of their system accounts, clear their desks, and secure all documents before leaving for the day. These policies reduce the risk of dumpster diving attacks, in which an intruder raids desks or trash bins for valuable information. In addition, paper shredders should be used to destroy sensitive documents.

Procedural security also includes safeguarding certain procedures that would be valuable to an attacker. The most common approach is a *need-to-know* concept, where access is limited to employees who need the information to perform security-related tasks. Many firms also apply a set of classification levels for access to company documents. For example, highly sensitive technical documents might be available only to the IT support team, while user-related materials would be available to most company employees. If classification levels are used, they should be identified clearly and enforced consistently.

Procedural security must be supported by upper management and fully explained to all employees. The organization must provide training to explain the procedures and issue reminders from time to time that will make security issues a priority.

CASE IN POINT 12.4:   CHAIN LINK CONSULTING, INC.

Chain Link Consulting is an IT consulting firm that specializes in system security issues. The company's president has asked you to help her put together a presentation to a group of potential clients at a trade show meeting next month. First, she wants you to review system security issues, considering all six security levels. Then she wants you to come up with a list of ways that Chain Link could test a client's security practices, in order to get a real-world assessment of vulnerability.

To make matters more interesting, she told you it was OK to be creative in your recommendations, but not to propose any action that would be illegal or unethical. For example, it would be OK to pose as a job applicant with false references to see if they were being checked, but it would not be appropriate to pick a lock and enter the computer room.

Your report is due tomorrow. What will you suggest?

12.8 BACKUP AND RECOVERY

Every system must provide for data backup and recovery. Recall from Chapter 9 that backup refers to copying data at prescribed intervals, or continuously. **Recovery** involves restoring the data and restarting the system after an interruption. An overall backup and recovery plan that prepares for a potential disaster is called a **disaster recovery plan**.

The tragic events of September 11, 2001, and increased concern about global terrorism have led many companies to upgrade their backup and disaster recovery plans. Heightened focus on disaster recovery has spawned a whole new industry, which includes new tools and strategies. Many IT professionals feel that terrorism concerns have raised security awareness throughout the corporate world. Although they are separate topics, backup and disaster recovery issues usually are intertwined. The following sections cover these topics in more detail.

12.8.1 Backup Policies

The cornerstone of business data protection is a **backup policy**, which contains detailed instructions and procedures. An effective backup policy can help a firm continue business operations and survive a catastrophe. The backup policy should specify backup media, backup types, and retention periods.

BACKUP MEDIA: **Backup media** can include tape, hard drives, optical storage, and online storage. Physical backups must be carefully identified and stored in a secure location. **Offsiting** refers to the practice of storing backup media away from the main business location, in order to mitigate the risk of a catastrophic disaster, such as a flood, fire, or earthquake. Even if the operating system includes a backup utility, many system administrators prefer to use specialized third-party software that offers more options and better controls for large-scale operations.

In addition to onsite data storage, cloud-based storage is growing rapidly. Many companies use online backup and retrieval services offered by leading vendors. For a small- or medium-sized firm, this option can be cost effective and reliable.

BACKUP TYPES: Backups can be full, differential, incremental, or continuous. A **full backup** is a complete backup of every file on the system. Frequent full backups are time consuming and redundant if most files are unchanged since the last full backup. Instead of performing a full backup, another option is to perform a **differential backup**, which is faster because it backs up *only* the files that are new or changed since the last full backup. To restore the data to its original state, the last full backup is restored first, and then the last differential backup is restored. Many IT managers believe that a combination of full and differential backups is the best option because it uses the least amount of storage space and is simple.

The fastest method, called an **incremental backup**, only includes recent files that never have been backed up by any method. This approach, however, requires multiple steps to restore the data — one for each incremental backup.

Most large systems use **continuous backup**, which is a real-time streaming method that records all system activity as it occurs. This method requires hardware, software, and substantial network capacity. However, system restoration is rapid and effective because data is being captured in real time, as it occurs. Continuous backup often uses a **RAID (redundant array of independent disks)** system that mirrors the data. RAID systems are called **fault tolerant** because a failure of any one disk does not disable the system. Compared to one large drive, a RAID design offers better performance, greater capacity, and improved reliability. When installed on a server, a RAID array of multiple drives appears to the computer as a single logical drive. Figure 12-34 shows a comparison of various backup methods.

Comparison of Backup Methods

BACKUP TYPE	CHARACTERISTICS	PROS AND CONS	TYPICAL FREQUENCY
Full	Backs up all files.	Slowest backup time and requires the most storage space. Rapid recovery because all files are restored in a single step.	Monthly or weekly.
Differential	Only backs up files that are new or changed since the last full backup.	Faster than a full backup and requires less storage space. All data can be restored in just two steps by using the last full backup and the last differential backup.	Weekly or daily.
Incremental	Only backs up files that are new or changed since the last backup of any kind.	Fastest backup and requires the least storage space because it only saves files that have never been backed up. However, requires many restore steps — one for each incremental backup.	Daily or more often.
Continuous	Real-time, streaming method that records all system activity.	Very expensive hardware, software, and network capacity. Recovery is very fast because system can be restored to just before an interruption.	Usually only used by large firms and network-based systems.

FIGURE 12-34 Comparison of full, differential, incremental, and continuous backup methods.

RETENTION PERIODS: Backups are stored for a specific retention period after which they are either destroyed or the backup media is reused. Retention periods can be a specific number of months or years, depending on legal requirements and company policy. Stored media must be secured, protected, and inventoried periodically.

12.8.2 Business Continuity Issues

Global concern about terrorism has raised awareness levels and increased top management support for a business continuity strategy in the event of an emergency. A disaster recovery plan describes actions to be taken, specifies key individuals and rescue authorities to be notified, and spells out the role of employees in evacuation, mitigation, and recovery efforts. The disaster recovery plan should be accompanied by a test plan, which can simulate various levels of emergencies and record the responses, which can be analyzed and improved as necessary.

After personnel are safe, damage to company assets should be mitigated. The plan might require shutting down systems to prevent further data loss, or moving physical assets to a secure location. Afterward, the plan should focus on resuming business operations, including the salvaging or replacement of equipment and the recovery of backup data. The main objective of a disaster recovery plan is to restore business operations to pre-disaster levels.

Disaster recovery plans are often part of a larger **business continuity plan (BCP)**, which goes beyond a recovery plan, and defines how critical business functions can continue in the event of a major disruption. Some BCPs specify the use of a hot site. A **hot site** is an alternate IT location, anywhere in the world, that can support critical systems in the event of a power outage, system crash, or physical catastrophe. A hot site requires **data replication**, which means that any transaction on the primary system must be mirrored on the hot site. If the primary system becomes unavailable, the hot site will have the latest data and can function seamlessly, with no downtime.

Although hot sites are attractive backup solutions, they are very expensive. However, a hot site provides the best insurance against major business interruptions. In addition to hot sites, business insurance can be important in a worst-case scenario. Although expensive, business insurance can offset the financial impact of system failure and business interruption.

12.9 System Obsolescence

At some point, every system becomes obsolete. For example, in the 1960s, punched cards represented the cutting edge of data management. Data was stored by punching holes at various positions and was retrieved by machines that could sense the presence or absence of a punched hole. Most full-size cards stored only 80 characters, or bytes, so more than 12,000 cards would be needed to store a megabyte. Punched cards were even used as checks and utility bills. Today, this technology is obsolete.

Constantly changing technology means that every system has a limited economic life span. Analysts and managers can anticipate system obsolescence in several ways and it never should come as a complete surprise.

A system becomes obsolete when it no longer supports user needs, or when the platform becomes outmoded. The most common reason for discontinuing a system is that it has reached the end of its economically useful life, as indicated by the following signs:

- The system's maintenance history indicates that adaptive and corrective maintenance are increasing steadily.

- Operational costs or execution times are increasing rapidly, and routine perfective maintenance does not reverse or slow the trend.

- A software package is available that provides the same or additional services faster, better, and less expensively than the current system.

- New technology offers a way to perform the same or additional functions more efficiently.

- Maintenance changes or additions are difficult and expensive to perform.

- Users request significant new features to support business requirements.

Systems operation and support continue until a replacement system is installed. Toward the end of a system's operational life, users are unlikely to submit new requests for adaptive maintenance because they are looking forward to the new release. Similarly, the IT staff usually does not perform much perfective or preventive maintenance because the system will not be around long enough to justify the cost. A system in its final stages requires corrective maintenance only to keep the system operational.

User satisfaction typically determines the life span of a system. The critical success factor for any system is whether or not it helps users achieve their operational and business goals. All negative feedback should be investigated and documented, because it can be the first signal of system obsolescence.

At some point in a system's operational life, maintenance costs start to increase, users begin to ask for more features and capability, new systems requests are submitted, and the SDLC begins again.

12.10 FUTURE CHALLENGES AND OPPORTUNITIES

There is an old saying that the only constant in life is change. The same is true for information technology, except that the rate of change in IT seems to increase every year. Rapid change can present numerous challenges to organizations and individuals, but it can also offer exciting new opportunities. The secret to success is to be ready for the changes that are bound to occur and be proactive, not reactive.

No prudent professional would start a complex journey without a map and a plan. To navigate the future of information technology, companies require strategic plans, which were discussed in Chapter 2. An individual also needs a plan to reach to a specific goal or destination. This section discusses trends and predictions that will affect all IT professionals. To prepare for the challenges ahead, individuals will need to plan and develop their knowledge, skills, and credentials.

12.10.1 Trends and Predictions

Navigating an IT career can be compared to sailing a small ship in difficult seas. Even a very good captain with a clear map for guidance will be subjected to forces and circumstances that are sometimes beyond their control. What can be done is to understand these forces and try to prepare for them. Figure 12-35 describes some winds of change that may influence IT trends, including globalization, technology integration, service orientation, cloud computing, and the workplace of the future.

In addition to the trends described in Figure 12-35, most firms will face economic, social, and political uncertainty. Many IT experts believe that in this environment, the top priorities will be the safety and security of corporate operations, agility and the ability to quickly respond to changing market forces, and bottom-line TCO. Here are some examples of possible trends and developments over the next few years:

- Cybercrime will increase significantly, with negative financial, social, and national security implications.

- Smartphones and tablets will become the dominant computing platform for most users, bypassing the traditional PC or laptop as the device of choice.

- Software-as-a-service will become the norm, which will affect business models and consumer costs as the industry moves from a purchase to a leasing model for computer applications.

- Cloud computing will become the principal computing infrastructure for the enterprise, which in turn will enable software-as-a-service and lower TCO.

- Insourcing (the moving of jobs from off-shore locations back home) will increase, due to economic factors, such as higher wages in emerging markets, improved automation through the use of sophisticated manufacturing robots, security concerns from outsourced components (hardware and software) developed overseas, and political pressure to preserve jobs.

TREND	DESCRIPTION	IMPACT ON IT GENERALLY	IMPACT ON FUTURE SYSTEMS ANALYSTS
Globalization	New kinds of corporations will be globally integrated, driven by the Internet, and free of traditional trade barriers.	Language skills will be extremely important. Technology will open new opportunities for developing countries to compete more effectively. Knowledge workers will communicate and collaborate across borders and boundaries. Work will be done 24/7 across multiple time zones.	Systems analysts will be directly affected by global trends. They will probably work for more firms in their careers, be exposed to more information, need more technical skills, and see greater change than at any time in history.
Technology Integration	Powered by an enormous increase in computing power, new IT models will include networks with smart, interconnected devices such as communication systems, automobiles, entertainment, transportation infrastructure, and "smart" power grids.	New technology will drive major changes in how personal and business services are provided. Firms will compete in a global marketplace that will reward innovation, creativity, and positive societal outcomes.	The systems analyst will need a mix of business savvy and technical skills. He or she will have a unique opportunity to work at the intersection of business operations and IT. Synergy between technology growth and globalization will create jobs and opportunities for people with the right skills.
Service Orientation	A business model of computing where processing capabilities and data storage are leased (rented) instead of bought (owned). Computing capabilities are seen as services used on-demand, like electricity or water, rather than as managed programs.	Service orientation is a paradigm shift. It represents a maturing of the field, where end users no longer care about technical details as much as business functionality. IT systems will be built using SOA (service-oriented architecture) to enable current and new functionality to be delivered as services to customers.	Systems analysts will need to increase their business acumen to work effectively in a service-oriented IT environment. Technical skills will still be needed, but services are about fulfilling business requirements.
Cloud Computing	Cloud computing is a new model for delivering business and IT services. It will have a profound impact on business strategies, including product innovation, marketing, customer relationships, and social media. Cloud computing provides the IT infrastructure that enables service orientation.	The full potential of cloud computing will be realized by firms that can integrate cloud-based infrastructure, services, servers, data access, and a secure environment. Creativity and innovation will be rewarded, and competition will be intense. Cloud computing will lower TCO by reducing capital expenditures.	Like any new technology, systems development for cloud-based applications will be a challenge for some and an opportunity for others. Regardless of the development method or platform, an analyst will need business savvy and technical know-how to help an organization take full advantage of the cloud.
The Workplace	In the face of worldwide competition and enormous technology change, firms will stress innovation, vision, and the ability to adapt rapidly. The ability to think critically will be vital.	Successful IT workers must be able to innovate, analyze, communicate effectively, and "think outside the box." The winners will be those who can adapt to change and embrace new technology and new ways of doing business.	Students preparing for the workplace of tomorrow will need a strong skill set. Systems analysts will be expected to bring communications, modeling, problem-solving, decision making, and critical thinking skills to the workplace — and to be aware of ethical issues that might affect them.

FIGURE 12-35 Major trends and their impact on IT generally and on future systems analysts.

It is entirely possible that large enterprises would require suppliers to certify their security credentials and sourcing policies. Another issue might relate to the growth of cloud computing and large-scale data centers such as the one shown in Figure 12-36. Access controls and issues related to international law concerning ownership and surveillance of network activity between the data centers and customers around the world will become progressively more important as the digital life of companies and individuals are placed online.

FIGURE 12-36 The rapid growth of data centers and cloud computing has increased security and privacy concerns.

Oleksiy Mark/Shutterstock.com

It's also possible that large enterprises will require suppliers to certify their green credentials and sourcing policies. One issue might relate to the explosion of data storage and server farms, such as the one shown in Figure 12-36. These server farms can use massive amounts of electricity, for normal operation and for cooling, which affects the environment and the corporate bottom line.

12.10.2 Strategic Planning for IT Professionals

A systems analyst should think like a small business entrepreneur who has certain assets, potential liabilities, and specific goals. Individuals, like companies, must have a strategic plan. The starting point is to formulate an answer to the following question: Have career goals been set for the next year, the next three years, and the next five years?

Working backward from these goals, intermediate milestones can be developed. An analyst's career can be managed just as an IT project would be managed. The project management tools described in Chapter 3 can be used to construct a Gantt chart or a PERT/CPM chart using months (or years) as time units. Once the plan is developed, it should be monitored regularly to stay on track. As with an agile enterprise, progress towards satisfying career goals should be corrected as needed.

12.10.3 IT Credentials and Certification

In recent years, technical credentials and certification have become extremely important to IT employers and employees. In a broad sense, credentials include formal degrees, diplomas, or certificates granted by learning institutions to show that a certain level of education has been achieved. The term certification also has a special meaning that relates to specific hardware and software skills that can be measured and verified by examination. For example, a person might have a two- or four-year degree in Information Systems and possess an ISTQB foundation level certification shown in Figure 12-37, which attests to the person's software testing knowledge and skills.

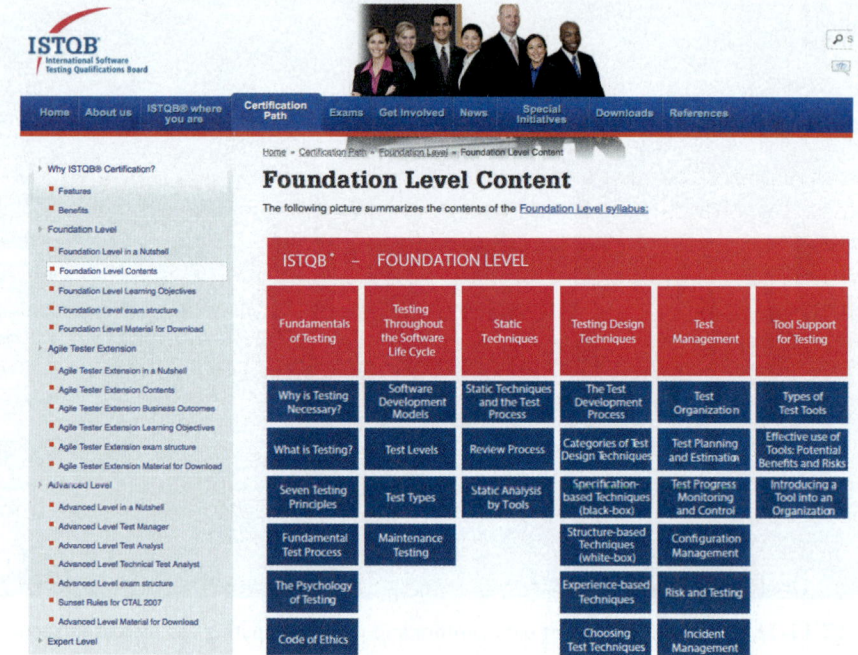

FIGURE 12-37 ISTQB has created a very successful scheme for certifying software testers worldwide.
Source: ISTQB

Rapid changes in the IT field require professionals adopt a life-long learning approach to managing their career. Even advanced degrees from universities have a short half-life, which means continuing education credits are needed to maintain competency. Many professional organizations offer continuing education courses and credentialed certificates, such as the ACM and the IEEE, as do IT industry leaders such as Microsoft, Cisco, and Oracle.

12.10.4 Critical Thinking Skills

In additional to technical skills, systems analysts must have soft skills, such as communications, interpersonal, and perceptive abilities. In fact, employers often lament the fact that their new hires are technically adept but lacking in these other areas. For a successful career, these areas must also be mastered, particularly for more senior leadership positions in the organization.

IT professionals also need critical thinking skills to succeed in the workplace. Perhaps the most important skill taught to students in school is how to learn, so that they can adapt to dynamic environments later in their career. For example, it's not so important for developers to know the latest programming languages as it is for them to be able to learn a new programming language very quickly.

The importance of critical thinking skills has been recognized for some time. They have been part of the higher cognitive levels of Bloom's taxonomy of learning objectives in education for many years. What has changed — particularly within information technology — is the relative importance of critical thinking skills for long-term career success.

Our digital society is inundated with massive amounts of data. Data mining, sophisticated algorithms, and technical innovation are important, but the most valuable asset is an employee who can solve problems. The IT community has become interested in critical thinking skills that can help a person find, organize, analyze, and use the information that he or she needs on the job. Many employers now seek critical thinkers who can locate data, identify important facts, and apply their knowledge in real-world decisions.

ETS Home > iSkills > About the iSkills Assessment

> About the iSkills Assessment
Test Content
Research
Product Tour
Request More Information
Test Administration
Scores and Reports
Off-Campus Testing
Case Studies
Pricing and Ordering
Related Products
Frequently Asked Questions

The iSkills™ Assessment

ETS has a long history of effectively helping institutions satisfy accreditation requirements and measure student performance. And, as the conversations around student learning outcomes and the shifting higher education landscape continue, it is important to work with a market leader who can provide valid and reliable data now and position you for the future.

Get the Valid, Actionable Data You Need to Demonstrate Critical Thinking in a Digital Environment

Your students need essential digital skills for the 21st century. You need an assessment that can measure and demonstrate student ability while optimizing your time and resources. The iSkills™ assessment from ETS is an outcomes-based assessment that measures the ability to think critically in a digital environment through a range of real-world tasks. This one-hour exam:

- Features **real-time, scenario-based tasks** that measure an individual's ability to navigate, understand and critically evaluate the variety of information available through digital technology
  - Tasks mirror the way individuals use information in academic, business and personal contexts
  - Test content is balanced among the humanities, social sciences, natural sciences, practical affairs and popular culture

FIGURE 12-38 Employers like to hire people who can think logically and effectively. The Educational Testing Service (ETS) measures critical thinking skills using an interactive test with realistic scenarios, and will provide certificates to students who are proficient.
Source: Educational Testing Service

Many training courses exist for technical skills, but developing critical thinking skills is equally important. Performing practice tasks that resemble actual workplace tasks can develop critical thinking skills. Studying systems analysis and design can help because it provides a solid foundation in techniques for developing models, organizing data, and recognizing patterns. Just as with hardware or software skills, formal certification is valuable in the job marketplace, but the greatest value is in learning the skills and using them to achieve career goals.

IT professionals also should be aware that the Educational Testing Service (ETS) provides assessment and certification of critical thinking skills, as shown in Figure 12-38. As stated on the ETS website (*www.ets.org*), "The scenario-based iSkill® test measures perception, organization, analysis, problem solving, and decision making." This is especially relevant for IT because the test lets students "demonstrate critical thinking in a digital environment."

Many instructors find that individual and team-based exercises can strengthen critical thinking skills. Examples include games, puzzles, brainstorming, creative problem-solving, decision tables, working with ethical questions, Boolean logic, Venn diagrams, and using cause-and-effect tools such as Pareto charts, X-Y diagrams, and fishbone diagrams, all of which are found in this textbook.

12.10.5 CyberEthics

As computers permeate more and more of our lives, the decisions made by IT professionals can have serious implications. Situations may arise involving ethical considerations that are not easy to resolve. Nevertheless, ethical, social, and legal aspects of IT are topics that today's systems analyst should be prepared to address.

In the two scenarios presented in the "Question of Ethics" section below, ask yourself what *you* would do? Where would you draw the line? How much would you be willing to risk doing what you thought was the right thing? The decisions you make could well affect your job and future employment (Scenario 1), but there are other situations where the implications can be even more severe (Scenario 2).

A QUESTION OF ETHICS

iStockphoto.com/faberfoto_it

SCENARIO 1: Jamie just completed a routine security audit on the company's information systems, and she found several areas of vulnerability. For example, file permissions have not been updated in some time, no comprehensive password policy exists, and network traffic is not fully encrypted. She noted these areas, among others, in a report to Tamika, her supervisor. The report included specific recommendations to fix the problems.

Tamika responded by saying that budgets are tight right now, and she could not approve Jamie's requests to resolve these issues. As an IT professional, Jamie is very uncomfortable with the risk level, but she has been unable to sway Tamika. When Jamie discussed the situation with her friend, Ethan, he said, "Why worry about it? If it's good enough for Tamika, it should be good enough for you."

What do you think of Ethan's advice, and why? Is this an ethical question? If Jamie still is uncomfortable, what are her options?

SCENARIO 2: Blake works for a large IT company. The company is presented with a legal directive from the federal government to divulge personal data regarding some of the company's customers who are suspected of wrongdoing.

Blake feels that this is a violation of the customers' privacy and is reluctant to comply with the request. His boss tells him the company has no choice; it must follow the law. Blake is told he can always choose to resign from the company if he feels so strongly about the situation.

Instead of complying or resigning, Blake goes public. He uses the media to advocate his point of view for freedom and privacy, even while knowing that his actions will have far-reaching consequences. Instead of just losing his job, Blake risks losing his freedom and his future.

Did Blake do the right thing? Is he a hero of free speech or a criminal (and possibly even a traitor)? What other options were available to him? What should the company have done when Blake went public? What should the government do?

12.11 CHAPTER SUMMARY

Systems support and security cover the period from the implementation of an information system until the system no longer is used. A systems analyst's primary involvement with an operational system is to manage and solve user support requests.

Corrective maintenance includes changes to correct errors. Adaptive maintenance satisfies new systems requirements, and perfective maintenance makes the system more efficient. Adaptive and perfective maintenance changes often are called enhancements. Preventive maintenance is performed to avoid future problems.

The typical maintenance process resembles a miniature version of the systems development life cycle. A systems request for maintenance work is submitted and evaluated. If it is accepted, the request is prioritized and scheduled for the IT group. The maintenance team then follows a logical progression of investigation, analysis, design, development, testing, and implementation.

Corrective maintenance projects occur when a user or an IT staff member reports a problem. Standard maintenance procedures usually are followed for relatively minor errors, but work often begins immediately when users report significant errors.

In contrast to corrective maintenance, adaptive, perfective, and preventive maintenance projects always follow the organization's standard maintenance procedures. Adaptive maintenance projects occur in response to user requests for improvements to meet changes in the business or operating environments. The IT staff usually initiates perfective maintenance projects to improve performance or maintainability. Automated program restructuring and reengineering are forms of perfective maintenance. In order to avoid future problems, IT staff perform preventive maintenance, which involves analysis of areas where trouble is likely to occur.

A maintenance team consists of one or more systems analysts and programmers. Systems analysts need the same talents and abilities for maintenance work as they use when developing a new system. Many IT departments are organized into separate new development and maintenance groups where staff members are rotated from one group to the other.

Configuration management is necessary to handle maintenance requests, to manage different versions of the information system, and to distribute documentation changes. Maintenance changes can be implemented as they are completed or a release methodology can be used in which all noncritical maintenance changes are collected and implemented simultaneously. A release methodology usually is cost effective and advantageous for users because they do not have to work with a constantly changing system. Systems analysts use functional, allocated, and product baselines as formal reference points to measure system characteristics at a specific time.

System performance measurements include response time, bandwidth, throughput, and turnaround time. Capacity management uses those measurements to forecast what is needed to provide future levels of service and support. Also, CASE tools that include system evaluation and maintenance features can be used during the systems operation, security, and support phase.

Security is a vital part of every information system. System security is dependent upon a comprehensive security policy that defines how organizational assets are to be protected and how attacks are to be responded to.

Risk management creates a workable security policy by identifying, analyzing, anticipating, and reducing risks to an acceptable level. Because information systems face a wide array of threats and attacks, six separate but interrelated security levels should be analyzed: physical security, network security, application security, file security, user security, and procedural security. Physical security concerns the physical environment, including critical equipment located in a computer room, as well as safeguards for servers and desktops throughout the company. Network security involves encryption techniques, as well as private networks and other protective measures, especially where wireless transmissions are concerned. Application security requires an understanding of services, hardening, application permissions, input validation techniques, software patches and updates, and software logs. File security involves the use of encryption and permissions, which can be assigned to individual users or to user groups. User security involves identity management techniques, a comprehensive password protection policy, an awareness of social engineering risks, and an effective means of overcoming user resistance. Procedural security involves managerial controls and policies that ensure secure operations.

Data backup and recovery issues include backup media, backup schedules, and retention periods, as well as backup designs such as RAID and cloud-based backups.

All information systems eventually become obsolete. The end of a system's economic life usually is signaled by rapidly increasing maintenance or operating costs, the availability of new software or hardware, or new requirements that cannot be achieved easily by the existing system. When a certain point is reached, an information system must be replaced, and the entire systems development life cycle begins again.

Many IT experts predict intense competition in the future, along with economic, political, and social uncertainty. Facing these challenges, top IT priorities will be the safety and security of corporate operations, environmental concerns, and bottom-line TCO.

An IT professional should have a strategic career plan that includes long-term goals and intermediate milestones. An important element of a personal strategic plan is the acquisition of IT credentials and certifications that document specific knowledge and skills. Many IT industry leaders offer certification. In addition to technical ability, other skills, such as critical thinking skills, also are extremely valuable.

Key Terms

acceptance One of four risk control strategies. In acceptance, the risk is accepted and nothing is done. Risk is usually accepted only if protection from risk is clearly not worth the expense.

adaptive maintenance Adds new capability and enhancements to an existing system.

administrator account An account that allows essentially unrestricted access to the application.

allocated baseline Documents the system at the end of the design phase and identifies any changes since the functional baseline. The allocated baseline includes testing and verification of all system requirements and features.

applications programmer A person who works on new systems development and maintenance.

archived The storage of previous version of a system when a new version is installed.

asset Hardware, software, data, networks, people, or procedures that provide tangible or intangible benefit to an organization.

attack A hostile act that targets an information system, or an organization itself.

automatic update service Enables an application to contact the vendor's server and check for a needed patch.

availability One of the three main elements of system security: confidentiality, integrity, and availability (CIA). Availability ensures that authorized users have timely and reliable access to necessary information.

avoidance One of four risk control strategies. In avoidance, adding protective safeguards eliminates the risk.

backup media Data storage options, including tape, hard drives, optical storage, and online storage.

backup policy Detailed instructions and procedures for all backups.

baseline A formal reference point that measures system characteristics at a specific time. Systems analysts use baselines as yardsticks to document features and performance during the systems development process.

benchmark testing A form of testing used by companies to measure system performance.

biometric scanning system Mapping an individual's facial features, handprint, or eye characteristics for identification purposes.

BIOS-level password A password that must be entered before the computer can be started. It prevents an unauthorized person from booting a computer by using a USB device or a CD-ROM. Also called a power-on password or a boot-level password.

boot-level password *See* **BIOS-level password**.

business continuity plan (BCP) A plan that defines how critical business functions can continue in the event of a major disruption.

capacity planning A process that monitors current activity and performance levels, anticipates future activity, and forecasts the resources needed to provide desired levels of service.

certification A credential an individual earns by demonstrating a certain level of knowledge and skill on a standardized test.

change control (CC) A process for controlling changes in system requirements during software development; also an important tool for managing system changes and costs after a system becomes operational.

CIA triangle The three main elements of system security: confidentiality, integrity, and availability.

confidentiality One of the three main elements of system security: confidentiality, integrity, and availability (CIA). Confidentiality protects information from unauthorized discloser and safeguards privacy.

configuration management (CM) A process for controlling changes in system requirements during the development phases of the SDLC. Configuration management also is an important tool for managing system changes and costs after a system becomes operational.

continuous backup A real-time streaming backup method that records all system activity as it occurs.

corrective maintenance Changes to the system to fix errors.

credentials Formal qualifications that include degrees, diplomas, or certificates granted by learning institutions to show that a certain level of education has been achieved.

critical risk When risks are categorized and prioritized, critical risks (those with the highest vulnerability and impact ratings) head the list.

critical thinking skills The ability to compare, classify, evaluate, recognize patterns, analyze cause and effect, and apply logic. Such skills are valued in the IT industry.

data replication In normal operating conditions, any transaction that occurs on the primary system must automatically propagate to the hot site.

database programmer A person who focuses on creating and supporting large-scale database systems.

denial of service (DOS) An online attack that occurs when an attacking computer makes repeated requests to a service or services running on certain ports.

differential backup A backup that includes only the files that have changed since the last full backup.

disaster recovery plan A documented procedure consisting of an overall backup and recovery plan.

distributed denial of service (DDOS) A service attack involving multiple attacking computers that can synchronize DOS attacks on a server.

dumpster diving Raiding desks or trash bins for valuable information.

enhancement A new feature or capability.

exploit An attack that takes advantage of a system vulnerability, often due to a combination of one or more improperly configured services.

fault management The timely detection and resolution of operational problems. Fault management includes monitoring a system for signs of trouble, logging all system failures, diagnosing the problem, and applying corrective action.

fault tolerant A system or application is said to be fault tolerant if the failure of one component does not disable the rest of the system or application.

firewall The main line of defense between a local network, or intranet, and the Internet.

full backup A complete backup of every file on the system.

functional baseline The configuration of the system documented at the beginning of the project. It consists of all the necessary system requirements and design constraints.

hardening Making a system more secure by removing unnecessary accounts, services, and features.

help desk A centralized resource staffed by IT professionals that provides users with the support they need to do their jobs. A help desk has three main objectives: to show people how to use system resources more effectively, to provide answers to technical or operational questions, and to make users more productive by teaching them how to meet their own information needs. Also called service desk or information center.

hot site A separate IT location, which might be in another state or even another country, that can support critical business systems in the event of a power outage, system crash, or physical catastrophe.

identity management Controls and procedures necessary to identify legitimate users and system components.

identity theft The stealing of personally identifying information online.

IEEE 802.11i A security standard for Wi-Fi wireless networks that uses the WPA2 protocol, currently the most secure encryption method for Wi-Fi networks.

incremental backup Saving a copy of only the files that have changed since the last full backup.

integrity One of the three main elements of system security: confidentiality, integrity, and availability (CIA). Integrity prevents unauthorized users from creating, modifying, or deleting information.

keystroke logger A device that can be inserted between a keyboard and a computer to record keystrokes.

log Record typically kept by operating systems and applications that documents all events, including dates, times, and other specific information. Logs can be important in understanding past attacks and preventing future intrusions.

maintenance activities Changing programs, procedures, or documentation to ensure correct system performance. Adapting the system to changing requirements; and making the system operate more efficiently. Those needs are met by corrective, adaptive, perfective, and preventive maintenance.

maintenance expenses Costs that vary significantly during the system's operational life and include spending to support maintenance activities.

maintenance release A formal release of a new system version that contains a number of changes.

maintenance release methodology A system of numbered releases used by organizations (especially software vendors) that helps organize maintenance changes and updates.

maintenance team One or more systems analysts and programmers working on product maintenance issues together.

malware Malicious software that might jeopardize the system's security or privacy.

metrics Workload measurements, also called metrics, include the number of lines printed, the number of records accessed, and the number of transactions processed in a given time period.

mitigation One of four risk control strategies. Mitigation reduces the impact of a risk by careful planning and preparation. For example, a company can prepare a disaster recovery plan to mitigate the effects of a natural disaster should one occur.

network Two or more devices that are connected for the purpose of sending, receiving, and sharing data.

network interface A combination of hardware and software that allows the computer to interact with the network.

network intrusion detection system (NIDS) Software that monitors network traffic to detect attempted intrusions or suspicious network traffic patterns, and sends alerts to network administrators. Can be helpful in documenting the efforts of attackers and analyzing network performance.

offsiting The practice of storing backup media away from the main business location, in order to mitigate the risk of a catastrophic disaster, such as a flood, fire, or earthquake.

operational costs Expenses that are incurred after a system is implemented and continue while the system is in use. Examples include system maintenance, supplies, equipment rental, and annual software license fees.

operational security Concerned with managerial policies and controls that ensure secure operations. Also called procedural security.

perfective maintenance Changes to a system to improve efficiency.

plain text Data that is not encrypted.

port A positive integer that is used for routing incoming traffic to the correct application on a computer.

port scan An attempt to detect the services running on a computer by trying to connect to various ports and recording the ports on which a connection was accepted.

power-on password *See* **BIOS-level password.**

pretexting Obtaining personal information under false pretenses.

preventive maintenance Changes to a system to reduce the possibility of future failure.

private key encryption A common encryption technology called public key encryption (PKE). The private key is one of a pair of keys, and it decrypts data that has been encrypted with the second part of the pair, the public key.

private network A dedicated connection, similar to a leased telephone line.

privilege escalation attack An unauthorized attempt to increase permission levels.

procedural security Concerned with managerial policies and controls that ensure secure operations. Also called operational security.

product baseline Describes the system at the beginning of operation. The product baseline incorporates any changes made since the allocated baseline and includes the results of performance and acceptance tests for the operational system.

programmer/analyst A designation for positions that require a combination of systems analysis and programming skills.

public key encryption (PKE) A common encryption technique. Each user on the network has a pair of keys: a public key and a private key. The public key encrypts data that can be decrypted with the private key.

RAID (redundant array of independent disks) A RAID system may be part of an organizations backup and recovery plans. A RAID system mirrors the data while processing continues. RAID systems are called fault tolerant, because a failure of any one disk does not disable the system.

recovery The process of restoring data and restarting a system after an interruption.

remote control software Applications that allow IT staff to take over a user's workstation and provide support and troubleshooting.

response time The overall time between a request for system activity and the delivery of the response. In the typical online environment, response time is measured from the instant the user presses the ENTER key or clicks a mouse button until the requested screen display appears or printed output is ready.

retention period Backups are stored for a specific retention period after which they are either destroyed or the backup media is reused.

risk In IT security, the impact of an attack multiplied by the likelihood of a vulnerability being exploited.

risk assessment Measures the likelihood and impact of risks.

risk control Develops safeguards that reduce the likelihood and impact of risks.

risk identification Listing each risk and assessing the likelihood that it could affect a project.

security hole Created by a combination of one or more improperly configured services.

security policy A plan that addresses the three main elements of system security: confidentiality, integrity, and availability.

security token A physical device that authenticates a legitimate user, such as a smart card or keychain device.

service An application that monitors, or listens on, a particular port.

service desk *See* **help desk.**

service pack A maintenance release supplied by commercial software suppliers.

social engineering An intruder uses social interaction to gain access to a computer system.

soft skills Communications, interpersonal skills, perceptive abilities, and critical thinking are soft skills. IT professionals must have soft skills as well as technical skills.

software reengineering Uses analytical techniques to identify potential quality and performance improvements in an information system.

superuser account A login account that allows essentially unrestricted access to the application.

system administrator A person who is responsible for the configuration management and maintenance of an organization's computer networks.

systems programmer A person who concentrates on operating system software and utilities.

tamper-evident case A case designed to show any attempt to open or unlock the case.

third-party software An application that is not developed in-house.

threat In risk management, an internal or external or external entity that could endanger an asset.

throughput A measurement of actual system performance under specific circumstances and is affected by network loads and hardware efficiency. Throughput, like bandwidth, is expressed as a data transfer rate, such as Kbps, Mbps, or Gbps.

transference One of four risk control strategies. In transference, risk is shifted to another asset or party, such as an insurance company.

tunnel A secure network connection established between the client and the access point of the local intranet.

turnaround time A measure applied to centralized batch processing operations, such as customer billing or credit card statement processing. Turnaround time measures the time between submitting a request for information and the fulfillment of the request. Turnaround time can also be used to measure the quality of IT support or services by measuring the time from a user request for help to the resolution of the problem.

unencrypted Data that is not encrypted.

uninterruptible power supply (UPS) Battery-powered backup power source that enables operations to continue during short-term power outages and surges.

Universal Security Slot (USS) Can be fastened to a cable lock or laptop alarm.

user rights User-specific privileges that determine the type of access a user has to a database, file, or directory. Also called permissions.

user training package The main objective of a user training package is to show users how the system can help them perform their jobs.

version control The process of tracking system releases.

virtual private network (VPN) Uses a public network to connect remote users securely. Allows a remote client to use a special key exchange that must be authenticated by the VPN.

vulnerability A security weakness or soft spot.

what-if analysis A feature of business support systems that allows analysis to define and account for a wide variety of issues (including issues not completely defined).

Wi-Fi Protected Access (WPA) A common method used to secure a wireless network. This approach requires each wireless client be configured manually to use a special, pre-shared key, rather than key pairs. The most recent and more secure version is WPA2.

Wired Equivalent Privacy (WEP) One of the earliest methods used to secure a wireless network, superseded by WPA and WPA2.

WPA2 A wireless security standard based on 802.11i that provides a significant increase in protection over WEP and WPA.

Chapter Exercises

Questions

1. Describe four types of system maintenance and provide two examples of each type.
2. As an IT manager, would you assign newly hired systems analysts to maintenance projects? Why or why not?
3. What is configuration management and why is it important?
4. Define the term *what-if analysis*. How could you use a spreadsheet in capacity planning?
5. What is a release methodology? Why is version control important?
6. Define the following terms: *response time*, *bandwidth*, *throughput*, and *turnaround time*. How are the terms related?
7. What are some key issues that you must address when considering data backup and recovery?
8. Explain the concept of risk management, including risk identification, assessment, and control.
9. What are the six security levels? Provide examples of threat categories, attacker profiles, and types of attacks.
10. Provide an example of technical obsolescence, and explain how it can be a threat to an information system.

Discussion Topics

1. Assume that your company uses a release methodology for its sales system. The current version is 5.5. Decide whether each of the following changes would justify a version 6.0 release, or be included in a version 5.6 update: (a) Add a new report, (b) add a web interface, (c) add data validation checks, (d) add an interface to the marketing system, and (e) change the user interface.
2. The four types of IT system maintenance also apply to other industries. Suppose you were in charge of aircraft maintenance for a small airline. What would be a specific example of each type of maintenance?
3. An IT manager assigns programmers and systems analysts to maintenance projects if they have less than two years of experience or if they received an average or lower rating in their last performance evaluation. Do you agree with this practice?
4. What are the most important IT security issues facing companies today? Have these changed in the last five years, and will they continue to change? How should companies prepare themselves for security threats and problems in the future?
5. Many people don't back up their data until it's too late. Once they go through a catastrophic loss of all their work, they tend to change their habits. What are some of the better ways to perform personal backups, such as cloud-based services?

Projects

1. Using the Internet, locate a software package designed to automate version control. List the key features and describe your findings in a brief memo.
2. Develop a process for managing change requests and design a form to handle a generic change request. The process should include a contingency plan for changes that must be resolved immediately.
3. Visit the IT department at your school or at a local company and find out whether performance measurements are used. Write a brief report describing your findings.
4. Explain how to use the Goal Seek feature in Microsoft Excel, and create a worksheet that demonstrates this feature.
5. Security breaches are in the news all the time. Document a recent hack involving the theft of employee information or customer data. Suggest ways the attack could have been avoided.

THE SYSTEMS ANALYST'S TOOLKIT

OBJECTIVE

Learn how to use communications tools, CASE tools, financial analysis tools, and Internet resource tools.

© 2008 Scott Adams, Inc./Dist. by UFC, INC.

The pointy-haired boss is implying that Dilbert's poor communication skills have negatively impacted the project team. In the last panel, Dogbert may just be mocking Dilbert, but there's no doubt that a systems analyst must have excellent communication skills to succeed. Fortunately, these are skills that can be learned, and the Systems Analyst's Toolkit can help.

The Systems Analyst's Toolkit presents a valuable set of skills and knowledge that can be used throughout the systems development process. The toolkit is analogous to a traditional toolbox that a craftsman would use to complete a project, full of the tools of the trade. But for the systems analyst, instead of a hammer and a screwdriver, the toolkit contains information technology tools and techniques that can help get the job done.

- Part A discusses communication tools that can help the analyst write clearly, speak effectively, and deliver powerful presentations.
- Part B describes CASE tools that can be used to design, construct, and document an information system.
- Part C demonstrates financial analysis tools that can used to measure project feasibility, develop accurate cost-benefit estimates, and make sound decisions.
- Part D describes Internet resource tools that can be used to locate information, obtain reference material, and monitor IT trends and developments.

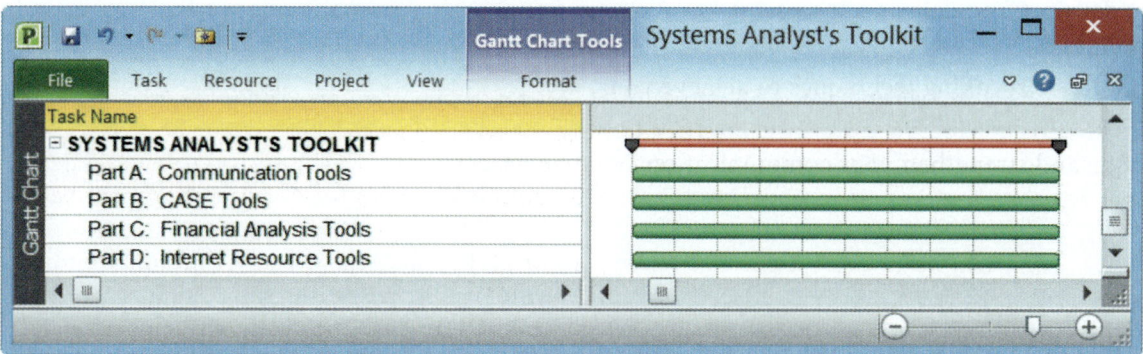

PART A Communication Tools

Part A of the Systems Analyst's Toolkit discusses communication tools that can help the analyst write clearly, speak effectively, and deliver powerful presentations.

LEARNING OBJECTIVES

When you finish this part of the Toolkit, you should be able to:

- List overall guidelines for successful communications
- Write effective letters, memos, and email messages
- Measure the readability of written material
- Organize and prepare written reports that are required during systems development
- Follow guidelines for effective oral communication
- Plan, develop, and deliver a successful presentation
- Use effective speaking techniques to achieve your objectives
- Manage and strengthen your communication skills

TOOLKIT CONTENTS

A.1 INTRODUCTION

A successful systems analyst must have good written and oral communication skills to perform his or her job effectively. Never underestimate the importance of effective communication, whether you are using a memo, email, an oral presentation, or a social networking site to convey your ideas. The following guidelines will help you prepare and deliver effective presentations. Remember, however, that nothing increases your ability to communicate better than practicing these skills.

A.2 SUCCESSFUL COMMUNICATION STRATEGIES

Successful communication does not just happen. Usually, it is the result of a specific strategy that includes careful planning, hard work, and practice. To be a successful communicator, you must consider five related questions about yourself, your audience, and your objectives: why, who, what, when, and how. You must also consider the cultural context of your communication. Above all, you must know your subject and have confidence in yourself.

A.2.1 Why, Who, What, When, and How

The **why, who, what, when, and how of communications** are important questions that you must answer before you communicate. These five questions are described in the following section.

WHY: Know *why* you are communicating and what you want to accomplish. Ask yourself the question, "Is this communication necessary, and what specific results am I seeking?" Your entire communication strategy depends on the results that you need.

WHO: Know *who* your targets are. Chapter 1 describes how information needs of users depend on their organizational and knowledge levels. When communicating with management, for example, sometimes a fine line exists between saying enough and saying too much. Each situation is different, so you must use good judgment and be alert for input from your audience.

WHAT: Know *what* is expected of you and when to go into detail. This is directly related to knowing who your targets are and the organizational and knowledge levels of your audience. For example, a vice president might expect less detail and more focus on how a project supports the company's strategic business goals. You must design your communications just as carefully as your systems project. For example, will the recipients expect you to address a specific issue or topic? Will they expect cost estimates or charts? Design your communications based on the answers to those questions.

WHEN: Know *when* to speak and *when* to remain silent and let others continue the discussion. To be an effective speaker, you must be a good listener — and use audience feedback to adjust your presentation. Good timing is an essential part of every presentation. Your delivery must be paced properly — too fast and you will lose your audience; too slow and they might become bored.

HOW: Know *how* to communicate effectively. You can strengthen your communication skills by using Toolkit suggestions, reflecting upon your own experiences, and observing successful and unsuccessful techniques used by others.

A.2.2 Cultural Context

Communication strategy is affected by the cultural context in which the communication takes place, as shown in Figure A-1. Cultural factors can include geography, background, educational level, and societal differences, among others. These differences must be considered when asking and answering the *why, who, what, when,* and *how* questions.

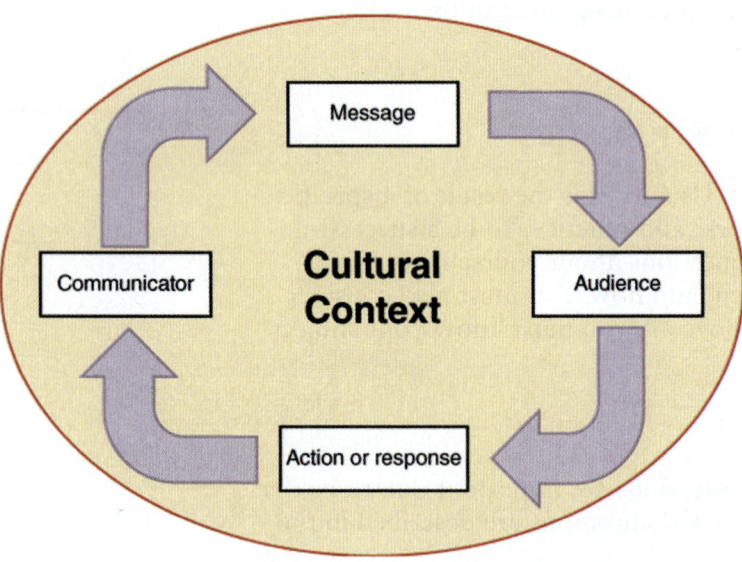

In addition to these factors, corporate culture is very important. A **corporate culture** includes the beliefs, rules, traditions, values, and attitudes that define a company and influence its way of doing business. To be successful, a systems analyst must understand and work within this culture. For example, if you speak to a group in a company that encourages a highly participative style, you might want to solicit feedback, invite audience comments, or conduct a poll during your presentation. Similarly, if the organization or group is very formal, or very informal, you might want to adjust your style accordingly.

FIGURE A-1 Every communication takes place within an overall cultural context.

A.2.3 Know Your Subject

No matter how well you plan your communication, you must know your subject inside and out. Your credibility and effectiveness will depend on whether others believe you and support your views. No one can know everything, so it is important to adopt a specific preparation strategy. For example, before a presentation, consider what others expect you to know and what questions they will ask. No matter how well you prepare, however, you will not have an answer for every question. Remember that it is better to say, "I don't know, but I'll find out and get back to you," rather than to guess.

A.3 WRITTEN COMMUNICATIONS

Good writing is important because others often judge you by your writing. If you make a mistake while speaking, your audience probably will forget it. Your written errors, however, might stay around for a long time. Grammatical, typographical, and spelling errors distract readers from your message. Your written communications will include email messages, memos, letters, workgroup communications, and formal reports.

A.3.1 Writing Style and Readability

If you have not taken a writing course, you should consider doing so. If you have a choice of courses, select one that focuses on business writing or technical writing. Any writing class, however, is worth the effort. Most bookstores and libraries have excellent books on effective communications, and many Internet sites offer writing guidelines, tips, and grammar rules. As you prepare written documents, keep in mind the following suggestions:

1. Know your audience. If you are writing for nontechnical readers, use terms that readers will understand.

2. Use **active voice** whenever possible. For example, the active voice sentence "Tom designed the system," is better than, "The system was designed by Tom," which is an example of **passive voice**.

3. Keep your writing clear, concise, and well organized. Each paragraph should present a single topic or idea.

4. Use an appropriate style. For example, use a conversational tone in informal documents and a business tone in formal documents.

5. Use lists. If a topic has many subtopics, a list can organize the material and make it easier to understand.

6. Use short, easy-to-understand words. Your objective is not to impress your audience with the size of your vocabulary.

7. Avoid repeating the same word too often. Use a thesaurus to locate synonyms for frequently repeated words. Many word processing programs include a thesaurus and other tools to help you write better.

8. Check your spelling. You can use the spell checker in your word processing program to check your spelling, but remember that a **spell checker** is a tool that identifies only words that do not appear in the program's dictionary. For example, a spell checker will not identify instances when you use the word *their*, instead of the word *there*.

9. Check your grammar. Most word processing programs include a **grammar checker**, which is a tool that can detect usage problems and offer suggestions. When you use a grammar checker, you can set various options to match the level and style of the writing and to highlight or ignore certain types of usage. For example, you can set the grammar checker in Microsoft Word to check grammar rules only, or you can configure it to check writing style, including gender-specific words, sentence fragments, and passive sentences. For more sophisticated grammar analysis, special-purpose tools, such as Grammarly shown in Figure A-2, can be used.

10. Review your work carefully. Then double-check it for spelling, grammatical, and typographical mistakes. If possible, ask a colleague to proofread your work and suggest improvements.

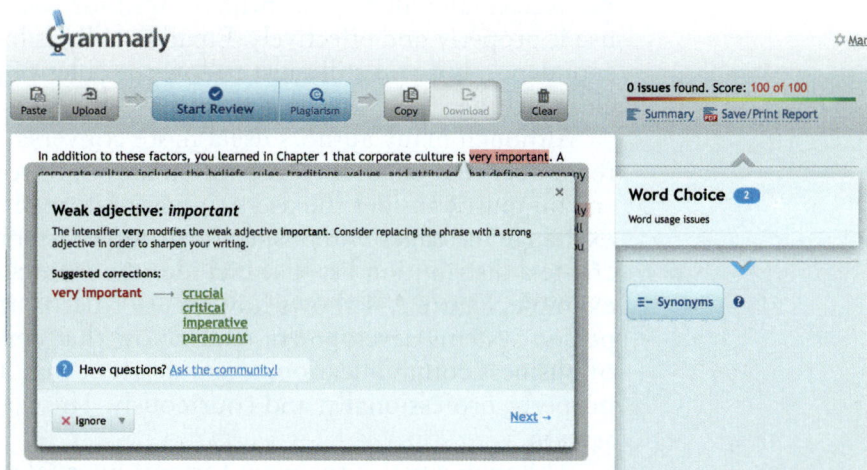

FIGURE A-2 Grammarly is a sophisticated tool for checking grammar that works with Microsoft Office or within a browser.
Source: Grammarly Inc.

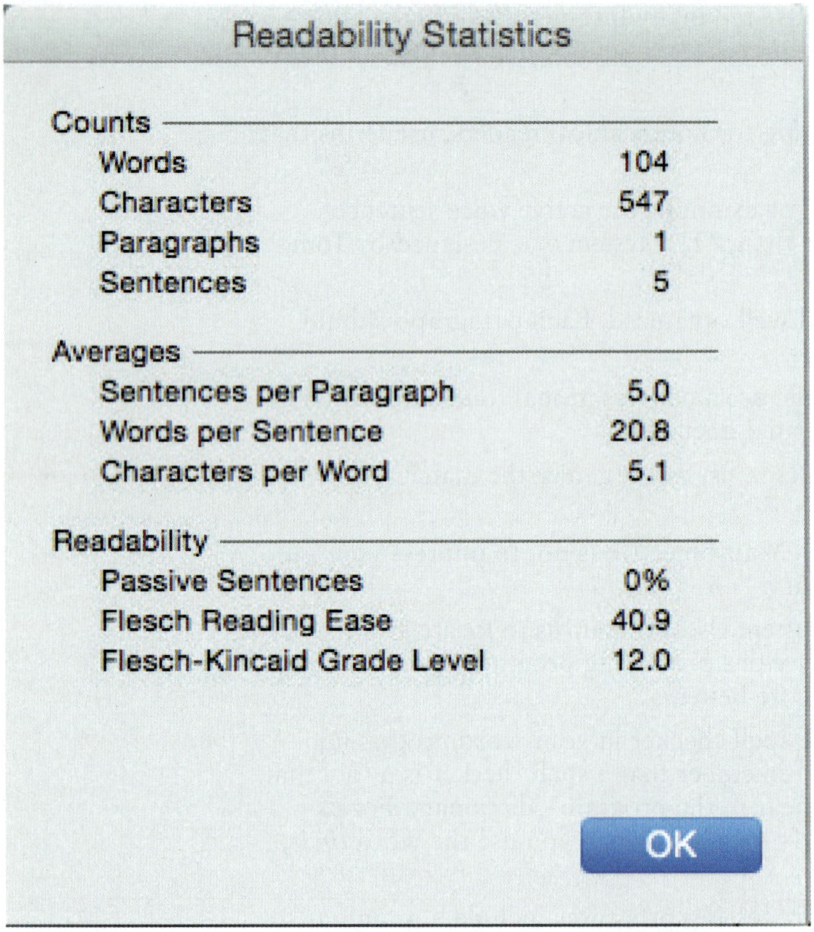

Readability Statistics

Counts
Words	104
Characters	547
Paragraphs	1
Sentences	5

Averages
Sentences per Paragraph	5.0
Words per Sentence	20.8
Characters per Word	5.1

Readability
Passive Sentences	0%
Flesch Reading Ease	40.9
Flesch-Kincaid Grade Level	12.0

OK

FIGURE A-3 Microsoft Word offers Readability Statistics that include the Flesch Reading Ease score and the Flesch-Kincaid Grade Level score.
Source: Microsoft Word 2011 for Mac

All writers must consider **readability**, which analyzes ease of comprehension by measuring specific characteristics of syllables, words, and sentences. Two popular readability measures are the Flesch Reading Ease score and the Flesch-Kincaid Grade Level score. Both scores can be calculated automatically using Microsoft Word, as shown in Figure A-3.

The **Flesch Reading Ease score** measures the average sentence length and the average number of syllables per word and rates the text on a 100-point scale. With this tool, the higher the score, the easier it is to understand. Microsoft suggests that for most standard documents, you should aim for a score of 60–70.

The **Flesch-Kincaid Grade Level score** uses the same variables but in a different formula that produces a rating keyed to a U.S. grade-school level. For example, a score of 8.0 would indicate material easily understood by a person at an eighth-grade reading level. With this tool, Microsoft suggests that for most standard documents, you should aim for a score of 7.0 to 8.0.

A.3.2 Email, Memos, and Letters

Because email will be your primary tool for written communication, it is important to use it properly and effectively. Email usually is less formal than other written correspondence, but you still must follow the rules of good grammar, correct spelling, and clear writing.

Although many authors use a more conversational style for email, you should remember that email messages often are forwarded to other recipients or groups, and so you must consider the users to whom it might be distributed. If you regularly exchange messages with a specific group of users, most email programs allow you to create a distribution list that includes the members and their email addresses. For example, Figure A-4 shows how to use Microsoft Outlook to send an email to a six-person systems development team. Now that email has become the standard method of business communication, it is important that all users know how to use email properly, professionally, and courteously. This topic is discussed in the following section.

Although email is the main form of internal communication, internal memos and announcements still are important, and external communications often require letters printed on company letterhead. Most companies use a standard format, or template, for internal memos and external letters. If your company stores those on a network, you can download and use the templates. If you want to create your own designs, you can use a word processor to create templates with specific layouts, fonts, and margin settings. A **template** gives your work a consistent look and makes your job easier. Most word processing programs also provide a feature that allows you to design your memos as forms and fill in the blanks as you work.

A.3.3 Social Media at Work

Social media is seeing explosive growth, which is certain to continue. This section focuses on just one aspect of this trend: social media in the office. It would be difficult to cite a communication method with greater potential benefits — and dangers — than the volatile mix of social networking and modern business settings. Many employees use social networking to advance their careers. Unfortunately, others have been reprimanded or worse for saying too much, or to the wrong people, or at the wrong time. An IT professional should consider the following issues:

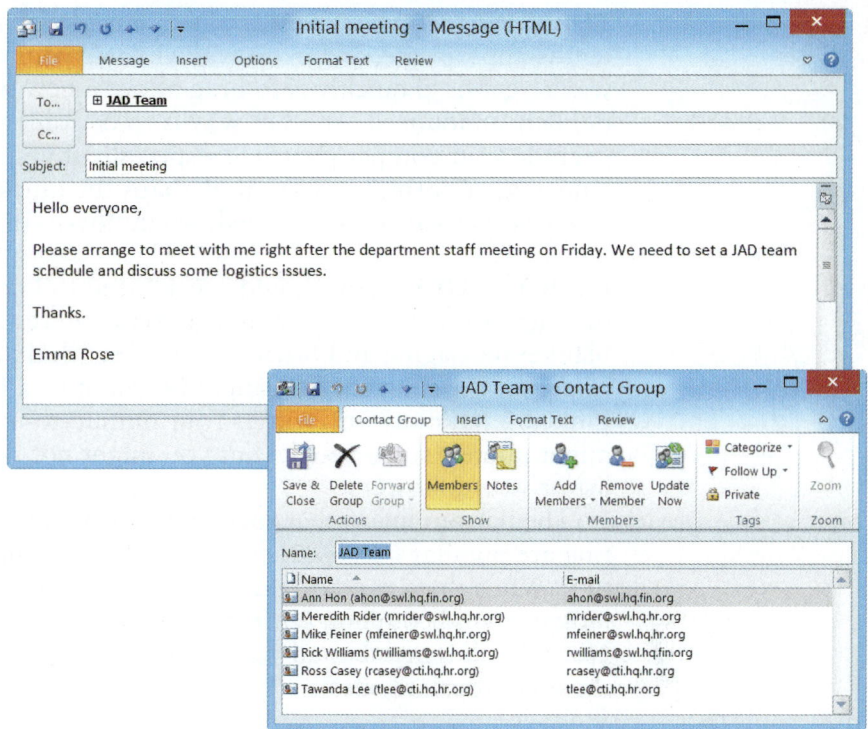

FIGURE A-4 Microsoft Outlook allows users to create distribution lists for sending email messages.

THE BACKDROP: Corporations are racing to embrace social media in their marketing plans. They have learned that they can create excitement, call attention to their products, and reach out to a young, active, socially aware market. In the corporate world, social media–driven event marketing has become a specialty unto itself, as you can see from visiting the Pepsi, NASCAR, or NFL sites; many of which sport multiple logos and links to Twitter and Facebook, among others. These trends are healthy, from an IT viewpoint because they demonstrate that technology and creativity have an important role in corporate strategy, and that is good news for systems analysts.

ADVANTAGES: IT professionals can use social media to network with others, find out about new technology, meet colleagues, discuss career issues, and maintain a web-based presence that would have been impossible just a few years ago. A person can gain credibility by sharing information and technical tips, posting how-to videos, or documenting an especially interesting assignment or challenge. However, any one of these activities could also have disastrous consequences.

RISKS: Drivers who are stopped for speeding often say "I didn't know I was going that fast." Similarly, employees who misuse social media usually plead ignorance. But there is a better way: know the rules, observe the rules, and when in doubt — don't!

Most firms have social media policies that govern workplace behavior. Some prohibit personal communications on company time or with company resources. Others use a case-by-case approach. Rather than guess your company's policy, you should find out exactly what is the policy and make sure you understand it clearly.

THREE WAYS TO GET FIRED: You must be absolutely sure that your message content is appropriate, and in no way violates your company's confidentiality policy. One way to get fired quickly is to brag about a new marketing strategy before it has been publicly announced. Another way is to be somewhere or do something that might degrade your company's image, especially if your employer can be identified by your nametag, uniform, or location. Perhaps the quickest way to get fired is to launch an angry verbal attack on your fellow employees or managers.

OTHER ISSUES: You should use a "need to know" approach, so you direct your messages to those who have a legitimate interest, and are people you trust. Avoid blanket messaging and broadcasting. Also think about whether the content is appropriate for the site you are using. For example, a funny joke might be out of place on LinkedIn but okay on Twitter. Your minute-to-minute experience at a rock concert might interest some people, but you might not want to send it to your entire contact list or your followers.

The bottom line is that social networking, instant messaging, and cell-phone texting are popular because they allow informal, interactive, and immediate communication. While these can be valuable collaboration tools, users should exercise good judgment and common sense, just as they would in any form of interpersonal contact. No one will remember all your excellent messages. They will, however, never forget the inappropriate ones.

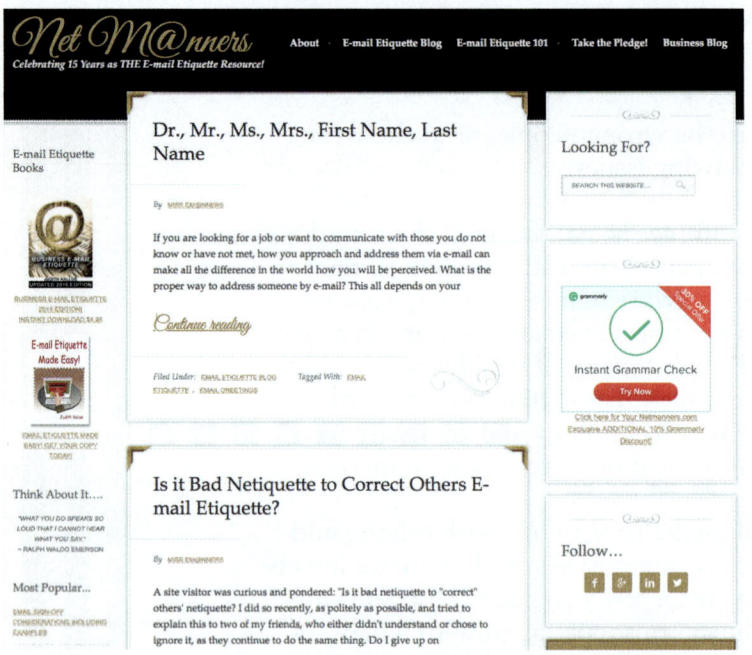

FIGURE A-5 The NetManners website offers netiquette guidelines, tips, and links.

Source: NetM@nners.com

A.3.4 Netiquette

Netiquette combines the words *Internet* and *etiquette*. With the explosive growth of social networking, netiquette is more important than ever. If you follow the guidelines in the preceding section, you can avoid major problems. But you should set your sights higher than that. An IT professional should have strong communication skills, and use good manners, proper style, and lots of common sense.

On the web, you can find many sources of information about netiquette. For example, the NetManners.com site shown in Figure A-5 offers many guidelines, tips, and links. Dale Carnegie, a famous educator and authority on interpersonal relations, said many years ago that others evaluate us based on "what we do, how we look, what we say, and how we say it."

All email users should be aware of some simple rules, most of which are nothing more than good manners and common sense. For example, an excellent starting point is to avoid sending material that is personal or confidential because your messages might be forwarded by others and distributed more widely than you intended. Another important rule is never to send or reply to an email when you are tired or upset. Instead, you can write a draft if you want to, but save the unsent message so you can review it later.

Here are some common rules and tips:

- Always fill in the subject field with a brief description of the contents.

- Be brief — in most cases, less is more.

- Be professional. Remember, if it has your name on it, it reflects on you personally and that often is how people will view your messages.

- Be sure to check your spelling.

- Don't forward jokes or chain letters without the permission of the recipient.

- Don't overuse humor or sarcasm that might work in a face-to-face situation but not in an email context.

- Don't type in all caps — it is like YELLING! It is also hard to read.

- Don't use colored fonts, background, or images in business email messages.

- Don't use the return receipt request feature unless there is a valid business reason to do so.

- If you have large attachment files, try to zip or compress them before sending.

- If you send a message to a group of people, especially if they don't know each other, use a blind copy (Bcc) for all of the recipients in order to shield the addresses from the entire group.

- Never give out personal contact information of others without their specific permission to do so.

- Never include personal information unless you are 100% sure of your recipient and no other means of communication would provide better privacy and security.

- Remember that there are copyright laws. You do not have an unrestricted right to do whatever you please with someone else's email message to you. Laws against discrimination and defamation can also apply to email messages.

- When replying, don't include all the earlier messages unless there is a reason to do so.

In addition to these guidelines, it is important to follow company policy regarding communications at work. Many firms restrict personal communications that involve company time or equipment, and courts have upheld an employer's right to limit or monitor such communications.

A.3.5 Workgroup Software

Many companies use **workgroup software**, often called **groupware**, because it enhances employee productivity and teamwork. In addition to basic email, workgroup software enables users to manage and share their calendars, task lists, schedules, contact lists, and documents.

Google Docs, which is shown in Figure A-6, offers free, cloud-based collaboration. Using this application, a team can work on centrally stored documents instead of emailing drafts back and forth. Teams can also use powerful multi-authoring software, such as Adobe Acrobat, to add revisions, notes, and comments to PDF documents.

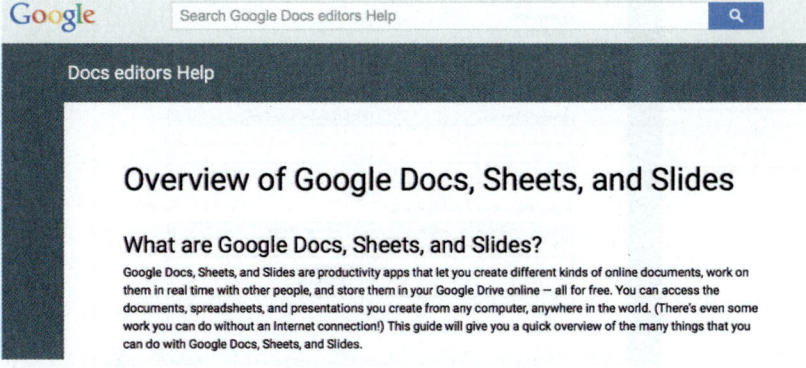

FIGURE A-6 Google Docs supports collaborative work on documents stored in the cloud.

Source: Google Inc.

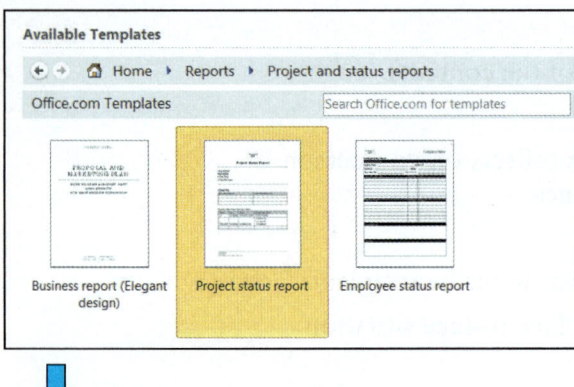

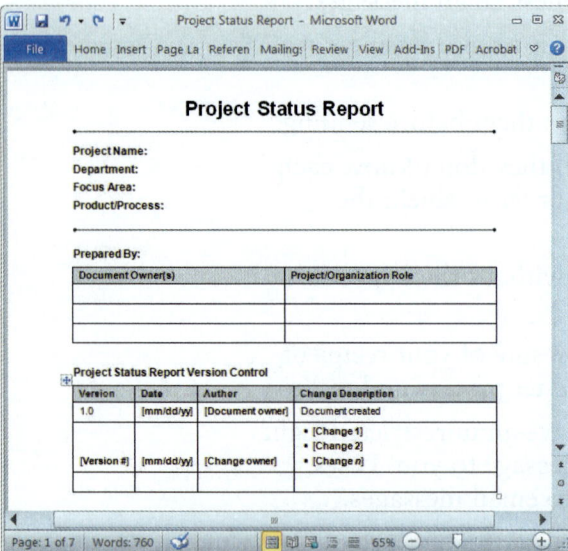

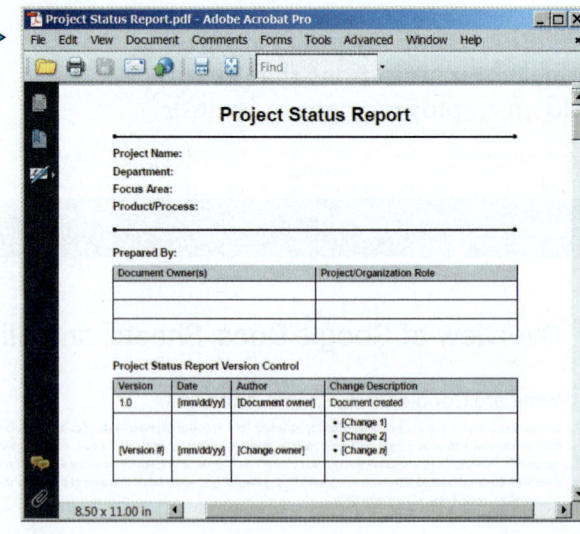

FIGURE A-7 A Microsoft Word report template can be transformed into an Adobe PDF form.

A.3.6 Reports

You must prepare many reports during systems development, including the preliminary investigation report, the system requirements document at the end of the systems analysis phase, the system design specification at the end of the system design phase, and the final report to management when the system goes into operation. You might also submit other reports, such as status reports, activity reports, proposals, and departmental business plans. You will create your reports as electronic documents, so you can attach them to emails.

When you create a report that will be delivered electronically, you should use the same high standards that apply to traditional printed materials. Notice that Microsoft Word provides many pre-made templates that you might be able to use for your report. Once you create a Word document, it is simple to transform it in to Adobe PDF format, as shown in Figure A-7. The PDF format offers several advantages. For example, PDF files are:

- *Very flexible.* You can work with pages as modules, and combine or extract them to create custom versions of your documents.

- *Totally compatible.* The PDF format travels well, and can be used and interchanged among virtually all devices, operating systems, applications, and hardware platforms.

- *More secure.* Unlike Microsoft Word, a PDF document can't readily be changed without leaving some trace, and the PDF format does not permit executable code, such as macros, to be embedded. However, no document is 100% secure. The PDF format might not deter a professional thief or intruder, but it can help with day-to-day office security concerns. Also, while the PDF format is not totally immune to malware and virus attacks, it is regarded as more resistant to these threats, compared to Word.

Whether you create the report using Microsoft Word, Adobe Acrobat, or some other program, your work must be professional, well organized, and well written. Experienced systems analysts know that when you put your name on a document, readers will see your work as a reflection of your personal skills and abilities. Also, for better or worse, the document will probably be around for a long time to come. With those thoughts in mind, you might want to review the written communication guidelines that appear elsewhere in this Toolkit.

Although most reports are delivered electronically, in some cases you must prepare printed versions. For example, suppose you had to submit a written system requirements document. You probably would create various sections, including an introduction, an executive summary, findings, recommendations, time and cost estimates, expected benefits, and an appendix containing relevant data.

INTRODUCTION: The introduction usually includes a title page, table of contents, and brief description of the proposal. The title page should be clean and neat and contain the name of the proposal, the subject, the date, and the names of the development team members. If the project already has a recognized name or acronym, you should use it. Also, you can include a table of contents when the report is long or includes many exhibits. Many word processing programs include a tool that can generate a table of contents automatically.

EXECUTIVE SUMMARY: The executive summary is used to summarize the entire project, including your recommendations, in several paragraphs. Generally, the executive summary should not exceed 200 words or one page.

FINDINGS: Use the findings section to describe the major conclusions that you or the team reached during the systems analysis phase. You can make the findings section detailed or summarized, depending on the project. You must explain the logical design of the new system in a way that nontechnical managers can understand clearly. With a management audience, the most important task is to explain how the proposed system supports the company's business needs.

RECOMMENDATIONS: The recommendations section presents the best system alternative, with a brief explanation that should mention economic, technical, operational, and schedule feasibility.

COSTS AND BENEFITS: In the costs and benefits section, you should list the advantages, disadvantages, costs, and benefits of each major system alternative. You should include a clear description of the financial analysis techniques you used. You might want to apply one or more of the financial analysis tools described in Part C of the Systems Analyst's Toolkit. You can use tables or graphs to support and clarify your alternatives when necessary.

APPENDIX: When you have a large number of supporting documents such as questionnaires or sampling results, you should put those items in an appendix located at the end of the document. Make sure you include only relevant information, and provide references for interested readers.

A.4 ORAL COMMUNICATIONS

An oral presentation is required at the end of the preliminary investigation and again at the conclusion of the systems analysis phase. You might need to give more than one presentation in some situations to present technical material to members of the IT department or to present an overview for top managers. When preparing an oral presentation, you should perform six important tasks: Define the audience, define the objectives for your presentation, organize the presentation, define any technical terms you will use, prepare your presentation aids, and practice your delivery.

A.4.1 Define the Audience

Before you develop a detailed plan for a management presentation, you must define the audience. Senior managers often prefer an executive summary rather than a detailed presentation, but that is not always the case, especially in smaller companies where top management is more involved in day-to-day activities. If you consider the expectations of your audience and design your presentation accordingly, you will improve your chances of success.

A.4.2 Define the Objectives

When you communicate, you should focus on your objectives. In the management presentation for the systems analysis phase, your goals are the following:

- Inform management of the status of the current system
- Describe your findings concerning the current system problems
- Explain the alternative solutions that you developed
- Provide detailed cost and time estimates for the alternative solutions
- Recommend the best alternative and explain the reasons for your selection

A.4.3 Organize the Presentation

Plan your presentation in three stages: the introduction, the information, and the summary. First, you should introduce yourself and describe your objectives. During the presentation, make sure that you discuss topics in a logical order. You should be as specific as possible when presenting facts — your listeners want to hear your views about what is wrong, how it can be fixed, how much it will cost, and when the objectives can be accomplished. In your summary, briefly review the main points, and then ask for questions.

A.4.4 Define Any Technical Terms

You should avoid specialized or technical terminology whenever possible. If your audience might be unfamiliar with a term that you plan to use, either define the term or find another way to say it so they will understand your material.

A.4.5 Prepare Presentation Aids

Much of what people learn is acquired visually, so you should use helpful, appropriate visual aids to help the audience follow the logic of your presentation and hold their attention. Visual aids can also direct audience attention away from you, which is helpful if you are nervous when you give the presentation. You can use a visual aid with an outline of topics that will help you stay on track. You can enhance the effect of your presentation with visual aids that use various media and software, as explained in the following sections.

VISUAL AIDS: Visual aids can help you display a graphical summary of performance trends, a series of cost-benefit examples, or a bulleted list of important points. You can use white-boards, flip charts, overhead trans-parencies, slides, films, and videotapes to enhance your presentation. When preparing your visual aids, make sure that the content is clear, readable, and easy to understand. Verify ahead of time that the audience can see the visual material from anywhere in the room. Remember that equipment can fail unexpectedly, so be prepared with an alternate plan.

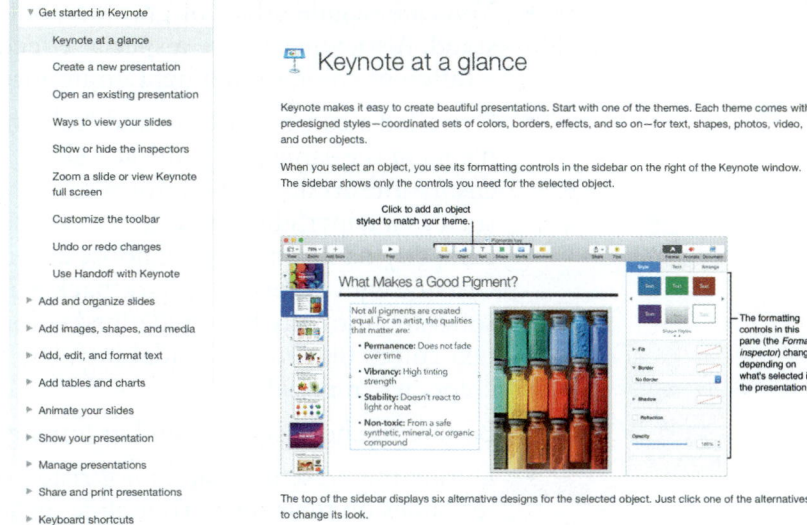

FIGURE A-8 Apple Keynote is an example of powerful presentation software.
Source: Apple Inc.

PRESENTATION SOFTWARE:
With a computer and a projection system, you can use **presentation software**, such as Apple Keynote or Microsoft PowerPoint, to create a multimedia slide show. As shown in Figure A-8, Apple offers many tips and techniques that can improve your Keynote presentations.

Preparing an effective slide presentation requires time and effort, and personal experience is the best teacher. There is no universal agreement about how to prepare a slide show, and many sources of information exist. Some overall guidelines include the following:

- Your first step (and perhaps the most important) is to prepare an overall outline that will be the foundation of your presentation. You should focus on the content and structure of your presentation before you consider visual issues.

- Remember that a fine line exists between providing too little information and too much.

- Display one topic per slide, and try to follow the rule often called the **7 by 7 rule**: no more than seven items per slide, and no more than seven words per item. Some presenters believe that a **6 by 6 rule** is even more effective.

- When displaying a list of items, consider using a series of slides to add each point sequentially, especially if you want to focus attention on the item being discussed.

- Use bullets rather than numbers, unless you are showing a specific sequence or order.

- Choose easily readable fonts. Use sans serif styles, such as Arial, for all body text. If you do use a serif style (such as Times Roman), apply it only in titles.

- Use appropriate point sizes for titles and body text. Your goal is to prepare slides that are readable and visually attractive. Although point size selection depends on individual judgment and experience, here are some suggestions to get you started: For titles, try either 40- or 36-point fonts; for body text, 32- or 24-point fonts usually work well.

- Select special effects carefully — too many graphics, colors, sounds, or other special effects will distract your audience.

- You can include tables or graphics, but keep them simple and easy to understand. Also, you can use a special effect, such as boldface, italic, underlining, or a different color, to highlight an important word or phrase.

- Strive for a consistent look and feel among your slides, and position visual elements in the same place on each slide. You should use a master template to ensure uniformity and conform to company-wide standards that might apply, such as a copyright notice, a confidentiality statement, or placement of the company name and logo. Choose colors carefully, and keep them consistent. Usually, light letters on a dark background are easiest to read. Presentation software normally has predefined color palettes that provide background and text colors that ensure readability. Use these palettes as a guideline for selecting colors when possible.

- Be sure to check spelling and grammar!

- During the presentation, do *not* read your slides to the audience! They can read the slides on their own. Your slide presentation is an outline that provides structure and emphasis — it is not the presentation itself.

- It is important to deliver a presentation that can be viewed easily from anywhere in the room. When setting up, consider the size of the room, the number of people attending, the size and location of your visual aids, and the characteristics of any projection equipment you will be using.

A.4.6 Practice

The most important part of your preparation is practice. You should rehearse several times to ensure that the presentation flows smoothly and the timing is correct. Practicing will make you more comfortable and build your confidence.

Do not be tempted to write a script. If you read your presentation, you will be unable to interact with your audience and adjust your content based on their reactions. Instead, prepare an outline of your presentation and practice from the outline. Then, when you deliver the actual presentation, you will not have to struggle to remember the exact words you planned to say, and you will be able to establish a good rapport with your audience.

A.4.7 The Presentation

When you deliver your presentation, the following pointers will help you succeed:

SELL YOURSELF AND YOUR CREDIBILITY: As a presenter, you must sell yourself and your credibility. A brilliant presentation will not convince top managers to approve the system if they are not sold on the person who gave the presentation. On the other hand, projects often are approved on the basis of the presenter's knowledge, commitment, and enthusiasm.

Your presentation must show confidence about the subject and your recommendations. You should avoid any conflicts with the people attending the presentation. If you encounter criticism or hostility, remain calm and stay focused on the issues — not the person making the comments. You will have a successful presentation only if you know the material thoroughly, prepare properly, and sell yourself and your credibility.

CONTROL THE PRESENTATION: During the presentation, you must control the discussion, maintain the pace of the presentation, and stay focused on the agenda —

especially when answering questions. Although you might be more familiar with the subject material, you should not display a superior attitude toward your listeners. Maintain eye contact with the audience and use some humor, but do not make a joke at someone else's expense.

ANSWER QUESTIONS APPROPRIATELY: Let your audience know whether you would prefer to take questions as you go along or have a question-and-answer session at the end. Sometimes the questions can be quite difficult. You must listen carefully and respond with a straightforward answer. Try to anticipate the questions your audience will ask so you can prepare your responses ahead of time.

When answering a difficult or confusing question, repeat the question in your own words to make sure that you understand it. For example, you can say, "If I understand your question, you are asking …" This will help avoid confusion and give you a moment to think on your feet. To make sure that you gave a clear answer, you can say, "Have I answered your question?" Allow follow-up questions when necessary.

USE EFFECTIVE SPEAKING TECHNIQUES: The delivery of your presentation is just as important as its content. You can strengthen your delivery by speaking clearly and confidently and projecting a relaxed approach. You must also control the pace of your delivery. If you speak too fast, you will lose the audience, and if the pace is too slow, people will lose their concentration and the presentation will not be effective.

Many speakers are nervous when facing an audience. If this is a problem for you, keep the following suggestions in mind:

- Control your environment. If you are most nervous when the audience is looking at you, use visual aids to direct their attention away from you. If your hands are shaking, do not

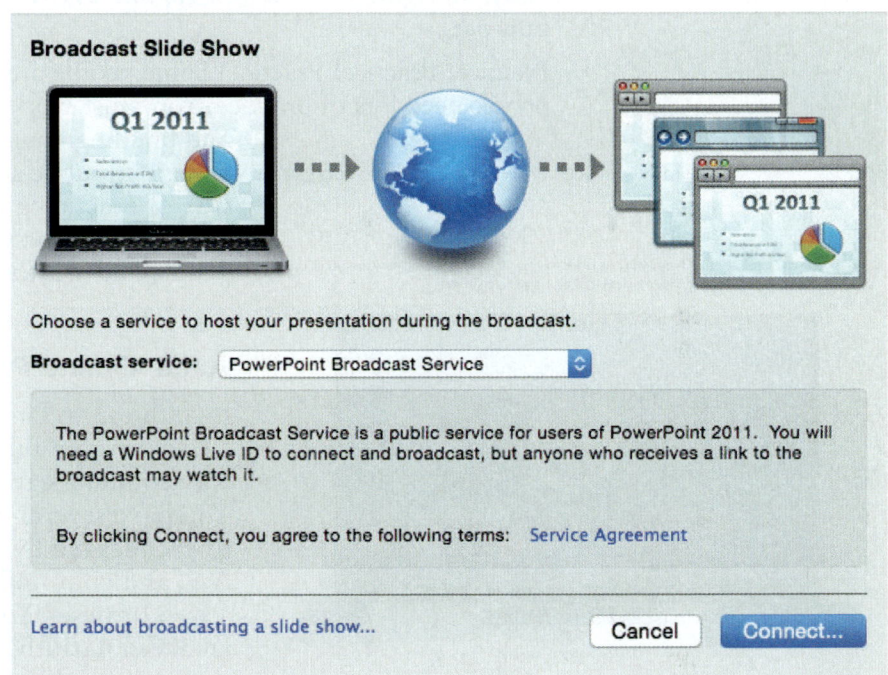

FIGURE A-9 Microsoft PowerPoint lets you broadcast your presentation to a remote audience.
Source: Microsoft PowerPoint 2011 for Mac

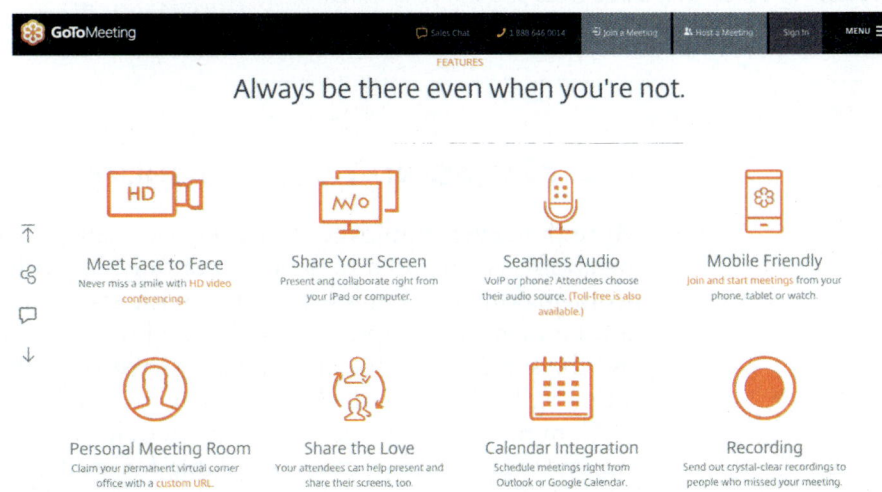

FIGURE A-10 GoToMeeting is a popular tool for holding online meetings and shared presentations.
Source: Citrix Systems, Inc.

hold your notes. If you are delivering a computer-based presentation, it is a good idea to use a handheld wireless device to control the slides. Concentrate on using a strong, clear voice. If your nervousness distracts you, take a deep breath and remind yourself that you really do know your subject.

- Turn your nervousness to your advantage. Many people do their best work when they are under a little stress. Think of your nervousness as normal pressure.

- Avoid meaningless filler words and phrases. Using words and phrases such as *okay*, *all right*, *you know*, *like*, *um*, and *ah* are distracting and serve no purpose.

- Practice! Practice! Practice! Some people are naturally gifted speakers, but most people need lots of practice. You must work hard at practicing your presentation and building your confidence. Many schools offer speech or public speaking courses that are an excellent way of practicing your skills. It can also be advantageous to preview your presentation with one or more people and ask for input.

FIGURE A-11 Skype is a free cross-platform communication and collaboration tool that is widely used.

Source: http://www.skype.com [owned by Microsoft]

A.4.8 Online Presentations

In addition to face-to-face meetings, you might have to deliver an **online presentation**, possibly with two-way communication between you and the audience. You have several options. You might use PowerPoint to broadcast a live presentation, as shown in Figure A-9, and your online audience would see the slides in a web browser. Your presentation could also include an audio narrative. If you want real-time participation, you might consider products such as Apple FaceTime, Cisco WebEx, Citrix GoToMeeting shown in Figure A-10, or Microsoft Skype shown in Figure A-11. These products can handle live audio and video, and allow you to deliver a fully interactive webinar.

A.5 MANAGING YOUR COMMUNICATION SKILLS

More than ever, employees must rely on their personal skills and experience. In an uncertain world and a turbulent economy, individuals should think of themselves as profit-making companies, complete with assets, liabilities, strengths, and areas for development. In Chapter 2, you learned that a company must have a strategic plan, and the same is true for an individual. Armed with a plan to improve your communication skills, you are much more likely to reach your full potential.

Communicating is like any other activity — the more you practice, the better you become. Many resources are available for students and IT professionals who want to improve their written and oral communication skills. For example, online learning websites such as SkillShare and Lynda offer a wide range of free and for-fee courses that can help you become a better writer, presenter, and public speaker. The Association for Computing Machinery (ACM) also offers many online courses and tutorials for members, including students and IT professionals.

Some people find it difficult to stand in front of a group and deliver a presentation or report. For many years, membership in Toastmasters, International has been a popular way to gain confidence, overcome stage fright, and develop public speaking skills. As shown in Figure A-12, Toastmasters offers a friendly environment where members critique each speech in a positive manner, note the strengths, and offer suggestions about what might be improved. This organization offers an excellent way to develop better public speaking skills.

FIGURE A-12 Toastmasters is one of the oldest organizations dedicated to helping individuals become more effective communicators.

Source: Toastmasters International.

A.6 Toolkit Summary

Your success as a systems analyst depends on your ability to communicate effectively. You must know why you are communicating, what you want to accomplish, who your targets are, what is expected of you, and when to go into detail. You must know your subject and how to use good written and oral communications techniques.

You will be judged by your written work, so it must be free of grammatical, spelling, and punctuation errors. You should write email, letters, and memos clearly, and the writing style should match the situation. Many firms have standard formats for letters and memos, and you can use templates to achieve consistency.

Social media is extremely popular because it allows informal, interactive, and immediate communication. While social media can be a valuable collaboration tool, users should exercise good judgment and common sense, just as they would in any form of interpersonal contact. They must understand clearly any workplace policies and rules that affect the use of social media, both on and off the job.

Your writing must be clear and understandable. You can use readability measurement tools such as the Flesch Reading Ease score and the Flesch-Kincaid Grade Level score.

You will prepare various reports during systems development, and the format will vary depending on the nature of the report. Your reports should have a cover memo and might include an introduction, an executive summary, findings, recommendations, time and cost estimates, expected benefits, and a data section.

In addition to written communications, you must communicate effectively in person. You might have to deliver several presentations to different audiences at different times during the SDLC. Presentations are an important form of oral communication, and you should follow specific guidelines in preparing your presentation. You prepare by defining your audience, identifying your objectives, and organizing the presentation itself. You also need to define technical terms and prepare visual aids to help your audience understand the material. Most important, you must practice your delivery to gain confidence and strengthen your presentation skills. You may also want to deliver your presentation through an online venue.

When you develop slide presentations, you should follow the 6 by 6 rule or 7 by 7 rule and other guidelines that will make your slides easy to read and understand. You should select fonts and point sizes carefully, and strive for a consistent look and feel throughout the presentation. Special effects can be interesting, but do not overuse them.

When you give the presentation, you are selling your ideas and your credibility. You must control the discussion, build a good rapport with the audience, answer all questions clearly and directly, and try to use good speaking techniques. Again, the best way to become a better speaker is to practice.

Every IT professional should have a strategic plan to manage and improve written and oral communication skills. Many online resources offer courses, tutorials, and support to help you develop the skills you will need in the workplace.

Key Terms

6 by 6 rule A presentation guideline no more than six items should be placed on each slide, and each item should have no more than six words.

7 by 7 rule A presentation guideline no more than seven items should be placed on each slide, and each item should have no more than seven words.

active voice Refers to using sentences where the actor is the subject of the sentence. For example, "Tom designed the system" is in active voice. Active voice is preferred in written communication.

corporate culture A set of beliefs, rules, traditions, values, and attitudes that define a company and influence its way of doing business.

Flesch-Kincaid Grade Level score Uses the same variables as the Flesch Reading Ease score, but in a different formula that produces a rating keyed to a U.S. grade-school level.

Flesch Reading Ease score Measures the average sentence length and the average number of syllables per word and rates the text on a 100-point scale, with higher ratings being easier to read.

grammar checker A software program that can detect usage problems and offer suggestions.

groupware Software that runs in the cloud or on a company intranet that enables users to share data, collaborate on projects, and work in teams, and may offer features in addition to basic email capability, such as calendars, task lists, schedules, contact lists, and document management. Also called workgroup software.

netiquette A term that combines the words *Internet* and *etiquette*. Encompasses web guidelines for protocol and courtesy. In many cases, FAQs describe the netiquette of a given newsgroup or site.

online presentation A presentation delivered to an online audience, usually through a web browser and/or a third-party application, such as Cisco's WebEx or Citrix's GoToMeeting.

oral presentation A presentation that is presented orally and is required at the end of the preliminary investigation and again at the conclusion of the systems analysis phase.

passive voice Refers to using sentences with the actor being the direct object. For example, "The system was designed by Tom" is in passive voice. Active voice is preferable to passive voice in written communication.

presentation software Applications used to create slides with sounds, animation, and graphics.

readability A measure of the ease of comprehension by analyzing specific characteristics of syllables, words, and sentences.

spell checker A component of most word processing programs, a spell checker is a tool that identifies words in a document that do not appear in the program's dictionary.

template A standard format for documents, presentations, and other output, with specific layouts, fonts, margin and other formatting settings. Templates are used to give work a consistent look.

visual aids Tools such as whiteboards, flip charts, overhead transparencies, slides, films, and videotapes used to enhance a presentation.

why, who, what, when, and how of communications Good communications must answer these basic questions: Why is one communicating? Who is the target audience? What is expected? When is detail required? How does one communicate effectively?

workgroup software *See* **groupware**.

Toolkit Exercises

Review Questions

1. What is a corporate culture, and why is it important? Describe the culture at a business where you have been employed.
2. Mention five specific techniques you can use to improve your written documents.
3. What techniques can help email communications? Provide specific examples.
4. Create a one-page document with at least five grammatical errors. Then run the Microsoft Word grammar checker and describe the results.
5. When preparing an oral presentation, what six tasks should you perform?
6. When you organize a presentation, what three stages do you plan?
7. Why are visual aids important? Give at least three examples of different types of visual aids, and explain how you would use each type in a presentation.
8. Based on your own experience, what tends to make a PowerPoint presentation stronger or weaker? Provide specific examples.
9. Name three specific strategies you can use if you get nervous during a presentation.
10. Why is practice so important when preparing a presentation? Provide a specific example from your own experience.

Discussion Topics

1. Most people agree that business email can be more conversational than formal written documents, but even email has its limits. As a manager, what guidance would you give people regarding email style and usage?
2. Is it possible to over communicate? For example, in Chapter 4 it was explained how to avoid leading questions, which might suggest an answer. Are there other examples, like newspaper headlines, where "less is more"?
3. Many articles stress the importance of body language. Think of examples where you noticed a person's body language. Did it relate to something they were trying to communicate — or something they were trying *not* to communicate?
4. Should email monitoring by an employer always be permissible, never permissible, or does the answer depend on specific factors? If so, what are they?
5. What new or additional skills should an analyst learn to effectively communicate in online meetings, such as those held using Cisco's WebEx or Citrix's GoToMeeting?

Projects

1. *The Elements of Style* by William Strunk, Jr. and E. B. White is a popular reference manual for proper English usage. The book identifies many words and phrases that are commonly misused, including *between* and *among*, *affect* and *effect*, *different from* and *different than*, *like* and *as*, and *infer* and *imply*. Review *The Elements of Style* or another source, and explain how these words should be used.
2. Using Microsoft PowerPoint, Apple Keynote, or another program, prepare a presentation on "How to Prepare an Effective Slide Presentation." Assume that your audience is familiar with presentation software but has no formal training.
3. As a training manual writer, choose a simple hardware or software task and write a two- or three-paragraph description of how to perform the task. Then use your word processing software to check the readability statistics. Try to keep the Flesch Reading Ease score above 60 and the Flesch-Kincaid Grade Level score to 8.0 or less.

4. View at least three examples of public speaking. You can investigate TV network news broadcasts, C-SPAN, or any other source. Describe each speaker's gestures, expressions, voice levels, inflections, timing, eye contact, and effectiveness.

5. Evaluate the collaborative support provided by the latest version of Microsoft Office. Suggest any improvements you feel would enhance group work, such as when multiple people are editing a Word document online.

B

CASE Tools

Part B of the Systems Analyst's Toolkit describes CASE tools that can be used to design, construct, and document an information system.

LEARNING OBJECTIVES

When you finish this part of the Toolkit, you should be able to:

- Explain CASE tools and the concept of a CASE environment
- Trace the history of CASE tools and their role in a fourth-generation environment
- Define CASE terms and concepts, including a repository, modeling tools, documentation tools, engineering tools, and construction tools
- Explain an integrated development environment (IDE) and application life cycle management (ALM) solutions
- Provide examples of CASE tool features
- Describe CASE tool trends, and how they relate to object-oriented analysis and agile methods

TOOLKIT CONTENTS

B.1 INTRODUCTION

Computer-aided systems engineering (CASE), also called computer-aided software engineering, is a technique that uses powerful software, called *CASE tools,* to help system developers design and construct information systems. In this part of the Systems Analyst's Toolkit, you will learn about the history, characteristics, and features of CASE tools. You will see specific examples of CASE tools and how they are used in various development tasks. In addition, you will learn about integrated software development environments and application life cycle management.

B.2 OVERVIEW OF CASE TOOLS

If you ask a carpenter for an example of a tool, the response might be a hammer, drill, or screwdriver. Put the same question to a chef, and the answer might be a measuring cup, knife, or spatula. Every type of work requires specific tools to do the job properly, and system development is no different. CASE tools can reduce costs, speed up development, and provide comprehensive documentation for future maintenance or enhancements.

Carnegie Mellon University's Software Engineering Institute (SEI) is a world leader in software engineering and development. SEI helps organizations improve their software capabilities and develop or acquire high-quality software. As shown in Figure B-1, the SEI is investigating the next generation of large-scale system-of-systems development. Powerful CASE tools continue to play critical roles in the development of such complex systems.

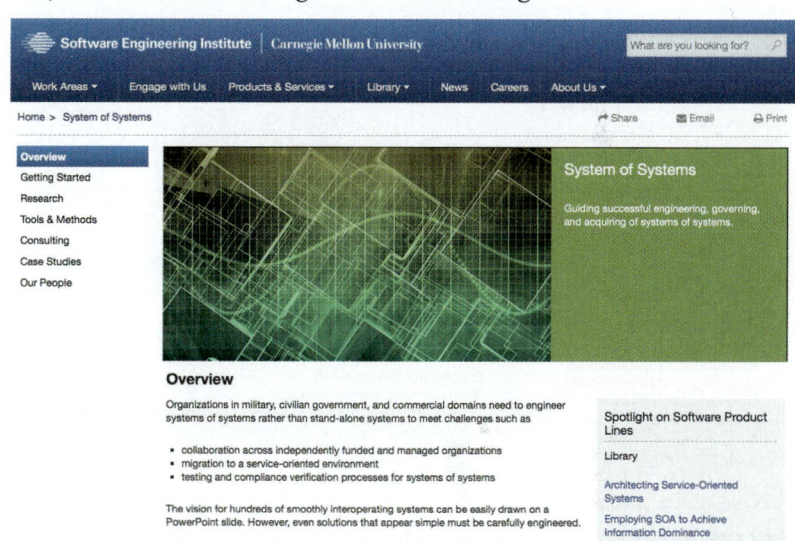

FIGURE B-1 Carnegie Mellon University's Software Engineering Institute is a world leader in software engineering research, including large-scale system-of-systems development as shown here.

Source: Carnegie Mellon University

B.2.1 CASE Tools History

As early as the 1960s, programmers used tools such as editors and code debuggers to write mainframe computer applications. Today, in our software-driven world, CASE tools have evolved into powerful resources that systems analysts need to build and maintain complex information systems.

Traditional code was written in procedural programming languages such as COBOL, which required a programmer to create a command for each processing step. In contrast, modern languages such as Java or Python are non-procedural programming languages, (also called event-driven programming languages) because instead of writing a series of instructions, a programmer defines the actions that the program must perform when certain events occur. Because non-procedural languages are object-oriented programming languages (OOPL), they make it easier to implement an object-oriented system design, as was explained in Chapter 6.

Part B CASE Tools

486   B.3 CASE Terms and Concepts

Another trend involves powerful programming languages called **fourth-generation languages (4GLs)** that are part of the **fourth-generation environment**, which was described in Chapter 7. In a fourth-generation environment that includes modern CASE tools, system developers can deliver high-quality software, shorten the timetable, and reduce expense.

One of the most vexing problems for CASE tools has always been integration. That is, how to make several CASE tools work well together. Since it's very rare for a single tool to solve all of the user's requirements, typically a federation of CASE tools must be used in a carefully orchestrated manner.

B.2.2 The Marketplace for CASE Tools

The CASE tool marketplace includes a wide variety of vendors and products, and no one tool dominates the market. You can search the web to locate CASE tool products and vendors, and even visit secondary sites such as Wikipedia to locate additional sources. Depending on their features, some CASE tools can cost thousands of dollars, while others are available as shareware, or even as freeware, such as Visual Paradigm's UML diagramming tool shown in Figure B-2.

How do you select a CASE tool? The answer depends on the type of project, its size and scope, possible budgetary and time constraints, and the preferences and experience of the system development team. After you study the terms, concepts, and examples in this part of the Toolkit, you will be able to evaluate various products and make an informed decision. The first step in learning about CASE tools is to understand basic CASE terms and concepts.

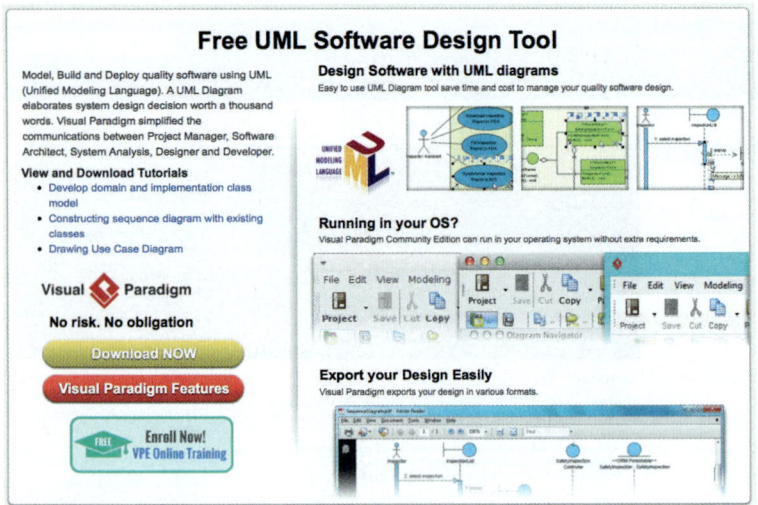

FIGURE B-2 Visual Paradigm offers a free UML diagramming tool.
Source: Visual Paradigm

B.3 CASE TERMS AND CONCEPTS

A typical CASE tool is actually a set of individual tools that share a repository of information. The important terms and concepts are explained in the following sections.

B.3.1 Repository

A **repository** is a database that serves as a central storage location for all information about the system being developed. Once a data element has been defined in the repository, it can be accessed and used by processes and other information systems. For example, sales processing, accounts receivable, and shipping systems all might require data about customers. After the CUSTOMER data element is entered in the repository, all three systems can share a consistent, up-to-date definition.

When a data element is defined in the repository, it is assigned a data type and format, a range of acceptable values, and one or more aliases. (An alias is an alternate name for a data element.) The repository can be searched, and all instances of the data element will be listed. For example, Figure B-3 shows a Visible Analyst search for the data element named CUSTOMER NUMBER. As the screens show, you can search the entire repository, or among specific types of diagrams, and the results will show all instances of the data element.

B.3.2 Individual Tools

An integrated set of CASE tools can be used to model, document, engineer, and construct the information system, as explained in the following sections.

MODELING TOOLS: Throughout the SDLC, system developers use modeling tools and diagrams to represent the system graphically. The textbook describes many examples, including Unified Modeling Language diagrams and functional decomposition diagrams (Chapter 4), data flow diagrams (Chapter 5), various object diagrams (Chapter 6), entity-relationship diagrams (Chapter 9), and structure charts (Chapter 10). Most popular CASE products offer

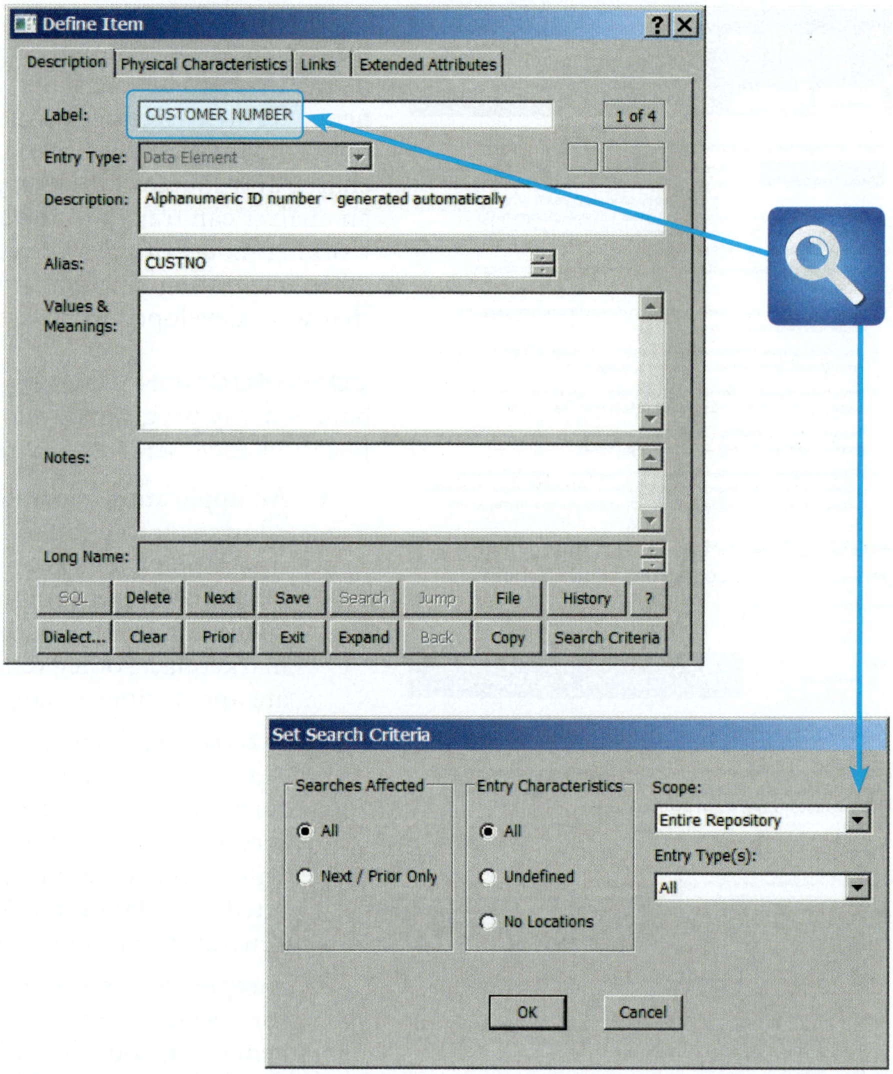

FIGURE B-3 A Visible Analyst repository search for the data element named CUSTOMER NUMBER. The results will show all instances of the data element.
Source: Visible Systems Corporation

these modeling tools, among others. One of the most important benefits of a **CASE environment** is that it provides an overall framework that allows a developer to create a series of graphical models based on data that has already been entered into a central repository.

DOCUMENTATION TOOLS: The main source of system documentation is the repository, which was explained in the previous section. In most CASE software, the repository automatically identifies the new entries and adds them to the database. In addition to the repository itself, many CASE products provide tools that check automatically for inconsistent or incomplete information in forms, reports, and diagrams. This is especially important in large, complex systems.

ENGINEERING TOOLS: Engineering tools include forward engineering and reverse engineering tools. **Forward engineering** means translating business processes and functions into applications. Some CASE tools allow you to build the system either by editing objects and code directly, or by modifying graphical representations such

Rational Rhapsody Architect for Software

Features   System requirements

Improve productivity, reuse and consistency with software visualization

Download the trial   IBM® Rational® Rhapsody® Architect for Software is an integrated development environment (IDE) for embedded software. Develop applications visually using industry-standard Unified Modeling Language (UML) diagrams. The visual programming environment integrates design and development functions, and facilitates team collaboration for better and faster results.

Rational Rhapsody Architect for Software helps you rapidly move from design to implementation.

- **Visual software development**—lets you visualize architecture and design with industry-standard UML diagrams.

- **Embedded software engineering**—moves you from design to implementation with real-time, automated, embedded software engineering.

- **Team collaboration**—helps you collaborate using model-based differencing and merging features including integration with IBM Rational Team Concert™.

- **Requirements traceability**—trace design to requirements to help you comply with standards such as DO-178B, ISO-26262 or IEC 61508.

- **Lifecycle support and add-on software**—integrates with other IBM Rational products for full product lifecycle development. Plus, you can extend the functionality of Rational Rhapsody Architect for Software with optional add-on software products.

FIGURE B-4 IBM Rational Rhapsody can generate source code from UML diagrams.
Source: IBM Corporation

SAP Crystal Reports	SAP Crystal Dashboard Design	SAP Crystal Server

SAP Crystal Reports

A robust production reporting tool, SAP Crystal Reports turns almost any data source into interactive, actionable information that can be accessed offline or online, from applications, portals and mobile devices.

Features & Benefits

SAP® Crystal Reports® software is the de facto standard in reporting. With SAP Crystal Reports 2013, you can create powerful, richly formatted, dynamic reports from virtually any data source, delivered in dozens of formats, in up to 24 languages. A robust production reporting tool, SAP Crystal Reports turns almost any data source into interactive, actionable information that can be accessed offline or online, from applications, portals and mobile devices.

Flexible, customizable report design
Create highly formatted, pixel-perfect reports quickly with SAP Crystal Reports' intuitive design interface and efficient workflows.

Broad data connectivity .
Connect to information sources spread across the organization directly. Data sources include: Native, ODBC, OLE DB, and JDBC connectivity to relational, OLAP, Web services, XML, enterprise data sources, and salesforce.com..

Powerful report delivery options
Deliver personalized reports to your business users' preferred destination in their preferred language and format.

Expanded support for Excel
XLSX export takes full advantage of the updated Excel file format by allowing more data to be exported to a single worksheet, without spanning multiple worksheets.

Mobile interactivity
Interactive reports are now available through your mobile devices.

SAP Crystal Dashboard Design software, Adobe Flex, Adobe Flash and HTML 5 integration
Enable SAP Crystal Reports developers to produce powerful "mash-ups" pulling data from various sources.

FIGURE B-5 SAP Crystal Reports is a popular report generator that can display business analytics and support decision making.
Source: SAP SE

as DFDs and UML diagrams. As explained in Chapter 1, CASE tools such as Visible Analyst allow you to develop a business model that can be translated into information system components. **Reverse engineering** allows you to examine an existing application and break it down into a series of diagrams, structure charts, and source code. Using a reverse engineering CASE tool, an analyst can transform existing application source code into a working model of the system. This can be especially important when integrating new systems with legacy systems or systems that were developed in different environments.

CONSTRUCTION TOOLS: A full-featured CASE tool can handle many program development tasks, such as generating application code, screens, and reports.

- An **application generator**, also called a **code generator**, allows you to develop computer programs rapidly by translating a logical model directly into code. As shown in Figure B-4, IBM Rational Rhapsody can generate source code from UML diagrams. In this crowded CASE tool marketplace, other vendors offer products that can generate applications in languages such as C, C++, and Java.

- A **screen generator**, or **form painter**, is an interactive tool that helps you design a custom interface, create screen forms, and handle data entry format and procedures. The screen generator allows you to control how the screen will display captions, data fields, data, and other visual attributes. Modern CASE tools usually include a screen generator that interacts with the data dictionary.

- A **report generator**, also called a **report writer**, is a tool for designing formatted reports rapidly. Using a report generator, you can modify a report easily at any stage of the design process. When you are satisfied with the report layout, the report writer creates a report definition and program code that actually produces the report. You can also input sample field values to create a mock-up report for users to review and approve.

SAP Crystal Reports, shown in Figure B-5, is a very popular report generator. According to SAP, Crystal Reports is a user-friendly, scalable tool that can display business analytics and support decision-making. **Business analytics**, which are discussed in Chapter 9, can measure past performance, help managers understand business trends, and monitor current operations.

B.4 DEVELOPMENT ENVIRONMENTS

A **development environment** refers to the mix of software tools, methods, and physical resources that an IT team uses to create an information system. Systems development is dynamic, and analysts should be aware of emerging trends, such as the integrated development environment (IDE), and various application life cycle management (ALM) solutions. These concepts are described in the following sections.

B.4.1 Integrated Development Environments

Although generic CASE tools can be used to plan and design any type of information system, it usually is easier to use an IDE, which uses built-in tools provided by the software vendor. For example, Oracle provides Oracle Designer, which is packaged with Oracle's application software. According to the company, Oracle Designer models business processes, data entities, and relationships — and easily can transform the models into applications.

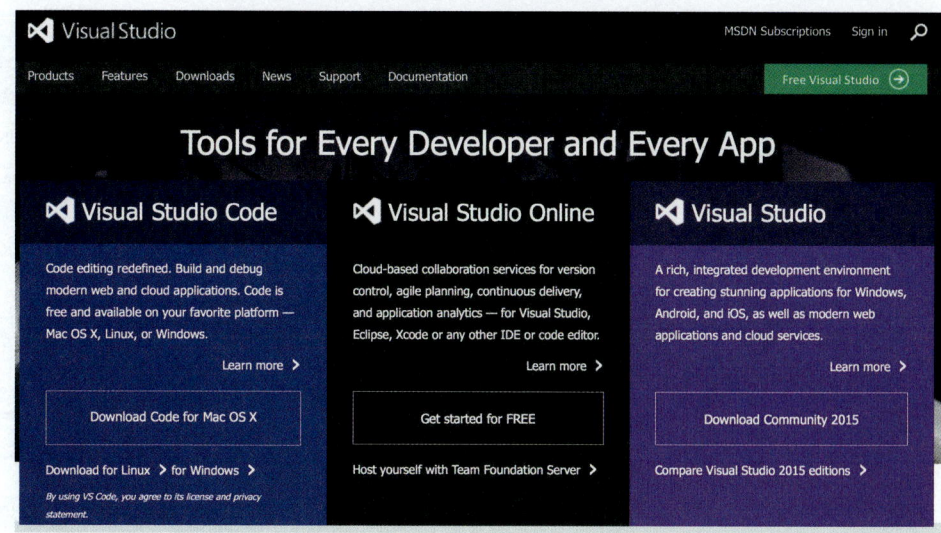

FIGURE B-6 Microsoft's Visual Studio includes development tools for traditional applications, mobile apps, and cloud-based solutions.
Source: Microsoft Corporation.

Microsoft's Visual Studio, shown in Figure B-6, is a popular commercial IDE for traditional applications, mobile apps, and cloud-based solutions. Eclipse is another well-known IDE, but it is free, open-source, and community-supported, as shown in Figure B-7. Xcode is a free IDE for all of Apple's platforms, as shown in Figure B-8, tailored to the Swift programming language.

B.4.2 Application Life Cycle Management Environments

Many vendors of traditional IDEs, including HP, now offer new **application life cycle management (ALM)** tools, as shown in Figure B-9. Although no standard definition exists, ALM generally refers to a start-to-finish approach to planning, designing, developing, deploying, managing, and maintaining an information system.

ALM can be seen as part of a broader concept known as **product life cycle management (PLM)**. According to the Florida Institute of Technology, PLM is "an integrated, information-driven approach — one that comprises people, processes and

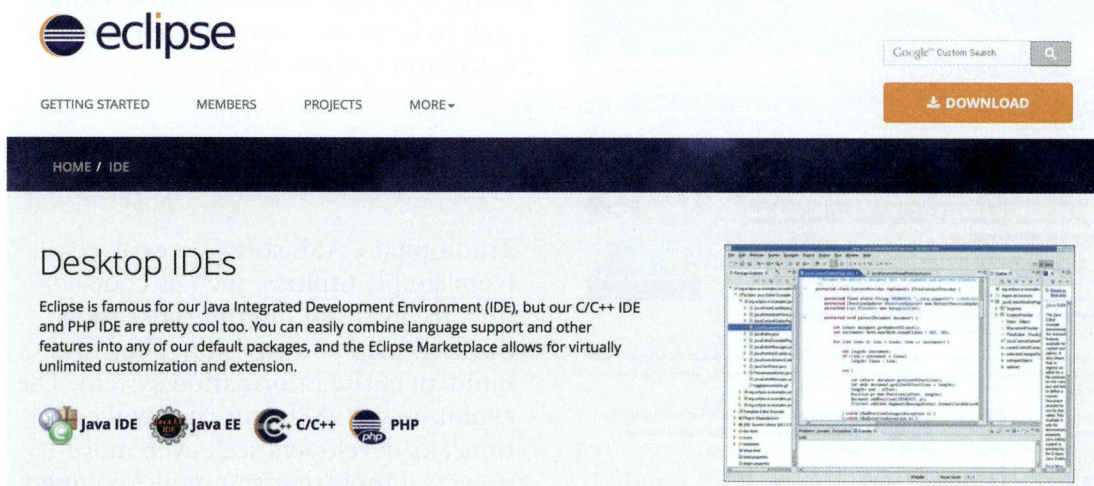

FIGURE B-7 Eclipse is a free, open-source, community-supported IDE.
Source: The Eclipse Foundation.

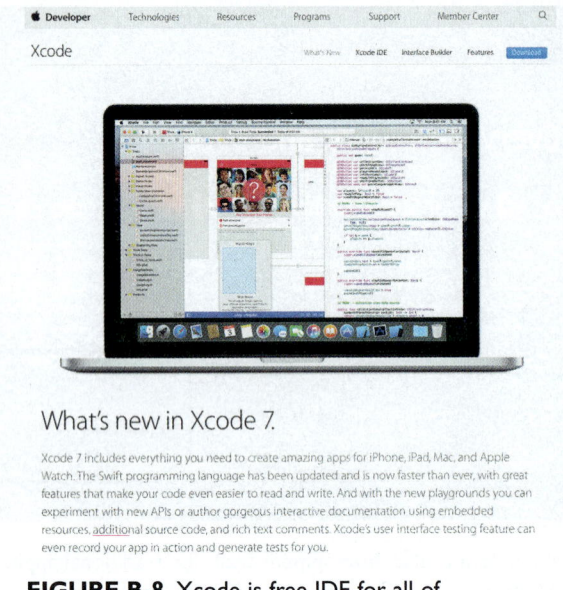

FIGURE B-8 Xcode is free IDE for all of Apple's platforms.
Source: Apple Inc.

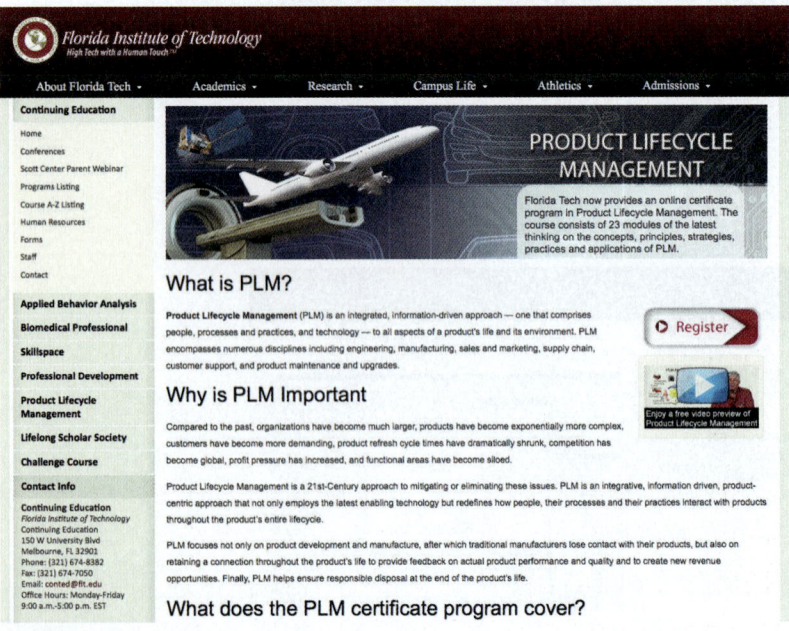

FIGURE B-9 HP provides a full range of application lifecycle management software solutions.
Source: Hewlett Packard Enterprise Development LP.

practices, and technology — to all aspects of a product's life and its environment." As shown in Figure B-10, analysts can now avail themselves of tailored courses to learn more about PLM tools and practices in the context of information systems.

B.4.3 Pros and Cons of Integrated Development Tools

In a specific software environment, an integrated development tool is highly effective because it is built into the vendor's software package. The only possible disadvantage is that each IDE is different, and requires a learning curve and skills that might or might not be readily transferable. In contrast, non-specific CASE tools such as Visible Analyst can be used in any development environment. Given the dynamic changes in IT, a systems analyst should seek to learn as many development and CASE tools as possible.

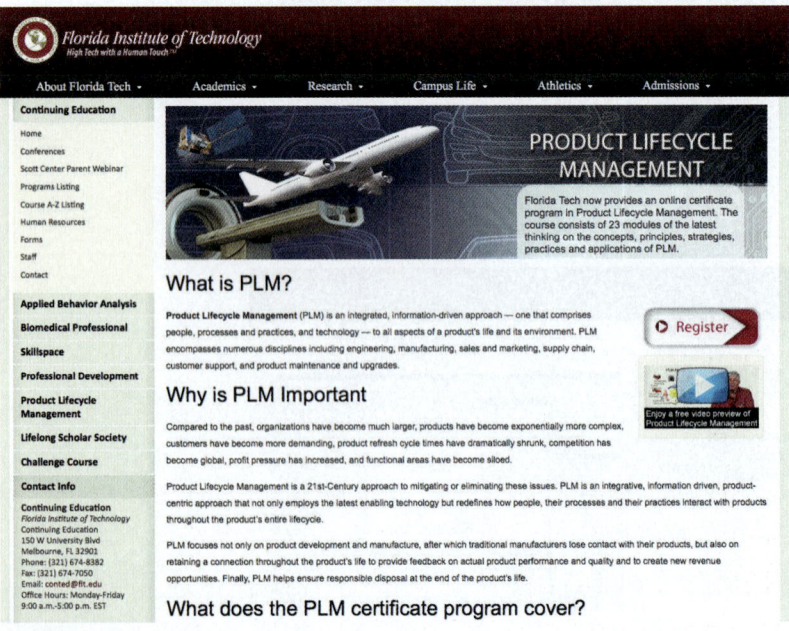

FIGURE B-10 PLM encompasses numerous disciplines, and is broader than ALM.
Source: Florida Institute of Technology.

B.5 CASE Tool Trends

Traditional CASE software evolved from simple utilities, such as code editors, to powerful multipurpose tools that can help you envision, plan, and build an entire information system. The evolution of CASE software will continue, as developers seek even more powerful tools that can model complex business processes and integrate with customer and supplier systems.

Just as modern spacecraft could not have been built without specialized, high-technology tools, future software will be planned, constructed, and maintained with a new generation of CASE tools. The following sections discuss CASE tool trends and method-specific tools.

B.5.1 New Products and Features

CASE tool vendors constantly offer more features and greater flexibility. One example is a framework to help transform business processes into an information system. A **framework** organizes and documents system development tasks. For example, the Zachman Framework shown in Figure B-11 arranges traditional fact-finding questions into a useful matrix. The vertical axis shows five development stages and stakeholder roles, while the horizontal axis displays six essential fact-finding questions.

In each of the 30 "cells," Visible Analyst suggests specific tools, diagrams, and methods to document the development process. Perhaps the most powerful feature is that all the data is integrated and stored automatically in a central repository, which can easily be viewed and updated.

As software becomes more powerful and complex, the lines between traditional CASE tools and other modeling tools continue to blur. For example, Microsoft Visio can model networks, business processes, and many types of special diagrams as shown in Figure B-12.

Another trend is the increasing use of completely online, cloud-based development environments. The Heroku platform, shown in Figure B-13, is an example of a suite of tools and PaaS support for developing and deploying modern applications.

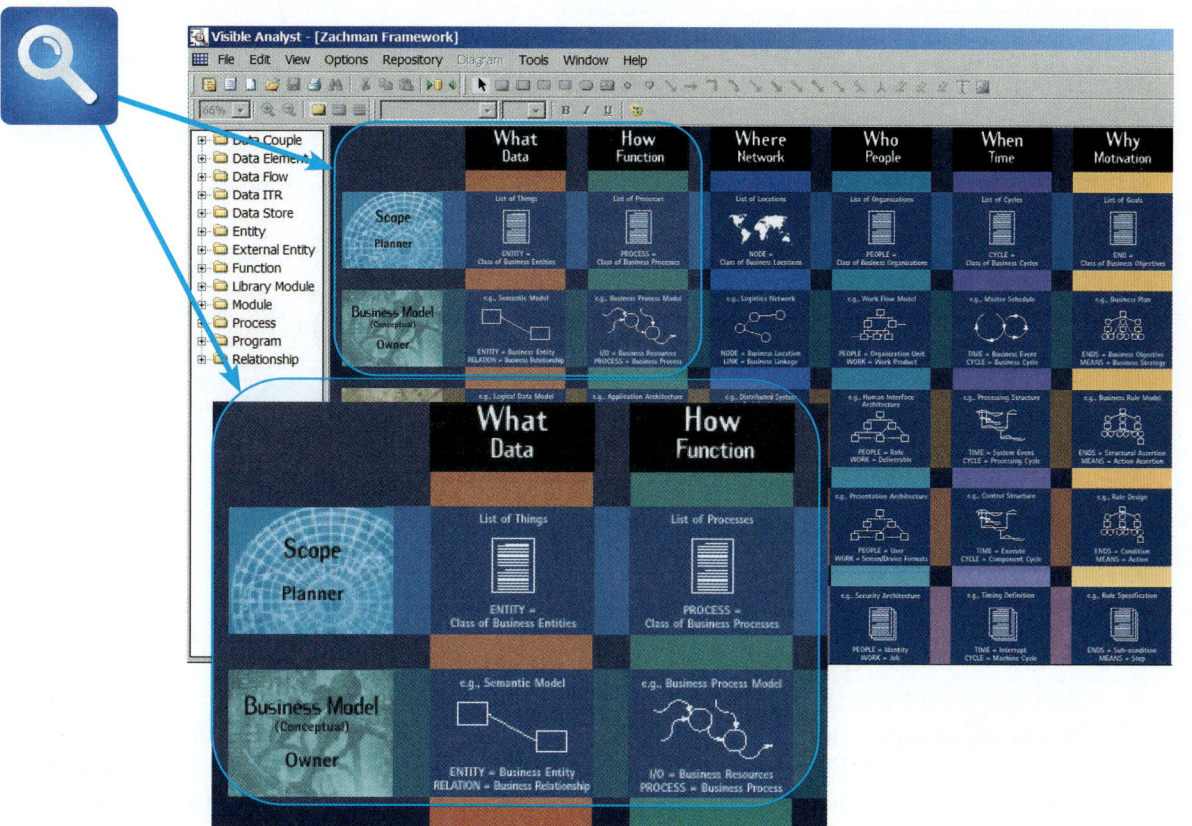

FIGURE B-11 The Zachman Framework in Visible Analyst provides an easy-to-follow matrix that helps system developers work on specific areas, and then integrate the results into an overall model.

Source: Visible Systems Corporation

Microsoft Visio Professional 2013 makes it easier than ever for individuals and teams to create and share professional, versatile diagrams that simplify complex information. It includes all of the functionality of Visio Standard 2013 as well as updated shapes, templates, and styles; enhanced support for team collaboration, including the ability for several people to work on a single diagram at the same time; and the ability to link diagrams to data. Visio Professional 2013 also adds additional stencils for business and engineering diagrams; process diagrams (including Business Process Model and Notation [BPMN] 2.0); maps and floor plans; network diagrams; and software and database diagrams.

Get a jump start on your diagram

Take advantage of over 60 built-in templates, many with updated shapes. Visio Professional includes all of the stencils in Visio Standard and adds:

- Additional business diagrams, such as ITIL (Information Technology Infrastructure Library), PivotDiagram, Six Sigma, and value stream map
- Engineering diagrams, such as electrical, circuits, and systems
- Additional flowcharts, such as IDEF0 (Integration Definition for Process Modeling) and Microsoft SharePoint workflows
- Additional process diagrams, such as BPMN 1.2 and BPMN 2.0 and SharePoint workflow
- Maps and floor plans, such as HVAC (heating, ventilation, and air conditioning), plumbing and piping plan, and space plan
- Additional network diagrams, such as Active Directory, detailed network, and rack
- Software and database diagrams, such as database notation, website map, and UML (Unified Modeling Language)

FIGURE B-12 Microsoft Visio can create many different types of diagrams.
Source: Microsoft Corporation.

The Heroku Platform

Heroku is a cloud platform based on a managed container system, with integrated data services and a powerful ecosystem, for deploying and running modern apps. The Heroku developer experience is an app-centric approach for software delivery, integrated with today's most popular developer tools and workflows.

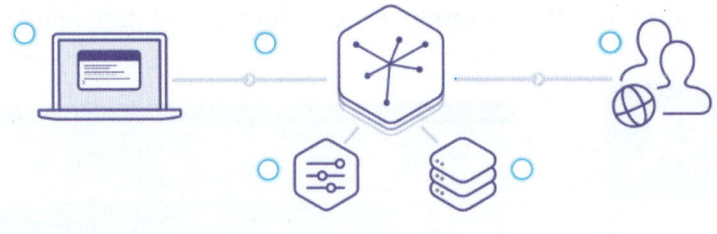

 Heroku Runtime

Heroku runs your apps inside dynos — smart containers on a reliable, fully managed runtime environment. Developers deploy their code written in Node, Ruby, Java, PHP, Python, Go, Scala, or Clojure to a build system

 Heroku Developer Experience (DX)

The Heroku Developer Experience is an app-centric approach to software delivery so developers can focus on creating, releasing, and updating applications, without being distracted

 Data Services and Ecosystem

Heroku Elements let developers extend their apps with Add-ons, customize their application stack with Buildpacks and jumpstart their projects with Buttons. Add-ons are 3rd party cloud

FIGURE B-13 The Heroku platform in the cloud.
Source: Salesforce.com

B.5.2 Method-Specific CASE Tools

As Chapter 11 explains, each systems development approach has a set of tools that has worked especially well for that method. For example, structured development relies heavily on DFDs and structure charts. Object-oriented methods use a variety of diagrams, such as use case, class, sequence, and state transition diagrams. Agile methods tend to use spiral or other iterative models. Chapter 1 describes several method-specific modeling tools. In addition to these tools, system developers also use multipurpose tools to help them translate the system logic into properly functioning program modules. These generic tools include entity-relationship diagrams, flow-charts, pseudocode, decision tables, and decision trees.

Structured analysis is a traditional approach that is time-tested and easy to understand. Structured modeling tools are described in detail in Chapter 5. However, as Chapter 1 points out, **object-oriented analysis and design (OOAD)** is very popular. Widespread use of object-oriented languages has spurred interest in O-O CASE and UML-based modeling tools, which provide seamless development from planning to actual coding. Other O-O features include modular design and reusable code, which can reduce costs and speed up development. Object-oriented analysis and design tools and techniques are described in Chapter 6.

The most recent trend is the popularity of agile methods. Chapter 11 includes a detailed description of an agile project, including the iterative cycles and the intense contact between developers and users. Agile developers use a wide range of modeling tools, including CASE tools. However, many agile teams find that simple whiteboard sketching works best for them.

Although it is difficult to predict the future, it seems clear that CASE tools will continue to evolve and become more powerful. At the same time, system developers will sometimes choose simpler, low-tech methods and techniques as modeling tools.

B.6 TOOLKIT SUMMARY

CASE stands for computer-aided systems engineering. CASE tools are software programs that system developers use to help them design and construct information systems. CASE tools can reduce costs, speed up development, and provide comprehensive documentation that can be used for future maintenance or enhancements.

Older systems used program code that was written in procedural languages such as COBOL, which required a programmer to create code statements for each processing step. Modern languages such as C++ and Java are non-procedural, or event-driven, languages because a programmer defines the actions that the program must perform when certain events occur.

Non-procedural languages, called 4GLs, are object-oriented programming languages (OOPL). 4GLs are important components of a fourth-generation environment that allows system developers to develop accurate prototypes, cut development time, and reduce expense.

A repository is a database that serves as a central storage location for all information about the system being developed. Once a data element has been defined in the repository, it can be accessed and used by processes and other information systems. An alias is an alternative name for a data element. The repository can be searched, and all instances of the data element will be listed.

An integrated set of CASE tools can be used to model, document, engineer, and construct the information system. Modeling tools represent the system graphically by using various types of diagrams, including data flow diagrams (DFDs), Unified Modeling Language (UML) diagrams, functional decomposition diagrams, structure charts, and network diagrams.

The main source of system documentation is the repository, which identifies new elements and adds them to the database. Additional documentation is provided by tools that check automatically for inconsistent or incomplete information in forms, reports, and diagrams.

Forward engineering means translating business processes and functions into applications. Reverse engineering allows you to examine an existing application and break it down into a series of diagrams, structure charts, and, in some cases, source code.

A CASE tool can handle many program development tasks, such as generating application code, screens, and reports.

An IDE uses a built-in CASE tool that a software vendor includes to make it easier to plan, construct, and maintain a specific software product. Examples of IDEs include Oracle Designer and Microsoft Visual Studio.

Many vendors, including IBM and Microsoft, are calling attention to application ALM concepts and tools. ALM refers to a start-to-finish approach to planning, designing, developing, deploying, managing, and maintaining an information system.

Two trends seem clear: CASE tool vendors will continue to add powerful new features, and cloud-based toolsets will continue to grow in popularity.

Key Terms

application generator A tool that supports the rapid development of computer programs by translating a logical model directly into code. Also called a code generator.

application life cycle management (ALM) A start-to-finish approach to planning, designing, developing, deploying, managing, and maintaining an information system, using specialized software tools.

business analytics Using software to measure past performance to help managers understand business trends and monitor current operations.

CASE environment More than just a set of CASE tools. A CASE environment includes any use of computer-based support in the software development process.

code generator *See* application generator.

development environment The mix of software tools, methods, and physical resources that an IT team uses to create an information system.

event-driven programming language Instead of writing a series of sequential instructions, a programmer defines the actions that the program must perform when certain events occur. Also called non-procedural programming language.

form painter *See* screen generator.

forward engineering Translating business processes and functions into applications.

fourth-generation environment A term used to describe an efficient software development environment that is created through the use of powerful CASE tools, application generators, report generators, screen generators, and fourth-generation languages (4GLs) during prototyping.

fourth-generation languages (4GLs) Non-procedural programming languages that are especially valuable in implementing an object-oriented system design.

framework Conceptual structure that organizes and documents system development tasks.

non-procedural programming language *See* event-driven programming language.

object-oriented analysis and design (OOAD) A technique used to create objects called actors, which represent the human users who will interact with the system.

object-oriented programming languages (OOPL) Non-procedural programming languages that are especially valuable in implementing an object-oriented system design.

procedural programming language A programming language that requires a programmer to create code statements for each processing step.

product life cycle management (PLM) A system that integrates all aspects of a product, its data, and its users across the SDLC in a large enterprise setting.

report generator A tool for designing formatted reports rapidly. Also called a report writer.

report writer *See* report generator.

repository A database that serves as a central storage location for all information about a system being developed.

reverse engineering A process that lets the analyst examine an existing application and break it down into a series of diagrams, structure charts, and, in some cases, source code.

screen generator An interactive tool that helps you design a custom interface, create screen forms, and handle data entry format and procedures. Also called a form painter.

Toolkit Exercises

Review Questions

1. Define CASE, CASE tools, and a CASE environment.
2. Explain the difference between procedural and non-procedural languages.
3. Describe 4GLs and their characteristics.
4. Define a repository, and explain its role in the systems development process.
5. What are forward and reverse engineering tools, and how are they used?
6. Provide an example of an application generator and a screen generator.
7. How is a report generator used, and what is a mock-up report?
8. Explain the concept of an integrated development environment and provide two examples of IDEs.
9. Explain the concept of an application life cycle management environment and provide two examples of ALMs.
10. What is the emerging role of object-oriented analysis and design methods? Agile methods?

Discussion Topics

1. Would a systems analyst be better off in a position where he or she works with an IDE, or where generic CASE tools are used? Explain your answer.
2. Visit the websites for Microsoft Visual Studio and Eclipse. If you could choose only one of these development environments, which one would you select, and why?
3. If you were a programmer, would you prefer to work with procedural or non-procedural languages? Explain your reasons.
4. Some analysts believe that if the trend toward more powerful CASE tools continues, many tedious development tasks might be performed automatically. Is there a limit to the capabilities of future CASE software? Could describing a business operation and specifying certain inputs and outputs design a complete information system? Explain your answer.
5. What are some of the advantages and disadvantages of cloud-based development environments like Heroku?

Projects

1. Search the Internet for a simple, user-friendly CASE tool that you would recommend for your school's computer lab. Visit the vendor's site and learn all you can about the product. Write a brief report that describes your experience.
2. Visit *www.visual-paradigm.com*. Locate and download the Community Edition, which is free, or a 30-day trial edition. Experiment with the program and write a brief report that describes your experience.
3. Search the Internet and locate an example of a screen generator. Visit the vendor's site and learn all you can about the product. Write a brief report that describes your experience.
4. Go to the SEI's website on System of Systems at *http://www.sei.cmu.edu/sos/*. Document the main differences for a system analyst working at this scale, and

describe the role CASE tools could play across the SDLC to help the analyst function effectively in such a complex environment.

5. Try out the Heroku cloud-based platform by developing and deploying a simple application of your choosing. Write a report comparing your experiences with this style of development versus a more traditional approach using tools such as Microsoft Visual Studio or Eclipse.

PART C

Financial Analysis Tools

Part C of the Systems Analyst's Toolkit demonstrates financial analysis tools that can used to measure project feasibility, develop accurate cost-benefit estimates, and make sound decisions.

LEARNING OBJECTIVES

When you finish this part of the Toolkit, you should be able to:

- Define economic feasibility
- Classify costs and benefits into various categories, including tangible or intangible, direct or indirect, fixed or variable, and developmental or operational
- Understand chargeback methods and how they are used
- Use payback analysis to calculate the length of time that it takes for a project to pay for itself
- Use return on investment analysis to measure a project's profitability
- Use present value analysis to determine the value of a future project measured in current dollars

TOOLKIT CONTENTS

C.1 INTRODUCTION

Part C of the Systems Analyst's Toolkit shows how to use various tools to calculate a project's costs and benefits. A systems analyst needs to know how to calculate costs and benefits when conducting preliminary investigations, evaluating IT projects, and making recommendations to management.

Financial analysis tools are important throughout the systems development life cycle. For example, in Chapter 2 it was explained that economic feasibility depends on a comparison of costs and benefits. A project is economically feasible if the future benefits outweigh the estimated costs of developing or acquiring the new system. In Chapter 7 it was explained that when development strategies are analyzed, financial analysis tools and techniques are used to examine various options. Then, as described in Chapter 12, these tools are again used to recognize the end of a system's useful life.

C.2 DESCRIBING COSTS AND BENEFITS

A systems analyst must review a project's costs and benefits at the end of each SDLC phase so management can decide whether or not to continue the project. Before the economic analysis tools described in this section of the Toolkit can be used, how to identify and classify all costs and benefits must be understood.

As described in Chapter 2, economic feasibility means that the projected benefits of the proposed system outweigh the projected costs. When economic feasibility has been determined, the project's benefits compared to the project's total cost of ownership (TCO) must be considered, which includes ongoing support and maintenance costs, as well as acquisition costs.

Figure C-1 shows a TCO calculator to compare the costs of running applications on-premises or in the cloud using Amazon.com's AWS infrastructure. Because migrating to the cloud is a complex activity, such calculators can greatly help the systems analyst make informed decisions. Google, IBM, Microsoft, and other vendors provide similar TCO guidance related to the cloud and other types of large-scale IT projects.

AWS Total Cost of Ownership (TCO) Calculator

Use this calculator to compare the cost of running your applications in an on-premises or traditional hosting environment to AWS. Describe your on-premises or hosting environment configuration to produce a detailed cost comparison with AWS.

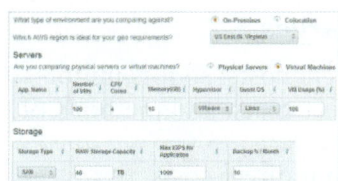

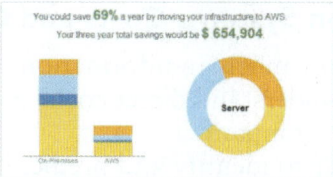

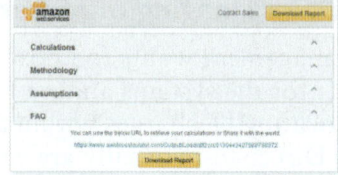

1. Describe your existing or planned on-premises or hosting infrastructure in four steps, or enter detailed configurations.

2. Get an instant summary report which shows you the three year TCO comparison by cost categories.

3. Download a full report including detailed cost breakdowns, Methodology, Assumptions, and FAQ or store the report in Amazon S3 for sharing with others.

FIGURE C-1 Amazon.com offers a calculator to compare the TCO of running applications on-premises or in the cloud using AWS.

Source: Amazon Web Services, Inc.

C.2.1 Cost Classifications

Costs can be classified as tangible or intangible, direct or indirect, fixed or variable, and developmental or operational. As Chapter 2 explained, tangible costs are costs that can be assigned a specific dollar value. Examples of tangible costs include employee salaries, hardware and software purchases, and office supplies. Tangible costs also include the interest charges that firms must pay when they need to borrow money for working capital or to finance new projects. In times of high interest rates, these costs can be significant and must be considered.

In contrast, intangible costs are costs whose dollar value cannot be calculated easily. The cost of customer dissatisfaction, lower employee morale, and reduced information availability are examples of intangible costs.

If the analyst examines an intangible item carefully, however, it sometimes is possible to estimate a dollar value. For example, users might dislike a system because it is difficult to learn. Their dissatisfaction is an intangible cost, but if it translates into an increase in errors that must be corrected, a tangible dollar cost could be assigned. It is preferable to work with tangible costs whenever possible.

Direct costs are costs that can be associated with the development of a specific system. Examples of direct costs include the salaries of project team members and the purchase of hardware that is used only for the new system. In contrast, indirect costs, or overhead expenses, cannot be attributed to the development of a particular information system. The salaries of network administrators, copy machine rentals, and insurance expenses are examples of indirect costs.

Fixed costs are costs that are relatively constant and do not depend on a level of activity or effort. Many fixed costs recur regularly, such as salaries and hardware rental charges. Variable costs are costs that vary depending on the level of activity. The costs of printer paper, supplies, and telephone charges are examples of variable costs.

Developmental costs are incurred only once, at the time the system is developed or acquired. Those costs might include salaries of people involved in systems development, software purchases, initial user training, and the purchase of necessary hardware or furniture. Operational costs, covered in Chapter 12, are incurred after the system is implemented and continue while the system is in use. Examples of operational costs include system maintenance, ongoing training, annual software license fees, and communications expense.

Some costs apply to more than one category of expenses. For example, overtime pay for clerical staff during the systems analysis phase would be classified as developmental, variable, and direct. A monthly fee for maintaining the company's website would be regarded as operational, fixed, and indirect.

C.2.2 Managing Information Systems Costs and Charges

Management wants to know how much an information system costs, so it is important for the systems analyst to understand direct costs, indirect costs, and methods of allocating IT charges within the company.

Direct costs usually are easier to identify and predict than indirect costs. For example, the salaries of project team members and the purchase of hardware, software, and supplies for the new system are direct costs. After a new information system goes into operation, other direct costs might include the lease of system-specific hardware or software.

Many IT department costs cannot be attributed directly to a specific information system or user group. Those indirect costs can include general hardware and software acquisition expenses, facility maintenance, air conditioning, security, rent, insurance, and general supplies, and the salaries of operations, technical support, and information center personnel.

A chargeback method is a technique that uses accounting entries to allocate the indirect costs of running the IT department. Most organizations adopt one of four chargeback methods: no charge, a fixed charge, a variable charge based on resource usage, or a variable charge based on volume.

1. No charge method. Some organizations treat information systems department indirect expenses as a necessary cost of doing business, and IT services are seen as benefiting the entire company. Thus, indirect IT department costs are treated as general organizational costs and are not charged to other departments. In this case, the information systems department is called a cost center because it generates accounting charges with no offsetting credits for IT services.

2. Fixed charge method. With this method, the indirect IT costs are divided among all the other departments in the form of a fixed monthly charge. The monthly charge might be the same for all departments or based on a relatively constant factor, such as department size or number of workstations. By using a fixed charge approach, all indirect costs are charged to other departments, and the IT group is regarded as a profit center. A profit center is a department that is expected to break even or show a profit. Under the profit center concept, company departments purchase services from the IT department and receive accounting charges that represent the cost of providing the services.

3. Variable charge method based on resource usage. Resource allocation is the charging of indirect costs based on the resources used by an information system. The allocation might be based on connect time, server processing time, network resources required, printer use, or a combination of similar factors. Connect time is the total time that a user is connected actively to a remote server — some Internet service providers use this as a basis for charges. In a client/server system, server processing time is the time that the server actually responds to client requests for processing. The amount a particular department is charged will vary from month to month, depending not only on that department's resource usage but also on the total resource usage. The IT department is considered a profit center when an organization uses the resource allocation method.

4. Variable charge method based on volume. The indirect IT department costs are allocated to other departments based on user-oriented activity, such as the number of transactions or printing volume. As with the resource allocation method, a department's share of the costs varies from month to month, depending on the level of activity. In this case, the IT department is considered a profit center.

C.2.3 Benefit Classifications

In addition to classifying costs, the benefits that the company expects from a project must be classified. Like costs, benefits can be classified as tangible or intangible, fixed or variable, and direct or indirect. Another useful benefit classification relates to the nature of the benefit: positive benefits versus cost-avoidance benefits. Positive benefits increase revenues, improve services, or otherwise contribute to the organization as a direct result of the new information system. Examples of positive benefits include improved information availability, greater flexibility, faster service to customers, higher employee morale, and better inventory management.

In contrast, **cost-avoidance benefits** refer to expenses that would be necessary if the new system were not installed. Examples of cost-avoidance benefits include handling the work with current staff instead of hiring additional people, not having to replace existing hardware or software, and avoiding problems that otherwise would be faced with the current system. Cost-avoidance benefits are just as important as positive benefits, and both types must be considered when performing cost-benefit analysis.

C.3 COST-BENEFIT ANALYSIS

Cost-benefit analysis is the process of comparing the anticipated costs of an information system to the anticipated benefits. Cost-benefit analysis is performed throughout the SDLC to determine the economic feasibility of an information system project and to compare alternative solutions. Many cost-benefit analysis techniques exist. This section covers discussion of three of the most common methods: payback analysis, return on investment analysis, and present value analysis. Each of the approaches analyzes cost-benefit figures differently, but the objective is the same: to provide reliable information for making decisions.

C.3.1 Payback Analysis

Payback analysis is the process of determining how long it takes an information system to pay for itself. The time it takes to recover the system's cost is called the **payback period**. To perform a payback analysis, the following steps are executed:

1. Determine the initial development cost of the system.
2. Estimate annual benefits.
3. Determine annual operating costs.
4. Find the payback period by comparing total development and operating costs to the accumulated value of the benefits produced by the system.

When the system costs over the potential life of the system are plotted, typically there is a curve similar to the one shown in Figure C-2. After the system is

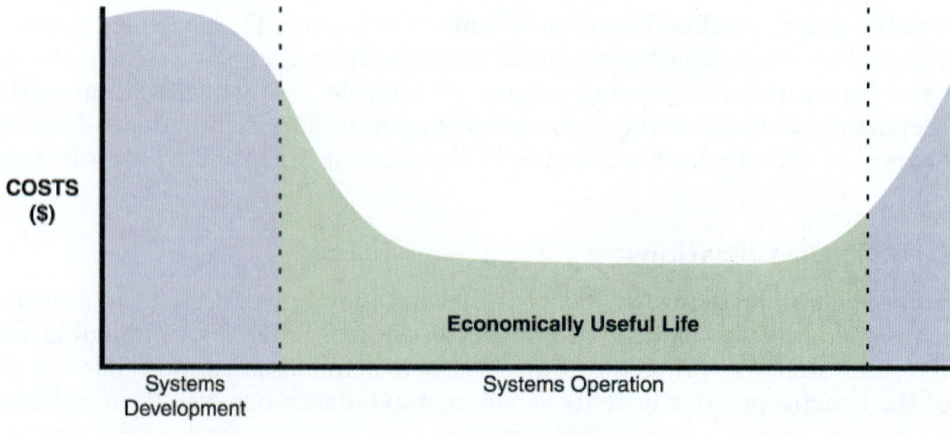

FIGURE C-2 The costs of a typical system vary over time. At the beginning, system costs are high due to initial development expenses. Costs then drop during systems operation. Maintenance costs begin to increase until the system reaches the end of its economically useful life.

operational, costs decrease rapidly and remain relatively low for a period of time. Eventually, as the system requires more maintenance, costs begin to increase. The period between the beginning of systems operation and the point when operational costs are rapidly increasing is called the **economically useful life** of the system.

When the benefits provided by an information system are plotted against time, the resulting curve usually resembles the one shown in the upper graph in Figure C-3. Benefits start to appear when the system becomes operational, might increase for a time, and then level off or start to decline.

When conducting a payback analysis, the time it takes for the accumulated benefits of an information system to equal the accumulated costs of developing and operating the system are calculated.

In the lower graph in Figure C-3, the cost and benefit curves are plotted together. The dashed line indicates the payback period. Notice that the payback period is not the point when current benefits equal current costs, where the two lines cross. Instead, the payback period compares accumulated costs and benefits. If current costs and benefits are graphed, the payback period corresponds to the time at which the areas under the two curves are equal.

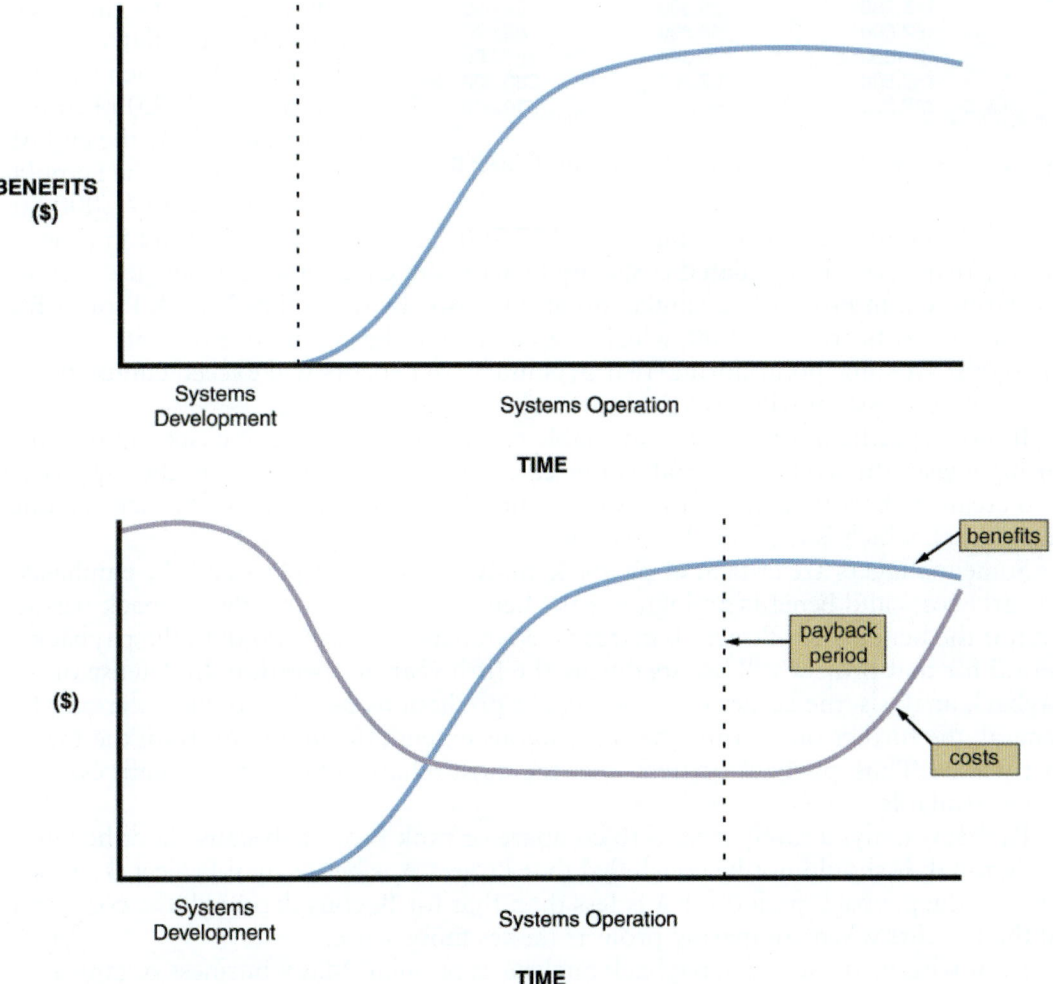

FIGURE C-3 Benefits of an information system change over time, as shown in the upper graph. The lower graph shows costs and benefits plotted on the same graph. The dashed line indicates the payback period, when accumulated benefits equal accumulated costs.

PAYBACK ANALYSIS EXAMPLES

PROJECT A:

YEAR	COSTS	CUMULATIVE COSTS	BENEFITS	CUMULATIVE BENEFITS
0	60,000	60,000	3,000	3,000
1	17,000	77,000	28,000	31,000
2	18,500	95,500	31,000	62,000
3	19,200	114,700	34,000	96,000
4	21,000	135,700	36,000	132,000
5	22,000	157,700	39,000	171,000
6	23,300	181,000	42,000	213,000

PROJECT B:

YEAR	COSTS	CUMULATIVE COSTS	BENEFITS	CUMULATIVE BENEFITS
0	80,000	80,000	——	——
1	40,000	120,000	6,000	6,000
2	25,000	145,000	26,000	32,000
3	22,000	167,000	54,000	86,000
4	24,000	191,000	70,000	156,000
5	26,500	217,500	82,000	238,000
6	30,000	247,500	92,000	330,000

FIGURE C-4 Payback analysis data for two information systems: Project A and Project B.

Consider the example shown in Figure C-4, which contains two cost-benefit tables. The tables show the anticipated annual costs, cumulative costs, annual benefits, and cumulative benefits for two information systems projects. Year 0 (zero) corresponds to the year in which systems development begins. The development of Project A takes less than one year, so some benefits are realized in Year 0. Systems development for Project B requires more than one year, so the benefits do not begin until some time in Year 1.

In Project A, by the end of Year 4, the cumulative costs are $135,700, which slightly exceeds the $132,000 cumulative benefits. By the end of Year 5, however, the cumulative benefits of $171,000 far exceed the cumulative costs, which are $157,700. Therefore, at some point in time during Year 5, the accumulated costs and benefits are equal, and the payback period is established. In Project B, a similar situation exists. By the end of Year 4, Project B's cumulative costs are $191,000, which is greater than the cumulative benefits of $156,000. At some point during Year 5, cumulative benefits will exceed cumulative costs, and the system will have paid for itself.

If more specific information is available regarding the timing of costs and benefits during a year, the payback period can be calculated more precisely. Another approach is to create a chart that shows the exact point when cumulative benefits exceed cumulative costs, which is explained in Section C.3.2.

Some managers are critical of payback analysis because it places all the emphasis on early costs and benefits and ignores the benefits received after the payback period. Even if the benefits for Project B in Year 6 soared as high as $500,000, the payback period for that project still occurs during the fifth year of operation. In defense of payback analysis, the earlier cost and benefit predictions usually are more certain. In general, the further out in time that projections extend, the more uncertain the forecast will be. Thus, payback analysis uses the most reliable of cost and benefit estimates available.

Payback analysis rarely is used to compare or rank projects because later benefits are ignored. It should not be concluded that Project A is better than Project B simply because the payback period for A is less than that for B; considering all the costs and all the benefits when comparing projects makes more sense.

Even with its drawbacks, payback analysis is popular. Many business organizations establish a minimum payback period for approved projects. If company policy requires a project to begin paying for itself within three years, then neither project in Figure C-4 would be approved, though both are economically feasible because total benefits exceed total costs.

C.3.2 Using a Spreadsheet to Compute Payback Analysis

A spreadsheet can be used to record and calculate accumulated costs and benefits, as shown in Figure C-5. The first step is to design the worksheet and label the rows and columns. After entering the cost and benefit data for each year, the formulas are entered. For payback analysis, a formula is needed to display cumulative totals, year by year. For example, the first year in the cumulative costs column is the same as Year 0 costs, so the formula in cell C6 is =B6. The cumulative cost total for the second year is Year 0 cumulative total + Year 1 costs, so the formula for cell C7 is =C6 + B7, and so on. The first worksheet shows the initial layout and the second worksheet shows the finished spreadsheet.

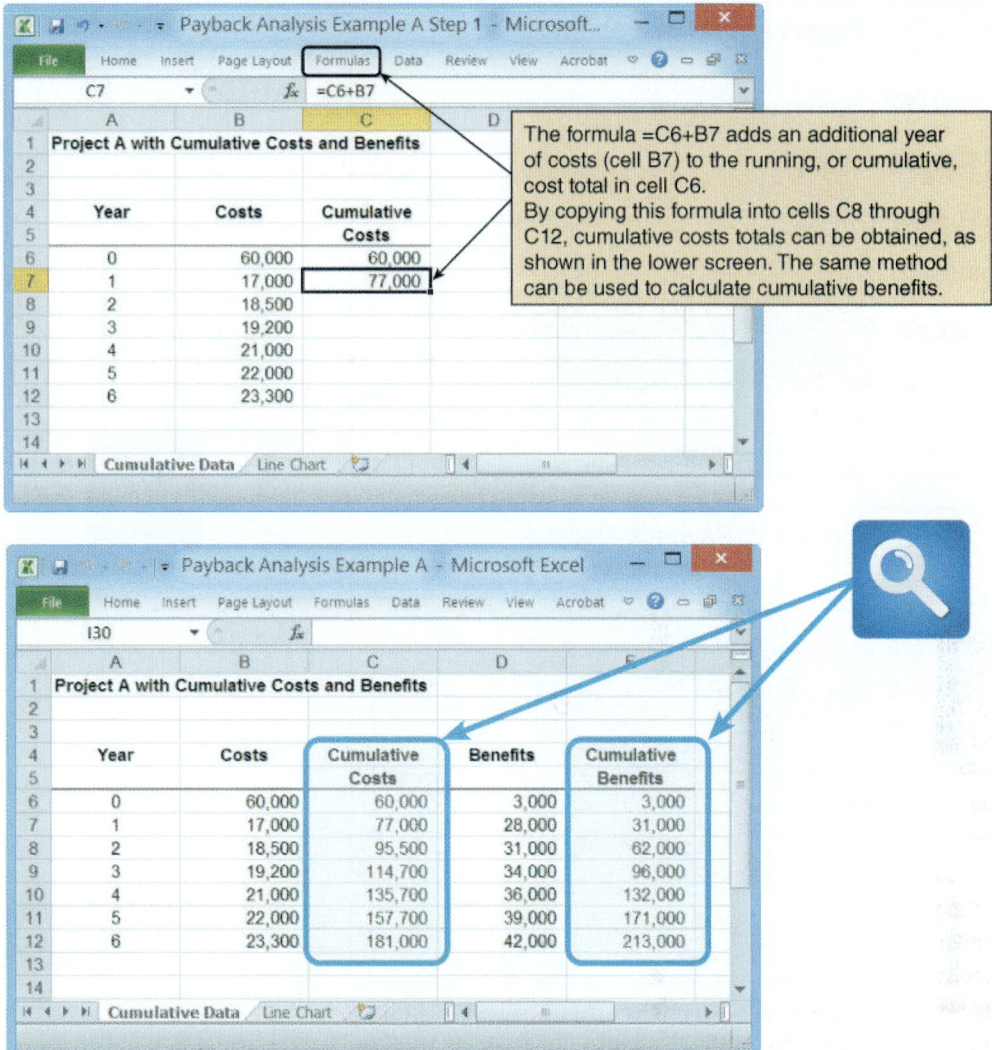

FIGURE C-5 A Microsoft Excel worksheet displays payback analysis data for Project A in the upper screen. When cumulative cost and benefit formulas are entered, the finished worksheet in the lower screen appears.

After verifying that the spreadsheet operates properly, a line chart is created that displays the cumulative costs, benefits, and payback period, which is identified by the intersection of the cost and benefit lines, as shown in Figure C-6.

C.3.3 Return on Investment Analysis

Return on investment (ROI) is a percentage rate that measures profitability by comparing the total net benefits (the return) received from a project to the total costs (the investment) of the project. ROI is calculated as follows:

$$\text{ROI} = (\text{total benefits} - \text{total costs}) / \text{total costs}$$

Return on investment analysis considers costs and benefits over a longer time span than payback analysis. ROI calculations usually are based on total costs and benefits for a period of five to seven years. For example, Figure C-7 shows the ROI calculations for Project A and Project B. The ROI for Project A is 17.7%, and the ROI for Project B is 33.3%.

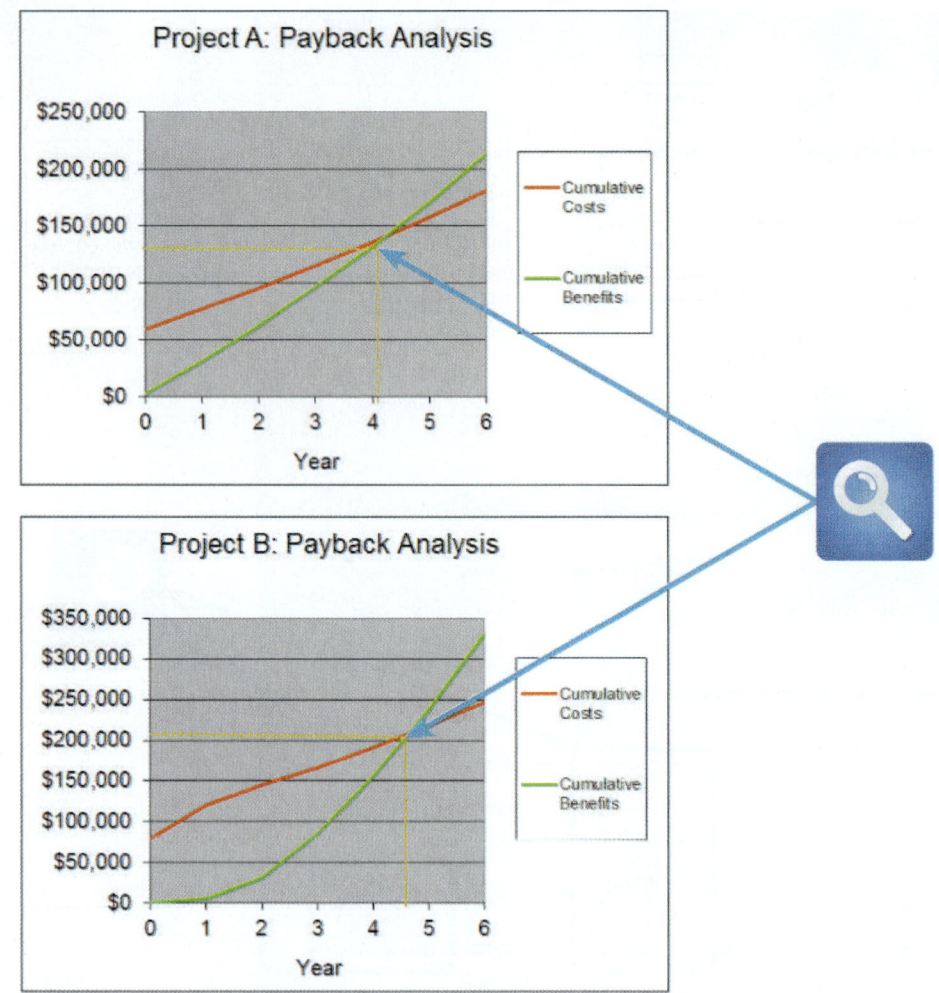

FIGURE C-6 Microsoft Excel can be used to show the payback period by creating a chart of cumulative costs and benefits. Note that Project A has a shorter payback period than Project B.

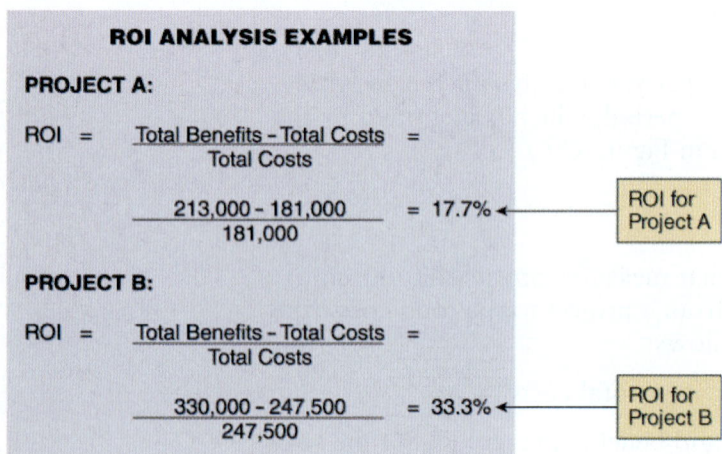

FIGURE C-7 Return on investment analysis for Projects A and B shown in Figure C-4.

In many organizations, projects must meet or exceed a minimum ROI. This minimum ROI can be an estimate of the return the organization would receive from investing its money in other investment opportunities, such as treasury bonds, or it can be a higher rate that the company requires for all new projects. If a company requires a minimum ROI of 15%, for example, then both Projects A and B would meet the criterion.

ROI can also be used for ranking projects. If Projects A and B represent two different proposed solutions for a single information systems project, then the solution represented by Project B is better than the Project A solution. If Projects A and B represent two different information systems projects, and if the organization has sufficient resources to pursue only one of the two projects, then Project B is the better choice.

Critics of return on investment analysis raise two points. First, ROI measures the overall rate of return for the total period, and annual return rates can vary considerably. Two projects with the same ROI might not be equally desirable if the benefits of one project occur significantly earlier than the benefits of the other project. The second criticism is that the ROI technique ignores the timing of the costs and benefits. This concept is called the time value of money, and is explained in the section on the present value analysis method.

C.3.4 Using a Spreadsheet to Compute ROI

A spreadsheet can be used to calculate the ROI. To do so for Project A, first set up the worksheet and enter the cost and benefit data. Cumulative columns can be used (as was done for payback analysis), but two overall totals are also needed (one for costs and one for benefits), as shown in Figure C-8.

The last step is to add a formula to calculate the ROI percentage rate, which is displayed in cell E13 in Figure C-8. As stated previously, the ROI calculation is total benefits minus total costs, divided by total costs. Therefore, the formula that displays the ROI percentage in cell E13 is = (E11 − C11) / C11.

A major advantage of using a spreadsheet is if the data changes, the worksheet can be modified and a new result calculated instantly.

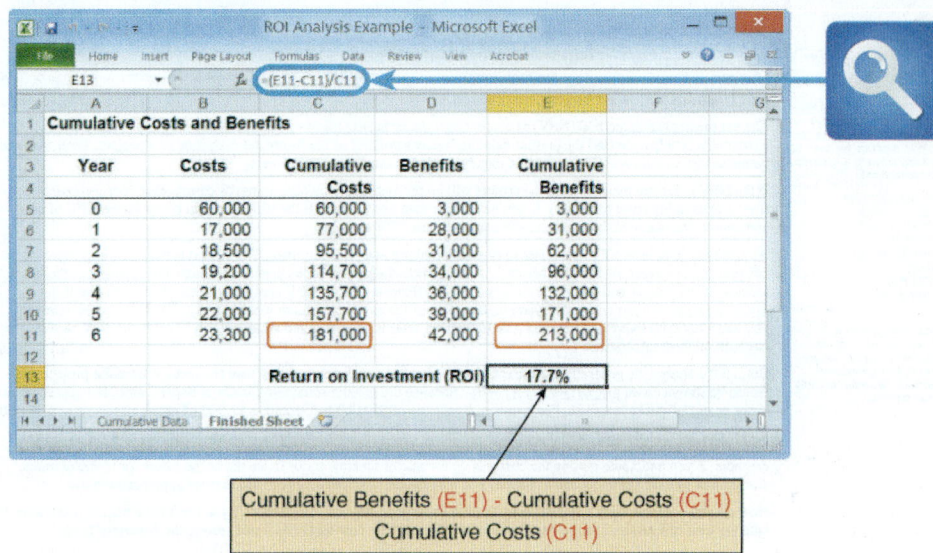

FIGURE C-8 Sample ROI worksheet. Notice that cell E13 contains the ROI formula.

C.3.5 Present Value Analysis

A dollar today is worth more than a dollar received a year from today. A dollar in hand can be invested now and it will grow in value. For example, most people would rather have $100 right now rather than the promise of a dollar a year from now. If the $100 was invested today in a mutual fund that has an annual return of 8%, one year from now there would be $108 instead of $100.

ROI can also be approached from a different direction. For example, instead of asking, "How much will $100 be worth a year from now?" ask instead, "How much should be invested today, at 8%, in order to have $100 a year from now?" This concept is known as the **time value of money**, as shown in Figure C-9, and it is the basis of the technique called **present value analysis**.

The **present value** of a future dollar is the amount of money that, when invested today at a specified interest rate, grows to exactly one dollar at a certain point in the future. The specified interest rate is called the discount rate. In present value analysis, a company uses a discount rate that represents the rate of return if the money is put into relatively risk-free investments, such as bonds, instead of being invested in the project.

Most companies require a rate of return that is higher than the discount rate because of the degree of risk in any project compared with investing in a bond. Companies often reject projects that seem attractive because the risk is not worth the potential reward.

To help the analyst perform present value analysis, adjustment factors for various interest rates and numbers of years are calculated and printed in tables called **present value tables**. Figure C-9 shows a portion of a present value table, including values for 10 years at various discount rates.

PERIODS	6%	8%	10%	12%	14%
1	0.943	0.926	0.909	0.893	0.877
2	0.890	0.857	0.826	0.797	0.769
3	0.840	0.794	0.751	0.712	0.675
4	0.792	0.735	0.683	0.636	0.592
5	0.747	0.681	0.621	0.567	0.519
6	0.705	0.630	0.564	0.507	0.456
7	0.665	0.583	0.513	0.452	0.400
8	0.627	0.540	0.467	0.404	0.351
9	0.592	0.500	0.424	0.361	0.308
10	0.558	0.463	0.386	0.322	0.270

FIGURE C-9 Portion of a present value table showing adjustment factors for various time periods and discount rates. Values in the table are calculated using the formula shown in the text. Notice how the factors decrease as time and percentage increase.

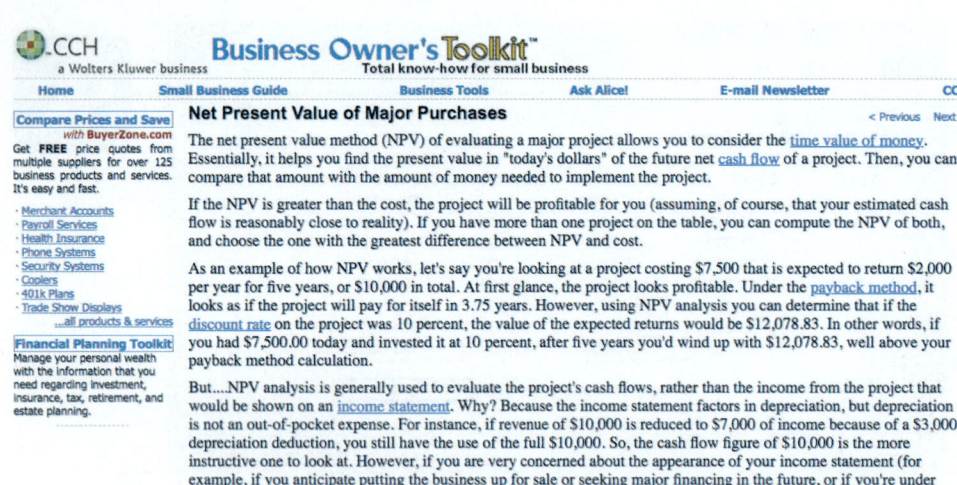

FIGURE C-10 The CCH Business Owner's Toolkit offers a small business guide and a wide range of financial tools, including guidance on calculating net present value.

Source: CCH Incorporated.

To use a present value table, locate the value in the column with the appropriate discount rate and the row for the appropriate number of years. For example, to calculate the present value of $1 at 12% for five years, look down the 12% column in Figure C-9 until reaching the row representing five years. The table value is 0.567. To determine what the present value of $3,000 will be in five years with a discount rate of 12%, multiply the present value factor from the table by the dollar amount; that is, PV = $3,000 × 0.567 × $1,701.

Many finance and accounting books contain comprehensive present value tables. This information can be obtained on the Internet, as shown in Figure C-10.

To perform present value analysis, the cost and benefit figures must be time-adjusted. First, multiply each of the projected benefits and costs by the proper present value factor, which depends on when the cost will be incurred or the benefit will be received. The second step is to sum all the time-adjusted benefits and time-adjusted costs. Then, calculate the net present value (NPV) of the project, which is the total present value of the benefits minus the total present value of the costs. Figure C-11 shows the calculation of net present value for two sample projects.

In theory, any project with a positive NPV is economically feasible because the project will produce a larger return than would be achieved by investing the same amount of money in a discount rate investment. Remember that risks are associated with any project, however, and management typically insists on a substantially higher return for high-risk projects. For example, both projects in Figure C-11 have positive net present values and appear economically worthwhile.

Suppose, however, that it was known one of the projects had a 90% probability of achieving its goals, while the other project had only a 70% chance. To be attractive, the project with the higher risk would have to offer a corresponding higher reward. Chapter 3 explains how project managers evaluate risks.

Net present value can also be used to compare and rank projects. All things being equal, the project with the highest net present value is the best investment. Figure C-11 shows that Project B is a better investment than Project A because it has a higher net present value.

Present value analysis provides solutions to the shortcomings of payback analysis and return on investment analysis. Unlike payback analysis, present value analysis considers all the costs and benefits, and not just the earlier values. In addition, present value analysis takes into account the timing of costs and benefits, so their values can be adjusted by the discount rate that provides a common yardstick and recognizes the time value of money. Even so, companies often use all three methods to get more input for making decisions. Sometimes a project will score higher on one method of analysis and lower on another.

NET PRESENT VALUE EXAMPLES

PROJECT A:

	Year 0	Year 1	Year 2	Year 3	Year 4	Year 5	Year 6	Total
Benefits:	3,000	28,000	31,000	34,000	36,000	39,000	42,000	
Present Value Factor (12%):	1.000	0.893	0.797	0.712	0.636	0.567	0.507	
Present Value:	3,000	25,004	24,707	24,208	22,896	22,113	21,294	143,222
Costs:	60,000	17,000	18,500	19,200	21,000	22,000	23,300	
Present Value Factor (12%):	1.000	0.893	0.797	0.712	0.636	0.567	0.507	
Present Value:	60,000	15,181	14,745	13,670	13,356	12,474	11,813	141,239
Net Present Value:								1,983

PROJECT B:

	Year 0	Year 1	Year 2	Year 3	Year 4	Year 5	Year 6	Total
Benefits:	——	6,000	26,000	54,000	70,000	82,000	92,000	
Present Value Factor (12%):	——	0.893	0.797	0.712	0.636	0.567	0.507	
Present Value:	——	5,358	20,722	38,448	44,520	46,494	46,644	202,186
Costs:	80,000	40,000	25,000	22,000	24,000	26,500	30,000	
Present Value Factor (12%):	1.000	0.893	0.797	0.712	0.636	0.567	0.507	
Present Value:	80,000	35,720	19,925	15,664	15,264	15,026	15,210	196,809
Net Present Value:								5,377

FIGURE C-11 Net present value analysis for Project A and Project B. The tables use discount factors from external sources, such as the CCH website shown in Figure C-10.

C.3.6 Using a Spreadsheet to Calculate Present Value

There are two ways to calculate present value using a spreadsheet program, such as Microsoft Excel. The discount adjustment factors can be entered from an external table, and a simple formula used to apply the factors. However, many analysts find it easier to use a built-in NPV formula that handles the calculations. The two methods are described in the following sections. The example shows costs and benefits for a proposed information system with a one-year development period, a three-year useful life, and a 6% discount rate.

USING EXTERNAL FACTORS: The first method is to create a spreadsheet similar to Figure C-12. Starting with the estimated benefits, enter adjustment factors in cells C5, D5, and E5. Then create formulas in cells C6, D6, and E6 that multiply the three factors times the dollar amounts for each year, with a total shown in column F. The same thing is done for the estimated costs. Finally, when the total costs are subtracted from total benefits, the net present value for the proposed system displays in cell F12.

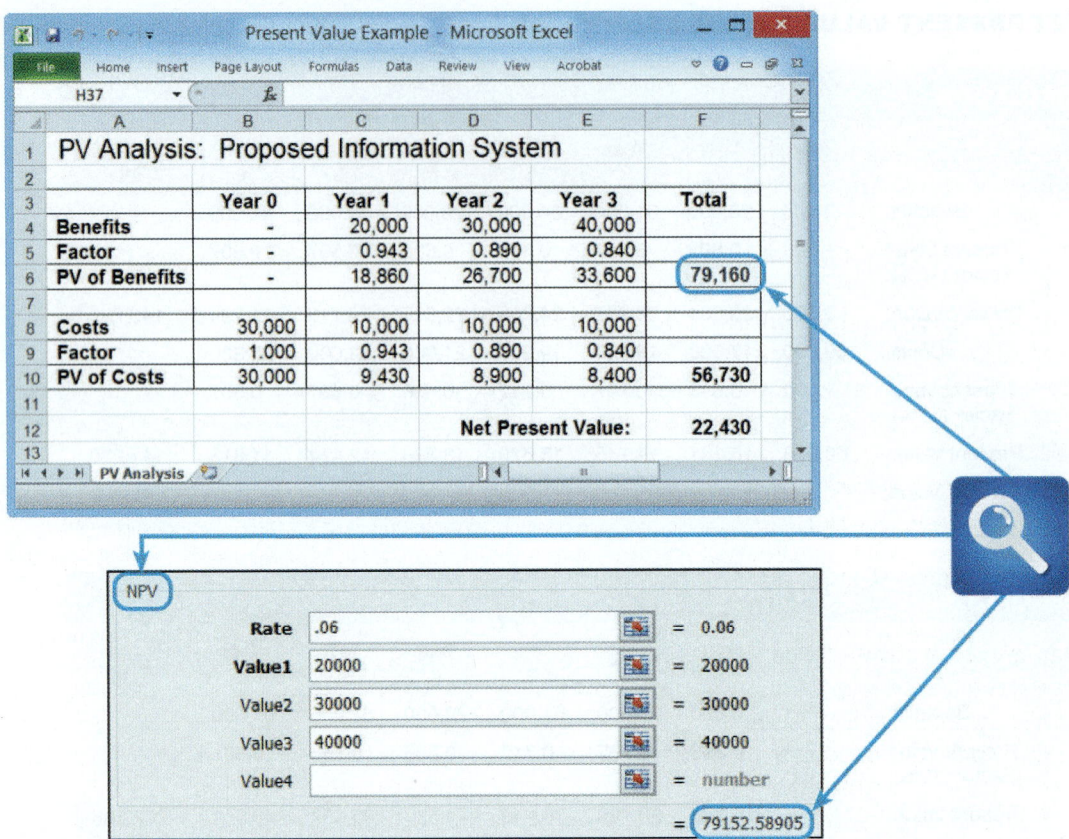

FIGURE C-12 The top screen shows how to use discount factors to calculate present value in a Microsoft Excel spreadsheet. In this case, the present value of benefits is $79,160. The bottom screen shows an example of the NPV function, which is a menu-driven formula that is built into Excel. The slight difference between the values is because Excel uses more decimal places.

USING A BUILT-IN FORMULA: The second method, which is shown in the bottom screen in Figure C-12, uses a built-in spreadsheet function to calculate present value. Enter the amounts, the discount rate, and number of time periods, and the program does the rest. Using this approach, four steps are performed, starting with the benefits.

1. First, create a spreadsheet similar to the upper screen in Figure C-12, but do not enter any factors or formulas — just the year-by-year cost and benefit amounts.

2. Next, select cell F6 and click the Function button on the formula bar. Select the NPV function, and a dialog box similar to the bottom of Figure C-12 appears. A discount rate of 6% is being used, so enter .06 in the Rate box.

3. Now enter the three benefit amounts: 20,000 for Value1, 30,000 for Value2, and 40,000 for Value3 and click the OK button (not shown in the figure).

4. At this point, a present value appears in cell F6. Now follow the same method to enter the cost amounts. When the PV of costs is subtracted from the PV of benefits, the result is the net present value, or NPV. Notice there is a slight difference in the two methods because Excel uses more decimal places. The difference is not significant.

C.4 Toolkit Summary

A systems analyst must be concerned with economic feasibility throughout the SDLC, and especially during the systems planning and systems analysis phases. A project is economically feasible if the anticipated benefits exceed the expected costs. When a project is reviewed, various feasibility and cost analysis tools are used.

Project costs are classified as tangible or intangible, direct or indirect, fixed or variable, and developmental or operational. Tangible costs are those that have a specific dollar value, whereas intangible costs involve items that are difficult to measure in dollar terms, such as employee dissatisfaction. Direct costs can be associated with a particular information system, while indirect costs refer to overhead expenses that cannot be allocated to a specific project. Fixed costs remain the same regardless of activity levels, while variable costs are affected by the degree of system activity. Developmental costs are one-time systems development expenses, while operational costs continue during the systems operation and use phase.

Every company must decide how to charge or allocate information systems costs and the chargeback method. Common chargeback approaches are no charge, a fixed charge, a variable charge based on resource usage, or a variable charge based on volume.

Some companies use a no charge approach because IT services benefit the overall organization. This method treats the IT group for accounting purposes as a cost center that offers services without charge. In contrast, if management imposes charges on other departments, the IT department is regarded as a profit center that sells services that otherwise would have to be purchased from outside the company.

System benefits must also be classified. Many benefit categories are similar to costs: tangible or intangible, fixed or variable, and direct or indirect. Benefits can also be classified as positive benefits that result in direct dollar savings or cost-avoidance benefits that allow the firm to avoid costs that they would otherwise have incurred.

Cost-benefit analysis involves three common approaches: payback analysis, ROI analysis, and present value analysis. Spreadsheet programs can be used to help work with those methods.

Payback analysis determines the time it takes for a system to pay for itself, which is called the payback period. In payback analysis, the total development and operating costs are compared to total benefits. The payback period is the point at which accumulated benefits equal accumulated costs. A disadvantage of this method is that payback analysis analyzes only costs and benefits incurred at the beginning of a system's useful life.

Return on investment (ROI) analysis measures a system by comparing total net benefits (the return) to total costs (the investment). The result is a percentage figure that represents a rate of return that the system offers as a potential investment. Many organizations set a minimum ROI that all projects must match or exceed and use ROI to rank several projects. Although ROI provides additional information compared with payback analysis, ROI expresses only an overall average rate of return that might not be accurate for a given time period. Also, ROI does not recognize the time value of money.

Present value analysis adjusts the value of future costs and benefits to account for the time value of money. By measuring all future costs and benefits in current dollars, systems can be compared more accurately and consistently. Present value analysis uses mathematical factors that can be derived or found in published tables. Spreadsheet functions can also be used to calculate present value. Many companies use present value analysis to evaluate and rank projects.

Key Terms

chargeback method A technique that uses accounting entries to allocate the indirect costs of running the IT department. Most organizations adopt one of four chargeback methods: no charge, a fixed charge, a variable charge based on resource usage, or a variable charge based on volume.

connect time The total time that a user is connected actively to a remote server. Some Internet service providers use this as a basis for charges.

cost center An element that generates charges with no offsetting credits.

cost-avoidance benefits Expenses that would be necessary if the new system is not installed. Examples include handling the work with existing staff, and not replacing existing hardware or software.

cost-benefit analysis The process of comparing the anticipated costs of an information system to the anticipated benefits.

developmental costs Expenses incurred only once, at the time a system is developed or acquired. Examples include salaries of people involved in system development or initial user training.

direct costs Expenses associated with the development of a specific system. Examples include the salaries of project team members and the purchase of hardware that is used only for the new system.

economically useful life The period between the beginning of systems operation and the point when operational costs are rapidly increasing.

fixed charge method A method of determining the indirect costs of running an IT department in which the indirect IT costs are divided among all the other departments in the form of a fixed monthly charge.

fixed costs Expenses that are relatively constant and do not depend on a level of activity or effort. Many fixed costs recur regularly, such as salaries and hardware rental charges.

indirect costs Expenses that cannot be attributed to the development of a particular information system. The salaries of network administrators and copy machine rentals are examples of indirect costs. Also called overhead expenses.

no charge method A method of determining the indirect costs of running an IT department in which in which an organization treats information systems department indirect expenses as a necessary cost of doing business.

overhead expenses *See* indirect costs.

payback period The time it takes to recover a system's cost.

positive benefits Increases in revenues, improvements in services, or other contributions to the organization as a direct result of the new information system. Examples include improved information availability, faster customer service, and higher employee morale.

present value The amount of money that, when invested today at a specified interest rate, grows to exactly one dollar at a certain point in the future.

present value analysis A technique that allows analysts to plan for future growth goals based on present value.

present value tables Third-party tables used to help analysts perform value analysis.

profit center A department expected to break even, or show a profit.

resource allocation A method of determining the indirect costs of running an IT department in which the charging of indirect costs is based on the resources used by an information system.

server processing time The time that the server actually requires to respond to client requests for processing.

time value of money A concept that recognizes that a given sum of money, over time, historically will increase in value.

variable charge method based on resource usage A method of determining the indirect costs of running an IT department based on allocation of resources, such as connect time, server processing time, network resources required, printer use, or a combination of similar factors.

variable charge method based on volume A method of determining the indirect costs of running an IT department in which the indirect information systems department costs are allocated to other departments based on user-oriented activity, such as the number of transactions or printing volume.

variable costs Expenses that vary depending on the level of activity. For example, the costs of printer paper or telephone line charges are variable costs.

Toolkit Exercises

Review Questions

1. How do you know if a project is economically feasible? Why is TCO important?
2. Describe each cost classification and include two examples.
3. What are four chargeback methods? In your view, is one more "fair" than another?
4. Describe each benefit classification and include two examples.
5. What formula do you use to calculate the payback period?
6. What formula do you use to calculate ROI?
7. Would the formulas in questions 5 and 6 also apply to heavy equipment, such as a bulldozer? Why or why not?
8. Define the term *present value*, and provide an example.
9. What is the meaning of the phrase, *time value of money*?
10. What are the two ways of using a spreadsheet to calculate present value?

Discussion Topics

1. Suppose your supervisor asks you to inflate the benefit figures for an IT proposal in order to raise the priority of his or her favorite project. Would this be ethical? Does internal cost-benefit analysis affect company shareholders? Why or why not?
2. In this Toolkit Part, you learned how to use payback analysis, ROI, and NPV to assess IT projects. Could these tools also be used in your personal life? Give an example of how you might use each one to help you make a financial decision.
3. Is there a role for intuition in the decision-making process, or should all judgments be made strictly on the numbers? Explain your answer.
4. The time value of money can be an important factor when analyzing a project's NPV. Is the time value of money just as important in periods of low inflation as it is in periods of high inflation? Explain your answer.
5. Why is it difficult to assign a dollar figure to an intangible cost? Can it ever be done? Explain your answer, and provide an example.

Projects

1. Suppose you are studying two hardware lease proposals. Option 1 costs $4,000, but requires that the entire amount be paid in advance. Option 2 costs $5,000, but the payments can be made $1,000 now and $1,000 per year for the next four years. If you do an NPV analysis assuming a 14% discount rate, which proposal is less expensive? What happens if you use an 8% rate?
2. Assume the following facts:

   • A project will cost $45,000 to develop.

   • When the system becomes operational after a one-year development period, operational costs will be $9,000 during each year of the system's five-year useful life.

   • The system will produce benefits of $30,000 in the first year of operation, and this figure will increase by a compound 10% each year.

   What is the payback period for this project?

3. Using the same facts as in Project 2, what is the ROI for this project?
4. Using the same facts as in Project 2, what is the NPV for this project?
5. Explore the TCO calculator shown in Figure C-1 that Amazon.com provides for estimating value in migrating to the cloud using their AWS infrastructure for a hypothetical product. Comment on the usefulness of such a tool to the systems analyst.

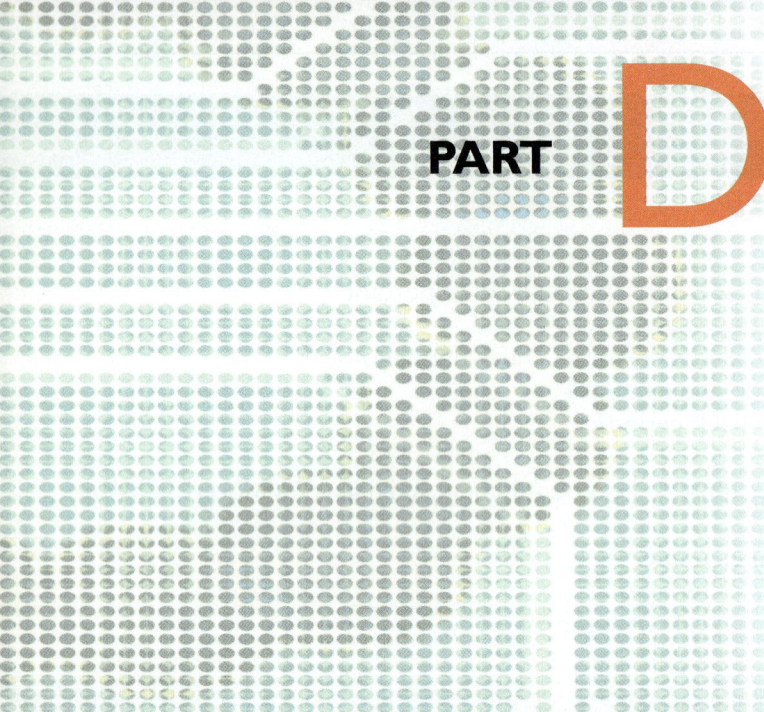

PART D

Internet Resource Tools

Part D of the Systems Analyst's Toolkit describes Internet resource tools that can be used to locate information, obtain reference material, and monitor IT trends and developments.

LEARNING OBJECTIVES

When you finish this part of the Toolkit, you should be able to:

- Describe the characteristics of the Internet and the web

- Plan an Internet search strategy, review your information requirements, use the proper search tools and techniques, evaluate the results, and consider copyright and data integrity issues

- Use search engines, subject directories, and the invisible web to locate the information you require

- Demonstrate advanced search techniques, including Boolean logic and Venn diagrams

- Describe Internet communication channels, including social networking, forums, newsletters, blogs, podcasts, videos, webinars, mailing lists, chat rooms, instant messaging, and text messaging

- Provide examples of IT community resources of value to a systems analyst

- Explain the benefits and disadvantages of online learning opportunities

TOOLKIT CONTENTS

D.1 INTRODUCTION

As a systems analyst, you rely on your knowledge, skills, and experience. Fortunately, you have access to the Internet, where an enormous storehouse of information is available to you at little or no cost. The Internet is a worldwide network that integrates many thousands of other networks, which in turn link millions of government, business, educational, and personal users around the globe. The Internet can assist you with technical problems and can help you advance your career by offering access to training, education, and communication with other IT professionals.

The Internet allows you to visit the World Wide Web, usually referred to as the web, which contains billions of text and multimedia documents called webpages. A collection of related webpages is called a website and is stored on a computer called a web server. A web browser, or browser, is a software program that allows you to access and display webpages that are delivered to you by a web server. Microsoft Edge and Internet Explorer, Mozilla Firefox, Google Chrome, and Apple Safari are popular browsers that offer powerful graphic interfaces to help you navigate the web.

This Toolkit Part begins with a step-by-step plan for Internet research, followed by a summary of search basics and a detailed discussion of search engines, subject directories, and the invisible web. Internet communications tools are covered next, including social networking, forums, newsletters, blogs, podcasts, RSS feeds, webinars, mailing lists, web-based discussion groups, chat rooms, and instant messaging. The last section presents valuable online resources available within the IT community.

D.2 PLANNING AN INTERNET RESEARCH STRATEGY

An Internet research strategy is necessary to avoid frustration and wasted time. A pilot or ship captain would not begin a journey without knowing the destination. Similarly, you can use a four-step plan to navigate efficiently and confidently toward your objectives:

1. Review your information requirements.
2. Use the proper search tools and techniques.
3. Evaluate the results.
4. Consider copyright and data integrity issues.

Over time, you will gain experience and develop your own preferences for using the Internet. You should remember that each research situation is unique, and several tools and techniques might be necessary to achieve the results you seek.

Step 1: Review Your Information Requirements

The first step to finding information online is to make sure you really understand what you are seeking. You need to think about the topic to ensure that you are casting an appropriate net. For example, a supervisor might ask you to help decide between two specific CASE products. Your initial inclination might be to find a review of various CASE applications. Upon reflection, however, you realize it would be more useful to understand CASE tools in a general sense before comparing specific products. Therefore, you decide to start with a more generalized search instead of going directly to vendor sites.

Step 2: Use the Proper Search Tools and Techniques

Once you feel that you understand the information required, it is time to pick an initial tool. At this point, you face some choices. Should you use search engines or subject directories? Should you seek commercial sites, IT publications, professional associations, forums, or other areas to explore? What about social networking?

As you gain experience, you will be able to handle a wide range of Internet tools and resources. As with most skills, the more you use them, the more expertise you acquire. In time, you probably will develop your own list of favorite tools and resources.

Step 3: Evaluate the Results

By definition, the Internet is essentially open and unregulated. On the plus side, a huge diversity of information is available. The quality of content, however, varies greatly. Unlike published journals or textbooks, almost anyone can post content on the web. This means that the searcher must review the information very carefully. Questions to ask when accessing content include the following:

SOURCE: Is the author identifiable? Does the author have expertise on the subject? You might need to trace back through website addresses or URLs to find biographical information, or do a separate search on the author's name.

ACCURACY: Does the information come from a commercial source that is offering its own solution? Is it from an association with an inherent bias? Often, it is very difficult to find completely objective information. Identifying biases and finding information from a variety of sources are ways to address this problem.

SCOPE: Is the information specific enough? If not, you should narrow and refine your search and seek additional resources until you locate the information you need. When you use a search engine, one way to do this is to perform a subsearch using the results of the initial search as a starting point.

CURRENCY: How old is the information? Is the topic static or dynamic? In the IT world, technology changes very quickly. If you locate information that appears to be out of date, you might seek more recent data to ensure that your results are valid.

LOOK AND FEEL: Is the information easy to access and navigate? If the site is designed in a logical manner and offers value-added links to worthwhile pages and resources, do not be overly concerned with style — some excellent material is created by authors and producers who focus on content, not design.

If you find the content useful, be sure to credit the source properly when you use it. You must observe legal and ethical standards when you deal with Internet material. To learn more about proper citation and to view specific examples of how to cite electronic material, you can visit the collection of student research resources at *www.aresearchguide.com*.

Step 4: Consider Copyright and Data Integrity Issues

Before you copy or download your search results, you must ensure that you legally can use the material and that the content is safe and free of threats.

The first issue involves copyright law. Many people regard the web as a public domain, but in reality, it is more like a book or a CD. In other words, you might own a CD, but you do not own the material on that CD — you only possess a license to use the content in certain ways. On the web, you should look for copyright notices and restrictions. If in doubt, you might have to contact the copyright holder to seek permission.

The second issue involves data integrity. It is important to protect your network and computer system from any unwanted viruses or malware, which is malicious software that might jeopardize your security or privacy. Unlike intellectual content, which is easy to evaluate, it is impossible for you to determine the integrity and validity of the internal file structure and format without a virus detection tool. Many thousands of viruses are identified each day. Viruses and other intrusions cost businesses many millions of dollars in lost data and additional effort. Without proper protection, you run the risk of not only corrupting your own files or hard drive but also bringing your entire company network down.

If the information is legally usable and safe, you can save it to your hard drive or network, depending on the content and purpose. The information you find may be in one of many formats, including word-processing documents, spreadsheets, and databases; Adobe PDF files; and multimedia material with file extensions such as .jpg, .mp3, .flv, and .mov.

You can download files directly to your hard drive from many websites. If this option is not offered explicitly, you can try right-clicking a link or embedded object to display a list of choices that includes downloading the selected information.

The following sections discuss search engines, subject directories, the invisible web, and other Internet tools in more detail.

D.3 SEARCH BASICS

As you journey on the Internet, you will use various navigation tools and techniques. To reach your destination, you must know how to use search engines, subject directories, and a collection of searchable databases called the invisible web.

A search engine is an application that uses keywords and phrases to locate information on the Internet. Meta-search engines are tools that can apply multiple search engines simultaneously. For most people, search engines are the workhorses of information gathering. Search engines employ a variety of approaches to gathering information, and although they are extremely valuable, users should be aware of potential problems. For example, search results can be affected if the search engine permits commercial users to achieve higher priority based on payment of fees. Also, search engines access only a portion of the Internet.

A subject directory or topic directory is a website that allows you to find information by using a hierarchy, starting with a general heading and proceeding to more specific topics. A subject directory is an excellent starting point when you want an overview of a topic before proceeding to specific websites. Typically, a subject directory is created by an editorial staff that visits, evaluates, and organizes the sites into various categories and subcategories.

The invisible web, also called the deep web or hidden web, refers to a vast collection of documents, databases, and webpages that are usually not detected by search engines, but can be accessed using other tools and techniques. The invisible web is a huge information storehouse, many times larger than the searchable web, and includes thousands of university, scientific, and government libraries.

The following sections cover search engines, subject directories, and the invisible web in more detail.

D.4 SEARCH ENGINES

A search engine often is the best starting point for gathering information. A well-planned search will narrow the range of content to a manageable level and will allow you to explore the choices or execute a subsearch within the focused results. As with any tool, it is important to understand the intended use and limitations of a search engine before applying it to a task.

Although many search engines exist, Google dominates the market, particularly in the all-important mobile space, as shown in the netmarketshare.com graph in Figure D-1. Google's appeal includes a robust package of features that users can access easily, and Google works hard to make its users feel like family members. However, when a single firm dominates a market, there is a risk that the firm's name can become a generic verb, such as "*You can Google it.*"

Mobile/Tablet Search Engine Market Share

September, 2015

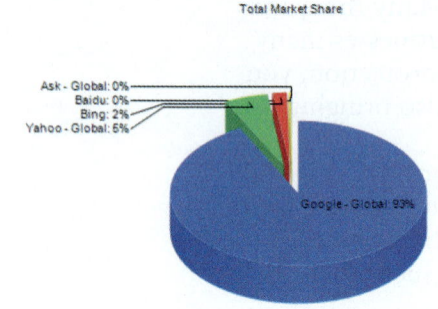

Search Engine	Total Market Share
Google - Global	92.22%
Yahoo - Global	5.37%
Bing	1.76%
Baidu	0.23%
Ask - Global	0.07%
AOL - Global	0.02%

FIGURE D-1 The chart shows the dominant market share enjoyed by Google on mobile devices.
Source: Netmarketshare

D.4.1 Search Engine Concepts

Search engines use a specialized computer program called a **spider** or **crawler** that travels from site to site **indexing**, or cataloging, the contents of the pages based on **keywords**. The results are compiled into a database, so what you are searching is not the web itself but the contents of the search engine's database.

No single search engine can catalog the shifting contents of the web, and even the most powerful engines do not cover all web content. If a particular site is not widely linked, or its author does not submit it to major search engines, then the material is invisible to them. Also, any website that requires a visitor to type in data, such as a name, cannot be accessed by search engines.

Although search engine indexes are incomplete and often dated, they are capable of delivering an overwhelming number of results, or **hits**. The *real* issue is quality versus quantity. When comparing search engines, it is important to know the company's policy toward allowing commercial sites to boost their ranking in a **pay for performance** arrangement. Links that are subsidized by companies are called **sponsored links**.

Not all search engines work the same way. By understanding the underlying algorithms, or specific rules, that drive these information engines, it is possible to better target your search. For example, some sites, like Google, rank their pages by analyzing the number of other sites that link to that page. Other search engines organize results differently.

INDEXED SEARCH ENGINES: Google and Bing are **indexed search engines** that organize and rank the results of a search. Although they have much in common, each tool has its own search algorithms, features, and user interface.

META-SEARCH ENGINES: A meta-search engine, such as Dogpile shown in Figure D-2, collects search results from various search engines. You only have to enter your search term once, and the system will sort the results (eliminating duplicates) for you.

D.4.2 Search Techniques

Consider the following suggestions when you begin a search:

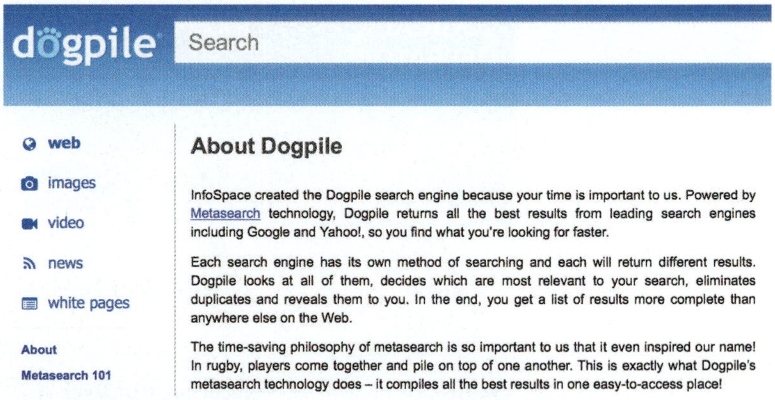

- Refine your topic. Unless you limit the scope of your search, the number of results might overwhelm you. If you are looking for general information on a broad topic, consider a subject directory site.

- Translate your question into an effective search query. Searches are executed on keywords. You will improve your success if you pick the proper keywords. Try to find unique words or phrases and avoid those with multiple uses. For example, a search for the term *hard drive* might produce information about a computer hardware device or a difficult auto trip. Also consider using advanced search techniques, which are described in the following section.

- Review the search results and evaluate the quality of the results. If the search needs refinement or additional material, you can either use the site's advanced search techniques or select a different Internet resource altogether.

- It is important to organize the results of your search so you can recognize and revisit important sites. Some search engines offer a personalized search history, which you can review and edit for this purpose. Many people find that the easiest solution is to create favorites or bookmarks in their browser for sites visited in important searches, using a set of folders and subfolders. If you do this, you can wait until you start the search, or you can create your filing system ahead of time.

To be effective, you should understand the mechanics of the search engine, use proper spelling, find unique phrases, and experiment with a variety of approaches. If you are consistently returning too many results, try using topic-specific terms and advanced search techniques. Conversely, if too few results are returned, eliminate the least important terms or concepts, broaden your subject, or use more general vocabulary when you select terms.

FIGURE D-2 Dogpile is an example of a meta-search engine.
Source: InfoSpace, LLC

D.4.3 Advanced Search Techniques

Many search engines offer powerful advanced search features that allow you to refine and control the type of information returned from searches. These features can include the option to search within returned results and the ability to search within specific areas, such as forums. Perhaps the most powerful advanced feature is the option to use Boolean logic.

Boolean logic is a system named after British mathematician George Boole and refers to the relationships among search terms. You can use various combinations of the logical operators OR, AND, and NOT to improve your search success greatly. Figure D-3 illustrates the use of the operators with search terms. The graphics shown in the figure are called Venn diagrams. A Venn diagram uses circular symbols to illustrate Boolean logic. Venn diagrams are named after John Venn, a nineteenth-century scholar who devised a scheme for visualizing logical relationships. In the sample diagrams, the shaded area indicates the results of the search.

LOGICAL OPERATORS	EXAMPLE	VENN DIAGRAM (SHADED AREA INDICATES RETURNED RESULTS)
A **or** B	Baseball **or** Football	Baseball 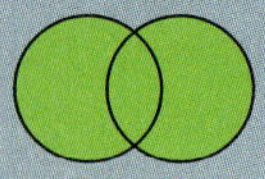 / Football
A **and** B	Baseball **and** Football	Baseball  / Football
A **not** B	Internet **not** Web	Internet 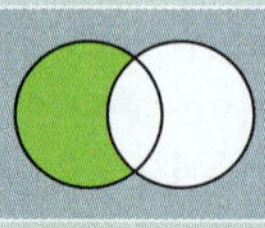 / Web
A **or** B **or** C	Colorado **or** Mining **or** Gold	Colorado  / Mining / Gold
A **and** B **and** C	Colorado **and** Mining **and** Gold	Colorado 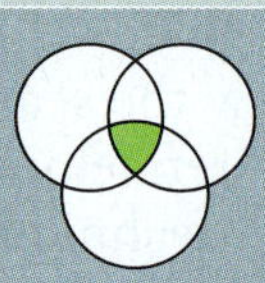 / Mining / Gold
A **and** B **not** C	Colorado **and** Mining **not** Gold	Colorado 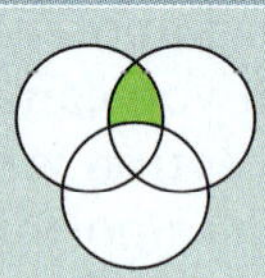 / Mining / Gold

FIGURE D-3 Examples of logical operators OR, AND, and NOT. The shaded areas represent the returned results. OR is the most inclusive term, returning results if any of the terms appear. AND requires all keywords to appear. NOT excludes results even if they are found in the same document.

To learn more about how logical operators work, consider the following diagrams in Figure D-3:

OR: The first diagram at the top of Figure D-3 shows that the OR term will retrieve all results containing either term. Notice that the shaded area includes both circles. The OR operator can be used when you need a wide search net.

AND: The second diagram in Figure D-3 shows that the AND term will retrieve only those results in which all terms linked by the AND operator are present. Notice that the shaded area includes only the overlapping portion of the two circles. The more terms or concepts combined in an AND search, the fewer pages will be returned. The AND operator often is used to narrow a set of search results.

NOT: The third diagram in Figure D-3 shows how the NOT operator can be used to exclude certain records. In this diagram, consider the closely related terms, *Internet* and *web*. It is likely that these terms both appear in many webpages. The NOT operator will strip out the results containing the unwanted term. For example, the search string "Internet NOT web" will return only those pages with the term *Internet*. You should use the NOT operator carefully, because the term you want to exclude may be intertwined with the term you seek in many documents that would be useful to you.

The last three diagrams in Figure D-3 illustrate other combinations of logical operators where three search terms are involved.

USING PHRASES: Suppose you want to find sites that sell board games that require players to use strategy, such as Monopoly®. In your search, you could specify both terms, *strategy* AND *game*, but your results probably would include many documents that describe game strategies used in various sports, which is not what you are seeking. A better approach might be to search using the phrase "strategy game" enclosed in quotes. A phrase is more specific than an AND operator because it specifies an exact placement of terms. In this example, the phrase "strategy game" will not retrieve any documents unless they contain that exact phrase.

The implementation of Boolean logic varies by search engine. Some engines require the use of full Boolean searching using the complete operators (OR, AND, NOT) in the search window. Others use implied Boolean logic with keyword searching. In implied Boolean logic, symbols are used to represent Boolean operators, such as a plus sign (+) for AND, and a minus sign (-) for NOT. If two search terms are entered in the search window with a space between them, some search engines may assume an OR; others assume an AND. You need to consult the site's Help files to understand the underlying rules.

USING FILL-IN FORMS: Most search engines provide an advanced search feature that offers a fill-in form similar to the Google example shown in Figure D-4. Many users find it easier to fill in a form than to work with Boolean operators. The examples in Figure D-4 include sample search terms, and on its site, Google offers many more advanced search samples and tips. Notice that the Google website also offers advanced search tips.

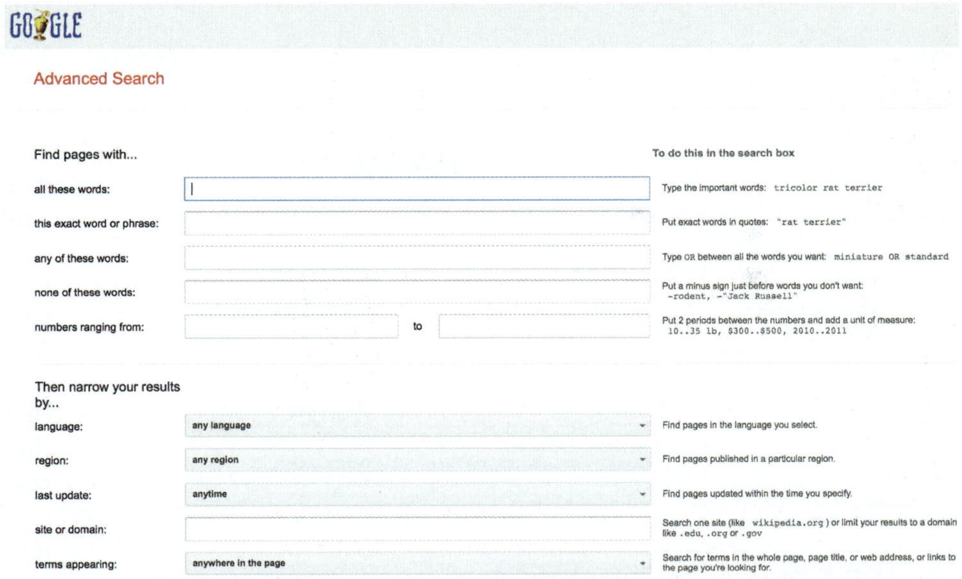

FIGURE D-4 Google offers advanced search capabilities with many user-selectable criteria.
Source: Google Inc.

D.4.4 Search Checklist

Many people find it helpful to prepare for an Internet search by using a checklist similar to the following:

- Does the topic have any unique words, phrases, or acronyms? If so, use these terms in the search.

- Do any of the search terms have other spellings or names? If so, include these with an OR operator in the search.

- Are certain additional words or phrases likely to appear in any web document? If so, consider adding an AND operator to narrow the search.

- Is there any unrelated material that my search terms might pick up? If so, consider using the NOT operator to exclude these documents.

- Are any organizations, publications, or institutions likely to have an interest in my topic? If so, try to locate their websites and then conduct a further search using the site indexes and databases available on the site.

- Is the search returning results too numerous to examine? If so, keep adding additional terms to narrow the search and reduce the number of hits until a reasonable number is achieved.

D.5 SUBJECT DIRECTORIES

A subject directory collects and organizes websites in a top-down format, based on subjects and topics. An analogy might be a corporate organization chart, where you could go to the top person for an overview, then visit with lower-level employees to obtain specific information about their areas.

A subject directory is an excellent tool when you want general information about a topic before plunging into an array of specific websites. Yahoo! offers a popular subject directory that serves as a **portal**, or entrance to other Internet resources. Other academic and professional directories target the specific needs of researchers and users who concentrate on particular subjects.

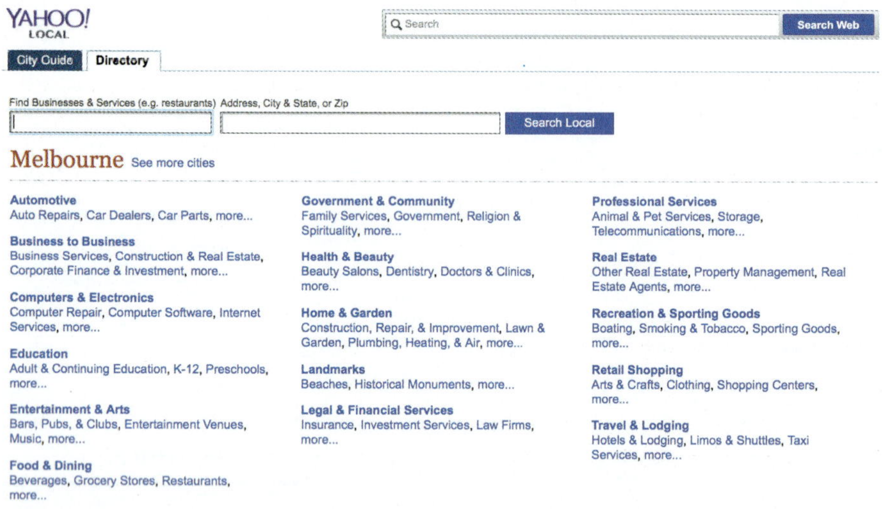

Many subject directories have changed to provide localized search capabilities. For example, Yahoo!'s subject directory *http://dir.yahoo.com* shown in Figure D-5 displays a searchable subject directory of resources available in the Melbourne, Florida area.

The main advantage of a subject directory is that it provides an overview when you are not sure of the size and scope of your topic. Later, when you have a better understanding of your subject, you can use a search engine to seek additional information and examples.

FIGURE D-5 Yahoo! provides a searchable subject directory of resources available in your local area. In this case, in and around Melbourne, Florida.

Source: Yahoo Inc.

Subject directories also have shortcomings. Many subject directories use human expertise to formulate the subject organization and determine the placement of links. This process involves subjective decisions that might affect the quality of search results. Some subject directories are updated continually; others might not be current. Also, unlike a search engine, a subject directory forces you to work your way through a series of levels, rather than using specific words and phrases to locate directly the material you seek.

D.6 THE INVISIBLE WEB

Everyone is familiar with what is called the **visible web**, which refers to websites that are indexed by the major search engines and are publicly accessible. As discussed earlier, much more information is available on the Internet that is not indexed. This valuable information source includes numerous text, graphics, and data files stored in collections that are unreachable by search engines.

The invisible web includes searchable databases that contain an enormous amount of information in university and government libraries, as well as thousands of specialized databases that are maintained by institutions and organizations around the world. The Library of Congress is one such example, as shown in Figure D-6. Much of the invisible web is open to the public, but some databases are password protected. Many sites allow guest access, but only members of a specific group can access some areas.

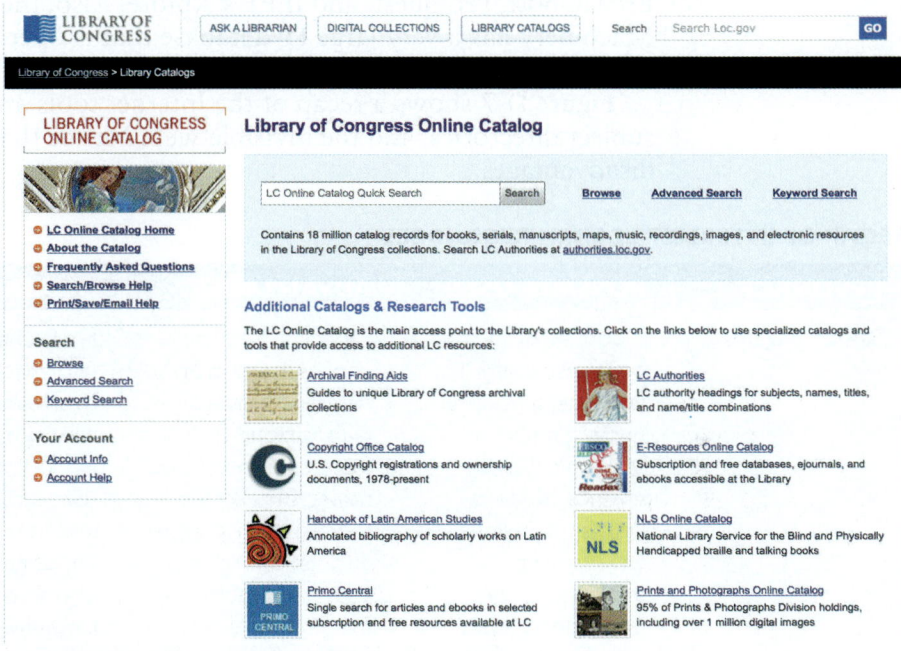

FIGURE D-6 The Library of Congress online catalog lets you search its vast collection of resources.
Source: Library of Congress

D.6.1 Invisible Web Examples

A few examples of information on the invisible web include the following:

- *Specialized topic databases:* subject-specific collections of information, such as corporate financial filings and reports, genealogy records, or Ellis Island immigration data

- *Hardware and software vendors:* searchable technical support databases for large sites, such as Microsoft's or Oracle's knowledge bases

- *Publications:* databases of published and archived articles

- *Libraries:* searchable catalogs for thousands of libraries, including the Library of Congress and numerous university and institutional libraries

- *Government databases:* census data, statutes, patents, copyrights, and trademarks

- *Auction sites:* searchable listings of items, bidders, and sellers

- *Locators:* telephone numbers, addresses, and email addresses

- *Career opportunities:* job listings and résumé postings

D.6.2 Navigation Tools for the Invisible Web

You can access the invisible web in several ways. One approach is to use a search engine to locate a portal, or entrance, to a searchable database by including the word *database* as a required search term. For example, if you are searching for information about printer drivers, you could specify "printer drivers AND database". The additional term will narrow the search results and increase the likelihood of finding searchable collections of printer drivers.

Another way to navigate the invisible web is to use a **proprietary database**; your school or local library probably subscribes to several. Popular examples include EBSCOhost, ProQuest, and IEEE's Xplore. Also, the Association for Computing Machinery has a very large IT database that is open to its members, including students who can join for a modest fee.

Figure D-7 shows a recap of the Internet tools and resources: search engines, subject directories, and the invisible web. Notice that each has advantages and disadvantages.

RECAP OF INTERNET SEARCH RESOURCES

RESOURCE	POSSIBLE USES	ADVANTAGES	DISADVANTAGES	NOTES
Search Engines	Good initial starting point, especially if you have an overall understanding of the topic. Search engines can lead you to important government, professional, or commercial sites.	Flexibility. You can choose from many different engines with various features. Some allow newsgroup access as well. Meta-search engines can return and rank results from multiple sources. Advanced search techniques can be used.	Frequently produces information overload. Can return many irrelevant or out-of-date links. Without a refined search, it is impossible to examine results carefully. Some sites allow companies to improve their hits by "pay for performance."	You can improve search effectiveness significantly by using advanced search techniques based on logical operators.
Subject Directories	Good way to get a broad overview of a topic before accessing specific sites.	With a subject directory, you can maintain broader focus and perspective, and work from the general to the specific without getting lost in a maze of websites.	Material is organized by human intervention; quality, currency, and accuracy might vary.	Once you work your way through the various levels, you might be able to bookmark the resource for more direct future access.
Invisible Web	Information from nonindexed databases and searchable directories such as company financial reports, library holdings, industry reports, and government information.	Very diverse resource. Many more pages on the web are non-indexed rather than indexed.	Can be difficult to access unless you know where to look. Navigating a searchable database can be more difficult than using a traditional search engine, because no common interface exists.	Portal sites are available to help you navigate the invisible Web. You can use a general search engine to locate searchable databases by searching a subject term and the word *database*.

FIGURE D-7 A recap of the three main Internet search resources: search engines, subject directories, and the invisible web. Notice that each option has advantages and disadvantages.

D.7 INTERNET COMMUNICATION CHANNELS

Suppose that you are asked to analyze your organization's malware protection requirements. As part of your research, you would want to learn about relevant news, developments, and the latest malware threats. You might also want to suggest several specific products. Assume that you performed your research using a search engine. Now you want to check your conclusions by getting feedback from other IT professionals. There are many Internet resources available to you, available through a variety of communication channels. You can consider using social networking, forums, newsletters, blogs, podcasts, webinars, mailing lists, chat rooms, and instant messaging. Several of these channels, including podcasts, webinars, and web-based discussion groups, were discussed in Chapter 11.

D.7.1 Social Networking

As Figure D-8 illustrates, **social networking** allows you to connect to an extended set of family, friends, and professional acquaintances. The "social" aspect refers to sharing of experiences and other personal items or activities that you find important. The "networking" aspect lets you build social connections in the traditional sense, with the exception that you communicate with your contacts online.

Social networking sites such as Facebook, Twitter, and LinkedIn have gained enormous popularity in recent years. Facebook is well suited to personal connections while LinkedIn is used primarily for professional networks. Twitter limits messages ("tweets") to 140 characters, which helps keep communication brief and to the point.

As a systems analyst, social networks are an excellent way to stay informed and to extend your sphere of influence. Twitter "tweets" and Facebook updates have largely replaced RSS (Really Simple Syndication) feeds for many in IT by providing constant updates to events of interest. However, the updates can also become a distraction if they are not used judiciously in the workplace.

D.7.2 Forums

Most people are familiar with bulletin boards they see at school, at work, and in their communities. Using thumbtacks or tape, people post information and read what others have posted. A forum, or newsgroup, is the electronic equivalent of the everyday bulletin board. Forums offer online discussions that address every conceivable subject and interest area. A forum can put you in touch with the knowledge, experience, and opinions of a large online community.

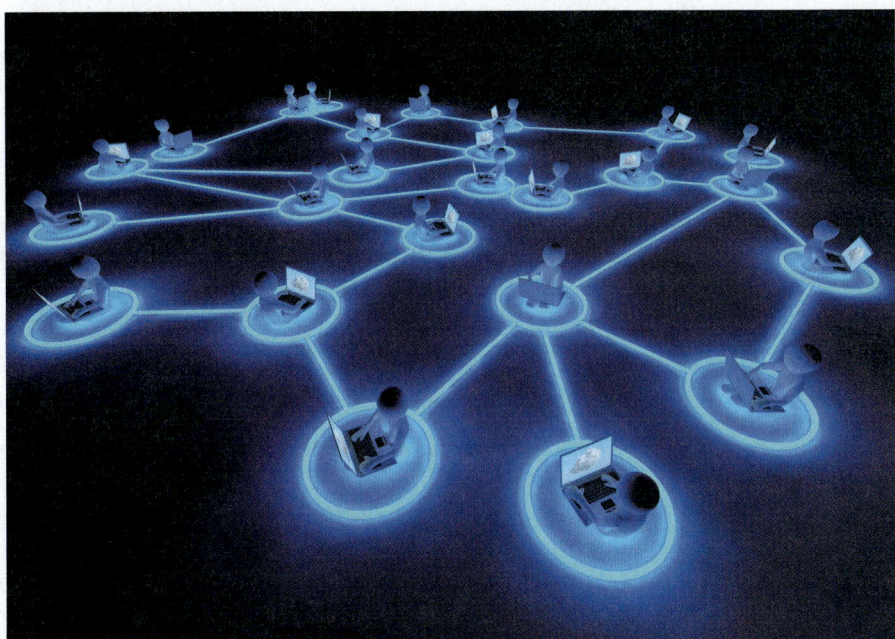

FIGURE D-8 Social networks let IT professionals connect with colleagues from around the world to share expertise and experience.

De Mango/Shutterstock.com

Yahoo! and Google allow users to join thousands of groups, and to create new ones if they wish. The Google site in Figure D-9 shows Google Groups, which offers a user-friendly interface and many social media features. Because of its dominant role in the search engine market, Google users have another benefit: in addition to recent content, they can search literally millions of postings that go back many years.

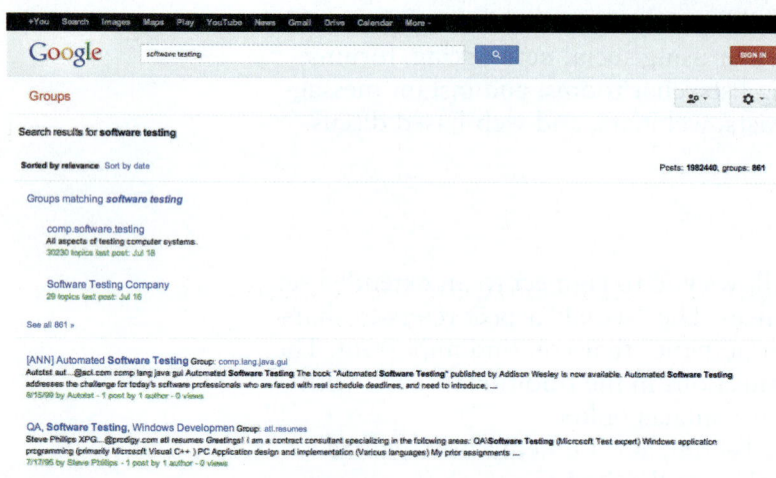

FIGURE D-9 Google Groups allows you to participate in numerous discussion groups on every imaginable topic, and to create new groups.
Source: Google Inc.

To understand how forums work, consider the following example. In your research on malware protection, which was mentioned in the previous section, assume that you have narrowed the product choices down to two. You are having trouble, however, differentiating between them and would like feedback from current users. You might want to visit individual product sites for user testimonials, but you would be unlikely to find a negative opinion on a vendor's site. You could chose to send a query to people you know using your social networks, but you want to survey a variety of users that goes beyond your connections.

At this point, you might decide to tap into an appropriate newsgroup and see if there have been any postings that are relevant to you. Some forums are moderated, in which articles are sent to a person who approves them before they are posted for the group. A few forums still allow anonymous posts, but most now require valid login credentials, either with an account specific to the forum, or through a trusted third party such as Facebook. A valid login means the forum owners can trace the posts back to the originator, which tends to reduce that amount of "flaming" (poor online behavior involving denigrating other users), and maintain a more polite and professional online atmosphere.

Before you post, you should read the **FAQs (Frequently Asked Questions)** associated with each newsgroup. FAQs are a common method of providing guidance on questions that users are likely to ask. In many cases, FAQs describe the particular netiquette, or web guidelines for protocol and courtesy, that exist on a particular newsgroup or site. You can learn more about netiquette in Part A of the Systems Analyst's Toolkit.

D.7.3 Newsletters, Blogs, Podcasts, and Videos

Newsletters are a convenient way to keep current on topics of interest. Many online magazines and other groups offer free email newsletters to subscribers interested in specific topics. For example, as shown in Figure D-10, CNET readers can access a wide range of IT-related newsletters, many of which are delivered as short videos.

A *blog* is a web-based log, or journal. Many computer industry experts update their blogs daily, which you valuable information for a systems analyst. You might also consider writing your own blog — it's a great way to help your career and maybe even help other people in your field.

A **podcast** is an audio blog. Podcasts are like radio shows that you can listen to at any time and anywhere. You can subscribe to them though services such as Apple's iTunes, which will download the latest episodes of the podcast to your computer, your smartphone, or your tablet. You can also listen to the podcasts as they stream over the Internet, without downloading the whole show. Podcasts are great ways to make productive use of down time, such as during a commute to work or while exercising. Many tools are now available to help you record and upload your own podcasts.

Google's YouTube is one of the most popular online video services. You can subscribe to YouTube channels that offer material ranging from entertaining to instructive. You can also create your own YouTube videos and upload them for others to view. Videos are a great way to communicate visual ideas, how-to lessons, and graphical concepts to other IT professionals.

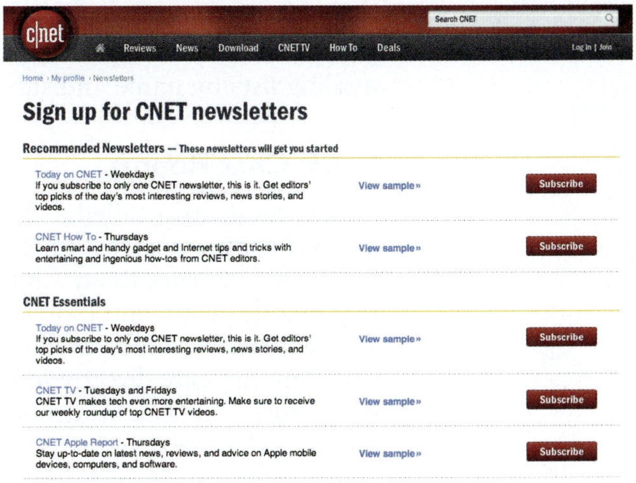

FIGURE D-10 CNET offers numerous free newsletters, many of which are delivered in video format.

Source: CBS Interactive Inc.

D.7.4 RSS Feeds

The term **RSS** stands for **Really Simple Syndication**. RSS is an older format for publishing frequently updated content to users who subscribe to an RSS download, also called a feed, an **RSS feed**, or a **web feed**. Web publishers such as Yahoo!, Google, CNN, MSNBC, and many other newspapers, magazines, vendors, and blogs use RSS feeds to distribute news and updates to subscribers, who can read the content with software called an **RSS reader**, a **feed reader**, or an **aggregator**.

D.7.5 Mailing Lists

A **mailing list** is similar to a newsgroup in that it provides a forum for people who want to exchange information about specific topics. Like a newsgroup, users can post messages and view postings made by others. However, instead of a bulletin board approach, a mailing list uses email to communicate with users. A computer called a **list server (listserv)** directs email to people who subscribe to, or join, the mailing list.

When a person subscribes to a list, he or she can receive email messages as they are posted. Subscribers can also receive a collection of messages called a **digest**, which contains a summary of the postings for a specific time interval (e.g., daily). Many mailing lists are associated with websites where users can search message archives.

A systems analyst would be interested in mailing lists that focus on information technology. To locate IT-related mailing lists, you can visit the websites of professional organizations,

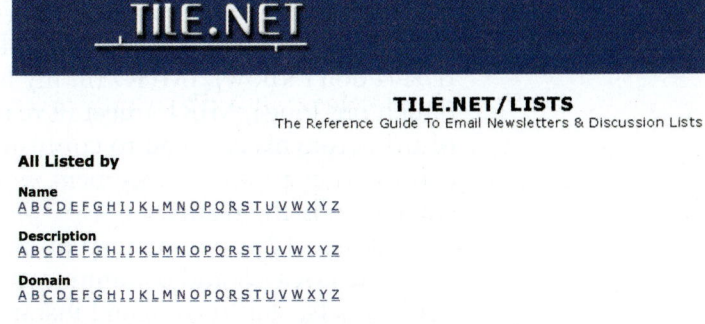

FIGURE D-11 Tile.net is an example of a website that organizes mailing lists by name and subject.

Source: Tile.net

and you can try adding the phrase "mailing list" or "listserv" to your search topic. Also, as shown in Figure D-11, you can visit websites such as tile.net that organize mailing lists by name and subject.

D.7.6 Chat Rooms

A chat room, also called a channel, is an online meeting place where users can interact and converse in real time. The chat room concept originated with IRC, which stands for Internet Relay Chat. IRC is a multichannel system supported by servers that enable group and individual conversations to occur on a worldwide basis.

Chat rooms can be used in conjunction with webinars. Instructors and students can communicate directly in chat rooms, with can help clarify question presented in the lecture material. Students can also use chat rooms to discuss common matters amongst themselves.

D.7.7 Instant Messaging and Text Messaging

Instant messaging (IM) allows online users to exchange messages immediately, even while they are working in another program or application. Users are alerted that other members of their group are available online, and users can send and receive messages or enter into a chat with other users.

Although instant messaging began as a popular feature in home-oriented services, such as AOL and Yahoo!, it has become an important business communications tool, and many firms such as IBM encourage the use of IM tools as a means of communication between employees who may be working in geographically different locations and time zones.

Corporate use of IM, however, raises serious security and privacy concerns because it is relatively uncontrolled. Also, certain industries such as banking and healthcare must observe legal regulations that govern all their communications, including IM, which must be logged and documented. Instant messages can be subject to freedom of information access requests just as emails and documents are.

Unauthorized instant messaging and exchange of files can compromise corporate security. Applications such as Skype and other computer-based voice and video channels add a burden to network bandwidth and efficiency. To combat these threats, firms often monitor IM communication channels to limit risk to the company.

Many people use text messaging (also known as texting) to send brief written messages from one mobile phone or wireless device to another. Users can also send text messages from a computer to a handheld device. The popularity of IM and texting has given rise to hundreds of abbreviations that reduce message size and speed up the communication process. Some well-known examples include HTH (hope that helps), IDK (I don't know), IMHO (in my humble opinion), JSYK (just so you know), LOL (laugh out loud), MIRL (meet in real life), and TYIA (thank you in advance). Overuse of IM acronyms can lead to confusing communications, just as overuse of uncommon acronyms in a written document would require a glossary to make the text understandable by the reader.

Figure D-12 shows a recap of online IT channels that can assist a systems analyst in online research and communication: social networking sites, forums, newsletters, mailing lists, chat rooms, and instant messaging. Notice that each resource has advantages and disadvantages.

RECAP OF INTERNET COMMUNICATION CHANNELS

RESOURCE	POSSIBLE USES	ADVANTAGES	DISADVANTAGES	NOTES
Social Networking Sites	Communicating with others who share similar interests.	Opens up new resources that can help you personally and professionally.	Your network can become too large and impersonal. Too much activity can be distracting.	Extremely convenient, popular, and no subscription fees.
Forums	Answers to technical questions, advice, and support.	Can find information on every conceivable subject — good place to exchange views with other analysts.	Cumbersome to search through message threads. Need to assess quality of information carefully.	Some major search engines allow newsgroup access.
Newsletters, Blogs, and Podcasts	Good way to follow trends and developments regarding specific IT topics.	Most newsletters, blogs, and podcasts are free to users who can subscribe to specific topics.	Not interactive, and the amount of information can be overwhelming. Difficult to filter irrelevant items.	Some newsletters, blogs, and podcasts are published daily; others weekly or monthly.
RSS Feeds	Provide news and updates for readers of online newspapers, magazines, and blogs.	Convenient way to keep posted on virtually any topic of interest.	Unless topics are specific, the volume of information might be difficult to sift through.	Rapid growth is expected to continue as more users discover this valuable resource.
Webinars	Internet-based training that can provide an interactive experience.	Users can plan, schedule, and pre-register for online sessions.	Only available when scheduled — otherwise not interactive.	Very popular technique because of convenience and cost-effectiveness.
Mailing Lists	Members can exchange information with others about specific topic of interest.	Messages arrive by email, rather than in the form of bulletin board postings.	Amount of material might be difficult to read and analyze.	Some mailing lists, or listservs, allow members to search archived messages.
Web Discussion Groups	Members form a web-based community regarding topics of common interest.	Combine many convenient features of forums and mailing lists.	Although free, these groups usually must be accessed through a Web portal.	Web discussion groups offer a mix of features and convenience.
Chat Rooms	Online meeting places where users can interact and converse.	Many IT chat rooms attract professionals who are willing to help each other solve problems.	Discussions take place in real time, which might not be convenient. Dialog might be unfocused and irrelevant to your needs.	Many large vendors, such as Microsoft, offer technical chat rooms.
Instant Messaging and Text Messaging	Users can exchange messages immediately, either online or by cell phone.	Highly efficient means of real-time communication on topics of interest. Good way to collaborate on team projects.	Can be distracting to a busy user, and sheer volume of nonessential messages can be a problem.	IM and text messaging have moved beyond the personal desktop and are acceptable business communication tools.

FIGURE D-12 A recap of Internet communication channels that can assist a systems analyst in online research and communication. Notice that each option has advantages and disadvantages.

D.8 INFORMATION TECHNOLOGY COMMUNITY RESOURCES

If you were asked to check a stock price or research the weather in a distant city for a business trip, you probably would not use a search engine. Instead, you would visit a favorite site you use regularly to access specific information. Similarly, when you require IT information, you can access a huge assortment of sites and resources that can be called the information technology (IT) community. This vast collection includes many sites that IT professionals can use to research specific questions or obtain background information. As a systems analyst, you are a member of this community. Like most communities, it offers you resources and support, including answers to technical questions, updates on new products and services, and information about training opportunities. The IT community includes numerous publications and online magazines, searchable databases, web-based discussion groups, and mailing lists.

Four important components of the IT community are corporate resources, government resources, professional resources, and online learning resources, which are described in the following sections.

D.8.1 Corporate Resources

Corporate resources can provide general IT knowledge and background, as well as help solve specific business challenges. It is very important to evaluate corporate content carefully, because companies develop some websites with an interest in selling you a specific solution or product.

If you are looking for help on a software application, it is a good idea to start by reviewing the software documentation. In many cases, technical support is included free of charge for a specific period of time. If you are working with an application with expired technical support, the software provider's website will describe support options that are available to you, including various fees and charges. Common problems often are addressed in the FAQ section.

An important corporate resource to systems analysts is their own internal company website or intranet. An intranet must be easy to access and provide access to valuable information. Companies increasingly are using intranets as a means of sharing information and working toward common solutions. Intranets can contain company policies and procedures, lessons-learned files, and financial information. They also enable employees to access and update their personal benefit information. In many organizations, the intranet is reducing the volume of paper memos and reports by serving as an enterprise-wide library and clearinghouse.

D.8.2 Government Resources

The IT needs of the federal government are enormous. Not surprisingly, a number of excellent federal IT resources are available on the Internet. Many sites offer comprehensive, nonbiased information and valuable advice for IT professionals. For example, recent U.S. General Accounting Office (GAO) reports on the IT industry have covered everything from an analysis of the information security practices to a framework for assessing IT investments. Additionally, government sites can provide information on federal, state, and local business policies and regulations. The General Services Administration (GSA) site depicted in Figure D-13 is a good source for federal policies and regulations, especially for firms that do business with the government.

D.8.3 Personal and Professional Resources

Most individuals have friends, acquaintances, and other people who they know or would like to meet. Whether the communication channel involves email, chats, forums, or social networking, the goal is to expand contacts and opportunities. Some observers have compared social networks to small virtual communities or neighborhoods, where people can meet and share information. Their objectives might be personal, or might relate to technical matters, career topics, or professional growth.

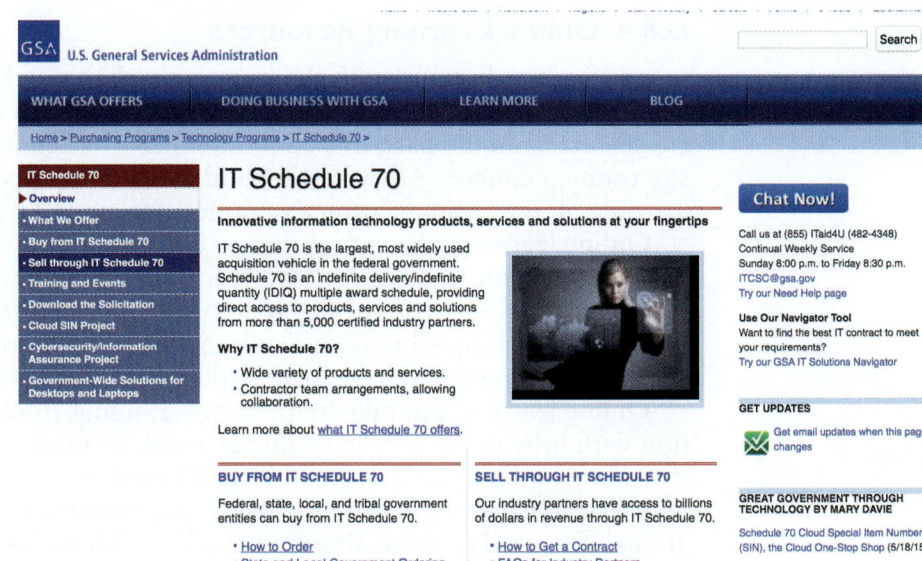

FIGURE D-13 The GSA site contains information about federal IT policies, news, and related links. The screen shows a sample from the IT Regulations, Guidelines, and Laws section.
Source: U.S. General Services Administration

In addition to social networking, a systems analyst can consider membership in one or more IT-related associations. Many organizations focus on a specific topic such as project management, software engineering, or information security. Membership in some associations is free or relatively inexpensive, and employers often subsidize professional memberships that are directly related to a person's job duties. The links provided by these sites often are quite useful. Professional organizations, such as the **Information Technology Association of America (ITAA)** or the **Association for Computing Machinery (ACM)**, which is shown in Figure D-14, also sponsor seminars and training. Many associations offer electronic newsletters that relate to your area of interest and are delivered to you by email on a periodic basis.

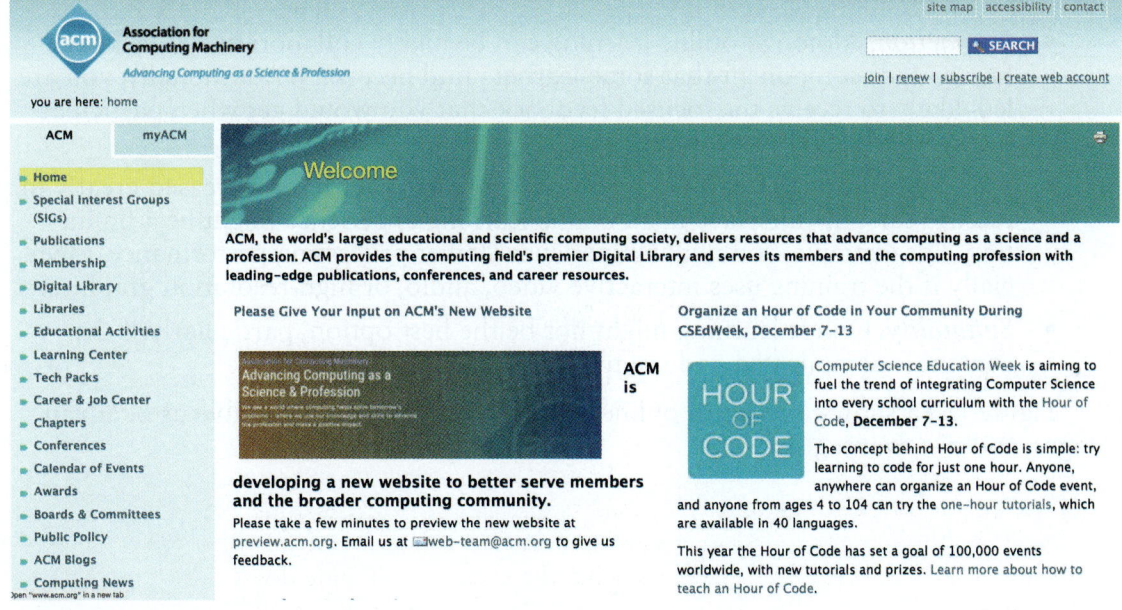

FIGURE D-14 The ACM website is one of many resources that a systems analyst can use to keep up with current issues, trends, and opportunities.
Source: ACM, Inc.

D.8.4 Online Learning Resources

It is difficult to keep up with the constantly changing IT landscape. Targeted professional development is a way for IT workers to remain focused and current in their chosen areas. In the past, this goal often meant attending lengthy and expensive off-site training courses. Advances in bandwidth and processing power have made online learning an increasingly attractive option for many IT professionals.

Online learning, also referred to as e-learning, is a term that refers to the delivery of educational or training content over the public Internet or an intranet. You can locate learning opportunities by searching the web or through various professional associations. Many schools and colleges have seen a tremendous increase in demand for online learning and have increased their course offerings accordingly.

Online learning can take many forms, ranging from individual self-paced instruction with little or no instructor involvement, to interactive, instructor-led groups with streaming audio and video capability. When choosing an online learning method, your learning goals and the quality of the content are the most important considerations. You need to think about your personal learning preferences. For example, you might learn better in a collaborative environment rather than working alone. If that is the case, consider options that include an interactive peer community. The following are some advantages and disadvantages that apply to the use of online resources:

BENEFITS OF ONLINE LEARNING: Benefits of online learning include the following:

- *Convenient.* You can participate in training when and where you want.
- *Economical.* Online learning options generally are less expensive than traditional face-to-face learning.
- *Customizable.* Generally, you can tailor the learning experience to your interests and needs.

DISADVANTAGES OF ONLINE LEARNING: Disadvantages of online learning include the following:

- *Interaction.* Although online learning can be highly collaborative, it lacks the face-to-face component that some learners find necessary. Additionally, you are less likely to receive the focused feedback that you would get when participating in traditional classroom training.
- *Interface.* Although bandwidth and computing power have increased greatly in recent years, the interface in an online learning experience might be a limitation. For example, you might experience slower processing performance, especially if the training uses interactive video, audio, or high-resolution graphics.
- *Suitability.* Online learning might not be the best option, particularly if the content is complicated and unfamiliar to you.

Figure D-15 shows a recap of online IT resources, including possible uses, advantages, and disadvantages.

RECAP OF ONLINE IT RESOURCES

RESOURCE	POSSIBLE USES	ADVANTAGES	DISADVANTAGES	NOTES
Corporate Resources	Specific technical hardware or software help, training opportunities.	First stop for troubleshooting proprietary software or hardware.	Very often an agenda is associated with the site — for example, advocating a particular product or service.	Vendor sites contain valuable specific product or solution information (check the site's FAQs). Many offer newsletters for interested visitors.
Government Resources	Information on IT regulations.	Wide variety of general topics, from congressional studies to industry-relevant government regulations.	Not all information can be accessed via the Web — sometimes sites refer to a document number for ordering. Information tends to be general and not always relevant.	Suggested sites: Library of Congress, General Accounting Office, Government Computer News.
Personal and Professional Resources	A combination of social networking, access to professional sites, and membership in IT organizations can expand personal and professional resources related to IT ethics, technical issues, and career opportunities.	Social networking is fun because it involves person-to-person contact. IT industry-related sites often provide valuable links and information on training opportunities.	Social networking is not a precise tool for specific issues. Conversely, many IT sites are too specialized to be of general interest.	Some IT sites can serve as portals to a collection of online resources.
Online Learning Resources	An IT professional needs to stay current in a constantly changing technology environment. Online learning can provide job-specific skills and support for career advancement.	Convenient, economical, and customizable. You can participate in training when and where you want, and online learning options are generally less expensive than traditional face-to-face learning.	Online learning lacks the face-to-face component that some learners find necessary. Learners are less likely to receive focused feedback. Also, the interface in an online learning experience might be a limitation. Online learning might not be the best option if the content is complicated and unfamiliar.	When considering online learning, you must know your personal learning style. You should examine the entire range of options, from individual self-paced instruction with little or no instructor involvement, to inter-active, instructor-led classes.

FIGURE D-15 A recap of online resources that a systems analyst can use to keep up with current issues and trends in IT. Notice that each resource has advantages and disadvantages.

D.9 TOOLKIT SUMMARY

The Internet is a worldwide network that integrates many thousands of other networks, which in turn link millions of government, business, educational, and personal users around the globe. The Internet can assist you in your daily work by helping you solve technical problems and in the ongoing development of your career by providing access to training and professional education.

The Internet allows access to the World Wide Web, usually called the web, which refers to the global collection of electronic documents stored on the Internet. These documents are referred to as webpages, which are organized and stored on individual websites.

An Internet research strategy should use a four-step approach: review your information requirements, use the proper search tools and techniques, evaluate the results, and consider copyright and data integrity issues. Many people find it helpful to prepare for an Internet search by using a checklist to identify key terms, phrases, and characteristics of the topic.

The primary research tools include search engines, subject directories, and a collection of searchable database resources called the invisible web. A search engine uses keywords and phrases to locate information on the Internet and list the results of the search. Users should be aware that results can be affected if the search engine permits commercial users to achieve higher priority based on payment of fees. Also, search engines access only a portion of the Internet. Meta-search engines are tools that can apply multiple search engines simultaneously.

A subject directory is a website that allows you to access topics by using a hierarchy, starting with general headings and proceeding to more specific topics. A subject directory is an excellent starting point when you want an overview of a particular topic before proceeding to specific websites.

The invisible web, or hidden web, describes numerous text, graphics, and data files stored in collections that are unreachable by search engines.

Many analysts use social networking as a primary online tool to expand personal and professional contacts and communication. Other Internet tools that might be of value to a systems analyst are forums, newsletters, blogs, podcasts, RSS feeds, webinars, mailing lists, web-based discussion groups, chat rooms, and instant messaging. Forums, or newsgroups, are online discussion groups that address every conceivable subject and interest area. Numerous commercial and nonprofit groups that offer membership subscriptions to users who are interested in specific topics publish newsletters. A mailing list, or listserv, allows subscribing members to post and receive messages forwarded to them by a list server. A web-based discussion group, usually accessed through a portal such as Yahoo!, combines features of forums and mailing lists for its members. A chat room is an online meeting place where users can interact and converse in real time. Instant messaging allows online users to exchange messages immediately, even while they are working in another program or application.

When an IT professional needs to research a topic or seek background information, he or she can turn to an assortment of sites and resources called the information technology (IT) community. The IT community includes corporate, government, professional, and online learning resources.

Professional development through online learning is a way for IT workers to remain current in their chosen areas. Online learning refers to the delivery of educational or training content over the Internet or an intranet. Online learning is convenient, economical, and customizable. Some disadvantages, however, include a lack of face-to-face interaction, limitations of the interface, and the fact that not everyone works well with this type of training.

Key Terms

advanced search An advanced search can include the option to search within returned results and the ability to search within specific areas, such as websites.

aggregator Client software or web application that aggregates syndicated web content such as blogs, podcasts, and RSS feeds in a single location for easy viewing. Also called feed reader or RSS reader.

AND The AND operator often is used to narrow a set of search results by requiring all operands to be true.

Association for Computing Machinery (ACM) A professional association for the computing field that sponsors seminars and training and has a website where members can keep up with current issues, trends, and opportunities.

Boolean logic A system named after British mathematician George Boole and refers to the relationships among search terms based on logical operators, such as OR, AND, and NOT.

browser A web browser, or browser, is a software program that lets users access and display webpages that are delivered by a web server.

channel An online meeting place where users can interact and converse in real time. Also called a chat room.

chat room *See* channel.

crawler Search engines use a specialized computer program called a spider or crawler that travels from site to site indexing, or cataloging, the contents of the pages based on keywords. Also called spider.

deep web The terms *invisible web, hidden web,* or *deep web* are used to describe this valuable information source, which includes numerous text, graphics, and data files stored in collections that are unreachable by search engines.

digest The format of an online mailing list.

e-learning A term that refers to the delivery of educational or training content over the public Internet or intranet. Also referred to as online learning.

FAQs (frequently asked question) A common method of providing guidance on questions that users are likely to ask.

feed reader *See* aggregator.

hidden web *See* deep web.

hits Search engine results.

implied Boolean logic In implied Boolean logic, symbols are used to represent Boolean operators, such as a plus sign (+) for AND, and a minus sign (–) for NOT.

indexed search engine An indexed search engine organizes and ranks the results of a search.

indexing Search engines use a specialized computer program called a spider that travels from site to site indexing, or cataloging, the contents of the pages based on keywords.

Information Technology Association of America (ITAA) A professional organization that sponsors seminars and training.

information technology (IT) community A collection of like-minded IT professionals who share expertise and resources.

instant messaging (IM) Allows online users to exchange messages immediately, even while they are working in another program or application.

Internet A worldwide network that integrates many thousands of other networks, which in turn link millions of government, business, educational, and personal users around the globe.

Internet Relay Chat (IRC) The chat room concept originated with Internet Relay Chat, or IRC. IRC is a multichannel system supported by servers that enable group and individual conversations to occur on a worldwide basis.

invisible web *See* deep web.

keywords Words used by a spider to catalog or index pages from websites.

list server A computer that directs email to people who subscribe to, or join, a particular mailing list.

listserv *See* mailing list.

logical operators The logical operators OR, AND, and NOT are used to create combinations of search terms to improve search success greatly.

mailing list Similar to a newsgroup in that it provides a forum for people who want to exchange information about specific topics. Also called a listserv.

meta-search engine A tool that can use multiple search engines simultaneously.

newsletters Publications by numerous commercial and nonprofit groups that offer membership subscriptions to users who are interested in specific topics.

NOT The NOT operator can be used to exclude certain records in a search.

online learning *See* e-learning.

OR The OR operator can be used to include search results of more than one query.

pay for performance An arrangement between a search engine company and a commercial site that boosts a sites ranking in search results in return for a fee.

phrase A phrase is more specific than an AND operator, because it specifies an exact placement of terms.

podcast A web-based broadcast that allows a user to receive audio or multimedia files using music player software such as iTunes, and listen to them on a PC or download them to a portable MP3 player or smart phone.

portal An entrance to a multifunction website. After entering a portal, a user can navigate to a destination, using various tools and features provided by the portal designer.

proprietary database A database that can be accessed for a fee or by subscription only, such as ProQuest or IEEE's Xplore.

RSS (Really Simple Syndication) A format for publishing frequently updated content to users who subscribe to an RSS download, also called a feed, RSS feed, or a web feed.

RSS feed Data format for providing users with frequently updated web content on all kinds of topics, available by subscription. Also called a feed or web feed.

RSS reader *See* aggregator.

search engine An application that uses keywords and phrases to locate information on the Internet and list the results of the search.

social networking Using online communication channels such as Facebook, Twitter, and LinkedIn to connect to personal and professional contacts and groups.

spider *See* crawler.

sponsored link A subsidized link, paid for by a company or individual to make the link more prominent on a website.

subject directory A website that structures topics in a hierarchy, starting with general headings and proceeding to more specific topics. Also called topic directory.

subsearch A focused search that can include the option to search within returned results and the ability to search within specific areas, such as newsgroups.

text messaging Sending text messages via cell phone. Also called texting.

texting *See* text messaging.

topic directory *See* subject directory.

Venn diagram A diagram that uses circular symbols to illustrate Boolean logic. Venn diagrams are named after John Venn, a nineteenth-century scholar who devised a scheme for visualizing logical relationships.

visible web Refers to websites that are indexed by major search engines and are publicly accessible.

web The Internet allows you to visit the World Wide Web, usually referred to as the web, which contains billions of text and multimedia documents called webpages.

web browser An application that enables the user to navigate, or browse the Internet and display webpages on a local computer.

web feed *See* RSS feed.

web server A computer that is used to store and house websites.

webpage Text and multimedia documents that are found on the web.

website A collection of related webpages.

World Wide Web *See* web.

Toolkit Exercises

Review Questions

1. Are the Internet and the World Wide Web one and the same? Why or why not?
2. How do search engines differ from subject directories? Is one approach better than the other? Why or why not?
3. What is the invisible web, and how large is it?
4. How would you plan an Internet research strategy?
5. How would you assess the *quality* of Internet research results?
6. What are sponsored links? Could they affect the quality of your search results? How?
7. What is Boolean logic? Provide three examples using everyday terms.
8. What do Venn diagrams display, and why is the information valuable?
9. Describe social networking, forums, newsletters, blogs, podcasts, RSS feeds, webinars, mailing lists, web-based discussion groups, chat rooms, and instant messaging. How can these tools be used in Internet research?
10. What is the information technology community, and what resources does it offer?

Discussion Topics

1. The textbook explains that some companies pay to obtain a higher ranking when search results are displayed. Is this good, is it bad, or does it not matter to you as a user? Explain your position.
2. Some people rely heavily on social networking, instant messaging, and texting to communicate with friends and business colleagues. Others find these methods distracting. Do you use social networking, instant messaging, or texting? Why or why not?
3. Could Boolean logic and Venn diagrams be useful in everyday life? How might they be used?
4. The Internet has affected many aspects of our society. What are the most important benefits of the Internet, and what problems has it created?
5. The invisible web can be used for criminal activity, since information about users and their actions in this environment is harder to uncover by law enforcement personnel. Do you think using the dark web should be made illegal, to address this phenomenon? Why or why not?

Projects

1. Use a search engine and enter the following words: *presidential candidates in 2016*. Run the search and notice how many results appear. Now place quotation marks around the phrase and run the search again. Explain the difference in the results.
2. Will the search phrase *commercial television* return the same results as the phrase *television commercial*? Experiment with a search engine, and explain the results you obtain.
3. Use LinkedIn to find out more about systems analysis interest groups. If there is a local group in your area, consider attending one of their meetings and writing a report on the experience.
4. Perform research on the web to learn more about RSS feeds. Then write a practical, step-by-step guide for users who want to set up RSS feeds of their own.
5. Setup your own Facebook page to reflect your professional activities as a systems analyst. Remember that this is a business-oriented web presence, which should describe your career, not your personal life.

GLOSSARY

1:1 A type of entity relationship. A one-to-one relationship, abbreviated 1:1, exists when exactly one of the second entity occurs for each instance of the first entity.

1:M A type of entity relationship. A one-to-many relationship, abbreviated 1:M, exists when one occurrence of the first entity can be related to many occurrences of the second entity, but each occurrence of the second entity can be associated with only one occurrence of the first entity.

6 by 6 rule A presentation guideline no more than six items should be placed on each slide, and each item should have no more than six words.

7 by 7 rule A presentation guideline no more than seven items should be placed on each slide, and each item should have no more than seven words.

802.11 A family of wireless network specifications developed by the IEEE.

802.11ac An IEEE wireless network specification, approved in 2014, that uses expanded multiple-input/multiple output (MIMO) technology to achieve theoretical speeds of nearly 7 Gbps while increasing the wireless range, and is backward-compatible with 802.11 a, b, g, and n.

802.11b An IEEE wireless network specification introduced in 1999, based on a frequency of 2.4 GHz, and maximum bandwidth of 11 Mbps. Replaced by 802.11g.

802.11g An IEEE wireless network specification introduced in 2003 based on a frequency of 2.4 GHz and maximum bandwidth of 54 Mbps; compatible with and replaced 802.11b, and has been superseded by the 802.11n standard.

802.11n An IEEE wireless network specification adopted in 2009 that uses multiple-input/multiple output (MIMO) technology to achieve speeds of 200+ Mbps while increasing the wireless range, and is backward-compatible with 802.11 a, b, and g.

802.16 Specifications developed by the IEEE for broadband wireless communications over MANs (metropolitan area networks). *See also* Wi-Max.

abbreviation code Alphabetic abbreviation. For example, standard state codes include NY for New York, ME for Maine, and MN for Minnesota.

absolute date The total number of days from some specific base date. To calculate the number of days between two absolute dates, subtract one date from the other. For example, using a base date of January 1, 1900, September 27, 2012, has an absolute date value of 41179 and July 13, 2011, has an absolute date of 40737. If the earlier date value is subtracted from the later one, the result is 442 days.

acceptance One of four risk control strategies. In acceptance, the risk is accepted and nothing is done. Risk is usually accepted only if protection from risk is clearly not worth the expense.

acceptance test Testing involves the entire information system, including all typical processing situations. During an acceptance test, users enter data, including samples of actual, or live data, perform queries, and produce reports to simulate actual operating conditions. All processing options and outputs are verified by users and the IT project development team to ensure that the system functions correctly. Sometimes known as a system test.

access point A central wireless device that provides network services to wireless clients.

action code Indicates what action is to be taken with an associated item. For example, a student records program might prompt a user to enter or click an action code such as D (to display the student's record), A (to add a record), and X (to exit the program).

active voice Refers to using sentences where the actor is the subject of the sentence. For example, "Tom designed the system" is in active voice. Active voice is preferred in written communication.

activity Any work that has a beginning and an end, and requires the use of company resources including people, time, and/or money. Examples include conducting a series of interviews, designing a report, selecting software, waiting for the delivery of equipment, and training users. *See also* task.

activity diagram A diagram that resembles a horizontal flow chart that shows the actions and events as they occur. Activity diagrams show the order in which actions take place and identify the outcome.

actor An external entity with a specific role. In a use case model, actors are used to model interaction with the system.

adaptive maintenance Adds new capability and enhancements to an existing system.

adaptive method A systems development method that typically uses a spiral development model, which builds on a series of iterations, to make adapting to changes easier for all stakeholders.

administrator account An account that allows essentially unrestricted access to the application.

advanced search An advanced search can include the option to search within returned results and the ability to search within specific areas, such as websites.

aggregator Client software or web application that aggregates syndicated web content such as blogs, podcasts, and RSS feeds in a single location for easy viewing. *Also called* feed reader or RSS reader.

agile method Systems development method that attempts to develop a system incrementally, by building a series of prototypes and constantly adjusting them to user requirements. Related to adaptive method.

alias A term used in various data dictionaries to indicate an alternate name, or a name other than the standard data element name, that is used to describe the same data element.

allocated baseline Documents the system at the end of the design phase and identifies any changes since the functional baseline. The allocated baseline includes testing and verification of all system requirements and features.

alphabetic code Uses alphabet letters to distinguish one item from another based on a category, an abbreviation, or an easy-to-remember value, called a mnemonic code.

AND The AND operator often is used to narrow a set of search results by requiring all operands to be true.

app A software application that runs on a mobile device, such as a smartphone or tablet.

application Part of the information system, an application handles the input, manages the processing logic, and provides the required output.

application development The process of constructing the programs and code modules that are the building blocks of an information system. Application development is handled by an application development group within a traditional IT department that is composed of systems analysts and programmers who handle information system design, development, and implementation.

application generator A tool that supports the rapid development of computer programs by translating a logical model directly into code. Also called a code generator.

application life cycle management (ALM) A start-to-finish approach to planning, designing, developing, deploying, managing, and maintaining an information system, using specialized software tools.

application logic The underlying business rules or logic for an application.

application server A computer acting as "middlemen" between customers and an organization's databases and applications. Often used to facilitate complex business transactions.

application service provider (ASP) A firm that delivers a software application, or access to an application, by charging a usage or subscription fee.

application software Software programs, such as email, word processors, spreadsheets, and graphics packages, used by employees in typical office scenarios.

applications programmer A person who works on new systems development and maintenance.

archived The storage of previous version of a system when a new version is installed.

ASCII Stands for American Standard Code for Information Interchange, a data storage coding method used on most personal computers and workstations.

asset Hardware, software, data, networks, people, or procedures that provide tangible or intangible benefit to an organization.

Association for Computing Machinery (ACM) A professional association for the computing field that sponsors seminars and training and has a website where members can keep up with current issues, trends, and opportunities.

associative entity An entity that has its own set of attributes and characteristics. Associative entities are used to link between many-to-many (M:N) relationships.

attack A hostile act that targets an information system, or an organization itself.

attribute A single characteristic or fact about an entity. An attribute, or field, is the smallest piece of data that has meaning within an information system. For example, a Social Security number or company name could be examples of an attribute. In object-oriented analysis, an attribute is part of a class diagram that describes the characteristics of objects in the class. *Also known as* data element or data item.

audit fields Special fields within data records to provide additional control or security information. Typical audit fields include the date the record was created or modified, the name of the user who performed the action, and the number of times the record has been accessed.

audit log files Record details of all accesses and changes to a file or database and can be used to recover changes made since the last backup.

audit trail A record of the source of each data item and when it entered a system. In addition to recording the original source, an audit trail must show how and when data is accessed or changed, and by whom. All these actions must be logged in an audit trail file and monitored carefully.

authorization zone Part of a form that contains any required signatures.

automated fax A system that allows a customer to request a fax using email, the company website, or a telephone. The response is transmitted in a matter of seconds back to the user's fax machine.

automatic update service Enables an application to contact the vendor's server and check for a needed patch.

availability One of the three main elements of system security: confidentiality, integrity, and availability (CIA). Availability ensures that authorized users have timely and reliable access to necessary information.

avoidance One of four risk control strategies. In avoidance, adding protective safeguards eliminates the risk.

B2B (business-to-business) A commercial exchange (e.g., products or services) between businesses, typically enabled by the Internet or electronic means.

B2C (business-to-consumer) A commercial exchange (e.g., products or services) between businesses and consumers conducted over the Internet.

backup The process of saving a series of file or data copies to be retained for a specified period of time. Data can be backed up continuously, or at prescribed intervals.

backup media Data storage options, including tape, hard drives, optical storage, and online storage.

backup policy Detailed instructions and procedures for all backups.

balancing A process used to maintain consistency among an entire series of diagrams, including input and output data flows, data definition, and process descriptions.

bandwidth The amount of data that the system can handle in a fixed time period. Bandwidth requirements are expressed in bits per second (bps).

baseline A formal reference point that measures system characteristics at a specific time. Systems analysts use baselines as yardsticks to document features and performance during the systems development process.

Basic Service Set (BSS) A wireless network configuration in which a central wireless device called an access point is used to serve all wireless clients; also called infrastructure mode.

batch A group of data, usually inputted into an information system at the same time.

batch control A total used to verify batch input. Batch controls might check data items such as record counts and numeric field totals. For example, before entering a batch of orders, a user might calculate the total number of orders and the sum of all the order quantities. When the batch of orders is entered, the order system also calculates the same two totals. If the system totals do not match the input totals, then a data entry error has occurred.

batch input A process where data entry is performed on a specified time schedule, such as daily, weekly, monthly, or longer. For example, batch input occurs when a payroll department collects time cards at the end of the week and enters the data as a batch.

benchmark A measures of the time a package takes to process a certain number of transactions.

benchmark testing A form of testing used by companies to measure system performance.

best-case estimate The most optimistic outcome.

binary storage format A format that offers efficient storage of numeric data. For example, when numeric data types are specified using Microsoft Access, there are a variety of storage formats choices, including integer and long integer, among others.

biometric device A mechanism used to uniquely identify a person by a retina scan or by mapping a facial pattern.

biometric scanning systems Mapping an individual's facial features, handprint, or eye characteristics for identification purposes.

BIOS-level password A password that must be entered before the computer can be started. It prevents an unauthorized person from booting a computer by using a USB device or a CD-ROM. Also called a power-on password or a boot-level password.

bit The smallest unit of data is one binary digit.

black box A metaphor for a process or action that produces results in a non-transparent or non-observable manner. In data flow diagrams, a process appears as a black box where the inputs, outputs, and general function of the process are known, but the underlying details are not shown.

black hole A process that has no output.

block sequence code Cipher that uses blocks of numbers for different classifications.

blog An online journal. The term is a contraction of "web log."

Bluetooth A form of wireless transmission very popular for short-distance wireless communication that does not require high power.

Boolean logic A system named after British mathematician George Boole and refers to the relationships among search terms based on logical operators such as OR, AND, and NOT.

boot-level password *See* BIOS-level password.

bottom-up technique A method for analyzing a large, complex project as a series of individual tasks, called project tasks.

brainstorming A fact-finding technique for gaining information through the use of a small group discussion of a specific problem, opportunity, or issue.

bring your own device (BYOD) An equipment management model where employees are in charge of their devices (e.g., computers, tablets, smartphones) at work, not the IT department. This includes device selection and setup, program installation and updating, and network connectivity (including security).

Brooks' Law Frederick Brooks, an IBM engineer, observed that adding more manpower to a late software project only makes it later.

browser A web browser, or browser, is a software program that lets users access and display webpages that are delivered by a web server.

bug tracking software System developers use defect tracking software, sometimes called bug tracking software, to document and track program defects, code changes, and replacement code, called patches.

build or buy A choice between developing in-house software and purchasing software, often called a build or buy, or make or buy, decision.

bus network A computer network where a single communication path connects the mainframe computer, server, workstations, and peripheral devices. Information is transmitted in either direction from any workstation to another workstation, and any message can be directed to a specific device.

business analytics Using software to measure past performance to help managers understand business trends and monitor current operations.

business case Refers to the reasons, or justification, for a proposal.

business continuity plan (BCP) A plan that defines how critical business functions can continue in the event of a major disruption.

business logic Rules to determine how a system handles data and produces useful information, reflecting the operational requirements of the business. Examples include adding the proper amount of sales tax to invoices, calculating customer balances and finance charges, and determining whether a customer is eligible for a volume-based discount. *Also called* business rules.

business model A graphical representation of business functions that consist of business processes, such as sales, accounting, and purchasing.

business process A description of specific events, tasks, and desired results.

business process model (BPM) A graphical representation of one or more business processes.

business process modeling notation (BPMN) A standard set of shapes and symbols used to represent events, processes, and workflows in computer-based modeling tools.

business process outsourcing (BPO) The outsourcing of a basic business process. *See also* outsourcing.

business profile A definition of a company's overall functions, processes, organization, products, services, customers, suppliers, competitors, constraints, and future direction.

business rules How a system handles data and produces useful information. Business rules, also called business logic, reflect the operational requirements of the business. Examples include adding the proper amount of sales tax to invoices, calculating customer balances and finance charges, and determining whether a customer is eligible for a volume-based discount.

business support system Provide job-related information support to users at all levels of a company.

byte A group of eight bits is called a byte, or a character. A set of bytes forms a field, which is an individual fact about a person, place, thing, or event.

calendar control A calendar control allows the user to select a date that the system will display and store as a field value.

candidate key Sometimes it is possible to have a choice of fields or field combinations to use as the primary key. Any field that could serve as a primary key is called a candidate key.

Capability Maturity Model (CMM)® A model developed by SEI that integrates software and systems development into a process improvement framework.

Capability Maturity Model Integration (CMMI)® An SEI-developed process to improve quality, reduce development time, and cut costs. A CMM tracks an organization's software development goals and practices, using five maturity levels, from Level 1 (relatively unstable, ineffective software) to Level 5 (software that is refined, efficient, and reliable).

capacity planning A process that monitors current activity and performance levels, anticipates future activity, and forecasts the resources needed to provide desired levels of service.

cardinality A concept that describes how instances of one entity relate to instances of another entity. Described in entity-relationship diagrams by notation that indicates combinations that include zero or one-to-many, one-to-one, and many-to-many.

cardinality notation Code that shows relationships between entities.

CASE environment More than just a set of CASE tools. A CASE environment includes any use of computer-based support in the software development process.

case for action A part of the preliminary investigation report to management that summarizes project requests and makes specific recommendations.

CASE tool Powerful software used in computer-aided systems (or software) engineering (CASE) to help systems analysts develop and maintain information systems. *See also* computer-aided software engineering (CASE).

category codes Ciphers that identify a group of related items. For example, a local department store may use a two-character category code to identify the department in which a product is sold.

certification A credential an individual earns by demonstrating a certain level of knowledge and skill on a standardized test.

change control (CC) A process for controlling changes in system requirements during software development; also an important tool for managing system changes and costs after a system becomes operational.

channel An online meeting place where users can interact and converse in real time. Also called a chat room.

character A group of eight bits is called a character, or a byte. A set of bytes forms a field, which is an individual fact about a person, place, thing, or event.

character-based report A report created using a single mono-spaced character set.

chargeback method A technique that uses accounting entries to allocate the indirect costs of running the IT department. Most organizations adopt one of four chargeback methods: no charge, a fixed charge, a variable charge based on resource usage, or a variable charge based on volume.

chat room *See* channel.

check box Used to select one or more choices from a group. A check mark, or an X, represents selected options.

child In inheritance, a child is the object that derives one or more attributes from another object, called the parent.

child diagram The lower-level diagram in an exploded data flow diagram.

CIA triangle The three main elements of system security: confidentiality, integrity, and availability.

cipher code Use of a keyword to encode a number. A retail store, for example, may use a 10-letter word, such as CAMPGROUND, to code wholesale prices, where the letter C represents 1, A represents 2, and so on. Thus, the code, GRAND, would indicate that the store paid $562.90 for the item.

class A term used in object-oriented modeling to indicate a collection of similar objects.

class diagram A detailed view of a single use case, showing the classes that participate in the use case, and documenting the relationship among the classes.

clicks to close The average number of page views to accomplish a purchase or obtain desired information.

clickstream storage Recording web visitor behavior and traffic trends for later data mining. use.

client Workstation that users interact with in a client/server design. These workstations, or computers, are supplied data, processing services, or other support from other computers, called servers.

client/server architecture Generally refers to systems that divide processing between one or more networked clients and a central server. In a typical client/ server system, the client handles the entire user interface, including data entry, data query, and screen presentation logic. The server stores the data and provides data access and database management functions. Application logic is divided in some manner between the server and the clients.

closed-ended questions Queries that limit or restrict the range of responses. Used in the interview process when specific information or fact verification is desired.

cloud computing An online software and data environment in which applications and services are accessed and used through an Internet connection rather than on a local computer; refers to the cloud symbol for the Internet.

code A set of letters or numbers that represents a data item. Codes can be used to simplify output, input, and data formats.

code generator *See* application generator.

code review A review of a project team member's work by other members of the team to spot logic errors. Generally, systems analysts review the work of other systems analysts, and programmers review the work of other programmers, as a form of peer review. Structured walkthroughs should take place throughout the SDLC and are called requirements reviews, design reviews, code reviews, or testing reviews, depending on the phase in which they occur. *Also known as* a structured walkthrough.

coding The process of turning program logic into specific instructions that a computer system can execute.

cohesion A measure of a module's scope and processing characteristics. A module that performs a single function or task has a high degree of cohesion, which is desirable.

combination check A type of data validation check that is performed on two or more fields to ensure that they are consistent or reasonable when considered together. Even though all the fields involved in a combination check might pass their individual validation checks, the combination of the field values might be inconsistent or unreasonable.

combination key A type of data validation check that is performed on two or more fields to ensure that they are consistent or reasonable when considered together. Even though all the fields involved in a combination check might pass their individual validation checks, the combination of the field values might be inconsistent or unreasonable.

command button Onscreen button that initiates an action such as printing a form or requesting Help.

common field An attribute that appears in more than one entity. Common fields can be used to link entities in various types of relationships.

composite key Sometimes it is necessary for a primary key to consist of a combination of fields. In that case, the primary key is called a combination key, composite key, concatenated key, or multivalued key.

computer output to microfilm (COM) Scanning and storing images of paper documents. Often used by large firms to provide high-quality records management and archiving.

computer resources committee A group of key managers and users responsible for evaluating systems requests. The term *systems review committee* is also used.

computer-aided software engineering (CASE) A technique that uses powerful programs called CASE tools to provide an overall framework for systems development. The tools support a wide variety of design methodologies, including structured analysis and object-oriented analysis. Also referred to as computer-aided systems engineering.

computer-aided systems engineering (CASE) *See* computer-aided software engineering (CASE).

concatenated key *See* composite key.

concurrent task A task that can be completed at the same time as (in parallel with) another task.

condition A specified action or state in a structure chart.

confidentiality One of the three main elements of system security: confidentiality, integrity, and availability (CIA). Confidentiality protects information from unauthorized discloser and safeguards privacy.

configuration management (CM) A process for controlling changes in system requirements during the development phases of the SDLC. Configuration management also is an important tool for managing system changes and costs after a system becomes operational.

connect time The total time that a user is connected actively to a remote server. Some Internet service providers use this as a basis for charges.

constraint A requirement or a condition that the system must satisfy or an outcome that the system must achieve.

construction phase A phase that focuses on program and application development tasks similar to the SDLC.

context diagram A top-level view of an information system that shows the boundaries and scope.

context-sensitive A feature that is sensitive to the current conditions when it is invoked. For example, context-sensitive help offers assistance for a task in progress.

continuous backup A real-time streaming backup method that records all system activity as it occurs.

control break A control break usually causes specific actions to occur, such as printing subtotals for a group of records.

control break report A detail report that focuses on control breaks.

control couple In a structure chart, a control couple shows a message, also called a flag, which one module sends to another.

control field order In a control break report, the records are arranged or sorted in the same order as the control fields.

control module In a structure chart, a control module is a higher-level module that directs lower-level modules, called subordinate modules.

control structure Serve as building blocks for a process. Control structures have one entry and exit point. They may be completed in sequential order, as the result of a test or condition, or repeated until a specific condition changes. *Also called* logical structure.

corporate culture A set of beliefs, rules, traditions, values, and attitudes that define a company and influence its way of doing business.

corporate portal A website that provides various tools and features for an organization's customers, employees, suppliers, and the public.

corrective maintenance Changes to the system to fix errors.

cost center An element that generates charges with no offsetting credits.

cost-avoidance benefits Expenses that would be necessary if the new system is not installed. Examples include handling the work with existing staff, and not replacing existing hardware or software.

cost-benefit analysis The process of comparing the anticipated costs of an information system to the anticipated benefits.

coupling Measures relationships and interdependence among modules. The opposite of cohesion.

crawler Search engines use a specialized computer program called a spider or crawler that travels from site to site indexing, or cataloging, the contents of the pages based on keywords. *Also called* spider.

credentials Formal qualifications that include degrees, diplomas, or certificates granted by learning institutions to show that a certain level of education has been achieved.

critical path A series of events and activities with no slack time. If any activity along the critical path falls behind schedule, the entire project schedule is similarly delayed. As the name implies, a critical path includes all activities that are vital to the project schedule.

Critical Path Method (CPM) Shows a project as a network diagram. The activities are shown as vectors, and the events are displayed graphically as nodes. Although CPM developed separately from the Program Evaluation Review Technique (PERT), the two methods are essentially identical. *See also* PERT/CPM.

critical risk When risks are categorized and prioritized, critical risks (those with the highest vulnerability and impact ratings) head the list.

critical success factor Vital objective that must be achieved for the enterprise to fulfill its mission.

critical thinking skills The ability to compare, classify, evaluate, recognize patterns, analyze cause and effect, and apply logic. Such skills are valued in the IT industry.

crow's foot notation A type of cardinality notation. It is called crow's foot notation because of the shapes, which include circles, bars, and symbols, that indicate various possibilities. A single bar indicates one, a double bar indicates one and only one, a circle indicates zero, and a crow's foot indicates many.

customer Primary user of a system, service, or product.

customer relationship management (CRM) Many companies implement systems to integrate all customer-related events and transactions including marketing, sales, and customer service activities.

cutover phase A phase that resembles the final tasks in the SDLC implementation phase, including data conversion, testing, changeover to the new system, and user training.

data The raw material or basic facts used by information systems.

data conversion Existing data is loaded into the new system, transformed as needed. Depending on the system, data conversion can be done before, during, or after the operational environment is complete.

data couple In a structure chart, a data couple shows data that one module passes to another.

data dictionary A central storehouse of information about a system's data.

data element A single characteristic or fact about an entity. A data element, field, or attribute is the smallest piece of data that has meaning within an information system. For example, a Social Security number or company name could be examples of a data element. *Also called* data item.

data flow A path for data to move from one part of the information system to another.

data flow diagram (DFD) Graphical representation of the system, showing it stores, processes, and transforms data into useful information.

data frames Traffic on a computer network.

data item *See* data element.

data manipulation language (DML) A data manipulation language controls database operations, including storing, retrieving, updating, and deleting data. Most commercial DBMSs, such as Oracle and IBM's DB2, use a DML.

data mart A specialized database designed to serve the needs of a specific department, such as sales, marketing, or finance. Each data mart includes only the data that users in that department require to perform their jobs.

data mining Looking for meaningful patterns and relationships among data. For example, data mining software could help a consumer products firm identify potential customers based on their prior purchases.

data processing center A central location where physical data was delivered or transmitted in some manner and entered into the system. Users in the organization had no input or output capability, except for printed reports that were distributed by a corporate IT department.

data replication In normal operating conditions, any transaction that occurs on the primary system must automatically propagate to the hot site.

data repository A symbol used in data flow diagrams to represent a situation in which a system must retain data because one or more processes need to use that stored data at a later time. *Also known as* data store.

data security Protection of data from loss or damage and recovers data when it is lost or damaged.

data store *See* data repository.

data structure A meaningful combination of related data elements that is included in a data flow or retained in a data store. A framework for organizing and storing data.

data type check A type of data validation check that is used to ensure that a data item fits the required data type. For example, a numeric field must have only numbers or numeric symbols, and an alphabetic field can contain only the characters A through Z or the characters a through z.

data validation rule A mechanism to improve input quality by testing the data and rejecting any entry that fails to meet specified conditions.

data warehouse An integrated collection of data that can support management analysis and decision making.

database administrator (DBA) Someone who manages a database management system (DBMS). The DBA assesses overall requirements and maintains the database for the benefit of the entire organization rather than a single department or user.

database management system (DBMS) A collection of tools, features, and interfaces that enables users to add, update, manage, access, and analyze data in a database.

database programmer A person who focuses on creating and supporting large-scale database systems.

decision table A table that shows a logical structure, with all possible combinations of conditions and resulting actions.

decision tree A graphical representation of the conditions, actions, and rules found in a decision table.

decomposing Another way of conveying a process or system that has been broken down from a general, top-level view to more detail. The terms *exploded* and *partitioned* also can be used.

deep web The terms *invisible web*, *hidden web*, or *deep web* are used to describe this valuable information source, which includes numerous text, graphics, and data files stored in collections that are unreachable by search engines.

default value A value that a system displays automatically.

defect tracking software System developers use defect tracking software, sometimes called bug tracking software, to document and track program defects, code changes, and replacement code, called patches.

deliverable A polished, final product, suitable for its intended use. End products or deliverables often coincide with the completion of each SDLC phase.

denial of service (DOS) An online attack that occurs when an attacking computer makes repeated requests to a service or services running on certain ports.

dependent task A task is said to be dependent when it has to be completed in a serial sequence.

derivation code Combining data from different item attributes, or characteristics, to build the code. Most magazine subscription codes are derivation codes.

design prototyping Creating a prototype of user requirements, after which the prototype is discarded and implementation continues. *Also called* throwaway prototyping.

design review *See* structured walk-through.

design walkthrough A session with users to review the interface with a cross-section of people who will work with the new system. This is a continuation of the modeling and prototyping effort that began early in the systems development process.

desk checking The process of reviewing the program code to spot logic errors, which produce incorrect results.

detail report A detail report produces one or more lines of output for each record processed.

development environment The mix of software tools, methods, and physical resources that an IT team uses to create an information system.

developmental costs Expenses incurred only once, at the time a system is developed or acquired. Examples include salaries of people involved in system development or initial user training.

diagram 0 A diagram depicting the first level of detail below the initial context diagram. Diagram 0 (zero) zooms in on the context diagram and shows major processes, data flows, and data stores, as well as repeating the external entities and data flows that appear in the context diagram.

dialog box Allows a user to enter information about a task that a system will perform.

differential backup A backup that includes only the files that have changed since the last full backup.

digest The format of an online mailing list.

direct costs Expenses associated with the development of a specific system. Examples include the salaries of project team members and the purchase of hardware that is used only for the new system.

direct cutover The direct cutover approach causes the changeover from the old system to the new system to occur immediately when the new system becomes operational.

disaster recovery plan A documented procedure consisting of an overall backup and recovery plan.

discretionary project Where management has a choice in implementing a project, they are called discretionary. For example, creating a new report for a user is an example of a discretionary project.

diskless workstation A network terminal that supports a full-featured user interface, but limits the printing or copying of data, except to certain network resources that can be monitored and controlled more easily.

distributed database management system (DDBMS) A system for managing data stored at more than one location. Using a DDBMS offers several advantages: data stored closer to users can reduce network traffic; the system is scalable, so new data sites can be added without reworking the system design; and with data stored in various locations, the system is less likely to experience a catastrophic failure. A potential disadvantage of distributed data storage involves data security. It can be more difficult to maintain controls and standards when data is stored in various locations.

distributed denial of service (DDOS) A service attack involving multiple attacking computers that can synchronize DOS attacks on a server.

distributed system Company-wide systems that are connected by one or more LANs or WANs. The capabilities of a distributed system depend on the power and capacity of the underlying data communication network.

diverging data flow A data flow in which the same data travels to two or more different locations.

document review A review of baseline documentation. A useful fact-finding technique that helps an analyst understand how the current system is supposed to work.

documentation Material that explains a system, helps people interact with it, and includes program documentation, system documentation, operations documentation, and user documentation.

domain The set of values permitted for a data element.

dumpster diving Raiding desks or trash bins for valuable information.

duration The amount of time it will take to complete a task.

EBCDIC Stands for Extended Binary Coded Decimal Interchange Code, a coding method used on mainframe computers and some high-capacity servers.

ecommerce (electronic commerce) Transactions (e.g., buying and selling of goods and information) that occur on the Internet. Includes both business-to-consumer and business-to-business.

economic feasibility Achieved if the projected benefits of the proposed system outweigh the estimated costs involved in acquiring, installing, and operating it.

economically useful life The period between the beginning of systems operation and the point when operational costs are rapidly increasing.

economy of scale The inherent efficiency of high-volume processing on larger computers. Database design allows better utilization of hardware. If a company maintains an enterprise-wide database, processing is less expensive using a powerful mainframe server instead of using several smaller computers.

event A reference point that marks a major occurrence. Used to monitor progress and manage a project. *See also* milestone.

e-learning A term that refers to the delivery of educational or training content over the public Internet or intranet. Also referred to as online learning.

electronic data interchange (EDI) A process that involves the computer-to-computer transfer of data between companies.

electronic health record (EHR) An electronic record of a patient's health information generated as the patient encounters various health care providers and shared among multiple facilities and agencies.

electronic product code (EPC) Technology that uses RFID tags to identify and monitor the movement of each individual product, from the factory floor to the retail checkout counter.

electronic proof of delivery (EPOD) A supplier uses RFID tags on each crate, case, or shipping unit to create a digital shipping list to verify receipt of goods.

empowerment A business practice that places more responsibility and accountability throughout all levels of an organization.

encapsulation The idea that all data and methods are self-contained, as in a black box.

encryption A process where data is coded (converted into unreadable characters) so that only those with the required authorization can access the data (usually via decoding software).

engaged listening The ability to really concentrate on what someone is saying, and avoid the temptation to hear what is expected. Also includes noticing non-verbal communication.

enhancement A new feature or capability.

enterprise application Company-wide applications, such as order processing systems, payroll systems, and company communications networks.

enterprise computing Information systems that support company-wide data management requirements, such as airline reservations or credit card billing systems.

enterprise resource planning (ERP) A process that establishes an enterprise-wide strategy for IT resources. ERP defines a specific architecture, including standards for data, processing, network, and user interface design.

entity A person, place, thing, or event for which data is collected and maintained. For example, an online sales system may include entities named CUSTOMER, ORDER, PRODUCT, and SUPPLIER.

entity-relationship diagram (ERD) A graphical model of the information system that depicts the relationships among system entities.

evaluation and selection team A group of people involved in selecting hardware and software. The group includes systems analysts and users. A team approach ensures that critical factors are not overlooked and that a sound choice is made.

evaluation model A technique that uses a common yardstick to measure and compare vendor ratings.

event-driven programming language Instead of writing a series of sequential instructions, a programmer defines the actions that the program must perform when certain events occur. Also called non-procedural programming language.

exception report A document displaying only those records that meet a specific condition or conditions. Exception reports are useful when the user wants information only on records that might require action, but does not need to know the details.

existence check A type of data validation check that is used for mandatory data items. For example, if an employee record requires a Social Security number, an existence check would not allow the user to save the record until he or she enters a suitable value in the SSN field.

exploding A diagram is said to be exploded if it "drills down" to a more detailed or expanded view.

exploit An attack that takes advantage of a system vulnerability, often due to a combination of one or more improperly configured services.

Extended Service Set (ESS) A wireless network configuration made up of two or more Basic Service Set (BSS) networks, which allows wireless clients to roam from BSS to BSS.

extensibility Refers to a system's ability to expand, change, or downsize easily to meet the changing needs of a business enterprise. Also known as scalability.

FAQs (frequently asked questions) A common method of providing guidance on questions that users are likely to ask.

fat client A network design that locates all or most of the application processing logic at the client. Also called a thick client design.

fault management The timely detection and resolution of operational problems. Fault management includes monitoring a system for signs of trouble, logging all system failures, diagnosing the problem, and applying corrective action.

fault tolerant A system or application is said to be fault tolerant if the failure of one component does not disable the rest of the system or application.

faxback A system that allows a customer to request a fax using e-mail, the company website, or a telephone. The response is transmitted in a matter of seconds back to the user's fax machine.

feasibility study An initial investigation to clearly identify the nature and scope of the business opportunity or problem. Also called a preliminary investigation.

feed reader *See* aggregator.

field A single characteristic or fact about an entity. A field, or attribute, is the smallest piece of data that has meaning within an information system. For example, a Social Security number or company name could be examples of a field. The terms *data element, data item,* and *field* are used interchangeably.

file Each file or table contains data about people, places, things, or events that interact with the information system.

file-oriented system A file-oriented system, also called a file-processing system, stores and manages data in one or more separate files.

fill-in form A template used to collect data on the Internet or a company intranet.

finish day/date The day or date when a task is scheduled to be finished.

firewall The main line of defense between a local network, or intranet, and the Internet.

first normal form (1NF) A record is said to be in first normal form (1NF) if it does not contain a repeating group (a set of data items that can occur any number of times in a single record).

fishbone diagram An analysis tool that represents the possible causes of a problem as a graphical outline. *Also called* Ishikawa diagram.

fixed charge method A method of determining the indirect costs of running an IT department in which the indirect IT costs are divided among all the other departments in the form of a fixed monthly charge.

fixed costs Expenses that are relatively constant and do not depend on a level of activity or effort. Many fixed costs recur regularly, such as salaries and hardware rental charges.

fixed fee model A service model that charges a set fee based on a specified level of service and user support.

Flesch Reading Ease score Measures the average sentence length and the average number of syllables per word and rates the text on a 100-point scale, with higher ratings being easier to read.

Flesch-Kincaid Grade Level score Uses the same variables as the Flesch Reading Ease score, but in a different formula that produces a rating keyed to a U.S. grade-school level.

flowchart A diagram used to describe program logic that represents logical rules and interaction graphically using a series of symbols connected by arrows. Flowcharts can be useful in visualizing modular program designs.

focus In a sequence diagram, a focus indicates when an object sends or receives a message. It is indicated by a narrow vertical rectangle that covers the lifeline.

foreign key A field in one table that must match a primary key value in another table in order to establish the relationship between the two tables.

form filling A very effective method of online data entry where a blank form that duplicates or resembles the source document is completed on the screen. The user enters the data and then moves to the next field.

form layout The physical appearance and placement of data on a form. Form layout makes the form easy to complete and provides enough space, both vertically and horizontally, for users to enter the data.

form painter *See* screen generator.

forum An online discussion on a particular topic, where people meet, offer support, and exchange ideas.

forward engineering Translating business processes and functions into applications.

four-model approach A physical model of the current system, a logical model of the current system, a logical model of the new system, and a physical model of the new system are all developed.

fourth-generation environment A term used to describe an efficient software development environment that is created through the use of powerful CASE tools, application generators, report generators, screen generators, and fourth-generation languages (4GLs) during prototyping.

fourth-generation languages (4GLs) Non-procedural programming languages that are especially valuable in implementing an object-oriented system design.

framework Conceptual structure that organizes and documents system development tasks.

full backup A complete backup of every file on the system.

functional baseline The configuration of the system documented at the beginning of the project. It consists of all the necessary system requirements and design constraints.

functional decomposition diagram (FDD) A top-down representation of business functions and processes. Also called a structure chart.

functional primitive A single function that is not exploded further. The logic for functional primitives is documented in a data dictionary process description.

functionally dependent Functional dependence is an important concept for understanding the second normal form (2NF). The field X is said to be functionally dependent on the field Y if the value of X depends on the value of Y. For example, an order date is dependent on an order number; for a particular order number, there is only one value for the order date. In contrast, the product description is not dependent on the order number. For a particular order number, there might be several product descriptions, one for each item ordered.

Gane and Sarson A popular symbol set used in data flow diagrams. Processes, data flows, data stores, and external entities all have a unique symbol.

Gantt chart A horizontal bar chart that illustrates a schedule. Developed many years ago by Henry L. Gantt as a production control technique. Still are in common use today.

garbage in, garbage out (GIGO) The concept that the quality of the output is only as good as the quality of the input.

gateway (1) In business processing modeling notation, a fork in the process, allowing the flow to go one way or another. (2) A router or other network device used to connect to a larger, dissimilar type of network, such as the Internet.

Gbps (gigabits per second) A bandwidth or throughput measurement indicating billions of bits per second.

global outsourcing The practice of shifting IT development, support, and operations to other countries.

glueware *See* middleware.

grammar checker A software program that can detect usage problems and offer suggestions.

graphical user interface (GUI) The use of graphical objects and techniques allowing users to communicate with a system. A well-designed GUI can help users learn a new system rapidly, and work with the system effectively.

gray hole A process with an input obviously insufficient to generate the shown output.

groupware Software that runs in the cloud or on a company intranet that enables users to share data, collaborate on projects, and work in teams, and may offer features in addition to basic email capability, such as calendars, task lists, schedules, contact lists, and document management. *Also called* workgroup software.

hardening Making a system more secure by removing unnecessary accounts, services, and features.

hardware The physical layer of the information system, to include computers, networks, communications equipment, and other technology-based infrastructure.

hash totals Not meaningful numbers themselves, but are useful for comparison purposes. Also known as batch control totals.

Hawthorne Effect A phenomenon where employees who know they are being observed are more productive.

help desk A centralized resource staffed by IT professionals that provides users with the support they need to do their jobs. A help desk has three main objectives: to show people how to use system resources more effectively, to provide answers to technical or operational questions, and to make users more productive by teaching them how to meet their own information needs. *Also called* service desk or information center.

hidden web *See* deep web.

hierarchical network A network design where one computer (typically a mainframe) controls the entire network. Satellite computers or servers control lower levels of processing and network devices.

histogram A common tool for showing the distribution of questionnaire or sampling results. It takes the form of a vertical bar chart.

hits Search engine results.

horizontal application A software package that can be used by many different types of organizations.

horizontal system A basic system, such as an inventory or payroll package that is commonly used by a variety of companies.

hot site A separate IT location, which might be in another state or even another country, that can support critical business systems in the event of a power outage, system crash, or physical catastrophe.

HTTP/2 The second major version of the network protocol used by the web. Released as a standard in 2015.

hub The center of a star network. Switches in modern networks have largely replaced hubs.

human-computer interaction (HCI) A description of the relationship between computers and the people who use them to perform business-related tasks. HCI concepts apply to everything from a PC desktop to the main menu for a global network.

identity management Controls and procedures necessary to identify legitimate users and system components.

identity theft The stealing of personally identifying information online.

IEEE 802.11i A security standard for Wi-Fi wireless networks that uses the WPA2 protocol, currently the most secure encryption method for Wi-Fi networks.

implied Boolean logic In implied Boolean logic, symbols are used to represent Boolean operators, such as a plus sign (+) for AND, and a minus sign (-) for NOT.

incremental backup Saving a copy of only the files that have changed since the last full backup.

indexed search engine An indexed search engine organizes and ranks the results of a search.

indexing Search engines use a specialized computer program called a spider that travels from site to site indexing, or cataloging, the contents of the pages based on keywords.

indirect costs Expenses that cannot be attributed to the development of a particular information system. The salaries of network administrators and copy machine rentals are examples of indirect costs. *Also called* overhead expenses.

inference rule Instruction that directs a knowledge management system to identify data patterns and relationships.

informal structure An organization based on interpersonal relationships, which can develop from previous work assignments, physical proximity, unofficial procedures, or personal relationships.

information center (IC) A facility that supports users by training them on application software. User support specialists answer questions, troubleshoot problems, and serve as a clearinghouse for user problems and solutions. *Also known as* service desk or help desk.

information Data that has been changed into a useful form of output.

information system A combination of information technology, people, and data to support business requirements. The five key components are hardware, software, data, processes, and people.

information technology (IT) A combination of hardware, software, and telecommunications systems that support business operations, improve productivity, and help managers make decisions.

information technology (IT) community A collection of like-minded IT professionals who share expertise and resources.

Information Technology Association of America (ITAA) A professional organization that sponsors seminars and training.

infrastructure mode A wireless network configuration in which a central wireless device called an access point is used to serve all wireless clients; also called Basic Service Set (BSS).

inheritance A type of object relationship. Inheritance enables an object to derive one or more of its attributes from another object (e.g., an INSTRUCTOR object may inherit many traits from the EMPLOYEE object, such as hire date).

in-house software An information center or help desk within the IT department responsible for providing user support and offering services such as hotline assistance, training, and guidance to users who need technical help.

input Necessary data that enters a system, either manually or in an automated manner.

input control The necessary measures to ensure that input data is correct, complete, and secure. A systems analyst must focus on input control during every phase of input design, starting with source documents that promote data accuracy and quality.

input mask Template or pattern that makes it easier for users to enter data. Often used in automated forms to guide an unfamiliar user.

instance A specific member of a class.

instant messaging (IM) Allows online users to exchange messages immediately, even while they are working in another program or application.

Institute of Electrical and Electronics Engineers (IEEE) A professional organization that establishes standards for telecommunications.

intangible benefit Positive outcome that is difficult to measure in dollars. However, intangible benefits can be very important in the calculation of economic feasibility. An example of an intangible benefit might be a new website that improves a company's image.

intangible cost Item that is difficult to measure in dollar terms, such as employee dissatisfaction.

integrated development environment (IDE) A suite of integrated tools to make it easier to plan, construct, and maintain a specific software product. An IDE is designed to allow the easy integration of system components with less time being spent on developing code for interactive modules.

integration testing The testing two or more programs that depend on each other.

integrity One of the three main elements of system security: confidentiality, integrity, and availability (CIA). Integrity prevents unauthorized users from creating, modifying, or deleting information.

International Organization for Standardization (ISO) A network of national standards institutes from 140 countries working in partnership with international organizations, governments, industry, business and consumer representatives. The ISO acts as a bridge between public and private sectors.

Internet A worldwide network that integrates many thousands of other networks, which in turn link millions of government, business, educational, and personal users around the globe.

Internet business services (IBS) Services that provide powerful web-based support for transactions such as order processing, billing, and customer relationship management.

Internet operating system Part of the Web 2.0 model, an online computing environment created by online communities and services, based on layers of shared information that can contain text, sound bytes, images, and video clips.

Internet Relay Chat (IRC) The chat room concept originated with Internet Relay Chat, or IRC. IRC is a multi-channel system supported by servers that enable group and individual conversations to occur on a worldwide basis.

interview A planned meeting during which information is obtained from another person.

invisible web *See* deep web.

ISO 9000-3:2014 A set of guidelines established and updated by the International Organization for Standardization (ISO) to provide a quality assurance framework for developing and maintaining software.

iteration The completion of a process step that is repeated until a specific condition changes. 5

iteration cycle An agile development cycle that includes planning, designing, coding, and testing one or more features based on user stories. 1

iteration planning meeting In agile development, a meeting held at the beginning of each iteration cycle to break down user stories into specific tasks that are assigned to team members.

iterative An adaptive method typically uses a spiral development model, which builds on a series of iterations.

JDBC (Java database connectivity) A standard that enables Java applications to exchange data with any database that uses SQL statements and is ODBC-compliant.

joint application development (JAD) A popular systems development technique that uses a group of users, managers and IT professionals that work together to gather information, discuss business needs, and define the new system requirements.

just-in-time (JIT) The exchange or delivery of information when and where it is needed. For example, just-in-time inventory systems rely on computer-to-computer data exchange to minimize unnecessary inventory.

Kbps (kilobits per second) A bandwidth or throughput measurement indicating thousands of bits per second.

key fields Used during the systems design phase to organize, access, and maintain data structures. The four types of key fields are primary keys, candidate keys, foreign keys, and secondary keys.

keystroke logger A device that can be inserted between a keyboard and a computer to record keystrokes.

keywords Words used by a spider to catalog or index pages from websites.

knee of the curve A performance characteristic of a client/server computing environment. Client/server response times tend to increase gradually, and then rise dramatically as the system nears its capacity. The point where response times increase dramatically.

knowledge base A popular systems development technique that uses a group of users, managers, and IT professionals that work together to gather information, discuss business needs, and define the new system requirements.

leading questions Queries that suggests or favors a particular reply.

legacy data The data associated with an older, less technologically advanced legacy system.

legacy system An older system that is typically less technologically advanced than currently available systems.

leveling The process of drawing a series of increasingly detailed diagrams to reach the desired level of detail.

library module In a structure chart, a library module is a module that is reusable and can be invoked from more than one point in the chart.

lifeline In a sequence diagram, a lifeline is used to represent the time during which the object above it is able to interact with the other objects in the use case. An x marks the end of a lifeline.

limit check Occurs when a validation check involves a minimum or a maximum value, but not both. Checking that a payment amount is greater than zero, but not specifying a maximum value, is an example of a limit check.

list box An output mechanism that displays a list of choices that the user can select.

list server A computer that directs email to people who subscribe to, or join, a particular mailing list.

listserv *See* list server.

local area network (LAN) A network design that allows the sharing of data and hardware, such as printers and scanners. Advances in data communication technology have made it possible to create powerful networks that use satellite links, high-speed fiber-optic lines, or the Internet to share data.

log Record typically kept by operating systems and applications that documents all events, including dates, times, and other specific information. Logs can be important in understanding past attacks and preventing future intrusions.

logic error Mistakes in the underlying logic that produce incorrect results.

logical design The definition of an information system's functions and features, and the relationships among its components.

logical model Shows what a system must do, regardless of how it will be implemented physically.

logical operators The logical operators OR, AND, and NOT are used to create combinations of search terms to improve search success greatly.

logical record A logical record contains field values that describe a single person, place, thing, or event. Application programs *see* a logical record as a set of fields, regardless of how or where the data is stored physically.

logical storage Refers to information as seen through a user's eyes, regardless of how or where that information is organized or stored.

logical structure *See* control structure.

logical topology A view of a network that describes the way the components interact, rather than the actual network cabling and connections.

loop In a structure chart, a loop indicates that one or more modules are repeated.

looping Refers to a process step that is repeated until a specific condition changes. For example, a process that continues to print paychecks until it reaches the end of the payroll file is looping. Also known as repetition.

loosely coupled Modules that are relatively independent. Loosely coupled modules are easier to maintain and modify, because the logic in one module does not affect other modules.

M:N A type of entity relationship. A many-to-many relationship, abbreviated M:N, exists when one instance of the first entity can be related to many instances of the second entity, and one instance of the second entity can be related to many instances of the first entity.

mailing list Similar to a newsgroup in that it provides a forum for people who want to exchange information about specific topics.

mainframe architecture A system design where the server performs all the processing.

maintenance activities Changing programs, procedures, or documentation to ensure correct system performance. Adapting the system to changing requirements; and making the system operate more efficiently. Those needs are met by corrective, adaptive, perfective, and preventive maintenance.

maintenance agreement A specification of the conditions, charges, and time frame for users to contact the vendor for assistance when they have system problems or questions.

maintenance expenses Costs that vary significantly during the system's operational life and include spending to support maintenance activities.

maintenance release A formal release of a new system version that contains a number of changes.

maintenance release methodology A system of numbered releases used by organizations (especially software vendors) that helps organize maintenance changes and updates.

maintenance team One or more systems analysts and programmers working on product maintenance issues together.

make or buy The choice between developing in-house software and purchasing software often is called a make or buy, or build or buy, decision.

malware Malicious software that might jeopardize the system's security or privacy.

MAN (metropolitan area network) A network that uses 802.16 standards, which are broadband wireless communications protocols.

managed hosting An operation is managed by the outside firm, or host. Another term for Internet business services (IBS).

management information system (MIS) A computer-based information system used in business planning, control, decision making, and problem solving.

many-to-many relationship *See* M:N.

market basket analysis A type of analysis that can detect patterns and trends in large amounts of data.

Mbps (megabits per second) A bandwidth or throughput measurement indicating millions of bits per second.

menu bar A set of user-selectable software application options, usually located across the top of the screen.

mesh network A network design in which each node connects to every other node. While this design is very reliable, it is also expensive to install and maintain.

message An object-oriented command that tells an object to perform a certain method.

meta-search engine A tool that can use multiple search engines simultaneously.

method Defines specific tasks that an object must perform. Describes what and how an object does something.

methods In a class diagram, methods represent program logic.

metrics Workload measurements, also called metrics, include the number of lines printed, the number of records accessed, and the number of transactions processed in a given time period.

middleware Software that connects dissimilar applications and enables them to communicate and exchange data. For example, middleware can link a departmental database to a web server that can be accessed by client computers via the Internet or a company intranet.

milestone A reference point that marks a major occurrence. Used to monitor progress and manage a project. *See also* event.

mission statement A document or statement that describes the company for its stakeholders and briefly states the company's overall purpose, products, services, and values.

mission-critical system An information system that is vital to a company's operations.

mitigation One of four risk control strategies. Mitigation reduces the impact of a risk by careful planning and preparation. For example, a company can prepare a disaster recovery plan to mitigate the effects of a natural disaster should one occur.

mnemonic code Ciphers using a specific combination of letters that are easy to remember. Many three-character airport codes are mnemonic codes. For example, LAX represents Los Angeles.

mobile device Smartphones, tablets, and other computing devices that are not permanently tethered to a desk. They connect to the network wirelessly.

mock-up When designing a report, a sample report is prepared, which is a mock-up, or prototype, for users to review. The sample should include typical field values and contain enough records to show all the design features.

modeling A process that produces a graphical representation of a concept or process that systems developers can analyze, test, and modify.

modular design A design that can be broken down into logical blocks. Also known as partitioning or top-down design.

module Related program code organized into small units that are easy to understand and maintain. A complex program could have hundreds or even thousands of modules.

Moore's Law A prediction that computing power would double every 18 to 24 months due to increased miniaturization of electronic components.

multipath design A network design that relies on multiple data paths to increase bandwidth and range, using MIMO (multiple input/multiple output) technology.

multiple input/multiple output (MIMO) A wireless networking technology incorporated in the IEEE 802.11n and 802.11ac standards that uses multiple data streams and multiple antennas to achieve higher transmission speeds and substantially increase wireless range over earlier standards.

multivalued key Sometimes it is necessary for a primary key to consist of a combination of fields. In that case, the primary key is called a combination key, composite key, concatenated key, or multivalued key.

natural language A software feature that allows users to type commands or requests in normal English (or other language) phrases.

net present value (NPV) The total value of the benefits minus the total value of the costs, with both the costs and benefits being adjusted to reflect the point in time at which they occur.

net-centric computing A distributed environment where applications and data are downloaded from servers and exchanged with peers across a network on as as-needed basis.

netiquette A term that combines the words *Internet* and *etiquette*. Encompasses web guidelines for protocol and courtesy. In many cases, FAQs describe the netiquette of a given newsgroup or site.

network Two or more devices that are connected for the purpose of sending, receiving, and sharing data.

network diagram A PERT chart also is referred to as a network diagram.

network interface A combination of hardware and software that allows the computer to interact with the network.

network intrusion detection system (NIDS) Software that monitors network traffic to detect attempted intrusions or suspicious network traffic patterns, and sends alerts to network administrators. Can be helpful in documenting the efforts of attackers and analyzing network performance.

network topology The way a network is configured. LAN and WAN networks typically are arranged in one of four common patterns: hierarchical, bus, star, and ring.

newsgroup An online discussion on a particular topic, where people meet, offer support, and exchange ideas. The electronic equivalent of the physical bulletin board. Also called a forum.

newsletters Publications by numerous commercial and nonprofit groups that offer membership subscriptions to users who are interested in specific topics.

no charge method A method of determining the indirect costs of running an IT department in which in which an organization treats information systems department indirect expenses as a necessary cost of doing business.

node A physical device, wired or wireless, that can send, receive, or manage network data.

nondiscretionary project Where management has no choice in implementing a project, it is called nondiscretionary. For example, adding a report required by a new federal law.

nonkey field Any field that is not a primary key or a candidate key is called a nonkey field.

non-procedural programming language See event-driven programming language.

normalization A process by which analysts identify and correct inherent problems and complexities in their record designs.

NOT The NOT operator can be used to exclude certain records in a search.

n-tier design A multi-level design or architecture. For example, three-tier designs also are called n-tier designs, to indicate that some designs use more than one intermediate layer.

object In object-oriented analysis or programming, an object represents a real person, place, event, or transaction.

object model Describes objects, which combine data and processes. Object models are the end product of object-oriented analysis.

object-oriented (O-O) analysis The act of understanding an information system by identifying things called objects. An object represents a real person, place, event, or transaction. Object-oriented analysis is a popular approach that sees a system from the viewpoint of the objects themselves as they function and interact with the system.

object-oriented analysis and design (OOAD) A technique used to create objects called actors, which represent the human users who will interact with the system.

object-oriented development (OOD) The process of translating an object model directly into an object-oriented programming language.

object-oriented programming languages (OOPL) Non-procedural programming languages that are especially valuable in implementing an object-oriented system design.

observation A fact-finding technique where an analyst sees a system in action. Observation allows the verification of statements made in interviews.

ODBC (open database connectivity) An industry-standard protocol that makes it possible for software from different vendors to interact and exchange data.

offshore outsourcing The practice of shifting IT development, support, and operations to other countries.

offsiting The practice of storing backup media away from the main business location, in order to mitigate the risk of a catastrophic disaster such as a flood, fire, or earthquake.

one-to-many relationship See 1:M.

one-to-one relationship See 1:1.

online data entry A data entry method used for most business activity. The online method offers major advantages, including the immediate validation and availability of data.

online documentation Provides immediate help when users have questions or encounter problems.

online learning See e-learning.

online presentation A presentation delivered to an online audience, usually through a web browser and/or a third-party application, such as Cisco's WebEx or Citrix's GoToMeeting.

online system Handling transactions when and where they occur and providing output directly to users. Because it is interactive, online processing avoids delays and allows a constant dialog between the user and the system.

open source Software that is supported by a large group of users and developers. The source code is made freely available.

open-ended questions Queries that allows for a range of answers. They encourage spontaneous and unstructured responses, and are useful in understanding a larger process.

operational costs Expenses that are incurred after a system is implemented and continue while the system is in use. Examples include system maintenance, supplies, equipment rental, and annual software license fees.

operational environment The environment for the actual system operation. It includes hardware and software configurations, system utilities, and communications resources. Also called the production environment.

operational feasibility A system that that will be used effectively after it has been developed.

operational security Concerned with managerial policies and controls that ensure secure operations. Also called procedural security.

operations documentation Contains all the information needed for processing and distributing online and printed output.

option button Radio buttons that represent groups of options. The user can select only one option at a time; a selected option contains a black dot. See also radio button.

OR The OR operator can be used to include search results of more than one query.

oral presentation A presentation that is presented orally and is required at the end of the preliminary investigation and again at the conclusion of the systems analysis phase.

orphan An unassociated or unrelated record or field. An orphan could be created if a customer order was entered in an order table where that customer did not already exist in the customer table. Referential integrity would prevent the creation of this orphan.

OSI (Open Systems Interconnection) model Describes how data actually moves from an application on one computer to an application on another networked computer. The OSI consists of seven layers, and each layer performs a specific function.

output Electronic or printed information produced by an information system.

output control Methods to maintain output integrity and security. For example, every report should include an appropriate title, report number or code, printing date, and time period covered. Reports should have pages that are numbered consecutively, identified as Page xx of xx, and the end of the report should be labeled clearly.

output security Output security protects privacy rights and shields the organization's proprietary data from theft or unauthorized access.

outsourcing The transfer of information systems development, operation, or maintenance to an outside firm that provides these services, for a fee, on a temporary or long-term basis.

overhead expenses See indirect costs.

page footer Appears at the bottom of the page and is used to display the name of the report and the page number.

page header Appears at the top of the page and includes the column headings that identify the data.

pair programming A practice in Extreme Programming in which two programmers work on the same task on the same computer; one drives (programs) while the other navigates (watches).

parallel operation The parallel operation changeover method requires that both the old and the new information systems operate fully for a specified period. Data is input into both systems, and output generated by the new system is compared with the equivalent output from the old system.

parent In inheritance, a parent is the object from which the other object, the child, derives one or more attributes.

parent diagram The higher or more top-level diagram in an exploded data flow diagram.

Pareto chart A vertical bar graph named for a nineteenth-century economist. The bars, which represent various causes of a problem, are arranged in descending order, so the team can focus on the most important causes.

partitioning The breaking down of overall objectives into subsystems and modules.

passive voice Refers to using sentences with the actor being the direct object. For example, "The system was designed by Tom" is in passive voice. Active voice is preferable to passive voice in written communication.

patch Replacement code that is applied to fix bugs or security holes in software.

pay for performance An arrangement between a search engine company and a commercial site that boosts a sites ranking in search results in return for a fee.

payback analysis A determination of how long it takes an information system to pay for itself through reduced costs and increased benefits.

payback period The time it takes to recover a system's cost.

perfective maintenance Changes to a system to improve efficiency.

performance System characteristics such as speed, volume, capacity, availability, and reliability.

permissions User-specific privileges that determine the type of access a user has to a database, file, or directory. Also called user rights.

personal information manager (PIM) A tool that helps manage tasks and schedules. Many handheld devices also include this function.

person-day The amount of work that one person can complete in one day.

PERT/CPM The Program Evaluation Review Technique (PERT) was developed by the U.S. Navy to manage very complex projects, such as the construction of nuclear submarines. At approximately the same time, the Critical Path Method (CPM) was developed by private industry to meet similar project management needs. The important distinctions between the two methods have disappeared over time, and today the technique is called either PERT, CPM, or PERT/CPM.

phased operation The phased operation method allows a new system to be implemented in stages, or modules.

phrase A search phrase is more specific than an AND operator, because it specifies an exact placement of terms.

physical design A plan for the actual implementation of the system.

physical model A model that describes how a system will be constructed.

physical storage Information storage mechanism that is strictly hardware-related, because it involves the process of reading and writing binary data to physical media, such as a hard drive, flash drive, or DVD.

physical topology The connection structure of an actual network's cabling.

pilot operation The pilot operation changeover method involves implementing the complete new system at a selected location of the company.

pilot site In a pilot operation, the group that uses the new system first is called the pilot site.

plain text Data that is not encrypted.

platform A specific hardware and software configuration that supports IT business goals such as hardware connectivity and easy integration of future applications. *Also called* environment.

podcast A web-based broadcast that allows a user to receive audio or multimedia files using music player software such as iTunes, and listen to them on a PC or download them to a portable MP3 player or smart phone.

point-of-sale (POS) The part of an information system that handles daily sales transactions and maintains the online inventory file.

polymorphism The concept that a message gives different meanings to different objects (e.g., a GOOD NIGHT message might produce different results depending if it is received by a child or the family dog).

pool The overall diagram In business process modeling notation (BPMN).

port A positive integer that is used for routing incoming traffic to the correct application on a computer.

port protector Network-based security application that controls access to and from workstation interfaces.

port scan An attempt to detect the services running on a computer by trying to connect to various ports and recording the ports on which a connection was accepted.

portal An entrance to a multifunction website. After entering a portal, a user can navigate to a destination, using various tools and features provided by the portal designer.

positive benefits Increases in revenues, improvements in services, or other contributions to the organization as a direct result of the new information system. Examples include improved information availability, faster customer service, and higher employee morale.

post-implementation evaluation An assessment of the overall quality of the information system. The evaluation verifies that the new system meets specified requirements, complies with user objectives, and achieves the anticipated benefits. In addition, by providing feedback to the development team, the evaluation also helps improve IT development practices for future projects.

power-on password *See* BIOS-level password.

predecessor task A single prior task upon which two or more concurrent tasks depend.

preliminary investigation An initial analysis to clearly identify the nature and scope of the business opportunity or problem. Also called a feasibility study.

present value The amount of money that, when invested today at a specified interest rate, grows to exactly one dollar at a certain point in the future.

present value analysis A technique that allows analysts to plan for future growth goals based on present value.

present value tables Third-party tables used to help analysts perform value analysis.

presentation software Applications used to create slides with sounds, animation, and graphics.

pretexting Obtaining personal information under false pretenses.

preventive maintenance Changes to a system to reduce the possibility of future failure.

primary key A field or combination of fields that uniquely and minimally identifies a particular member of an entity. For example, in a customer table the customer number is a unique primary key because no two customers can have the same customer number. That key also is minimal because it contains no information beyond what is needed to identify the customer.

private key encryption A common encryption technology called public key encryption (PKE). The private key is one of a pair of keys, and it decrypts data that has been encrypted with the second part of the pair, the public key.

private network A dedicated connection, similar to a leased telephone line.

privilege escalation attack An unauthorized attempt to increase permission levels.

probable-case estimate The most likely outcome is called a probable case estimate.

procedural programming language A programming language that requires a programmer to create code statements for each processing step.

procedural security Concerned with managerial policies and controls that ensure secure operations. Also called operational security.

process Procedure or task that users, managers, and IT staff members perform. Also, the logical rules of a system that are applied to transform data into meaningful information. In data flow diagrams, a process receives input data and produces output that has a different content, form, or both.

process 0 In a data flow diagram, process 0 (zero) represents the entire information system, but does not show the internal workings.

process description A documentation of a functional primitive's details, which represents a specific set of processing steps and business logic.

process improvement The framework used to integrate software and systems development by a new SEI model, Capability Maturity Model Integration (CMMI).

product baseline Describes the system at the beginning of operation. The product baseline incorporates any changes made since the allocated baseline and includes the results of performance and acceptance tests for the operational system.

product life cycle management (PLM) A system that integrates all aspects of a product, its data, and its users across the SDLC in a large enterprise setting.

production environment The environment for the actual system operation. It includes hardware and software configurations, system utilities, and communications resources. Also called the operational environment.

productivity software Applications such as word processing, spreadsheet, database management, and presentation graphics programs.

product-oriented Companies that manufacture computers, routers, or microchips.

profit center A department expected to break even, or show a profit.

program documentation Preparation of program documentation starts in the systems analysis phase and continues during systems implementation. Systems analysts prepare overall documentation, such as process descriptions and report layouts, early in the SDLC. Programmers provide documentation by constructing modules that are well supported by internal and external comments and descriptions that can be understood and maintained easily.

Program Evaluation Review Technique (PERT) *See* PERT/CPM.

programmer/analyst A designation for positions that require a combination of systems analysis and programming skills.

project coordinator The person who handles administrative responsibilities for the development team and negotiates with users who might have conflicting requirements or want changes that would require additional time or expense.

project creep The process by which projects with very general scope definitions expand gradually, without specific authorization.

project leader The person charged with leading a project from a technical perspective.

project management The process of planning, scheduling, monitoring, controlling, and reporting upon the development of an information system.

project manager The person charged with managing a project from an administrative perspective.

project monitoring Guiding, supervising, and coordinating the project team's workload.

project planning Identifying project tasks and estimating completion time and costs.

project reporting Providing regular progress reports to management, users, and the project team itself.

project scheduling The creation of a specific timetable to facilitate completion of a project. Also involves selecting and staffing the project team and assigning specific tasks to team members.

project scope A specific determination of a project's boundaries or extent.

project triangle The three major components of a project: cost, scope, and time. A project manager tries to find the optimal balance among these factors.

properties In object-oriented (O-O) analysis, characteristics that objects inherit from their class or possess on their own.

proprietary database A database that can be accessed for a fee or by subscription only, such as ProQuest or IEEE's Xplore.

prototype An early, rapidly constructed working version of the proposed information system.

prototyping The method by which a prototype is developed. It involves a repetitive sequence of analysis, design, modeling, and testing. It is a common technique that can be used to design anything from a new home to a computer network.

proxy server A networking device that provides Internet connectivity for internal LAN users.

pseudocode A technique for representing program logic.

public key encryption (PKE) A common encryption technique. Each user on the network has a pair of keys: a public key and a private key. The public key encrypts data that can be decrypted with the private key.

qualitative risk analysis Evaluating risk by estimating the probability that it will occur and the degree of impact.

quality assurance (QA) A process or procedure for minimizing errors and ensuring quality in products. Poor quality can result from inaccurate requirements, design problems, coding errors, faulty documentation, and ineffective testing. A quality assurance (QA) team reviews and tests all applications and systems changes to verify specifications and software quality standards.

quantitative risk analysis Evaluating risk in terms of the actual impact in terms of dollars, time, project scope, or quality.

query by example (QBE) A language allows the user to provide an example of the data requested.

query language Allows a user to specify a task without specifying how the task will be accomplished. Some query languages use natural language commands that resemble ordinary English sentences.

questionnaire A document containing a number of standard questions that can be sent to many individuals. Also called a survey.

radio button *See* option button.

radio frequency identification (RFID) Technology that uses high-frequency radio waves to track physical objects.

RAID (redundant array of independent disks) A RAID system may be part of an organizations backup and recovery plans. A RAID system mirrors the data while processing continues. RAID systems are called fault-tolerant, because a failure of any one disk does not disable the system.

random sample A selection taken in a random, unplanned manner. For example, a random sample might be a sample that selects any 20 customers.

range check A type of data validation check that tests data items to verify that they fall between a specified minimum and maximum value. The daily hours worked by an employee, for example, must fall within the range of 0 to 24.

range-of-response questions Closed-ended questions that ask the person to evaluate something by providing limited answers to specific responses or on a numeric scale.

rapid application development (RAD) A team-based technique that speeds up information systems development and produces a functioning information system. RAD is similar in concept to joint application development (JAD), but goes further by including all phases of the System Development Life Cycle (SDLC).

readability A measure of the ease of comprehension by analyzing specific characteristics of syllables, words, and sentences.

reasonableness check A type of data validation check that identifies values that are questionable, but not necessarily wrong. For example, input payment values of $0.05 and $5,000,000.00 both pass a simple limit check for a payment value greater than zero, and yet both values could be errors.

record A set of related fields that describes one instance, or member of an entity, such as one customer, one order, or one product. A record might have one or dozens of fields, depending on what information is needed. Also called a tuple.

records retention policy Rules designed to meet all legal requirements and business needs for keeping records.

recovery procedure Process for restoring data and restarting a system after an interruption. Recovery procedures can be used to restore a file or database to its current state at the time of the last backup.

recovery The process of restoring data and restarting a system after an interruption.

referential integrity A type of validity check. Referential integrity is a set of rules that avoids data inconsistency and quality problems.

relational database A database in which tables are related by common fields, creating a unified data structure that provides improved data quality and access.

relational model A model used in relational databases. The relational model was introduced during the 1970s and became popular because it was flexible and powerful.

relationships Enable objects to communicate and interact as they perform the business functions and transactions required by a system. Relationships describe what objects need to know about each other, how objects respond to changes in other objects, and the effects of membership in classes, superclasses, and subclasses.

release plan In agile development, a plan that specifies when user stories will be implemented and the timing of the releases. Releases are relatively frequent, and each release is treated as a system prototype that can be tested and modified as needed.

remote control software Applications that allow IT staff to take over a user's workstation and provide support and troubleshooting.

repeating group A set of one or more fields that can occur any number of times in a single record, with each occurrence having different values.

report footer Appears at the end of the report, can include grand totals for numeric fields and other end-of-report information.

report generator A tool for designing formatted reports rapidly. *Also called* report writer.

report header Appears at the beginning of a report and identifies the report as well as the report title, date, and other necessary information.

report writer *See* report generator.

repository A database that serves as a central storage location for all information about a system being developed.

request for proposal (RFP) A written list of features and specifications given to prospective vendors before a specific product or package has been selected.

request for quotation (RFQ) Used to obtain a price quotation or bid on a specific product or package.

requirements modeling Used in the systems planning phase of the SDLC. It involves using various fact-finding techniques, such as interviews, surveys, observation, and sampling, to describe the current system and identify the requirements for the new system.

requirements planning phase A phase that combines elements of the systems planning and systems analysis phases of the SDLC.

research An important fact-finding technique that include the review of journals, periodicals, and books to obtain background information, technical material, and news about industry trends and developments.

resource allocation A method of determining the indirect costs of running an IT department in which the charging of indirect costs is based on the resources used by an information system.

response time The overall time between a request for system activity and the delivery of the response. In the typical online environment, response time is measured from the instant the user presses the ENTER key or clicks a mouse button until the requested screen display appears or printed output is ready.

retention period Backups are stored for a specific retention period after which they are either destroyed or the backup media is reused.

return on investment (ROI) A percentage rate that measures profitability by comparing the total net benefits (the return) received from a project to the total costs (the investment) of the project. ROI = (total benefits - total costs) / total costs.

reverse engineering A process that lets the analyst examine an existing application and break it down into a series of diagrams, structure charts, and, in some cases, source code.

RFID tag An input device used in source data automation.

ring network A network resembling a circle of computers that communicate with each other. A ring network often is used when processing is performed at local sites rather than at a central location.

risk (1) An event that could affect the project negatively; (2) the impact of an attack multiplied by the likelihood of a vulnerability being exploited.

risk assessment Measures the likelihood and impact of risks.

risk control Develops safeguards that reduce the likelihood and impact of risks.

risk identification Listing each risk and assessing the likelihood that it could affect a project.

risk management The process of identifying, evaluating, tracking, and controlling risks to minimize their impact.

risk management plan Includes a review of the project's scope, stakeholders, budget, schedule, and any other internal or external factors that might affect the project. The plan should define project roles and responsibilities, risk management methods and procedures, categories of risks, and contingency plans.

risk response plan A proactive effort to anticipate a risk and describe an action plan to deal with it. An effective risk response plan can reduce the overall impact by triggering a timely and appropriate action.

roaming A process that allows wireless clients to move from one access point to another, automatically associating with the stronger access point and allowing for uninterrupted service.

router A device that connects network segments, determines the most efficient data path, and guides the flow of data.

RSS (Really Simple Syndication) A format for publishing frequently updated content to users who subscribe to an RSS download, also called a feed, RSS feed, or a web feed.

RSS feed Data format for providing users with frequently updated web content on all kinds of topics, available by subscription. *Also called* a feed or web feed.

RSS reader *See* aggregator.

sampling A process where an analyst collects examples of actual documents, which could include records, reports, or various forms.

scalability A characteristic of a system, implying that the system can be expanded, modified, or downsized easily to meet the rapidly changing needs of a business enterprise.

scalable The ability of a system to expand to meet new business requirements and volumes.

scaling on demand The ability to match network resources to needs at any given time; a feature of cloud computing. For example, during peak loads, additional cloud servers might come on line automatically to support increased workloads.

scatter diagram A tool used by system analysts to graphically show the correlation between two variables. *Also called* XY chart.

schedule feasibility A project can be implemented in an acceptable time frame.

schema The complete definition of a database, including descriptions of all fields, records, and relationships.

screen generator An interactive tool that helps you design a custom interface, create screen forms, and handle data entry format and procedures. *Also called* form painter.

scroll bar In user interface design, a scroll bar allows the user to move through the available choices for an input field.

Scrum A popular technique for agile project management. Derived from a rugby term. In Scrum, team members play specific roles and interact in intense sessions.

search engine An application that uses keywords and phrases to locate information on the Internet and list the results of the search.

second normal form (2NF) A record design is in second normal form (2NF) if it is in 1NF and if all fields that are not part of the primary key are dependent on the entire primary key. If any field in a 1NF record depends on only one of the fields in a combination primary key, then the record is not in 2NF. A 1NF record with a primary key that is a single field is automatically in 2NF.

secondary key A field or combination of fields that can be used to access or retrieve records. Secondary key values are not unique. For example, to access records for only those customers in a specific postal code, the postal code field could be used as a secondary key.

security Hardware, software, and procedural controls that safeguard and protect a system and its data from internal or external threats.

security hole Created by a combination of one or more improperly configured services.

security policy A plan that addresses the three main elements of system security: confidentiality, integrity, and availability.

security token A physical device that authenticates a legitimate user, such as a smart card or keychain device.

selection A control structure in modular design, it is the completion of two or more process steps based on the results of a test or condition.

semantic web An evolution of the web where the documents shared on the Internet have semantics (meaning) and not just syntax (HTML markup). Sometimes called Web 3.0.

sequence The completion of steps in sequential order, one after another.

sequence check A type of data validation check that is used when the data must be in some predetermined sequence. If the user must enter work orders in numerical sequence, for example, then an out-of-sequence order number indicates an error. If the user must enter transactions chronologically, then a transaction with an out-of-sequence date indicates an error.

sequence code Numbers or letters assigned in a specific order. Sequence codes contain no additional information other than an indication of order of entry into a system.

sequence diagram A UML diagram that shows the timing of transactions between objects as they occur during system execution.

server Computer in a client/server design that supplies data, processing, and services to client workstations.

server farm A large concentration of networked computers working together.

server processing time The time that the server actually requires to respond to client requests for processing.

service An application that monitors, or listens on, a particular port.

service desk A centralized resource staffed by IT professionals that provides users with the support they need to do their jobs. *Also called* help desk.

service pack A maintenance release supplied by commercial software suppliers.

service provider A firm that offers outsourcing solutions. Two popular outsourcing options involve application service providers and firms that offer Internet business services.

service-oriented A company that primarily offers information or services, or sells goods produced by others.

service-oriented architecture (SOA) A way of engineering systems in which reusable business functionality is provided by services through well-defined interfaces. Technically, not software architecture but an architectural style.

significant digit code Cipher that distinguishes items by using a series of subgroups of digits. U.S. Postal Service zip codes, for example, are significant digit codes.

simulation A dress rehearsal for users and IT support staff. Organizations typically include all procedures, such as those that they execute only at the end of a month, quarter, or year, in their simulations.

sink An external entity that receives data from an information system.

site visit A trip to a physical location to observe a system in use at another location.

slack time The amount of time by which an event can be late without delaying the project. The difference between latest completion time (LCT) and earliest completion time (ECT).

social engineering An intruder uses social interaction to gain access to a computer system.

social networking Using online communication channels such as Facebook, Twitter, and LinkedIn to connect to personal and professional contacts and groups.

soft skills Communications, interpersonal skills, perceptive abilities, and critical thinking are soft skills. IT professionals must have soft skills as well as technical skills.

software A program run by computers for a specific function or task.

Software as a Service (SaaS) A model of software delivery in which functionality is delivered on-demand as a network-accessible service, rather than as a traditional software application that is downloaded and installed on the customer's computer.

software engineering A software development process that stresses solid design, effective structure, accurate documentation, and careful testing.

software license A legal agreement that gives users the right to use the software under certain terms and conditions.

software package Software that is purchased or leased from another firm. A commercially produced software product, or family of products.

software reengineering Uses analytical techniques to identify potential quality and performance improvements in an information system.

software requirements specification A document that contains the requirements for the new system, describes the alternatives that were considered, and makes a specific recommendation to management. It is the end product of the systems analysis phase. Sometimes also called a system requirements document.

software vendor Company that develops software for sale.

source An external entity that supplies data to an information system.

source data automation A popular online input method that combines online data entry and automated data capture using input devices such as magnetic data strips, or swipe scanners.

source document A form used to request and collect input data, trigger or authorize an input action, and provide a record of the original transaction. During the input design stage, you develop source documents that are easy to complete and inexpensive.

spell checker A component of most word processing programs, a spell checker is a tool that identifies words in a document that do not appear in the program's dictionary.

spider *See* crawler.

spiral model A development model with a series of iterations, or revisions, based on user feedback.

sponsored link A subsidized link, paid for by a company or individual to make the link more prominent on a website.

spontaneous generation An unexplained generation of data or information. With respect to data flow diagrams, processes cannot spontaneously generate data flows – they must have an input to have an output.

SQL (Structured Query Language) A query language that allows PC users to communicate with servers and mainframe computers.

stakeholder Anyone who is affected by the company's performance, such as customers, employees, suppliers, stockholders, and members of the community.

stand-alone When personal computers first appeared in large numbers in the 1990, users found that they could run their own word processing, spreadsheet, and database applications, without assistance from the IT group, in a mode called stand-alone computing.

standard notation format A representation that makes designing tables easier as it clearly shows a table's structure, fields, and primary key.

star network A network design with a central device and one or more workstations connected to it in a way that forms a star pattern.

start day/date The day or date when a task is scheduled to begin.

state An adjective that describes an object's current status (e.g., a student could be a CURRENT, FUTURE, or PAST student).

state transition diagram Shows how an object changes from one state to another, depending on the events that affect the object.

status flag In structured application development, an indicator that allows one module to send a message to another module.

storyboard Sketches used during prototyping to show the general screen layout and design.

strategic plan The long-range plan that defines the corporate mission and goals. Typically defined by top management, with input from all levels.

strategic planning The process of identifying long-term organizational goals, strategies, and resource.

stratified sample A set metric is collected across functional areas. For example, a certain percentage of transactions from every work shift, or five customers from each of four zip codes, could be a stratified sample.

structure chart A top-down representation of business functions and processes. Also called a functional decomposition diagram.

structured analysis A traditional systems development technique that uses phases to plan, analyze, design, implement, and support an information system. Processes and data are treated as separate components.

structured brainstorming A group discussion where each participant speaks when it is his or her turn, or passes.

structured English A subset of standard English that describes logical processes clearly and accurately.

structured walk-through A review of a project team member's work by other members of the team. Generally, systems analysts review the work of other systems analysts, and programmers review the work of other programmers, as a form of peer review. Should take place throughout the SDLC and are called requirements reviews, design reviews, code reviews, or testing reviews, depending on the phase in which they occur.

stub testing A form of testing where the programmer simulates each program outcome or result and displays a message to indicate whether or not the program executed successfully. Each stub represents an entry or exit point that will be linked later to another program or data file.

subclass A further division of objects in a class. Subclasses are more specific categories within a class.

subject directory A website that structures topics in a hierarchy, starting with general headings and proceeding to more specific topics. *Also called* topic directory.

subordinate module A lower-level module in a structure chart.

subschema A view of the database used by one or more systems or users. A subschema defines only those portions of the database that a particular system or user needs or is allowed to access.

subscription model A service model that charges a variable fee for an application based on the number of users or workstations that have access to the application.

subsearch A focused search that can include the option to search within returned results and the ability to search within specific areas, such as newsgroups.

successor task Each of the concurrent tasks of a predecessor task.

summary report A report used by individuals at higher levels in the organization that includes less detail than reports used by lower-level employees.

superclass A more generalized category to which objects may belong (e.g., a NOVEL class might belong to a superclass called BOOK).

superuser account A login account that allows essentially unrestricted access to the application.

supply chain A traditional systems development technique that uses phases to plan, analyze, design, implement, and support an information system. Processes and data are treated as separate components.

supply chain management (SCM) The coordination, integration, and management of materials, information, and finances as they move from suppliers to customers, both within and between companies. In a totally integrated supply chain, a customer order could cause a production planning system to schedule a work order, which in turn could trigger a call for certain parts from one or more suppliers.

survey A document containing a number of standard questions that can be sent to many individuals. Also called a questionnaire.

swim lanes In a business process diagram, the overall diagram is called a pool, and the designated customer areas are called swim lanes.

switch Central networking device in a star network, which manages the network and acts as a conduit for all network traffic.

switchboard The use of command buttons in a user interface to enable users to navigate a system and select from groups of related tasks.

SWOT analysis An examination of a company's strengths (S), weaknesses (W), opportunities (O), and threats (T).

syntax error Programming language grammar error.

system A set of related components that produces specific results.

system administrator A person who is responsible for the configuration management and maintenance of an organization's computer networks.

system architecture A translation of the logical design of an information system into a physical structure that includes hardware, software, network support, and processing methods.

system boundary Shows what is included and excluded from a system. Depicted by a shaded rectangle in use case diagrams.

system changeover The process of putting the new information system online and retiring the old system. Changeover can be rapid or slow, depending on the method.

system design specification A document that presents the complete design for the new information system, along with detailed costs, staffing, and scheduling for completing the next SDLC phase, systems implementation. Also called the technical design specification or the detailed design specification.

system documentation A description of a system's functions and how they are implemented. The analyst prepares most of the system documentation during the systems analysis and systems design phases. System documentation includes data dictionary entries, data flow diagrams, object models, screen layouts, source documents, and the systems request that initiated the project.

system prototyping Producing a full-featured, working model of the information system being developed.

system requirement A characteristic or feature that must be included in an information system to satisfy business requirements and be acceptable to users.

system requirements document A document that contains the requirements for the new system, describes the alternatives that were considered, and makes a specific recommendation to management. It is the end product of the systems analysis phase.

system software Programs that control the computer, including the operating system, device drivers that communicate with hardware, and low-level utilities.

system testing A form of testing involving an entire information system and includes all typical processing situations. During a system test, users enter data, including samples of actual, or live data, perform queries, and produce reports to simulate actual operating conditions. All processing options and outputs are verified by users and the IT project development team to ensure that the system functions correctly.

systematic sample A sample that occurs at a predetermined periodicity. For example, every tenth customer record might be selected as a systematic sample for review.

systems analysis and design The process of developing information systems that effectively use hardware, software, data, processes, and people to support the company's business objectives.

systems analysis phase The second SDLC phase. The purpose of this phase is to build a logical model of the new system.

systems analyst A person who plans, analyzes, and implements information systems. He or she may work internally within a company's IT department, or be hired by a company as an independent consultant.

systems design The goal of systems design is to build a system that is effective, reliable, and maintainable.

systems design phase The third SDLC phase. The purpose of systems design is to create a blueprint for the new system that will satisfy all documented requirements, whether the system is being developed in-house or purchased as a package.

systems development life cycle (SDLC) Activities and functions that systems developers typically perform, regardless of how those activities and functions fit into a particular methodology. The SDLC model includes five phases: 1. Systems planning, 2. Systems analysis, 3. Systems design, 4. Systems implementation, and 5. Systems support and security.

systems implementation phase The fourth phase of SDLC. During this phase the new system is constructed, programs are written, tested, and documented, and the system is installed.

systems planning phase The first phase of the SDLC. During this phase the systems project gets started. The project proposal is evaluated to determine its feasibility. The project management plan is formulated, with the help of CASE tools where appropriate.

systems programmer A person who concentrates on operating system software and utilities.

systems request A formal request to the IT department that describes problems or desired changes in an information system or business process. It might propose enhancements for an existing system, the correction of problems, or the development of an entirely new system.

systems review committee A group of key managers and users responsible for evaluating systems requests. The term *computer resources committee* is sometimes also used.

systems support and security phase During the systems support and security phase of the SDLC, the IT staff maintains, enhances, and protects the system.

table Each file or table contains data about people, places, things, or events that interact with the information system.

table design Specifies the fields and identifies the primary key in a particular table or file.

tamper-evident case A case designed to show any attempt to open or unlock the case.

tangible benefit Positive outcome that can be measured in dollars. It can result from a decrease in expenses, an increase in revenues, or both.

tangible cost Expense that has a specific dollar value. Examples include employee salaries and hardware purchases.

task Any work that has a beginning and an end, and requires the use of company resources including people, time, and/or money. Examples include conducting a series of interviews, designing a report, selecting software, waiting for the delivery of equipment, and training users. *See also* activity.

task box A component of a PERT/CPM chart that contains important scheduling and duration information about a task. Each task in a project is represented by its own task box in the PERT/CPM chart.

task group A task that represents several activities.

task ID A number or code that uniquely identifies a task.

task name A brief descriptive name for a task, which does not have to be unique in the project. For example, a task named Conduct Interviews might appear in several phases of the project.

task pattern A logical sequence of tasks in a work breakdown structure. Can involve sequential tasks, multiple successor tasks, and multiple predecessor tasks.

technical feasibility When an organization has the resources to develop or purchase, install, and operate the system.

technical support Technical support is necessary to support the wide variety of IT systems and users. It includes six main functions: application development, systems support, user support, database administration, network administration, and web support. These functions overlap considerably and often have different names in different companies.

template A standard format for documents, presentations, and other output, with specific layouts, fonts, margin and other formatting settings. Templates are used to give work a consistent look.

terminator A data flow diagram symbol that indicates a data origin or final destination. Also called an external entity.

test data The data used in unit testing. Test data should contain both correct data and erroneous data and should test all possible situations that could occur.

test environment The environment that analysts and programmers use to develop and maintain programs.

test plan A plan designed by a systems analyst that includes test steps and test data for integration testing and system testing.

test-driven development (TDD) An Extreme Programming (XP) concept that unit tests are designed before code is written, focusing on end results and preventing programmers from straying from their goals.

testing review *See* structured walk-through.

text messaging Sending text messages via cell phone. *Also called* texting.

texting *See* text messaging.

thick client A system design that locates most or all of the application processing logic at the client. Also called a fat client design.

thin client A system design that locates most or all of the processing logic at the server.

third normal form (3NF) A record design is in third normal form (3NF) if it is in 2NF and if no nonkey field is dependent on another nonkey field. A nonkey field is a field that is not a candidate key for the primary key.

third-party software An application that is not developed in-house.

threat In risk management, an internal or external or external entity that could endanger an asset.

three-tier design In a three-tier design, the user interface runs on the client and the data is stored on the server, just as in a two-tier design. A three-tier design also has a middle layer between the client and server that processes the client requests and translates them into data access commands that can be understood and carried out by the server.

throughput A measurement of actual system performance under specific circumstances and is affected by network loads and hardware efficiency. Throughput, like bandwidth, is expressed as a data transfer rate, such as Kbps, Mbps, or Gbps.

throwaway prototyping *See* design prototyping.

tightly coupled If modules are tightly coupled, one module refers to internal logic contained in another module.

time value of money A concept that recognizes that a given sum of money, over time, historically will increase in value.

toggle button A GUI element used to represent on or off status. Clicking the toggle button switches to the other status.

toolbar A GUI element that contains icons or buttons that represent shortcuts for executing common commands.

top-down approach A design approach, also called modular design, where the systems analyst defines the overall objectives of the system, and then breaks them down into subsystems and modules. This breaking-down process also is called partitioning.

topic directory *See* subject directory.

total cost of ownership (TCO) A number used in assessing costs, which includes ongoing support and maintenance costs, as well as acquisition costs.

totals zone If a form has data totals, they will appear in this section of the form.

training plan A successful information system requires training for users, managers, and IT staff members. The entire systems development effort can depend on whether or not people understand the system and know how to use it effectively. The training plan is a document that details these requirements.

train-the-trainer A strategy where one group of users has been trained and can assist others. Users often learn more quickly from coworkers who share common experience and job responsibilities.

transaction model A service model that charges a variable fee for an application based on the volume of transactions or operations performed by the application. *Also called* usage model.

transaction processing (TP) system Operational system used to process day-to-day recurring business transactions, such as customer billing.

transference One of four risk control strategies. In transference, risk is shifted to another asset or party, such as an insurance company.

transparent A network is transparent if a user sees the data as if it were stored on his or her own workstation.

transparent interface A user interface that users don't really notice; a user-friendly interface that does not distract the user and calls no attention to itself.

tunnel A secure network connection established between the client and the access point of the local intranet.

tuple A tuple (rhymes with couple), or record, is a set of related fields that describes one instance, or member of an entity, such as one customer, one order, or one product. A tuple might have one or dozens of fields, depending on what information is needed.

turnaround document Output document that is later entered back into the same or another information system. A telephone or utility bill, for example, might be a turnaround document printed by the company's billing system. When the bill is returned with payment, it is scanned into the company's accounts receivable system to record the payment accurately.

turnaround time A measure applied to centralized batch processing operations, such as customer billing or credit card statement processing. Turnaround time measures the time between submitting a request for information and the fulfillment of the request. Turnaround time also can be used to measure the quality of IT support or services by measuring the time from a user request for help to the resolution of the problem.

tutorial A series of online interactive lessons that present material and provide a dialog with users.

two-tier design A network design where the user interface resides on the client, all data resides on the server, and the application logic can run either on the server or on the client, or be divided between the client and the server.

unencrypted Data that is not encrypted.

Unicode A relatively recent coding method that represents characters as integers. Unlike EBCDIC and ASCII, which use eight bits for each character, Unicode requires 16 bits per character, which allows it to represent more than 65,000 unique characters.

Unified Modeling Language (UML) A widely used method of visualizing and documenting software systems design. UML uses object-oriented design concepts, but it is independent of any specific programming language and can be used to describe business processes and requirements generally

uninterruptible power supply (UPS) Battery-powered backup power source that enables operations to continue during short-term power outages and surges.

unit testing The testing of an individual program or module. The objective is to identify and eliminate execution errors that could cause the program to terminate abnormally, and logic errors that could have been missed during desk checking.

Universal Security Slot (USS) Can be fastened to a cable lock or laptop alarm.

unnormalized A record that contains a repeating group, which means that a single record has multiple occurrences of a particular field, with each occurrence having different values.

unstructured brainstorming A group discussion where any participant can speak at any time.

usability In user interface design, includes user satisfaction, support for business functions, and system effectiveness.

usability metrics Data that interface designers can obtain by using software that can record and measure user interactions with the system.

usage model *See* transaction model.

use case Represents the steps in a specific business function or process in UML.

use case description A description in UML that documents the name of the use case, the actor, a description of the use case, a step-by-step list of the tasks required for successful completion, and other key descriptions and assumptions.

use case diagram A visual representation that represents the interaction between users and the information system in UML.

user Stakeholder inside or outside the company who will interact with the system.

user application Programs that utilize standard business software, such as Microsoft Office, which has been configured in a specific manner to enhance user productivity.

user design phase In this phase, users interact with systems analysts and develop models and prototypes that represent all system processes, outputs, and inputs.

user documentation Instructions and information to users who will interact with the system. Includes user manuals, help screens, and tutorials.

user interface Includes screens, commands, controls, and features that enable users to interact more effectively with an application. *See also* graphical user interface (GUI).

user productivity system Application that provides employees of all levels a wide array of tools to improve job performance. Examples include email, word processing, graphics, and company intranets.

user rights User-specific privileges that determine the type of access a user has to a database, file, or directory. Also called permissions.

user story In agile development, a short, simple requirements definition provided by the customer. Programmers use user stories to determine a project's requirements, priorities, and scope.

user training package The main objective of a user training package is to show users how the system can help them perform their jobs.

user-centered A term that indicates the primary focus is upon the user. In a user-centered system, the distinction blurs between input, output, and the interface itself.

validity check A type of data validation check that is used for data items that must have certain values. For example, if an inventory system has 20 valid item classes, then any input item that does not match one of the valid classes will fail the check.

validity rules Checks that are applied to data elements when data is entered to ensure that the value entered is valid. For example, a validity rule might require that an employee's salary number be within the employer's predefined range for that position.

value-added reseller (VAR) A firm that enhances a commercial package by adding custom features and configuring it for a particular industry.

variable charge method based on resource usage A method of determining the indirect costs of running an IT department based on allocation of resources such as connect time, server processing time, network resources required, printer use, or a combination of similar factors.

variable charge method based on volume A method of determining the indirect costs of running an IT department in which the indirect information systems department costs are allocated to other departments based on user-oriented activity, such as the number of transactions or printing volume.

variable costs Expenses that vary depending on the level of activity. For example, the costs of printer paper or telephone line charges are variable costs.

Venn diagram Diagram that uses circular symbols to illustrate Boolean logic. Venn diagrams are named after John Venn, a nineteenth-century scholar who devised a scheme for visualizing logical relationships.

version control The process of tracking system releases.

vertical application A software package that has been developed to handle information requirements for a specific type of business.

vertical system A system designed to meet the unique requirements of a specific business or industry, such as a web-based retailer or auto-supply store.

virtual private network (VPN) Uses a public network to connect remote users securely. Allows a remote client to use a special key exchange that must be authenticated by the VPN.

visible web Refers to websites that are indexed by major search engines and are publicly accessible.

visual aids Tools such as whiteboards, flip charts, overhead transparencies, slides, films, and videotapes used to enhance a presentation.

vulnerability A security weakness or soft spot.

waterfall model The traditional model of software development. A graph that depicts the result of each SDLC phase flowing down into the next phase.

Web 2.0 A second generation of the web that enables people to collaborate, interact, and share information much more dynamically, based on continuously available user applications rather than static HTML webpages. Interactive experience is a hallmark of Web 2.0.

web browser An application that enables the user to navigate, or browse the Internet and display webpages on a local computer.

web feed *See* RSS feed.

web server A computer that is used to store and house websites.

web The Internet allows you to visit the World Wide Web, usually referred to as the web, which contains billions of text and multimedia documents called webpages.

web-based discussion group An online community that combines features of mailing lists and newsgroups.

webcast A one-way transmission of information or training materials, such as a Webinar session, available on demand or for a specific period to online participants.

web-centric A strategy or approach that emphasizes a high degree of integration with other web-based components. A web-centric architecture follows Internet design protocols and enables a company to integrate the new application into its ecommerce strategy.

webinar An Internet-based training session that provides an interactive experience. The word "webinar" combines the words "web" and "seminar."

webpage Text and multimedia documents that are found on the web.

website A collection of related webpages.

weight An important multiplier that managers factor into estimates so they can be analyzed.

what-if analysis A feature of business support systems that allows analysis to define and account for a wide variety of issues (including issues not completely defined).

why, who, what, when, and how of communications Good communications must answer these basic questions: Why is one communicating? Who is the target audience? What is expected? When is detail required? How does one communicate effectively?

wide area network (WAN) A network spanning long distances that can link users who are continents apart.

Wi-Fi (wireless fidelity) Family of popular IEEE local area network wireless networking standards, also known as 802.11, including 802.11a, b, g, and n. 802.11n is the most recent standard. 802.11ac and 802.11ad are proposed new standards.

Wi-Fi Alliance A nonprofit international association formed in 1999 to certify interoperability of wireless network products based on IEEE 802.11 specifications.

Wi-Fi Protected Access (WPA) A common method used to secure a wireless network. This approach requires each wireless client be configured manually to use a special, pre-shared key, rather than key pairs. The most recent and more secure version is WPA2.

wiki A web-based repository of information that anyone can access, contribute to, or modify.

Wi-Max IEEE 802.16 specifications, which are expected to enable wireless multimedia applications with a range of up to 30 miles. *See also* 802.16.

Wired Equivalent Privacy (WEP) One of the earliest methods used to secure a wireless network, superseded by WPA and WPA2.

wireless access point (WAP) A central wireless device that provides network services to wireless clients. Also called an access point.

wireless local area network (WLAN) A wireless network that is relatively inexpensive to install and is well-suited to workgroups and users who are not anchored to a specific desk or location.

work breakdown structure (WBS) A project broken down into a series of smaller tasks. *See also* Gantt chart; PERT/CPM chart.

workgroup software *See* groupware.

World Wide Web *See* web.

worst-case estimate The most pessimistic outcome.

WPA2 A wireless security standard based on 802.11i that provides a significant increase in protection over WEP and WPA.

XY chart A tool used by system analysts to graphically show the correlation between two variables. Also called a *scatter diagram*.

Y2K issue A problem faced by many firms in the year 2000 because their computer systems used only two digits to represent the year; most dates now use a four-digit format for the year (YYYYMMDD).

Yourdon A type of symbol set that is used in data flow diagrams. Processes, data flows, data stores, and external entities each have a unique symbol in the Yourdon symbol set.

Zachman Framework for Enterprise Architecture A model that asks the traditional fact-finding questions in a systems development context.

INDEX